Algorithms Illuminated
(Omnibus Edition)

In *Algorithms Illuminated*, Tim Roughgarden teaches the basics of algorithms in the most accessible way imaginable, with thorough coverage of asymptotic analysis, graph search and shortest paths, data structures, divide-and-conquer algorithms, greedy algorithms, dynamic programming, and NP-hard problems. Readers of this book will become better programmers; sharpen their analytical skills; learn to think algorithmically; acquire literacy with computer science's greatest hits; and ace their technical interviews.

Tim Roughgarden is a Professor of Computer Science at Columbia University. His research, teaching, and expository writings have been recognized by a Presidential Early Career Award for Scientists and Engineers, the ACM Grace Murray Hopper Award, the EATCS-SIGACT Gödel Prize, a Guggenheim Fellowship, the INFORMS Lanchester Prize, and a Tau Beta Pi Teaching Award. His other books include *Twenty Lectures on Algorithmic Game Theory* and *Beyond the Worst-Case Analysis of Algorithms*.

Praise for *Algorithms Illuminated*

"*Algorithms Illuminated* is academic gold for both students and instructors. The most incredible thing about this book is the way it reaches different types of learners. Beginning students love the approach of getting exposed to complex material slowly and methodically, with lots of intuition and illustrations; advanced students can focus their energy on the formal treatment, going back to the intuition as needed. I love this book because it makes very difficult concepts accessible to everyone."
    -Thomas Cook, *U.S. Military Academy at West Point*

"Tim Roughgarden's *Algorithms Illuminated* is a well-crafted, thorough, and engaging presentation of algorithms on a wide range of topics. The chapters on NP-hard problems are particularly remarkable, as they overturn the conventional wisdom that this topic is too hard for students to understand. I have found that my students really benefit from this approach and strongly recommend this book to others."
    -Avraham Leff, *Yeshiva College*

"In my experience, students find *Algorithms Illuminated* much more relatable and motivating to read than other algorithms books. The presentation style is very modern and honest: complicated ideas are broken down into digestible chunks with the explicit recognition that the reader is indeed facing deep content; pseudocode, proofs, and mathematical techniques are presented truthfully without hiding "technical/boring" details; and every problem is well motivated with the actual reasons why computer scientists care about it. The reader gets the feeling that the book is talking directly to them and inviting them to be part of the story, not just a guest who looks at the highlights and moves on."
    -Saray Shai, *Wesleyan University*

"This fabulous book is an ideal introduction to the design and analysis of algorithms. *Algorithms Illuminated* stands out for its accessible and readable style, with plenty of examples, quizzes and problems for students to check their understanding. The clarity of the exposition brings out the beautiful ideas at the core of the subject. I highly recommend *Algorithms Illuminated* to anyone starting out with algorithms!"
    -Mary Wootters, *Stanford University*

"Look through the Table of Contents and you might conclude that this is just another algorithms book. Don't be fooled. What makes this book special—what makes this book the first of its kind—is Tim Roughgarden's singular ability to weave algorithm design with pedagogical design. Learners need opportunities to check their understanding at key points, to study examples, to see algorithms in contexts that they care about, to confront the needed mathematical background buffered by these motivating contexts. It's all here, carried along by Roughgarden's enthusiasm not only for algorithms but also for the people who want to learn them."
    -Daniel Zingaro, *University of Toronto*

Algorithms Illuminated
(Omnibus Edition)

Tim Roughgarden

Soundlikeyourself Publishing

New York, NY

First Printing, 2022

Printed in the United States of America

First Omnibus Edition

Cover image:
Kazuya Akimoto, *Overlapped Blue Rectangles*, 2004
acrylics on board; 46 x 53 cm
© Kazuya Akimoto

Cover design by PixelStudio

ISBN: 978-0-9992829-8-4 (Hardback)

Library of Congress Control Number: 2017914282

Soundlikeyourself Publishing, LLC
P. O. Box 20113
New York, NY 10014-9992
soundlikeyourselfpublishing@gmail.com
www.algorithmsilluminated.org

To Emma and Marz

Contents

Preface   **xii**

I The Basics   **1**

1 Introduction   **2**
   1.1 Why Study Algorithms?   2
   1.2 Integer Multiplication   3
   1.3 Karatsuba Multiplication   6
   1.4 `MergeSort`: The Algorithm   10
   1.5 `MergeSort`: The Analysis   14
   1.6 Guiding Principles for the Analysis of Algorithms   20
   Problems   24

2 Asymptotic Notation   **27**
   2.1 The Gist   27
   2.2 Big-O Notation   33
   2.3 Two Basic Examples   35
   2.4 Big-Omega and Big-Theta Notation   37
   2.5 Additional Examples   40
   Problems   42

3 Divide-and-Conquer Algorithms   **45**
   3.1 The Divide-and-Conquer Paradigm   45
   3.2 Counting Inversions in $O(n \log n)$ Time   46
   3.3 Strassen's Matrix Multiplication Algorithm   53
   *3.4 An $O(n \log n)$-Time Algorithm for the Closest Pair   58
   Problems   68

4 The Master Method   **71**
   4.1 Integer Multiplication Revisited   71
   4.2 Formal Statement   73
   4.3 Six Examples   75
   *4.4 Proof of the Master Method   79
   Problems   87

5   QuickSort   90
    5.1   Overview   90
    5.2   Partitioning Around a Pivot Element   93
    5.3   The Importance of Good Pivots   98
    5.4   Randomized `QuickSort`   101
   *5.5   Analysis of Randomized `QuickSort`   104
   *5.6   Sorting Requires $\Omega(n \log n)$ Comparisons   112
    Problems   116

6   Linear-Time Selection   120
    6.1   The `RSelect` Algorithm   120
   *6.2   Analysis of `RSelect`   125
   *6.3   The `DSelect` Algorithm   129
   *6.4   Analysis of `DSelect`   132
    Problems   138

II   Graph Algorithms and Data Structures   141

7   Graphs: The Basics   142
    7.1   Some Vocabulary   142
    7.2   A Few Applications   143
    7.3   Measuring the Size of a Graph   144
    7.4   Representing a Graph   146
    Problems   151

8   Graph Search and Its Applications   153
    8.1   Overview   153
    8.2   Breadth-First Search and Shortest Paths   159
    8.3   Computing Connected Components   166
    8.4   Depth-First Search   170
    8.5   Topological Sort   174
   *8.6   Computing Strongly Connected Components   181
    8.7   The Structure of the Web   190
    Problems   193

9   Dijkstra's Shortest-Path Algorithm   198
    9.1   The Single-Source Shortest Path Problem   198
    9.2   Dijkstra's Algorithm   202
   *9.3   Why Is Dijkstra's Algorithm Correct?   204
    9.4   Implementation and Running Time   209
    Problems   210

10   The Heap Data Structure   214
    10.1   Data Structures: An Overview   214
    10.2   Supported Operations   216
    10.3   Applications   218

10.4 Speeding Up Dijkstra's Algorithm   222
*10.5 Implementation Details   226
Problems   235

11   Search Trees   **237**
11.1 Sorted Arrays   237
11.2 Search Trees: Supported Operations   239
*11.3 Implementation Details   241
*11.4 Balanced Search Trees   251
Problems   254

12   Hash Tables and Bloom Filters   **257**
12.1 Supported Operations   257
12.2 Applications   259
*12.3 Implementation: High-Level Ideas   263
*12.4 Further Implementation Details   273
12.5 Bloom Filters: The Basics   277
*12.6 Bloom Filters: Heuristic Analysis   282
Problems   286

III Greedy Algorithms and Dynamic Programming   **290**

13   Introduction to Greedy Algorithms   **291**
13.1 The Greedy Algorithm Design Paradigm   291
13.2 A Scheduling Problem   293
13.3 Developing a Greedy Algorithm   295
13.4 Proof of Correctness   299
Problems   303

14   Huffman Codes   **306**
14.1 Codes   306
14.2 Codes as Trees   309
14.3 Huffman's Greedy Algorithm   313
*14.4 Proof of Correctness   320
Problems   326

15   Minimum Spanning Trees   **328**
15.1 Problem Definition   328
15.2 Prim's Algorithm   331
*15.3 Speeding Up Prim's Algorithm via Heaps   335
*15.4 Prim's Algorithm: Proof of Correctness   340
15.5 Kruskal's Algorithm   346
*15.6 Speeding Up Kruskal's Algorithm via Union-Find   349
*15.7 Kruskal's Algorithm: Proof of Correctness   357
15.8 Application: Single-Link Clustering   358
Problems   362

16 Introduction to Dynamic Programming   **366**
   16.1 The Weighted Independent Set Problem   366
   16.2 A Linear-Time Algorithm for WIS in Paths   370
   16.3 A Reconstruction Algorithm   376
   16.4 The Principles of Dynamic Programming   377
   16.5 The Knapsack Problem   381
   Problems   388

17 Advanced Dynamic Programming   **392**
   17.1 Sequence Alignment   392
  *17.2 Optimal Binary Search Trees   400
   Problems   411

18 Shortest Paths Revisited   **415**
   18.1 Shortest Paths with Negative Edge Lengths   415
   18.2 The Bellman-Ford Algorithm   418
   18.3 The All-Pairs Shortest Path Problem   429
   18.4 The Floyd-Warshall Algorithm   430
   Problems   438

IV Algorithms for NP-Hard Problems   **441**

19 What Is NP-Hardness?   **442**
   19.1 MST vs. TSP: An Algorithmic Mystery   442
   19.2 Possible Levels of Expertise   446
   19.3 Easy and Hard Problems   448
   19.4 Algorithmic Strategies for NP-Hard Problems   453
   19.5 Proving NP-Hardness: A Simple Recipe   457
   19.6 Rookie Mistakes and Acceptable Inaccuracies   464
   Problems   467

20 Compromising on Correctness: Efficient Inexact Algorithms   **471**
   20.1 Makespan Minimization   471
   20.2 Maximum Coverage   481
  *20.3 Influence Maximization   490
   20.4 The 2-OPT Heuristic Algorithm for the TSP   497
   20.5 Principles of Local Search   502
   Problems   511

21 Compromising on Speed: Exact Inefficient Algorithms   **519**
   21.1 The Bellman-Held-Karp Algorithm for the TSP   519
  *21.2 Finding Long Paths by Color Coding   525
   21.3 Problem-Specific Algorithms vs. Magic Boxes   535
   21.4 Mixed Integer Programming Solvers   537
   21.5 Satisfiability Solvers   540
   Problems   545

22 Proving Problems NP-Hard   **551**
    22.1 Reductions Revisited   551
    22.2 3-SAT and the Cook-Levin Theorem   553
    22.3 The Big Picture   554
    22.4 A Template for Reductions   557
    22.5 Independent Set Is NP-Hard   558
 *22.6 Directed Hamiltonian Path Is NP-Hard   562
    22.7 The TSP Is NP-Hard   567
    22.8 Subset Sum Is NP-Hard   569
    Problems   574

23 P, NP, and All That   **577**
 *23.1 Amassing Evidence of Intractability   577
 *23.2 Decision, Search, and Optimization   579
 *23.3 $\mathcal{NP}$: Problems with Easily Recognized Solutions   580
 *23.4 The P $\neq$ NP Conjecture   584
 *23.5 The Exponential Time Hypothesis   587
 *23.6 NP-Completeness   590
    Problems   594

24 Case Study: The FCC Incentive Auction   **596**
    24.1 Repurposing Wireless Spectrum   596
    24.2 Greedy Heuristics for Buying Back Licenses   598
    24.3 Feasibility Checking   604
    24.4 Implementation as a Descending Clock Auction   609
    24.5 The Final Outcome   613
    Problems   615

A Quick Review of Proofs By Induction   **617**
    A.1 A Template for Proofs by Induction   617
    A.2 Example: A Closed-Form Formula   618
    A.3 Example: The Size of a Complete Binary Tree   618

B Quick Review of Discrete Probability   **620**
    B.1 Sample Spaces   620
    B.2 Events   621
    B.3 Random Variables   622
    B.4 Expectation   623
    B.5 Linearity of Expectation   624
    B.6 Example: Load Balancing   627

Epilogue: A Field Guide to Algorithm Design   **630**

Hints and Solutions   **632**

Index   **655**

Preface

This book has only one goal: *to teach the basics of algorithms in the most accessible way possible*. Think of it as a transcript of what an expert algorithms tutor would say to you over a year of one-on-one lessons. This book is inspired by my online algorithms courses that have been running regularly since 2012, which in turn are based on an undergraduate course that I taught many times at Stanford University. People of all ages, backgrounds, and walks of life are well represented in these online courses, with large numbers of students (high-school, college, etc.), software engineers (both current and aspiring), scientists, and professionals hailing from all corners of the world.

What We'll Cover

Algorithms Illuminated will transform you from an algorithms newbie (say, a rising third-year undergraduate) to a seasoned veteran with expertise comparable to graduates of the world's best computer science master's degree programs. Specifically, this book will help you master the following topics.

Asymptotic analysis and big-O notation. Asymptotic notation provides the basic vocabulary for discussing the design and analysis of algorithms. The key concept here is "big-O" notation, which is a modeling choice about the granularity with which we measure the running time of an algorithm. We'll see that the sweet spot for clear high-level thinking about algorithm design is to ignore constant factors and lower-order terms, and to concentrate on how an algorithm's performance scales with the size of the input.

Divide-and-conquer algorithms and the master method. There's no silver bullet in algorithm design, no single problem-solving method that cracks all computational problems. However, there are a few general algorithm design techniques that find successful application across a range of different domains. In the "divide-and-conquer" technique, the key idea is to break a problem into smaller subproblems, solve the subproblems recursively, and then quickly combine their solutions into one for the original problem. We'll see fast divide-and-conquer algorithms for sorting, integer and matrix multiplication, and a basic problem in computational geometry. We'll also cover the master method, which is a powerful tool for analyzing the running time of divide-and-conquer algorithms.

Randomized algorithms. A randomized algorithm "flips coins" as it runs, and its behavior can depend on the outcomes of these coin flips. Surprisingly often, randomization leads to simple, elegant, and practical algorithms. Among other randomized algorithms, we'll describe and analyze in detail the canonical example of randomized QuickSort.

Sorting and selection.   As a byproduct of studying the first three topics, we'll learn several famous algorithms for sorting and selection, including MergeSort, QuickSort, and linear-time selection (both randomized and deterministic). These computational primitives are so blazingly fast that they do not take much more time than that needed just to read the input. This book will help you cultivate a collection of such "for-free primitives," both to apply directly to data and to use as the building blocks for solutions to more difficult problems.

Graph search and applications.   Graphs model many different types of networks, including road networks, communication networks, social networks, and networks of dependencies between tasks. Graphs can get complex, but there are several blazingly fast primitives for reasoning about graph structure. We begin with linear-time algorithms for searching a graph, with applications ranging from network analysis to task sequencing.

Shortest paths.   In the shortest-path problem, the goal is to compute the best route in a network from point A to point B. The problem has obvious applications, like computing driving directions, and also shows up in disguise in many more general planning problems. We'll generalize one of our graph search algorithms and arrive at Dijkstra's famous shortest-path algorithm.

Data structures.   This book will turn you into an educated client of several different data structures for maintaining an evolving set of objects with keys. The primary goal is to develop your intuition about which data structure is the right one for your application. The optional advanced sections provide guidance in how to implement these data structures from scratch.

We first discuss heaps, which can quickly identify the stored object with the smallest key and are useful for sorting, implementing a priority queue, and implementing Dijkstra's algorithm in near-linear time. Search trees maintain a total ordering over the keys of the stored objects and support an even richer array of operations. Hash tables are optimized for super-fast lookups and are ubiquitous in modern programs. We'll also cover the bloom filter, a close cousin of the hash table that uses less space at the expense of occasional errors, and the union-find (disjoint-set) data structure.

Greedy algorithms and applications.   Greedy algorithms solve problems by making a sequence of myopic and irrevocable decisions. For many problems, they are easy to devise and often blazingly fast. Most greedy algorithms are not guaranteed to be correct, but we'll cover several killer applications that are exceptions to this rule. Examples include scheduling problems, optimal compression, and minimum spanning trees of graphs.

Dynamic programming and applications.   Few benefits of a serious study of algorithms rival the empowerment that comes from mastering dynamic programming. This design paradigm takes a lot of practice to perfect, but it has countless applications to problems that appear unsolvable using any simpler method. Our dynamic programming boot camp will double as a tour of some of the paradigm's killer applications, including the knapsack problem, the Needleman-Wunsch genome sequence alignment algorithm, Knuth's algorithm for optimal binary search trees, and the Bellman-Ford and Floyd-Warshall shortest-path algorithms.

Algorithmic tools for tackling NP-hard problems. Many real-world problems are "NP-hard" and appear unsolvable by always-correct and always-fast algorithms. When an NP-hard problem shows up in your own work, you must compromise on either correctness or speed. We'll see techniques old (like greedy algorithms) and new (like local search) for devising fast heuristic algorithms that are "approximately correct," with applications to scheduling, influence maximization in social networks, and the traveling salesman problem. We'll also cover techniques old (like dynamic programming) and new (like MIP and SAT solvers) for developing correct algorithms that improve dramatically over exhaustive search; applications here include the traveling salesman problem (again), finding signaling pathways in biological networks, and television station repacking in a recent and high-stakes spectrum auction in the United States.

Recognizing NP-hard problems. This book will also train you to quickly recognize an NP-hard problem so that you don't inadvertently waste time trying to design a too-good-to-be-true algorithm for it. You'll acquire familiarity with many famous and basic NP-hard problems, ranging from satisfiability to graph coloring to the Hamiltonian path problem. Through practice, you'll learn the tricks of the trade in proving problems NP-hard via reductions.

For a more detailed look into the book's contents, check out the "Upshot" sections that conclude each chapter and highlight the most important points. The "Field Guide to Algorithm Design" on page 630 provides a bird's-eye view of how to apply the algorithmic toolbox you'll acquire from this book to problems that you encounter in your own work.

The starred sections of the book are the most advanced ones. The time-constrained reader can skip these sections on a first reading without any loss of continuity.

Skills You'll Learn

Mastering algorithms takes time and effort. Why bother?

Become a better programmer. You'll learn several blazingly fast subroutines for processing data as well as several useful data structures for organizing data that you can deploy directly in your own programs. Implementing and using these algorithms will stretch and improve your programming skills. You'll also learn general algorithm design paradigms that are relevant to many different problems across different domains, as well as tools for predicting the performance of such algorithms. These "algorithmic design patterns" can help you come up with new algorithms for problems that arise in your own work.

Sharpen your analytical skills. You'll get lots of practice describing and reasoning about algorithms. Through mathematical analysis, you'll gain a deep understanding of the specific algorithms and data structures that this book covers. You'll acquire facility with several mathematical techniques that are broadly useful for analyzing algorithms.

Think algorithmically. After you learn about algorithms, you'll start seeing them everywhere, whether you're riding an elevator, watching a flock of birds, managing your investment portfolio, or even watching an infant learn. Algorithmic thinking is increasingly useful and prevalent in disciplines outside of computer science, including biology, statistics, and economics.

Literacy with computer science's greatest hits. Studying algorithms can feel like watching a highlight reel of many of the greatest hits from the last sixty years of computer science. No longer will you feel excluded at that computer science cocktail party when someone cracks a joke about Dijkstra's algorithm. After reading this book, you'll know exactly what they mean.

Ace your technical interviews. Over the years, countless students have regaled me with stories about how mastering the concepts in this book enabled them to ace every technical interview question they were ever asked.

Using this Book in a Course

All of this book's material has been battle-tested in a university setting—by yours truly at Stanford, and by many instructors at other schools. Parts I–III are tailor-made for serving as the primary text in an introductory undergraduate course on algorithms and data structures, focusing on the basics (Part I), graph algorithms and data structures (Part II), and greedy algorithms and dynamic programming (Part III). For example, I cover 75-80% of this content over nineteen 75-minute lectures; a semester-long course could accommodate the rest of it, or selected topics from Chapter 19 about NP-hard problems. Parts III and IV of the book form an ideal basis for a traditional master's level course on basic and advanced algorithms, emphasizing greedy algorithms and their applications, dynamic programming and its applications, the recognition of NP-hard problems, and algorithmic tools for tackling such problems.

Many chapters of this book are logically independent of each other. For example, the design paradigms of divide-and-conquer algorithms (Chapters 3–6), greedy algorithms (Chapters 13–15), and dynamic programming (Chapter 16–18) can be covered in any order. Similarly, data structures (Chapters 10–12) can be taught before or after basic graph algorithms (Chapters 7–9), with the exception of the heap-based implementation of Dijkstra's algorithm in Section 10.4.

As for prerequisites, students in an algorithms course generally have at least a little background in programming (including, for example, the use of arrays and recursion) and in mathematical reasoning (such as proofs by induction and by contradiction). Readers can level up their programming and mathematical skills with any number of free online resources (see www.algorithmsilluminated.org for specific recommendations). Appendices A and B also offer quick reviews of induction and discrete probability, respectively. Alternatively, readers without any programming experience can learn the basics of algorithm design and analysis from this book at the level of pseudocode descriptions (if not concrete implementations), and those with little mathematical background can focus squarely on algorithm design techniques (if not detailed algorithm analysis).

I've recorded over 200 YouTube videos that cover in detail every section of the book, as well as additional advanced content (on Karger's random contraction algorithm, path compression in disjoint set data structures, Johnson's all-pairs shortest-path algorithm, and more). These videos, which are catalogued at www.algorithmsilluminated.org, can serve an instructor in three different ways: (i) as part of a flipped classroom, with students watching lecture videos in advance of class time, which can then be used for discussion and problem-solving exercises; (ii) as a way to help students fill in missing prerequisites without taking up class time; and (iii) as supplementary material above and beyond what is covered during class time (perhaps for an honors section or extra credit).

Additional Features and Resources

This book is based on online courses that are currently running on the Coursera and EdX platforms. I've made several resources available to help you replicate as much of the online course experience as you like.

Videos.   If you're more in the mood to watch and listen than to read, check out the YouTube video playlists available at www.algorithmsilluminated.org. These videos feature yours truly teaching all the topics in this book, as well as additional advanced topics. I hope they exude a contagious enthusiasm for algorithms that, alas, is impossible to replicate fully on the printed page.

Quizzes.   How can you know if you're truly absorbing the concepts in this book? Over 100 quizzes with solutions and explanations are scattered throughout the text; when you encounter one, I encourage you to pause and think about the answer before reading on.

End-of-chapter problems.   At the end of each chapter, you'll find several relatively straightforward questions that test your understanding, followed by harder and more open-ended challenge problems. Hints or solutions to all of these problems (as indicated by an "*(H)*" or "*(S)*," respectively) are included at the end of the book. Readers can interact with me and each other about the end-of-chapter problems through the book's discussion forum (see below).

Programming problems.   Most of the chapters conclude with suggested programming projects whose goal is to help you develop a detailed understanding of an algorithm by creating your own working implementation of it. Data sets, along with test cases and their solutions, can be found at www.algorithmsilluminated.org.

Discussion forums.   A big reason for the success of online courses is the opportunities they provide for participants to help each other understand the course material and debug programs through discussion forums. Readers of this book have the same opportunity via the forums available at www.algorithmsilluminated.org.

Acknowledgments

This book would not exist without the passion and hunger supplied by the hundreds of thousands of participants in my algorithms courses over the years. I am particularly grateful to those who supplied detailed feedback on earlier drafts: Tonya Blust, Yuan Cao, Lauren Cowles, Leslie Damon, Tyler Dae Devlin, Roman Gafiteanu, Carlos Guia, Blanca Huergo, Jim Humelsine, Tim Kearns, Vladimir Kokshenev, Bayram Kuliyev, Patrick Monkelban, Kyle Schiller, Nissanka Wickremasinghe, Clayton Wong, Lexin Ye, Daniel Zingaro, several anonymous reviewers, and many pseudonymous contributors to the book's discussion forums. Thanks also to several experts who provided technical advice: Amir Abboud, Vincent Conitzer, Christian Kroer, Aviad Rubinstein, and Ilya Segal.

I always appreciate suggestions and corrections from readers. These are best communicated through the discussion forums mentioned above.

Tim Roughgarden
New York, NY
April 2022

Part I

The Basics

Chapter 1

Introduction

The goal of this chapter is to get you excited about the study of algorithms. We begin by discussing algorithms in general and why they're so important. Then we use the problem of multiplying two integers to illustrate how algorithmic ingenuity can improve on more straightforward or naive solutions. We then discuss the `MergeSort` algorithm in detail, for several reasons: it's a practical and famous algorithm that you should know; it's a good warm-up to get you ready for more intricate algorithms; and it's the canonical introduction to the "divide-and-conquer" algorithm design paradigm. The chapter concludes by describing several guiding principles for how we'll analyze algorithms throughout the rest of the book.

1.1 Why Study Algorithms?

Let me begin by justifying this book's existence and giving you some reasons why you should be highly motivated to learn about algorithms. So what is an algorithm, anyway? It's a set of well-defined rules—a recipe, in effect—for solving some computational problem. Maybe you have a bunch of numbers and you want to rearrange them so that they're in sorted order. Maybe you have a road map and you want to compute the shortest path from some origin to some destination. Maybe you need to complete several tasks before certain deadlines, and you want to know in what order you should finish the tasks so that you complete them all by their respective deadlines.

So why study algorithms?

Important for all other branches of computer science.   First, understanding the basics of algorithms and the closely related field of data structures is essential for doing serious work in pretty much any branch of computer science. For example, during my years as a professor at Stanford University, every degree the computer science department offered (B.S., M.S., and Ph.D.) required an algorithms course. To name just a few examples:

1. Routing protocols in communication networks piggyback on classical shortest-path algorithms.

2. Public-key cryptography relies on efficient number-theoretic algorithms.

3. Computer graphics requires the computational primitives supplied by geometric algorithms.

4. Database indices rely on balanced search tree data structures.

5. Computational biologists use dynamic programming algorithms to measure genome similarity.

6. Clustering algorithms are one of the most ubiquitous tools in unsupervised machine learning.

And the list goes on.

Driver of technological innovation.   Second, algorithms play a key role in modern technological innovation. To give just one obvious example, search engines use a tapestry of algorithms to efficiently compute the relevance of various Web pages to a given search query. The most famous such algorithm is the `PageRank` algorithm, which gave birth to Google. Indeed, in a December 2010 report to the United States White House, the President's council of advisers on science and technology wrote the following:

> "Everyone knows Moore's Law — a prediction made in 1965 by Intel co-founder Gordon Moore that the density of transistors in integrated circuits would continue to double every 1 to 2 years... in many areas, performance gains due to improvements in algorithms have vastly exceeded even the dramatic performance gains due to increased processor speed."[1]

Lens on other sciences.   Third, although this is beyond the scope of this book, algorithms are increasingly used to provide a novel "lens" on processes outside of computer science and technology. For example, the study of quantum computation has provided a new computational viewpoint on quantum mechanics. Price fluctuations in economic markets can be fruitfully viewed as an algorithmic process. Even evolution can be thought of as a surprisingly effective search algorithm.

Good for the brain.   Back when I was a student, my favorite classes were always the challenging ones that, after I struggled through them, left me feeling a few IQ points smarter than when I started. I hope this material provides a similar experience for you.

Fun!   Finally, I hope that by the end of the book you can see why the design and analysis of algorithms is simply fun. It's an endeavor that requires a rare blend of precision and creativity. It can certainly be frustrating at times, but it's also highly addictive. And let's not forget that you've been learning about algorithms since you were a little kid.

1.2   Integer Multiplication

1.2.1   Problems and Solutions

When you were in third grade or so, you probably learned an algorithm for multiplying two numbers—a well-defined set of rules for transforming an input (two numbers) into an output (their product). It's important to distinguish between two different things: the description of the *problem being solved*, and that of the *method of solution* (that is, the algorithm for the problem). In this book, we'll repeatedly follow the pattern of first introducing a computational problem (the inputs and desired output), and then describing one or more algorithms that solve the problem.

---

[1]Excerpt from Report to the President and Congress: Designing a Digital Future, December 2010 (page 71).

1.2.2   The Integer Multiplication Problem

In the integer multiplication problem, the input is two n-digit numbers, which we'll call x and y. The length n of x and y could be any positive integer, but I encourage you to think of n as large, in the thousands or even more.[2] (Perhaps you're implementing a cryptographic application that must manipulate very large numbers.) The desired output in the integer multiplication problem is the product $x \cdot y$.

Problem: Integer Multiplication

Input: Two n-digit nonnegative integers, x and y.

Output: The product $x \cdot y$.

1.2.3   The Grade-School Algorithm

Having defined the computational problem precisely, we describe an algorithm that solves it—the same algorithm you learned in third grade. We will assess the performance of this algorithm through the number of "primitive operations" it performs, as a function of the number of digits n in each input number. For now, let's think of a primitive operation as any of the following: (i) adding two single-digit numbers; (ii) multiplying two single-digit numbers; or (iii) adding a zero to the beginning or end of a number.

To jog your memory, consider the concrete example of multiplying $x = 5678$ and $y = 1234$ (so $n = 4$). See also Figure 1.1. The algorithm first computes the "partial product" of the first number and the last digit of the second number $5678 \cdot 4 = 22712$. Computing this partial product boils down to multiplying each of the digits of the first number by 4, and adding in "carries" as necessary.[3] When computing the next partial product ($5678 \cdot 3 = 17034$), we do the same thing, shifting the result one digit to the left, effectively adding a "0" at the end. And so on for the final two partial products. The final step is to add up all the partial products.

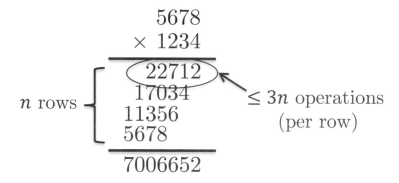

Figure 1.1: The grade-school integer multiplication algorithm.

---

[2]If you want to multiply numbers with different lengths (like 1234 and 56), a simple hack is to just add some zeros to the beginning of the smaller number (for example, treat 56 as 0056). Alternatively, the algorithms we'll discuss can be modified to accommodate numbers with different lengths.

[3]$8 \cdot 4 = 32$, carry the 3, $7 \cdot 4 = 28$, plus 3 is 31, carry the 3, . . .

Back in third grade, you probably accepted that this algorithm is *correct*, meaning that no matter what numbers x and y you start with, provided that all intermediate computations are done properly, it eventually terminates with the product $x \cdot y$ of the two input numbers. That is, you're never going to get a wrong answer, and the algorithm can't loop forever.

1.2.4   Analysis of the Number of Operations

Your third-grade teacher might not have discussed the number of primitive operations needed to carry out this procedure to its conclusion. To compute the first partial product, we multiplied 4 times each of the digits $5, 6, 7, 8$ of the first number. This is four primitive operations. Each carry might force us to add a single-digit number to a double-digit one, for another two primitive operations. In general, computing a partial product involves n multiplications (one per digit) and at most $2n$ additions (at most two per carry), for a total of at most $3n$ primitive operations. There's nothing special about the first partial product: every partial product requires at most $3n$ operations. Because there are n partial products—one per digit of the second number—computing all of them requires at most $n \cdot 3n = 3n^2$ primitive operations. We still have to add them all up to compute the final answer, but this takes a comparable number of operations (at most another $3n^2$, as you should check). Summarizing:

$$\textbf{total number of operations} \leq \underbrace{\textbf{constant}}_{\textbf{=6}} \cdot \textbf{n}^2.$$

Thinking about how the amount of work the algorithm performs *scales* as the input numbers grow bigger and bigger, we see that the work required grows quadratically with the number of digits. If you double the length of the input numbers, the work required jumps by a factor of 4. Quadruple their length and it jumps by a factor of 16, and so on.

1.2.5   Can We Do Better?

Depending on what type of third-grader you were, you might well have accepted this procedure as the unique or at least optimal way to multiply two numbers. If you want to be a serious algorithm designer, you'll need to grow out of that kind of obedient timidity. The classic algorithms book by Aho, Hopcroft, and Ullman, after iterating through a number of algorithm design paradigms, has this to say:

> "Perhaps the most important principle for the good algorithm designer is to refuse to be content."[4]

Or as I like to put it, every algorithm designer should adopt the mantra:

> *Can we do better?*

This question is particularly apropos when you're faced with a naive or straightforward solution to a computational problem. In the third grade, you might not have asked if one could do better than the straightforward integer multiplication algorithm. Now is the time to ask, and answer, this question.

---

[4] Alfred V. Aho, John E. Hopcroft, and Jeffrey D. Ullman, *The Design and Analysis of Computer Algorithms*, Addison-Wesley, 1974, page 70.

1.3   Karatsuba Multiplication

The algorithm design space is surprisingly rich, and there are certainly other interesting methods of multiplying two integers beyond what you learned in the third grade. This section describes a method called *Karatsuba multiplication*.[5]

1.3.1   A Concrete Example

To get a feel for Karatsuba multiplication, let's re-use our previous example with $x = 5678$ and $y = 1234$. We're going to execute a sequence of steps, quite different from the grade-school algorithm, culminating in the product $x \cdot y$. The sequence of steps should strike you as very mysterious, like pulling a rabbit out of a hat; later in the section we'll explain exactly what Karatsuba multiplication is and why it works. The key point to appreciate now is that there's a dazzling array of options for solving computational problems like integer multiplication.

First, to regard the first and second halves of x as numbers in their own right, we give them the names a and b (so $a = 56$ and $b = 78$). Similarly, c and d denote 12 and 34, respectively (Figure 1.2).

Figure 1.2: Thinking of four-digit numbers as pairs of two-digit numbers.

Next we'll perform a sequence of operations that involve only the double-digit numbers a, b, c, and d, and finally collect all the terms together in a magical way that results in the product of x and y.

Step 1:   Compute $a \cdot c = 56 \cdot 12$, which is 672 (as you're welcome to check).

Step 2:   Compute $b \cdot d = 78 \cdot 34 = 2652$.

The next two steps are still more inscrutable.

Step 3:   Compute $(a + b) \cdot (c + d) = 134 \cdot 46 = 6164$.

Step 4:   Subtract the results of the first two steps from the result of the third step: $6164 - 672 - 2652 = 2840$.

Finally, we add up the results of steps 1, 2, and 4, but only after adding four trailing zeroes to the answer in step 1 and two trailing zeroes to the answer in step 4.

[5]Discovered in 1960 by Anatoly Karatsuba, who at the time was a 23-year-old student.

Step 5:   Compute $10^4 \cdot 672 + 10^2 \cdot 2840 + 2652 = 6720000 + 284000 + 2652 = 7006652$.

This is exactly the same (correct) result computed by the grade-school algorithm in Section 1.2!

You should not have any intuition about what just happened. Rather, I hope that you feel some mixture of bafflement and intrigue, and appreciate the fact that there seem to be fundamentally different algorithms for multiplying integers than the one you learned as a kid. Once you realize how rich the space of algorithms is, you have to wonder: can we do better than the third-grade algorithm? Does the algorithm above already do better?

1.3.2   A Recursive Algorithm

Before tackling full-blown Karatsuba multiplication, let's explore a simpler recursive approach to integer multiplication.[6] A recursive algorithm for integer multiplication presumably involves multiplications of numbers with fewer digits (like 12, 34, 56, and 78 in the computation above).

In general, a number x with an even number n of digits can be expressed in terms of two $n/2$-digit numbers, its first half a and second half b:

$$x = 10^{n/2} \cdot a + b.$$

Similarly, we can write

$$y = 10^{n/2} \cdot c + d.$$

To compute the product of x and y, let's use the two expressions above and multiply out:

$$\begin{aligned} x \cdot y &= (10^{n/2} \cdot a + b) \cdot (10^{n/2} \cdot c + d) \\ &= 10^n \cdot (a \cdot c) + 10^{n/2} \cdot (a \cdot d + b \cdot c) + b \cdot d. \end{aligned} \tag{1.1}$$

Note that all of the multiplications in (1.1) are either between pairs of $n/2$-digit numbers or involve a power of 10.[7]

The expression (1.1) suggests a recursive approach to multiplying two numbers. To compute the product $x \cdot y$, we compute the expression (1.1). The four relevant products ($a \cdot c$, $a \cdot d$, $b \cdot c$, and $b \cdot d$) all concern numbers with fewer than n digits, so we can compute each of them recursively. Once our four recursive calls come back to us with their answers, we can compute the expression (1.1) in the obvious way: tack on n trailing zeroes to $a \cdot c$, add $a \cdot d$ and $b \cdot c$ (using grade-school addition) and tack on $n/2$ trailing zeroes to the result, and finally add these two expressions to $b \cdot d$.[8] We summarize this algorithm, which we'll call `RecIntMult`, in the following pseudocode.[9]

---

[6]I'm assuming you've heard of recursion as part of your programming background. A recursive procedure is one that invokes itself as a subroutine with a smaller input, until a base case is reached.

[7]For simplicity, we are assuming that n is a power of 2. A simple hack for enforcing this assumption is to add an appropriate number of leading zeroes to x and y, which at most doubles their lengths. Alternatively, when n is odd, it's also fine to break x and y into two numbers with almost equal lengths.

[8]Recursive algorithms also need one or more base cases, so that they don't keep calling themselves for the rest of time. Here, the base case is: if x and y are 1-digit numbers, multiply them in one primitive operation and return the result.

[9]In pseudocode, we use "=" to denote an equality test, and ":=" to denote a variable assignment.

RecIntMult

Input: two n-digit positive integers x and y.
Output: the product $x \cdot y$.
Assumption: n is a power of 2.

---

if $n = 1$ **then**   // base case
    compute $x \cdot y$ in one step and return the result
else   // recursive case
    $a, b :=$ first and second halves of x
    $c, d :=$ first and second halves of y
    recursively compute $ac := a \cdot c$, $ad := a \cdot d$, $bc := b \cdot c$, and
      $bd := b \cdot d$
    compute $10^n \cdot ac + 10^{n/2} \cdot (ad + bc) + bd$ using grade-school
    addition and return the result

Is the RecIntMult algorithm faster or slower than the grade-school algorithm? You shouldn't necessarily have any intuition about this question, and the answer will have to wait until Chapter 4.

1.3.3 Karatsuba Multiplication

Karatsuba multiplication is an optimized version of the RecIntMult algorithm. We again start from the expansion (1.1) of $x \cdot y$ in terms of a, b, c, and d. The RecIntMult algorithm uses four recursive calls, one for each of the products in (1.1) between $n/2$-digit numbers. But *we don't care about $a \cdot d$ or $b \cdot c$*, except inasmuch as we care about their sum $a \cdot d + b \cdot c$. With only three quantities that we care about—$a \cdot c$, $a \cdot d + b \cdot c$, and $b \cdot d$—can we get away with only three recursive calls? To see that we can, first use two recursive calls to compute $a \cdot c$ and $b \cdot d$, as before.

Step 1: Recursively compute $a \cdot c$.

Step 2: Recursively compute $b \cdot d$.

Instead of recursively computing $a \cdot d$ or $b \cdot c$, we recursively compute the product of $a + b$ and $c + d$.[10]

Step 3: Compute $a + b$ and $c + d$ using grade-school addition, and recursively compute $(a + b) \cdot (c + d)$.

The key trick in Karatsuba multiplication goes back to the early 19th-century mathematician Carl Friedrich Gauss, who was thinking about multiplying complex numbers. Subtracting the results of the first two steps from the result of the third step gives exactly what we want, the middle coefficient in (1.1) of $a \cdot d + b \cdot c$:

$$\underbrace{(a + b) \cdot (c + d)}_{=a \cdot c + a \cdot d + b \cdot c + b \cdot d} - a \cdot c - b \cdot d = a \cdot d + b \cdot c.$$

---

[10]The numbers $a + b$ and $c + d$ might have as many as $(n/2) + 1$ digits, but the algorithm still works fine.

Step 4: Subtract the results of the first two steps from the result of the third step to obtain $a \cdot d + b \cdot c$.

The final step computes (1.1), as in the `RecIntMult` algorithm.

Step 5: Compute (1.1) by adding up the results of steps 1, 2, and 4, after adding n trailing zeroes to the answer in step 1 and $n/2$ trailing zeroes to the answer in step 4.

Karatsuba

Input: two n-digit positive integers x and y.
Output: the product $x \cdot y$.
Assumption: n is a power of 2.

---

if $n = 1$ **then**   // base case
    compute $x \cdot y$ in one step and return the result
else   // recursive case
    $a, b :=$ first and second halves of x
    $c, d :=$ first and second halves of y
    compute $p := a + b$ and $q := c + d$ using grade-school addition
    recursively compute $ac := a \cdot c$, $bd := b \cdot d$, and $pq := p \cdot q$
    compute $adbc := pq - ac - bd$ using grade-school addition
    compute $10^n \cdot ac + 10^{n/2} \cdot adbc + bd$ using grade-school
      addition and return the result

Thus Karatsuba multiplication makes only three recursive calls! Saving a recursive call should save on the overall running time, but by how much? Is the `Karatsuba` algorithm faster than the grade-school multiplication algorithm? The answer is far from obvious, but it is an easy application of the tools you'll acquire in Chapter 4 for analyzing the running time of such "divide-and-conquer" algorithms.

On Pseudocode

This book explains algorithms using a mixture of high-level pseudocode and English (as in this section). I'm assuming that you have the skills to translate such high-level descriptions into working code in your favorite programming language. Several other books and resources on the Web offer concrete implementations of various algorithms in specific programming languages.

    The first benefit of emphasizing high-level descriptions over language-specific implementations is flexibility: while I assume familiarity with *some* programming language, I don't care which one. Second, this approach promotes the understanding of algorithms at a deep and conceptual level, unencumbered by low-level details. Seasoned programmers and computer scientists generally think and communicate about algorithms at a similarly high level.

Still, there is no substitute for the detailed understanding of an algorithm that comes from providing your own working implementation of it. I strongly encourage you to implement as many of the algorithms in this book as you have time for. (It's also a great excuse to pick up a new programming language!) For guidance, see the end-of-chapter Programming Problems and supporting test cases.

1.4 `MergeSort`: The Algorithm

This section and the next provide our first taste of analyzing the running time of a non-trivial algorithm—the famous `MergeSort` algorithm.

1.4.1 Motivation

`MergeSort` is a relatively ancient algorithm, and was certainly known to John von Neumann as early as 1945. Why begin a modern course on algorithms with such an old example?

Oldie but a goodie.   Despite being over 70 years old, `MergeSort` is still one of the methods of choice for sorting. It's used all the time in practice, and is the default sorting algorithm in a number of programming libraries.

Canonical divide-and-conquer algorithm.   The "divide-and-conquer" algorithm design paradigm is a general approach to solving problems, with applications in many different domains. The basic idea is to break your problem into smaller subproblems, solve the subproblems recursively, and finally combine the solutions to the subproblems into one for the original problem. `MergeSort` is an ideal introduction to the divide-and-conquer paradigm, the benefits it offers, and the analysis challenges it presents.

Calibrate your preparation.   Our `MergeSort` discussion will give you a good indication of whether your current skill set is a good match for this book. My assumption is that you have the programming and mathematical backgrounds to (with some work) translate the high-level idea of `MergeSort` into a working program in your favorite programming language and to follow our running time analysis of the algorithm. If this and the next section make sense, you're in good shape for the rest of the book.

Motivates guiding principles for algorithm analysis.   Our running time analysis of `MergeSort` exposes a number of more general guiding principles, such as the quest for running time bounds that hold for every input of a given size, and the importance of the rate of growth of an algorithm's running time (as a function of the input size).

Warm-up for the master method.   We'll analyze `MergeSort` using the "recursion tree method," which is a way of tallying up the operations performed by a recursive algorithm. Chapter 4 builds on these ideas and culminates with the "master method," a powerful and easy-to-use tool for bounding the running time of many different divide-and-conquer algorithms, including the `RecIntMult` and `Karatsuba` algorithms of Section 1.3.

1.4.2   Sorting

Look around and you'll notice that computers seem pretty good at sorting things instanta-neously. Think of the list of contacts on your phone. Are they listed in the order that you entered them? Of course not—that would be annoying, so they're instead sorted alphabet-ically for easy reference. Meanwhile, your favorite spreadsheet program has no trouble sorting a large file according to whatever criterion you want. How do they do it?

Here's a canonical version of the sorting problem:

Problem: Sorting

Input: An array of n numbers, in arbitrary order.

Output: An array of the same numbers, sorted from smallest to largest.

For example, given the input array

5	4	1	8	7	2	6	3

the desired output array is

1	2	3	4	5	6	7	8

In the example above, the eight numbers in the input array are distinct. Sorting isn't really any harder when there are duplicates, and it can even be easier. But to keep the discussion as simple as possible, let's assume—among friends—that the numbers in the input array are always distinct. I strongly encourage you to think about how our sorting algorithms need to be modified (if at all) to handle duplicates.[11]

If you don't care about optimizing the running time, it's not too difficult to come up with a correct sorting algorithm. Perhaps the simplest approach is to first scan through the input array to identify the minimum element and copy it over to the first element of the output array; then do another scan to identify and copy over the second-smallest element; and so on. This algorithm is called `SelectionSort`. You may have heard of `InsertionSort`, which can be viewed as a slicker implementation of the same idea of iteratively growing a prefix of the sorted output array. You might also know `BubbleSort`, in which you identify adjacent pairs of elements that are out of order, and perform repeated swaps until the entire array is sorted. All of these algorithms have quadratic running times, meaning that—analogous to the grade-school multiplication algorithm in Section 1.2.3—the number of operations performed on arrays of length n scales with n^2, the square of the input length.

---

[11]In practice, there is often data (called the *value*) associated with each number (which is called the *key*). For example, you might want to sort employee records (with the name, salary, etc.), using social security numbers as keys. We focus on sorting the keys, with the understanding that each key retains its associated data.

Can we do better? By using the divide-and-conquer algorithm design paradigm, the `MergeSort` algorithm improves dramatically over these more straightforward sorting algorithms.[12]

1.4.3 An Example

The easiest way to understand `MergeSort` is through a picture of a concrete example (Figure 1.3). We'll use the input array from Section 1.4.2.

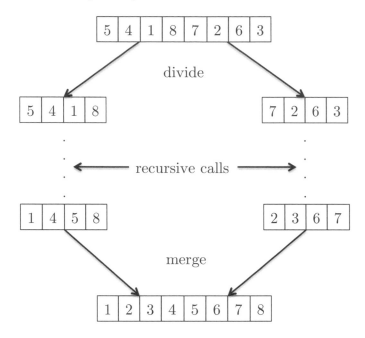

Figure 1.3: A bird's-eye view of `MergeSort` on a concrete example.

As a recursive divide-and-conquer algorithm, `MergeSort` calls itself on smaller arrays. The simplest way to decompose a sorting problem into smaller sorting problems is to break the input array in half. The first and second halves are each sorted recursively. For example, in Figure 1.3, the first and second halves of the input array are $[5, 4, 1, 8]$ and $[7, 2, 6, 3]$. By the magic of recursion (or induction, if you prefer), the first recursive call correctly sorts the first half, returning the array $[1, 4, 5, 8]$. The second recursive call returns the array $[2, 3, 6, 7]$. The final "merge" step combines these two sorted arrays of length 4 into a single sorted array of all 8 numbers. Details of this step are given below; the basic idea is to walk indices down each of the sorted subarrays, populating the output array from left to right in sorted order.

1.4.4 Pseudocode

The picture in Figure 1.3 suggests the following pseudocode, with two recursive calls and a merge step, for the general problem. As usual, our description cannot necessarily be translated line by line into working code (though it's pretty close).

---

[12]While generally dominated by `MergeSort`, `InsertionSort` is still useful in practice in certain cases, especially for small input sizes.

MergeSort

Input: array A of n distinct integers.
Output: array with the same integers, sorted from smallest to largest.

```
// ignoring base cases
```
$C :=$ recursively sort first half of A
$D :=$ recursively sort second half of A
return `Merge` (C,D)

There are several deliberate omissions from the pseudocode that deserve comment. As a recursive algorithm, there should also be one or more base cases, in which there is no further recursion and the answer is returned directly. So if the input array A contains only 0 or 1 elements, `MergeSort` returns it (it is already sorted). The pseudocode does not detail what "first half" and "second half" mean when n is odd, but the obvious interpretation (with one "half" having one more element than the other) works fine. Finally, the pseudocode ignores the implementation details of how to actually pass the two subarrays to their respective recursive calls. These details depend somewhat on the programming language. The point of high-level pseudocode is to ignore such details and focus on the concepts that transcend any particular programming language.

1.4.5 The `Merge` Subroutine

How should we implement the `Merge` step? At this point, the two recursive calls have done their work and we have in our possession two sorted subarrays C and D of length $n/2$. The idea is to traverse both the sorted subarrays in order and populate the output array from left to right in sorted order.[13]

Merge

Input: sorted arrays C and D (length $n/2$ each).
Output: sorted array B (length n).
Simplifying assumption: n is even.

---

1   $i := 1$
2   $j := 1$
3   **for** $k := 1$ to n **do**
4   **if** $C[i] < D[j]$ **then**
5         $B[k] := C[i]$ `// populate output array`
6         $i := i + 1$ `// increment i`
7   **else**   `// D[j] < C[i]`
8         $B[k] := D[j]$
9         $j := j + 1$

---

[13] Unless otherwise noted, we number our array entries beginning with 1 (rather than 0), and use the syntax "$A[i]$" for the ith entry of an array A. These details vary across programming languages.

We traverse the output array using the index k, and the sorted subarrays with the indices i and j. All three arrays are traversed from left to right. The for loop in line 3 implements the pass over the output array. In the first iteration, the subroutine identifies the minimum element in either C or D and copies it over to the first position of the output array B. The minimum element overall is either in C (in which case it's $C[1]$, because C is sorted) or in D (in which case it's $D[1]$, because D is sorted). Advancing the appropriate index (i or j) effectively removes from further consideration the element just copied, and the process is then repeated to identify the smallest element remaining in C or D (the second-smallest overall). In general, the smallest element not yet copied over to B is either $C[i]$ or $D[j]$; the subroutine explicitly checks to see which one is smaller and proceeds accordingly. Because every iteration copies over the smallest element still under consideration in C or D, the output array is indeed populated in sorted order.

As usual, our pseudocode is intentionally a bit sloppy, to emphasize the forest over the trees. A full implementation should also keep track of when the traversal of C or D falls off the end of the array, at which point the remaining elements of the other array are copied into the final entries of B (in order). Now is a good time to work through your own implementation of the `MergeSort` algorithm.

1.5 `MergeSort`: The Analysis

What's the running time of the `MergeSort` algorithm, as a function of the length n of the input array? Is it faster than more straightforward methods of sorting, such as `SelectionSort`, `InsertionSort`, and `BubbleSort`? By "running time," we mean the number of lines of code executed in a concrete implementation of the algorithm. Think of walking line by line through this implementation using a debugger, one "primitive operation" at a time. We're interested in the number of steps the debugger takes before the program completes.

1.5.1 Running Time of `Merge`

Analyzing the running time of the `MergeSort` algorithm is an intimidating task, as it's a recursive algorithm that calls itself over and over. So let's warm up with the simpler task of understanding the number of operations performed by a single invocation of the `Merge` subroutine when called on two sorted arrays of length $\ell/2$ each. We can do this directly, by inspecting the code in Section 1.4.5 (where n corresponds to ℓ). First, lines 1 and 2 each perform an initialization, and we'll count this as two operations. Then, we have a for loop that executes a total of ℓ times. Each iteration of the loop performs a comparison in line 4, an assignment in either line 5 or line 8, and an increment in either line 6 or line 9. The loop index k also needs to get incremented each loop iteration. This means that 4 primitive operations are performed for each of the ℓ iterations of the loop.[14] Totaling up, we conclude that the `Merge` subroutine performs at most $4\ell + 2$ operations to merge two sorted arrays of length $\ell/2$ each. Let me abuse our friendship further with a true but sloppy inequality that will make our lives easier: for every positive integer $\ell \geq 1$, we have $4\ell + 2 \leq 4\ell + 2\ell = 6\ell$.

---

[14]One could quibble with the choice of 4. Does comparing the loop index k to its upper bound also count as an additional operation each iteration, for a total of 5? Section 1.6 explains why such differences in accounting don't really matter. So let's agree, among friends, that it's 4 primitive operations per iteration.

That is, 6ℓ is also a valid upper bound on the number of operations performed by the Merge subroutine.

Lemma 1.1 (Running Time of Merge) *For every pair of sorted input arrays C, D of length $\ell/2$, the Merge subroutine performs at most 6ℓ operations.*

On Lemmas, Theorems, and the Like

In mathematical writing, the most important technical statements are labeled *theorems*. A *lemma* is a technical statement that assists with the proof of a theorem (much as Merge assists with the implementation of MergeSort). A *corollary* is a statement that follows immediately from an already-proven result, such as a special case of a theorem. We use the term *proposition* for stand-alone technical statements that are not particularly important in their own right.

1.5.2   Running Time of MergeSort

How can we go from the straightforward analysis of the Merge subroutine to an analysis of MergeSort, a recursive algorithm that spawns further invocations of itself? Especially terrifying is the rapid proliferation of recursive calls, the number of which is blowing up exponentially with the depth of the recursion. The one thing we have going for us is the fact that every recursive call is passed an input substantially smaller than the one we started with. There's a tension between two competing forces: on the one hand, the explosion of different subproblems that need to be solved; and on the other, the ever-shrinking inputs for which these subproblems are responsible. Reconciling these two forces will drive our analysis of MergeSort. In the end, we'll prove the following concrete and useful upper bound on the number of operations performed by MergeSort (across all its recursive calls).

Theorem 1.2 (Running Time of MergeSort) *For every input array of length $n \geq 1$, the MergeSort algorithm performs at most*

$$6n \log_2 n + 6n$$

operations, where $\log_2$ denotes the base-2 logarithm.

On Logarithms

Some people are unnecessarily frightened by the appearance of a logarithm, which is actually a very down-to-earth concept. For a positive integer n, $\log_2 n$ just means the following: type n into a calculator, and count the number of times you need to divide it by 2 before the result is 1 or less.[a] For example, it takes five divide-by-twos to bring 32 down to 1, so $\log_2 32 = 5$. Ten divide-by-twos bring 1024 down to 1, so $\log_2 1024 = 10$. These examples make it intuitively clear that $\log_2 n$ is much less than n (compare 10 vs. 1024), especially as n grows large. A plot confirms this intuition

---

(Figure 1.4).

---

[a]To be pedantic, $\log_2 n$ is not an integer if n is not a power of 2, and what we have described is really $\log_2 n$ rounded up to the nearest integer. We can ignore this minor distinction.

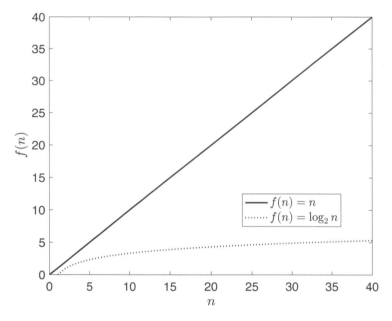

Figure 1.4: The base-2 logarithm function $f(n) = \log_2 n$ grows much more slowly than the linear function $f(n) = n$. Other logarithm bases lead to qualitatively similar pictures.

Theorem 1.2 is a win for the `MergeSort` algorithm and showcases the benefits of the divide-and-conquer algorithm design paradigm. We mentioned that the running times of simpler sorting algorithms, like `SelectionSort`, `InsertionSort`, and `BubbleSort`, depend *quadratically* on the input size n, meaning that the number of operations required scales as a constant times n^2. In Theorem 1.2, one of these factors of n is replaced by $\log_2 n$. As suggested by Figure 1.4, this means that `MergeSort` typically runs much faster than the simpler sorting algorithms, especially as n grows large.[15]

1.5.3   Proof of Theorem 1.2

We now do a full running time analysis of `MergeSort`, thereby substantiating the claim that a recursive divide-and-conquer approach results in a faster sorting algorithm than more straightforward methods. For simplicity, we assume that the input array length n is a power of 2. This assumption can be removed with minor additional work.

The plan for proving the running time bound in Theorem 1.2 is to use a *recursion tree*; see Figure 1.5.[16] The idea of the recursion tree method is to write out all the work done by a

---

[15]See Section 1.6.3 for further discussion of this point.

[16]For some reason, computer scientists seem to think that trees grow downward.

recursive algorithm in a tree structure, with nodes of the tree corresponding to recursive calls, and the children of a node corresponding to the recursive calls made by that node. This tree structure provides us with a principled way to tally up all the work done by MergeSort across all its recursive calls.

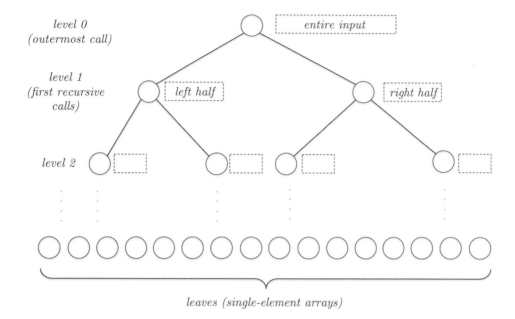

leaves (single-element arrays)

Figure 1.5: A recursion tree for MergeSort. Nodes correspond to recursive calls. Level 0 corresponds to the outermost call to MergeSort, level 1 to its recursive calls, and so on.

The root of the recursion tree corresponds to the outermost call to MergeSort, where the input is the original input array. We'll call this level 0 of the tree. Because each invocation of MergeSort spawns two recursive calls, the tree is binary (that is, with two children per node). Level 1 of the tree has two nodes, corresponding to the two recursive calls made by the outermost call, one for the left half of the input array and one for the right half. Each of the level-1 recursive calls itself makes two recursive calls, each operating on a distinct quarter of the original input array. This process continues until eventually the recursion bottoms out with arrays of length 1 (the base cases).

Quiz 1.1

Roughly how many levels does this recursion tree have, as a function of the length n of the input array?

    a) A constant number (independent of n)

    b) $\log_2 n$

    c) $\sqrt{n}$

d) n

(See Section 1.5.4 for the solution and discussion.)

This recursion tree suggests a particularly convenient way to account for the work done by `MergeSort`, which is level by level. To implement this idea, we need to understand two things: the number of distinct subproblems at a given recursion level j, and the length of the input to each of these subproblems.

Quiz 1.2

What is the pattern? Fill in the blanks in the following statement: at each level $j = 0, 1, 2, \ldots$ of the recursion tree, there are [blank] subproblems, each operating on a subarray of length [blank].

a) 2^j and 2^j, respectively

b) $n/2^j$ and $n/2^j$, respectively

c) 2^j and $n/2^j$, respectively

d) $n/2^j$ and 2^j, respectively

(See Section 1.5.4 for the solution and discussion.)

Let's now put this pattern to use and tally all the operations that `MergeSort` performs. We proceed level by level, so fix a level j of the recursion tree. How much work is done by the level-j recursive calls, not counting the work done by their recursive calls at deeper levels? Inspecting the `MergeSort` code, we see that it does only three things: make two recursive calls and invoke the `Merge` subroutine on the results. Thus, ignoring the work done by its recursive calls, the work done in a level-j subproblem is just the work performed by `Merge`. This we already understand from Lemma 1.1: at most 6ℓ operations, where ℓ is the length of the input array in this subproblem.

To put everything together, we can express the total work done by level-j recursive calls (not counting later recursive calls) as

$$\underbrace{\text{\# of level-}j\text{ subproblems}}_{=2^j} \times \underbrace{\text{work per level-}j\text{ subproblem}}_{=6n/2^j} .$$

Using the solution to Quiz 1.2, we know that the first term equals 2^j, and the input length in each such subproblem is $n/2^j$. Taking $\ell = n/2^j$, Lemma 1.1 implies that each level-j subproblem performs at most $6n/2^j$ operations. We conclude that at most

$$2^j \cdot \frac{6n}{2^j} = 6n$$

operations are performed across all the recursive calls at the jth recursion level.

Remarkably, our bound on the work done at a given level j is independent of j! That is, each level of the recursion tree contributes the same number of operations to the analysis. The reason for this is a perfect equilibrium between two competing forces—the number of subproblems doubles every level, while the amount of work performed per subproblem halves every level.

We're interested in the number of operations performed across *all* levels of the recursion tree. By the solution to Quiz 1.1, the recursion tree has $\log_2 n + 1$ levels (levels 0 through $\log_2 n$, inclusive). Using our bound of $6n$ operations per level, we can bound the total number of operations by

$$\underbrace{\text{number of levels}}_{=\log_2 n+1} \times \underbrace{\text{work per level}}_{\leq 6n} \leq 6n \log_2 n + 6n,$$

matching the bound claimed in Theorem 1.2. $\mathcal{QED}$[17]

On Primitive Operations

We measure the running time of an algorithm like MergeSort in terms of the number of "primitive operations" performed. Intuitively, a primitive operation performs a simple task (like adding, comparing, or copying) while touching a small number of simple variables (like 32-bit integers).[18] Warning: in some high-level programming languages, a single line of code can mask a large number of primitive operations. For example, a line of code that touches every element of a long array translates to a number of primitive operations proportional to the array's length.

1.5.4   Solutions to Quizzes 1.1–1.2

Solution to Quiz 1.1

Correct answer: (b). The correct answer is $\approx \log_2 n$. The reason is that the input size decreases by a factor of two with each level of the recursion. If the input length in level 0 is n, the level-1 recursive calls operate on arrays of length $n/2$, the level-2 recursive calls on arrays of length $n/4$, and so on. The recursion bottoms out at the base cases, with input arrays of length at most one, where there are no more recursive calls. How many levels of recursion are required? The number of times you need to divide n by 2 before obtaining a number that is at most 1. For n a power of 2, this is precisely the definition of $\log_2 n$. (More generally, it is $\log_2 n$ rounded up to the nearest integer.)

Solution to Quiz 1.2

Correct answer: (c). The correct answer is that there are 2^j distinct subproblems at recursion level j, and each operates on a subarray of length $n/2^j$. For the first point, start with level 0, where there is one recursive call. There are two recursive calls at level 1, and more generally, because MergeSort calls itself twice, the number of recursive calls at each level is double the number at the previous level. This successive doubling implies

---

[17]"Q.e.d." is an abbreviation for *quod erat demonstrandum* and means "that which was to be demonstrated." In mathematical writing, it is used at the end of a proof to mark its completion.

[18]More precise definitions are possible, but we won't need them.

that there are 2^j subproblems at each level j of the recursion tree. Similarly, because every recursive call gets only half the input of the previous one, after j levels of recursion the input length has dropped to $n/2^j$. Or for a different argument, we already know that there are 2^j subproblems at level j, and the original input array (of length n) is equally partitioned among these—exactly $n/2^j$ elements per subproblem.

1.6   Guiding Principles for the Analysis of Algorithms

With our first real algorithm analysis under our belt (`MergeSort`, in Theorem 1.2), it's the right time to take a step back and make explicit three assumptions that informed our running time analysis and interpretation of it. We will adopt these three assumptions as guiding principles for how to reason about algorithms, and use them to define what we actually mean by a "fast algorithm."

The goal of these principles is to identify a sweet spot for the analysis of algorithms, one that balances accuracy with tractability. Exact running time analysis is possible only for the simplest algorithms; more generally, compromises are required. On the other hand, we don't want to throw out the baby with the bathwater—we still want our mathematical analysis to have predictive power about whether an algorithm will be fast or slow in practice. Once we find the right balance, we'll be able to prove good running time guarantees for dozens of fundamental algorithms, and these guarantees will paint an accurate picture of which algorithms tend to run faster than others.

1.6.1   Principle #1: Worst-Case Analysis

Our running time bound of $6n \log_2 n + 6n$ in Theorem 1.2 holds for *every* input array of length n, no matter what its contents. We made no assumptions about the input beyond its length n. Hypothetically, if there was an adversary whose sole purpose in life was to concoct a malevolent input designed to make `MergeSort` run as slow as possible, the $6n \log_2 n + 6n$ bound would still apply. This type of analysis is called *worst-case analysis*, as it gives a running time bound that is valid even for the "worst" inputs.

Given how naturally worst-case analysis fell out of our analysis of `MergeSort`, you might well wonder what else we could do. One alternative approach is "average-case analysis," which analyzes the average running time of an algorithm under some assumption about the relative frequencies of different inputs. For example, in the sorting problem, we could assume that all input arrays are equally likely and then study the average running time of different sorting algorithms. A second alternative is to look only at the performance of an algorithm on a small collection of "benchmark instances" that are thought to be representative of "typical" or "real-world" inputs.

Both average-case analysis and the analysis of benchmark instances can be useful when you have domain knowledge about your problem, and some understanding of which inputs are more representative than others. Worst-case analysis, in which you make absolutely no assumptions about the input, is particularly appropriate for general-purpose subroutines designed to work well across a range of application domains. To be useful to as many people as possible, this book focuses on such general-purpose subroutines and, accordingly, uses worst-case analysis to judge algorithm performance.

As a bonus, worst-case analysis is usually much more tractable mathematically than its alternatives. This is one reason why worst-case analysis naturally popped out of our `MergeSort` analysis, even though we had no a priori focus on worst-case inputs.

1.6.2   Principle #2: Big-Picture Analysis

The second and third guiding principles are closely related. Let's call the second one *big-picture analysis* (warning: this is not a standard term). This principle states that we should not worry unduly about small constant factors or lower-order terms in running time bounds. We've already seen this philosophy at work in our analysis of `MergeSort`: when analyzing the running time of the `Merge` subroutine (Lemma 1.1), we first proved an upper bound of $4\ell + 2$ on the number of operations (where ℓ is the length of the output array) and then settled for the simpler upper bound of 6ℓ, even though it suffers from a larger constant factor. How do we justify being so fast and loose with constant factors?

Mathematical tractability.   The first reason for big-picture analysis is that it's way easier mathematically than the alternative of pinning down precise constant factors or lower-order terms. This point was already evident in our running time analysis of `MergeSort`.

Constants depend on environment-specific factors.   The second justification is less obvious but extremely important. At the level of granularity we'll use to describe algorithms, as with the `MergeSort` algorithm, it would be totally misguided to obsess over exactly what the constant factors are. For example, during our analysis of the `Merge` subroutine, there was ambiguity about exactly how many "primitive operations" are performed each loop iteration (4, 5, or something else?). Thus, different interpretations of the same pseudocode can lead to different constant factors. The ambiguity only increases once pseudocode gets translated into a concrete implementation in some high-level programming language, and then translated further into machine code—the constant factors will inevitably depend on the programming language used, the specific implementation, and the details of the compiler and processor. Our goal is to focus on properties of algorithms that transcend the details of the programming language and machine architecture, and these properties should be independent of small constant-factor changes in a running time bound.

Lose little predictive power.   The third justification is simply that we're going to be able to get away with it. You might be concerned that ignoring constant factors would lead us astray, tricking us into thinking that an algorithm is fast when it is actually slow in practice, or vice versa. Happily, this won't happen for the algorithms discussed in this book.[19] Even though we won't be keeping track of lower-order terms and constant factors, the qualitative predictions of our mathematical analysis will be highly accurate—when analysis suggests that an algorithm should be fast, it will in fact be fast in practice, and conversely. So while big-picture analysis does discard some information, it preserves what we really care about: accurate guidance about which algorithms tend to be faster than others.[20]

---

[19]With one possible exception, the deterministic linear-time selection algorithm in the optional Section 6.3.

[20]It's still useful to have a general sense of the relevant constant factors, however. For example, in the highly tuned versions of `MergeSort` that you'll find in many programming libraries, the algorithm switches from `MergeSort` over to `InsertionSort` (for its better constant factor) once the input array length becomes small (for example, at most seven elements).

1.6.3 Principle #3: Asymptotic Analysis

Our third and final guiding principle is to use *asymptotic analysis* and focus on the rate of growth of an algorithm's running time, as the input size n grows large. This bias toward large inputs was already evident when we interpreted our running time bound for MergeSort (Theorem 1.2), of $6n \log_2 n + 6n$ operations. We then cavalierly declared that MergeSort is "better than" simpler sorting methods with running time quadratic in the input size, such as InsertionSort. But is this really true?

For concreteness, suppose we have a sorting algorithm that performs at most $\frac{1}{2}n^2$ operations when sorting an array of length n, and consider the comparison

$$6n \log_2 n + 6n \quad \text{vs.} \quad \frac{1}{2}n^2.$$

Looking at the behavior of these two functions in Figure 1.6, we see that $\frac{1}{2}n^2$ is the smaller expression when n is small (at most 90 or so), while $6n \log_2 n + 6n$ is smaller for all larger n. So when we say that MergeSort is faster than simpler sorting methods, what we really mean is that it is faster on *sufficiently large instances*.

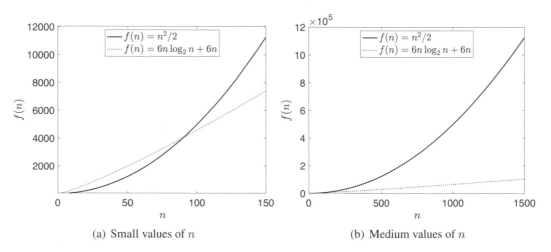

(a) Small values of n (b) Medium values of n

Figure 1.6: The function $\frac{1}{2}n^2$ grows much more quickly than $6n \log_2 n + 6n$ as n grows large. The scales of the x- and y-axes in (b) are one and two orders of magnitude, respectively, bigger than those in (a).

Why should we care more about large instances than small ones? Because large instances are the only ones that require algorithmic ingenuity. Almost any sorting method you can think of would sort an array of length 1000 instantaneously on a modern computer—there's no need to learn about divide-and-conquer algorithms.

Given that computers are constantly getting faster, you might wonder if all computational problems will eventually become trivial to solve. In fact, faster computers make asymptotic analysis more relevant than ever! Our computational ambitions have always grown with our computational power, so as time goes on, we tackle larger and larger problem sizes. And the gulf in performance between algorithms with different asymptotic running times only becomes wider as inputs grow larger. For example, Figure 1.6(b) shows the difference between the functions $6n \log_2 n + 6n$ and $\frac{1}{2}n^2$ for larger (but still modest) values of n, and by the time $n = 1500$ there is roughly a factor-10 difference between them. If we scaled n up by another factor of 10, or 100, or 1000 to start reaching interesting problem sizes, the difference between the two functions would be huge.

For a different way to think about asymptotic analysis, suppose you have a fixed time budget, like an hour or a day. How does the solvable problem size scale with additional computing power? With an algorithm that runs in time proportional to the input size, a four-fold increase in computing power lets you solve problems four times as large as before. With an algorithm that runs in time proportional to the square of the input size, you would be able to solve only problems that are twice as large as before.

1.6.4   What Is a "Fast" Algorithm?

Our three guiding principles lead us to the following definition of a "fast algorithm":

> A *"fast algorithm" is an algorithm whose worst-case running time grows slowly with the input size.*

Our first guiding principle, that we want running time guarantees that do not assume any domain knowledge, is the reason why we focus on the worst-case running time of an algorithm. Our second and third guiding principles, that constant factors are language- and machine-dependent and that large problems are the interesting ones, are the reasons why we focus on the rate of growth of the running time of an algorithm.

What do we mean that the running time of an algorithm "grows slowly"? For almost all of the problems we'll discuss, the holy grail is a *linear-time algorithm*, meaning an algorithm with running time proportional to the input size. Linear time is even better than our bound on the running time of MergeSort, which is proportional to $n \log_2 n$ and hence modestly super-linear. We will succeed in designing linear-time algorithms for some problems but not for others. In any case, it is the best-case scenario to which we will aspire.

For-Free Primitives

You can think of an algorithm with a linear or near-linear running time as a primitive that can be used essentially "for free"—the amount of time required barely exceeds what you need to read the input. Sorting is a canonical example of a for-free primitive, and we will also learn several others. When you have such a blazingly fast primitive that is relevant to your problem, why not use it? For example, you can always sort your data in a preprocessing step, even if you're not quite sure how it will help later. One of the goals of this book is to stock your algorithmic toolbox with as many for-free primitives as possible, ready to be applied at will.

The Upshot

☆ An algorithm is a set of well-defined rules for solving some computational problem.

☆ The number of primitive operations performed by the algorithm you learned in grade school to multiply two n-digit integers scales as a quadratic function of the number n.

☆ Karatsuba multiplication is a recursive algorithm for integer multiplication, and it uses Gauss's trick to save one recursive call over a more straightforward recursive algorithm.

☆ Seasoned programmers and computer scientists generally think and communicate about algorithms using high-level descriptions rather than detailed implementations.

☆ The `MergeSort` algorithm is a "divide-and-conquer" algorithm that splits the input array into two halves, recursively sorts each half, and combines the results using the `Merge` subroutine.

☆ Ignoring constant factors and lower-order terms, the number of operations performed by `MergeSort` to sort n elements grows like the function $n \log_2 n$. The analysis uses a recursion tree to conveniently organize the work done by all the recursive calls.

☆ Because the function $\log_2 n$ grows slowly with n, `MergeSort` is typically faster than simpler sorting algorithms, which all require a quadratic number of operations. For large n, the improvement is dramatic.

☆ Three guiding principles for the analysis of algorithms are: (i) worst-case analysis, to promote general-purpose algorithms that work well with no assumptions about the input; (ii) big-picture analysis, which balances predictive power with mathematical tractability by ignoring constant factors and lower-order terms; and (iii) asymptotic analysis, which is a bias toward large inputs, which are the inputs that require algorithmic ingenuity.

☆ A "fast algorithm" is an algorithm whose worst-case running time grows slowly with the input size.

☆ A "for-free primitive" is an algorithm that runs in linear or near-linear time, barely more than what is required to read the input.

Test Your Understanding

Problem 1.1 *(S)* Suppose we run `MergeSort` on the following input array:

5	3	8	9	1	7	0	2	6	4

Fast forward to the moment after the two outermost recursive calls complete, but before the final `Merge` step. Thinking of the two 5-element output arrays of the recursive calls as a glued-together 10-element array, which number is in the 7th position?

Problem 1.2 *(H)* Consider the following modification to the `MergeSort` algorithm: divide the input array into thirds (rather than halves), recursively sort each third, and finally combine the results using a three-way `Merge` subroutine. What is the running time of this algorithm as a function of the length n of the input array, ignoring constant factors and lower-order terms?

    a) n

    b) $n \log n$

    c) $n(\log n)^2$

    d) $n^2 \log n$

Problem 1.3 *(H)* Suppose you are given k sorted arrays, each with n elements, and you want to combine them into a single array of kn elements. One approach is to use the `Merge` subroutine from Section 1.4.5 repeatedly, first merging the first two arrays, then merging the result with the third array, then with the fourth array, and so on until you merge in the kth and final input array. What is the running time taken by this successive merging algorithm, as a function of k and n, ignoring constant factors and lower-order terms?

    a) $n \log k$

    b) nk

    c) $nk \log k$

    d) $nk \log n$

    e) nk^2

    f) $n^2 k$

Problem 1.4 *(S)* Consider again the problem of merging k sorted length-n arrays into a single sorted length-kn array. Consider the algorithm that first divides the k arrays into $k/2$ pairs of arrays, and uses the `Merge` subroutine to combine each pair, resulting in $k/2$ sorted length-$2n$ arrays. The algorithm repeats this step until there is only one length-kn sorted array. What is the running time of this procedure, as a function of k and n, ignoring constant factors and lower-order terms?

    a) $n \log k$

    b) nk

    c) $nk \log k$

    d) $nk \log n$

e) nk^2

f) n^2k

Problem 1.5 *(S)* The following problems all concern an input array of integers, possibly with duplicate entries. Which of them can be solved using a single invocation of a sorting subroutine followed by a single pass over the sorted array? (Choose all that apply.)

a) Compute the minimum gap between any pair of array elements.

b) Compute the number of distinct integers contained in the array.

c) Compute a "de-duplicated" version of the input array, meaning an output array that contains exactly one copy of each of the distinct integers in the input array.

d) Compute the mode (the most frequently appearing integer) of the array. If there is a tie and there are two or more modes, the algorithm should return all of them.

e) For this part, assume that the array's integers are distinct and that the array has odd length. Compute the median of the array—the "middle element," with the number of other elements less than it equal to the number of other elements greater than it.

Challenge Problems

Problem 1.6 *(H)* Intuitively, every algorithm that checks whether an array A of n integers contains a given integer t must examine every array element and therefore requires at least n primitive operations. Suppose now that the input includes not one but k integers $t_1, t_2, \ldots, t_k$, and the goal is to identify which of the t_i's appear in A. Does every algorithm for this problem require at least kn operations? Does the answer depend on k?

Problem 1.7 *(H)* You are given as input an unsorted array of n distinct numbers, where n is a power of 2. Give an algorithm that identifies the second-largest number in the array while using at most $n + \log_2 n - 2$ comparisons.

Programming Problems

Problem 1.8 Implement Karatsuba's integer multiplication algorithm in your favorite programming language.[21] To get the most out of this problem, your program should invoke the language's multiplication operator only on pairs of single-digit numbers.

For a concrete challenge, what's the product of the following two 64-digit numbers?[22]

3141592653589793238462643383279502884197169399375105820974944592

2718281828459045235360287471352662497757247093699959574966967627

---

[21] Food for thought: does it make your life easier if the number of digits of each integer is a power of 2?

[22] If you need help or want to compare notes with other readers, visit the discussion forums at www.algorithmsilluminated.org.

Chapter 2

Asymptotic Notation

This chapter develops the mathematical formalism that encodes our guiding principles for the analysis of algorithms (Section 1.6). The goal is to identify a sweet spot of granularity for reasoning about algorithms—we want to suppress second-order details like constant factors and lower-order terms, and focus on how the running time of an algorithm scales as the input size grows. This is done formally through big-O notation and its relatives—concepts that belong in the vocabulary of every serious programmer and computer scientist.

2.1 The Gist

Before getting into the mathematical formalism of asymptotic notation, let's make sure the topic is well motivated, that you have a strong sense of what it's trying to accomplish, and that you've seen a couple of simple and intuitive examples.

2.1.1 Motivation

Asymptotic notation provides the basic vocabulary for discussing the design and analysis of algorithms. It's important that you know what programmers mean when they say that one piece of code runs in "big-O of n time," while another runs in "big-O of n-squared time."

This vocabulary is so ubiquitous because it identifies the right "sweet spot" for reasoning about algorithms. Asymptotic notation is coarse enough to suppress all the details you want to ignore—details that depend on the choice of architecture, the choice of programming language, the choice of compiler, and so on. On the other hand, it's precise enough to make useful comparisons between different high-level algorithmic approaches to solving a problem, especially on larger inputs (the inputs that require algorithmic ingenuity). For example, asymptotic analysis helps us differentiate between better and worse approaches to sorting, better and worse approaches to multiplying two integers, and so on.

2.1.2 The High-Level Idea

If you ask a practicing programmer to explain the point of asymptotic notation, they are likely to say something like the following:

Asymptotic Notation in Seven Words

suppress constant factors and lower-order terms

too system-dependent   *irrelevant for large inputs*

We'll see that there's more to asymptotic notation than just these seven words, but ten years from now, if you remember only seven words about it, these are good ones.

When analyzing the running time of an algorithm, why would we want to throw away information like constant factors and lower-order terms? Lower-order terms, by definition, become increasingly irrelevant as you focus on large inputs, which are the inputs that require algorithmic ingenuity. Meanwhile, the constant factors are generally highly dependent on the details of the environment. If we don't want to commit to a specific programming language, architecture, or compiler when analyzing an algorithm, it makes sense to use a formalism that does not focus on constant factors.

For example, remember when we analyzed `MergeSort` (Sections 1.4–1.5)? We gave an upper bound on its running time of

$$6n \log_2 n + 6n$$

primitive operations, where n is the length of the input array. The lower-order term here is the $6n$, as n grows more slowly than $n \log_2 n$, so it will be suppressed in asymptotic notation. The leading constant factor of 6 also gets suppressed, leaving us with the much simpler expression of $n \log n$. We would then say that the running time of `MergeSort` is "big-O of $n \log n$," written $O(n \log n)$, or that `MergeSort` is an "$O(n \log n)$-time algorithm."[1] Intuitively, saying that something is $O(f(n))$ for a function $f(n)$ means that $f(n)$ is what you're left with after suppressing constant factors and lower-order terms.[2] This "big-O notation" buckets algorithms into groups according to their asymptotic worst-case running times—the linear ($O(n)$)-time algorithms, the $O(n \log n)$-time algorithms, the quadratic ($O(n^2)$)-time algorithms, the constant ($O(1)$)-time algorithms, and so on.

To be clear, I'm certainly not claiming that constant factors never matter in algorithm design. Rather, when you want to make a comparison between fundamentally different ways of solving a problem, asymptotic analysis is often the right tool for understanding which one is going to perform better, especially on reasonably large inputs. Once you've figured out the best high-level algorithmic approach to a problem, you might well want to work harder to improve the leading constant factor, and perhaps even the lower-order terms. By all means, if the future of your start-up depends on how efficiently you implement a particular piece of code, have at it and make it as fast as you can.

2.1.3   Four Examples

We conclude this section with four very simple examples. They are so simple that, if you have any prior experience with big-O notation, you should probably just skip straight to Section 2.2 to start learning the mathematical formalism. But if these concepts are completely new to you, these simple examples should get you properly oriented.

Consider first the problem of searching an array for a given integer t. Let's analyze the straightforward algorithm that performs a linear scan through the array, checking each entry to see if it is the desired integer t.

---

[1]When ignoring constant factors, we don't even need to specify the base of the logarithm (as different logarithmic functions differ only by a constant factor). See Section 4.2.2 for further discussion.

[2]For example, even the function $10^{100} \cdot n$ is technically $O(n)$. In this book, we will only study running time bounds in which the suppressed constant factor is reasonably small.

Searching One Array

Input: array A of n integers, and an integer t.
Output: Whether or not A contains t.

```
for i := 1 to n do // check each array entry in turn
    if A[i] = t then                          // found it!
        return TRUE
return FALSE      // exhausted all possibilities
```

We haven't formally defined what big-O notation means yet, but from our intuitive discussion so far you might be able to guess the asymptotic running time of the code above.

Quiz 2.1

What is the asymptotic running time of the code above for searching one array, as a function of the array length n?

a) $O(1)$

b) $O(\log n)$

c) $O(n)$

d) $O(n^2)$

(See Section 2.1.4 for the solution and discussion.)

Our final three examples concern different ways of combining two loops. First, let's think about one loop followed by another. Suppose we're now given two integer arrays A and B, both of length n, and we want to know whether a target integer t is in either one. Let's again consider the straightforward algorithm, in which we search through A, and if we fail to find t in A, we then search through B. If we don't find t in B either, we return false.

Searching Two Arrays

Input: arrays A and B of n integers each, and an integer t.
Output: Whether or not A or B contains t.

```
for i := 1 to n do                  // search first array
    if A[i] = t then
        return TRUE
for i := 1 to n do                  // search second array
    if B[i] = t then
        return TRUE
return FALSE
```

What, in big-O notation, is the running time of this longer piece of code?

Quiz 2.2

What is the asymptotic running time of the code above for searching two arrays, as a function of the array lengths n?

a) $O(1)$

b) $O(\log n)$

c) $O(n)$

d) $O(n^2)$

(See Section 2.1.4 for the solution and discussion.)

Next let's look at a more interesting example of two loops that are nested, rather than in sequence. Suppose we want to check whether or not two given arrays of length n have a number in common. The simplest solution is to check all possibilities. That is, for each index i into the array A and each index j into the array B, we check if $A[i]$ is the same number as $B[j]$. If it is, we return true. If we exhaust all the possibilities without ever finding equal elements, we can safely return false.

Checking for a Common Element

Input: arrays A and B of n integers each.
Output: Whether or not there is an integer t contained in both A and B.

```
// outer loop
for i := 1 to n do
    // inner loop
    for j := 1 to n do
        if A[i] = B[j] then
            return TRUE
return FALSE
```

The question is the usual one: in big-O notation, what is the running time of this piece of code?

Quiz 2.3

What is the asymptotic running time of the code above for checking for a common element, as a function of the array lengths n?

a) $O(1)$

b) $O(\log n)$

c) $O(n)$

d) $O(n^2)$

(See Section 2.1.4 for the solution and discussion.)

Our final example again involves nested loops, but this time we're looking for duplicate entries in a single array A, rather than in two different arrays. Here's the piece of code we're going to analyze.

Checking for Duplicates

Input: array A of n integers.
Output: Whether or not A contains an integer more than once.

```
for i := 1 to n do
    for j := i + 1 to n do
        if A[i] = A[j] then
            return TRUE
return FALSE
```

There are two small differences between this piece of code and the previous one. The first and more obvious change is that we're comparing the ith element of A to the jth element of A, rather than to the jth element of some other array B. The second and more subtle change is that the inner loop now begins at the index $i + 1$ rather than the index 1. Why not start at 1, like before? Because then it would also return true in the very first iteration (because clearly $A[1] = A[1]$), whether or not the array has any duplicate entries! Correctness could be salvaged by skipping all the iterations in which i and j are equal, but this would still be wasteful: each pair of elements $A[h]$ and $A[k]$ of A would be compared to each other twice (once when $i = h$ and $j = k$ and once when $i = k$ and $j = h$), while the code above compares them only once.

The question is the usual one: in big-O notation, what is the running time of this piece of code?

Quiz 2.4

What is the asymptotic running time of the code above for checking for duplicates, as a function of the array length n?

a) $O(1)$

b) $O(\log n)$

c) $O(n)$

d) $O(n^2)$

(See Section 2.1.4 for the solution and discussion.)

These basic examples should have given you a strong intuitive sense of how big-O notation is defined and what it is trying to accomplish. Next we move on to both the mathematical development of asymptotic notation and some more interesting algorithms.

2.1.4   Solutions to Quizzes 2.1–2.4

Solution to Quiz 2.1

Correct answer: (c). The correct answer is $O(n)$. Equivalently, we say that the algorithm has running time *linear in* n. Why is that true? The exact number of operations performed depends on the input—whether or not the target t is contained in the array A and, if so, where in the array it lies. In the worst case, when t is not in the array, the code will do an unsuccessful search, scanning through the entire array (over n loop iterations) and returning false. The key observation is that the code performs a constant number of operations for each entry of the array (comparing $A[i]$ with t, incrementing the loop index i, etc.). Here "constant" means some number independent of n, like 2 or 3. We could argue about exactly what this constant is in the code above, but whatever it is, it is conveniently suppressed in the big-O notation. Similarly, the code does a constant number of operations before the loop begins and after it ends, and whatever the exact constant may be, it constitutes a lower-order term that is suppressed in the big-O notation. Because ignoring constant factors and lower-order terms leaves us with a bound of n on the total number of operations, the asymptotic running time of this code is $O(n)$.

Solution to Quiz 2.2

Correct answer: (c). The answer is the same as before, $O(n)$. The reason is that the worst-case number of operations performed (in an unsuccessful search) is twice that of the previous piece of code—first we search the first array, and then the second array. This extra factor of 2 contributes only to the leading constant in the running time bound and is therefore suppressed when we use big-O notation. So this algorithm, like the previous one, is a linear-time algorithm.

Solution to Quiz 2.3

Correct answer: (d). This time, the answer has changed. For this piece of code, the running time is not $O(n)$, but is $O(n^2)$. ("Big-O of n squared," also called a "quadratic-time algorithm.") So with this algorithm, if you multiply the lengths of the input arrays by 10, the running time will go up by a factor of 100 (rather than a factor of 10 for a linear-time algorithm).

   Why does this code have a running time of $O(n^2)$? The code again does a constant number of operations for each loop iteration (that is, for each choice of the indices i and j) and a constant number of operations outside the loops. What's different is that there's now a total of n^2 iterations of this double for loop—one for each choice of $i \in \{1, 2, \ldots, n\}$ and $j \in \{1, 2, \ldots, n\}$. In our first example, there were only n iterations of a single for loop. In our second example, because the first for loop completed before the second one began, we had only $2n$ iterations overall. Here, for *each* of the n iterations of the outer for loop, the code performs n iterations of the inner for loop. This gives $n \times n = n^2$ iterations in all.

Solution to Quiz 2.4

Correct answer: (d). The answer to this question is the same as the last one, $O(n^2)$. The running time is again proportional to the number of iterations of the double for loop (with a constant number of operations per iteration). So how many iterations are there? The answer is roughly $n^2/2$. One way to see this is to remember that this piece of code does roughly half the work of the previous one (because it considers only the pairs i, j with $i < j$, and not those with $i \geq j$). A second way is to observe that there is exactly one iteration for each subset $\{i, j\}$ of two distinct indices from $\{1, 2, \ldots, n\}$, and there are precisely $\binom{n}{2} = \frac{n(n-1)}{2}$ such subsets.[3]

2.2   Big-O Notation

This section presents the formal definition of big-O notation. We begin with a definition in plain English, illustrate it pictorially, and finally give the mathematical definition.

Pep Talk

It is totally normal to feel confused the first time you see the mathematical definition of big-O notation. Confusion should not discourage you. It does not represent an intellectual failure on your part, only an opportunity to get even smarter.

2.2.1   English Definition

Big-O notation concerns functions $T(n)$ defined on the positive integers $n = 1, 2, \ldots$. For us, $T(n)$ will almost always denote a bound on the worst-case running time of an algorithm, as a function of the size n of the input. What does it mean to say that $T(n) = O(f(n))$, for some "canonical" function $f(n)$, like n, $n \log n$, or n^2? Here's the definition in English.

Big-O Notation (English Version)

$T(n) = O(f(n))$ if and only if $T(n)$ is eventually bounded above by a constant multiple of $f(n)$.

2.2.2   Pictorial Definition

See Figure 2.1 for a pictorial illustration of the definition of big-O notation. The x-axis corresponds to the parameter n, the y-axis to the value of a function. Let $T(n)$ be the function corresponding to the solid line, and $f(n)$ the lower dashed line. $T(n)$ is not bounded above by $f(n)$, but multiplying $f(n)$ by 3 results in the upper dashed line, which does lie above $T(n)$ once we go far enough to the right on the graph, after the "crossover point" at n_0. Because $T(n)$ is indeed eventually bounded above by a constant multiple of $f(n)$, we can say that $T(n) = O(f(n))$.

---

[3] $\binom{n}{2}$ is pronounced "n choose 2," and is also sometimes referred to as a "binomial coefficient." See also the solution to Quiz 3.1.

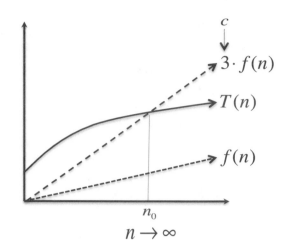

Figure 2.1: A picture illustrating when $T(n) = O(f(n))$. The constant c quantifies the "constant multiple" of $f(n)$, and the constant n_0 quantifies "eventually."

2.2.3   Mathematical Definition

Here is the mathematical definition of big-O notation, the definition you should use in formal proofs.

Big-O Notation (Mathematical Version)

$T(n) = O(f(n))$ if and only if there exist positive constants c and n_0 such that

$$T(n) \leq c \cdot f(n) \tag{2.1}$$

for all $n \geq n_0$.

This is a direct translation of the English definition in Section 2.2.1. The inequality in (2.1) expresses that $T(n)$ should be bounded above by a multiple of $f(n)$ (with the constant c specifying the multiple). The "for all $n \geq n_0$" expresses that the inequality only needs to hold eventually, once n is sufficiently large (with the constant n_0 specifying how large). For example, in Figure 2.1, the constant c corresponds to 3, while n_0 corresponds to the crossover point between the functions $T(n)$ and $c \cdot f(n)$.

A game-theoretic view.   If you want to prove that $T(n) = O(f(n))$, for example to prove that the asymptotic running time of an algorithm is linear in the input size (corresponding to $f(n) = n$), then your task is to choose the constants c and n_0 so that (2.1) holds whenever $n \geq n_0$. One way to think about this is game-theoretically, as a contest between you and an opponent. You go first, and have to commit to constants c and n_0. Your opponent goes second and can choose any integer n that is at least n_0. You win if (2.1) holds, your opponent wins if the opposite inequality $T(n) > c \cdot f(n)$ holds.

   If $T(n) = O(f(n))$, then there are constants c and n_0 such that (2.1) holds for all $n \geq n_0$, and you have a winning strategy in this game. Otherwise, no matter how you choose c

and n_0, your opponent can choose a large enough $n \geq n_0$ to flip the inequality and win the game.

A Word of Caution

When we say that c and n_0 are constants, we mean they *cannot depend on n*. For example, in Figure 2.1, c and n_0 are fixed numbers (like 3 or 1000), and we then consider the inequality (2.1) as n grows arbitrarily large (looking rightward on the graph toward infinity). If you ever find yourself saying "take $n_0 = n$" or "take $c = \log_2 n$" in an alleged big-O proof, you need to start over with choices of c and n_0 that are independent of n.

2.3   Two Basic Examples

Having slogged through the formal definition of big-O notation, let's look at a couple of examples. These examples won't provide us with any insights we don't already have, but they serve as an important sanity check that big-O notation is achieving its intended goal, of suppressing constant factors and lower-order terms. They are also a good warm-up for the less obvious examples we will encounter later.

2.3.1   Degree-k Polynomials are $O(n^k)$

Our first formal claim is that if $T(n)$ is a polynomial with some degree k, then $T(n) = O(n^k)$.

Proposition 2.1 *Suppose*

$$T(n) = a_k n^k + \cdots + a_1 n + a_0,$$

where $k \geq 0$ is a nonnegative integer and the a_i's are real numbers (positive or negative). Then $T(n) = O(n^k)$.

Proposition 2.1 says that with a polynomial, in big-O notation, all you need to worry about is the highest degree that appears in the polynomial. Thus, big-O notation really is suppressing constant factors and lower-order terms.

Proof of Proposition 2.1: To prove this proposition, we need to use the mathematical definition of big-O notation (Section 2.2.3). To satisfy the definition, it's our job to find a pair of positive constants c and n_0 (each independent of n), with c quantifying the constant multiple of n^k and n_0 quantifying "sufficiently large n." To keep things easy to follow but admittedly mysterious, let's pull values for these constants out of a hat: $n_0 = 1$ and c equal to the sum of absolute values of the coefficients:[4]

$$c = |a_k| + \cdots + |a_1| + |a_0|.$$

---

[4]Recall that the *absolute value* $|x|$ of a real number x equals x when $x \geq 0$ and $-x$ when $x \leq 0$. In particular, $|x|$ is always nonnegative.

Both of these numbers are independent of n. We now need to show that these choices of constants satisfy the definition, meaning that $T(n) \leq c \cdot n^k$ for all $n \geq n_0 = 1$.

To verify this inequality, fix an arbitrary positive integer $n \geq n_0 = 1$. We need a sequence of upper bounds on $T(n)$, culminating in an upper bound of $c \cdot n^k$. First let's apply the definition of $T(n)$:

$$T(n) = a_k n^k + \cdots + a_1 n + a_0.$$

If we take the absolute value of each coefficient a_i on the right-hand side, the expression only becomes larger. ($|a_i|$ is at least as big as a_i and, because n^i is positive, $|a_i| n^i$ is then at least as big as $a_i n^i$.) This means that

$$T(n) \leq |a_k| n^k + \cdots + |a_1| n + |a_0|.$$

Why is this step useful? Now that the coefficients are nonnegative, we can use a similar trick to turn the different powers of n into a common power of n. Because $n \geq 1$, n^k is at least as big as n^i for every $i \in \{0, 1, 2, \ldots, k\}$. Because $|a_i|$ is nonnegative, $|a_i| n^k$ is at least as big as $|a_i| n^i$. This means that

$$T(n) \leq |a_k| n^k + \cdots + |a_1| n^k + |a_0| n^k = \underbrace{(|a_k| + \cdots + |a_1| + |a_0|)}_{=c} \cdot n^k.$$

This inequality holds for every $n \geq n_0 = 1$, which is exactly what we wanted to prove. $\mathcal{QED}$

How do you know how to choose the constants c and n_0? The usual approach is to reverse engineer them. This involves going through a derivation like the one above and figuring out on-the-fly the choices of constants that let you push the proof through. We'll see some examples of this method in Section 2.5.

2.3.2 Degree-k Polynomials Are Not $O(n^{k-1})$

Our second example is really a non-example: a degree-k polynomial is $O(n^k)$, but is not generally $O(n^{k-1})$.

Proposition 2.2 *Let $k \geq 1$ be a positive integer and define $T(n) = n^k$. Then $T(n)$ is not $O(n^{k-1})$.*

Proposition 2.2 implies that polynomials with distinct degrees are distinct with respect to big-O notation. (If this weren't true, something would be wrong with our definition of big-O notation!)

Proof of Proposition 2.2: The best way to prove that one function is not big-O of another is usually with a proof by contradiction. In this type of proof, you assume the *opposite* of what you want to prove, and then build on this assumption with a sequence of logically correct steps that culminates in a patently false statement. Such a contradiction implies that the assumption can't be true, and this proves the desired statement.

So, assume that n^k is in fact $O(n^{k-1})$; we proceed to derive a contradiction. What does it mean if $n^k = O(n^{k-1})$? That n^k is eventually bounded by a constant multiple of n^{k-1}. That is, there are positive constants c and n_0 such that

$$n^k \leq c \cdot n^{k-1}$$

for all $n \geq n_0$. Because n is a positive number, we can cancel n^{k-1} from both sides of this inequality to derive

$$n \leq c$$

for all $n \geq n_0$. This inequality asserts that the constant c is bigger than every positive integer, a patently false statement (for a counterexample, take $c + 1$, rounded up to the nearest integer). This shows that our original assumption that $n^k = O(n^{k-1})$ cannot be correct, and we can conclude that n^k is not $O(n^{k-1})$. $\mathcal{QED}$

2.4   Big-Omega and Big-Theta Notation

Big-O notation is by far the most important and ubiquitous concept for discussing the asymptotic running time of algorithms. A couple of its close relatives, the big-omega and big-theta notations, are also worth knowing. If big-O is analogous to "less than or equal to ($\leq$)," then big-omega and big-theta are analogous to "greater than or equal to ($\geq$)," and "equal to ($=$)," respectively. Let's now treat them a little more precisely.

2.4.1   Big-Omega Notation

The formal definition of big-omega notation parallels that of big-O notation. In English, we say that one function $T(n)$ is big-omega of another function $f(n)$ if and only if $T(n)$ is eventually bounded *below* by a constant multiple of $f(n)$. In this case, we write $T(n) = \Omega(f(n))$. As before, we use two constants c and n_0 to quantify "constant multiple" and "eventually."

Big-Omega Notation (Mathematical Version)

$T(n) = \Omega(f(n))$ if and only if there exist positive constants c and n_0 such that

$$T(n) \geq c \cdot f(n)$$

for all $n \geq n_0$.

You can imagine what the corresponding picture looks like:

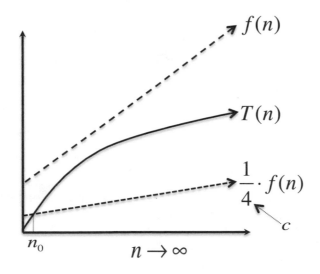

$T(n)$ again corresponds to the function with the solid line. The function $f(n)$ is the upper dashed line. This function does not bound $T(n)$ from below, but if we multiply it by the constant $c = \frac{1}{4}$, the result (the lower dashed line) does bound $T(n)$ from below for all n past the crossover point at n_0. Thus $T(n) = \Omega(f(n))$.

2.4.2 Big-Theta Notation

Big-theta notation, or simply theta notation, is analogous to "equal to." Saying that $T(n) = \Theta(f(n))$ means that both $T(n) = \Omega(f(n))$ and $T(n) = O(f(n))$. Equivalently, $T(n)$ is eventually sandwiched between two different constant multiples of $f(n)$.[5]

Big-Theta Notation (Mathematical Version)

$T(n) = \Theta(f(n))$ if and only if there exist positive constants c_1, c_2, and n_0 such that

$$c_1 \cdot f(n) \leq T(n) \leq c_2 \cdot f(n)$$

for all $n \geq n_0$.

A Word of Caution

Algorithm designers often use big-O notation even when big-theta notation would be more accurate. This book will follow that tradition. For example, consider a subroutine that scans an array of length n, performing a constant number of operations per entry (like the Merge subroutine in Section 1.4.5). The running time of such a subroutine is obviously $\Theta(n)$, but it's common to only mention that it is $O(n)$.[6] Why so sloppy? Because as algorithm designers, we're often single-mindedly focused on upper bounds—guarantees about how long our algorithms could possibly run.

The next quiz checks your understanding of big-O, big-omega, and big-theta notation.

Quiz 2.5

Let $T(n) = \frac{1}{2}n^2 + 3n$. Which of the following statements are true? (There might be more than one correct answer.)

    a) $T(n) = O(n)$

---

[5]Proving this equivalence amounts to showing that one version of the definition is satisfied if and only if the other one is. If $T(n) = \Theta(f(n))$ according to the second definition, then the constants c_2 and n_0 prove that $T(n) = O(f(n))$, while the constants c_1 and n_0 prove that $T(n) = \Omega(f(n))$. In the other direction, suppose you can prove that $T(n) = O(f(n))$ using the constants c_2 and n_0' and $T(n) = \Omega(f(n))$ using the constants c_1 and n_0''. Then $T(n) = \Theta(f(n))$ according to the second definition, with constants c_1, c_2, and $n_0 = \max\{n_0', n_0''\}$.

[6]Similarly, the bounds of $O(n)$ in Quizzes 2.1–2.2 and $O(n^2)$ in Quizzes 2.3–2.4 would more accurately be stated as $\Theta(n)$ and $\Theta(n^2)$, respectively.

b) $T(n) = \Omega(n)$

c) $T(n) = \Theta(n^2)$

d) $T(n) = O(n^3)$

(See Section 2.4.5 for the solution and discussion.)

2.4.3   Little-O Notation

There's one final piece of asymptotic notation, "little-o notation," that you see from time to time. If big-O notation is analogous to "less than or equal to," little-o notation is analogous to "strictly less than." In other words, $T(n) = o(f(n))$ means that the function $T(n)$ grows strictly more slowly than $f(n)$.[7]

Little-O Notation (Mathematical Version)

$T(n) = o(f(n))$ if and only if for every positive constant $c > 0$, there exists a choice of n_0 such that

$$T(n) \le c \cdot f(n) \tag{2.2}$$

for all $n \ge n_0$.

Proving that one function is big-O of another requires only two constants c and n_0, chosen once and for all. To prove that one function is little-o of another, we have to prove something stronger, that for *every* constant c, no matter how small, $T(n)$ is eventually bounded above by the constant multiple $c \cdot f(n)$. Importantly, in the definition of little-o notation, the constant n_0 chosen to quantify "eventually" can depend on c (but not on n), with smaller constants c generally requiring bigger constants n_0. For example, for every positive integer k, $n^{k-1} = o(n^k)$.[8]

2.4.4   Where Does Notation Come From?

Asymptotic notation was not invented by computer scientists—it has been used in number theory since around the turn of the 20th century. Donald E. Knuth, the grandfather of the formal analysis of algorithms, proposed using it as the standard language for discussing rates of growth, and in particular for algorithm running times.

"On the basis of the issues discussed here, I propose that members of SIGACT,[9] and editors of computer science and mathematics journals, adopt the O, Ω,

---

[7]Similarly, there is a "little-omega" notation that corresponds to "strictly greater than," but we won't have occasion to use it. There is no "little-theta" notation.

[8]Here's the proof. Fix an arbitrary constant $c > 0$. In response, choose n_0 to be $1/c$, rounded up to the nearest integer. Then for all $n \ge n_0$, $n_0 \cdot n^{k-1} \le n^k$ and hence $n^{k-1} \le \frac{1}{n_0} \cdot n^k \le c \cdot n^k$, as required.

[9]SIGACT is the special interest group of the ACM (Association for Computing Machinery) that concerns theoretical computer science, and in particular the analysis of algorithms.

and Θ notations as defined above, unless a better alternative can be found reasonably soon."[10]

2.4.5   Solution to Quiz 2.5

Correct answers: (b),(c),(d). The final three responses are all correct, and hopefully the intuition for why is clear. $T(n)$ is a quadratic function. The linear term $3n$ doesn't matter for large n, so we should expect that $T(n) = \Theta(n^2)$ (answer (c)). This automatically implies that $T(n) = \Omega(n^2)$ and hence $T(n) = \Omega(n)$ also (answer (b)). Note that $\Omega(n)$ is not a particularly impressive lower bound on $T(n)$, but it is a legitimate one nonetheless. Similarly, $T(n) = \Theta(n^2)$ automatically implies that $T(n) = O(n^2)$ and hence also $T(n) = O(n^3)$ (answer (d)).[11]

Proving these statements formally boils down to exhibiting appropriate constants to satisfy the definitions. For example, taking $n_0 = 1$ and $c = \frac{1}{2}$ proves (b). Taking $n_0 = 1$ and $c = 4$ proves (d). Combining these constants ($n_0 = 1$, $c_1 = \frac{1}{2}$, $c_2 = 4$) proves (c). The argument in the proof of Proposition 2.2 can be used to prove formally that (a) is not a correct answer.

2.5   Additional Examples

This section is for readers who want additional practice with asymptotic notation. Other readers can skip the three additional examples here and proceed straight to Chapter 3.

2.5.1   Adding a Constant to an Exponent

First we have another example of a proof that one function is big-O of another.

Proposition 2.3 *If*
$$T(n) = 2^{n+10},$$
then $T(n) = O(2^n)$.

That is, adding a constant to the exponent of an exponential function does not change its asymptotic rate of growth.

Proof of Proposition 2.3: To satisfy the mathematical definition of big-O notation (Section 2.2.3), we need to exhibit a suitable pair of positive constants c and n_0 (each independent of n), such that $T(n)$ is at most $c \cdot 2^n$ for all $n \geq n_0$. In the proof of Proposition 2.1 we pulled these two constants out of a hat; here, let's reverse engineer them.

We're looking for a derivation that begins with $T(n)$ on the left-hand side, followed by a sequence of only-larger numbers, culminating in a constant multiple of 2^n. How would

---

[10]Donald E. Knuth, "Big Omicron and Big Omega and Big Theta," *SIGACT News*, Apr.-June 1976, page 23. Reprinted in *Selected Papers on Analysis of Algorithms* (Center for the Study of Language and Information, 2000).

[11]The fact that $T(n)$ can be both $O(n^2)$ and $O(n^3)$ is no different from the fact that "$5 \leq 5$" and "$5 \leq 10$" are both true statements about integers. The big-O and big-theta notations are often conflated in casual conversation but, technically, big-O notation indicates only an upper bound on the rate of growth of a function, and not necessarily a tight upper bound.

such a derivation begin? The "10" in the exponent is annoying, so a natural first step is to separate it out:

$$T(n) = 2^{n+10} = 2^{10} \cdot 2^n = 1024 \cdot 2^n.$$

Now we're in good shape; the right-hand side is a constant multiple of 2^n, and the derivation suggests that we should take $c = 1024$. Given this choice of c, we have $T(n) \le c \cdot 2^n$ for all $n \ge 1$, so we can take $n_0 = 1$. This pair of constants certifies that $T(n)$ is indeed $O(2^n)$. $\mathcal{QED}$

2.5.2   Multiplying an Exponent by a Constant

Next is another non-example, showing that one function is *not* big-O of another.

Proposition 2.4 *If*

$$T(n) = 2^{10n},$$

then $T(n)$ is not $O(2^n)$.

That is, multiplying the exponent of an exponential function by a constant changes its asymptotic rate of growth.

Proof of Proposition 2.4: As with Proposition 2.2, the usual way to prove that one function is not big-O of another is by contradiction. So assume the opposite of the statement in the proposition, that $T(n)$ is in fact $O(2^n)$. By the definition of big-O notation, this means there are positive constants c and n_0 such that

$$2^{10n} \le c \cdot 2^n$$

for all $n \ge n_0$. Because 2^n is a positive number, we can cancel it from both sides of this inequality to derive

$$2^{9n} \le c$$

for all $n \ge n_0$. But this inequality is patently false: the right-hand side is a fixed constant (independent of n), while the left-hand side goes to infinity as n grows large. This shows that our assumption that $T(n) = O(2^n)$ cannot be correct, and we can conclude that 2^{10n} is not $O(2^n)$. $\mathcal{QED}$

2.5.3   Maximum vs. Sum

Our final example uses big-theta notation (Section 2.4.2), the asymptotic version of "equal to." This example shows that, when using asymptotic notation, there's no difference between taking the pointwise maximum of two nonnegative functions and taking their sum.

Proposition 2.5 *Let f and g denote functions from the positive integers to the nonnegative real numbers, and define*

$$T(n) = \max\{f(n), g(n)\}$$

for each $n \ge 1$. Then $T(n) = \Theta(f(n) + g(n))$.

One consequence of Proposition 2.5 is that an algorithm that performs a constant number (meaning independent of n) of $O(f(n))$-time subroutines itself runs in $O(f(n))$ time. The solution to Quiz 2.2 can be viewed as a simple special case of this fact.

Proof of Proposition 2.5: Recall that $T(n) = \Theta(f(n))$ means that $T(n)$ is eventually sandwiched between two different constant multiples of $f(n)$. To make this precise, we need to exhibit three constants: the usual constant n_0, and the constants c_1 and c_2 corresponding to the smaller and larger multiples of $f(n)$. Let's reverse engineer values for these constants.

Consider an arbitrary positive integer n. We have

$$\max\{f(n), g(n)\} \le f(n) + g(n),$$

because the right-hand side is just the left-hand side plus a nonnegative number ($f(n)$ or $g(n)$, whichever is smaller). Similarly,

$$2 \cdot \max\{f(n), g(n)\} \ge f(n) + g(n),$$

because the left-hand side is two copies of the larger of $f(n), g(n)$ and the right-hand side is one copy of each. Putting these two inequalities together, we see that

$$\frac{1}{2}\left(f(n) + g(n)\right) \le \max\{f(n), g(n)\} \le f(n) + g(n) \tag{2.3}$$

for every $n \ge 1$. Thus $\max\{f(n), g(n)\}$ is indeed wedged between two different multiples of $f(n) + g(n)$. Formally, choosing $n_0 = 1$, $c_1 = \frac{1}{2}$, and $c_2 = 1$ shows (by (2.3)) that $\max\{f(n), g(n)\} = \Theta(f(n) + g(n))$. $\mathcal{QED}$

The Upshot

☆ The purpose of asymptotic notation is to suppress constant factors (which are too system-dependent) and lower-order terms (which are irrelevant for large inputs).

☆ A function $T(n)$ is said to be "big-O of $f(n)$," written "$T(n) = O(f(n))$," if it is eventually (for sufficiently large n) bounded above by a constant multiple of $f(n)$. That is, there are positive constants c and n_0 such that $T(n) \le c \cdot f(n)$ for all $n \ge n_0$.

☆ A function $T(n)$ is "big-omega of $f(n)$," written "$T(n) = \Omega(f(n))$," if it is eventually bounded below by a constant multiple of $f(n)$.

☆ A function $T(n)$ is "big-theta of $f(n)$," written "$T(n) = \Theta(f(n))$," if both $T(n) = O(f(n))$ and $T(n) = \Omega(f(n))$.

☆ A big-O statement is analogous to "less than or equal to," big-omega to "greater than or equal to," and big-theta to "equal to."

Test Your Understanding

Problem 2.1 *(S)* Let f and g be non-decreasing real-valued functions defined on the positive integers, with $f(n)$ and $g(n)$ at least 2 for all $n \geq 1$. Assume that $f(n) = O(g(n))$, and let c be a positive constant. Is $f(n) \cdot \log_2(f(n)^c) = O(g(n) \cdot \log_2(g(n)))$?

a) Yes, for all such f, g, and c

b) Never, no matter what f, g, and c are

c) Sometimes yes, sometimes no, depending on the constant c

d) Sometimes yes, sometimes no, depending on the functions f and g

Problem 2.2 *(H)* Assume again two positive non-decreasing functions f and g such that $f(n) = O(g(n))$. Is $2^{f(n)} = O(2^{g(n)})$? (Multiple answers may be correct; choose all that apply.)

a) Yes, for all such f and g

b) Never, no matter what f and g are

c) Sometimes yes, sometimes no, depending on the functions f and g

d) Yes whenever $f(n) \leq g(n)$ for all sufficiently large n

Problem 2.3 *(S)* Arrange the following functions in order of increasing growth rate, with $g(n)$ following $f(n)$ in your list if and only if $f(n) = O(g(n))$.

a) $\sqrt{n}$

b) 10^n

c) $n^{1.5}$

d) $2^{\sqrt{\log_2 n}}$

e) $n^{5/3}$

Problem 2.4 *(S)* Arrange the following functions in order of increasing growth rate, with $g(n)$ following $f(n)$ in your list if and only if $f(n) = O(g(n))$.

a) $n^2 \log_2 n$

b) 2^n

c) 2^{2^n}

d) $n^{\log_2 n}$

e) n^2

Problem 2.5 *(S)* Arrange the following functions in order of increasing growth rate, with $g(n)$ following $f(n)$ in your list if and only if $f(n) = O(g(n))$.

a) $2^{\log_2 n}$

b) $2^{2^{\log_2 n}}$

c) $n^{5/2}$

d) 2^{n^2}

e) $n^2 \log_2 n$

Problem 2.6 *(S)* Let $f(n), g(n)$ denote functions from the positive integers to the positive real numbers. Prove that $f(n) = O(g(n))$ if and only if $g(n) = \Omega(f(n))$.

Challenge Problems

Problem 2.7 *(S)* Let $T(n), f(n)$ denote two functions from the positive integers to the positive real numbers. Recall the formal definitions of big-O (Section 2.2.3) and little-o (Section 2.4.3) notation.

(a) Suppose we replace the inequality (2.1) in the definition of big-O notation with a strict inequality $(T(n) < c \cdot f(n))$ and leave the definition otherwise unchanged. Prove that $T(n) = O(f(n))$ under this alternative definition if and only if $T(n) = O(f(n))$ under the original definition.

(b) Suppose we replace the inequality (2.2) in the definition of little-o notation with a strict inequality $(T(n) < c \cdot f(n))$ and leave the definition otherwise unchanged. Prove that $T(n) = o(f(n))$ under this alternative definition if and only if $T(n) = o(f(n))$ under the original definition.

(c) Big-O and little-o notation supposedly correspond to the concepts of "less than or equal to" and "strictly less than," respectively. How do you reconcile this statement with parts (a) and (b), which seem to show that in asymptotic notation there's no difference between them?

Chapter 3

Divide-and-Conquer Algorithms

This chapter provides practice with the divide-and-conquer algorithm design paradigm through applications to three basic problems. Our first example is an algorithm for counting the number of inversions in an array (Section 3.2). This problem is related to measuring similarity between two ranked lists, which is relevant for making good recommendations to someone based on your knowledge of their and others' preferences (called "collaborative filtering").[1] Our second divide-and-conquer algorithm is Strassen's mind-blowing recursive algorithm for matrix multiplication, which improves over the obvious iterative method (Section 3.3). The third algorithm, which is advanced and optional material, is for a fundamental problem in computational geometry: computing the closest pair of points in the plane (Section 3.4).

3.1   The Divide-and-Conquer Paradigm

You've seen the canonical example of a divide-and-conquer algorithm, `MergeSort` (Section 1.4). More generally, the divide-and-conquer algorithm design paradigm has three conceptual steps.

The Divide-and-Conquer Paradigm

1. *Divide* the input into smaller subproblems.

2. *Conquer* the subproblems recursively.

3. *Combine* the solutions for the subproblems into a solution for the original problem.

For example, in `MergeSort`, the "divide" step splits the input array into its left and right halves, the "conquer" step uses two recursive calls to sort the left and right subarrays, and the "combine" step is implemented by the `Merge` subroutine (Section 1.4.5). In `MergeSort` and many other divide-and-conquer algorithms, it is the last step that requires the most ingenuity. There are also divide-and-conquer algorithms in which the cleverness is in the first step (see `QuickSort` in Chapter 5) or in the specification of the recursive calls (see Section 3.2).

Confronted with a new problem, how can you know if there's a good divide-and-conquer algorithm for it? In general, this design paradigm is well suited to computational problems for which there's an obvious way to split the input into smaller subproblems that do not

---

[1]The presentation in Section 3.2 draws inspiration from that in the book *Algorithm Design*, by Jon Kleinberg and Éva Tardos (Pearson, 2005).

interfere with each other. The lion's share of applications concern splitting an array into two halves (as in `MergeSort`, Section 3.2, and Problems 3.3–3.4), but we'll also see applications involving numbers (Section 1.3 and Problem 3.1), matrices (Section 3.3 and Problem 3.5), and points in the plane (Section 3.4 and Problem 3.7).[2]

3.2 Counting Inversions in $O(n \log n)$ Time

3.2.1 The Problem

This section studies the problem of computing the number of inversions in an array. An *inversion* of an array is a pair of elements that are "out of order," meaning that the element that occurs earlier in the array is bigger than the one that occurs later.

Problem: Counting Inversions

Input: An array A of distinct integers.

Output: The number of inversions of A—the number of pairs (i, j) of array indices with $i < j$ and $A[i] > A[j]$.

For example, an array A that is in sorted order has no inversions. You should convince yourself that the converse is also true: Every array that is not in sorted order has at least one inversion.

3.2.2 An Example

Consider the following array of length 6:

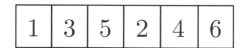

How many inversions does this array have? One that jumps out is the 5 and 2 (corresponding to $i = 3$ and $j = 4$). There are exactly two other out-of-order pairs: the 3 and the 2, and the 5 and the 4.

Quiz 3.1

What is the largest-possible number of inversions a 6-element array can have?

a) 15

b) 21

c) 36

---
[2]Full disclosure: For plenty of important problems out there in the wild, the divide-and-conquer paradigm offers no help. Later parts of this book cover additional algorithm design paradigms, such as greedy algorithms and dynamic programming, that you can resort to if the divide-and-conquer approach fails.

d) 64

(See Section 3.2.13 for the solution and discussion.)

3.2.3   Collaborative Filtering

Why would you want to count the number of inversions in an array? One reason is to compute a numerical similarity measure that quantifies how close two ranked lists are to each other. For example, suppose I ask you and a friend to rank, from favorite to least favorite, ten movies that you have both seen. Are your tastes "similar" or "different"? One way to answer this question quantitatively is through the following 10-element array A: $A[1]$ contains your friend's ranking of your favorite movie in their list, $A[2]$ your friend's personal ranking of your second-favorite movie, ..., and $A[10]$ your friend's personal ranking of your least favorite movie. So if your favorite movie is *Star Wars* but your friend has it only fifth in their list, then $A[1] = 5$. If your rankings are identical, this array will be sorted and have no inversions. The more inversions the array has, the more pairs of movies on which you disagree about their relative merits, and the more different your preferences.

One reason you might want a similarity measure between rankings is to do *collaborative filtering*, a technique for generating recommendations. How do Web sites come up with suggestions for products, movies, songs, news stories, and so on? In collaborative filtering, the idea is to identify other users who have similar preferences, and to recommend to you things that have been popular with them. Thus collaborative filtering algorithms require a formal notion of "similarity" between users, and the problem of computing inversions captures some of the essence of this problem.

3.2.4   Exhaustive Search

How quickly can we compute the number of inversions in an array? If we're feeling unimaginative, there's always exhaustive search.

Exhaustive Search for Counting Inversions

Input: array A of n distinct integers.
Output: the number of inversions of A.

$numInv := 0$
for $i := 1$ to $n - 1$ **do**
    for $j := i + 1$ to n **do**
        if $A[i] > A[j]$ **then**
            $numInv := numInv + 1$
    return $numInv$

This is certainly a correct algorithm. What about its running time? From the solution to Quiz 3.1, we know that the number of loop iterations grows quadratically with the length n of the input array. Because the algorithm performs a constant number of operations in each loop iteration, its asymptotic running time is $\Theta(n^2)$. Remember the mantra of a seasoned algorithm designer:

can we do better?

3.2.5   A Divide-and-Conquer Approach

The answer is yes, and the solution will be a divide-and-conquer algorithm that runs in $O(n \log n)$ time, a big improvement over the exhaustive search algorithm. The "divide" step will be exactly as in the `MergeSort` algorithm, with one recursive call for the left half of the array and one for the right half. To understand the residual work that needs to be done outside the two recursive calls, let's classify the inversions (i, j) of an array A of length n into one of three types:

1. *left inversion*: an inversion with i, j both in the first half of the array (i.e., $i, j \le \frac{n}{2}$);[3]

2. *right inversion*: an inversion with i, j both in the second half of the array (i.e., $i, j > \frac{n}{2}$);

3. *split inversion*: an inversion with i in the left half and j in the right half (i.e., $i \le \frac{n}{2} < j$).

For example, in the six-element array in Section 3.2.2, all three of the inversions are split inversions.

The first recursive call, on the first half of the input array, recursively counts all the left inversions (and nothing else). Similarly, the second recursive call counts all the right inversions. The remaining task is to count the inversions not counted by either recursive call—the split inversions. This is the "combine" step of the algorithm, and we will need to implement a special linear-time subroutine for it, analogous to the `Merge` subroutine in the `MergeSort` algorithm.

3.2.6   High-Level Algorithm

Our divide-and-conquer approach translates to the following pseudocode; the subroutine `CountSplitInv` is, as of now, unimplemented.

CountInv

Input: array A of n distinct integers.
Output: the number of inversions of A.

---

if $n = 0$ or $n = 1$ **then**   // base cases
    return 0
else
    $leftInv :=$ `CountInv`(first half of A)
    $rightInv :=$ `CountInv`(second half of A)
    $splitInv :=$ `CountSplitInv`(A)
    return $leftInv + rightInv + splitInv$

---

[3]The abbreviation "i.e." stands for *id est*, and means "that is."

The first and second recursive calls count the number of left and right inversions. Provided the subroutine CountSplitInv correctly computes the number of split inversions, CountInv correctly computes the total number of inversions.

3.2.7   Key Idea: Piggyback on MergeSort

Counting the number of split inversions of an array in linear time is an ambitious goal. There can be a lot of split inversions: If A consists of the numbers $\frac{n}{2} + 1, \ldots, n$ in order, followed by the numbers $1, 2, \ldots, \frac{n}{2}$ in order, there are $n^2/4$ split inversions. How could we ever count a quadratic number of things with only a linear amount of work?

The inspired idea is to design our recursive inversion-counting algorithm so that it piggybacks on the MergeSort algorithm. This involves demanding more from our recursive calls, in service of making it easier to count the number of split inversions. Each recursive call will be responsible not only for counting the number of inversions in the array that it is given, but also for returning a sorted version of the array. We already know (from Theorem 1.2) that sorting is a for-free primitive (see page 23), running in $O(n \log n)$ time, so if we're shooting for a running time bound of $O(n \log n)$, there's no reason not to sort. And we'll see that the task of merging two sorted subarrays is tailor-made for uncovering all the split inversions of an array.

Here is the revised version of the pseudocode in Section 3.2.6, which counts inversions while also sorting the input array.

Sort-and-CountInv

Input: array A of n distinct integers.
Output: sorted array B with the same integers, and the number of inversions of A.

---

if $n = 0$ or $n = 1$ **then**   // base cases
    return $(A, 0)$
else
    $(C, leftInv) := $ Sort-and-CountInv(first half of A)
    $(D, rightInv) := $ Sort-and-CountInv(second half of A)
    $(B, splitInv) := $ Merge-and-CountSplitInv(C, D)
    return $(B, leftInv + rightInv + splitInv)$

We still need to implement the Merge-and-CountSplitInv subroutine. We know how to merge two sorted lists in linear time, but how can we piggyback on this work to also count the number of split inversions?

3.2.8   Merge Revisited

To see why merging sorted subarrays naturally uncovers split inversions, let's revisit the pseudocode for the Merge subroutine.

Merge

Input: sorted arrays C and D (length $n/2$ each).
Output: sorted array B (length n).
Simplifying assumption: n is even.

$i := 1, j := 1$
for $k := 1$ to n **do**
    if $C[i] < D[j]$ **then**
        $B[k] := C[i], i := i + 1$
    else $// \; D[j] < C[i]$
        $B[k] := D[j], j := j + 1$

To review, the Merge subroutine walks one index down each of the sorted subarrays in parallel (i for C and j for D), populating the output array (B) from left to right in sorted order (using the index k). At each iteration of the loop, the subroutine identifies the smallest element that it hasn't yet copied over to B. Because C and D are sorted, and all the elements before $C[i]$ and $D[j]$ have already been copied over to B, the only two candidates for the smallest-remaining element are $C[i]$ and $D[j]$. The subroutine determines which of the two is smaller and then copies it over to the next position of the output array.

What does the Merge subroutine have to do with counting the number of split inversions? Let's start with the special case of an array A that has no split inversions at all—every inversion of A is either a left or a right inversion.

Quiz 3.2

Suppose the input array A has no split inversions. What is the relationship between the sorted subarrays C and D?

a) C has the smallest element of A, D the second-smallest, C the third-smallest, and so on.

b) All the elements of C are less than all the elements of D.

c) All the elements of C are greater than all the elements of D.

d) There is not enough information to answer this question.

(See Section 3.2.13 for the solution and discussion.)

After solving Quiz 3.2, you can see that Merge has a particularly boring execution on an array with no split inversions. Because every element of C is smaller than every element of D, the smallest remaining element is always in C (until no elements of C remain). Thus the Merge subroutine simply concatenates C and D—it will first copy over all of C, and then all of D. This suggests that, perhaps, split inversions have something to do with the number of elements remaining in C when an element of D is copied over to the output array.

3.2.9   `Merge` and Split Inversions

To build our intuition further, let's think about running the `MergeSort` algorithm on the six-element array $A = \{1, 3, 5, 2, 4, 6\}$ from Section 3.2.2; see also Figure 3.1. The left and right halves of this array are already sorted, so there are no left inversions or right inversions, and the two recursive calls return 0. In the first iteration of the `Merge` subroutine, the first element of C (the 1) is copied over to B. This tells us nothing about any split inversions, and indeed there are no split inversions that involve this element. In the second iteration, however, the 2 is copied over to the output array, even though C still contains the elements 3 and 5. This exposes two of the split inversions of A—the two such inversions that involve the 2. In the third iteration, the 3 is copied over from C and there are no further split inversions that involve this element. When the 4 is copied over from D, the array C still contains a 5, and this copy exposes the third and final split inversion of A (involving the 5 and the 4).

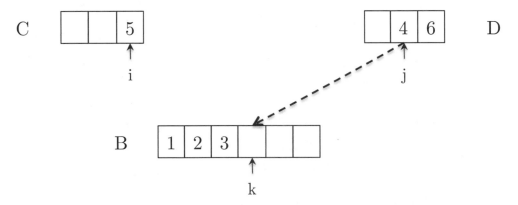

Figure 3.1: The fourth iteration of the `Merge` subroutine with the sorted input subarrays $\{1, 3, 5\}$ and $\{2, 4, 6\}$. Copying the 4 from D, with the 5 still in C, exposes the split inversion involving these two elements.

The following lemma states that the pattern in the example above holds in general: The number of split inversions that involve an element y of the second subarray D is precisely the number of elements remaining in C in the iteration of the `Merge` subroutine in which y is copied to the output array.

Lemma 3.1 (Identifying Split Inversions in `Merge`) *Let A be an array, and C and D sorted versions of the first and second halves of A. An element x from the first half of A and an element y from the second half of A form a split inversion if and only if, in the `Merge` subroutine with inputs C and D, y is copied to the output array before x.*

Proof: Because the output array is populated from left to right in sorted order, the smaller of x or y is copied over first. Because x is in the first half of A and y in the second half, x and y form a split inversion if and only if $x > y$, and this is true if and only if y is copied over to the output array before x. $\mathcal{QED}$

3.2.10   `Merge-and-CountSplitInv`

With the insight provided by Lemma 3.1, we can extend the implementation of `Merge` to an implementation of `Merge-and-CountSplitInv`. We maintain a running count of the split inversions, and every time an element is copied over from the second subarray D to the output array B, we increment the running count by the number of elements remaining in the first subarray C.[4]

Merge-and-CountSplitInv

Input: sorted arrays C and D (of length $n/2$ each).
Output: sorted array B (of length n) and the number of split inversions.
Simplifying assumption: n is even.

$i := 1, j := 1, splitInv := 0$
for $k := 1$ to n **do**
    if $C[i] < D[j]$ **then**
        $B[k] := C[i], i := i + 1$
    else $// \ \ D[j] < C[i]$
        $B[k] := D[j], j := j + 1$
        $splitInv := splitInv + \underbrace{(\frac{n}{2} - i + 1)}_{\text{\# left in } C}$
return $(B, splitInv)$

3.2.11 Correctness

Correctness of `Merge-and-CountSplitInv` follows from Lemma 3.1. Every split inversion involves exactly one element y from the second subarray, and this inversion is counted exactly once, when y is copied over to the output array. Correctness of the entire `Sort-and-CountInv` algorithm (Section 3.2.7) follows: the first recursive call correctly computes the number of left inversions, the second recursive call the number of right inversions, and `Merge-and-CountSplitInv` the remaining (split) inversions.

3.2.12 Running Time

We can also analyze the running time of the `Sort-and-CountInv` algorithm by piggybacking on the analysis we already did for the `MergeSort` algorithm. First consider the running time of a single invocation of the `Merge-and-CountSplitInv` subroutine, given two subarrays of length $\ell/2$ each. Like the `Merge` subroutine, it performs a constant number of operations per loop iteration, plus a constant number of additional operations, for a running time of $O(\ell)$.

Looking back at our running time analysis of the `MergeSort` algorithm in Section 1.5, we can see that there were three important properties of the algorithm that led to the running time bound of $O(n \log n)$. First, each invocation of the algorithm makes two recursive calls. Second, the length of the input is divided in half with each level of recursion. Third, the amount of work done in a recursive call, not counting work done by later recursive calls, is

---

[4]As with `Merge`, a full implementation should also keep track of when the traversal of C or D falls off the end of the array.

linear in the size of that call's input. Because the `Sort-and-CountInv` algorithm shares these three properties, the analysis in Section 1.5 carries over, again giving a running time bound of $O(n \log n)$.

Theorem 3.2 (Counting Inversions) *For every input array* A *of length* $n \geq 1$, *the* `Sort-and-CountInv` *algorithm correctly computes the number of inversions of* A *and runs in* $O(n \log n)$ *time.*

3.2.13   Solutions to Quizzes 3.1–3.2

Solution to Quiz 3.1

Correct answer: (a). The correct answer to this question is 15. The maximum-possible number of inversions is at most the number of ways of choosing $i, j \in \{1, 2, \ldots, 6\}$ with $i < j$. The latter quantity is denoted $\binom{6}{2}$, for "6 choose 2." In general, $\binom{n}{2} = \frac{n(n-1)}{2}$, and so $\binom{6}{2} = 15$.[5] In a six-element array $[6, 5, \ldots, 1]$ sorted in reverse order, every pair of elements is out of order, and so this array achieves 15 inversions.

Solution to Quiz 3.2

Correct answer: (b). In an array with no split inversions, everything in the first half is less than everything in the second half. If there *was* an element $A[i]$ in the first half (with $i \in \{1, 2, \ldots, \frac{n}{2}\}$) greater than an element $A[j]$ in the second half (with $j \in \{\frac{n}{2} + 1, \frac{n}{2} + 2, \ldots, n\}$), (i, j) would constitute a split inversion.

3.3   Strassen's Matrix Multiplication Algorithm

This section applies the divide-and-conquer algorithm design paradigm to the problem of multiplying matrices, culminating in Strassen's amazing subcubic-time matrix multiplication algorithm. This algorithm is a canonical example of the magic and power of clever algorithm design—of how algorithmic ingenuity can improve over straightforward solutions, even for extremely fundamental problems.

3.3.1   Matrix Multiplication

Suppose $\mathbf{X}$ and $\mathbf{Y}$ are $n \times n$ matrices of integers—n^2 entries in each. In the product $\mathbf{Z} = \mathbf{X} \cdot \mathbf{Y}$, the entry z_{ij} in the ith row and jth column of $\mathbf{Z}$ is defined as the dot product of the ith row of $\mathbf{X}$ and the jth column of $\mathbf{Y}$ (Figure 3.2).[6] That is,

$$z_{ij} = \sum_{k=1}^{n} x_{ik} y_{kj}. \tag{3.1}$$

---

[5]There are $n(n-1)$ ways to choose (i, j) so that $i \neq j$ (n choices for i, then $n - 1$ for j). By symmetry, $i < j$ in exactly half of these.

[6]To compute the *dot product* of two length-n vectors $\mathbf{a} = (a_1, a_2, \ldots, a_n)$ and $\mathbf{b} = (b_1, b_2, \ldots, b_n)$, add up the results of multiplying componentwise. Or in symbols, $\mathbf{a} \cdot \mathbf{b} = \sum_{k=1}^{n} a_k b_k$.

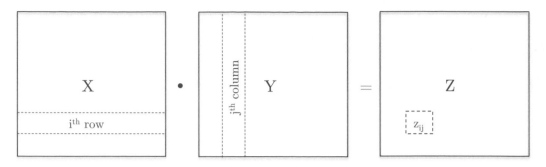

Figure 3.2: The (i, j) entry of the matrix product $\mathbf{X} \cdot \mathbf{Y}$ is the dot product of the ith row of $\mathbf{X}$ and the jth column of $\mathbf{Y}$.

3.3.2   Example ($n = 2$)

Let's drill down on the $n = 2$ case. We can describe two 2×2 matrices using eight parameters:

$$\underbrace{\begin{bmatrix} a & b \\ c & d \end{bmatrix}}_{\mathbf{X}} \quad \text{and} \quad \underbrace{\begin{bmatrix} e & f \\ g & h \end{bmatrix}}_{\mathbf{Y}}.$$

In the matrix product $\mathbf{X} \cdot \mathbf{Y}$, the upper-left entry is the dot product of the first row of $\mathbf{X}$ and the first column of $\mathbf{Y}$, or $ae + bg$. In general, for $\mathbf{X}$ and $\mathbf{Y}$ as above,

$$\mathbf{X} \cdot \mathbf{Y} = \begin{bmatrix} ae + bg & af + bh \\ ce + dg & cf + dh \end{bmatrix}. \tag{3.2}$$

3.3.3   The Straightforward Algorithm

Now let's think about algorithms for computing the product of two matrices.

Problem: Matrix Multiplication

Input: Two $n \times n$ integer matrices, $\mathbf{X}$ and $\mathbf{Y}$.[7]

Output: The matrix product $\mathbf{X} \cdot \mathbf{Y}$.

The input size is proportional to n^2, the number of entries in each of $\mathbf{X}$ and $\mathbf{Y}$. Because we presumably have to read the input and write out the output, the best we can hope for is an algorithm with running time $O(n^2)$—linear in the input size, and quadratic in the dimension. How close can we get to this best-case scenario?

Translating the mathematical definition into code gives a straightforward algorithm for matrix multiplication.

---

[7]The algorithms we discuss can also be extended to multiply non-square matrices, but we'll stick with the square case for simplicity.

Straightforward Matrix Multiplication

Input: $n \times n$ integer matrices $\mathbf{X}$ and $\mathbf{Y}$.
Output: $\mathbf{Z} = \mathbf{X} \cdot \mathbf{Y}$.

```
for i := 1 to n do              // loop over rows of X
    for j := 1 to n do          // loop over columns of Y
        Z[i][j] := 0
        for k := 1 to n do          // compute dot product
            Z[i][j] := Z[i][j] + X[i][k] · Y[k][j]
    return Z
```

What is the running time of this algorithm?

Quiz 3.3

What is the asymptotic running time of the straightforward algorithm for matrix multiplication, as a function of the matrix dimension n? You can assume that the addition or multiplication of two matrix entries is a constant-time operation.

a) $\Theta(n \log n)$

b) $\Theta(n^2)$

c) $\Theta(n^3)$

d) $\Theta(n^4)$

(See Section 3.3.7 for the solution and discussion.)

3.3.4   A Divide-and-Conquer Approach

The question is, as always, *can we do better?* Everyone's first reaction is that matrix multiplication should, essentially by definition, require cubic (that is, $\Omega(n^3)$) time. But perhaps we're emboldened by the success of the `Karatsuba` algorithm for integer multiplication (Section 1.3), a clever divide-and-conquer algorithm that improves over the straightforward grade-school algorithm. (We haven't actually proved this yet, but we will in Section 4.3.) Could a similar approach work for multiplying matrices?

To apply the divide-and-conquer paradigm (Section 3.1), we need to figure out how to divide the input into smaller subproblems and how to combine the solutions of these subproblems into a solution for the original problem. The simplest way to divide a square matrix into smaller square submatrices is to slice it in half, both vertically and horizontally. In other words, write

$$\mathbf{X} = \begin{bmatrix} \mathbf{A} & \mathbf{B} \\ \mathbf{C} & \mathbf{D} \end{bmatrix} \quad \text{and} \quad \mathbf{Y} = \begin{bmatrix} \mathbf{E} & \mathbf{F} \\ \mathbf{G} & \mathbf{H} \end{bmatrix}, \tag{3.3}$$

where $\mathbf{A}, \mathbf{B}, \ldots, \mathbf{H}$ are all $\frac{n}{2} \times \frac{n}{2}$ matrices.[8]

---

[8] As usual, we're assuming that n is even for convenience. And as usual, it doesn't really matter.

One cool thing about matrix multiplication is that equal-size blocks behave just like individual entries. That is, for $\mathbf{X}$ and $\mathbf{Y}$ as above, we have

$$\mathbf{X} \cdot \mathbf{Y} = \begin{bmatrix} \mathbf{A} \cdot \mathbf{E} + \mathbf{B} \cdot \mathbf{G} & \mathbf{A} \cdot \mathbf{F} + \mathbf{B} \cdot \mathbf{H} \\ \mathbf{C} \cdot \mathbf{E} + \mathbf{D} \cdot \mathbf{G} & \mathbf{C} \cdot \mathbf{F} + \mathbf{D} \cdot \mathbf{H} \end{bmatrix}, \tag{3.4}$$

completely analogous to the equation (3.2) for the $n = 2$ case. (This follows from the definition of matrix multiplication, as you should check.) In equation (3.4), adding two matrices means adding them entrywise—the (i, j) entry of $\mathbf{K} + \mathbf{L}$ is the sum of the (i, j) entries of $\mathbf{K}$ and $\mathbf{L}$. The decomposition and computation in (3.4) translates naturally to a recursive algorithm for matrix multiplication, which we'll call RecMatMult.

RecMatMult

Input: $n \times n$ integer matrices $\mathbf{X}$ and $\mathbf{Y}$.
Output: $\mathbf{Z} = \mathbf{X} \cdot \mathbf{Y}$.
Assumption: n is a power of 2.

---

if $n = 1$ **then**   // base case
    return the 1×1 matrix with entry $\mathbf{X}[1][1] \cdot \mathbf{Y}[1][1]$

$\mathbf{A}, \mathbf{B}, \mathbf{C}, \mathbf{D} :=$ submatrices of $\mathbf{X}$ as in (3.3)
$\mathbf{E}, \mathbf{F}, \mathbf{G}, \mathbf{H} :=$ submatrices of $\mathbf{Y}$ as in (3.3)

// eight recursive calls
recursively compute matrix products in right-hand side of (3.4)

// constant number of matrix additions
complete computation of the right-hand side of (3.4), return result

---

The running time of the RecMatMult algorithm is not immediately obvious. What is clear is that there are eight recursive calls, each on an input of half the dimension. Other than making these recursive calls, the only work required is the matrix additions in (3.4). Because an $n \times n$ matrix has n^2 entries, and the number of operations needed to add two matrices is proportional to the number of entries, a recursive call on a pair of $\ell \times \ell$ matrices performs $\Theta(\ell^2)$ operations, not counting the work done by its own recursive calls.

Disappointingly, this recursive algorithm turns out to have a running time of $\Theta(n^3)$, the same as the straightforward algorithm.[9] Has all our work been for naught? Remember that in the integer multiplication problem, the key to beating the grade-school algorithm was Gauss's trick, which reduced the number of recursive calls from four to three (Section 1.3.3). Is there an analog of Gauss's trick for matrix multiplication, one that allows us to reduce the number of recursive calls from eight to seven?

3.3.5 Saving a Recursive Call

The high-level plan of the Strassen algorithm is to save one recursive call relative to the RecMatMult algorithm, in exchange for a constant number of additional matrix additions and subtractions.

---

[9]This fact follows from the "master method," which is explained in the next chapter.

Strassen (Very High-Level Description)

Input: $n \times n$ integer matrices $\mathbf{X}$ and $\mathbf{Y}$.
Output: $\mathbf{Z} = \mathbf{X} \cdot \mathbf{Y}$.
Assumption: n is a power of 2.

```
// base case
```
if $n = 1$ **then**
    return the 1×1 matrix with entry $\mathbf{X}[1][1] \cdot \mathbf{Y}[1][1]$

```
// recursive case
```
$\mathbf{A}, \mathbf{B}, \mathbf{C}, \mathbf{D} :=$ submatrices of $\mathbf{X}$ as in (3.3)
$\mathbf{E}, \mathbf{F}, \mathbf{G}, \mathbf{H} :=$ submatrices of $\mathbf{Y}$ as in (3.3)

```
// seven recursive calls
```
recursively compute seven (cleverly chosen) products involving
$\mathbf{A}, \mathbf{B}, \ldots, \mathbf{H}$

```
// constant number of matrix additions and
  subtractions
```
return the appropriate (cleverly chosen) additions and subtractions of
the matrices computed in the previous step

Saving one of the eight recursive calls is a big win. It doesn't merely reduce the running time of the algorithm by 12.5%. The recursive call is saved over and over again, so the savings are compounded and—spoiler alert!—this results in an asymptotically superior running time. We'll see the exact running time bound in Section 4.3, but for now the important thing to know is that saving a recursive call yields an algorithm that runs in subcubic time.

This concludes all the high-level points you should know about Strassen's matrix multiplication algorithm. Are you in disbelief that it's possible to improve over the obvious algorithm? Or curious about exactly how the products, additions, and subtractions are chosen? If so, the next section is for you.

3.3.6   The Details

Let $\mathbf{X}$ and $\mathbf{Y}$ denote the two $n \times n$ input matrices, and define $\mathbf{A}, \mathbf{B}, \ldots, \mathbf{H}$ as in (3.3). Here are the seven recursive matrix multiplications performed by Strassen's algorithm:

$$\mathbf{P}_1 = \mathbf{A} \cdot (\mathbf{F} - \mathbf{H})$$
$$\mathbf{P}_2 = (\mathbf{A} + \mathbf{B}) \cdot \mathbf{H}$$
$$\mathbf{P}_3 = (\mathbf{C} + \mathbf{D}) \cdot \mathbf{E}$$
$$\mathbf{P}_4 = \mathbf{D} \cdot (\mathbf{G} - \mathbf{E})$$
$$\mathbf{P}_5 = (\mathbf{A} + \mathbf{D}) \cdot (\mathbf{E} + \mathbf{H})$$
$$\mathbf{P}_6 = (\mathbf{B} - \mathbf{D}) \cdot (\mathbf{G} + \mathbf{H})$$
$$\mathbf{P}_7 = (\mathbf{A} - \mathbf{C}) \cdot (\mathbf{E} + \mathbf{F}).$$

After spending $\Theta(n^2)$ time performing the necessary matrix additions and subtractions, $\mathbf{P}_1, \mathbf{P}_2, \ldots, \mathbf{P}_7$ can be computed using seven recursive calls on pairs of $\frac{n}{2} \times \frac{n}{2}$ matrices. But is this really enough information to reconstruct the matrix product of $\mathbf{X}$ and $\mathbf{Y}$ in $\Theta(n^2)$ time? The following amazing equation gives an affirmative answer:

$$\mathbf{X} \cdot \mathbf{Y} = \left[\begin{array}{c|c} \mathbf{A} \cdot \mathbf{E} + \mathbf{B} \cdot \mathbf{G} & \mathbf{A} \cdot \mathbf{F} + \mathbf{B} \cdot \mathbf{H} \\ \hline \mathbf{C} \cdot \mathbf{E} + \mathbf{D} \cdot \mathbf{G} & \mathbf{C} \cdot \mathbf{F} + \mathbf{D} \cdot \mathbf{H} \end{array} \right]$$

$$= \left[\begin{array}{c|c} \mathbf{P}_5 + \mathbf{P}_4 - \mathbf{P}_2 + \mathbf{P}_6 & \mathbf{P}_1 + \mathbf{P}_2 \\ \hline \mathbf{P}_3 + \mathbf{P}_4 & \mathbf{P}_1 + \mathbf{P}_5 - \mathbf{P}_3 - \mathbf{P}_7 \end{array} \right].$$

The first equation is copied from (3.4). For the second equation, we need to check that the equality holds in each of the four quadrants. To quell your disbelief, check out the crazy cancellations in the upper-left quadrant:

$$\begin{aligned} \mathbf{P}_5 + \mathbf{P}_4 - \mathbf{P}_2 + \mathbf{P}_6 = \ & (\mathbf{A} + \mathbf{D}) \cdot (\mathbf{E} + \mathbf{H}) + \mathbf{D} \cdot (\mathbf{G} - \mathbf{E}) \\ & - (\mathbf{A} + \mathbf{B}) \cdot \mathbf{H} + (\mathbf{B} - \mathbf{D}) \cdot (\mathbf{G} + \mathbf{H}) \\ = \ & \mathbf{A} \cdot \mathbf{E} + \mathbf{A} \cdot \mathbf{H} + \mathbf{D} \cdot \mathbf{E} + \mathbf{D} \cdot \mathbf{H} + \mathbf{D} \cdot \mathbf{G} \\ & - \mathbf{D} \cdot \mathbf{E} - \mathbf{A} \cdot \mathbf{H} - \mathbf{B} \cdot \mathbf{H} + \mathbf{B} \cdot \mathbf{G} \\ & + \mathbf{B} \cdot \mathbf{H} - \mathbf{D} \cdot \mathbf{G} - \mathbf{D} \cdot \mathbf{H} \\ = \ & \mathbf{A} \cdot \mathbf{E} + \mathbf{B} \cdot \mathbf{G}. \end{aligned}$$

The computation for the lower-right quadrant is similar, and equality is easy to see in the other two quadrants. So the `Strassen` algorithm really can multiply matrices with only seven recursive calls and $\Theta(n^2)$ additional work![10]

3.3.7 Solution to Quiz 3.3

Correct answer: (c). The correct answer is $\Theta(n^3)$. There are three nested for loops. This results in n^3 inner loop iterations (one for each choice of $i, j, k \in \{1, 2, \ldots, n\}$), and the algorithm performs a constant number of operations in each iteration (one multiplication and one addition). Alternatively, for each of the n^2 entries of $\mathbf{Z}$, the algorithm spends $\Theta(n)$ time evaluating (3.1).

*3.4   An $O(n \log n)$-Time Algorithm for the Closest Pair

Our final example of a divide-and-conquer algorithm is a very cool algorithm for the closest pair problem, in which you're given n points in the plane and want to figure out the pair of points that are closest to each other. This is our first taste of computational geometry,

---

[10]Of course, checking that the algorithm works is a lot easier than coming up with it in the first place. And how did Volker Strassen ever come up with it, back in 1969? Here's what he said (in a personal communication, June 2017):

> "The way I remember it, I had realized that a faster noncommutative algorithm for some small case would give a better exponent. I tried to prove that the straightforward algorithm is optimal for 2×2 matrices. To simplify matters I worked modulo 2, and then discovered the faster algorithm combinatorially."

an area of computer science that studies algorithms for reasoning about and manipulating geometric objects. Computational geometry has applications in robotics, computer vision, and computer graphics.[11]

3.4.1 The Problem

The closest pair problem concerns points $(x, y) \in \mathbb{R}^2$ in the plane. To measure the distance between two points $p_1 = (x_1, y_1)$ and $p_2 = (x_2, y_2)$, we use the usual Euclidean (straight-line) distance:

$$d(p_1, p_2) = \sqrt{(x_1 - x_2)^2 + (y_1 - y_2)^2}. \tag{3.5}$$

Problem: Closest Pair

Input: $n \geq 2$ points $p_1 = (x_1, y_1), p_2 = (x_2, y_2), \ldots, p_n = (x_n, y_n)$ in the plane.

Output: The pair p_i, p_j of distinct points with smallest Euclidean distance $d(p_i, p_j)$.

For convenience, we'll assume that no two points have the same x-coordinate or the same y-coordinate. You should think about how to extend the algorithm from this section to accommodate ties.[12]

The closest pair problem can be solved in quadratic time using exhaustive search—that is, by computing the distance between each of the $\Theta(n^2)$ pairs of points one by one, and returning the closest of them. For example, if the input comprises the four points $(1, 8)$, $(2, 5)$, $(4, 7)$, and $(6, 3)$, the distances between them are

Point	$(1, 8)$	$(2, 5)$	$(4, 7)$	$(6, 3)$
$(1, 8)$	0	$\sqrt{10}$	$\sqrt{10}$	$\sqrt{50}$
$(2, 5)$	$\sqrt{10}$	0	$\sqrt{8}$	$\sqrt{20}$
$(4, 7)$	$\sqrt{10}$	$\sqrt{8}$	0	$\sqrt{20}$
$(6, 3)$	$\sqrt{50}$	$\sqrt{20}$	$\sqrt{20}$	0

and the closest pair of distinct points consists of $(2, 5)$ and $(4, 7)$.

For the problem of counting inversions (Section 3.2), we were able to improve over the quadratic-time exhaustive search algorithm with a divide-and-conquer algorithm. Can we also do better here?

3.4.2 Does Sorting Help?

If we're happy with a running time of $O(n \log n)$—and we are, because that would be much faster than exhaustive search—one of our first instincts should be to turn to everyone's

---

[11]Starred sections like this one are the more difficult sections, and they can be skipped on a first reading.

[12]In a real-world implementation, a closest pair algorithm would not bother to compute the square root in (3.5)—the pair of points with the smallest Euclidean distance is the same as the one with the smallest squared Euclidean distance, and the latter distance is easier to compute.

favorite for-free primitive, sorting. For example, the one-dimensional version of the closest pair problem, in which the input points are points on the real line rather than in the plane, can be solved using a single invocation of a sorting subroutine followed by a single pass over the sorted points (see also Problem 1.5).

How can we sort points in the plane, which have two coordinates? The two obvious ways are by x-coordinate and by y-coordinate. For example, the four points above would be listed in the order

$$[(1,8),(2,5),(4,7),(6,3)]$$

if sorted by x-coordinate and in the order

$$[(6,3),(2,5),(4,7),(1,8)]$$

if sorted by y-coordinate.

Focusing on only one coordinate at a time can be misleading, however. In our running example, while the points $(1,8)$ and $(2,5)$ are closest in x-coordinate and the points $(4,7)$ and $(1,8)$ are closest in y-coordinate, it's the points $(2,5)$ and $(4,7)$ that constitute the actual closest pair. Can we somehow synthesize the information contained in the two one-dimensional orderings to identify the closest pair?

3.4.3 A Divide-and-Conquer Approach

We can improve over exhaustive search with a divide-and-conquer approach. First, in a preprocessing step, the input points are sorted (using MergeSort), once by x-coordinate and once again by y-coordinate; for our running example, this creates two copies of the point set, $P_x = [(1,8),(2,5),(4,7),(6,3)]$ and $P_y = [(6,3),(2,5),(4,7),(1,8)]$. The high-level plan is then analogous to the one that worked so well for counting inversions (see Section 3.2):

  (i) split the input points into a "left half" and "right half";

 (ii) recursively examine pairs of points in the left half;

(iii) recursively examine pairs of points in the right half;

(iv) use a bespoke subroutine to examine pairs of points split between the left and right halves.

Here "left half" and "right half" refer to the first and second halves of the list P_x of points sorted by x-coordinate. Call the three types of point pairs *left pairs*, *right pairs*, and *split pairs*.

For example, with the points $[(1,8),(2,5),(4,7),(6,3)]$ sorted by x-coordinate, $(1,8)$ and $(2,5)$ form a left pair, $(4,7)$ and $(6,3)$ form a right pair, and $(2,5)$ and $(4,7)$ form a split pair.

The following pseudocode summarizes the high-level plan; the bespoke subroutine ClosestSplitPair is, as of now, unimplemented.

ClosestPair (Preliminary Version)

Input: two copies P_x and P_y of a set P of $n \geq 2$ points in the plane, the first copy sorted by x-coordinate and the second copy by y-coordinate.

Output: the pair p_i, p_j of distinct points with the smallest Euclidean distance between them.

```
// base case of <= 3 points omitted
```
1 $L_x :=$ left half of P, sorted by x-coordinate
2 $L_y :=$ left half of P, sorted by y-coordinate
3 $R_x :=$ right half of P, sorted by x-coordinate
4 $R_y :=$ right half of P, sorted by y-coordinate

```
// best left pair
```
5 $(l_1, l_2) := \texttt{ClosestPair}(L_x, L_y)$

```
// best right pair
```
6 $(r_1, r_2) := \texttt{ClosestPair}(R_x, R_y)$

```
// best split pair
```
7 $(s_1, s_2) := \texttt{ClosestSplitPair}(P_x, P_y)$

8 return best of (l_1, l_2), (r_1, r_2), (s_1, s_2)

In the omitted base case, when there are two or three input points, the algorithm computes the closest pair by exhaustive search. With only a constant number of points, exhaustive search requires only a constant ($O(1)$) number of operations.

Every recursive call expects as input two copies of the same point set, one sorted by x-coordinate and the other by y-coordinate; this is the reason for the computation of the four lists L_x, L_y, R_x, and R_y. These lists can be constructed in linear ($O(n)$) time from the two given sorted copies of the input point set (P_x and P_y). The lists L_x and R_x are exactly the first and second halves of P_x. The last point of L_x (or the first point of R_x) then indicates which x-coordinates belong to the left half of P and which belong to the right half. To compute L_y and R_y in linear time, the algorithm can then perform a single pass over P_y, putting each point at the end of L_y or R_y, according to the point's x-coordinate. This pass correctly partitions the point set P into its left and right halves while retaining the ordering of each by y-coordinate. In our running four-point example:

$$L_x = [(1,8), (2,5)], R_x = [(4,7), (6,3)], L_y = [(2,5), (1,8)], R_y = [(6,3), (4,7)].$$

Provided we implement the `ClosestSplitPair` subroutine correctly, the algorithm is guaranteed to compute the closest pair of points—the three subroutine calls in lines 5–7 cover all the possibilities for where the closest pair might lie, and line 8 explicitly computes and returns the best of the last three candidates left standing.

Quiz 3.4

If we implement the `ClosestSplitPair` subroutine in $O(n)$ time, what will be the running time of the `ClosestPair` algorithm? (Choose the smallest correct bound.)

a) $O(n)$

b) $O(n \log n)$

c) $O(n(\log n)^2)$

d) $O(n^2)$

(See Section 3.4.9 for the solution and discussion.)

3.4.4 A Subtle Tweak

The solution to Quiz 3.4 makes our goal clear: We want an $O(n)$-time implementation of the `ClosestSplitPair` subroutine, leading to an overall running time bound of $O(n \log n)$.

We'll design a slightly weaker subroutine that is adequate for our purposes. Here's the key observation:

We rely on the `ClosestSplitPair` subroutine to correctly identify the closest split pair only when it is also the closest pair overall.

If the closest pair is a left or right pair, `ClosestSplitPair` might as well return garbage—line 8 of the pseudocode in Section 3.4.3 will ignore its suggested point pair anyway, in favor of the actual closest pair computed by one of the recursive calls. Our algorithm will make crucial use of this relaxed correctness requirement.

To implement this idea, we'll pass to the `ClosestSplitPair` subroutine the distance δ between the closest pair that is a left or right pair; the subroutine then knows that it has to worry only about split pairs with interpoint distance less than δ. In other words, we replace lines 7–8 of the pseudocode in Section 3.4.3 with the following.

`ClosestPair` (Addendum)

7 $\delta := \min\{d(l_1, l_2), d(r_1, r_2)\}$
8 $(s_1, s_2) := $ `ClosestSplitPair`(P_x, P_y, δ)
9 return best of $(l_1, l_2), (r_1, r_2), (s_1, s_2)$

3.4.5 `ClosestSplitPair`

We now supply an implementation of the `ClosestSplitPair` subroutine that runs in linear time and correctly computes the closest pair whenever it is a split pair. You may not believe that the following pseudocode satisfies these requirements, but it does. The high-level idea is to perform exhaustive search over a cleverly restricted set of point pairs.

ClosestSplitPair

Input: two copies P_x and P_y of a set P of $n \geq 2$ points in the plane, the first sorted by x-coordinate and the second by y-coordinate; and a parameter δ.

Output: the closest pair, provided it is a split pair.

```
      // compute median x-coordinate
1  x̄ := largest x-coordinate in left half
      // identify points near left/right boundary
2  Sy := list of points q₁, q₂, ..., qₗ with x-coordinate
          between x̄ − δ and x̄ + δ, sorted by y-coordinate
```

3 $closestDistance := \delta$ // distance to beat

4 $closestSplitPair := \emptyset$

5 **for** $i := 1$ to $\ell - 1$ **do**   // each point near boundary

6   **for** $j := i + 1$ to $\min\{i + 7, \ell\}$ **do**   // check next 7

7   **if** $d(q_i, q_j) < closestDistance$ **then**

8              $closestDistance := d(q_i, q_j)$

9              $closestSplitPair := (q_i, q_j)$

10 **return** $closestSplitPair$

In line 1 the subroutine identifies the rightmost point in the left half of the point set, which defines the "median x-coordinate" $\bar{x}$. A pair of points is a split pair if and only if one point has x-coordinate at most $\bar{x}$ and the other greater than $\bar{x}$. Because $\bar{x}$ is the x-coordinate of the $(n/2)$th entry of the list P_x, it can be retrieved in constant (that is, $O(1)$) time. In line 2 the subroutine performs a filtering step, discarding all points except those lying in the vertical strip of width 2δ centered at $\bar{x}$ (Figure 3.3). The set S_y can be computed in linear time by scanning through P_y and removing any points with an x-coordinate outside the range of interest.[13] Lines 5–9 perform the cleverly restricted exhaustive search, examining only pairs of points such that: (i) both points lie in the width-2δ vertical strip; and (ii) among such points, have near-consecutive y-coordinates (with at most six other such points between them). The subroutine returns the closest of all such point pairs.[14]

The subroutine performs a constant number of operations per loop iteration, along with $O(n)$ work outside the double for loop. Because of the mysterious "7" in the inner for loop, the number of loop iterations is at most $7\ell \leq 7n$ and we can conclude that the subroutine runs in $O(n)$ time, as desired. But why on earth should it find the closest pair? How can we justify examining only a linear number of the quadratically many point pairs? How do we know that the subroutine didn't miss out on the true closest pair?

---

[13]This step is the reason why we sorted the point set by y-coordinate once and for all in a preprocessing step. Because we're shooting for a linear-time subroutine, there's no time to sort them now!

[14]Or, if there is no such pair of points at distance less than δ, the subroutine returns the empty set. In this case, in ClosestPair, the final comparison in line 9 is between only the point pairs returned by the two recursive calls.

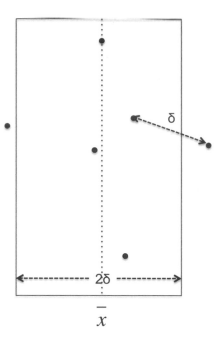

Figure 3.3: The `ClosestSplitPair` subroutine. The list S_y is the set of points enclosed by the vertical strip, ordered by y-coordinate. The parameter δ denotes the smallest distance between a left pair or a right pair of points. The split pairs have one point on either side of the dotted line.

3.4.6   Correctness

The following lemma, which is a bit shocking, guarantees that when the closest pair is a split pair, its points appear nearly consecutively in the filtered set S_y.

Lemma 3.3 (`ClosestSplitPair` Examines All Relevant Pairs) *Suppose (p, q) is a split pair with $d(p, q) < \delta$, where δ is the smallest distance between a left pair or right pair of points. Then, in the `ClosestSplitPair` subroutine:*

  (a) p and q will be included in the set S_y;

  (b) at most six points of S_y will have a y-coordinate in between those of p and q.

Lemma 3.3 is far from obvious, and we prove it in the next two sections. For now, we note that this lemma implies that the `ClosestSplitPair` subroutine does its job.

Corollary 3.4 (Correctness of `ClosestSplitPair`) *Whenever the closest pair is a split pair, the `ClosestSplitPair` subroutine returns it.*

Proof: Assume that the closest pair (p, q) is a split pair, and so $d(p, q) < \delta$, where δ is the minimum distance between a left or right pair. Then, Lemma 3.3 ensures that both p and q belong to the set S_y in the `ClosestSplitPair` subroutine, and that there are at most six points of S_y between them in y-coordinate. Because the subroutine exhaustively searches over all pairs of points that satisfy these two properties, it will compute the closest such pair, which must be the actual closest pair (p, q). $\mathcal{QED}$

Pending the proof of Lemma 3.3, we now have a correct and blazingly fast algorithm for the closest pair problem.

Theorem 3.5 (Computing the Closest Pair) *For every set P of $n \geq 2$ points in the plane, the* `ClosestPair` *algorithm correctly computes the closest pair of P and runs in $O(n \log n)$ time.*

Proof: We have already argued the running time bound: The algorithm spends $O(n \log n)$ time in its preprocessing step, and the rest of the algorithm has the same asymptotic running time as `MergeSort` (with two recursive calls each on half the input, plus linear additional work), which is also $O(n \log n)$.

For correctness, if the closest pair is a left pair, it is returned by the first recursive call (line 5 in Section 3.4.3). If it is a right pair, it is returned by the second recursive call (line 6). If it is a split pair, then Corollary 3.4 guarantees that it is returned by the `ClosestSplitPair` subroutine. The closest pair is, therefore, always among the final three candidates examined by the algorithm (in line 9 in Section 3.4.4), and will be returned as the final answer. $\mathcal{QED}$

3.4.7   Proof of Lemma 3.3(a)

Part (a) of Lemma 3.3 is the easier part to prove. Assume that there is a split pair (p, q) with $d(p, q) < \delta$, where p and q belong to the left and right halves of the point set, respectively, and δ is the minimum distance between a left or right pair. Write $p = (x_1, y_1)$ and $q = (x_2, y_2)$, and let $\bar{x}$ denote the x-coordinate of the rightmost point of the left half of the point set. Because p and q are in the left and right halves, respectively, we have

$$x_1 \leq \bar{x} < x_2.$$

At the same time, because p and q are close, x_1 and x_2 cannot be very different. Formally, because the Euclidean distance between p and q is less than δ, they differ by less than δ in each of their coordinates:

$$|x_1 - x_2|, |y_1 - y_2| < \delta. \tag{3.6}$$

Why is this true? Because if, say, $|x_1 - x_2| \geq \delta$, the Euclidean distance (3.5) between p and q would be at least $\sqrt{(x_1 - x_2)^2} \geq \sqrt{\delta^2} = \delta$, a contradiction.

Because $x_1 \leq \bar{x}$ and x_2 is at most δ larger than x_1, we have $x_2 \leq \bar{x} + \delta$ (Figure 3.4).[15] Similarly, because $x_2 \geq \bar{x}$ and x_1 is at most δ smaller than x_2, we have $x_1 \geq \bar{x} - \delta$. In particular, p and q both have x-coordinates that are wedged in between $\bar{x} - \delta$ and $\bar{x} + \delta$. All such points, including p and q, belong to the list S_y.

3.4.8   Proof of Lemma 3.3(b)

Recall our standing assumptions: There is a split pair (p, q), with $p = (x_1, y_1)$ in the left half of the point set and $q = (x_2, y_2)$ in the right half, such that $d(p, q) < \delta$, where δ is the minimum distance between a left or right pair. Lemma 3.3(b) asserts that p and q not only

---

[15] Imagine that p and q are people tied at the waist by a rope of length δ. The point p can travel only as far rightward as $\bar{x}$, which limits q's travels to $\bar{x} + \delta$.

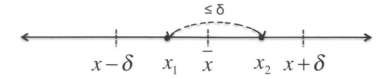

Figure 3.4: Proof of Lemma 3.3(a). Both p and q have x-coordinates between $\bar{x} - \delta$ and $\bar{x} + \delta$.

appear in the list S_y (as proved in part (a)), but that they are nearly consecutive, with at most six other points of S_y possessing a y-coordinate between y_1 and y_2.

For the proof, in our minds (not in the actual algorithm!), we draw eight boxes in the plane in a 2×4 pattern, where each box has side length $\delta/2$ (Figure 3.5). There are two columns of boxes on either side of $\bar{x}$, the median x-coordinate. The bottom of the boxes is aligned with the lower of the points p and q, at the y-coordinate $\min\{y_1, y_2\}$.

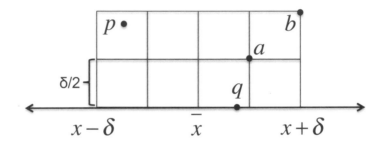

Figure 3.5: Proof of Lemma 3.3(b). The points p and q inhabit two of these eight boxes, and there is at most one point in each box.

From part (a), we know that both p and q have x-coordinates between $\bar{x} - \delta$ and $\bar{x} + \delta$. For concreteness, suppose q has the smaller y-coordinate; the other case is analogous. Thus, q appears at the bottom of some box in the bottom row (in the right half). Because p's y-coordinate can be only δ larger than q's (see (3.6)), p also appears in one of the boxes (in the left half). Every point of S_y with y-coordinate between p and q has: (i) x-coordinate between $\bar{x} - \delta$ and $\bar{x} + \delta$ (the requirement for membership in S_y); and (ii) y-coordinate between y_2 and $y_1 < y_2 + \delta$. Hence, every such point lies in one of the eight boxes.

The worry is that there are lots of points in these boxes that have y-coordinate between y_1 and y_2. To show that this can't happen, let's prove that each box contains at most one point. Then, the eight boxes include at most eight points (including p and q), and there can be only six points of S_y in between p and q in y-coordinate.[16]

Why does each box contain at most one point? This is the part of the argument that uses our observation in Section 3.4.4 and the fact that δ is the smallest distance between a left pair or a right pair. To derive a contradiction, suppose that some box has two points, a and b

---

[16]If a point has x-coordinate exactly $\bar{x}$, count it toward the box to its left. Other points on the boundary of multiple boxes can be assigned arbitrarily to one of them.

(one of which might be p or q). This point pair is either a left pair (if the points are in the first two columns) or a right pair (if they are in the last two). The farthest apart that a and b can be is at opposite corners of their box (Figure 3.5), in which case, by the Pythagorean theorem[17], the distance between a and b is $\sqrt{2} \cdot \frac{\delta}{2} < \delta$. But this contradicts the assumption that the distance between every left and right pair of points is at least δ! This contradiction implies that each of the eight boxes in Figure 3.5 contains at most one point, completing the proof. $\mathcal{QED}$

3.4.9   Solution to Quiz 3.4

Correct answer: (b). The correct answer is $O(n \log n)$. $O(n)$ is not correct because, among other reasons, the `ClosestPair` algorithm already spends $\Theta(n \log n)$ time in its preprocessing step creating the sorted lists P_x and P_y. The upper bound of $O(n \log n)$ follows from the exact same argument as for `MergeSort`: the `ClosestPair` algorithm makes two recursive calls, each on an input of half the size, and performs $O(n)$ work outside its recursive calls. (Recall that lines 1–4 and 8 can be implemented in $O(n)$ time, and for this quiz we are assuming that `ClosestSplitPair` also runs in linear time.) This pattern perfectly matches the one we already analyzed for `MergeSort` in Section 1.5, so we know that the total number of operations performed is $O(n \log n)$. Because the preprocessing step also runs in $O(n \log n)$ time, the final running time bound is $O(n \log n)$.

The Upshot

☆ A divide-and-conquer algorithm divides the input into smaller sub-problems, conquers the subproblems recursively, and combines the subproblem solutions into a solution for the original problem.

☆ Computing the number of inversions in an array is relevant for measuring similarity between two ranked lists. The exhaustive search algorithm for the problem runs in $\Theta(n^2)$ time for arrays of length n.

☆ There is a divide-and-conquer algorithm that piggybacks on `MergeSort` and computes the number of inversions in an array in $O(n \log n)$ time.

☆ Strassen's subcubic-time divide-and-conquer algorithm for matrix multiplication is a mind-blowing example of how algorithmic ingenuity can improve over straightforward solutions. The key idea is to save a recursive call over a simpler divide-and-conquer algorithm, analogous to Karatsuba multiplication.

☆ In the closest pair problem, the input is n points in the plane, and the goal is to compute the pair of points with smallest Euclidean distance between them. The exhaustive search algorithm runs in $\Theta(n^2)$ time.

---

[17]For a right triangle, the sum of the squared lengths of the sides equals the squared length of the hypotenuse.

> ☆ There is a sophisticated divide-and-conquer algorithm that solves the closest pair problem in $O(n \log n)$ time.

Test Your Understanding

Problem 3.1 *(H)* Consider the following pseudocode for calculating a^b, where a and b are positive integers:[18]

FastPower

Input: positive integers a and b.
Output: a^b.

---

if $b = 1$ **then**
    return a
else
    $c := a \cdot a$
    $ans := \text{FastPower}(c, \lfloor b/2 \rfloor)$
if b is odd **then**
    return $a \cdot ans$
else
    return ans

Assume for this problem that each multiplication and division can be performed in constant time. What is the asymptotic running time of this algorithm, as a function of b?

a) $\Theta(\log b)$

b) $\Theta(\sqrt{b})$

c) $\Theta(b)$

d) $\Theta(b \log b)$

Problem 3.2 *(S)* Consider using the `Strassen` algorithm to multiply the following two matrices:

$$\begin{bmatrix} 1 & 2 \\ 3 & 4 \end{bmatrix} \quad \text{and} \quad \begin{bmatrix} 5 & 6 \\ 7 & 8 \end{bmatrix}.$$

In this case, what are the matrices $\mathbf{P}_1$–$\mathbf{P}_7$ defined in Section 3.3.6?

---

[18]The notation $\lfloor x \rfloor$ denotes the "floor" function, which rounds its argument down to the nearest integer.

Challenge Problems

Problem 3.3 *(H)* You are given a *unimodal* array of n distinct elements, meaning that its entries are in increasing order up until its maximum element, after which its elements are in decreasing order. Give an algorithm to compute the maximum element of a unimodal array that runs in $O(\log n)$ time.

Problem 3.4 *(H)* You are given a sorted (from smallest to largest) array A of n distinct integers which can be positive, negative, or zero. Design the fastest algorithm you can for deciding whether there is an index i such that $A[i] = i$.

Problem 3.5 *(H)* In the matrix-vector multiplication problem, the input is an $n \times n$ integer matrix $\mathbf{A}$ and a length-n integer vector $\mathbf{x}$. The goal is to compute their product $\mathbf{A} \cdot \mathbf{x}$, which is the length-$n$ vector containing the dot product of $\mathbf{x}$ with each of the rows of $\mathbf{A}$. For example,

$$\begin{bmatrix} 1 & 2 \\ 3 & 4 \end{bmatrix} \cdot \begin{bmatrix} 5 \\ 6 \end{bmatrix} = \begin{bmatrix} 1 \cdot 5 + 2 \cdot 6 \\ 3 \cdot 5 + 4 \cdot 6 \end{bmatrix} = \begin{bmatrix} 17 \\ 39 \end{bmatrix}.$$

Matrix-vector multiplication requires $\Omega(n^2)$ operations in general, but there are important-in-practice examples of matrices $\mathbf{A}$ for which it can be done much faster by a divide-and-conquer approach.

Here are the first three *Hadamard matrices*:

$$\mathbf{H}_1 = \begin{bmatrix} 1 \end{bmatrix}, \ \mathbf{H}_2 = \begin{bmatrix} 1 & 1 \\ 1 & -1 \end{bmatrix}, \ \mathbf{H}_3 = \begin{bmatrix} 1 & 1 & 1 & 1 \\ 1 & -1 & 1 & -1 \\ 1 & 1 & -1 & -1 \\ 1 & -1 & -1 & 1 \end{bmatrix}.$$

In general, the kth Hadamard matrix $\mathbf{H}_k$ is derived from the previous one $\mathbf{H}_{k-1}$ according to

$$\mathbf{H}_k = \left[\begin{array}{c|c} \mathbf{H}_{k-1} & \mathbf{H}_{k-1} \\ \hline \mathbf{H}_{k-1} & -\mathbf{H}_{k-1} \end{array} \right].$$

Give an $O(n \log n)$-time algorithm that accepts as input an integer vector $\mathbf{x}$ of length n, with $n = 2^k$ a power of two, and outputs the matrix-vector product $\mathbf{H}_k \cdot \mathbf{x}$. You can assume for this problem that every arithmetic operation can be performed in constant time.[19]

Problem 3.6 *(H)* (Difficult.) You are given an n-by-n grid of distinct numbers. A number is a *local minimum* if it is smaller than all its neighbors. (A *neighbor* of a number is one immediately above, below, to the left, or to the right. Most numbers have four neighbors; numbers on the side have three; the four corners have two.) Use the divide-and-conquer algorithm design paradigm to compute a local minimum with only $O(n)$ comparisons between pairs of numbers. (Note: because there are n^2 numbers in the input, you cannot afford to look at all of them.)

---

[19]The *Fast Fourier Transform (FFT)* is an ultra-famous $O(n \log n)$-time algorithm that works in exactly the same way, except with the similarly recursively defined "Fourier matrix" $\mathbf{F}_k$ playing the role of the Hadamard matrix $\mathbf{H}_k$. For example, if $\mathbf{x}$ represents 2^k evenly-spaced samples of an audio signal over a period of time, the FFT $\mathbf{F}_k \cdot \mathbf{x}$ re-expresses the signal as the sum of its frequencies, facilitating signal manipulations such as noise reduction.

Problem 3.7 *(H)* (Difficult.) In the *all-nearest-neighbors* problem, the input is a set $P = \{p_1, p_2, \ldots, p_n\}$ of $n \geq 2$ points in the plane, and the goal is to compute, for every point $p_i \in P$, the point $p_j \in P$ that minimizes the Euclidean distance $d(p_i, p_j)$ defined in (3.5). (Of course, p_i and p_j are required to be distinct.)

Give an $O(n \log n)$-time algorithm for this problem. You can assume that the input points have distinct x-coordinates and distinct y-coordinates.

Programming Problems

Problem 3.8 Implement in your favorite programming language the `CountInv` algorithm from Section 3.2 for counting the number of inversions of an array. (See `www.algorithmsilluminated.org` for test cases and challenge data sets.)

Chapter 4

The Master Method

This chapter presents a "black-box" method for determining the running time of recursive algorithms—plug in a few key characteristics of the algorithm, and out pops an upper bound on the algorithm's running time. This "master method" applies to most of the divide-and-conquer algorithms you'll ever see, including Karatsuba's integer multiplication algorithm (Section 1.3) and Strassen's matrix multiplication algorithm (Section 3.3).[1] This chapter also illustrates a more general theme in the study of algorithms: properly evaluating novel algorithmic ideas often requires non-obvious mathematical analysis.

After introducing recurrences in Section 4.1, we give a formal statement of the master method (Section 4.2) and look at six example applications (Section 4.3). Section 4.4 covers the proof of the master method, with an emphasis on the meaning behind its famous three cases. The proof builds nicely on our analysis of the `MergeSort` algorithm back in Section 1.5.

4.1 Integer Multiplication Revisited

To motivate the master method, let's review what we know about integer multiplication (Sections 1.2–1.3). The problem is to multiply two n-digit numbers, where the primitive operations are the addition or multiplication of two single-digit numbers. The iterative grade-school algorithm requires $\Theta(n^2)$ operations to multiply two n-digit numbers. Can we do better with a divide-and-conquer approach?

4.1.1 The `RecIntMult` Algorithm

The `RecIntMult` algorithm from Section 1.3 creates smaller subproblems by breaking the given n-digit numbers x and y into their first and second halves:

$$x = 10^{n/2} \cdot a + b$$

and

$$y = 10^{n/2} \cdot c + d,$$

where a, b, c, d are $n/2$-digit numbers (assuming n is even, for simplicity). For example, if $x = 1234$, then $a = 12$ and $b = 34$. We can expand the product $x \cdot y$ as

$$x \cdot y = 10^n \cdot (a \cdot c) + 10^{n/2} \cdot (a \cdot d + b \cdot c) + b \cdot d, \tag{4.1}$$

which shows that multiplying two n-digit numbers reduces to multiplying four pairs of $n/2$-digit numbers, plus $O(n)$ additional operations (for appending zeroes appropriately and grade-school addition).

---

[1]The master method is also called the "master theorem."

The way to describe this pattern formally is by a *recurrence*. Let $T(n)$ denote the maximum number of operations used by this recursive algorithm to multiply two n-digit numbers—this is the quantity that we seek to bound from above. A recurrence expresses a running time bound $T(n)$ in terms of the number of operations performed by recursive calls. The recurrence for the RecIntMult algorithm is

$$T(n) \quad \leq \quad \underbrace{4 \cdot T\left(\frac{n}{2}\right)}_{\text{work done by recursive calls}} \quad + \quad \underbrace{O(n)}_{\text{work done outside recursive calls}} \quad .$$

Like a recursive algorithm, a recurrence also needs one or more base cases, which state what $T(n)$ is for values of n that are too small to trigger any recursive calls. Here, the base case is when $n = 1$; because the algorithm performs a single multiplication in this case, $T(1) = 1$.

4.1.2 The Karatsuba Algorithm

Karatsuba's recursive algorithm for integer multiplication uses a trick due to Gauss to save one recursive call. The trick is to recursively compute the products of a and c, b and d, and $a + b$ and $c + d$, and extract the middle coefficient $ad + bc$ of (4.1) via the computation $(a + b)(c + d) - ac - bd$. These calculations provide enough information to compute the right-hand side of (4.1) with $O(n)$ additional primitive operations.

Quiz 4.1

Which recurrence best describes the running time of the Karatsuba algorithm for integer multiplication?

a) $T(n) \leq 2 \cdot T\left(\frac{n}{2}\right) + O(n^2)$

b) $T(n) \leq 3 \cdot T\left(\frac{n}{2}\right) + O(n)$

c) $T(n) \leq 3 \cdot T\left(\frac{n}{2}\right) + O(n^2)$

d) $T(n) \leq 4 \cdot T\left(\frac{n}{2}\right) + O(n)$

(See below for the solution and discussion.)

Correct answer: (b). The only change from the RecIntMult algorithm is that the number of recursive calls has dropped by one. It's true that the amount of work done outside the recursive calls is larger in the Karatsuba algorithm, but only by a constant factor that gets suppressed in the big-O notation. The appropriate recurrence for the Karatsuba algorithm is therefore

$$T(n) \quad \leq \quad \underbrace{3 \cdot T\left(\frac{n}{2}\right)}_{\text{work done by recursive calls}} \quad + \quad \underbrace{O(n)}_{\text{work done outside recursive calls}} \quad ,$$

again with the base case $T(1) = 1.$[2]

---

[2] Technically, the recursive call on $a + b$ and $c + d$ might involve $(\frac{n}{2} + 1)$-digit numbers. Among friends, let's ignore this—it doesn't matter in the final analysis.

4.1.3   Comparing the Recurrences

At the moment, we don't know the running time of `RecIntMult` or `Karatsuba`, but inspecting their recurrences suggests that the latter is at least as fast as the former. Meanwhile, we saw in Section 1.5 that the running time of `MergeSort` is governed by a similar recurrence with still one fewer recursive call:

$$T(n) \;\leq\; \underbrace{2 \cdot T\left(\frac{n}{2}\right)}_{\text{work done by recursive calls}} + \underbrace{O(n)}_{\text{work done outside recursive calls}} \;,$$

where n is the length of the array to be sorted. This fact suggests that our running time bounds for both the `RecIntMult` and `Karatsuba` algorithms cannot be better than our bound for `MergeSort`, which is $O(n \log n)$. Beyond these clues, we really have no idea what the running time of either algorithm is. Enlightenment awaits with the master method, discussed next.

4.2   Formal Statement

The master method is exactly what you'd want for analyzing recursive algorithms. It takes as input the recurrence for the algorithm and—boom—spits out as output an upper bound on the running time of the algorithm.

4.2.1   Standard Recurrences

We'll discuss a version of the master method that handles what we'll call "standard recurrences," which have three free parameters and the following form.[3]

Standard Recurrence Format

Base case: $T(n)$ is at most a constant for all sufficiently small n.[4]

General case: for larger values of n,

$$T(n) \leq a \cdot T\left(\frac{n}{b}\right) + O(n^d).$$

Parameters:

- a = number of recursive calls

- b = input size shrinkage factor

- d = exponent in running time of the "combine step"

The base case of a standard recurrence asserts that once the input size is so small that no recursive calls are needed, the problem can be solved in $O(1)$ time. This will be the

---

[3]This presentation of the master method draws inspiration from Chapter 2 of *Algorithms*, by Sanjoy Dasgupta, Christos Papadimitriou, and Umesh Vazirani (McGraw-Hill, 2006).

[4]Formally, there exist positive integers n_0 and c, independent of n, such that $T(n) \leq c$ for all $n \leq n_0$.

case for all the applications we consider. The general case assumes that the algorithm makes a recursive calls, each on a subproblem with size a b factor smaller than its input, and does $O(n^d)$ work outside these recursive calls. For example, in the MergeSort algorithm, there are two recursive calls ($a = 2$), each on an array of half the size of the input ($b = 2$), and $O(n)$ work is done outside the recursive calls ($d = 1$). In general, a can be any positive integer, b can be any real number bigger than 1 (if $b \leq 1$ then the algorithm won't terminate), and d can be any nonnegative real number, with $d = 0$ indicating only constant ($O(1)$) work beyond the recursive calls. As usual, we ignore the detail that n/b might need to be rounded up or down to an integer—and as usual, it doesn't affect our final conclusions. Never forget that a, b, and d should be *constants*—numbers that are independent of the input size n.[5] Typical values for these parameters are 0 (for d), 1 (for a and d), 2, and other small integers (primarily for a). If you ever find yourself saying something like "apply the master method with $a = n$ or $b = \frac{n}{n-1}$," you're using it incorrectly.

One restriction in standard recurrences is that every recursive call is on a subproblem of the same size. For example, an algorithm that recurses once on the first third of an input array and once on the rest would lead to a non-standard recurrence. Most (but not all) natural divide-and-conquer algorithms lead to standard recurrences. For example, in the MergeSort algorithm, both recursive calls operate on problems with size half that of the input array. In our recursive integer multiplication algorithms, recursive calls are always given numbers with half as many digits.[6]

4.2.2 Statement and Discussion of the Master Method

We can now state the master method, which provides an upper bound on a standard recurrence as a function of the parameters a, b, and d.

Theorem 4.1 (Master Method) *If $T(n)$ is defined by a standard recurrence, with parameters $a \geq 1$, $b > 1$, and $d \geq 0$, then*

$$T(n) = \begin{cases} O(n^d \log n) & \textit{if } a = b^d & \text{[Case 1]} \\ O(n^d) & \textit{if } a < b^d & \text{[Case 2]} \\ O(n^{\log_b a}) & \textit{if } a > b^d & \text{[Case 3].} \end{cases} \qquad (4.2)$$

What's up with the three cases, and why are the relative values of a and b^d so important? In the second case, could the running time of the whole algorithm really be only $O(n^d)$, when the outermost recursive call already does $O(n^d)$ work? And what's the deal with the exotic-looking running time bound in the third case? By the end of this chapter you'll learn satisfying answers to all of these questions, and the statement of the master method will seem like the most natural thing in the world.[7]

---

[5]There are also the constants suppressed in the base case and in the "$O(n^d)$" term, but the conclusion of the master method does not depend on their values.

[6]There are more general versions of the master method that accommodate a wider range of recurrences, but the simple version here is sufficient for almost any divide-and-conquer algorithm that you're likely to encounter in the wild.

[7]The bounds in Theorem 4.1 have the form $O(f(n))$ rather than $\Theta(f(n))$ because in our recurrence we assume only an upper bound on $T(n)$. If we replace "$\leq$" with "$=$" and $O(n^d)$ with $\Theta(n^d)$ in the definition of a standard recurrence, the bounds in Theorem 4.1 hold with $O(\cdot)$ replaced by $\Theta(\cdot)$. See also Problem 4.6.

> ### More On Logarithms
>
> Another puzzling aspect of Theorem 4.1 concerns the inconsistent use of logarithms. The third case carefully states that the logarithm in question is base-b—the number of times you can divide n by b before the result is at most 1. Meanwhile, the first case does not specify the base of the logarithm at all. The reason is that *any two logarithmic functions differ only by a constant factor*. For example, the base-2 logarithm always exceeds the natural logarithm (i.e., the base-e logarithm, where $e = 2.718\ldots$) by a factor of $1/\ln 2 \approx 1.44$. In the first case of the master method, changing the base of the logarithm changes only the constant factor that is conveniently suppressed in the big-O notation. In the third case, the logarithm appears in the exponent, where different constant factors translate to very different running time bounds (like n^2 vs. n^{100})!

4.3   Six Examples

The master method (Theorem 4.1) is hard to get your head around the first time you see it. Let's instantiate it in six different examples.

4.3.1   `MergeSort` Revisited

As a sanity check, let's revisit an algorithm whose running time we already know, `MergeSort`.   To apply the master method, all we need to do is identify the values of the three free parameters: a, the number of recursive calls; b, the factor by which the input size shrinks prior to the recursive calls; and d, the exponent in the bound on the amount of work done outside the recursive calls.[8] In `MergeSort`, there are two recursive calls, so $a = 2$. Each recursive call receives half of the input array, so $b = 2$ as well. The work done outside these recursive calls is dominated by the `Merge` subroutine, which runs in linear time (Section 1.5.1), and so $d = 1$. Thus

$$a = 2 = 2^1 = b^d,$$

putting us in the first case of the master method. Plugging in the parameters, Theorem 4.1 tells us that the running time of `MergeSort` is $O(n^d \log n) = O(n \log n)$, thereby replicating our analysis in Section 1.5.

4.3.2   Binary Search

For our second example, consider the problem of searching a sorted array for a given element. Think, for example, of searching for your own name in an alphabetical list in a large book. (Readers of at least a certain age might be reminded of a phone book.) You could search linearly starting from the beginning, but this would squander the advantage that the list is

---

[8]All the recurrences that we consider have a base case in the form required for standard recurrences, and we won't discuss them from here on out.

in alphabetical order. A smarter approach is to look in the middle of the book and recurse on either its first half (if the name in the middle comes after your own) or its second half (otherwise). This algorithm, translated to the problem of searching a sorted array, is known as *binary search*.[9]

What's the running time of binary search? This question is easy enough to answer directly, but let's see how the master method handles it.

Quiz 4.2

What are the respective values of a, b, and d for the binary search algorithm?

a) $1, 2, 0$ [case 1]

b) $1, 2, 1$ [case 2]

c) $2, 2, 0$ [case 3]

d) $2, 2, 1$ [case 1]

(See Section 4.3.7 for the solution and discussion.)

4.3.3 Recursive Integer Multiplication

Now we get to the good stuff, divide-and-conquer algorithms for which we don't yet know a running time bound. Let's begin with the `RecIntMult` algorithm for integer multiplication. We saw in Section 4.1 that the appropriate recurrence for this algorithm is

$$T(n) \leq 4 \cdot T\left(\frac{n}{2}\right) + O(n),$$

and so $a = 4$, $b = 2$, and $d = 1$. Thus

$$a = 4 > 2 = 2^1 = b^d,$$

putting us in the third case of the master method. In this case, we obtain the exotic-looking running time bound of $O(n^{\log_b a})$. For our parameter values, this is $O(n^{\log_2 4}) = O(n^2)$. Thus the `RecIntMult` algorithm matches but does not outperform the iterative grade-school algorithm for integer multiplication (which uses $\Theta(n^2)$ operations).

4.3.4 Karatsuba Multiplication

A divide-and-conquer approach to integer multiplication pays off only once Gauss's trick is used to save a recursive call. As we saw in Section 4.1, the running time of the `Karatsuba` algorithm is governed by the recurrence

$$T(n) \leq 3 \cdot T\left(\frac{n}{2}\right) + O(n),$$

---

[9]If you haven't walked through the code of this algorithm before, look it up in your favorite introductory programming book or online tutorial.

which differs from the previous recurrence only in that a has dropped from 4 to 3 (b is still 2, d is still 1). We expect the running time to be somewhere between $O(n \log n)$ (the bound when $a = 2$, as in `MergeSort`) and $O(n^2)$ (the bound when $a = 4$, as in `RecIntMult`). If the suspense is killing you, the master method offers a quick resolution. We have

$$a = 3 > 2 = 2^1 = b^d,$$

and so we are still in the third case of the master method, but with an improved running time bound: $O(n^{\log_b a}) = O(n^{\log_2 3}) = O(n^{1.59})$. Thus saving a recursive call leads to a fundamentally better running time, and the integer multiplication algorithm that you learned in the third grade is not the fastest possible![10]

4.3.5   Matrix Multiplication

Section 3.3 considered the problem of multiplying two $n \times n$ matrices. As with integer multiplication, we discussed three algorithms—a straightforward iterative algorithm, the straightforward recursive `RecMatMult` algorithm, and the ingenious `Strassen` algorithm. The iterative algorithm uses $\Theta(n^3)$ operations (Quiz 3.3). The `RecMatMult` algorithm breaks each of the two input matrices into four $\frac{n}{2} \times \frac{n}{2}$ matrices (one for each quadrant), performs the corresponding eight recursive calls on smaller matrices, and combines the results appropriately (using straightforward matrix addition). The `Strassen` algorithm cleverly identifies seven pairs of $\frac{n}{2} \times \frac{n}{2}$ matrices whose products suffice to reconstruct the product of the original input matrices.

Quiz 4.3

What running time bounds does the master method provide for the `RecMatMult` and `Strassen` algorithms, respectively?

   a) $O(n^3)$ and $O(n^2)$

   b) $O(n^3)$ and $O(n^{\log_2 7})$

   c) $O(n^3)$ and $O(n^3)$

   d) $O(n^3 \log n)$ and $O(n^3)$

(See Section 4.3.7 for the solution and discussion.)

4.3.6   A Fictitious Recurrence

In our five examples thus far, two recurrences have fallen in the first case of the master method, and the rest in the third case. There are also naturally occurring recurrences that fall in the second case. For example, suppose we have a divide-and-conquer algorithm that

---

[10]Fun fact: In the Python programming language, the built-in subroutine for multiplying integer objects uses the grade-school algorithm for integers with at most 70 digits, and the `Karatsuba` algorithm otherwise.

operates like `MergeSort`, except that the algorithm works harder outside the recursive calls, doing a quadratic rather than linear amount of work. That is, consider the recurrence

$$T(n) \le 2 \cdot T\left(\frac{n}{2}\right) + O(n^2).$$

Here, we have

$$a = 2 < 4 = 2^2 = b^d,$$

putting us squarely in the second case of the master method, for a running time bound of $O(n^d) = O(n^2)$. This might seem counterintuitive; given that the `MergeSort` algorithm does linear work outside the two recursive calls and has a running time of $O(n \log n)$, you might expect that a quadratic-time combine step would lead to a running time of $O(n^2 \log n)$. The master method shows this to be an overestimate, and provides the better upper bound of $O(n^2)$. Remarkably, this means that the total running time of the algorithm is dominated by the work done in the outermost call—all subsequent recursive calls only increase the total number of operations performed by a constant factor.[11]

4.3.7   Solutions to Quizzes 4.2–4.3

Solution to Quiz 4.2

Correct answer: (a). Binary search recurses on either the left half of the input array or the right half (never both), so there is only one recursive call ($a = 1$). This recursive call is on half of the input array, so b is again equal to 2. Outside the recursive call, all binary search does is a single comparison (between the middle element of the array and the element being searched for) to determine whether to recurse on the left or the right half of the array. This translates to $O(1)$ work outside the recursive call, so $d = 0$. Because $a = 1 = 2^0 = b^d$, we are again in the first case of the master method, and we get a running time bound of $O(n^d \log n) = O(\log n)$.

Solution to Quiz 4.3

Correct answer: (b). Let's start with the `RecMatMult` algorithm (Section 3.3.4). Let $T(n)$ denote the maximum number of primitive operations that the algorithm uses to multiply two $n \times n$ matrices. The number a of recursive calls is 8. Each of these calls is on a pair of $\frac{n}{2} \times \frac{n}{2}$ matrices, so $b = 2$. The work done outside the recursive calls involves a constant number of matrix additions, and these require $O(n^2)$ time (constant time for each of the n^2 matrix entries). Thus the recurrence is

$$T(n) \le 8 \cdot T\left(\frac{n}{2}\right) + O(n^2),$$

and because

$$a = 8 > 4 = 2^2 = b^d,$$

we are in the third case of the master method, which gives a running time bound of $O(n^{\log_b a}) = O(n^{\log_2 8}) = O(n^3)$.

---

[11]We'll see another example of case 2 of the master method when we discuss linear-time selection in Chapter 6.

The only difference between the recurrence for the `Strassen` algorithm and the recurrence above is that the number a of recursive calls drops from 8 to 7. It's true that the `Strassen` algorithm does more matrix additions and subtractions than `RecMatMult`, but only by a constant factor, and hence d is still equal to 2. Thus

$$a = 7 > 4 = 2^2 = b^d.$$

We are still in the third case of the master method, but with an improved running time bound: $O(n^{\log_b a}) = O(n^{\log_2 7}) = O(n^{2.81})$. Thus the `Strassen` algorithm really is asymptotically superior to the straightforward iterative algorithm![12]

*4.4   Proof of the Master Method

This section proves the master method (Theorem 4.1): If $T(n)$ is governed by a standard recurrence, of the form

$$T(n) \le a \cdot T\left(\frac{n}{b}\right) + O(n^d),$$

then

$$T(n) = \begin{cases} O(n^d \log n) & \text{if } a = b^d & \text{[Case 1]} \\ O(n^d) & \text{if } a < b^d & \text{[Case 2]} \\ O(n^{\log_b a}) & \text{if } a > b^d & \text{[Case 3]}. \end{cases}$$

It's important to remember the meanings of the three free parameters:

Parameter	Meaning
a	number of recursive calls
b	factor by which input size shrinks in recursive call
d	exponent of work done outside recursive calls

4.4.1   Preamble

The proof of the master method is important not because we care about formality for its own sake, but because it provides the fundamental explanation for why things are the way they are—for example, why the master method has three cases. With this in mind, you should distinguish between two types of content in the proof. At a couple points we will resort to algebraic computations to understand what's going on. These calculations are worth seeing once in your life, but they are not particularly important to remember in the long term. What is worth remembering is the conceptual meaning of the three cases of the master method. The proof will use the recursion tree approach that served us so well for analyzing the `MergeSort` algorithm (Section 1.5), and the three cases correspond to three different types of recursion trees. If you can remember the meaning of the three cases, there is no need to memorize the running times in the master method—you will be able to reverse engineer them as needed from your conceptual understanding of it.

---

[12]There is a long line of research papers that devise increasingly sophisticated matrix multiplication algorithms with ever-better worst-case asymptotic running times (albeit with large constant factors that preclude practical implementations). The current world record is a running time bound of roughly $O(n^{2.3729})$, and for all we know there could be an $O(n^2)$-time algorithm waiting to be discovered.

For the formal proof, we should explicitly write out all the constant factors in the recurrence:

Base case: $T(1) \leq c$.

General case: for $n > 1$,

$$T(n) \leq a \cdot T\left(\frac{n}{b}\right) + cn^d. \tag{4.3}$$

For simplicity we're assuming that the constant n_0 specifying when the base case kicks in is 1; the proof for a different constant n_0 is pretty much the same. We can assume that the suppressed constants in the base case and the $O(n^d)$ term in the general case are equal to the same number c; if they were different constants, we could simply work with the larger of the two. Finally, let's focus on the case in which n is a power of b. The proof for the general case is similar, with no additional conceptual content, but it is more tedious.

4.4.2   Recursion Trees Revisited

The high-level plan for the proof is as natural as could be: generalize the recursion tree argument for `MergeSort` (Section 1.5) so that it accommodates other values of the key parameters a, b, and d. Recall that a recursion tree provides a principled way to keep track of all the work done by a recursive algorithm, across all its recursive calls. Nodes of the tree correspond to recursive calls, and the children of a node correspond to the recursive calls made by that node (Figure 4.1). The root (level 0) of the recursion tree corresponds to the outermost call to the algorithm, level 1 has a nodes corresponding to its recursive calls, and so on. The leaves at the bottom of the tree correspond to recursive calls where the base case is triggered.

As in our analysis of `MergeSort`, we'd like to account level-by-level for the work performed by a recursive algorithm. This plan requires understanding two things: the number of distinct subproblems at a given recursion level j, and the length of the input to each of these subproblems.

Quiz 4.4

What is the pattern? Fill in the blanks in the following statement: at each level $j = 0, 1, 2, \ldots$ of the recursion tree, there are [blank] subproblems, each operating on a subarray of length [blank].

a) a^j and n/a^j, respectively

b) a^j and n/b^j, respectively

c) b^j and n/a^j, respectively

d) b^j and n/b^j, respectively

(See Section 4.4.10 for the solution and discussion.)

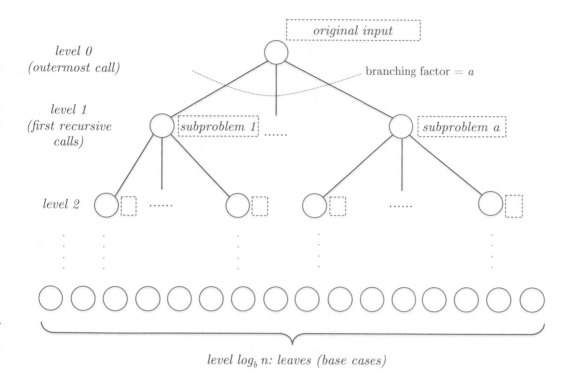

Figure 4.1: The recursion tree corresponding to a standard recurrence. Nodes correspond to recursive calls. Level 0 corresponds to the outermost call, level 1 to its recursive calls, and so on.

4.4.3   Work Performed at a Single Level

Inspired by our `MergeSort` analysis, the plan is to count the total number of operations performed by the level-j subproblems in a divide-and-conquer algorithm, and then add up over all the levels. So zoom in on a recursion level j. By the solution to Quiz 4.4, there are a^j different subproblems at level j, each with an input with size n/b^j. We care about the size of a subproblem only inasmuch as it determines the amount of work the recursive call performs. Our recurrence (4.3) asserts that the work performed in a level-j subproblem, not counting the work performed in its recursive calls, is at most a constant times the input size raised to the d power: $c(n/b^j)^d$. Adding up over all a^j of the level-j subproblems gives an upper bound on the amount of work performed at level j of the recursion tree:

$$\text{work at level } j \leq \underbrace{a^j}_{\text{\# of subproblems}} \cdot \overbrace{c \cdot \underbrace{\left[\frac{n}{b^j}\right]^d}_{\substack{\text{input} \\ \text{size}}}}^{\text{work per subproblem}}.$$

Let's simplify this expression by separating out the parts that depend on the level j and the parts that don't:

$$\text{work at level } j \leq cn^d \cdot \left[\frac{a}{b^d}\right]^j.$$

The right-hand side marks the grand entrance of the critical ratio a/b^d. Given that the value of a versus b^d is exactly what dictates the relevant case of the master method, we shouldn't be surprised that this ratio shows up explicitly in the analysis.

4.4.4   Summing over the Levels

How many levels are there? The input size is initially n and drops by a factor of b with each level. Because we're assuming that n is a power of b and that the base case kicks in when the input size is 1, the last level corresponds exactly to the number of times you need to divide n by b to reach 1, also known as $\log_b n$. Summing over all the levels $j = 0, 1, 2, \ldots, \log_b n$, we obtain the following inscrutable upper bound on the running time (using that cn^d is independent of j and can be yanked out front):

$$\text{total work} \le cn^d \cdot \sum_{j=0}^{\log_b n} \left[\frac{a}{b^d}\right]^j. \tag{4.4}$$

Believe it or not, we've reached an important milestone in the proof of the master method. The right-hand side of the inequality (4.4) probably looks like alphabet soup, but with the proper interpretation, it holds the keys that unlock a deep understanding of the master method.

4.4.5   Good vs. Evil: The Need for Three Cases

Next we'll attach some semantics to the running time bound in (4.4) and develop some intuition about why the running time bounds in the master method are what they are.

Why is the ratio of a vs. b^d so important? Fundamentally, this comparison represents a tug-of-war between the forces of good and the forces of evil. Evil is represented by a, the *rate of subproblem proliferation (RSP)*—with every level of recursion, the number of subproblems explodes by an a factor, and this is a little scary. Good takes the form of b^d, the *rate of work shrinkage (RWS)*—the good news is that with every level of recursion, the amount of work per subproblem decreases by a factor of b^d.[13] The key question then is: which side wins, the forces of good or the forces of evil? The three cases of the master method correspond exactly to the three possible outcomes of this tug-of-war: a draw $(RSP = RWS)$; a victory for good $(RSP < RWS)$; or a victory for evil $(RSP > RWS)$.

To understand this point better, spend some time thinking about the amount of work done at each level of a recursion tree (as in Figure 4.1). When is the amount of work performed increasing with the recursion tree level j? When is it decreasing? Is it ever the same at every level?

Quiz 4.5

Which of the following statements are true? (Choose all that apply.)

---

[13]Why b^d instead of b? Because b is the rate at which the *input size* shrinks, and we care about the input size only inasmuch as it determines the amount of work performed. For example, in a divide-and-conquer algorithm with a quadratic-time combine step ($d = 2$), when the input size is cut in half ($b = 2$), only 25% as much work is needed to solve each smaller subproblem (because $b^d = 4$).

a) If $RSP < RWS$ then the amount of work performed is decreasing with the recursion level j.

b) If $RSP > RWS$ then the amount of work performed is increasing with the recursion level j.

c) No conclusions can be drawn about how the amount of work varies with the recursion level j unless $RSP = RWS$.

d) If $RSP = RWS$ then the amount of work performed is the same at every recursion level.

(See Section 4.4.10 for the solution and discussion.)

4.4.6   Forecasting the Running Time Bounds

We now understand why the master method has three cases. There are three fundamentally different types of recursion trees—with the work-per-level staying the same, decreasing, or increasing—and the relative sizes of a (the RSP) and b^d (the RWS) determine the recursion tree type of a divide-and-conquer algorithm.

Even better, we now have enough intuition to accurately forecast the running time bounds that appear in the master method. Consider the first case, when $a = b^d$ and the algorithm performs the same amount of work at every level of its recursion tree. We certainly know how much work is done at the root, in level 0—$O(n^d)$, as explicitly specified in the recurrence. With $O(n^d)$ work per level, and with $1 + \log_b n = O(\log n)$ levels, we should expect a running time bound of $O(n^d \log n)$ in this case (cf., case 1 of Theorem 4.1).[14]

In the second case, $a < b^d$ and the forces of good are victorious—the amount of work performed is decreasing with the level. Thus more work is done at level 0 than at any other level. The simplest and best outcome we could hope for is that the work done at the root dominates the running time of the algorithm. Because $O(n^d)$ work is done at the root, this best-case scenario would translate to an overall running time of $O(n^d)$ (cf., case 2 of Theorem 4.1).

In the third case, when subproblems proliferate even faster than the work-per-subproblem shrinks, the amount of work performed is increasing with the recursion level, with the most work being done at the leaves of the tree. Again, the simplest- and best-case scenario would be that the running time is dominated by the work done at the leaves. A leaf corresponds to a recursive call in which the base case is triggered, so the algorithm performs only $O(1)$ operations per leaf. How many leaves are there? From the solution to Quiz 4.4, we know that there are a^j nodes at each level j. The leaves are at the last level $j = \log_b n$, so there are $a^{\log_b n}$ leaves. Thus, the best-case scenario translates to a running time bound of $O(a^{\log_b n})$.

The remaining mystery is the connection between our forecast running time bound for the third case of the master method ($O(a^{\log_b n})$) and the actual bound that appears in Theorem 4.1 ($O(n^{\log_b a})$). The connection is... they are exactly the same! The identity

$$\underbrace{a^{\log_b n}}_{\text{more intuitive}} = \underbrace{n^{\log_b a}}_{\text{easier to apply}}$$

---

[14]The abbreviation "cf." stands for *confer* and means "compare to."

probably looks like a rookie mistake made by a freshman algebra student, but it's actually true.[15] Thus the running time bound of $O(n^{\log_b a})$ simply says that the work performed at the leaves of the recursion tree dominates the computation, with the bound stated in a form convenient for plugging in parameters (as for the integer and matrix multiplication algorithms analyzed in Section 4.3).

4.4.7   The Final Calculations: Case 1

We still need to check that our intuition in the previous section is actually correct, and the way to do this is through a formal proof. The culmination of our previous calculations was the following scary-looking upper bound on the running time of a divide-and-conquer algorithm, as a function of the parameters a, b, and d:

$$\text{total work} \le cn^d \cdot \sum_{j=0}^{\log_b n} \left[\frac{a}{b^d}\right]^j. \tag{4.5}$$

We obtained this bound by zooming in on a particular level j of the recursion tree (with its a^j subproblems and $c(n/b^j)^d$ work-per-subproblem) and then summing up over the levels.

When the forces of good and evil are in perfect equilibrium (i.e., $a = b^d$) and the algorithm performs the same amount of work at every level, the right-hand side of (4.5) simplifies dramatically:

$$cn^d \cdot \sum_{j=0}^{\log_b n} \underbrace{\left[\underbrace{\frac{a}{b^d}}_{=1}\right]^j}_{=1 \text{ for each } j} = cn^d \cdot \underbrace{(1+1+\cdots+1)}_{1 + \log_b n \text{ times}},$$

which is $O(n^d \log n)$.[16]

4.4.8   Detour: Geometric Series

Our hope is that for the second and third types of recursion trees (decreasing- and increasing-work-per-level, respectively), the overall running time is dominated by the work performed at the most difficult level (the root and the leaves, respectively). Making this hope real requires understanding geometric series, which are expressions of the form $1 + r + r^2 + \cdots + r^k$ for some real number r and nonnegative integer k. (For us, r will be the critical ratio a/b^d.) Whenever you see a parameterized expression like this, it's a good idea to keep a couple of canonical parameter values in mind. For example, if $r = 2$, it's a sum of positive powers of 2: $1 + 2 + 4 + 8 + \cdots + 2^k$. When $r = \frac{1}{2}$, it's a sum of negative powers of 2: $1 + \frac{1}{2} + \frac{1}{4} + \frac{1}{8} + \cdots + \frac{1}{2^k}$.

---

[15]To verify it, simply take the logarithm base-b of both sides: $\log_b(a^{\log_b n}) = \log_b n \cdot \log_b a = \log_b a \cdot \log_b n = \log_b(n^{\log_b a})$. (Because $\log_b$ is a strictly increasing function, the only way $\log_b x$ and $\log_b y$ can be equal is if x and y are equal.)

[16]Remember, because different logarithmic functions differ by a constant factor, there is no need to specify the base of this logarithm.

When $r \neq 1$, there is a useful closed-form formula for a geometric series:[17]

$$1 + r + r^2 + \cdots + r^k = \frac{1 - r^{k+1}}{1 - r}. \tag{4.6}$$

Two consequences of this formula are important for us. First, when r is positive and less than 1,

$$1 + r + r^2 + \cdots + r^k \leq \frac{1}{1 - r} = \text{a constant (independent of } k\text{)}.$$

Thus *every geometric series with $r \in (0, 1)$ is dominated by its first term*—the first term is 1 and the sum is only $O(1)$. For example, it doesn't matter how many powers of $\frac{1}{2}$ you add up, the resulting sum is never more than 2.

Second, when $r > 1$,

$$1 + r + r^2 + \cdots + r^k = \frac{r^{k+1} - 1}{r - 1} \leq \frac{r^{k+1}}{r - 1} = r^k \cdot \frac{r}{r - 1}.$$

Thus *every geometric series with $r > 1$ is dominated by its last term*—the last term is r^k while the sum is at most a constant factor $(r/(r - 1))$ times this. For example, if you sum up the powers of 2 up to 1024, the resulting sum is less than 2048.

4.4.9   The Final Calculations: Cases 2 and 3

Returning to our analysis of (4.5), suppose that $a < b^d$. In this case, the proliferation in subproblems is drowned out by the savings in work-per-subproblem, and the number of operations performed is decreasing with the recursion tree level. Set $r = a/b^d$; because a, b, and d are constants (independent of the input size n), so is r. Because r is positive and less than 1, the geometric series in (4.5) is at most the constant $1/(1 - r)$, and the bound in (4.5) becomes

$$cn^d \cdot \underbrace{\sum_{j=0}^{\log_b n} r^j}_{=O(1)} = O(n^d),$$

with the big-O notation on the right-hand side suppressing the constant factor $c/(1 - r)$. This confirms our hope that, with the second type of recursion tree, the total amount of work performed is dominated by the work done at the root.

For the final case, suppose that $a > b^d$, with the proliferation of subproblems outpacing the per-subproblem work shrinkage. Set $r = a/b^d$. Because r is now greater than 1, the last term of the geometric series dominates and the bound in (4.5) becomes

$$cn^d \cdot \underbrace{\sum_{j=0}^{\log_b n} r^j}_{=O(r^{\log_b n})} = O(n^d \cdot r^{\log_b n}) = O\left(n^d \cdot \left(\tfrac{a}{b^d}\right)^{\log_b n}\right). \tag{4.7}$$

---

[17]To verify this identity, simply multiply both sides by $1 - r$: $(1 - r)(1 + r + r^2 + \cdots + r^k) = 1 - r + r - r^2 + r^2 - r^3 + r^3 - \cdots - r^{k+1} = 1 - r^{k+1}$.

This looks messy until we notice some remarkable cancellations. Because exponentiation base-b and the logarithm base-b are inverse operations, we can write

$$(b^{-d})^{\log_b n} = b^{-d \log_b n} = (b^{\log_b n})^{-d} = n^{-d}.$$

Thus the $(1/b^d)^{\log_b n}$ term in (4.7) cancels out the n^d term, leaving us with an upper bound of $O(a^{\log_b n})$. This confirms our hope that the total running time in this case is dominated by the work done at the leaves of the recursion tree. Because $a^{\log_b n}$ is the same as $n^{\log_b a}$, we have completed the proof of the master method. $\mathcal{QED}$

4.4.10   Solutions to Quizzes 4.4–4.5

Solution to Quiz 4.4

Correct answer: (b). First, by definition, the "branching factor" of the recursion tree is a—every recursive call that doesn't trigger the base case makes a new recursive calls. This means the number of distinct subproblems gets multiplied by a with each level. Because there is 1 subproblem at level 0, there are a^j subproblems at level j.

For the second part of the solution, again by definition, the subproblem size decreases by a factor of b with each level. Because the problem size is n at level 0, all subproblems at level j have size n/b^j.[18]

Solution to Quiz 4.5

Correct answers: (a),(b),(d). First suppose that $RSP < RWS$, and so the forces of good are more powerful than the forces of evil—the shrinkage in work done per subproblem more than makes up for the increase in the number of subproblems. In this case, the algorithm does less work with each successive recursion level. Thus the first statement is true (and the third statement is false). The second statement is true for similar reasons—if subproblems grow so rapidly that they outpace the savings-per-subproblem, then each recursion level requires more work than the previous one. In the final statement, when $RSP = RWS$, there is a perfect equilibrium between the forces of good and evil. Subproblems are proliferating, but our savings in work-per-subproblem are increasing at exactly the same rate. The two forces cancel out, and the work done at each level of the recursion tree remains the same.

The Upshot

☆ A recurrence expresses a running time bound $T(n)$ in terms of the number of operations performed by recursive calls.

☆ A standard recurrence $T(n) \le aT(\frac{n}{b}) + O(n^d)$ is defined by three parameters: the number a of recursive calls, the input size shrinkage factor b, and the exponent d in the running time of the combine step.

---

[18]Unlike in our `MergeSort` analysis, the fact that the number of subproblems at level j is a^j does not imply that the size of each subproblem is n/a^j. In `MergeSort`, the inputs to the level-j subproblems form a partition of the original input. This is not the case in many of our other divide-and-conquer algorithms. For example, in our recursive integer and matrix multiplication algorithms, parts of the original input are reused across different recursive calls.

☆ The master method provides an asymptotic upper bound for every standard recurrence, as a function of a, b, and d: $O(n^d \log n)$ if $a = b^d$, $O(n^d)$ if $a < b^d$, and $O(n^{\log_b a})$ if $a > b^d$.

☆ Special cases include an $O(n \log n)$ time bound for MergeSort, an $O(n^{1.59})$ time bound for Karatsuba, and an $O(n^{2.81})$ time bound for Strassen.

☆ The proof of the master method generalizes the recursion tree argument used to analyze MergeSort.

☆ The quantities a and b^d represent the forces of evil (the rate of subproblem proliferation) and the forces of good (the rate of work shrinkage).

☆ The three cases of the master method correspond to three different types of recursion trees: those with the per-level work performed the same at each level (a tie between good and evil), decreasing with the level (when good wins), and increasing with the level (when evil wins).

☆ Properties of geometric series imply that the work done at the root of the recursion tree (which is $O(n^d)$) dominates the overall running time in the second case, while the work done at the leaves (which is $O(a^{\log_b n}) = O(n^{\log_b a})$) dominates in the third case.

Test Your Understanding

Problem 4.1 *(S)* Recall the master method (Theorem 4.1) and its three parameters a, b, and d. Which of the following is the best interpretation of b^d?

a) The rate at which the total work is growing (per level of recursion).

b) The rate at which the number of subproblems is growing (per level of recursion).

c) The rate at which the subproblem size is shrinking (per level of recursion).

d) The rate at which the work-per-subproblem is shrinking (per level of recursion).

Problem 4.2 *(S)* Which of the following statements about the master method are true? (Choose all that apply.)

a) A standard recurrence with $a = 1$ always falls into case 2 of the master method.

b) A standard recurrence with $a = 1$ never falls into case 3 of the master method.

c) A standard recurrence with $a > b$ never falls into case 2 of the master method.

d) A standard recurrence with $a > b$ always falls into case 3 of the master method.

Problem 4.3 *(S)* This and the next two questions will give you further practice with the master method. Suppose the running time $T(n)$ of an algorithm is bounded by a standard recurrence with $T(n) \leq 7 \cdot T(\frac{n}{3}) + O(n^2)$. Which of the following is the smallest correct upper bound on the asymptotic running time of the algorithm?

a) $O(n \log n)$

b) $O(n^2)$

c) $O(n^2 \log n)$

d) $O(n^{2.81})$

Problem 4.4 *(S)* Suppose the running time $T(n)$ of an algorithm is bounded by a standard recurrence with $T(n) \leq 9 \cdot T(\frac{n}{3}) + O(n^2)$. Which of the following is the smallest correct upper bound on the asymptotic running time of the algorithm?

a) $O(n \log n)$

b) $O(n^2)$

c) $O(n^2 \log n)$

d) $O(n^{3.17})$

Problem 4.5 *(S)* Suppose the running time $T(n)$ of an algorithm is bounded by a standard recurrence with $T(n) \leq 5 \cdot T(\frac{n}{3}) + O(n)$. Which of the following is the smallest correct upper bound on the asymptotic running time of the algorithm?

a) $O(n^{\log_5 3})$

b) $O(n \log n)$

c) $O(n^{\log_3 5})$

d) $O(n^{5/3})$

e) $O(n^2)$

f) $O(n^{2.59})$

Challenge Problems

Problem 4.6 *(H)* Let $T(n)$ be a recurrence that satisfies $T(1) = 1$ and, for larger values of n,

$$T(n) \geq a \cdot T\left(\frac{n}{b}\right) + \Omega(n^d),$$

where as usual a is a positive integer, $b > 1$, and $d \geq 0$. (For simplicity, you can restrict your attention to values of n that are powers of b.) Prove that

$$T(n) = \begin{cases} \Omega(n^d \log n) & \text{if } a = b^d \\ \Omega(n^d) & \text{if } a < b^d \\ \Omega(n^{\log_b a}) & \text{if } a > b^d. \end{cases}$$

Problem 4.7 *(S)* Suppose the running time $T(n)$ of an algorithm is bounded by the (non-standard!) recurrence with $T(1) = 1$ and $T(n) \leq T(\lfloor \sqrt{n} \rfloor) + 1$ for $n > 1$.[19] Which of the following is the smallest correct upper bound on the asymptotic running time of the algorithm? (Note that the master method does not apply!)

a) $O(1)$

b) $O(\log \log n)$

c) $O(\log n)$

d) $O(\sqrt{n})$

---

[19] As in Problem 3.1, $\lfloor x \rfloor$ denotes the "floor" function, which rounds its argument down to the nearest integer.

Chapter 5

QuickSort

This chapter covers `QuickSort`, a first-ballot hall-of-fame algorithm. After giving a high-level overview of how the algorithm works (Section 5.1), we discuss how to partition an array around a "pivot element" in linear time (Section 5.2) and how to choose a good pivot element (Section 5.3). Section 5.4 introduces randomized `QuickSort`, and Section 5.5 proves that its asymptotic average running time is $O(n \log n)$ for n-element arrays. Section 5.6 wraps up our sorting discussion with a proof that no "comparison-based" sorting algorithm can have a running time faster than $O(n \log n)$.

5.1   Overview

Ask a professional computer scientist or programmer to list their top 10 algorithms, and you'll find `QuickSort` on many lists (including mine). Why is this? We already know one blazingly fast sorting algorithm (`MergeSort`)—why do we need another?

On the practical side, `QuickSort` is competitive with and often superior to `MergeSort`, and for this reason is the default sorting method in many programming libraries. The big win for `QuickSort` over `MergeSort` is that it runs *in place*—it operates on the input array only through repeated swaps of pairs of elements, and for this reason needs to allocate only a minuscule amount of additional memory for intermediate computations. On the aesthetic side, `QuickSort` is a remarkably beautiful algorithm, with an equally beautiful running time analysis.

5.1.1   Sorting

The `QuickSort` algorithm solves the problem of sorting an array, the same problem we tackled in Section 1.4.

Problem: Sorting

Input: An array of n numbers, in arbitrary order.

Output: An array of the same numbers, sorted from smallest to largest.

So if the input array is

3	8	2	5	1	4	7	6

then the correct output array is

| 1 | 2 | 3 | 4 | 5 | 6 | 7 | 8 |

As in our `MergeSort` discussion, let's assume for simplicity that the input array has distinct elements, with no duplicates.[1]

5.1.2   Partitioning Around a Pivot

`QuickSort` is built around a fast subroutine for "partial sorting," whose responsibility is to partition an array around a "pivot element."

Step 1: Choose a pivot element.   First, choose one element of the array to act as a *pivot element*. Section 5.3 will obsess over exactly how this should be done. For now, let's be naive and blindly use the first element of the array (above, the "3").

Step 2: Rearrange the input array around the pivot.   Given the pivot element p, the next task is to arrange the elements of the array so that everything before p in the array is less than p, and everything after p is greater than p. For example, with the input array above, here's one legitimate way of rearranging the elements:

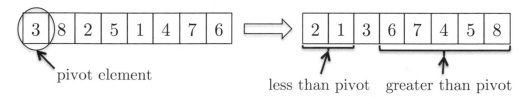

This example makes clear that the elements before the pivot do not need to be placed in the correct relative order (the "1" and "2" are reversed), and similarly for the elements after the pivot. This partitioning subroutine places the (non-pivot) elements of the array into two buckets, one for the elements smaller than the pivot and the other for those greater than the pivot.

Here are the two key facts about this partition subroutine.

Fast.   The partition subroutine has a blazingly fast implementation, running in linear ($O(n)$) time. Even better, and key to the practical utility of `QuickSort`, the subroutine can be implemented in place, with next to no memory beyond that occupied by the input array.[2] Section 5.2 describes this implementation in detail.

Significant progress.   Partitioning an array around a pivot element makes progress toward sorting the array. First, the pivot element winds up in its rightful position, meaning the same position as in the sorted version of the input array (with all smaller elements before it and all larger elements after it). Second, partitioning reduces the sorting problem to two smaller sorting problems: sorting the elements less than the pivot (which conveniently occupy their

---

[1]In the unlikely event that you're tasked with coding up a robust implementation of `QuickSort`, be warned that handling ties correctly and efficiently is a bit tricky, more so than in `MergeSort`. For a detailed discussion, see Section 2.3 of *Algorithms (Fourth Edition)*, by Robert Sedgewick and Kevin Wayne (Addison-Wesley, 2011).

[2]This contrasts with `MergeSort` (Section 1.4), which repeatedly copies elements over from one array to another.

own subarray) and the elements greater than the pivot (also in their own subarray). After recursively sorting the elements in each of these two subarrays, the algorithm is done![3]

5.1.3 High-Level Description

In the following high-level description of the QuickSort algorithm, the "first part" and "second part" of the array refer to the elements less than and greater than the pivot element, respectively:

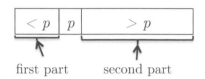

first part   second part

QuickSort (High-Level Description)

Input: array A of n distinct integers.
Postcondition: elements of A are sorted from smallest to largest.

---

  if $n \leq 1$ **then**   // base case-already sorted
     return
choose a pivot element p // to-be-implemented
partition A around p // to-be-implemented
recursively sort first part of A
recursively sort second part of A

While both MergeSort and QuickSort are divide-and-conquer algorithms, the order of operations is different. In MergeSort, the recursive calls are performed first, followed by the combine step, Merge. In QuickSort, the recursive calls occur after partitioning, and their results don't need to be combined at all![4]

5.1.4 Looking Ahead

Our remaining to-do list is:

1. (Section 5.2) How do we implement the partitioning subroutine?

2. (Section 5.3) How should we choose the pivot element?

3. (Sections 5.4 and 5.5) What's the running time of QuickSort?

---

[3]One of the subproblems might be empty, if the minimum or maximum element is chosen as the pivot. In this case, the corresponding recursive call can be skipped.

[4]QuickSort was invented by Tony Hoare, in 1959, when he was only 25 years old. Hoare went on to make numerous fundamental contributions in programming languages and was awarded the ACM Turing Award—the equivalent of the Nobel Prize in computer science—in 1980.

Another question is: "are we really sure that `QuickSort` always correctly sorts the input array?" I've been giving short shrift to formal correctness arguments thus far because students generally have strong and accurate intuition about why divide-and-conquer algorithms are correct. (Compare this to understanding the running times of divide-and-conquer algorithms, which are usually far from obvious!) If you have any lingering concerns, it is straightforward to argue formally the correctness of `QuickSort` using a proof by induction.[5]

5.2   Partitioning Around a Pivot Element

Next we fill in the details about how to partition an array around a pivot element p, meaning rearranging the array so that it looks like this:

5.2.1   The Easy Way Out

It's easy to come up with a linear-time partitioning subroutine if we don't care about allocating additional memory. One approach is to do a single scan over the input array A and copy over its non-pivot elements one by one into a new array B of the same length, populating B both from its front (for elements less than p) and its back (for elements bigger than p). The pivot element can be copied into the remaining entry of B after all the non-pivot elements have been processed. For our running example input array, here's a snapshot from the middle of this computation:

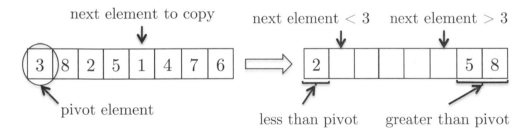

Because this subroutine does only $O(1)$ work for each of the n elements in the input array, its running time is $O(n)$.

---

[5]Following the template for induction proofs reviewed in Appendix A, let $P(n)$ denote the statement "for every input array of length n, `QuickSort` correctly sorts it." The base case ($n = 1$) is uninteresting: an array with 1 element is necessarily sorted, and so `QuickSort` is automatically correct in this case. For the inductive step, fix an arbitrary positive integer $n \geq 2$. We're allowed to assume the inductive hypothesis (i.e., $P(k)$ is true for all $k < n$), meaning that `QuickSort` correctly sorts every array with fewer than n elements.

After the partitioning step, the pivot element p is in the same position as it is in the sorted version of the input array. The elements before p are exactly the same as those before p in the sorted version of the input array (possibly in the wrong relative order), and similarly for the elements after p. Thus the only remaining tasks are to reorganize the elements before p in sorted order, and similarly for the elements after p. Because both recursive calls are on subarrays of length at most $n - 1$ (if nothing else, p is excluded), the inductive hypothesis implies that both calls sort their subarrays correctly. This concludes the inductive step and the formal proof of correctness for the `QuickSort` algorithm.

5.2.2   In-Place Implementation: The High-Level Plan

How do we partition an array around a pivot element while allocating almost no additional memory? Our high-level approach will be to do a single scan through the array, swapping pairs of elements as needed so that the array is properly partitioned by the end of the pass.

Assume that the pivot element is the first element of the array; this can always be enforced (in $O(1)$ time) by swapping the pivot element with the first element of the array in a preprocessing step. As we scan and transform the input array, we will take care to ensure that it has the following form:

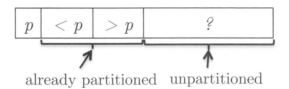

That is, the subroutine maintains the following invariant:[6] the first element is the pivot element; next are the non-pivot elements that have already been processed, with all such elements less than the pivot preceding all such elements greater than the pivot; followed by the not-yet-processed non-pivot elements, in arbitrary order.

If we succeed with this plan, then at the conclusion of the linear scan we will have transformed the array so that it looks like this:

To complete the partitioning, we can swap the pivot element with the last element less than it:

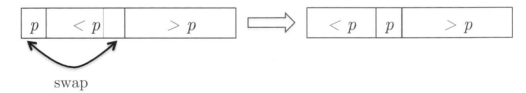

5.2.3   Example

Next we'll step through the in-place partitioning subroutine on a concrete example. It may seem weird to go through an example of a program before you've seen its code, but trust me: this is the shortest path to understanding the subroutine.

Based on our high-level plan, we expect to keep track of two boundaries: the boundary between the non-pivot elements we've already looked at and those we haven't, and within the first group, the boundary between the elements less than the pivot and those greater than the pivot. We'll use the indices j and i, respectively, to keep track of these two boundaries. Our desired invariant can then be rephrased as:

---
[6] An *invariant* of an algorithm is a property that is always true at prescribed points of its execution (like at the end of every loop iteration).

Invariant: all elements between the pivot and i are less than the pivot, and all elements between i and j are greater than the pivot.

Both i and j are initialized to the boundary between the pivot element and the rest. There are then no elements between the pivot and j, and the invariant holds vacuously:

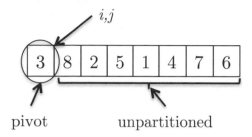

pivot   unpartitioned

Each iteration, the subroutine looks at one new element, and increments j. Additional work may or may not be required to maintain the invariant. The first time we increment j in our example, we get:

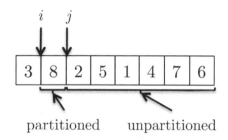

partitioned   unpartitioned

There are no elements between the pivot and i, and the only element between i and j (the "8") is greater than the pivot, so the invariant still holds.

Now the plot thickens. After incrementing j a second time, there is an element between i and j that is less than the pivot (the "2"), a violation of the invariant. To restore the invariant, we swap the "8" with the "2," and also increment i, so that it is wedged between the "2" and the "8" and again delineates the boundary between processed elements less than and greater than the pivot:

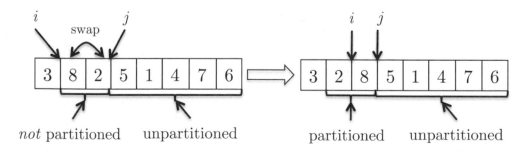

not partitioned   unpartitioned   partitioned   unpartitioned

The third iteration is similar to the first. We process the next element (the "5") and increment j. Because the new element is greater than the pivot, the invariant continues to hold and there is nothing more to do:

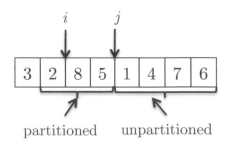

The fourth iteration is similar to the second. Incrementing j ushers in an element less than the pivot (the "1") between i and j, which violates the invariant. But restoring the invariant is easy enough—simply swap the "1" with the first element greater than the pivot (the "8"), and increment i to reflect the new boundary between processed elements less than and greater than the pivot:

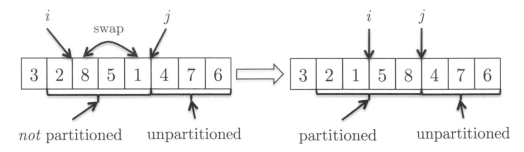

The last three iterations process elements that are larger than the pivot, so nothing needs to be done beyond incrementing j. After all the elements have been processed and everything after the pivot has been partitioned, we conclude with the final swap of the pivot element and the last element smaller than it:

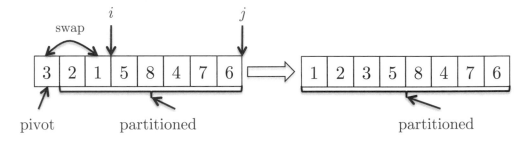

As required, in the final array, all the elements less than the pivot come before it, and all the elements greater than the pivot come after it. It is a coincidence that the "1" and "2" are in sorted order. The elements after the pivot are obviously not in sorted order.

5.2.4   Pseudocode for `Partition`

The pseudocode for the `Partition` subroutine is exactly what you'd expect after the example.[7]

---

[7]If you look at other textbooks or on the Web, you'll see a number of variants of this subroutine that differ in the details. (There's even a version performed by Hungarian folk dancers! See https://www.youtube.com/watch?v=ywWBy6J5gz8.) These variants are equally suitable for our purposes.

Partition

Input: array A of n distinct integers, left and right endpoints
$\ell, r \in \{1, 2, \ldots, n\}$ with $l \leq r$.

Postcondition: elements of the subarray $A[\ell], A[\ell + 1], \ldots, A[r]$ are
partitioned around $A[\ell]$.

Output: final position of pivot element.

$p := A[\ell]$
$i := \ell + 1$
for $j := \ell + 1$ **to** r **do**
    if $A[j] < p$ **then**   // if $A[j] > p$ do nothing
        swap $A[j]$ and $A[i]$
        $i := i + 1$ // restores invariant
  swap $A[\ell]$ and $A[i - 1]$ // place pivot correctly
  return $i - 1$ // report final pivot position

The Partition subroutine takes as input an array A but operates only on the subarray of elements $A[\ell], \ldots, A[r]$, where ℓ and r are given parameters. Looking ahead, each recursive call to QuickSort will be responsible for a specific subarray of the original input array, and the parameters ℓ and r specify the corresponding endpoints.

As in the example, the index j keeps track of which elements have been processed, while i keeps track of the boundary between processed elements that are less than and greater than the pivot (with $A[i]$ the leftmost processed element greater than the pivot, if any). Each iteration of the for loop processes a new element. Like in the example, when the new element $A[j]$ is greater than the pivot, the invariant holds automatically and there's nothing to do. Otherwise, the subroutine restores the invariant by swapping $A[j]$, the new element, and $A[i]$, the leftmost element greater than the pivot, and incrementing i to update the boundary between elements less than and greater than the pivot.[8,9] The final step, as previously advertised, swaps the pivot element into its rightful position, trading places with the rightmost element that is less than it. The Partition subroutine concludes by reporting this position back to the invocation of QuickSort that called it.

This implementation is blazingly fast. It performs only a constant number of operations for each element $A[\ell], A[\ell + 1], \ldots, A[r]$ of the relevant subarray, and so runs in time linear in the length of this subarray. Importantly, the subroutine operates on this subarray in place,

---

[8]No swap is necessary if no elements greater than the pivot have yet been encountered—the subarray of processed elements is trivially partitioned. But the extra swap is harmless (as you should verify), so we'll stick with our simple pseudocode.

[9]Why does this swap and increment always restore the invariant? The invariant held before the most recent increment of j (by induction, if you want to be formal about it). This means that all the elements $A[\ell + 1], \ldots, A[i - 1]$ are less than the pivot and all the elements $A[i], \ldots, A[j - 1]$ are greater than the pivot. The only problem is that $A[j]$ is less than the pivot. After swapping $A[i]$ with $A[j]$, the elements $A[\ell + 1], \ldots, A[i]$ and $A[i + 1], \ldots, A[j]$ are less than and greater than the pivot, respectively. After incrementing i, $A[\ell + 1], \ldots, A[i - 1]$ and $A[i], \ldots, A[j]$ are less than and greater than the pivot, respectively, which restores the invariant.

without allocating any additional memory beyond the $O(1)$ amount needed to keep track of variables like i and j.

5.2.5 Pseudocode for QuickSort

We now have a full description of the QuickSort algorithm, modulo the subroutine ChoosePivot that chooses a pivot element.

QuickSort

Input: array A of n distinct integers, left and right endpoints $\ell, r \in \{1, 2, \ldots, n\}$.
Postcondition: elements of the subarray $A[\ell], A[\ell+1], \ldots, A[r]$ are sorted from smallest to largest.

---

if $\ell \geq r$ **then**   // 0- or 1-element subarray
    return
$i := \text{ChoosePivot}(A, \ell, r)$ // to-be-implemented
swap $A[\ell]$ and $A[i]$ // make pivot first
$j := \text{Partition}(A, \ell, r)$ // j =new pivot position
$\text{QuickSort}(A, \ell, j-1)$ // recurse on first part
$\text{QuickSort}(A, j+1, r)$ // recurse on second part

The function call $\text{QuickSort}(A, 1, n)$ can then be used to sort your favorite n-element array A.[10]

5.3   The Importance of Good Pivots

Is QuickSort a fast algorithm? The bar is high: Simple sorting algorithms like InsertionSort run in quadratic ($O(n^2)$) time, and we already know one sorting algorithm (MergeSort) that runs in $O(n \log n)$ time. The answer to this question depends on how we implement the ChoosePivot subroutine, which chooses one element from a designated subarray. For QuickSort to be quick, it's important that "good" pivot elements are chosen, meaning pivot elements that result in two subproblems of approximately the same size.

5.3.1   Naive Implementation of ChoosePivot

In our overview of QuickSort we mentioned a naive implementation of the ChoosePivot subroutine, which always picks the first element.

---

[10]The array A is always passed by reference, meaning that all function calls operate directly on the original copy of the input array.

ChoosePivot (Naive Implementation)

Input: array A of n distinct integers, left and right endpoints
$\ell, r \in \{1, 2, \ldots, n\}$.
Output: an index $i \in \{\ell, \ell + 1, \ldots, r\}$.

---

return ℓ

Is this naive implementation already good enough?

Quiz 5.1

What is the running time of the QuickSort algorithm, with the naive implementation of ChoosePivot, when the n-element input array is already sorted?

a) $\Theta(n)$

b) $\Theta(n \log n)$

c) $\Theta(n^2)$

d) $\Theta(n^3)$

(See Section 5.3.3 for the solution and discussion.)

5.3.2   Overkill Implementation of ChoosePivot

Quiz 5.1 paints a worst-case picture of what can happen in QuickSort, with only one element removed per recursive call. What would be the *best-case* scenario? The most perfectly balanced split is achieved by the *median* element of the array, meaning the element for which the same number of other elements are less than it and greater than it.[11] So if we want to work really hard for our pivot element, we can compute the median element of the given subarray.

ChoosePivot (Overkill Implementation)

Input: array A of n distinct integers, left and right endpoints
$\ell, r \in \{1, 2, \ldots, n\}$.
Output: an index $i \in \{\ell, \ell + 1, \ldots, r\}$.

---

return position of the median element of $\{A[\ell], \ldots, A[r]\}$

---

[11]For example, the median of an array containing $\{1, 2, 3, \ldots, 9\}$ would be 5. For an even-length array, there are two legitimate choices for the median, and either is fine for our purposes. So in an array that contains $\{1, 2, 3, \ldots, 10\}$, either 5 or 6 can be considered the median element.

We'll see in the next chapter that the median element of an array can be computed in time linear in the array length; let's take this fact on faith for the following quiz.[12] Is there any reward for working hard to compute an ideal pivot element?

Quiz 5.2

What is the running time of the QuickSort algorithm, with the overkill implementation of ChoosePivot, on an arbitrary n-element input array? Assume that the ChoosePivot subroutine runs in $\Theta(n)$ time.

   a) Insufficient information to answer

   b) $\Theta(n)$

   c) $\Theta(n \log n)$

   d) $\Theta(n^2)$

(See Section 5.3.3 for the solution and discussion.)

5.3.3   Solutions to Quizzes 5.1–5.2

Solution to Quiz 5.1

Correct answer: (c). The combination of naively chosen pivots and an already-sorted input array causes QuickSort to run in $\Theta(n^2)$ time, which is much worse than MergeSort and no better than simple algorithms such as InsertionSort. What goes wrong? The Partition subroutine in the outermost call to QuickSort, with the first (smallest) element as the pivot, does nothing: It sweeps over the array, and because it only encounters elements greater than the pivot, it never swaps any pair of elements. After this call to Partition completes, the picture is:

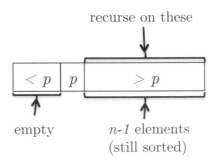

In the non-empty recursive call, the pattern recurs: the subarray is already sorted, the first (smallest) element is chosen as the pivot, and there is one empty recursive call and one recursive call that is passed a subarray of $n - 2$ elements. And so on.

In the end, the Partition subroutine is invoked on subarrays of length $n, n - 1, n - 2, \ldots, 2$. Because the work done in one call to Partition is proportional to the length of

---

[12]You do at this point know an $O(n \log n)$-time algorithm for computing the median of an array. (Hint: Sort!)

the call's subarray, the total amount of work done by `QuickSort` in this case is proportional to

$$\underbrace{n + (n - 1) + (n - 2) + \cdots + 1}_{=\Theta(n^2)}$$

and hence is quadratic in the input length n.[13]

Solution to Quiz 5.2

Correct answer: (c). In this best-case scenario, `QuickSort` runs in $\Theta(n \log n)$ time. The reason is that its running time is governed by the exact same recurrence that governs the running time of `MergeSort`. That is, if $T(n)$ denotes the running time of this implementation of `QuickSort` on arrays of length n, then

$$T(n) = \underbrace{2 \cdot T\left(\frac{n}{2}\right)}_{\text{as pivot = median}} + \underbrace{\Theta(n)}_{\text{ChoosePivot \& Partition}} .$$

The primary work done by a call to `QuickSort` outside its recursive calls occurs in its `ChoosePivot` and `Partition` subroutines. We're assuming that the former is $\Theta(n)$, and Section 5.2 proves that the latter is also $\Theta(n)$. Because we're using the median element as the pivot element, we get a perfect split of the input array and each recursive call gets a subarray with at most $\frac{n}{2}$ elements:

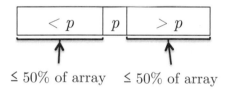

$$\leq 50\% \text{ of array} \quad \leq 50\% \text{ of array}$$

Applying the master method (Theorem 4.1) with $a = b = 2$ and $d = 1$ then gives $T(n) = \Theta(n \log n)$.[14]

5.4   Randomized `QuickSort`

Choosing the first element of a subarray as the pivot takes only $O(1)$ time but can cause `QuickSort` to run in $\Theta(n^2)$ time. Choosing the median element as the pivot guarantees an overall running time of $\Theta(n \log n)$ but is much more time-consuming (if still linear-time). Can we have the best of both worlds? Is there a simple and lightweight way to choose a pivot element that leads to a roughly balanced split of the array? The answer is yes, and the key idea is to use *randomization*.

---

[13] A quick way to see that $n + (n - 1) + (n - 2) + \cdots + 1 = \Theta(n^2)$ is to note that it is at most n^2 (each of the n terms is at most n) and at least $n^2/4$ (each of the first $n/2$ terms is at least $n/2$).

[14] Technically, we're using here a variant of the master method that works with Θ-notation rather than O-notation, but otherwise is the same as Theorem 4.1. See also Problem 4.6.

5.4.1 Randomized Implementation of ChoosePivot

A *randomized algorithm* is one that "flips coins" as it proceeds, and can make decisions based on the outcomes of these coin flips. If you run a randomized algorithm on the same input over and over, you will see different behavior on different runs. All major programming languages include libraries that make it easy to pick random numbers at will, and randomization is a tool that should be in the toolbox of every serious algorithm designer.

Why on earth would you want to inject randomness into your algorithm? Aren't algorithms just about the most deterministic thing you can think of? As it turns out, there are dozens of computational problems for which randomized algorithms are faster, more effective, or easier to code than their deterministic counterparts.[15]

The simplest way to incorporate randomness into QuickSort, which turns out to be extremely effective, is to always choose pivot elements *uniformly at random*.

ChoosePivot (Randomized Implementation)

Input: array A of n distinct integers, left and right endpoints $\ell, r \in \{1, 2, \ldots, n\}$.
Output: an index $i \in \{\ell, \ell+1, \ldots, r\}$.

---

return an element of $\{\ell, \ell+1, \ldots, r\}$, chosen uniformly at random

---

For example, if $\ell = 41$ and $r = 50$, then each of the 10 elements $A[41], \ldots, A[50]$ has a 10% chance of being chosen as the pivot element.[16]

5.4.2 Running Time of Randomized QuickSort

The running time of randomized QuickSort, with pivot elements chosen at random, is not always the same. There is always some chance, however remote, that the algorithm always picks the minimum element of the remaining subarray as the pivot element, leading to the $\Theta(n^2)$ running time observed in Quiz 5.1.[17] There's a similarly remote chance that the algorithm gets incredibly lucky and always selects the median element of a subarray as the pivot, resulting in the $\Theta(n \log n)$ running time seen in Quiz 5.2. So the algorithm's running time fluctuates between $\Theta(n \log n)$ and $\Theta(n^2)$—which occurs more frequently, the best-case scenario or the worst-case scenario? Amazingly, the performance of QuickSort is almost always close to its best-case performance.

Theorem 5.1 (Running Time of Randomized QuickSort) *For every input array of length $n \geq 1$, the average running time of randomized QuickSort is $O(n \log n)$.*

---

[15]It took computer scientists a while to figure this out, with the floodgates opening in the mid-1970s with fast randomized algorithms for testing whether an integer is prime.

[16]An equally effective way of using randomness is to randomly shuffle the input array in a preprocessing step and then run the naive implementation of QuickSort.

[17]For even modest values of n, there's a bigger probability that you'll be struck by a meteor while reading this!

The word "average" in the theorem statement refers to the randomness in the QuickSort algorithm itself. Theorem 5.1 does *not* assume that the input array is random. Randomized QuickSort is a general-purpose algorithm (cf., Section 1.6.1): no matter what your input array is, if you run the algorithm on it over and over again, the average running time will be $O(n \log n)$, good enough to qualify as a for-free primitive. In principle randomized QuickSort can run in $\Theta(n^2)$ time, but you will almost always observe a running time of $O(n \log n)$ in practice. Two added bonuses: The constant hidden in the big-O notation in Theorem 5.1 is reasonably small (like in MergeSort), and the algorithm doesn't spend time allocating and managing additional memory (unlike MergeSort).

5.4.3   Intuition: Why Are Random Pivots Good?

To understand deeply why QuickSort is so quick, there's no substitute for studying the proof of Theorem 5.1, which is explained in Section 5.5. In preparation for that proof, and also as a consolation prize for the reader who is too time-limited to absorb Section 5.5, we next develop intuition about why Theorem 5.1 should be true.

The first insight is that, to achieve a running time of $O(n \log n)$ as in the best-case scenario of Quiz 5.2, it's overkill to use the median element as the pivot element. Suppose we instead use an "approximate median," meaning some element that gives us a 25%-75% split or better. Equivalently, this is an element that is greater than at least 25% of the other elements and also less than at least 25% of the other elements. The picture after partitioning around such a pivot element is:

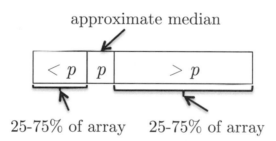

If every recursive call chooses a pivot element that is an approximate median in this sense, the running time of QuickSort is still $O(n \log n)$. We cannot derive this fact directly from the master method (Theorem 4.1), because using a non-median results in subproblems with unequal sizes. But it is not hard to generalize the analysis of MergeSort (Section 1.5) so that it also applies here.[18]

The second insight is that while you'd have to get incredibly lucky to choose the median element in randomized QuickSort (only a 1 in n chance), you have to be only slightly

---

[18]Draw out the recursion tree of the algorithm. Whenever QuickSort calls itself recursively on two subproblems, the subproblems involve different elements (those less than the pivot, and those greater than it). This means that, for every recursion level j, there are no overlaps between the subarrays of different level-j subproblems, and so the sum of subarray lengths of level-j subproblems is at most n. The total work done at this level (by calls to Partition) is linear in the sum of the subarray lengths. Thus, like MergeSort, the algorithm performs $O(n)$ work per recursion level. How many levels are there? With pivot elements that are approximate medians, at most 75% of the elements are passed to the same recursive call, and so the subproblem size is divided by at least 4/3 with each level. This means there are at most $\log_{4/3} n = O(\log n)$ levels in the recursion tree, and so $O(n \log n)$ work is done in all.

lucky to choose an approximate median. For example, consider a length-100 array that contains the elements $\{1, 2, 3, \ldots, 100\}$ in some order. Any number between 26 and 75, inclusive, is an approximate median, with at least 25 elements less than it and 25 elements greater than it. This is 50% of the numbers in the array! So QuickSort has a 50-50 chance of randomly choosing an approximate median, as if it were trying to guess the outcome of a fair coin flip. This means we expect roughly half of the calls to QuickSort to use approximate medians, and we can hope that the $O(n \log n)$ running time analysis in the previous paragraph continues to hold, perhaps with twice as many levels as before.

Make no mistake: This is not a formal proof, only a heuristic argument that Theorem 5.1 might plausibly be true. If I were you, given the central position of QuickSort in the design and analysis of algorithms, I would demand an indisputable argument that Theorem 5.1 really is true.

*5.5   Analysis of Randomized QuickSort

Randomized QuickSort seems like a great idea, but how do we really know it will work well? More generally, when you come up with a new algorithm in your own work, how do you know whether it's brilliant or whether it stinks? One useful but ad hoc approach is to code up the algorithm and try it on a bunch of different inputs. Another approach is to develop intuition about why the algorithm should work well, as in Section 5.4.3 for randomized QuickSort. But thoroughly understanding what makes an algorithm good or bad often requires mathematical analysis. This section will give you such an understanding of why QuickSort is so quick.

This section assumes familiarity with the concepts from discrete probability that are reviewed in Appendix B: sample spaces, events, random variables, expectation, and linearity of expectation.

5.5.1   Preliminaries

Theorem 5.1 asserts that for every input array of length $n \geq 1$, the average running time of randomized QuickSort (with pivot elements chosen uniformly at random) is $O(n \log n)$. Let's begin by translating this assertion into a formal statement in the language of discrete probability.

Fix for the rest of the analysis an arbitrary input array A of length n. Recall that a sample space is the set of all possible outcomes of some random process. In randomized QuickSort, all the randomness is in the random choices of pivot elements in the different recursive calls. Thus we take the sample space Ω as the set of all possible outcomes of random choices in QuickSort (i.e., all pivot sequences).

Recall that a random variable is a numerical measurement of the outcome of a random process—a real-valued function defined on Ω. The random variable we care about is the number RT of primitive operations (i.e., lines of code) performed by randomized QuickSort. This is a well-defined random variable because, whenever all the pivot element choices are pre-determined (i.e., $\omega \in \Omega$ is fixed), QuickSort has some fixed running time $RT(\omega)$. Ranging over all possible pivot sequences ω, $RT(\omega)$ ranges from $\Theta(n \log n)$ to $\Theta(n^2)$ (see Section 5.3).

We can get away with analyzing a simpler random variable that counts only comparisons and ignores the other types of primitive operations performed. Let C denote the random variable equal to the number of comparisons between pairs of input elements performed by `QuickSort` with a given sequence of pivot choices. Looking back over the pseudocode, we see that these comparisons occur in exactly one place: the line "if $A[j] < p$" in the `Partition` subroutine (Section 5.2.4), which compares the current pivot element to some other element of the input subarray.

The following lemma shows that comparisons dominate the overall running time of `QuickSort`, meaning that the latter is larger than the former by only a constant factor. This implies that, to prove an upper bound of $O(n \log n)$ on the expected running time of `QuickSort`, we need only prove an upper bound of $O(n \log n)$ on the expected number of comparisons made.

Lemma 5.2 (Comparisons Dominate the Work in `QuickSort`) *There is a constant $a > 0$ such that, for every input array A of length at least 2 and every pivot sequence ω,*

$$RT(\omega) \leq a \cdot C(\omega).$$

We include the proof for the skeptics; skip it if you find Lemma 5.2 intuitively obvious.

Proof of Lemma 5.2: First, in every call to `Partition`, the pivot element is compared exactly once to every other element in the given subarray. Thus the number of comparisons in the call is linear in the subarray length and, by inspection of the pseudocode in Section 5.2.4, the total number of operations in the call is at most a constant times this. By inspection of the pseudocode in Section 5.2.5, randomized `QuickSort` performs only a constant number of operations in each recursive call outside the `Partition` subroutine.[19] There are at most n recursive calls to `QuickSort` in all—each input array element can be chosen as the pivot only once before being excluded from all future recursive calls—and so the total work outside calls to `Partition` is $O(n)$. Summing over all the recursive calls, the total number $RT(\omega)$ of operations is at most a constant times the number $C(\omega)$ of comparisons, plus $O(n)$. Because $C(\omega)$ is always at least proportional to n, the additional $O(n)$ work can be absorbed into the constant factor a of the lemma statement, and this completes the proof. $\mathcal{QED}$

The rest of this section concentrates on bounding the expected number of comparisons.

Theorem 5.3 (Comparisons in Randomized `QuickSort`) *For every input array of length $n \geq 1$, the expected number of comparisons between input array elements in randomized `QuickSort` is at most*

$$2(n-1)\ln n = O(n \log n).$$

By Lemma 5.2, Theorem 5.3 implies Theorem 5.1, with a different constant factor hidden in the big-O notation.

---

[19]This statement assumes that choosing a random pivot element counts as one primitive operation. The proof remains valid even if choosing a random pivot requires $\Theta(\log n)$ primitive operations (as you should check), and this covers typical practical implementations of random number generators.

5.5.2   A Decomposition Blueprint

The master method (Theorem 4.1) resolved the running time of every divide-and-conquer algorithm we've studied up to this point, but there are two reasons why it doesn't apply to randomized `QuickSort`. First, the running time of the algorithm corresponds to a random recurrence or a random recursion tree, and the master method works with deterministic recurrences. Second, the two subproblems that are solved recursively (elements less than the pivot and elements greater than the pivot) do not generally have the same size. We need a new idea.[20]

To prove Theorem 5.3, we'll follow a decomposition blueprint that is useful for analyzing the expectation of complicated random variables. The first step is to identify the (possibly complicated) random variable Y that you care about; for us, this is the number C of comparisons between input array elements made by randomized `QuickSort`, as in Theorem 5.3. The second step is to express Y as the sum of simpler random variables, ideally indicator (i.e., 0-1) random variables $X_1, \ldots, X_m$:

$$Y = \sum_{\ell=1}^{m} X_\ell.$$

We are now in the wheelhouse of linearity of expectation, which states that the expectation of a sum of random variables equals the sum of their expectations (Theorem B.1). The third step of the blueprint uses this property to reduce the computation of the expectation of Y to that of the simple random variables:

$$\mathbf{E}[Y] = \mathbf{E}\left[\sum_{\ell=1}^{m} X_\ell\right]$$
$$= \sum_{\ell=1}^{m} \mathbf{E}[X_\ell].$$

When the X_ℓ's are indicator random variables, their expectations are particularly easy to compute via the definition (B.1):

$$\mathbf{E}[X_\ell] = \underbrace{0 \cdot \mathbf{Pr}[X_\ell = 0]}_{=0} + 1 \cdot \mathbf{Pr}[X_\ell = 1]$$
$$= \mathbf{Pr}[X_\ell = 1].$$

The final step computes the expectations of the simple random variables and adds up the results.[21]

---

[20]There are generalizations of the master method that address both these issues, but they are somewhat complicated and outside the scope of this book.

[21]The randomized load-balancing analysis in Section B.6 is a simple example of this blueprint in action.

A Decomposition Blueprint

1. Identify the random variable Y that you care about.

2. Express Y as a sum of indicator (i.e., 0-1) random variables $X_1, \ldots, X_m$:

$$Y = \sum_{\ell=1}^{m} X_\ell.$$

3. Apply linearity of expectation:

$$\mathbf{E}[Y] = \sum_{\ell=1}^{m} \mathbf{Pr}[X_\ell = 1].$$

4. Compute each of the $\mathbf{Pr}[X_\ell = 1]$'s and add up the results to obtain $\mathbf{E}[Y]$.

5.5.3   Applying the Blueprint

To apply the decomposition blueprint to the analysis of randomized `QuickSort`, we need to decompose the random variable C that we really care about into simpler (ideally 0-1) random variables. The key idea is to break down the total comparison count according to the pair of input array elements getting compared.

To make this precise, let z_i denote the ith-smallest element in the input array, also known as the *ith order statistic*. For example, in the array

$$\boxed{6} \ \boxed{8} \ \boxed{9} \ \boxed{2}$$

z_1 refers to the "2," z_2 the "6," z_3 the "8," and z_4 the "9." Note that z_i does *not* denote the element in the ith position of the (unsorted) input array, but rather the element in this position of the sorted version of the input array.

For every pair of array indices $i, j \in \{1, 2, \ldots, n\}$ with $i < j$, we define a random variable X_{ij} as follows:

> for every fixed choice of pivots ω, $X_{ij}(\omega)$ is the number of times the elements z_i and z_j get compared in `QuickSort` when the pivots are specified by ω.

For the input array above, for example, $X_{1,3}$ is the number of times the `QuickSort` algorithm compares the "2" with the "8." We don't care about the X_{ij}'s per se, except inasmuch as they add up to the random variable C that we do care about.

The point of this definition is to implement the second step of the decomposition blueprint. Because each comparison involves exactly one pair of input array elements,

$$C(\omega) = \sum_{i=1}^{n-1} \sum_{j=i+1}^{n} X_{ij}(\omega)$$

for every $\omega \in \Omega$. The fancy-looking double sum on the right-hand side is simply iterating over all pairs (i, j) with $i < j$, and all this equation says is that the X_{ij}'s account for all the comparisons made by the QuickSort algorithm.

Quiz 5.3

Fix two different elements of the input array, say z_i and z_j. How many times might z_i and z_j be compared with each other during the execution of QuickSort?

   a) exactly once

   b) 0 or 1 times

   c) 0, 1, or 2 times

   d) any number between 0 and $n - 1$ is possible

(See Section 5.5.6 for the solution and discussion.)

The solution to Quiz 5.3 shows that all of the X_{ij}'s are indicator random variables. We can therefore apply the third step of our decomposition blueprint to obtain

$$\mathbf{E}[C] = \sum_{i=1}^{n-1} \sum_{j=i+1}^{n} \mathbf{E}[X_{ij}] = \sum_{i=1}^{n-1} \sum_{j=i+1}^{n} \mathbf{Pr}[X_{ij} = 1]. \tag{5.1}$$

To compute what we really care about, the expected number $\mathbf{E}[C]$ of comparisons, all we need to do is understand the $\mathbf{Pr}[X_{ij} = 1]$'s! Each of these numbers is the probability that some z_i and z_j are compared to each other at some point in randomized QuickSort, and the next order of business is to nail down these numbers.[22]

5.5.4 Computing Comparison Probabilities

There is a satisfying formula for the probability that two input array elements get compared in randomized QuickSort.

Lemma 5.4 (Comparison Probability) *If z_i and z_j denote the ith and jth smallest elements of the input array, with $i < j$, then*

$$\mathbf{Pr}[z_i, z_j \text{ get compared in randomized QuickSort}] = \frac{2}{j - i + 1}.$$

For example, if z_i and z_j are the minimum and maximum elements ($i = 1$ and $j = n$), then they are compared with probability only $\frac{2}{n}$. If there are no elements with value between z_i and z_j ($j = i + 1$), then z_i and z_j are always compared to each other.

---

[22]Section B.5 makes a big deal of the fact that linearity of expectation applies even to random variables that are not independent (i.e., when knowledge of one random variable tells you something about the others). This fact is crucial for us here, because the X_{ij}'s are not independent. For example, if I tell you that $X_{1n} = 1$, you know that either z_1 or z_n was chosen as the pivot element in the outermost call to QuickSort (why?), and this in turn makes it much more likely that a random variable of the form X_{1j} or X_{jn} also equals 1.

Fix z_i and z_j with $i < j$, and consider the pivot z_k chosen in the first call to QuickSort. What are the different scenarios?

Four QuickSort Scenarios

1. The chosen pivot is smaller than both z_i and z_j ($k < i$). Both z_i and z_j are passed to the second recursive call.

2. The chosen pivot is greater than both z_i and z_j ($k > j$). Both z_i and z_j are passed to the first recursive call.

3. The chosen pivot is between z_i and z_j ($i < k < j$). Elements z_i and z_j are then passed to the first and second recursive calls, respectively.

4. The chosen pivot is either z_i or z_j ($k \in \{i, j\}$). The pivot is excluded from both recursive calls; the other element is passed to the first (if $k = j$) or second (if $k = i$) recursive call.

We have two things going for us. First, remember that every comparison involves the current pivot element. Thus z_i and z_j are compared in the outermost call to QuickSort if and only if one of them is chosen as the pivot element (scenario 4). Second, in scenario 3, not only will z_i and z_j not be compared now, but they will never again appear together in the same recursive call and so cannot be compared in the future. For example, in the array

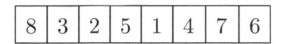

with $z_i = 3$ and $z_j = 7$, if any of the elements $\{4, 5, 6\}$ are chosen as the pivot element, then z_i and z_j are sent to different recursive calls, never to meet again. For example, if the "6" is chosen, the picture is:

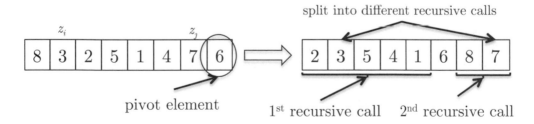

Scenarios 1 and 2 are a holding pattern: z_i and z_j haven't been compared yet, but it's still possible they will be compared in the future. During this holding pattern, z_i and z_j, and all of the elements $z_{i+1}, \ldots, z_{j-1}$ with values in between z_i and z_j, lead parallel lives and keep getting passed to the same recursive call. Eventually, their collective journey is interrupted by a recursive call to QuickSort in which one of the elements $z_i, z_{i+1}, \ldots, z_{j-1}, z_j$ is chosen as the pivot element, triggering either scenario 3 or scenario 4.[23]

---

[23] If nothing else, previous recursive calls eventually whittle the subarray down to only the elements $\{z_i, z_{i+1}, \ldots, z_{j-1}, z_j\}$.

Fast forwarding to this recursive call, which is where the action is, scenario 4 (and a comparison between z_i and z_j) is triggered if z_i or z_j is the chosen pivot, while scenario 3 (and no such comparison, ever) is triggered if any one of $z_{i+1}, \ldots, z_{j-1}$ is chosen as the pivot. So there are two bad cases (z_i and z_j) out of the $j - i + 1$ options ($z_i, z_{i+1}, \ldots, z_{j-1}, z_j$). Because randomized QuickSort always chooses pivot elements uniformly at random, by symmetry:

> *each element of $\{z_i, z_{i+1}, \ldots, z_{j-1}, z_j\}$ is equally likely to be the first pivot element chosen from the set.*

Putting everything together,

$$\mathbf{Pr}[z_i, z_j \text{ get compared at some point in randomized QuickSort}]$$

is the same as

$$\mathbf{Pr}[z_i \text{ or } z_j \text{ is chosen as a pivot before any of } z_{i+1}, \ldots, z_{j-1}],$$

which is

$$\frac{\text{number of bad cases}}{\text{total number of options}} = \frac{2}{j - i + 1}.$$

This completes the proof of Lemma 5.4. *QED*

Returning to our formula (5.1) for the expected number of comparisons made by randomized QuickSort, we obtain a shockingly exact expression:

$$\mathbf{E}[C] = \sum_{i=1}^{n-1} \sum_{j=i+1}^{n} \mathbf{Pr}[X_{ij} = 1] = \sum_{i=1}^{n-1} \sum_{j=i+1}^{n} \frac{2}{j - i + 1}. \tag{5.2}$$

To prove Theorem 5.3, all that's left to show is that the right-hand side of (5.2) is in fact $O(n \log n)$.

5.5.5 Final Calculations

It's easy to prove an upper bound of $O(n^2)$ on the right-hand side of (5.2): There are at most n^2 terms in the double sum, and each of these has value at most $\frac{1}{2}$ (achieved when $j = i+1$). But we're after a much better upper bound of $O(n \log n)$, and we'll have to be smarter to get it, by exploiting the fact that most of the quadratically many terms are much smaller than $\frac{1}{2}$.

Consider one of the inner sums in (5.2), for a fixed value of i:

$$\sum_{j=i+1}^{n} \frac{2}{j - i + 1} = 2 \cdot \underbrace{\left(\frac{1}{2} + \frac{1}{3} + \cdots + \frac{1}{n - i + 1} \right)}_{n - i \text{ terms}}.$$

We can bound each of these sums from above by the largest such sum, which occurs when $i = 1$:

$$\sum_{i=1}^{n-1} \sum_{j=i+1}^{n} \frac{2}{j - i + 1} \leq \sum_{i=1}^{n-1} \underbrace{\sum_{j=2}^{n} \frac{2}{j}}_{\text{independent of } i} = 2(n - 1) \cdot \sum_{j=2}^{n} \frac{1}{j}. \tag{5.3}$$

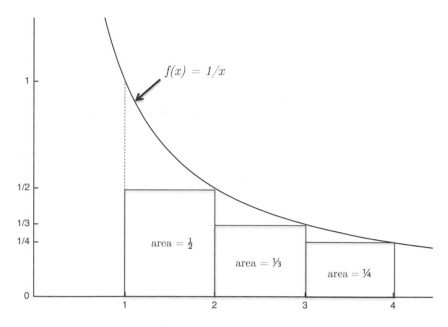

Figure 5.1: Each term of the sum $\sum_{j=2}^{n} 1/j$ can be identified with a rectangle of width 1 (between x-coordinates $j-1$ and j) and height $1/j$ (between y-coordinates 0 and $1/j$). The graph of the function $f(x) = 1/x$ kisses the northeastern corner of each of these rectangles, and so the area under the curve (i.e., the integral) is an upper bound on the area of the rectangles.

And how big is $\sum_{j=2}^{n} \frac{1}{j}$? Let's look at a picture. Viewing the terms of the sum as rectangles in the plane as in Figure 5.1, we see that we can bound this sum from above by the area under the curve $f(x) = \frac{1}{x}$ between the points 1 and n, also known as the integral $\int_{1}^{n} \frac{dx}{x}$. If you remember a little bit of calculus, you'll recognize the solution to this integral as the natural logarithm $\ln x$ (i.e., $\ln x$ is the function whose derivative is $\frac{1}{x}$):

$$\sum_{j=2}^{n} \frac{1}{j} \leq \int_{1}^{n} \frac{1}{x}\, dx = \ln x \Big|_{1}^{n} = \ln n - \underbrace{\ln 1}_{=0} = \ln n. \tag{5.4}$$

Chaining together the equations and inequalities in (5.2)–(5.4), we have

$$\mathbf{E}[C] = \sum_{i=1}^{n-1} \sum_{j=i+1}^{n} \frac{2}{j-i+1} \leq 2(n-1) \cdot \sum_{j=2}^{n} \frac{1}{j} \leq 2(n-1)\ln n.$$

Thus the expected number of comparisons made by randomized `QuickSort`—and also its expected running time, by Lemma 5.2—really is $O(n \log n)$! $\mathcal{QED}$

5.5.6   Solution to Quiz 5.3

Correct answer: (b). If either z_i or z_j is chosen as the pivot element in the outermost call to `QuickSort`, then z_i and z_j will get compared in the first call to `Partition`. (Remember that the pivot element is compared to every other element in the subarray.) If i and j differ by more than 1, it is also possible that z_i and z_j never get compared at all (see also Section 5.5.4). For example, the minimum and maximum elements will not be compared to each other unless one of them is chosen as the pivot element in the outermost recursive call (do you see why?).

Finally, as one would expect from a good sorting algorithm, z_i and z_j will never be compared to each other more than once (which would be redundant). Every comparison involves the current pivot element, so the first time z_i and z_j are compared in some call (if ever), one of them must be the pivot element. Because the pivot element is excluded from all future recursive calls, z_i and z_j never again appear together in the same recursive call (let alone get compared to each other).

*5.6   Sorting Requires $\Omega(n \log n)$ Comparisons

Is there a sorting algorithm faster than `MergeSort` and `QuickSort`, with running time better than $\Theta(n \log n)$? It's intuitively clear that an algorithm has to look at every input element once, but this implies only a linear lower bound of $\Omega(n)$. This optional section shows that we *can't* do better for sorting—the `MergeSort` and `QuickSort` algorithms achieve the best-possible asymptotic running time.

5.6.1   Comparison-Based Sorting Algorithms

Here's the formal statement of the $\Omega(n \log n)$ lower bound for general-purpose sorting.

Theorem 5.5 (Lower Bound for Sorting) *There is a constant $c > 0$ such that, for every $n \geq 1$, every comparison-based sorting algorithm performs at least $c \cdot n \log_2 n$ operations on some length-n input array.*

By a "comparison-based sorting algorithm," we mean an algorithm that accesses the input array only via comparisons between pairs of elements, and never directly accesses the value of an element. Comparison-based sorting algorithms are general-purpose, in that they make no assumptions about the input elements other than that they belong to some totally ordered set. You can think of a comparison-based sorting algorithm as interacting with the input array through an API that supports only one operation: given two indices i and j (each between 1 and the array length n), the operation reports whether the ith element is smaller than, equal to, or larger than the jth element.[24]

For example, the `MergeSort` algorithm is a comparison-based sorting algorithm—it doesn't care if it's sorting integers or fruits (assuming we agreed on a total ordering of all possible fruits, such as alphabetical).[25] So are `SelectionSort`, `InsertionSort`, `BubbleSort`, and `QuickSort`.

---

[24] For example, the default sorting routine in the Unix operating system works this way. The only requirement is a user-defined function for comparing pairs of input array elements.

[25] For an analogy, compare Sudoku and KenKen puzzles. Sudoku puzzles need only a notion of equality between different objects, and would make perfect sense with the digits 1–9 replaced by nine different fruits. KenKen puzzles involve arithmetic and hence need numbers—what would be the sum of a pluot and a mangosteen?

5.6.2   Faster Sorting Under Stronger Assumptions

The best way to understand comparison-based sorting is to look at some non-examples. Here are three famous sorting algorithms that make assumptions about the input but in exchange beat the $\Omega(n \log n)$ lower bound in Theorem 5.5.

BucketSort.   The `BucketSort` algorithm is useful in practice for numerical data, especially when it is spread out uniformly over a known range. For example, suppose the input array has n elements between 0 and 1 that are roughly evenly spread out. In our minds, we divide the interval $[0, 1]$ into n "buckets," the first reserved for input elements between 0 and $\frac{1}{n}$, the second for elements between $\frac{1}{n}$ and $\frac{2}{n}$, and so on. The first step of the `BucketSort` algorithm does a single linear-time pass over the input array and places each element in its bucket. *This is not a comparison-based step*—the `BucketSort` algorithm looks at the actual value of an input element to identify which bucket it belongs to. It matters whether the value of an input element is .17 or .27, even if we hold the relative ordering of the elements fixed.

   If the elements are roughly evenly spread out, the population of every bucket is small. The second step of the algorithm sorts the elements inside each bucket separately (for example, using `InsertionSort`). Provided there are few elements in every bucket, this step also runs in linear time (with a constant number of operations performed per bucket). Finally, the sorted lists of the different buckets are concatenated, from the first to the last. This step also runs in linear time. We conclude that linear-time sorting is possible under a strong assumption on the input data.

CountingSort.   The `CountingSort` algorithm is a variation on the same idea. Here, we assume that there are only k different possible values of each input element (known in advance), such as the integers $\{1, 2, \ldots, k\}$. The algorithm sets up k buckets, one for each possible value, and in a single pass through the input array places each element in the appropriate bucket. The output array is simply the concatenation of these buckets (in order). `CountingSort` runs in linear time when $k = O(n)$, where n is the length of the input array. For the same reasons as `BucketSort`, it is not a comparison-based algorithm.

RadixSort.   The `RadixSort` algorithm is an extension of `CountingSort` that gracefully handles n-element integer input arrays with reasonably large numbers represented in binary (a string of 0s and 1s, or "bits"). The first step of `RadixSort` considers only the block of the $\log_2 n$ least significant bits of the input numbers, and sorts them accordingly. Because $\log_2 n$ bits can encode only n different values—corresponding to the numbers $0, 1, 2, \ldots, n - 1$, written in binary—the `CountingSort` algorithm can be used to implement this step in linear time. The `RadixSort` algorithm then re-sorts all the elements using the block of the next-least significant $\log_2 n$ bits, and so on until all the bits of the input have been processed. For this algorithm to sort correctly, it's important to implement the `CountingSort` subroutine so that it is *stable*, meaning that it preserves the relative order of different elements with the same value.[26]   The `RadixSort` algorithm runs in linear time provided the input array contains only integers between 0 and n^k for some constant k.

---

[26]Not all sorting algorithms are stable. For example, `QuickSort` is not a stable sorting algorithm (do you see why?).

These three sorting algorithms demonstrate how additional assumptions about the input data (like being not-too-large integers) enable techniques beyond comparisons (like bucketing) and algorithms that are faster than $\Theta(n \log n)$ time. Theorem 5.5 states that such improvements are impossible for general-purpose comparison-based sorting algorithms. Let's see why.

5.6.3   Proof of Theorem 5.5

Fix an arbitrary deterministic comparison-based sorting algorithm.[27]

Zero comparisons.   First imagine an algorithm that makes *zero* comparisons. Because the algorithm can learn about the input only through comparisons, it knows absolutely nothing about it. For example, such an algorithm has no idea whether the input is

$$\boxed{1\ 2\ 3\ 4} \quad \text{or} \quad \boxed{4\ 3\ 2\ 1}$$

To be correct in the first case, the algorithm's output array must be the same as the input array. Because the algorithm doesn't know which case it's in, its output array must then also be the same as the (unsorted) input array in the second case. This argument shows that every comparison-based sorting algorithm that makes zero comparisons behaves incorrectly for at least one of these two cases.

One comparison.   Now consider an algorithm that makes *one* comparison—say of the first and second input array elements. Such an algorithm can distinguish between the two cases above, and execute differently in each case. But it still has no clue whether the input is

$$\boxed{1\ 2\ 3\ 4} \quad \text{or} \quad \boxed{1\ 2\ 4\ 3}$$

Because the algorithm executes identically in these two cases, it must be incorrect in at least one of them. If its output array doesn't equal the input array in these cases, then it's incorrect in the first scenario; otherwise, it's incorrect in the second scenario.

Two comparisons.   An algorithm that makes *two* comparisons is able to learn something about every element of a length-4 array, for example by comparing the first and second elements and then the third and fourth elements. This still isn't enough, as the algorithm can't tell if the input is

$$\boxed{1\ 2\ 3\ 4} \quad \text{or} \quad \boxed{1\ 3\ 2\ 4}$$

If the algorithm could access the *values* of the input array elements, it could distinguish between these two inputs. But as a comparison-based algorithm, it learns nothing beyond the facts that the first element is smaller than the second and the third element is smaller than the fourth. The algorithm executes identically in the two cases, and can be correct in only one of them.

---
[27]Similar arguments apply to randomized comparison-based sorting algorithms, and no such algorithm has expected running time better than $\Theta(n \log n)$. See also Problems 5.6–5.7.

k **comparisons.**   Consider the general case of an algorithm that always makes at most k comparisons. The general pattern is: If two different input arrays lead to the same answers to all k comparisons, then the algorithm cannot distinguish between them and it executes identically in both cases (and incorrectly in at least one of them). Because there are 2^k possible sets of answers to the algorithm's k comparisons, the algorithm can distinguish between at most 2^k different inputs and execute in at most 2^k different ways (Figure 5.2).

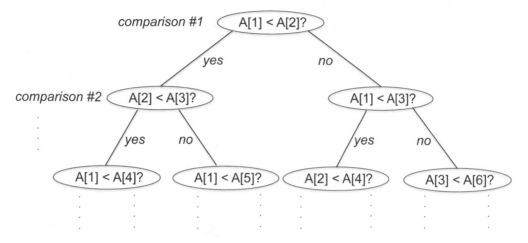

Figure 5.2: A comparison-based sorting algorithm that makes at most k comparisons can execute in at most 2^k different ways.

There are $n! = n \cdot (n-1) \cdots 2 \cdot 1$ different length-n input arrays that contain the numbers $\{1, 2, 3 \ldots, n\}$, and a correct sorting algorithm must distinguish all of them.[28] Thus, the maximum number k of comparisons made by a correct comparison-based sorting algorithm must satisfy

$$2^k \geq \underbrace{n!}_{n \cdot (n-1) \cdots 2 \cdot 1} \geq \left(\frac{n}{2}\right)^{n/2},$$

where we have used the fact that the first $n/2$ terms of $n \cdot (n-1) \cdots 2 \cdot 1$ are all at least $\frac{n}{2}$. Taking the logarithm base-2 of both sides shows that

$$k \geq \frac{n}{2} \log_2 \left(\frac{n}{2}\right) = \Omega(n \log n).$$

This completes the proof of Theorem 5.5. $\mathcal{QED}$

The Upshot

☆ The famous `QuickSort` algorithm has three high-level steps: first, it chooses one element p of the input array to act as a "pivot element"; second, its `Partition` subroutine rearranges the array so that

---

[28]There are n choices for the location of the "1," $n-1$ remaining choices for the location of the "2," and so on.

elements smaller than and greater than p come before it and after it, respectively; third, it recursively sorts the two subarrays on either side of the pivot.

☆ The `Partition` subroutine can be implemented to run in linear time and in place, meaning with negligible auxiliary memory. As a consequence, `QuickSort` also runs in place.

☆ The correctness of the `QuickSort` algorithm does not depend on how pivot elements are chosen, but its running time does.

☆ The worst-case scenario is a running time of $\Theta(n^2)$, where n is the length of the input array. This occurs when the input array is already sorted and the first element is always used as the pivot element.

☆ The best-case scenario is a running time of $\Theta(n \log n)$. This occurs when the median element is always used as the pivot.

☆ In randomized `QuickSort`, the pivot element is always chosen uniformly at random. Its running time can be anywhere from $\Theta(n \log n)$ to $\Theta(n^2)$, depending on its random coin flips.

☆ The average running time of randomized `QuickSort` is $\Theta(n \log n)$, only a small constant factor worse than its best-case running time.

☆ Intuitively, choosing a random pivot is a good idea because there's a 50% chance of getting a 25%-75% or better split of the input array.

☆ The formal analysis uses a decomposition blueprint that expresses a complicated random variable as a sum of 0-1 random variables and then applies linearity of expectation.

☆ The key insight is that the ith- and jth-smallest elements of the input array get compared in `QuickSort` if and only if one of them is chosen as a pivot before an element with value strictly in between them is chosen as a pivot.

☆ A comparison-based sorting algorithm is a general-purpose algorithm that accesses the input array only by comparing pairs of elements, and never directly uses the value of an element.

☆ No comparison-based sorting algorithm has a worst-case asymptotic running time better than $O(n \log n)$.

Test Your Understanding

Problem 5.1 *(S)* Which of the following statements are true? (Choose all that apply.)

a) QuickSort should always be preferred over MergeSort in practice.

b) MergeSort should always be preferred over QuickSort in practice.

c) The $\Omega(n \log n)$ sorting lower bound for length-n arrays can be overcome using randomization.

d) The $\Omega(n \log n)$ sorting lower bound can be overcome when all array elements are known to be integers between 1 and n^{10}.

Problem 5.2 *(S)* Recall the Partition subroutine employed by QuickSort (Section 5.2). You are told that the following array has just been partitioned around some pivot element:

3	1	2	4	5	8	7	6	9

Which of the elements could have been the pivot element? (List all that apply; there could be more than one possibility.)

Problem 5.3 *(S)* Let α be some constant, independent of the input array length n, strictly between 0 and $\frac{1}{2}$. What is the probability that, with a randomly chosen pivot element, the Partition subroutine produces a split in which the size of both the resulting subproblems is at least α times the size of the original array?

a) α

b) $1 - \alpha$

c) $1 - 2\alpha$

d) $2 - 2\alpha$

Problem 5.4 *(H)* Let α be some constant, independent of the input array length n, strictly between 0 and $\frac{1}{2}$. Assume you achieve the approximately balanced splits from the preceding problem in every recursive call—so whenever a recursive call is given an array of length k, each of its two recursive calls is passed a subarray with length between αk and $(1 - \alpha)k$. How many successive recursive calls can occur before triggering the base case? Equivalently, which levels of the algorithm's recursion tree can contain leaves? Express your answer as a range of possible numbers d, from the minimum to the maximum number of recursive calls that might be needed.

a) $0 \le d \le -\frac{\ln n}{\ln \alpha}$

b) $-\frac{\ln n}{\ln \alpha} \le d \le -\frac{\ln n}{\ln(1-\alpha)}$

c) $-\frac{\ln n}{\ln(1-\alpha)} \le d \le -\frac{\ln n}{\ln \alpha}$

d) $-\frac{\ln n}{\ln(1-2\alpha)} \le d \le -\frac{\ln n}{\ln(1-\alpha)}$

Problem 5.5 *(S)* Define the recursion depth of QuickSort as the maximum number of successive recursive calls it makes before hitting the base case—equivalently, the deepest level of its recursion tree. In randomized QuickSort, the recursion depth is a random variable, depending on the pivots chosen. What are the minimum- and maximum-possible recursion depths of randomized QuickSort?

a) minimum: $\Theta(1)$; maximum: $\Theta(n)$

b) minimum: $\Theta(\log n)$; maximum: $\Theta(n)$

c) minimum: $\Theta(\log n)$; maximum: $\Theta(n \log n)$

d) minimum: $\Theta(\sqrt{n})$; maximum: $\Theta(n)$

Challenge Problems

Problem 5.6 *(H)* Consider the $n!$ different arrays consisting of the numbers $\{1, 2, \ldots, n\}$ in some order. Prove that every deterministic comparison-based sorting algorithm has an average running time of $\Omega(n \log n)$ on these $n!$ inputs.

Problem 5.7 *(H)* Prove that for every randomized comparison-based sorting algorithm, there is a length-n array for which its expected running time is $\Omega(n \log n)$. (In fact, this lower bound holds even on average over the $n!$ inputs considered in the previous problem.)

Programming Problems

Problem 5.8 Implement the QuickSort algorithm in your favorite programming language. Experiment with the performance of different ways of choosing the pivot element.

One approach is to keep track of the number of comparisons between input array elements made by QuickSort.[29] For several different input arrays, determine the number of comparisons made with the following implementations of the ChoosePivot subroutine:

1. Always use the first element as the pivot.

2. Always use the last element as the pivot.

3. Use a random element as the pivot. (In this case you should run the algorithm 10 times on a given input array and average the results.)

4. Use the *median-of-three* as the pivot element. The goal of this rule is to do a little extra work to get much better performance on input arrays that are nearly sorted or reverse sorted.

   In more detail, this implementation of ChoosePivot considers the first, middle, and final elements of the given array. (For an array with even length $2k$, use the kth element for the "middle" one.) It then identifies which of these three elements is the

---

[29]There's no need to count the comparisons one by one. When there is a recursive call on a subarray of length m, you can simply add $m - 1$ to your running total of comparisons. (Recall that the pivot element is compared to each of the other $m - 1$ elements in the subarray in this recursive call.)

median (i.e., the one whose value is in between the other two), and returns this as the pivot.[30]

For example, with the input array

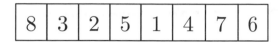

the subroutine would consider the first (8), middle (5), and last (6) elements. It would return 6, the median of the set $\{5, 6, 8\}$, as the pivot element.

See www.algorithmsilluminated.org for test cases and challenge data sets.

---

[30]A careful analysis would keep track of the comparisons made in identifying the median of the three candidate elements, in addition to the comparisons made in calls to Partition.

Chapter 6

Linear-Time Selection

This chapter studies the *selection problem*, where the goal is to identify the ith-smallest element of an unsorted array. It's easy to solve this problem in $O(n \log n)$ time using sorting, but we can do better. Section 6.1 describes an extremely practical randomized algorithm, very much in the spirit of randomized `QuickSort`, that runs in *linear* time on average. Section 6.2 provides the elegant analysis of this algorithm—there's a cool way to think about the algorithm's progress in terms of a simple coin-flipping experiment, and then linearity of expectation (yes, it's back...) seals the deal.

Theoretically inclined readers might wonder whether the selection problem can be solved in linear time without resorting to randomization. Section 6.3 describes a famous deterministic algorithm for the problem, one that has more Turing Award-winning authors than any other algorithm I know of. It is deterministic (i.e., no randomization allowed) and based on an ingenious "median-of-medians" idea for guaranteeing good pivot choices. Section 6.4 proves the linear running time bound, which is not so easy!

This chapter assumes that you remember the `Partition` subroutine from Section 5.2 that partitions an array around a pivot element in linear time, as well as the intuition for what makes a pivot element good or bad (Section 5.3).

6.1 The `RSelect` Algorithm

6.1.1 The Selection Problem

In the *selection problem*, the input is the same as for the sorting problem—an array of n numbers—along with an integer $i \in \{1, 2, \ldots, n\}$. The goal is to identify the ith *order statistic*—the ith-smallest entry in the array.

Problem: Selection

Input: An array of n numbers, in arbitrary order, and an integer $i \in \{1, 2, \ldots, n\}$.

Output: The ith-smallest element of A.

As usual, we assume for simplicity that the input array has distinct elements, with no duplicates.

For example, if the input array is

and the value of i is 2, the correct output is 6. If i were 3, the correct output would be 8, and so on.

When $i = 1$, the selection problem is simply the problem of computing the minimum element of an array. This is easy to do in linear time—make one pass through the array and remember the smallest element seen. Similarly, the case of finding the maximum element ($i = n$) is easy. But what about for values of i in the middle? For example, what if we want to compute the middle element—the *median*—of an array?

To be precise, for an array with odd length n, the median is the ith order statistic with $i = (n + 1)/2$. For an array with even length n, let's agree to define the median as the smaller of the two possibilities, which corresponds to $i = n/2$.[1]

6.1.2   Reduction to Sorting

We already know a fast algorithm for the selection problem, which piggybacks on our fast sorting algorithms.

Reducing Selection to Sorting

Input: array A of n distinct numbers, and an integer $i \in \{1, 2, \ldots, n\}$.
Output: the ith order statistic of A.

$B := \text{MergeSort}(A)$
return $B[i]$

After sorting the input array, we certainly know where to find the ith smallest element—it's hanging out in the ith position of the sorted array. Because MergeSort runs in $O(n \log n)$ time (Theorem 1.2), so does this two-step algorithm.[2]

But remember the mantra of any algorithm designer worth their salt: *can we do better?* Can we design an algorithm for the selection problem that is even faster than $O(n \log n)$ time? The best we can hope for is linear time ($O(n)$)—if we don't even take the time to look at each element in the array, there's no hope of always correctly identifying, say, the minimum element. We also know from Theorem 5.5 that any algorithm that uses a sorting subroutine is stuck with a worst-case running time of $\Omega(n \log n)$.[3] So if we *can* get a running time better than $O(n \log n)$ for the selection problem, we'll have proved that *selection is fundamentally easier than sorting*. Accomplishing this requires ingenuity—piggybacking on our sorting algorithms won't cut it.

---

[1]Why would you want to compute the median element of an array? After all, the *mean* (i.e., average) is easy enough to compute in linear time—sum up all the array elements in a single pass and divide by n. One reason is to compute a summary statistic of an array that is more robust than the mean. For example, one badly corrupted element, such as a data entry error, can totally screw up the mean of an array, but generally has little effect on the median.

[2]A computer scientist would call this a *reduction* from the selection problem to the sorting problem. A reduction absolves you from developing a new algorithm from scratch, and instead allows you to stand on the shoulders of existing algorithms. In addition to their practical utility, reductions are an extremely fundamental concept in computer science, and we will discuss them at length in later parts of the book (especially Part IV).

[3]Assuming that we restrict ourselves to comparison-based sorting algorithms, as in Section 5.6.

6.1.3   A Divide-and-Conquer Approach

The randomized linear-time selection algorithm `RSelect` follows the template that proved so successful in randomized `QuickSort`: Choose a random pivot element, partition the input array around the pivot, and recurse appropriately. The next order of business is to understand the appropriate recursion for the selection problem.

Recall what the `Partition` subroutine in Section 5.2 does: Given an array and a choice of pivot element, it rearranges the elements of the array so that everything less than and greater than the pivot appears before and after the pivot, respectively.

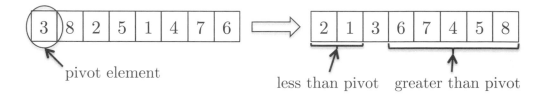

Thus the pivot element ends up in its rightful position, after all the elements less than it and before all the elements greater than it.

`QuickSort` recursively sorts the subarray of elements less than the pivot element, and also the subarray of elements greater than the pivot. What is the analog for the selection problem?

Quiz 6.1

Suppose we are looking for the 5th order statistic in an input array of 10 elements. Suppose that after partitioning the array, the pivot element ends up in the third position. On which side of the pivot element should we recurse, and what order statistic should we look for?

   a) The 3rd order statistic on the left side of the pivot.

   b) The 2nd order statistic on the right side of the pivot.

   c) The 5th order statistic on the right side of the pivot.

   d) We might need to recurse on both the left and the right sides of the pivot.

(See Section 6.1.6 for the solution and discussion.)

6.1.4   Pseudocode for `RSelect`

Our pseudocode for the `RSelect` algorithm follows the high-level description of `QuickSort` in Section 5.1, with two changes. First, we commit to using random pivot elements rather than having a generic `ChoosePivot` subroutine. Second, `RSelect` makes only one recursive call, while `QuickSort` makes two. This difference is the primary reason to hope that `RSelect` might be even faster than randomized `QuickSort`.

RSelect

Input: array A of $n \geq 1$ distinct numbers, and an integer
$\quad i \in \{1, 2, \ldots, n\}$.
Output: the ith order statistic of A.

---

if $n = 1$ **then**   // base case
$\quad$ return $A[1]$

choose pivot element p uniformly at random from A
partition A around p
$j := p$'s position in partitioned array
if $j = i$ **then**   // you got lucky!
$\quad$ return p
else if $j > i$ **then**
$\quad$ return RSelect(first part of A, i)
else   // $j < i$
$\quad$ return RSelect(second part of A, $i - j$)

Partitioning the input array around the pivot element p splits the array into three pieces, leading to three cases in the RSelect algorithm:

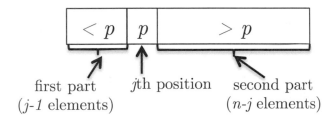

Because the pivot element p assumes its rightful position in the partitioned array, if it's in the jth position, it must be the jth order statistic. If by dumb luck the algorithm was looking for the jth order statistic (that is, $i = j$), it's done. If the algorithm is searching for a smaller number (that is, $i < j$), it must belong to the first part of the partitioned array. In this case, recursing only throws out elements bigger than the jth (and hence the ith) order statistic, so the algorithm is still looking for the ith-smallest element among those in the first subarray. In the final case ($i > j$), the algorithm is looking for a number larger than the pivot element, and the recursion mimics the solution to Quiz 6.1. The algorithm recurses on the second part of the partitioned array, throwing out the pivot element and the $j - 1$ elements smaller than it from further consideration. Because the algorithm was originally looking for the ith-smallest element, it's now looking for the $(i - j)$th-smallest element among those that remain.

$\quad$ The RSelect algorithm can be implemented to work in place, without allocating significant additional memory. The in-place implementation uses left and right endpoints to keep track of the current subarray, like in the pseudocode for QuickSort in Section 5.2.5. See also Programming Problem 6.7.

6.1.5   Running Time of `RSelect`

Like randomized `QuickSort`, the running time of the `RSelect` algorithm depends on the pivots it chooses. What's the worst that could happen?

Quiz 6.2

What is the running time of the `RSelect` algorithm if pivot elements are always chosen in the worst possible way?

a) $\Theta(n)$

b) $\Theta(n \log n)$

c) $\Theta(n^2)$

d) $\Theta(2^n)$

(See Section 6.1.6 for the solution and discussion.)

We now know that the `RSelect` algorithm does not run in linear time for all possible choices of pivot elements, but could it run in linear time on average over its random choices of pivots? Let's start with a more modest goal: are there *any* choices of pivots for which `RSelect` runs in linear time?

What makes a good pivot? The answer is the same as for `QuickSort` (see Section 5.3): Good pivots guarantee that recursive calls receive significantly smaller subproblems. The best-case scenario is a pivot element that gives the most balanced split possible, with two subarrays of equal length.[4] This scenario occurs when the median element is chosen as the pivot. It may seem circular to explore this scenario, as we might well be trying to compute the median in the first place! But it's still a useful thought experiment to understand the best-possible running time that `RSelect` can have (which had better be linear!).

Let $T(n)$ denote the running time of `RSelect` on arrays of length n. If the algorithm magically always chooses the median element of the current subarray, every recursive call will perform work linear in its subarray (mostly in the `Partition` subroutine) and make one recursive call on a subarray of half the size:

$$T(n) \le \underbrace{T\left(\frac{n}{2}\right)}_{\text{as pivot = median}} + \underbrace{O(n)}_{\texttt{Partition, etc.}} .$$

This recurrence is right in the wheelhouse of the master method (Theorem 4.1): Because there is one recursive call ($a = 1$), the subproblem size drops by a factor of 2 ($b = 2$), and linear work is done outside the recursive call ($d = 1$), $1 = a < b^d = 2$ and the second case of the master method tells us that $T(n) = O(n)$. This is an important sanity check: If `RSelect` gets sufficiently lucky, it runs in linear time.

So is the running time of `RSelect` typically closer to its best-case performance of $\Theta(n)$ or its worst-case performance of $\Theta(n^2)$? With the success of randomized `QuickSort`

---

[4]We're ignoring the lucky case in which the chosen pivot is exactly the order statistic being searched for—this is unlikely to happen before the last few recursive calls of the algorithm.

under our belt, we might hope that typical executions of RSelect have performance close to the best-case scenario. And indeed, while in principle RSelect can run in $\Theta(n^2)$ time, you will almost always observe a running time of $O(n)$ in practice.

Theorem 6.1 (Running Time of RSelect) *For every input array of length $n \geq 1$, the average running time of RSelect is $O(n)$.*

Section 6.2 provides the proof of Theorem 6.1.

Amazingly, the average running time of RSelect is only a constant factor larger than the time needed to read the input! Because sorting requires $\Omega(n \log n)$ time (Section 5.6), Theorem 6.1 shows that selection is fundamentally easier than sorting.

The same comments about the average running time of randomized QuickSort (Theorem 5.1) apply here. The RSelect algorithm is general-purpose in that the running time bound applies to all possible inputs and the "average" refers only to the random pivot elements chosen by the algorithm. Like with QuickSort, the constant hidden in the big-O notation in Theorem 6.1 is reasonably small and the algorithm can be implemented to work in place.

6.1.6   Solution to Quizzes 6.1–6.2

Solution to Quiz 6.1

Correct answer: (b). After partitioning the array, we know that the pivot element is in its rightful position, with all smaller numbers before it and larger numbers after it. Because the pivot element wound up in the third position of the array, it is the third-smallest element. We're looking for the fifth-smallest element, which is larger. We can therefore be sure that the 5th order statistic is in the second subarray, and we need to recurse only once. What order statistic are we looking for in the recursive call? Originally we were looking for the fifth-smallest, but now we've thrown out the pivot element and the two elements smaller than it. Because $5 - 3 = 2$, we're now looking for the second-smallest element among those passed to the recursive call.

Solution to Quiz 6.2

Correct answer: (c). The worst-case running time of RSelect is the same as for randomized QuickSort. The bad example is the same as in Quiz 5.1: suppose the input array is already sorted, and the algorithm repeatedly picks the first element as the pivot. In every recursive call, the first part of the subarray is empty while the second part includes everything save the current pivot. Thus the subarray length of each recursive call is only one less than the previous one. The work done in each recursive call (mostly by the Partition subroutine) is linear in its subarray length. When computing the median element, there are $\approx n/2$ recursive calls, each with a subarray of length at least $n/2$, and so the overall running time is $\Theta(n^2)$.

*6.2   Analysis of RSelect

One way to prove the linear expected running time bound for the RSelect algorithm (Theorem 6.1) is to follow the same decomposition blueprint that worked so well for analyzing randomized `QuickSort` (Section 5.5), with indicator random variables that track comparisons. For `RSelect`, we can also get away with a simpler instantiation of the decomposition blueprint that formalizes the intuition from Section 5.4.3: (i) random pivots are likely to be pretty good; and (ii) pretty good pivots make rapid progress.

6.2.1   Tracking Progress via Phases

We've already noted that a call to `RSelect` does $O(n)$ work outside of its recursive call, primarily in its call to `Partition`. That is, there is a constant $c > 0$ such that

> (*) for every input array of length n, `RSelect` performs at most cn operations outside of its recursive call.

Because `RSelect` always makes only one recursive call, we can track its progress by the length of the subarray that it is currently working on, which shrinks in size over time. For simplicity, we'll use a coarser version of this progress measure.[5] Suppose the outer call to `RSelect` is given an array of length n. For an integer $j \geq 0$, we say that a recursive call to `RSelect` is in *phase j* if the length of its subarray is between

$$\left(\frac{3}{4}\right)^{j+1} \cdot n \text{ and } \left(\frac{3}{4}\right)^{j} \cdot n.$$

For example, the outermost call to `RSelect` is always in phase 0, as are any subsequent recursive calls that operate on at least 75% of the original input array. Recursive calls on subarrays that contain between $(\frac{3}{4})^2 \approx 56\%$ and 75% of the original elements belong to phase 1, and so on. By phase $j \approx \log_{4/3} n$, the subarray has size at most 1 and there are no further recursive calls.

For each integer $j \geq 0$, let X_j denote the random variable equal to the number of phase-j recursive calls. X_j can be as small as 0, because a phase might get skipped entirely, and certainly can't be bigger than n, the maximum number of recursive calls made by `RSelect`. By (*), `RSelect` performs at most

$$c \cdot \underbrace{\left(\frac{3}{4}\right)^{j} \cdot n}_{\substack{\text{max subarray length} \\ \text{(phase } j\text{)}}}$$

operations in each phase-j recursive call. We can then decompose the running time of `RSelect` across the different phases:

$$\text{running time of RSelect} \quad \leq \quad \sum_{j \geq 0} \underbrace{X_j}_{\substack{\text{\# calls} \\ \text{(phase } j\text{)}}} \cdot \underbrace{c \left(\frac{3}{4}\right)^{j} n}_{\substack{\text{work per call} \\ \text{(phase } j\text{)}}}$$

$$= \quad cn \sum_{j \geq 0} \left(\frac{3}{4}\right)^{j} X_j.$$

---

[5] A more refined analysis can be carried out to prove a smaller constant factor in the running time bound.

This upper bound on the running time of RSelect is a complicated random variable, but it is a weighted sum of simpler random variables (the X_j's). Your automatic response at this point should be to apply linearity of expectation (Theorem B.1), to reduce the computation of the complicated random variable to those of the simpler ones:

$$\mathbf{E}[\text{running time of RSelect}] \leq cn \sum_{j \geq 0} \left(\frac{3}{4}\right)^j \mathbf{E}[X_j]. \tag{6.1}$$

So what is $\mathbf{E}[X_j]$?

6.2.2   Reduction to Coin Flipping

We have two things going for us in bounding the expected number $\mathbf{E}[X_j]$ of phase-j recursive calls. First, whenever we pick a pretty good pivot, we proceed to a later phase. As in Section 5.4.3, define an *approximate median* of a subarray as an element that is greater than at least 25% of the other elements in the subarray and also less than at least 25% of the other elements. The picture after partitioning around such a pivot element is:

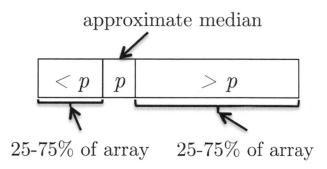

No matter which case is triggered in RSelect, the recursive call gets a subarray of length at most $\frac{3}{4}$ times that of the previous call, and therefore belongs to a later phase. This argument proves the following proposition.

Proposition 6.2 (Approximate Medians Make Progress) *If a phase-j recursive call chooses an approximate median as the pivot element, then the next recursive call belongs to phase $j + 1$ or later.*

Second, as proved in Section 5.4.3, a recursive call has a decent chance of picking an approximate median.

Proposition 6.3 (Approximate Medians Are Abundant) *A call to RSelect chooses an approximate median as the pivot element with probability at least 50%.*

For example, in an array that contains the elements $\{1, 2, \ldots, 100\}$, each of the fifty elements between 26 and 75, inclusive, is an approximate median.

Propositions 6.2 and 6.3 let us substitute a simple coin-flipping experiment for the number of phase-j recursive calls. Suppose you have a fair coin, equally likely to be heads or tails. Flip the coin repeatedly, stopping the first time you get "heads," and let N be the number of coin flips performed (including the last flip). Think of "heads" as corresponding to choosing an approximate median (and ending the experiment).

Proposition 6.4 (Reduction to Coin Flipping) *For each phase* $j = 0, 1, 2, \ldots$, $\mathbf{E}[X_j] \leq$ $\mathbf{E}[N]$.

Proof: There are two differences between the random variables X_j and N, both of which push the expected value of the former lower than that of the latter. First, there might be no phase-j recursive calls (if the phase is skipped entirely), while there is always at least one coin flip (the first one). Second, each coin flip has exactly a 50% chance of ending the experiment (if it comes up heads). Meanwhile, Propositions 6.2 and 6.3 imply that a phase-j recursive call ends the phase with probably 50% or more—choosing an approximate median as the pivot element guarantees the end of the phase, and in many cases other pivot elements work as well. $\mathcal{QED}$

The random variable N is called a *geometric random variable with parameter* $\frac{1}{2}$. Looking up its expectation in a textbook or on the Web, we find that $\mathbf{E}[N] = 2$. Alternatively, a sneaky way to see this is to write the expected value of N in terms of itself. The key idea is to exploit the fact that the random experiment is memoryless: If the first coin flip comes up "tails," the rest of the experiment is a copy of the original one. In math, whatever the expected value of N might be, it must satisfy the relationship

$$\mathbf{E}[N] = \underbrace{1}_{\text{first flip}} + \underbrace{\frac{1}{2}}_{\mathbf{Pr}[\text{tails}]} \cdot \underbrace{\mathbf{E}[N]}_{\text{further coin flips}} .$$

The unique value for $\mathbf{E}[N]$ that satisfies this equation is 2.[6]

Proposition 6.4 implies that this value is an upper bound on what we care about, the expected number of phase-j recursive calls.

Corollary 6.5 (Two Calls Per Phase) *For every* j, $\mathbf{E}[X_j] \leq 2$.

6.2.3 Putting It All Together

We can now use the upper bound in Corollary 6.5 on the $\mathbf{E}[X_j]$'s to simplify our upper bound (6.1) on the expected running time of `RSelect`:

$$\mathbf{E}[\text{running time of } \texttt{RSelect}] \leq cn \sum_{j \geq 0} \left(\frac{3}{4}\right)^j \mathbf{E}[X_j] \leq 2cn \sum_{j \geq 0} \left(\frac{3}{4}\right)^j .$$

The sum $\sum_{j \geq 0} \left(\frac{3}{4}\right)^j$ looks messy, but it's a beast we've already tamed. When proving the master method (Section 4.4), we took a detour to discuss geometric series (Section 4.4.8), and derived the exact formula (4.6):

$$1 + r + r^2 + \cdots + r^k = \frac{1 - r^{k+1}}{1 - r}$$

for every real number $r \neq 1$ and nonnegative integer k. When r is positive and less than 1, this quantity is at most $\frac{1}{1-r}$, no matter how big k is. Plugging in $r = \frac{3}{4}$, we have

$$\sum_{j \geq 0} \left(\frac{3}{4}\right)^j \leq \frac{1}{1 - \frac{3}{4}} = 4,$$

---

[6]Strictly speaking, we should also rule out the possibility that $\mathbf{E}[N] = +\infty$ (which is not hard to do).

and so
$$\mathbf{E}[\text{running time of RSelect}] \le 8cn = O(n).$$

This completes the analysis of RSelect and the proof of Theorem 6.1. *QED*

*6.3   The DSelect Algorithm

The RSelect algorithm runs in expected linear time for every input, where the expectation is over the random choices made by the algorithm. Is randomization required for linear-time selection?[7] This section and the next resolve this question with a deterministic linear-time algorithm for the selection problem.

For the sorting problem, the $O(n \log n)$ average running time of randomized QuickSort is matched by that of the deterministic MergeSort algorithm, and both QuickSort and MergeSort are useful algorithms in practice. In contrast, while the deterministic linear-time selection algorithm described in this section works OK in practice, it is not competitive with the RSelect algorithm. The two reasons for this are the larger constant factors in the running time and the work performed by DSelect allocating and managing additional memory. Still, the ideas in the algorithm are so cool that I can't help but tell you about them.

6.3.1   The Big Idea: Median-of-Medians

The RSelect algorithm is fast because random pivot elements tend to be pretty good, yielding a roughly balanced split of the input array after partitioning, and because pretty good pivots lead to rapid progress. But suppose we're not allowed to use randomization. How can we compute a pretty good pivot element without doing too much work?

The big idea in deterministic linear-time selection is to use the "median-of-medians" as a proxy for the true median. The algorithm treats the input array elements like sports teams and runs a two-round knockout tournament, the champion of which is the pivot element; see also Figure 6.1.

The first round is the group stage, with the elements in positions 1–5 of the input array the first group, the elements in positions 6–10 the second group, and so on. The first-round winner of a group of 5 is defined as the median element of the group (i.e., the third-smallest). Because there are $\approx n/5$ groups of 5, there are $\approx n/5$ first-round winners. (As usual, we ignore fractions for simplicity.) The tournament champion is then defined as the median of the first-round winners.

6.3.2   Pseudocode for DSelect

How do we actually compute the median-of-medians? Implementing the first stage of the knockout tournament is easy, because each median computation involves only 5 elements. For example, each such computation can be done naively (checking, for each of the 5 possibilities, whether it's the middle element), or by using our reduction to sorting (Section 6.1.2). To implement the second stage, we compute the median of the $\approx n/5$ first-round winners *recursively*.

---

[7]Understanding the power of randomness in computation more generally is a deep question and continues to be a topic of active research in theoretical computer science.

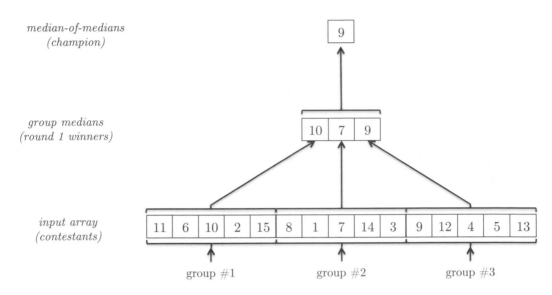

Figure 6.1: Computing a pivot element with a two-round knockout tournament. In this example, the chosen pivot is not the median of the input array, but it is pretty close.

DSelect

Input: array A of $n \geq 1$ distinct numbers, and an integer $i \in \{1, 2, \ldots, n\}$.

Output: the ith order statistic of A.

---

1 **if** $n = 1$ **then**   // base case
2   return $A[1]$

3 **for** $h := 1$ to $n/5$ **do**   // first-round winners
4       $C[h] :=$ middle element from the hth group of 5
5 $p := \mathtt{DSelect}(C, n/10)$ // median-of-medians
6 partition A around p
7 $j := p$'s position in partitioned array
8 **if** $j = i$ **then**   // you got lucky!
9   return p
10 **else if** $j > i$ **then**
11   return $\mathtt{DSelect}$(first part of A, i)
12 **else**   // $j < i$
13   return $\mathtt{DSelect}$(second part of A, $i - j$)

Lines 1–2 and 6–13 are identical to $\mathtt{RSelect}$. Lines 3–5 are the only new part of the algorithm; they compute the median-of-medians of the input array, replacing the line in $\mathtt{RSelect}$ that chooses a pivot element at random.

Lines 3 and 4 compute the first-round winners of the knockout tournament, with the middle element of each group of 5 computed naively or using a sorting algorithm, and copy these winners over into a new array C.[8] Line 5 computes the tournament champion by recursively computing the median of C; because C has length $\approx n/5$, this is the $(n/10)$th order statistic of C. No randomization is used in any step of the algorithm.

6.3.3   Understanding DSelect

It may seem dangerously circular to recursively call DSelect while computing the pivot element. To understand what's going on, let's first be clear on the total number of recursive calls.

Quiz 6.3

How many recursive calls does a single call to DSelect typically make?

   a) 0

   b) 1

   c) 2

   d) 3

(See below for the solution and discussion.)

Correct answer: (c). Putting aside the base case and the lucky case in which the pivot element happens to be the desired order statistic, the DSelect algorithm makes two recursive calls. To see why, don't overthink it; simply inspect the pseudocode for DSelect line by line. There is one recursive call on line 5, and one more on either line 11 or 13.

There are two common points of confusion about these two recursive calls. First, isn't the fact that the RSelect algorithm makes only one recursive call the reason it runs faster than our sorting algorithms? Isn't the DSelect algorithm giving up this improvement by making two recursive calls? Section 6.4 shows that, because the extra recursive call in line 5 needs to solve only a relatively small subproblem (with 20% of the elements of the original array), we can still rescue the linear-time analysis.

Second, the two recursive calls play fundamentally different roles. The goal of the recursive call in line 5 is to identify a good pivot element for the current recursive call. The goal of the recursive call in line 11 or 13 is the usual one, to recursively solve the smaller residual problem left by the current recursive call. Nevertheless, the recursive structure in DSelect is squarely in the tradition of all the other divide-and-conquer algorithms we've studied: Each recursive call makes a small number of further recursive calls on strictly smaller subproblems, and does some amount of additional work. If we weren't worried about an algorithm like MergeSort or QuickSort running forever, we shouldn't be worried about DSelect either.

---

[8]This auxiliary array is why the DSelect algorithm, unlike RSelect, fails to run in place.

6.3.4 Running Time of `DSelect`

The `DSelect` algorithm is not merely a well-defined program that completes in a finite amount of time—it runs in *linear* time, performing only a constant factor more work than necessary to read the input.

Theorem 6.6 (Running Time of `DSelect`) *For every input array of length $n \geq 1$, the running time of `DSelect` is $O(n)$.*

Unlike the running time of `RSelect`, which can in principle be as bad as $\Theta(n^2)$, the running time of `DSelect` is always $O(n)$. Still, you should prefer `RSelect` to `DSelect` in practice, because the former runs in place and the constant hidden in the "$O(n)$" average running time in Theorem 6.1 is smaller than the constant hidden in Theorem 6.6.

A Computer Science Superteam

One of the goals of this book is to make famous algorithms seem so simple (at least in hindsight) that you feel like you could have come up with them yourself, had you been in the right place at the right time. Almost nobody feels this way about the `DSelect` algorithm, which was devised by a computer science superteam of five researchers, four of whom have been recognized with the ACM Turing Award (all for different things!), the equivalent of the Nobel Prize for computer science.[9] So don't despair if it's hard to imagine coming up with the `DSelect` algorithm, even on your most creative days—it's also hard to imagine beating Roger Federer (let alone five of him) on the tennis court!

---

*6.4   Analysis of `DSelect`

Could the `DSelect` algorithm really run in linear time? It seems to do an extravagant amount of work, with two recursive calls and significant extra work outside the recursive calls. Every other algorithm we've seen with two or more recursive calls has running time $\Theta(n \log n)$ or worse.

6.4.1   Work Outside the Recursive Calls

Let's start by understanding the number of operations performed by a call to `DSelect` outside its recursive calls. The two steps that require significant work are computing the

---

[9] The algorithm and its analysis were published in the paper "Time Bounds for Selection," by Manuel Blum, Robert W. Floyd, Vaughan Pratt, Ronald L. Rivest, and Robert E. Tarjan (*Journal of Computer and System Sciences*, 1973). (It was very unusual to see papers with five authors back then.) In chronological order: Floyd won the Turing Award in 1978 for contributions to algorithms and also programming languages and compilers; Tarjan was recognized in 1986 (along with John E. Hopcroft) for his work on algorithms and data structures; Blum was awarded it in 1995, largely for his contributions to cryptography; and Rivest, whom you may know as the "R" in the RSA cryptosystem, won it in 2002 (with Leonard Adleman and Adi Shamir) for his work on public-key cryptography. Meanwhile, Pratt is famous for accomplishments that run the gamut from primality testing algorithms to the co-founding of Sun Microsystems!

first-round winners (lines 3–4) and partitioning the input array around the median-of-medians (line 6). As in QuickSort or RSelect, the second step runs in linear time. What about the first step?

Focus on a particular group of 5 elements. Because this is only a constant number of elements (independent of the input array length n), computing the median takes constant time. For example, suppose we do this computation by reducing to sorting (Section 6.1.2), say using MergeSort. We understand well the amount of work performed by MergeSort (Theorem 1.2): at most

$$6m(\log_2 m + 1)$$

operations to sort an array of length m. You might be worried about the fact that the MergeSort algorithm does not run in linear time. But we're invoking it only for constant-size subarrays ($m = 5$), and as a result it performs a constant number of operations (at most $6 \cdot 5 \cdot (\log_2 5 + 1) \leq 120$) per subarray. Summing over the $n/5$ groups of 5 that need to be sorted, this is at most $120 \cdot \frac{n}{5} = 24n = O(n)$ operations in all. We conclude that, outside its recursive calls, the DSelect algorithm performs only a linear amount of work.

6.4.2   A Rough Recurrence

In Chapter 4 we analyzed divide-and-conquer algorithms using recurrences, which express a running time bound $T(n)$ in terms of the number of operations performed by recursive calls. Let's try the same approach here, letting $T(n)$ denote the maximum number of operations that the DSelect algorithm performs on an input array of length n. When $n = 1$ the DSelect algorithm simply returns the sole array element, so $T(1) = 1$. For larger n, the DSelect algorithm makes one recursive call in line 5, another recursive call in line 11 or 13, and performs $O(n)$ additional work (for partitioning, and computing and copying over the first-round winners). This translates to a recurrence of the form

$$T(n) \leq T\big(\underbrace{\text{size of subproblem \#1}}_{=n/5}\big) + T\big(\underbrace{\text{size of subproblem \#2}}_{=?}\big) + O(n).$$

To evaluate the running time of DSelect, we need to understand the sizes of the subproblems solved by its two recursive calls. The size of the first subproblem (line 5) is $n/5$, the number of first-round winners. We don't know the size of the second subproblem—it depends on which element ends up being the pivot, and on whether the order statistic sought is less than or greater than this pivot. This indeterminacy in subproblem size is why we didn't use recurrences to analyze the QuickSort and RSelect algorithms.

In the special case in which the true median element of the input array is chosen as the pivot, the second subproblem is guaranteed to comprise at most $n/2$ elements. The median-of-medians is generally not the true median (Figure 6.1). Is it close enough to guarantee an approximately balanced split of the input array, and hence a not-too-big subproblem in line 11 or 13?

6.4.3   The 30-70 Lemma

The heart of the analysis of DSelect is the following lemma, which quantifies the payoff of the hard work done to compute the median-of-medians: This pivot element guarantees a split of 30%-70% or better of the input array.

Lemma 6.7 (30-70 Lemma) *For every input array of length $n \geq 2$, the subarray passed to the recursive call in line 11 or 13 of* DSelect *has length at most $\frac{7}{10}n$.*[10]

The 30-70 Lemma lets us substitute "$\frac{7}{10}n$" for "?" in the rough recurrence above: for every $n \geq 2$,

$$T(n) \leq T\left(\frac{1}{5} \cdot n\right) + T\left(\frac{7}{10} \cdot n\right) + O(n). \tag{6.2}$$

We first prove the 30-70 Lemma, and then prove that the recurrence (6.2) implies that DSelect is a linear-time algorithm.

Proof of Lemma 6.7: Let $k = n/5$ denote the number of groups of 5, and hence the number of first-round winners. Define x_i as the ith-smallest of the first-round winners. Equivalently, $x_1, x_2 \ldots, x_k$ denote the first-round winners, indexed in increasing order. The tournament champion, the median-of-medians, is $x_{k/2}$ (or $x_{\lceil k/2 \rceil}$, if k is odd).[11]

The plan is to argue that $x_{k/2}$ is bigger than at least 60% of the elements in at least 50% of the groups of 5, and is smaller than at least 60% of the elements in at least 50% of the groups. Then at least $60\% \cdot 50\% = 30\%$ of the input array elements would be smaller than the median-of-medians, and at least 30% would be larger:

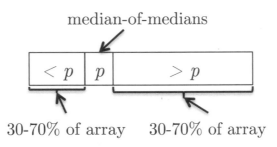

To implement this plan, consider the following thought experiment. In our minds (not in the actual algorithm!), we lay out all the input array elements in a two-dimensional grid format. There are five rows, and each of the $n/5$ columns corresponds to one of the groups of 5. Within each column, we lay out the 5 elements in sorted order from bottom to top. Finally, we lay out the columns so that the first-round winners (i.e., the elements in the middle row) are in sorted order from left to right. For example, if the input array is

11	6	10	2	15	8	1	7	14	3	9	12	4	5	13

then the corresponding grid is

---

[10]Strictly speaking, because one of the "groups of 5" could have fewer than five elements (if n is not a multiple of 5), the $\frac{7}{10}n$ should be $\frac{7}{10}n + 2$, rounded up to the nearest integer. We'll ignore the "+2" for the same reason we ignore fractions—it is a detail that complicates the analysis in an uninteresting way and has no real effect on the bottom line.

[11]The notation $\lceil x \rceil$ denotes the "ceiling" function, which rounds its argument up to the nearest integer.

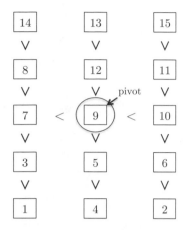

with the pivot, the median-of-medians, in the center position.

Key Observation

Because the middle row is sorted from left to right, and each column is sorted from bottom to top, *all the elements to the left and down from the pivot are less than the pivot, and all the elements to the right and up from the pivot are greater than the pivot.*

In our example, the pivot is the "9," the elements to the left and down are $\{1, 3, 4, 5, 7\}$, and the elements to the right and up are $\{10, 11, 12, 13, 15\}$.[12] Thus at least 6 elements will be excluded from the subarray passed to the next recursive call—the pivot element 9 and either $\{10, 11, 12, 13, 15\}$ (in line 11) or $\{1, 3, 4, 5, 7\}$ (in line 13). Either way, the next recursive call receives at most 9 elements, and 9 is less than 70% of 15.

The argument for the general case is the same. Figure 6.2 depicts what the grid looks like for an arbitrary input array. Because the pivot element is the median of the elements in the middle row, at least 50% of the columns are to the left of the one that contains the pivot (counting also the pivot's own column). In each of these columns, at least 60% of the elements (the three smallest of the five) are no larger than the column's median and hence no larger than the median-of-medians. Thus at least 30% of the input array elements are no larger than the pivot element (counting the pivot itself), and all of these would be excluded from the recursive call in line 13. Similarly, at least 30% of the elements are no smaller than the pivot element (counting the pivot itself), and these would be excluded from the recursive call in line 11. This completes the proof of the 30-70 lemma. *Q.E.D.*

6.4.4   Solving the Recurrence

The 30-70 Lemma implies that the input size shrinks by a constant factor with every recursive call of `DSelect`, and this bodes well for a linear running time. But is it a Pyrrhic victory? Does the cost of computing the median-of-medians outweigh the benefits of partitioning around a pretty good pivot? Answering these questions, and completing the proof of Theorem 6.6, requires figuring out the solution to the recurrence in (6.2).

---

[12]Elements to the left and up or to the right and down could be less than or greater than the pivot.

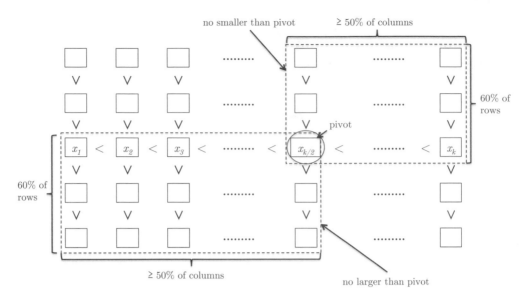

Figure 6.2: Proof of the 30-70 Lemma. Imagine the input array elements laid out in a grid format. Each column corresponds to a group of 5, sorted from bottom to top. Columns are sorted in order of their middle elements. The picture assumes that k is even; for k odd, the "$x_{k/2}$" should be replaced by "$x_{\lceil k/2 \rceil}$." Elements to the southwest of the median-of-medians are less than it; those to the northeast are greater than it. As a result, at least $60\% \cdot 50\% = 30\%$ of the elements are excluded from each of the two possible recursive calls.

Because the DSelect algorithm performs a linear ($O(n)$) amount of work outside its recursive calls (computing first-round winners, partitioning the array, etc.), there is a constant $c > 0$ such that, for every $n \geq 2$,

$$T(n) \leq T\left(\frac{1}{5} \cdot n\right) + T\left(\frac{7}{10} \cdot n\right) + cn, \tag{6.3}$$

where $T(n)$ is an upper bound on the running time of DSelect on length-n arrays. We can assume that $c \geq 1$ (as increasing c cannot invalidate the inequality (6.3)). Also, $T(1) = 1$. As we'll see, the crucial property of this recurrence is that $\frac{1}{5} + \frac{7}{10} < 1$.

We leaned on the master method (Chapter 4) to evaluate all the recurrences we've encountered so far—for MergeSort, Karatsuba, Strassen, and more, we simply plugged in the three relevant parameters (a, b, and d) and out popped an upper bound on the algorithm's running time. Unfortunately, the two recursive calls in DSelect have different input sizes, and this rules out applying Theorem 4.1. While it's possible to generalize the recursion tree argument in Theorem 4.1 to accommodate the recurrence in (6.3), for variety's sake, and to add another tool to your toolbox, we proceed instead with a different method.[13]

---

[13]For a heuristic argument, think about the first pair of recursive calls to DSelect—the two nodes in level 1 of the algorithm's recursion tree. One has 20% of the input array elements, the other at most 70%, and the work done at this level is linear in the sum of the two subproblem sizes. Thus the amount of work done at level 1 is at most 90% of that done at level 0, and so on at subsequent levels. This resembles the second case of the master method, in which the work-per-level drops by a constant factor each level. This analogy suggests that the $O(n)$ work performed at the root should dominate the running time (cf., Section 4.4.6).

6.4.5   The Guess-and-Check Method

The *guess-and-check* method for evaluating recurrences is as ad hoc as it sounds, but it's also extremely flexible and applies to arbitrarily crazy recurrences.

Step 1: Guess.   Guess a function $f(n)$ which you suspect satisfies $T(n) = O(f(n))$.

Step 2: Check.   Prove by induction on n that $T(n)$ really is $O(f(n))$.

In general, the guessing step is a bit of a dark art. In our case, because we're trying to prove a linear running time bound, we'll guess that $T(n) = O(n)$.[14] That is, we guess that there is a constant $\ell > 0$ (independent of n) such that

$$T(n) \leq \ell \cdot n \tag{6.4}$$

for every positive integer n. If true, because ℓ is a constant, this would imply our hope that $T(n) = O(n)$.

When verifying (6.4), we are free to choose ℓ however we want, as long as it is independent of n. Similar to asymptotic notation proofs, the usual way to figure out the appropriate constant is to reverse engineer it (cf., Section 2.5). Here, we'll take $\ell = 10c$, where c is the constant factor in the recurrence (6.3). (Because c is a constant, so is ℓ.) Where did this number come from? It's the smallest constant for which the inequality (6.5) below is valid.

We prove (6.4) by induction. In the language of Appendix A, $P(n)$ is the assertion that $T(n) \leq \ell \cdot n = 10c \cdot n$. For the base case, we need to prove directly that $P(1)$ is true, meaning that $T(1) \leq 10c$. The recurrence explicitly says that $T(1) = 1$ and $c \geq 1$, so certainly $T(1) \leq 10c$.

For the inductive step, fix an arbitrary positive integer $n \geq 2$. We need to prove that $T(n) \leq \ell \cdot n$. The inductive hypothesis states that $P(1), P(2), \ldots, P(n-1)$ are all true, meaning that $T(k) \leq \ell \cdot k$ for all $k < n$. To prove $P(n)$, follow your nose.

First, the recurrence (6.3) decomposes $T(n)$ into three terms:

$$T(n) \leq \underbrace{T\left(\frac{1}{5} \cdot n\right)}_{\substack{\leq \ell \cdot \frac{n}{5} \\ \text{(ind. hyp.)}}} + \underbrace{T\left(\frac{7}{10} \cdot n\right)}_{\substack{\leq \ell \cdot \frac{7n}{10} \\ \text{(ind. hyp.)}}} + cn.$$

We can't directly manipulate any of these terms, but we can apply the inductive hypothesis, once with $k = n/5$ and once with $k = 7n/10$:

$$T(n) \leq \ell \cdot \frac{n}{5} + \ell \cdot \frac{7n}{10} + cn.$$

Grouping terms,

$$T(n) \leq n \underbrace{\left(\frac{9}{10}\ell + c\right)}_{\substack{=\ell \\ \text{(as } \ell = 10c)}} = \ell \cdot n. \tag{6.5}$$

This proves the inductive step, which verifies that $T(n) = O(n)$ and completes the proof that the ingenious `DSelect` algorithm runs in linear time (Theorem 6.6). $\mathcal{QED}$

---

[14]"Hope and check" might be a more apt description for us!

The Upshot

☆ The goal in the selection problem is to compute the ith-smallest element of an unsorted array.

☆ The selection problem can be solved in $O(n \log n)$ time, where n is the length of the input array, by sorting the array and then returning the ith element.

☆ The problem can also be solved by partitioning the input array around a pivot element, as in `QuickSort`, and recursing once on the relevant side. The `RSelect` algorithm always chooses the pivot element uniformly at random.

☆ The running time of `RSelect` varies from $\Theta(n)$ to $\Theta(n^2)$, depending on the pivots chosen.

☆ The average running time of `RSelect` is $\Theta(n)$. The proof uses a reduction to a coin-flipping experiment.

☆ The big idea in the deterministic `DSelect` algorithm is to use the "median-of-medians" as the pivot element: Break the input array into groups of 5, directly compute the median of each group, and recursively compute the median of these $n/5$ first-round winners.

☆ The 30-70 Lemma shows that the median-of-medians guarantees a 30%-70% or better split of the input array.

☆ The analysis of `DSelect` shows that the work spent in the recursive call to compute the median-of-medians is outweighed by the benefit of a 30%-70% split, resulting in a linear running time.

Test Your Understanding

Problem 6.1 *(S)* Which of the following statements are true? (Choose all that apply.)

a) If the sorting problem can be solved in $T(n)$ time, then the selection problem can be solved in $O(T(n))$ time.

b) If the selection problem can be solved in $T(n)$ time, then the sorting problem can be solved in $O(T(n))$ time.

c) Using randomization does not improve the best asymptotic worst-case running time of algorithms for the selection problem.

d) Using randomization does not improve the practicality of algorithms for the selection problem.

Problem 6.2 *(S)* Let α be some constant, independent of the input array length n, strictly between $\frac{1}{2}$ and 1. Suppose you are using the RSelect algorithm to compute the median element of a length-n array. What is the probability that the first recursive call is passed a subarray of length at most αn?

a) $1 - \alpha$

b) $\alpha - \frac{1}{2}$

c) $1 - \frac{\alpha}{2}$

d) $2\alpha - 1$

Problem 6.3 *(S)* Let α be some constant, independent of the input array length n, strictly between $\frac{1}{2}$ and 1. Assume that every recursive call to RSelect makes progress as in the preceding problem—so whenever a recursive call is given an array of length k, its recursive call is passed a subarray with length at most αk. What is the maximum number of successive recursive calls that can occur before triggering the base case?

a) $-\frac{\ln n}{\ln \alpha}$

b) $-\frac{\ln n}{\alpha}$

c) $-\frac{\ln n}{\ln(1-\alpha)}$

d) $-\frac{\ln n}{\ln(\frac{1}{2}+\alpha)}$

Challenge Problems

Problem 6.4 *(H)* Suppose we modify the DSelect algorithm by breaking the elements into groups of 7, rather than groups of 5. (Use the median-of-medians as the pivot element, as before.) Does this modified algorithm also run in $O(n)$ time? What if we use groups of 3?

Problem 6.5 *(H)* You are given as input an unsorted array of n integers, possibly with duplicate entries. Give a deterministic $O(n)$-time algorithm that identifies every value appearing more than $n/4$ times in the array (if any). (In this and the next problem, feel free to use any algorithm from this chapter as a subroutine.)

Problem 6.6 *(S)* In this problem, the input is an unsorted array of n distinct elements $x_1, x_2, \ldots, x_n$ with positive weights $w_1, w_2, \ldots, w_n$. Let W denote the sum $\sum_{i=1}^{n} w_i$ of the weights. Define a *weighted median* as an element x_k for which the total weight of all elements with value less than x_k (i.e., $\sum_{x_i < x_k} w_i$) is at most $W/2$, and also the total weight of elements with value larger than x_k (i.e., $\sum_{x_i > x_k} w_i$) is at most $W/2$. Observe that there is either one or two weighted medians. Give a deterministic linear-time algorithm for computing a weighted median of the input array.

Programming Problems

Problem 6.7 Implement in your favorite programming language the `RSelect` algorithm from Section 6.1. Your implementation should operate in place, using an in-place implementation of `Partition` (which you might have implemented for Problem 5.8) and passing indices through the recursion to keep track of the still-relevant portion of the original input array. (See `www.algorithmsilluminated.org` for test cases and challenge data sets.)

Part II

Graph Algorithms and Data Structures

Chapter 7

Graphs: The Basics

This short chapter explains what graphs are, what they are good for, and the most common ways to represent them in a computer program. The next two chapters cover a number of famous and useful algorithms for reasoning about graphs.

7.1 Some Vocabulary

When you hear the word "graph," you probably think about an x-axis, a y-axis, and so on (Figure 7.1(a)). To an algorithms person, a *graph* can also mean a representation of the relationships between pairs of objects (Figure 7.1(b)).

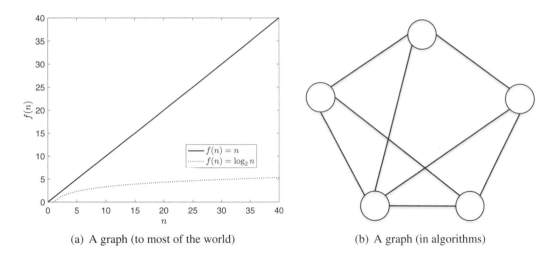

(a) A graph (to most of the world)   (b) A graph (in algorithms)

Figure 7.1: In algorithms, a graph is a representation of a set of objects (such as people) and the pairwise relationships between them (such as friendships).

The second type of graph has two ingredients—the objects being represented, and their pairwise relationships. The former are called the *vertices* (singular: vertex) or the *nodes* of the graph.[1] The pairwise relationships translate to the *edges* of the graph. We usually denote the vertex and edge sets of a graph by V and E, respectively, and sometimes write $G = (V, E)$ to mean the graph G with vertices V and edges E.

There are two flavors of graphs, directed and undirected. Both types are important and ubiquitous in applications, so you should know about both of them. In an *undirected* graph, each edge corresponds to an unordered pair $\{v, w\}$ of vertices, which are called the

---

[1]Having two names for the same thing can be annoying, but both terms are in widespread use and you should be familiar with them. For the most part, we'll stick with "vertices" throughout this book.

endpoints of the edge (Figure 7.2(a)). In an undirected graph, an edge with endpoints v and w can be denoted by (v, w) or by (w, v)—there is no difference between the two. In a *directed* graph, each edge (v, w) is an ordered pair, with the edge traveling from the first vertex v (called the *tail*) to the second w (the *head*); see Figure 7.2(b).[2]

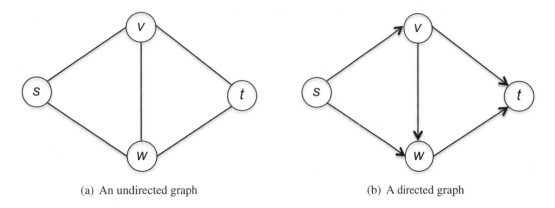

(a) An undirected graph   (b) A directed graph

Figure 7.2: Graphs with four vertices and five edges. The edges of undirected and directed graphs are unordered and ordered vertex pairs, respectively.

7.2   A Few Applications

Graphs are a fundamental concept, and they show up all the time in computer science, biology, sociology, economics, and so on. Here arc a few of the countless examples.

Road networks.   When an app on your smartphone computes driving directions, it searches through a graph that represents the road network, with vertices corresponding to intersections and edges corresponding to individual road segments.

The World Wide Web.   The Web can be modeled as a directed graph, with the vertices corresponding to individual Web pages, and the edges corresponding to hyperlinks, directed from the page containing the hyperlink to the destination page.

Social networks.   A social network can be represented as a graph whose vertices correspond to individuals and edges to some type of relationship. For example, an edge could indicate a friendship between its endpoints, or that one of its endpoints is a follower of the other. Among the currently popular social networks, which ones are most naturally modeled as an undirected graph, and which ones as a directed graph? (There are interesting examples of both.)

Precedence constraints.   Graphs are also useful in problems that lack an obvious network structure. For example, imagine that you have to complete a bunch of tasks, subject to precedence constraints—perhaps you're a first-year university student, planning which courses to take and in which order. One way to tackle this problem is to apply the topological sorting algorithm described in Section 8.5 to the following directed graph: there is one vertex

---

[2]Directed edges are sometimes called *arcs*, but we won't use this terminology in this book.

for each course that your major requires, with an edge directed from course A to course B whenever A is a prerequisite for B.

7.3   Measuring the Size of a Graph

Continuing in the tradition of Part I, we'll analyze the running time of different algorithms as a function of the input size. When the input is a single array, as for a sorting algorithm, there is an obvious way to define the "input size," as the array's length. When the input involves a graph, we must specify exactly how the graph is represented and what we mean by its "size."

7.3.1   The Number of Edges in a Graph

Two parameters control a graph's size—the number of vertices and the number of edges. Here is the most common notation for these quantities.

Notation for Graphs

For a graph $G = (V, E)$ with vertex set V and edge set E:

- $n = |V|$ denotes the number of vertices; and

- $m = |E|$ denotes the number of edges.[3]

The next quiz asks you to think about how the number m of edges in an undirected graph can depend on the number n of vertices. For this question, we'll assume that there's at most one undirected edge between each pair of vertices—no "parallel edges" are allowed. We'll also assume that the graph is "connected." We'll define this concept formally in Section 8.3; intuitively, it means that the graph is "in one piece," with no way to break it into two parts without any edges crossing between the parts. The graphs in Figures 7.1(b) and 7.2(a) are connected, while the graph in Figure 7.3 is not.

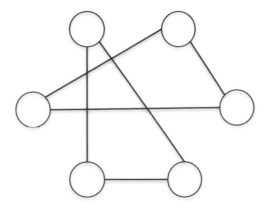

Figure 7.3: An undirected graph that is not connected.

---

[3]For a finite set S, $|S|$ denotes the number of elements in S.

Quiz 7.1

Consider an undirected graph with n vertices and no parallel edges. Assume that the graph is connected, meaning "in one piece." What are the minimum and maximum numbers of edges, respectively, that the graph could have?

   a) $n - 1$ and $\frac{n(n-1)}{2}$

   b) $n - 1$ and n^2

   c) n and 2^n

   d) n and n^n

(See Section 7.3.3 for the solution and discussion.)

7.3.2   Sparse vs. Dense Graphs

Now that Quiz 7.1 has you thinking about how the number of edges of a graph can vary with the number of vertices, we can discuss the distinction between *sparse* and *dense* graphs. The difference is important because some data structures and algorithms are better suited for sparse graphs, and others for dense graphs.

Let's translate the solution to Quiz 7.1 into asymptotic notation.[4] First, if an undirected graph with n vertices is connected, the number of edges m is at least linear in n (that is, $m = \Omega(n)$).[5] Second, if the graph has no parallel edges, then $m = O(n^2)$.[6] We conclude that the number of edges in a connected undirected graph with no parallel edges is somewhere between linear and quadratic in the number of vertices.

Informally, a graph is *sparse* if the number of edges is relatively close to linear in the number of vertices, and *dense* if this number is closer to quadratic in the number of vertices. For example, graphs with n vertices and $O(n \log n)$ edges are usually considered sparse, while those with $\Omega(n^2 / \log n)$ edges are considered dense. "Partially dense" graphs, like those with $\approx n^{3/2}$ edges, may be considered either sparse or dense, depending on the specific application.

7.3.3   Solution to Quiz 7.1

Correct answer: (a). In a connected undirected graph with n vertices and no parallel edges, the number m of edges is at least $n - 1$ and at most $n(n-1)/2$. To see why the lower bound is correct, consider a graph $G = (V, E)$. As a thought experiment, imagine building up G one edge at a time, starting from the graph with vertices V and no edges. Initially, before any edges are added, each of the n vertices is completely isolated, so the graph trivially has n distinct "pieces." Adding an edge (v, w) has the effect of fusing the piece containing v with the piece containing w (Figure 7.4). Thus, each edge addition decreases the number

---

[4]See Chapter 2 for the definitions of big-O, big-Omega, and big-Theta notation.

[5]If the graph need not be connected, there could be as few as zero edges.

[6]If parallel edges are allowed, a graph with at least two vertices can have an arbitrarily large number of edges.

of pieces by at most 1.[7] To get down to a single piece from n pieces, you need to add at least $n - 1$ edges. There are plenty of connected graphs that have n vertices and only $n - 1$ edges—these are called *trees* (Figure 7.5).

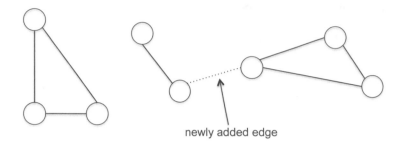

newly added edge

Figure 7.4: Adding a new edge fuses the pieces containing its endpoints into a single piece. In this example, the number of different pieces drops from three to two.

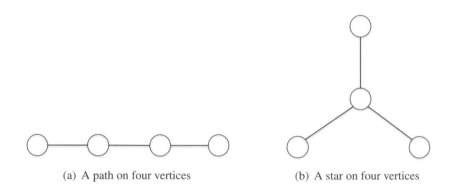

(a) A path on four vertices   (b) A star on four vertices

Figure 7.5: Two connected undirected graphs with four vertices and three edges.

The maximum number of edges in a graph with no parallel edges is achieved by the *complete graph*, with every possible edge present. Because there are $\binom{n}{2} = \frac{n(n-1)}{2}$ pairs of vertices in an n-vertex graph, this is also the maximum number of edges. For example, when $n = 4$, the maximum number of edges is $\binom{4}{2} = 6$ (Figure 7.6).[8]

7.4   Representing a Graph

There is more than one way to encode a graph for use in an algorithm. In this book, we'll work primarily with the "adjacency list" representation of a graph (Section 7.4.1), but you should also be aware of the "adjacency matrix" representation (Section 7.4.2).

---

[7]If both endpoints of the edge are already in the same piece, the number of pieces doesn't decrease at all.

[8]$\binom{n}{2}$ is pronounced "n choose 2," and is also sometimes referred to as a "binomial coefficient"; see also the solution to Quiz 3.1. To see why the number of ways to choose an unordered pair of distinct objects from a set of n objects is $n(n-1)/2$, think about choosing the first object (from the n options) and then a second, distinct object (from the $n - 1$ remaining options). The $n(n - 1)$ resulting outcomes produce each pair (x, y) of objects twice (once with x first and y second, once with y first and x second), so there must be $n(n-1)/2$ pairs in all.

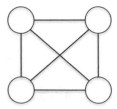

Figure 7.6: The complete graph on four vertices has $\binom{4}{2} = 6$ edges.

7.4.1   Adjacency Lists

The *adjacency list* representation of graphs is the dominant one that we'll use in this book.

Ingredients for Adjacency Lists

1. An array containing the graph's vertices.

2. An array containing the graph's edges.

3. For each edge, a pointer to each of its two endpoints.

4. For each vertex, a pointer to each of the incident edges.

The adjacency list representation boils down to two arrays (or linked lists, if you prefer): one for keeping track of the vertices, and one for the edges. These two arrays cross-reference each other in the natural way, with each edge associated with pointers to its endpoints and each vertex with pointers to the edges for which it is an endpoint.[9]

For a directed graph, each edge keeps track of which endpoint is the tail and which endpoint is the head. Each vertex v maintains two arrays of pointers, one for the outgoing edges (for which v is the tail) and one for the incoming edges (for which v is the head).

What are the memory requirements of the adjacency list representation?

Quiz 7.2

How much space does the adjacency list representation of a graph require, as a function of the number n of vertices and the number m of edges?

a) $\Theta(n)$

b) $\Theta(m)$

c) $\Theta(m + n)$

d) $\Theta(n^2)$

---

[9]By a *pointer*, we mean a reference to an object (as opposed to the object itself). For example, if you pass an object to a subroutine in Python or Java, it works only with a pointer to that object (as opposed to with its own local copy).

(See Section 7.4.4 for the solution and discussion.)

7.4.2   The Adjacency Matrix

Consider an undirected graph $G = (V, E)$ with n vertices and no parallel edges, and label its vertices $1, 2, 3, \ldots, n$. The *adjacency matrix* representation of G is a square $n \times n$ matrix A—equivalently, a two-dimensional array—with only zeroes and ones as entries. Each entry A_{ij} is defined as

$$A_{ij} = \begin{cases} 1 & \text{if edge } (i, j) \text{ belongs to } E \\ 0 & \text{otherwise.} \end{cases}$$

Thus, an adjacency matrix maintains one bit for each pair of vertices, which keeps track of whether or not the edge is present (Figure 7.7).

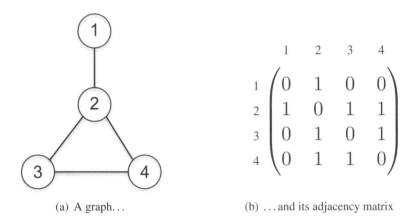

(a) A graph...   (b) ...and its adjacency matrix

Figure 7.7: The adjacency matrix of a graph maintains one bit for each vertex pair, indicating whether or not there is an edge connecting the two vertices.

It's easy to add bells and whistles to the adjacency matrix representation of a graph:

- *Parallel edges.* If a graph can have multiple edges with the same pair of endpoints, then A_{ij} can be defined as the number of edges with endpoints i and j.

- *Weighted graphs.* Similarly, if each edge (i, j) has a weight w_{ij}—perhaps representing a cost or a distance—then each entry A_{ij} stores w_{ij}.

- *Directed graphs.* For a directed graph G, each entry A_{ij} of the adjacency matrix is defined as

$$A_{ij} = \begin{cases} 1 & \text{if edge } (i, j) \text{ belongs to } E \\ 0 & \text{otherwise,} \end{cases}$$

  where "edge (i, j)" now refers to the edge directed from i to j. Every undirected graph has a symmetric adjacency matrix, while a directed graph usually has an asymmetric adjacency matrix.

What are the memory requirements of an adjacency matrix?

Quiz 7.3

How much space does the adjacency matrix of a graph require, as a function of the number n of vertices and the number m of edges?

a) $\Theta(n)$

b) $\Theta(m)$

c) $\Theta(m + n)$

d) $\Theta(n^2)$

(See Section 7.4.4 for the solution and discussion.)

7.4.3   Comparing the Representations

Confronted with two different ways to represent a graph, you're probably wondering: Which is better? The answer, as it so often is with such questions, is "it depends." First, it depends on the density of your graph—on how the number m of edges compares to the number n of vertices. The moral of Quizzes 7.2 and 7.3 is that the adjacency matrix is an efficient way to encode a dense graph but is wasteful for a sparse graph. Second, it depends on which operations you want to support. On both counts, adjacency lists make more sense for the algorithms and applications described in this book.

Most of our graph algorithms will involve exploring a graph. Adjacency lists are perfect for graph exploration—you arrive at a vertex, and the adjacency list immediately indicates your options for the next step.[10] Adjacency matrices do have their applications, but we won't see them in this book.[11]

Much of the modern-day interest in fast graph primitives is motivated by massive sparse networks. Consider, for example, the Web graph (Section 7.2), in which vertices correspond to Web pages and directed edges to hyperlinks. It's hard to get an exact measurement of the size of this graph, but a conservative lower bound on the number of vertices is 10 billion, or 10^{10}. Storing and reading through an array of this length already requires significant computational resources, but it is well within the limits of what modern computers can do. The size of the adjacency matrix of this graph, however, is proportional to 100 quintillion (10^{20}). This is way too big to store or process with today's technology. But the Web graph is sparse—the average number of outgoing edges from a vertex is well under 100. The memory requirements of the adjacency list representation of the Web graph are therefore proportional to 10^{12} (a trillion). This may be too big for your laptop, but it's within the capabilities of state-of-the-art data-processing systems.[12]

---

[10]If you had access to only the adjacency matrix of a graph, how long would it take you to figure out which edges are incident to a given vertex?

[11]For example, you can count the number of common neighbors of each pair of vertices in one fell swoop by squaring the graph's adjacency matrix.

[12]For example, the essence of Google's original `PageRank` algorithm for measuring Web page importance relied on efficient search in the Web graph.

7.4.4 Solutions to Quizzes 7.2–7.3

Solution to Quiz 7.2

Correct answer: (c). The adjacency list representation requires space linear in the size of the graph (meaning the number of vertices plus the number of edges), which is ideal.[13] Seeing this is a little tricky. Let's step through the four ingredients one by one. The vertex and edge arrays have lengths n and m, respectively, and so require $\Theta(n)$ and $\Theta(m)$ space. The third ingredient associates two pointers with each edge (one for each endpoint). These $2m$ pointers contribute an additional $\Theta(m)$ to the space requirement.

The fourth ingredient might make you nervous. After all, each of the n vertices can participate in as many as $n-1$ edges—one per other vertex—seemingly leading to a bound of $\Theta(n^2)$. This quadratic bound would be accurate in a very dense graph, but is overkill in sparser graphs. The key insight is: *For every vertex→edge pointer in the fourth ingredient, there is a corresponding edge→vertex pointer in the third ingredient.* If the edge e is incident to the vertex v, then e has a pointer to its endpoint v, and, conversely, v has a pointer to the incident edge e. We conclude that the pointers in the third and fourth ingredients are in one-to-one correspondence, and so they require exactly the same amount of space, namely $\Theta(m)$. The final scorecard is:

	vertex array	$\Theta(n)$
	edge array	$\Theta(m)$
	pointers from edges to endpoints	$\Theta(m)$
+	pointers from vertices to incident edges	$\Theta(m)$
	total	$\Theta(m+n)$.

The bound of $\Theta(m+n)$ applies whether or not the graph is connected, and whether or not it has parallel edges.[14]

Solution to Quiz 7.3

Correct answer: (d). The straightforward way to store an adjacency matrix is as an $n \times n$ two-dimensional array of bits. This uses $\Theta(n^2)$ space, albeit with a small hidden constant. For a dense graph, in which the number of edges is itself close to quadratic in n, the adjacency matrix requires space close to linear in the size of the graph. For sparse graphs, however, in which the number of edges is closer to linear in n, the adjacency matrix representation is highly wasteful.[15]

The Upshot

☆ A graph is a representation of the pairwise relationships between objects, such as friendships in a social network, hyperlinks between

---

[13]Caveat: The leading constant factor here is larger than that for the adjacency matrix by an order of magnitude.

[14]If the graph is connected, then $m \geq n-1$ (by Quiz 7.1), and we could write $\Theta(m)$ in place of $\Theta(m+n)$.

[15]This waste can be reduced by using tricks for storing and manipulating sparse matrices, meaning matrices with lots of zeroes. For instance, both Matlab and Python's SciPy package support sparse matrix representations.

Web pages, or dependencies between tasks.

☆ A graph comprises a set of vertices and a set of edges. Edges are unordered in undirected graphs and ordered in directed graphs.

☆ A graph is sparse if the number of edges m is close to linear in the number of vertices n, and dense if m is close to quadratic in n.

☆ The adjacency list representation of a graph maintains vertex and edge arrays, cross-referencing each other in the natural way, and requires space linear in the total number of vertices and edges.

☆ The adjacency matrix representation of a graph maintains one bit per pair of vertices to keep track of which edges are present, and requires space quadratic in the number of vertices.

☆ The adjacency list representation is the preferred one for sparse graphs, and for applications that involve graph exploration.

Test Your Understanding

Problem 7.1 *(S)* Consider a directed graph with n vertices and no parallel edges. What is the maximum numbers of edges that the graph could have?

a) $n(n-1)/2$

b) $n^2/2$

c) $n(n-1)$

d) n^2

Problem 7.2 *(S)* Let $G = (V, E)$ be an undirected graph. By the *degree* of a vertex $v \in V$, we mean the number of edges in E that are incident to v (i.e., that have v as an endpoint). What is the sum of the degrees of all of G's vertices, as a function of n and m? (As usual, in this and subsequent problems, n and m denote the number of vertices and edges, respectively.)

a) m

b) $m + n$

c) $2m$

d) n^2

Problem 7.3 *(S)* For each of the following conditions on a graph $G = (V, E)$, is the condition satisfied only by dense graphs, only by sparse graphs, or by both some sparse and some dense graphs? Assume that the number n of vertices is large (say, at least 10,000).

a) At least one vertex of G has degree at most 10.

b) Every vertex of G has degree at most 10.

c) At least one vertex of G has degree $n - 1$.

d) Every vertex of G has degree $n - 1$.

Problem 7.4 *(S)* Consider an undirected graph $G = (V, E)$ that is represented as an adjacency matrix. Given a vertex $v \in V$, how many operations are required to identify the edges incident to v? (Let k denote the number of such edges.)

a) $\Theta(1)$

b) $\Theta(k)$

c) $\Theta(n)$

d) $\Theta(m)$

Problem 7.5 *(S)* Consider a directed graph $G = (V, E)$ that is represented with adjacency lists, except with each vertex storing only an array of its outgoing edges (and *not* its incoming edges). Given a vertex $v \in V$, how many operations are required to identify the incoming edges of v? (Let k denote the number of such edges.)

a) $\Theta(1)$

b) $\Theta(k)$

c) $\Theta(n)$

d) $\Theta(m)$

Chapter 8

Graph Search and Its Applications

This chapter is all about fundamental primitives for graph search and their applications. One very cool aspect of this material is that all the algorithms that we'll cover are blazingly fast (linear time with small constants), and it can be quite tricky to understand why they work! The culmination of this chapter—computing the strongly connected components of a directed graph with only two passes of depth-first search (Section 8.6)—vividly illustrates how fast algorithms often require deep insight into the problem structure.

We begin with an overview section (Section 8.1), which covers some reasons why you should care about graph search, a general strategy for searching a graph without doing any redundant work, and a high-level introduction to the two most important search strategies, breadth-first search (BFS) and depth-first search (DFS). Sections 8.2 and 8.3 describe BFS in more detail, including applications to computing shortest paths and the connected components of an undirected graph. Sections 8.4 and 8.5 drill down on DFS and how to use it to compute a topological ordering of a directed acyclic graph (equivalently, to sequence tasks while respecting precedence constraints). Section 8.6 uses DFS to compute the strongly connected components of a directed graph in linear time. Section 8.7 explains how this fast graph primitive can be used to explore the structure of the Web.

8.1   Overview

This section provides a bird's-eye view of algorithms for graph search and their applications.

8.1.1   Some Applications

Why would we want to search a graph, or to figure out if there's a path from point A to point B? Here are a few of the many reasons.

Checking connectivity. In a physical network, such as a road network or a network of computers, an important sanity check is that you can get anywhere from anywhere else. That is, for every choice of a point A and a point B, there should be a path in the network from the former to the latter.

Connectivity can also be important in abstract (non-physical) graphs that represent pairwise relationships between objects. One network that's fun to play with is the movie network, in which vertices correspond to movie actors, and two actors are connected by an undirected edge whenever they appeared in the same movie.[1] For example, how many "degrees of separation" are there between different actors? The most famous statistic of this type is the *Bacon number*, which is the minimum number of hops through the movie

---

[1] https://oracleofbacon.org/

network needed to reach the fairly ubiquitous actor Kevin Bacon.[2] So, Kevin Bacon himself
has a Bacon number of 0, every actor who has appeared in a movie with Kevin Bacon has
a Bacon number of 1, every actor who has appeared with an actor whose Bacon number
is 1 (and does not have a Bacon number of 0 or 1) has a Bacon number of 2, and so on. For
example, Jon Hamm—perhaps best known as Don Draper from the cable television series
Mad Men—has a Bacon number of 2. Hamm never appeared in a movie with Bacon, but he
did have a bit part in the Colin Firth vehicle *A Single Man*, and Firth and Bacon co-starred in
Atom Egoyan's *Where the Truth Lies* (Figure 8.1).[3]

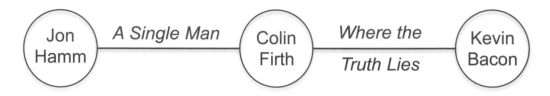

Figure 8.1: A snippet of the movie network, showing that Jon Hamm's Bacon number is at most 2.

Shortest paths.   The Bacon number concerns the *shortest* path between two vertices of the
movie network, meaning the path using the fewest number of edges. We'll see in Section 8.2
that a graph search strategy known as breadth-first search naturally computes shortest paths.

Plenty of other problems boil down to a shortest-path computation, where the definition
of "short" depends on the application (minimizing time for driving directions, or money for
airline tickets, and so on). Dijkstra's shortest-path algorithm, the subject of Chapter 9, builds
on breadth-first search to solve more general shortest-path problems.

Planning.   A path in a graph need not represent a physical path through a physical network.
More abstractly, a path is a sequence of decisions taking you from one state to another. Graph
search algorithms can be applied to such abstract graphs to compute a plan for reaching a
goal state from an initial state.

For example, imagine you want to use an algorithm to solve a Sudoku puzzle. Think of
the graph in which vertices correspond to partially completed Sudoku puzzles (with some
of the 81 squares blank, but no rules of Sudoku violated), and directed edges correspond
to filling in one new entry of the puzzle (subject to the rules of Sudoku). The problem of
computing a solution to the puzzle is exactly the problem of computing a directed path from
the vertex corresponding to the initial state of the puzzle to the vertex corresponding to the
completed puzzle.[4]

For another example, using a robotic hand to grasp a coffee mug is essentially a planning
problem. In the associated graph, vertices correspond to the possible configurations of the
hand, and edges correspond to small and realizable changes in the configuration.

---

[2]The Bacon number is a riff on the older concept of the *Erdös number*, named after the famous mathematician
Paul Erdös, which measures the number of degrees of separation from Erdös in the co-authorship graph (in
which vertices are researchers, and there is an edge between each pair of researchers who have co-authored a
paper).

[3]There are also lots of other two-hop paths between Bacon and Hamm in the movie network.

[4]Because this graph is too big to write down explicitly, practical Sudoku solvers incorporate some additional
ideas.

Connected components. We'll also see algorithms that build on graph search to compute the connected components (the "pieces") of a graph. Defining and computing the connected components of an undirected graph is relatively easy (Section 8.3). For directed graphs, even defining what a "connected component" should mean is a little subtle. Section 8.6 defines them and shows how to use depth-first search (Section 8.4) to compute them efficiently. We'll also see applications of depth-first search to sequencing tasks (Section 8.5) and to understanding the structure of the Web graph (Section 8.7).

8.1.2   For-Free Graph Primitives

The examples in Section 8.1.1 demonstrate that graph search is a fundamental and widely applicable primitive. I'm happy to report that, in this chapter, all our algorithms will be blazingly fast, running in just $O(m + n)$ time with small constant factors, where m and n denote the number of edges and vertices of the graph. That's only a constant factor larger than the amount of time required to read the input![5] These algorithms are "for-free primitives" (see page 23)—whenever you have graph data, you should immediately consider applying one or more of these primitives to glean information about what it looks like.[6]

8.1.3   Generic Graph Search

The point of a graph search algorithm is to solve the following problem.

Problem: Graph Search

Input: An undirected or directed graph $G = (V, E)$, and a starting vertex $s \in V$.

Goal: Identify the vertices of V reachable from s in G.

By a vertex v being "reachable," we mean that there is a sequence of edges in G that travels from s to v. If G is a directed graph, all the path's edges should be traversed in the forward (outgoing) direction. For example, in Figure 8.2(a), the set of reachable vertices (from s) is $\{s, u, v, w\}$. In the directed version of the graph in Figure 8.2(b), there is no directed path from s to w, and only the vertices s, u, and v are reachable from s via a directed path.[7]

The two graph search strategies that we'll focus on—breadth-first search and depth-first search—are different ways of instantiating a generic graph search algorithm. The generic algorithm systematically finds all the reachable vertices, taking care to avoid exploring anything twice. It maintains an extra variable with each vertex that keeps track of whether or not it has already been explored, planting a flag the first time that vertex is reached. The main loop's responsibility is to reach a new unexplored vertex in each iteration.

---

[5]In graph search and connectivity problems, there is no reason to expect that the input graph is connected. In the disconnected case, in which m might be much smaller than n, the size of a graph is $\Theta(m + n)$ but not necessarily $\Theta(m)$.

[6]Can we do better? No, up to the hidden constant factor: Every correct algorithm must at least read the entire input in some cases.

[7]In general, most of the algorithms and arguments in this chapter apply equally well to undirected and directed graphs. The big exception is computing connected components, which is a trickier problem in directed graphs than in undirected graphs.

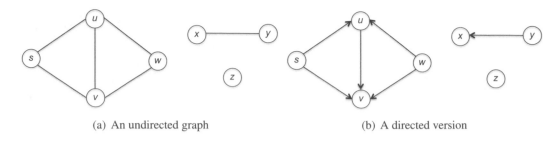

(a) An undirected graph   (b) A directed version

Figure 8.2: In (a), the set of vertices reachable from s is $\{s, u, v, w\}$. In (b), it is $\{s, u, v\}$.

GenericSearch

Input: graph $G = (V, E)$ and a vertex $s \in V$.
Postcondition: a vertex is reachable from s if and only if it is marked as "explored."

---

mark s as explored, all other vertices as unexplored
while there is an edge $(v, w) \in E$ with v explored and w unexplored
do
    choose some such edge (v, w) `// underspecified`
    mark w as explored

The algorithm is essentially the same for both directed and undirected graphs. In the directed case, the edge (v, w) chosen in an iteration of the while loop should be directed from an explored vertex v to an unexplored vertex w.

For example, in the graph in Figure 8.2(a), initially only our home base s is marked as explored. In the first iteration of the while loop, two edges meet the loop condition: (s, u) and (s, v). The GenericSearch algorithm chooses one of these edges—(s, u), say—and marks u as explored. In the second iteration of the loop, there are now three choices: (s, v), (u, v), and (u, w). The algorithm might choose (u, w), in which case w is marked as explored. With one more iteration (after choosing either (s, v), (u, v), or (w, v)), v is marked as explored. At this point, the edge (x, y) has two unexplored endpoints and the other edges have two explored endpoints, and the algorithm halts. As one would hope, the vertices marked as explored—s, u, v, and w—are precisely the vertices reachable from s.

This generic graph search algorithm is underspecified, as multiple edges (v, w) can be eligible for selection in an iteration of the while loop. Breadth-first search and depth-first search correspond to two specific decisions about which edge to explore next. No matter how this choice is made, the GenericSearch algorithm is guaranteed to be correct (in both undirected and directed graphs).

Proposition 8.1 (Correctness of Generic Graph Search) *At the conclusion of the* GenericSearch *algorithm, a vertex $v \in V$ is marked as explored if and only if there is a path from s to v in G.*

Section 8.1.5 provides a formal proof of Proposition 8.1; feel free to skip it if the proposition seems intuitively obvious.

What about the running time of the `GenericSearch` algorithm? The algorithm explores each edge at most once—after an edge (v, w) has been explored for the first time, both v and w are marked as explored and the edge will not be considered again. This suggests that it should be possible to implement the algorithm in linear time, as long as we can quickly identify an eligible edge (v, w) in each iteration of the while loop. We'll see how this works in detail for breadth-first search and depth-first search in Sections 8.2 and 8.4, respectively.

8.1.4   Breadth-First and Depth-First Search

Every iteration of the `GenericSearch` algorithm chooses an edge that is "on the frontier" of the explored part of the graph, with one endpoint explored and the other unexplored (Figure 8.3). There can be many such edges, and to specify the algorithm fully we need a method for choosing one of them. We'll focus on the two most important strategies: breadth-first search and depth-first search. Both are excellent ways to explore a graph, and each has its own set of applications.

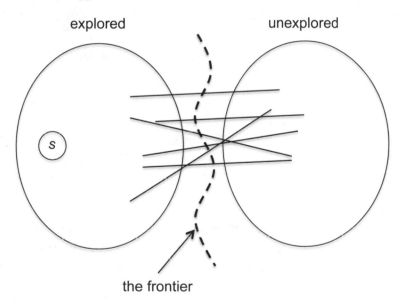

Figure 8.3: Every iteration of the `GenericSearch` algorithm chooses an edge "on the frontier," with one endpoint explored and the other unexplored.

Breadth-first search (BFS).   The high-level idea of *breadth-first search*—or *BFS* to its friends—is to explore the vertices of a graph cautiously, in "layers." Layer 0 consists only of the starting vertex s. Layer 1 contains the vertices that neighbor s, meaning the vertices v such that (s, v) is an edge of the graph (directed from s to v, in the case that G is directed). Layer 2 comprises the neighbors of layer-1 vertices that do not already belong to layer 0 or 1, and so on. In Sections 8.2 and 8.3, we'll see:

- how to implement BFS in linear time using a queue (first-in first-out) data structure;

- how to use BFS to compute (in linear time) the length of a shortest path between one vertex and all other vertices, with the layer-i vertices being precisely the vertices at distance i from s;

- how to use BFS to compute (in linear time) the connected components of an undirected graph.

Depth-first search (DFS).   *Depth-first search—DFS to its friends—*is perhaps even more important. DFS employs a more aggressive strategy for exploring a graph, very much in the spirit of how you might explore a maze, going as deeply as you can and backtracking only when absolutely necessary. In Sections 8.4–8.7, we'll see:

- how to implement DFS in linear time using either recursion or an explicit stack (last-in first-out) data structure;

- how to use DFS to compute (in linear time) a topological ordering of the vertices of a directed acyclic graph, a useful primitive for task sequencing problems;

- how to use DFS to compute (in linear time) the "strongly connected components" of a directed graph, with applications to understanding the structure of the Web.

8.1.5   Correctness of the `GenericSearch` Algorithm

We now prove Proposition 8.1, which states that at the conclusion of the `GenericSearch` algorithm with input graph $G = (V, E)$ and starting vertex $s \in V$, a vertex $v \in V$ is marked as explored if and only if there is a path from s to v in G. As usual, if G is a directed graph, the $s \rightsquigarrow v$ path should also be directed, with all edges traversed in the forward direction.

The "only if" direction of the proposition should be intuitively clear: The only way that the `GenericSearch` algorithm discovers new vertices and marks them as explored is by following paths from s.[8]

The "if" direction asserts the less obvious fact that the `GenericSearch` algorithm doesn't miss anything—it finds every vertex that it could conceivably discover. For this direction, we'll use a proof by contradiction. (That is, we'll assume the opposite of what we want to prove, derive a mathematical contradiction, and conclude that the original statement must be true.)

Assume that there is a path from s to v in the graph G, but the `GenericSearch` algorithm somehow misses it and concludes with the vertex v marked as unexplored. Let $S \subseteq V$ denote the vertices of G marked as explored by the algorithm. The vertex s belongs to S (by the first line of the algorithm), and the vertex v does not (by assumption). Because the $s \rightsquigarrow v$ path travels from a vertex inside S to one outside S, at least one edge e of the path has one endpoint u in S and the other w outside S (with e directed from u to w in the case that G is directed); see Figure 8.4. But this, my friends, is impossible: The edge e would be eligible for selection in the while loop of the `GenericSearch` algorithm, and the algorithm would have explored at least one more vertex, rather than giving up! There's no way that the `GenericSearch` algorithm could have halted at this point, so we've reached a contradiction. This contradiction concludes the proof of Proposition 8.1. *QED*

---

[8]If we wanted to be pedantic about it, we'd prove this direction by induction on the number of loop iterations.

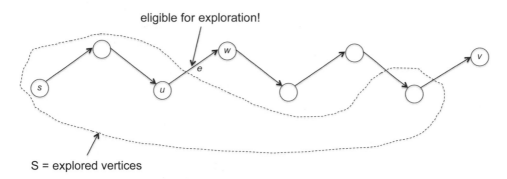

Figure 8.4: Proof of Proposition 8.1. As long as the GenericSearch algorithm has not yet discovered all the reachable vertices, there is an eligible edge along which it can explore further.

8.2   Breadth-First Search and Shortest Paths

Let's drill down on our first specific graph search strategy, *breadth-first search*.

8.2.1   High-Level Idea

Breadth-first search explores the vertices of a graph in layers, in order of increasing distance from the starting vertex. Layer 0 contains the starting vertex s and nothing else. Layer 1 is the set of vertices that are one hop away from s—that is, s's neighbors. These are the vertices that are explored immediately after s in breadth-first search. For example, in the graph in Figure 8.5, a and b are the neighbors of s and constitute layer 1. In general, the vertices in a layer i are those that neighbor a vertex in layer $i - 1$ and that do not already belong to one of the layers $0, 1, 2, \ldots, i - 1$. Breadth-first search explores all of layer-i vertices immediately after completing its exploration of layer-$(i - 1)$ vertices. (Vertices not reachable from s do not belong to any layer.) For example, in Figure 8.5, the layer-2 vertices are c and d, as they neighbor layer-1 vertices but do not themselves belong to layer 0 or 1. (The vertex s is also a neighbor of a layer-1 vertex, but it already belongs to layer 0.) The last layer of the graph in Figure 8.5 comprises only the vertex e.

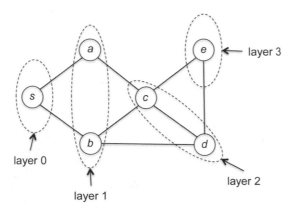

Figure 8.5: Breadth-first search discovers vertices in layers. The layer-i vertices are the neighbors of the layer-$(i - 1)$ vertices that do not appear in any earlier layer.

Quiz 8.1

Consider a connected undirected graph (with every vertex reachable from every other vertex) with $n \geq 2$ vertices. What are the minimum and maximum number of different layers that the graph could have, respectively?

    a) 1 and $n - 1$

    b) 2 and $n - 1$

    c) 1 and n

    d) 2 and n

(See Section 8.2.6 for the solution and discussion.)

8.2.2 Pseudocode for BFS

Implementing breadth-first search in linear time requires a simple "first-in first-out" data structure known as a *queue*. BFS uses a queue to keep track of which vertices to explore next. If you're unfamiliar with queues, now is a good time to read up on them in your favorite introductory programming book (or on Wikipedia). The gist is that a queue is a data structure for maintaining a list of objects, and you can remove stuff from the front or add stuff to the back in constant time.[9]

BFS

Input: graph $G = (V, E)$ in adjacency-list representation, and a vertex $s \in V$.

Postcondition: a vertex is reachable from s if and only if it is marked as "explored."

---

1 mark s as explored, all other vertices as unexplored
2 $Q :=$ a queue data structure, initialized with s
3 **while** Q is not empty **do**
4   remove the vertex from the front of Q, call it v
5   **for** each edge (v, w) in v's adjacency list **do**
6   **if** w is unexplored **then**
7   mark w as explored
8   add w to the end of Q

Each iteration of the while loop explores one new vertex. In line 5, BFS iterates through all the edges incident to the vertex v (if G is undirected) or through all the outgoing edges

---

[9]You may never need to implement a queue from scratch, as they are built in to most modern programming languages. If you do, you can use a doubly linked list. Or, if you have advance knowledge of the maximum number of objects that might ever get inserted (which is $|V|$, in the case of BFS), you can get away with a fixed-length array and a couple of indices (which keep track of the front and back of the queue).

from v (if G is directed).[10] Unexplored neighbors of v are added to the end of the queue and are marked as explored; they will eventually be processed in later iterations of the algorithm.

8.2.3   An Example

Let's see how our pseudocode works for the graph in Figure 8.5, numbering the vertices in order of insertion into the queue (equivalently, in order of exploration). The starting vertex s is always the first to be explored. The first iteration of the while loop extracts s from the queue Q and the subsequent for loop examines the edges (s, a) and (s, b), in whatever order these edges appear in s's adjacency list. Because neither a nor b is marked as explored, both get inserted into the queue. Let's say that edge (s, a) came first and so a is inserted before b. The current state of the graph and the queue is now:

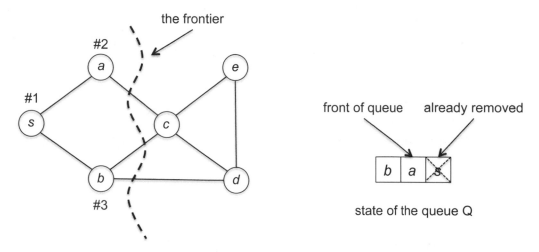

The next iteration of the while loop extracts the vertex a from the front of the queue, and considers its incident edges (s, a) and (a, c). It skips over the former after double-checking that s is already marked as explored, and adds the (previously unexplored) vertex c to the end of the queue. The third iteration extracts the vertex b from the front of the queue and adds vertex d to the end (because s and c are already marked as explored, they are skipped over). The new picture is:

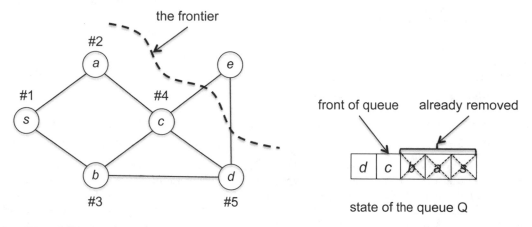

---

[10]This is the step in which it's so convenient to have the input graph represented via adjacency lists.

In the fourth iteration, the vertex c is removed from the front of the queue. Of its neighbors, the vertex e is the only one not encountered before, and it is added to the end of the queue. The final two iterations extract d and then e from the queue, and verify that all of their neighbors have already been explored. The queue is then empty, and the algorithm halts. The vertices are explored in order of the layers, with the layer-i vertices explored immediately after the layer-$(i-1)$ vertices (Figure 8.6).

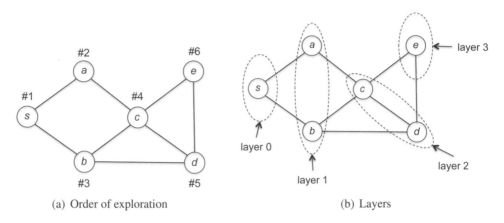

(a) Order of exploration   (b) Layers

Figure 8.6: In breadth-first search, the layer-i vertices are explored immediately after the layer-$(i-1)$ vertices.

8.2.4   Correctness and Running Time

Breadth-first search discovers all the vertices reachable from the starting vertex, and it runs in linear time. The more refined running time bound in Theorem 8.2(c) below will come in handy for our linear-time algorithm for computing connected components (described in Section 8.3).

Theorem 8.2 (Properties of BFS) *For every undirected or directed graph $G = (V, E)$ in adjacency-list representation and for every starting vertex $s \in V$:*

(a) *At the conclusion of BFS, a vertex $v \in V$ is marked as explored if and only if there is a path from s to v in G.*

(b) *The running time of BFS is $O(m + n)$, where $m = |E|$ and $n = |V|$.*

(c) *The running time of lines 2–8 of BFS is $O(m_s + n_s)$, where m_s and n_s denote the number of edges and vertices, respectively, reachable from s in G.*

Proof: Part (a) follows from the guarantee in Proposition 8.1 for the generic graph search algorithm GenericSearch, of which BFS is a special case.[11] Part (b) follows from

---

[11] Formally, BFS is equivalent to the version of GenericSearch in which, in every iteration of the latter's while loop, the algorithm chooses the eligible edge (v, w) for which v was discovered the earliest, breaking ties among v's eligible edges according to their order in v's adjacency list. If that sounds too complicated, you can alternatively check that the proof of Proposition 8.1 holds verbatim also for breadth-first search. Intuitively, breadth-first search discovers vertices only by exploring paths from s; and as long as it hasn't explored every vertex on a path, the "next vertex" on the path is guaranteed to be in the queue awaiting future exploration.

part (c), as the overall running time of BFS is simply the running time of lines 2–8 plus the $O(n)$ time needed for the initialization in line 1.

We can prove part (c) by inspecting the pseudocode. The initialization in line 2 takes $O(1)$ time. In the main while loop, the algorithm only ever encounters the n_s vertices that are reachable from s. Because no vertex is explored twice, each such vertex is added to the end of the queue and removed from the front of the queue exactly once. Each of these operations takes $O(1)$ time—this is the whole point of the first-in first-out queue data structure—and so the total amount of time spent in lines 3–4 and 7–8 is $O(n_s)$. Each of the m_s edges (v, w) reachable from s is processed in line 5 at most twice—once when v is explored, and once when w is explored.[12] Thus the total amount of time spent in lines 5–6 is $O(m_s)$, and the overall running time for lines 2–8 is $O(m_s + n_s)$. $\mathcal{QED}$

8.2.5   Shortest Paths

The properties in Theorem 8.2 are not unique to breadth-first search—for example, they also hold for depth-first search. What *is* unique about BFS is that, with just a couple extra lines of code, it efficiently computes shortest-path distances.

Problem Definition

Fix a graph $G = (V, E)$. For a pair $v, w \in V$ of vertices, by $dist(v, w)$ we mean the fewest number of edges in a path from v to w in G. If G contains no paths from v to w, $dist(v, w)$ is defined as $+\infty$.[13] For example, in the graph

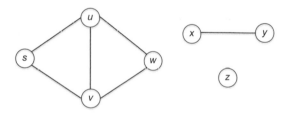

$dist(s, s) = 0$, $dist(s, u) = dist(s, v) = 1$, $dist(s, w) = 2$, and $dist(s, x) = dist(s, y) = dist(s, z) = +\infty$.

Problem: Shortest Paths (Unit Edge Lengths)

Input: An undirected or directed graph $G = (V, E)$, and a starting vertex $s \in V$.

Output: $dist(s, v)$ for every vertex $v \in V$.[14]

For example, if G is the movie network and s is the vertex corresponding to Kevin Bacon, the problem of computing shortest paths is precisely the problem of computing everyone's

---

[12]If G is a directed graph, each edge is processed at most once, when its tail is explored.

[13]If G is directed, all edges should be traversed in the forward direction.

[14]The phrase "unit edge lengths" in the problem statement refers to the assumption that each edge of G contributes 1 to the length of a path. Chapter 9 generalizes BFS to compute shortest paths in graphs in which each edge has its own nonnegative length.

Bacon number (Section 8.1.1). The basic graph search problem (Section 8.1.3) corresponds to the special case of identifying all the vertices v with $dist(s, v) \neq +\infty$.

Pseudocode

To compute shortest paths, we add two lines to the basic BFS algorithm (lines 2 and 9 below); these increase the algorithm's running time by a small constant factor. Line 2 initializes preliminary estimates of vertices' shortest-path distances—0 for s, and $+\infty$ for the other vertices, which might not even be reachable from s. Line 9 executes whenever a vertex w is discovered for the first time, and computes w's final shortest-path distance as one more than that of the vertex v that triggered w's discovery.

Augmented-BFS

Input: graph $G = (V, E)$ in adjacency-list representation, and a
vertex $s \in V$.
Postcondition: for every vertex $v \in V$, the value $l(v)$ equals the true
shortest-path distance $dist(s, v)$.

---

1 mark s as explored, all other vertices as unexplored
2 $l(s) := 0, l(v) := +\infty$ for every $v \neq s$
3 $Q :=$ a queue data structure, initialized with s
4 **while** Q is not empty **do**
5   remove the vertex from the front of Q, call it v
6   **for** each edge (v, w) in v's adjacency list **do**
7   **if** w is unexplored **then**
8   mark w as explored
9              $l(w) := l(v) + 1$
10   add w to the end of Q

Example and Analysis

In our running example (Figure 8.6), the first iteration of the while loop discovers the vertices a and b. Because s triggered their discovery and $l(s) = 0$, the algorithm reassigns $l(a)$ and $l(b)$ from $+\infty$ to 1:

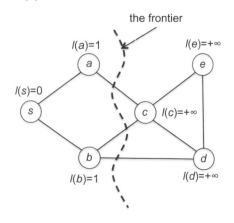

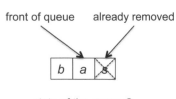

state of the queue Q

The second iteration of the while loop processes the vertex a, leading to c's discovery. The algorithm reassigns $l(c)$ from $+\infty$ to $l(a) + 1$, which is 2. Similarly, in the third iteration, $l(d)$ is set to $l(b) + 1$, which is also 2:

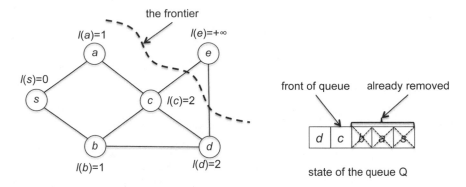

The fourth iteration discovers the final vertex e via the vertex c, and sets $l(e)$ to $l(c) + 1$, which is 3. At this point, for every vertex v, $l(v)$ equals the true shortest-path distance $dist(s, v)$, which also equals the number of the layer that contains v (Figure 8.6). These properties hold in general, not only for this example.

Theorem 8.3 (Properties of Augmented-BFS) *For every undirected or directed graph $G = (V, E)$ in adjacency-list representation and for every starting vertex $s \in V$:*

(a) *At the conclusion of* Augmented-BFS, *for every vertex $v \in V$, the value of $l(v)$ equals the length $dist(s, v)$ of a shortest path from s to v in G (or $+\infty$, if no such path exists).*

(b) *The running time of* Augmented-BFS *is $O(m + n)$, where $m = |E|$ and $n = |V|$.*

Because the asymptotic running time of the Augmented-BFS algorithm is the same as that of BFS, part (b) of Theorem 8.3 follows from the latter's running time guarantee (Theorem 8.2(b)). Part (a) follows from two observations. First, the vertices v with $dist(s, v) = i$ are precisely the vertices in the ith layer of the graph—this is why we defined layers the way we did. Second, for every layer-i vertex w, Augmented-BFS eventually sets $l(w) = i$ (because w is discovered via a layer-$(i - 1)$ vertex v with $l(v) = i - 1$). For vertices not in any layer—that is, not reachable from s—both $dist(s, v)$ and $l(v)$ are $+\infty$.[15]

8.2.6   Solution to Quiz 8.1

Correct answer: (d). A connected undirected graph with $n \geq 2$ vertices has at least two layers and at most n layers. When $n \geq 2$, there cannot be fewer than two layers because s is the only vertex in layer 0. Complete graphs have only two layers (Figure 8.7(a)). There cannot be more than n layers, as layers are disjoint and contain at least one vertex each. Path graphs have n layers (Figure 8.7(b)).

---

[15]If you're hungry for a more rigorous proof, then proceed—in the privacy of your own home—by induction on the number of while loop iterations performed by the Augmented-BFS algorithm. Alternatively, Theorem 8.3(a) is a special case of the correctness of Dijkstra's shortest-path algorithm, as proved in Section 9.3.

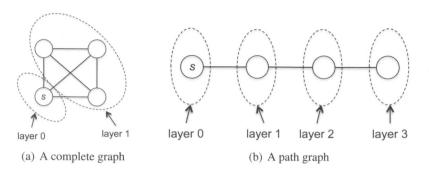

(a) A complete graph   (b) A path graph

Figure 8.7: A connected n-vertex graph can have anywhere from two to n layers.

8.3   Computing Connected Components

In this section, $G = (V, E)$ will always denote an *undirected* graph. Section 8.6 addresses the more difficult case of directed graphs.

8.3.1   Connected Components

An undirected graph $G = (V, E)$ naturally falls into "pieces," which are called *connected components* (Figure 8.8). More formally, a connected component is a maximal subset $S \subseteq V$ of vertices such that there is a path from any vertex in S to any other vertex in S. For example, the connected components of the graph in Figure 8.8 are $\{1, 3, 5, 7, 9\}$, $\{2, 4\}$, and $\{6, 8, 10\}$.[16]

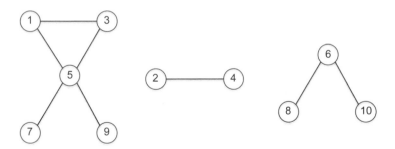

Figure 8.8: A graph with vertex set $\{1, 2, 3, \ldots, 10\}$ and three connected components.

---

[16]Still more formally, the connected components of a graph can be defined as the *equivalence classes* of a suitable *equivalence relation*. Equivalence relations are usually covered in a first course on proofs or on discrete mathematics. A *relation* on a set X of objects specifies, for each pair $x, y \in X$ of objects, whether or not x and y are related. (If so, we write $x \sim y$.) For connected components, the relevant relation (on the set V) is "$v \sim_G w$ if and only if there is a path between v and w in G." An *equivalence* relation satisfies three properties. First, it is *reflexive*, meaning that $x \sim x$ for every $x \in X$. (Satisfied by $\sim_G$, as the empty path connects a vertex with itself.) Second, it is *symmetric*, with $x \sim y$ if and only if $y \sim x$. (Satisfied by $\sim_G$, as G is undirected.) Finally, it is *transitive*, meaning that $x \sim y$ and $y \sim z$ implies that $x \sim z$. (Satisfied by $\sim_G$, as you can paste together a path between vertices u and v and a path between vertices v and w to get a path between u and w.) An equivalence relation partitions the set of objects into equivalence classes, with each object related to all the objects in its class, and only to these. The equivalence classes of the relation $\sim_G$ are the connected components of G.

The goal of this section is to use breadth-first search to compute the connected components of a graph in linear time.[17]

Problem: Undirected Connected Components

Input: An undirected graph $G = (V, E)$.

Goal: Identify the connected components of G.

Next, let's double-check your understanding of the definition of connected components.

Quiz 8.2

Consider an undirected graph with n vertices and m edges. What are the minimum and maximum number of connected components that the graph could have, respectively?

a) 1 and $n - 1$

b) 1 and n

c) 1 and $\max\{m, n\}$

d) 2 and $\max\{m, n\}$

(See Section 8.3.6 for the solution and discussion.)

8.3.2   Applications

There are several reasons why you might be interested in the connected components of a graph.

Detecting network failures.   One obvious application is checking whether a network, such as a road or communication network, has become disconnected.

Data visualization.   Another application is in graph visualization—if you're trying to draw or otherwise visualize a graph, presumably you want to display the different components separately.

Clustering.   Suppose you have a collection of objects that you care about, with each pair annotated as either "similar" or "dissimilar." For example, the objects could be documents (like crawled Web pages or news stories), with similar objects corresponding to near-duplicate documents (perhaps differing only in a timestamp or a headline). Or the objects could be genomes, with two genomes deemed similar if a small number of mutations can transform one into the other.

Now form an undirected graph $G = (V, E)$, with vertices corresponding to objects and edges corresponding to pairs of similar objects. Intuitively, each connected component of

---

[17]Other graph search algorithms, including depth-first search, can be used to compute connected components in exactly the same way.

this graph represents a set of objects that share much in common. For example, if the objects are crawled news stories, one might expect the vertices of a connected component to be variations on the same story reported on different Web sites. If the objects are genomes, a connected component might correspond to different individuals belonging to the same species.

8.3.3   The UCC Algorithm

Computing the connected components of an undirected graph easily reduces to breadth-first search (or other graph search algorithms, such as depth-first search). The idea is to use an outer loop to make a single pass over the vertices, invoking BFS as a subroutine whenever the algorithm encounters a vertex that it has never seen before. This outer loop ensures that the algorithm looks at every vertex at least once. Vertices are initialized as unexplored before the outer loop, and not inside a call to BFS. The algorithm also maintains a field $cc(v)$ for each vertex v, to remember which connected component contains it. By identifying each vertex of V with its position in the vertex array, we can assume that $V = \{1, 2, 3, \ldots, n\}$.

UCC

Input: undirected graph $G = (V, E)$ in adjacency-list representation, with $V = \{1, 2, 3, \ldots, n\}$.
Postcondition: for every $u, v \in V$, $cc(u) = cc(v)$ if and only if u, v are in the same connected component.

```
mark all vertices as unexplored
numCC := 0
for i := 1 to n do                    // try all vertices
    if i is unexplored then           // avoid redundancy
        numCC := numCC + 1            // new component
        // call BFS starting at i (lines 2-8)
        Q := a queue data structure, initialized with i
        while Q is not empty do
            remove the vertex from the front of Q, call it v
            cc(v) := numCC
            for each (v, w) in v's adjacency list do
                if w is unexplored then
                    mark w as explored
                    add w to the end of Q
```

8.3.4   An Example

Let's trace the UCC algorithm's execution on the graph in Figure 8.8. The algorithm marks all vertices as unexplored and starts the outer for loop with vertex 1. This vertex has not been seen before, so the algorithm invokes BFS from it. Because BFS finds everything reachable from its starting vertex (Theorem 8.2(a)), it discovers all the vertices in $\{1, 3, 5, 7, 9\}$, and sets their cc-values to 1. One possible order of exploration is:

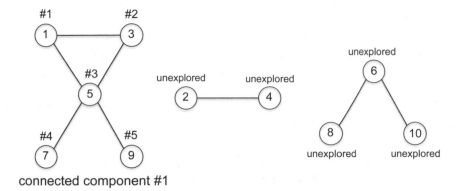

connected component #1

Once this call to BFS completes, the algorithm's outer for loop marches on and considers vertex 2. This vertex was not discovered by the first call to BFS, so BFS is invoked again, this time with vertex 2 as the starting vertex. After discovering vertices 2 and 4 (and setting their *cc*-values to 2), this call to BFS completes and the UCC algorithm resumes its outer for loop. Has the algorithm seen vertex 3 before? Yup, in the first BFS call. What about vertex 4? Yes again, this time in the second BFS call. Vertex 5? Been there, done that in the first BFS call. But what about vertex 6? Neither of the previous BFS calls discovered this vertex, so BFS is called again with vertex 6 as the starting vertex. This third call to BFS discovers the vertices in $\{6, 8, 10\}$, and sets their *cc*-values to 3:

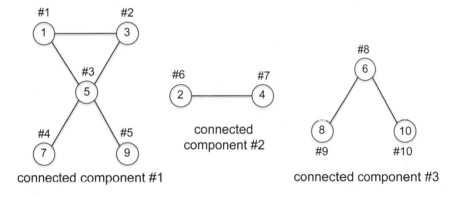

connected component #1   connected component #3

Finally, the algorithm verifies that the remaining vertices (7, 8, 9, and 10) have already been explored and halts.

8.3.5   Correctness and Running Time

The UCC algorithm correctly computes the connected components of an undirected graph, and does so in linear time.

Theorem 8.4 (Properties of UCC) *For every undirected graph $G = (V, E)$ in adjacency-list representation:*

(a) *At the conclusion of UCC, for every pair u, v of vertices, $cc(u) = cc(v)$ if and only if u and v belong to the same connected component of G.*

(b) *The running time of UCC is $O(m + n)$, where $m = |E|$ and $n = |V|$.*

Proof: For correctness, the first property of breadth-first search (Theorem 8.2(a)) implies that each call to BFS with a starting vertex i will discover the vertices in i's connected component and nothing more. The UCC algorithm gives these vertices a common *cc*-value. Because no vertex is explored twice, each call to BFS identifies a new connected component, with each component having a different *cc*-value. The outer for loop ensures that every vertex is visited at least once, so the algorithm will discover every connected component.

The running time bound follows from our refined running time analysis of BFS (Theorem 8.2(c)). Each call to BFS from a vertex i runs in $O(m_i + n_i)$ time, where m_i and n_i denote the number of edges and vertices, respectively, in i's connected component. As BFS is called only once for each connected component, and each vertex or edge of G participates in exactly one component, the combined running time of all the BFS calls is $O(\sum_i m_i + \sum_i n_i) = O(m + n)$. The initialization and additional bookkeeping performed by the algorithm requires only $O(n)$ time, so the final running time is $O(m + n)$. $\mathcal{QED}$

8.3.6   Solution to Quiz 8.2

Correct answer: (b). A graph with one connected component is one in which you can get from anywhere to anywhere else. Path graphs and complete graphs (Figure 8.7) are two examples. At the other extreme, in a graph with no edges, each vertex is in its own connected component, for a total of n. There cannot be more than n connected components, as they are disjoint and each contains at least one vertex.

8.4   Depth-First Search

Why do we need another graph search strategy? After all, breadth-first search seems pretty awesome—it finds all the vertices reachable from the starting vertex in linear time, and can even compute shortest-path distances along the way.

There's another linear-time graph search strategy, *depth-first search (DFS)*, which comes with its own impressive catalog of applications (not already covered by BFS). For example, we'll see how to use DFS to compute in linear time a topological ordering of the vertices of a directed acyclic graph, as well as the connected components (appropriately defined) of a directed graph.

8.4.1   An Example

If breadth-first search is the cautious and tentative exploration strategy, depth-first search is its more aggressive cousin, always exploring from the most recently discovered vertex and backtracking only when necessary (like exploring a maze). Before we describe the full pseudocode for DFS, let's illustrate how it works on the same running example used in Section 8.2 (Figure 8.9).

Like BFS, DFS marks a vertex as explored the first time it discovers it. Because it begins its exploration at the starting vertex s, for the graph in Figure 8.9, the first iteration of DFS examines the edges (s, a) and (s, b), in whatever order these edges appear in s's adjacency list. Let's say (s, a) comes first, leading DFS to discover the vertex a and mark it as explored. The second iteration of DFS is where it diverges from BFS—rather than considering next s's other layer-1 neighbor b, DFS immediately proceeds to exploring the neighbors of a. (It will

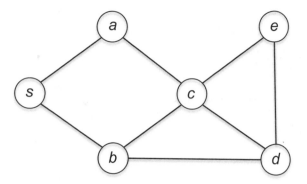

Figure 8.9: Running example for depth-first search.

eventually get back to exploring (s, b).) Perhaps from a it checks s first (which is already marked as explored) and then discovers the vertex c, which is where it travels next:

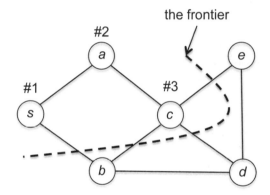

Then DFS examines in some order the neighbors of c, the most recently discovered vertex. To keep things interesting, let's say that DFS discovers d next, followed by e:

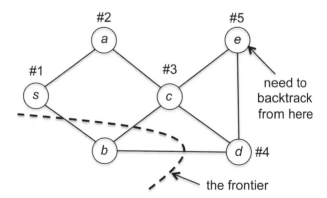

From e, DFS has nowhere to go—both of e's neighbors are already marked as explored. DFS is forced to retreat to the previous vertex, namely d, and resume exploring the rest of its neighbors. From d, DFS will discover the final vertex b (perhaps after checking c and finding it marked as explored). Once at b, the dominoes fall quickly. DFS discovers that all of b's neighbors have already been explored, and must backtrack to the previously visited vertex, which is d. Similarly, because all of d's remaining neighbors are already marked as explored, DFS must rewind further, to c. DFS then retreats further to a (after checking that all of c's remaining neighbors are marked as explored), then to s. It finally stops once it checks s's remaining neighbor (which is b) and finds it marked as explored.

8.4.2   Pseudocode for DFS

Iterative Implementation

One way to think about and implement DFS is to start from the code for BFS and make two changes: (i) swap in a stack data structure (which is last-in first-out) for the queue (which is first-in first-out); and (ii) postpone checking whether a vertex has already been explored until after removing it from the data structure.[18]

DFS (Iterative Version)

Input: graph $G = (V, E)$ in adjacency-list representation, and a
    vertex $s \in V$.
Postcondition: a vertex is reachable from s if and only if it is
    marked as "explored."

---

mark all vertices as unexplored
$S :=$ a stack data structure, initialized with s
while S is not empty **do**
    remove ("pop") the vertex v from the front of S
    if v is unexplored **then**
        mark v as explored
        for each edge (v, w) in v's adjacency list **do**
            add ("push") w to the front of S

As usual, the edges processed in the for loop are the edges incident to v (if G is an undirected graph) or the edges outgoing from v (if G is a directed graph).

For example, in the graph in Figure 8.9, the first iteration of DFS's while loop pops the vertex s and pushes its two neighbors onto the stack in some order, say, with b first and a second. Because a was the last to be pushed, it is the first to be popped, in the second iteration of the while loop. This causes s and c to be pushed onto the stack, let's say with c first. The vertex s is popped in the next iteration; because it has already been marked as explored, the algorithm skips it. Then c is popped, and all of its neighbors (a, b, d, and e) are pushed onto the stack, joining the first occurrence of b. If d is pushed last, and also b is pushed before e when d is popped in the next iteration, then we recover the order of exploration from Section 8.4.1 (as you should check).

---

[18] A *stack* is a "last-in first-out" data structure—like those stacks of upside-down trays at a cafeteria—that is typically studied in a first programming course (along with queues, see footnote 9). A stack maintains a list of objects, and you can add an object to the beginning of the list (a "push") or remove one from the beginning of the list (a "pop") in constant time.

Recursive Implementation

Depth-first search also has an elegant recursive implementation.

DFS (Recursive Version)

Input: graph $G = (V, E)$ in adjacency-list representation, and a
vertex $s \in V$.
Postcondition: a vertex is reachable from s if and only if it is
marked as "explored."

```
// all vertices unexplored before outer call
mark s as explored
for each edge (s, v) in s's adjacency list do
    if v is unexplored then
        DFS (G, v)
```

In this implementation, all recursive calls to DFS have access to the same set of global
variables which track the vertices that have been marked as explored (with all vertices initially
unexplored). The aggressive nature of DFS is perhaps more obvious in this implementation—
the algorithm immediately recurses on the first unexplored neighbor that it finds, before
considering the remaining neighbors.[19] In effect, the explicit stack data structure in the
iterative implementation of DFS is being simulated by the program stack of recursive calls
in the recursive implementation.[20]

8.4.3   Correctness and Running Time

Depth-first search is just as correct and just as blazingly fast as breadth-first search, for the
same reasons (cf., Theorem 8.2).

Theorem 8.5 (Properties of DFS) *For every undirected or directed graph $G = (V, E)$ in
adjacency-list representation and for every starting vertex $s \in V$:*

 (a) *At the conclusion of DFS, a vertex $v \in V$ is marked as explored if and only if there is
     a path from s to v in G.*

 (b) *The running time of DFS is $O(m + n)$, where $m = |E|$ and $n = |V|$.*

Part (a) holds because depth-first search is a special case of the generic graph search algorithm
GenericSearch (see Proposition 8.1).[21] Part (b) holds because DFS examines each edge

---

[19] As stated, the two versions of DFS explore the edges in a vertex's adjacency list in opposite orders. (Do
you see why?) If one of the versions is modified to iterate backward through a vertex's adjacency list, then the
iterative and recursive implementations explore the vertices in the same order.

[20] Pro tip: If your computer runs out of memory while executing the recursive version of DFS, you should
either switch to the iterative version or increase the program stack size in your programming environment.

[21] Formally, DFS is equivalent to the version of GenericSearch in which, in every iteration of the latter's
while loop, the algorithm chooses the eligible edge (v, w) for which v was discovered most recently. Ties
among v's eligible edges are broken according to their order (for the recursive version) or their reverse order (for
the iterative version) in v's adjacency list.

at most twice (once from each endpoint) and, because the stack supports pushes and pops in $O(1)$ time, performs a constant number of operations per edge examination (for $O(m)$ total). The initialization requires $O(n)$ time.[22]

8.5   Topological Sort

Depth-first search is perfectly suited for computing a topological ordering of a directed acyclic graph. "What's that and who cares," you say?

8.5.1   Topological Orderings

Imagine that you have a bunch of tasks to complete, and there are *precedence constraints*, meaning that you cannot start some of the tasks until you have completed others. Think, for example, about the courses in a university degree program, some of which are prerequisites for others. One application of topological orderings is to sequencing tasks so that all precedence constraints are respected.

Topological Orderings

Let $G = (V, E)$ be a directed graph. A *topological ordering* of G is an assignment of every vertex $v \in V$ to a different number $f(v)$ such that:

for every $(v, w) \in E$, $f(v) < f(w)$.

The function f effectively orders the vertices, from the vertex with the smallest f-value to the one with the largest. The condition asserts that all of G's (directed) edges should travel forward in the ordering, with the label of the tail of an edge smaller than that of its head.

Quiz 8.3

How many different topological orderings does the following graph have? Use only the labels $\{1, 2, 3, 4\}$.

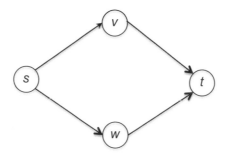

a) 0

b) 1

---

[22]The refined bound in Theorem 8.2(c) also holds for DFS (for the same reasons), which means DFS can substitute for BFS in the linear-time UCC algorithm for computing connected components in Section 8.3.

c) 2

d) 3

(See Section 8.5.7 for the solution and discussion.)

You can visualize a topological ordering by plotting the vertices in order of their f-values. In a topological ordering, all edges of the graph are directed from left to right. Figure 8.10 plots the topological orderings identified in the solution to Quiz 8.3.

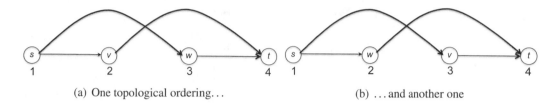

(a) One topological ordering...   (b) ...and another one

Figure 8.10: A topological ordering effectively plots the vertices of a graph on a line, with all edges going from left to right.

When the vertices of a graph represent tasks and the directed edges represent precedence constraints, topological orderings correspond exactly to the different ways to sequence the tasks while respecting the precedence constraints.

8.5.2   When Does a Topological Ordering Exist?

Does every graph have a topological ordering? No way. Think about a graph consisting solely of a directed cycle (Figure 8.11(a)). No matter what vertex ordering you choose, traversing the edges of the cycle takes you back to the starting point, which is possible only if some edges go backward in the ordering (Figure 8.11(b)).

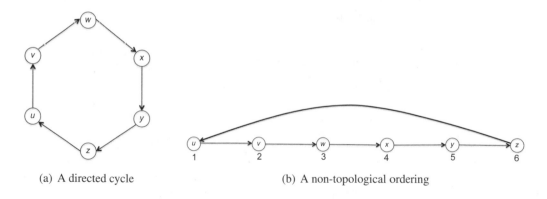

(a) A directed cycle   (b) A non-topological ordering

Figure 8.11: A graph with a directed cycle has no topological ordering.

More generally, it is impossible to topologically order the vertices of a graph that contains a directed cycle. Equivalently, it is impossible to sequence a set of tasks when their dependencies are circular.

Happily, directed cycles are the only obstruction to topological orderings. A directed graph with no directed cycles is called—wait for it—a *directed acyclic graph*, or simply a *DAG*. For example, the graph in Figure 8.10 is directed acyclic; the one in Figure 8.11 is not.

Theorem 8.6 (Every DAG Has a Topological Ordering) *Every directed acyclic graph has at least one topological ordering.*

To prove this theorem, we'll need the following lemma about source vertices. A *source vertex* of a directed graph is a vertex with no incoming edges. (Analogously, a *sink vertex* is one with no outgoing edges.) For example, s is the unique source vertex in the graph in Figure 8.10; the directed cycle in Figure 8.11 has no source vertices.

Lemma 8.7 (Every DAG Has a Source) *Every directed acyclic graph has at least one source vertex.*

Lemma 8.7 is true because if you keep following incoming edges backward out of an arbitrary vertex of a directed acyclic graph, you're bound to eventually reach a source vertex. (Otherwise, you would produce a cycle, which is impossible.) See also Figure 8.12.[23]

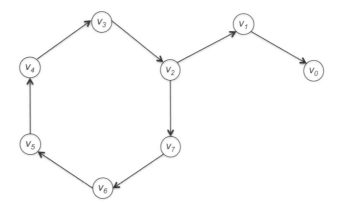

Figure 8.12: A graph with no source vertex. Tracing incoming edges back from the vertex v_0 exposes a directed cycle (from v_2 back to itself).

We can prove Theorem 8.6 by populating a topological ordering from left to right with successively extracted source vertices.[24]

Proof of Theorem 8.6: Let G be a directed acyclic graph with n vertices. The plan is to assign f-values to vertices in increasing order, from 1 to n. Which vertex has earned the

[23]More formally, pick a vertex v_0 of a directed acyclic graph G; if it's a source vertex, we're done. If not, it has at least one incoming edge (v_1, v_0). If v_1 is a source vertex, we're done. Otherwise, there is an incoming edge of the form (v_2, v_1) and we can iterate again. After iterating up to n times, where n is the number of vertices, we either find a source vertex or produce a sequence of n edges $(v_n, v_{n-1}), (v_{n-1}, v_{n-2}), \ldots, (v_1, v_0)$. Because there are only n vertices, there's at least one repeat vertex in the sequence $v_n, v_{n-1}, \ldots, v_0$. But if $v_j = v_i$ with $j > i$, then the edges $(v_j, v_{j-1}), \ldots, (v_{i+1}, v_i)$ form a directed cycle, contradicting the assumption that G is directed acyclic. (In Figure 8.12, $i = 2$ and $j = 8$, with vertex v_2 visited twice.)

[24]Alternatively, following outgoing edges rather than incoming edges in the proof of Lemma 8.7 shows that every DAG has at least one sink vertex, and we can populate a topological ordering from right to left with successively extracted sink vertices.

right to wear 1 as its f-value? It had better be a source vertex—if a vertex with an incoming edge was assigned the first position, the incoming edge would go backward in the ordering. So, let v_1 be a source vertex of G—one exists by Lemma 8.7—and assign $f(v_1) = 1$. If there are multiple source vertices, pick one arbitrarily.

Next, obtain the graph G' from G by removing v_1 and all its (outgoing) edges. Because G is directed acyclic, so is G'—deleting stuff can't create new cycles. We can therefore recursively compute a topological ordering of G', using the labels $\{2, 3, 4, \ldots, n\}$, with every edge in G' traveling forward in the ordering. (Because each recursive call is on a smaller graph, the recursion eventually stops with a single-vertex graph.) The only edges in G that are not also in G' are the (outgoing) edges of v_1; as $f(v_1) = 1$, these also travel forward in the ordering.[25] $\mathcal{QED}$

8.5.3   Computing a Topological Ordering

Theorem 8.6 implies that it makes sense to ask for a topological ordering of a directed graph if and only if the graph is directed acyclic.

Problem: Topological Sort

Input: A directed acyclic graph $G = (V, E)$.

Output: A topological ordering of the vertices of G.

The proofs of Lemma 8.7 and Theorem 8.6 naturally lead to an algorithm. For an n-vertex directed acyclic graph in adjacency-list representation, the former proof gives an $O(n)$-time subroutine for finding a source vertex. The latter proof computes a topological ordering with n invocations of this subroutine, plucking off a new source vertex in each iteration.[26] The running time of this algorithm is $O(n^2)$, which is linear time for the densest graphs (with $m = \Theta(n^2)$ edges) but not for sparser graphs (for which n^2 could be way bigger than m). Next up: a slicker solution via depth-first search, resulting in a linear-time ($O(m + n)$) algorithm.[27]

8.5.4   Topological Sort via DFS

The slick way to compute a topological ordering is to augment depth-first search in two small ways. For simplicity, we'll start from the recursive implementation of DFS in Section 8.4. The first addition is an outer loop that makes a single pass over the vertices, invoking DFS as a subroutine whenever a previously unexplored vertex is discovered. This ensures that every vertex is eventually discovered and assigned a label. The global variable *curLabel* keeps track of where we are in the topological ordering. Our algorithm will compute an ordering

---

[25] If you prefer a formal proof of correctness, proceed in the privacy of your own home by induction on the number of vertices.

[26] For the graph in Figure 8.10, this algorithm might compute either of the two topological orderings, depending on which of v, w is chosen as the source vertex in the second iteration, after s has been removed.

[27] With some cleverness, the algorithm implicit in the proofs of Lemma 8.7 and Theorem 8.6 can also be implemented in linear time (Problem 8.11).

in reverse order (from right to left), so $curLabel$ counts down from the number of vertices to 1.

TopoSort

Input: directed acyclic graph $G = (V, E)$ in adjacency-list representation.

Postcondition: the f-values of vertices constitute a topological ordering of G.

```
mark all vertices as unexplored
curLabel := |V|            // keeps track of ordering
for every v ∈ V do
    if v is unexplored then // not seen in a prior DFS
        DFS-Topo (G, v)
```

Second, we must add a line of code to DFS that assigns an f-value to a vertex v. The right time to do this is immediately upon completion of the DFS call initiated at v.

DFS-Topo

Input: graph $G = (V, E)$ in adjacency-list representation, and a vertex $s \in V$.

Postcondition: every vertex reachable from s is marked as "explored" and has an assigned f-value.

```
mark s as explored
for each edge (s, v) in s's outgoing adjacency list do
    if v is unexplored then
        DFS-Topo (G, v)
f(s) := curLabel           // s's position in ordering
curLabel := curLabel − 1     // work right-to-left
```

8.5.5 An Example

Suppose the input graph is the graph in Quiz 8.3. The TopoSort algorithm initializes the global variable $curLabel$ to the number of vertices, which is 4. The outer loop in TopoSort iterates through the vertices in an arbitrary order; let's assume this order is v, t, s, w. In the first iteration, because v is not marked as explored, the algorithm invokes the DFS-Topo subroutine with starting vertex v. The only outgoing edge from v is (v, t), and the next step is to recursively call DFS-Topo with starting vertex t. This call returns immediately (as t has no outgoing edges), at which point $f(t)$ is set to 4 and $curLabel$ is decremented from 4 to 3. Next, the DFS-Topo call at v completes (as v has no other outgoing edges), at which point $f(v)$ is set to 3 and $curLabel$ is decremented from 3 to 2. At this point, the TopoSort algorithm resumes its linear scan of the vertices in its outer loop. The next vertex is t; because t has already been marked as explored in the first call to DFS-Topo, the TopoSort algorithm skips it. Because the next vertex (which is s) has not yet been explored, the algorithm invokes DFS-Topo from s. From s, DFS-Topo skips v (which is already marked as explored) and recursively calls DFS-Topo at the newly discovered vertex w. The call at w completes immediately (the only outgoing edge is to the previously explored vertex t), at which point $f(w)$ is set to 2 and $curLabel$ is decremented from 2 to 1. Finally, the DFS-Topo call at vertex s completes, and $f(s)$ is set to 1. The resulting topological ordering is the same as that in Figure 8.10(b).

Quiz 8.4

What happens when the TopoSort algorithm is run on a graph with a directed cycle?

a) The algorithm might or might not loop forever.

b) The algorithm always loops forever.

c) The algorithm always halts, and may or may not successfully compute a topological ordering.

d) The algorithm always halts, and never successfully computes a topological ordering.

(See Section 8.5.7 for the solution and discussion.)

8.5.6   Correctness and Running Time

The TopoSort algorithm correctly computes a topological ordering of a directed acyclic graph, and does so in linear time.

Theorem 8.8 (Properties of TopoSort) *For every directed acyclic graph* $G = (V, E)$ *in adjacency-list representation:*

(a) *At the conclusion of* TopoSort, *every vertex v has been assigned an f-value, and these f-values constitute a topological ordering of G.*

(b) *The running time of* TopoSort *is* $O(m + n)$, *where* $m = |E|$ *and* $n = |V|$.

Proof: The TopoSort algorithm runs in linear time for the usual reasons. It explores each edge only once (from its tail), and therefore performs only a constant number of operations for each vertex or edge. This implies an overall running time of $O(m + n)$.

For correctness, first note that DFS-Topo will be called from each vertex $v \in V$ exactly once, when v is encountered for the first time, and that v is assigned a label when this call completes. Thus, every vertex receives a label, and by decrementing the $curLabel$ variable with every label assignment, the algorithm ensures that each vertex v gets a distinct label $f(v)$ from the set $\{1, 2, \ldots, |V|\}$. To see why these labels constitute a topological ordering, consider an arbitrary edge (v, w); we must argue that $f(v) < f(w)$. There are two cases, depending on which of v, w the algorithm discovers first.[28]

---

[28] Both cases are possible, as we saw in Section 8.5.5.

If v is discovered before w, then DFS-Topo is invoked with starting vertex v before w has been marked as explored. As w is reachable from v (via the edge (v, w)), this call to DFS-Topo eventually discovers w and recursively calls DFS-Topo at w. By the last-in first-out nature of recursive calls, the call to DFS-Topo at w completes before that at v. Because labels are assigned in decreasing order, w is assigned a larger f-value than v, as required.

Second, suppose w is discovered by the TopoSort algorithm before v. Because G is a directed acyclic graph, there is no path from w back to v; otherwise, combining such a path with the edge (v, w) would produce a directed cycle (Figure 8.13). Thus, the call to DFS-Topo starting at w cannot discover v and completes with v still unexplored. Once again, the DFS-Topo call at w completes before that at v and hence $f(v) < f(w)$. $\mathcal{QED}$

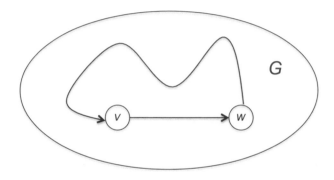

Figure 8.13: A directed acyclic graph cannot contain both an edge (v, w) and a path from w back to v.

8.5.7   Solution to Quizzes 8.3–8.4

Solution to Quiz 8.3

Correct answer: (c). Figure 8.14 shows two different topological orderings of the graph—you should check that these are the only ones.

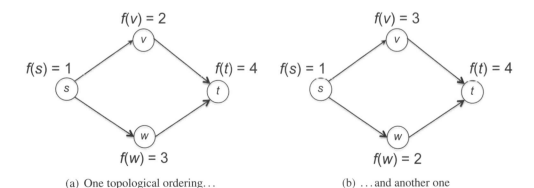

(a) One topological ordering...   (b) ...and another one

Figure 8.14: Two topological orderings of the graph in Quiz 8.3.

Solution to Quiz 8.4

Correct answer: (d). The algorithm always halts: There are only $|V|$ iterations of the outer loop, and each iteration either does nothing or invokes depth-first search (with minor additional bookkeeping). Depth-first search always halts, whether or not the input graph is directed acyclic (Theorem 8.5), and so `TopoSort` does as well. Any chance it halts with a topological ordering? No way—it is impossible to topologically sort the vertices of any graph with a directed cycle (recall Section 8.5.2).

*8.6   Computing Strongly Connected Components

Next we'll learn an even more interesting application of depth-first search: computing the strongly connected components of a directed graph. Our algorithm will be as blazingly fast as in the undirected case (Section 8.3), although less straightforward. Computing strongly connected components is a more challenging problem than topological sorting, and one pass of depth-first search won't be enough. So, we'll use two![29]

8.6.1   Defining Strongly Connected Components

What do we even mean by a "connected component" of a directed graph? For example, how many connected components does the graph in Figure 8.15 have?

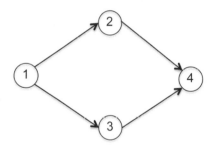

Figure 8.15: How many connected components?

It's tempting to say that this graph has one connected component—if it were a physical object, with the edges corresponding to strings tying the vertices together, we could pick it up and it would hang together in one piece. But remember how we defined connected components in the undirected case (Section 8.3), as maximal regions within which you can get from anywhere to anywhere else. There is no way to "move to the left" in the graph in Figure 8.15, so it's not the case that you can get from anywhere to anywhere else.

A *strongly connected component* or *SCC* of a directed graph is a maximal subset $S \subseteq V$ of vertices such that there is a directed path from any vertex in S to any other vertex in S.[30]

---

[29] Actually, there *is* a somewhat tricky way to compute the strongly connected components of a directed graph with only one pass of depth-first search; see the paper "Depth-First Search and Linear Graph Algorithms," by Robert E. Tarjan (*SIAM Journal on Computing*, 1973).

[30] As with connected components in undirected graphs (footnote 16), the strongly connected components of a directed graph G are precisely the equivalence classes of an equivalence relation $\sim_G$, where $v \sim_G w$ if and only if there are directed paths from v to w and from w to v in G. The proof that $\sim_G$ is an equivalence relation mirrors that in the undirected case (footnote 16).

For example, the strongly connected components of the graph in Figure 8.16 are $\{1, 3, 5\}$, $\{11\}$, $\{2, 4, 7, 9\}$, and $\{6, 8, 10\}$. Within each component, it's possible to get from anywhere to anywhere else (as you should check). Each component is maximal subject to this property, as there's no way to "move to the left" from one SCC to another.

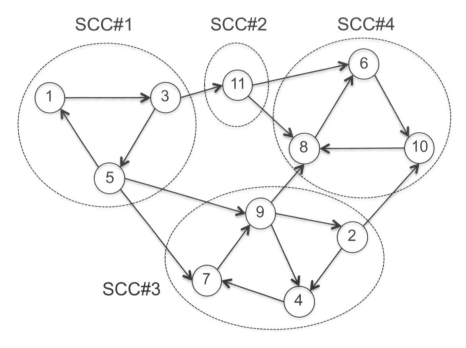

Figure 8.16: A graph with vertex set $\{1, 2, 3, \ldots, 11\}$ and four strongly connected components.

The relationships between the four SCCs of the graph in Figure 8.16 resemble those between the four vertices in the graph in Figure 8.15. More generally, if you squint, *every* directed graph can be viewed as a directed acyclic graph built up from its SCCs.

Proposition 8.9 (The SCC Meta-Graph Is Directed Acyclic) *Let $G = (V, E)$ be a directed graph. Define the corresponding* meta-graph $H = (X, F)$ *with one meta-vertex $x \in X$ per SCC of G and a meta-edge (x, y) in F whenever there is an edge in G from a vertex in the SCC corresponding to x to one in the SCC corresponding to y. Then H is a directed acyclic graph.*

For example, the directed acyclic graph in Figure 8.15 is the meta-graph corresponding to the directed graph in Figure 8.16.

Proof of Proposition 8.9: If the meta-graph H had a directed cycle with $k \geq 2$ meta-vertices, the corresponding cycle of allegedly distinct SCCs $S_1, S_2, \ldots, S_k$ in G would collapse to a single SCC: You can already travel freely within each of the S_i's, and the cycle then permits travel between any pair of the S_i's. $\mathcal{QED}$

Proposition 8.9 implies that every directed graph can be viewed at two levels of granularity. Zooming out, you focus only on the (acyclic) relationships among its SCCs; zooming in to a specific SCC reveals its fine-grained structure.

Quiz 8.5

Consider a directed acyclic graph with n vertices and m edges. What are the minimum and maximum number of strongly connected components that the graph could have, respectively?

    a) 1 and 1

    b) 1 and n

    c) 1 and m

    d) n and n

(See Section 8.6.7 for the solution and discussion.)

8.6.2   Why Depth-First Search?

To see why graph search might help in computing strongly connected components, let's return to the graph in Figure 8.16. Suppose we invoke depth-first search (or breadth-first search, for that matter) from the vertex 6. The algorithm will find everything reachable from 6 and nothing more, discovering $\{6, 8, 10\}$, which is exactly one of the strongly connected components. But if we instead initiate a graph search from vertex 1, all the vertices (not only $\{1, 3, 5\}$) are discovered and we learn nothing about the component structure.

The take-away is that graph search can uncover strongly connected components, provided you start from the right place. Intuitively, we want to first discover a "sink SCC," meaning an SCC with no outgoing edges (like SCC#4 in Figure 8.16), and then work backward. In terms of the meta-graph in Proposition 8.9, it seems we want to discover the SCCs in reverse topological order, plucking off sink SCCs one by one. We've already seen in Section 8.5 that topological orderings are right in the wheelhouse of depth-first search, and this is the reason why our algorithm will use two passes of depth-first search. The first pass computes a magical ordering in which to process the vertices, and the second follows this ordering to discover the SCCs one by one. This two-pass strategy is known as *Kosaraju's algorithm*.[31]

For shock value, here's what Kosaraju's algorithm looks like from 30,000 feet:

Kosaraju (High-Level)

1. Let G^{rev} denote the input graph G with the direction of every edge reversed.

2. Call DFS from every vertex of G^{rev}, processed in arbitrary order, to compute a position $f(v)$ for each vertex v.

3. Call DFS from every vertex of G, processed from the first to the last position, to compute the identity of each vertex's strongly connected component.

---

[31]This algorithm first appeared in an unpublished paper by S. Rao Kosaraju in 1978. Micha Sharir also discovered it (sometimes called the Kosaraju-Sharir algorithm) and published it in the paper "A Strong-Connectivity Algorithm and Its Applications in Data Flow Analysis" (*Computers & Mathematics with Applications*, 1981).

You might have at least a little intuition for the second and third steps of Kosaraju's algorithm. The second step presumably is similar to the `TopoSort` algorithm from Section 8.5, with the goal of processing the SCCs of the input graph in the third step in reverse topological order. (Caveat: We studied the `TopoSort` algorithm only in DAGs, and here we have a general directed graph.) The third step is hopefully analogous to the `UCC` algorithm from Section 8.3 for undirected graphs. (Caveat: In undirected graphs, the order in which you process the vertices doesn't matter; in directed graphs, as we've seen, it does.) But what's up with the first step? Why does the first pass work with the reversal of the input graph?

8.6.3   Why the Reversed Graph?

Suppose we instead invoke the `TopoSort` algorithm from Section 8.5 on the original input graph $G = (V, E)$. Recall that this algorithm has an outer for loop that makes a pass over the vertices of G in an arbitrary order; initiates depth-first search whenever it encounters a not-yet-explored vertex; and assigns a position $f(v)$ to a vertex v when the depth-first search initiated at v completes. The positions are assigned in decreasing order, from $|V|$ down to 1.

The `TopoSort` algorithm was originally motivated by the case of a directed acyclic input graph, but it can be used to compute vertex positions for an arbitrary directed graph (Quiz 8.4). We're hoping these vertex positions are somehow helpful for quickly identifying a good starting vertex for our second depth-first search pass, ideally a vertex in a sink SCC of G, with no outgoing edges. There's reason for optimism: With a directed acyclic graph G, the vertex positions constitute a topological ordering (Theorem 8.8), and the vertex in the last position must be a sink vertex of G, with no outgoing edges. (Any such edges would travel backward in the ordering.) Perhaps with a general directed graph G, the vertex in the last position always belongs to a sink SCC?

An Example

Sadly, no. For example, suppose we run the `TopoSort` algorithm on the graph in Figure 8.16. Suppose that we process the vertices in increasing order, with vertex 1 considered first. (In this case, all the vertices are discovered in the first iteration of the outer loop.) Suppose further that depth-first search traverses edge $(3, 5)$ before $(3, 11)$, $(5, 7)$ before $(5, 9)$, $(9, 4)$ before $(9, 2)$, and $(9, 2)$ before $(9, 8)$. In this case, you should check that the vertex positions wind up being:

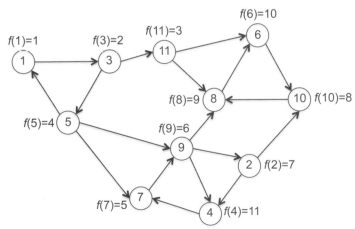

Against our wishes, the vertex in the last position (vertex 4) does not belong to the sink SCC. The one piece of good news is that the vertex in the *first* position (vertex 1) belongs to a source SCC (meaning an SCC with no incoming edges).

What if we instead process the vertices in descending order? If depth-first search traverses edge $(11, 6)$ before $(11, 8)$ and edge $(9, 2)$ before $(9, 4)$, then (as you should check) the vertex positions are:

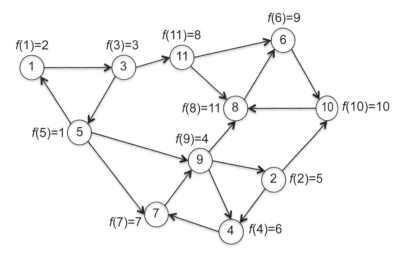

This time, the vertex in the last position is in the sink SCC, but we know this doesn't happen in general. More intriguingly, the vertex in the first position belongs to the source SCC, albeit a different vertex from this SCC than last time. Any chance this property could hold in general?

The First Vertex Resides in a Source SCC

In fact, something stronger is true: If we label each SCC of G with the smallest position of one of its vertices, these labels constitute a topological ordering of the meta-graph of SCCs defined in Proposition 8.9.

Theorem 8.10 (Topological Ordering of the SCCs) *Let G be a directed graph, with the vertices ordered arbitrarily, and for each vertex $v \in V$ let $f(v)$ denote the position of v computed by the* TopoSort *algorithm. Let S_1, S_2 denote two SCCs of G, and suppose G has an edge (v, w) with $v \in S_1$ and $w \in S_2$. Then,*

$$\min_{x \in S_1} f(x) < \min_{y \in S_2} f(y).$$

Proof: The proof is similar to the correctness of the TopoSort algorithm (Theorem 8.8, which is worth re-reading now). Let S_1, S_2 denote two SCCs of G, and consider two cases.[32] First, suppose that the TopoSort algorithm discovers and initiates depth-first search from a vertex s of S_1 before any vertex of S_2. Because there is an edge from a vertex v in S_1 to a vertex w in S_2 and S_1 and S_2 are SCCs, every vertex of S_2 is reachable from s—to reach some vertex $y \in S_2$, paste together a $s \rightsquigarrow v$ path within S_1, the edge (v, w), and a

---

[32]Both cases are possible, as we saw in the preceding example.

$w \rightsquigarrow y$ path within S_2. By the last-in first-out nature of recursive calls, the depth-first search initiated at s will not complete until after all the vertices of S_2 have been fully explored. Because vertex positions are assigned in decreasing order, s's position will be smaller than that of every vertex of S_2.

For the second case, suppose the `TopoSort` algorithm discovers a vertex $s \in S_2$ before any vertex of S_1. Because G's meta-graph is directed acyclic (Proposition 8.9), there is no directed path from s to any vertex of S_1. (Such a path would collapse S_1 and S_2 into a single SCC.) Thus, the depth-first search initiated at s completes after discovering all the vertices of S_2 (and possibly other stuff) and none of the vertices of S_1. In this case, *every* vertex of S_1 is assigned a position smaller than that of every vertex of S_2. $\mathcal{QED}$

Theorem 8.10 implies that the vertex in the first position always resides in a source SCC, just as we hoped. For consider the vertex v with $f(v) = 1$, inhabiting the SCC S. If S were not a source SCC, with an incoming edge from a different SCC S', then by Theorem 8.10 the smallest vertex position in S' would be less than 1, which is impossible.

Summarizing, after one pass of depth-first search, we can immediately identify a vertex in a source SCC. The only problem? We want to identify a vertex in a *sink* SCC. The fix? *Reverse the graph first.*

Reversing the Graph

Quiz 8.6

Let G be a directed graph and G^{rev} a copy of G with the direction of every edge reversed. How are the SCCs of G and G^{rev} related? (Choose all that apply.)

    a) In general, they are unrelated.

    b) Every SCC of G is also an SCC of G^{rev}, and conversely.

    c) Every source SCC of G is also a source SCC of G^{rev}.

    d) Every sink SCC of G becomes a source SCC of G^{rev}.

(See Section 8.6.7 for the solution and discussion.)

The following corollary rewrites Theorem 8.10 for the reversed graph, using the solution to Quiz 8.6.

Corollary 8.11 (First Vertex Resides in a Sink SCC) *Let G be a directed graph, with the vertices ordered arbitrarily, and for each vertex $v \in V$ let $f(v)$ denote the position of v computed by the* `TopoSort` *algorithm on the reversed graph G^{rev}. Let S_1, S_2 denote two SCCs of G, and suppose G has an edge (v, w) with $v \in S_1$ and $w \in S_2$. Then,*

$$\min_{x \in S_1} f(x) > \min_{y \in S_2} f(y). \tag{8.1}$$

In particular, the vertex in the first position resides in a sink SCC of G, and is the perfect starting point for a second depth-first search pass.

8.6.4   Pseudocode for Kosaraju

We now have all our ducks in a row: We run one pass of depth-first search (via TopoSort) on the reversed graph, which computes a magical ordering in which to visit the vertices, and a second pass (via the DFS-Topo subroutine) to discover the SCCs in reverse topological order, peeling them off one by one like the layers of an onion. Here's the pseudocode:

Kosaraju

Input: directed graph $G = (V, E)$ in adjacency-list representation, with $V = \{1, 2, 3, \ldots, n\}$.
Postcondition: for every $v, w \in V$, $scc(v) = scc(w)$ if and only if v, w are in the same SCC of G.

$G^{rev} := G$ with all edges reversed
mark all vertices of G^{rev} as unexplored

```
// first pass of depth-first search
// (computes f(v)'s, the magical ordering)
```
TopoSort (G^{rev})

```
// second pass of depth-first search
// (finds SCCs in reverse topological order)
```
mark all vertices of G as unexplored
$numSCC := 0$ // global variable
for each $v \in V$, in increasing order of $f(v)$ **do**
    if v is unexplored **then**
        $numSCC := numSCC + 1$
        // assign scc-values (details below)
        DFS-SCC (G, v)

Three implementation details:[33]

1. The most obvious way to implement the algorithm is to literally make a second copy of the input graph, with all edges reversed, and feed it to the TopoSort subroutine. A smarter implementation runs the TopoSort algorithm *backward* in the original input graph, by replacing the clause "each edge (s, v) in s's outgoing adjacency list" in the DFS-Topo subroutine of Section 8.5 with "each edge (v, s) in s's incoming adjacency list."

2. For best results, the first pass of depth-first search should export an array that contains the vertices (or pointers to them) in order of their positions, so that the second pass can process them with a simple array scan. This adds only constant overhead to the TopoSort subroutine (as you should check).

3. The DFS-SCC subroutine is the same as DFS, with one additional line of bookkeeping:

---

[33]To really appreciate these, it's best to implement the algorithm yourself (see Programming Problem 8.13).

DFS-SCC

Input: directed graph $G = (V, E)$ in adjacency-list representation,
  and a vertex $s \in V$.
Postcondition: every vertex reachable from s is marked as
  "explored" and has an assigned scc-value.

---

mark s as explored
$scc(s) := numSCC$ `// global variable above`
for each edge (s, v) in s's outgoing adjacency list **do**
    if v is unexplored **then**
        DFS-SCC (G, v)

8.6.5   An Example

Let's verify on our running example that we get what we want—that the second pass of depth-first search discovers the SCCs in reverse topological order. Suppose the graph in Figure 8.16 is the reversal G^{rev} of the input graph. We computed in Section 8.6.3 two ways in which the TopoSort algorithm might assign f-values to the vertices of this graph; let's use the first one. Here's the (unreversed) input graph with its vertices annotated with these vertex positions:

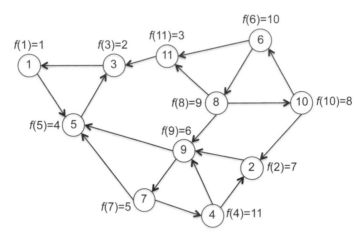

The second pass iterates through the vertices in increasing order of vertex position. Thus, the first call to DFS-SCC is initiated at the vertex in the first position (which happens to be vertex 1); it discovers the vertices 1, 3, and 5 and marks them as the vertices of the first SCC. The algorithm proceeds to consider the vertex in the second position (vertex 3); it was already explored by the first call to DFS-SCC and is skipped. The vertex in the third position (vertex 11) has not yet been discovered and is the next starting point for DFS-SCC. The only outgoing edge of this vertex travels to an already-explored vertex (vertex 3), so 11 is the only member of the second SCC. The algorithm skips the vertex in the fourth position (vertex 5, already explored) and next initiates DFS-SCC from vertex 7, the vertex in the fifth position. This search discovers the vertices 2, 4, 7, and 9 (the other outgoing edges are to the already-explored vertex 5) and classifies them as the third SCC. The algorithm skips vertex 9 and then vertex 2, and finally invokes DFS-SCC from vertex 10 to discover the final SCC (comprising the vertices 6, 8, and 10).

8.6.6   Correctness and Running Time

The Kosaraju algorithm is correct and blazingly fast for every directed graph, not merely for our running example.

Theorem 8.12 (Properties of Kosaraju) *For every directed graph* $G = (V, E)$ *in adjacency-list representation:*

(a) *At the conclusion of* Kosaraju, *for every pair* v, w *of vertices,* $scc(v) = scc(w)$ *if and only if* v *and* w *belong to the same strongly connected component of* G.

(b) *The running time of* Kosaraju *is* $O(m + n)$, *where* $m = |E|$ *and* $n = |V|$.

We've already discussed all the ingredients needed for the proof. The algorithm can be implemented in $O(m + n)$ time, with a small hidden constant factor, for the usual reasons. Each of the two passes of depth-first search does a constant number of operations per vertex or edge, and the extra bookkeeping increases the running time by only a constant factor.

The algorithm also correctly computes all the SCCs: Each time it initiates a new call to DFS-SCC, the algorithm discovers exactly one new SCC, which is a sink SCC relative to the graph of not-yet-explored vertices (that is, an SCC in which all outgoing edges lead to already-explored vertices).[34]

8.6.7   Solutions to Quizzes 8.5–8.6

Solution to Quiz 8.5

Correct answer: (d). In a directed acyclic graph $G = (V, E)$, every vertex is in its own strongly connected component (for a total of $n = |V|$ SCCs). To see this, fix a topological ordering of G (Section 8.5.1), with each vertex $v \in V$ assigned a distinct label $f(v)$. (One exists, by Theorem 8.6.) Edges of G travel only from smaller to larger f-values, so for every pair $v, w \in V$ of vertices, there is either no $v \rightsquigarrow w$ path (if $f(v) > f(w)$) or no $w \rightsquigarrow v$ path (if $f(w) > f(v)$) in G. This precludes two vertices from inhabiting the same SCC.

Solution to Quiz 8.6

Correct answers: (b),(d). Two vertices v, w of a directed graph are in the same strongly connected component if and only if there is both a directed path P_1 from v to w and a directed path P_2 from w to v. This property holds for v and w in G if and only if it holds

---

[34]For a more formal proof, consider a call to the DFS-SCC subroutine with a starting vertex v that belongs to an SCC S. Corollary 8.11 implies that directed paths out of v can reach only SCCs containing at least one vertex assigned a position earlier than v's. Because the Kosaraju algorithm processes vertices in order of position, all the vertices in SCCs reachable from v have already been explored by the algorithm. (Remember that once the algorithm finds one vertex from an SCC, it finds them all.) Thus, the edges going out of S reach only already-explored vertices. This call to DFS-SCC discovers the vertices of S and nothing more, as there are no available avenues for it to trespass on other SCCs. As every call to DFS-SCC discovers a single SCC and every vertex is eventually considered, the Kosaraju algorithm correctly identifies all the SCCs.

in G^{rev}—in the latter, using the reversed version of P_1 to get from w to v and the reversed version of P_2 to get from v to w. We can conclude that the SCCs of G and G^{rev} are exactly the same. Source SCCs of G (with no incoming edges) become sink SCCs of G^{rev} (with no outgoing edges), and sink SCCs become source SCCs. More generally, there is an edge from a vertex in SCC S_1 to a vertex SCC S_2 in G if and only if there is a corresponding edge from a vertex in S_2 to a vertex in S_1 in G^{rev} (Figure 8.17).[35]

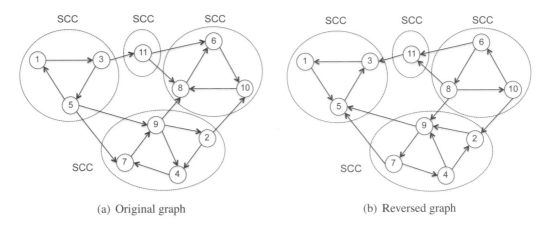

(a) Original graph   (b) Reversed graph

Figure 8.17: A graph and its reversal have the same strongly connected components.

8.7   The Structure of the Web

You now know a collection of for-free graph primitives. If you have graph data, you can apply these blazingly fast algorithms even if you're not sure how you'll use the results. For example, with a directed graph, why not compute its strongly connected components to get a sense of what it looks like? Next, we explore this idea in a huge and hugely interesting directed graph, the *Web graph*.

8.7.1   The Web Graph

In the Web graph, vertices correspond to Web pages, and edges to hyperlinks. This graph is directed, with an edge pointing from the page that contains the link to the landing page for the link. For example, my home page corresponds to a vertex in this graph, with outgoing edges corresponding to links to pages that list my books, my courses, and so on. There are also incoming edges corresponding to links to my home page, perhaps from my co-authors or lists of instructors of online courses (Figure 8.18).

While the Web's origins date back to roughly 1990, the Web really started to explode about five years later. By the year 2000 (still the Stone Age in Internet years), the Web graph was already so big as to defy imagination, and researchers were keenly interested in understanding its structure.[36] This section describes a famous study from that time that

---

[35]That is, the meta-graph of G^{rev} (Proposition 8.9) is simply the meta-graph of G with every edge reversed.

[36]Constructing this graph requires crawling (a big chunk of) the Web by repeatedly following hyperlinks, and this is a significant engineering feat in its own right.

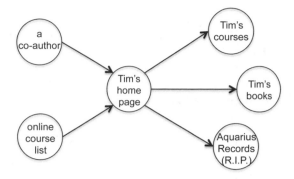

Figure 8.18: A minuscule piece of the Web graph.

explored the structure of the Web graph by computing its strongly connected components.[37] The graph had more than 200 million vertices and 1.5 billion edges, so linear-time algorithms were absolutely essential![38]

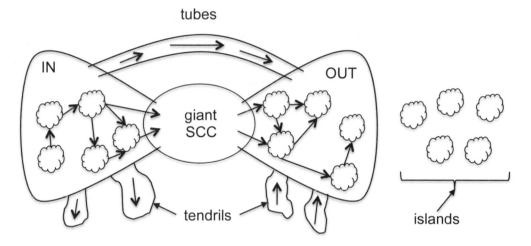

Figure 8.19: Visualizing the Web graph as a "bow tie." Roughly the same number of Web pages belong to the giant SCC, to IN, to OUT, and to the rest of the graph.

8.7.2   The Bow Tie

The Broder et al. study computed the strongly connected components of the Web graph, and explained its findings using the "bow tie" depicted in Figure 8.19. The knot of the bow tie is the biggest strongly connected component of the graph, comprising roughly 28% of its vertices. The title "giant" is well earned by this SCC, as the next-largest SCC was over two

---

[37]This study is described in the very readable paper "Graph Structure in the Web," by Andrei Broder, Ravi Kumar, Farzin Maghoul, Prabhakar Raghavan, Sridhar Rajagopalan, Raymie Stata, Andrew Tomkins, and Janet Wiener (*Computer Networks*, 2000). Google barely existed at this time, and the study used data from Web crawls by the search engine Alta Vista (which is now long since defunct).

[38]The study pre-dates modern massive data processing frameworks like MapReduce and Hadoop, and this was an intimidating input size at the time.

orders of magnitude smaller.[39] The giant SCC can be interpreted as the core of the Web, with every page reachable from every other page by a sequence of hyperlinks.

The smaller SCCs can be placed into a few categories. From some, it's possible to reach the giant SCC (but not vice versa); this is the left ("IN") part of the bow tie. For example, a newly created Web page with a link to some page in the giant SCC would appear in this part. Symmetrically, the "OUT" part is all the SCCs reachable from the giant SCC, but not vice versa. One example of an SCC in this part is a corporate Web site for which the company policy dictates that all hyperlinks from its pages stay within the site. There's also some other weird stuff: "tubes," which travel from IN to OUT, bypassing the giant SCC; "tendrils," which are reachable from IN or which can reach OUT (but not belonging to the giant SCC); and "islands" of Web pages that cannot reach or be reached from almost any other part of the Web.

8.7.3   Main Findings

Perhaps the most surprising finding of the study is that the giant SCC, the IN part, the OUT part, and the weird stuff all have roughly the same size (with ≈ 24–28% of the vertices each). Before this study, many people expected the giant SCC to be much bigger than only 28% of the Web. A second interesting finding is that the giant SCC is internally richly connected: It has roughly 56 million Web pages, but you typically need to follow fewer than 20 hyperlinks to get from one to another.[40] The rest of the Web graph is more poorly connected, with long paths often necessary to get from one vertex to another.

You'd be right to wonder whether any of these findings are an artifact of the now prehistoric snapshot of the Web graph that the experiment used. While the exact numbers have changed over time as the Web graph has grown and evolved, more recent follow-up studies re-evaluating the structure of the Web graph suggest that Broder et al.'s qualitative findings remain accurate.[41]

The Upshot

☆ Breadth-first search (BFS) explores a graph cautiously, in layers.

☆ BFS can be implemented in linear time using a queue data structure.

☆ BFS can be used to compute the lengths of shortest paths between a starting vertex and all other vertices in linear time.

☆ A connected component of an undirected graph is a maximal subset

---

[39]Remember that all it takes to collapse two SCCs into one is one edge in each direction. Intuitively, it would be pretty weird if two massive SCCs somehow avoided this.

[40]The presence of ubiquitous short paths is also known as the "small world property," which is closely related to the popular phrase "six degrees of separation."

[41]There continues to be lots of cool research about the Web graph and other information networks; for example, about how the Web graph evolves over time, on the dynamics of how information spreads through such a graph, and on how to identify "communities" or other meaningful fine-grained structure. Blazingly fast graph primitives play a crucial role in much of this research. For an introduction to these topics, check out the textbook *Networks, Crowds, and Markets: Reasoning About a Highly Connected World*, by David Easley and Jon Kleinberg (Cambridge University Press, 2010).

of vertices such that there is a path between each pair of its vertices.

☆ An efficient graph search algorithm like BFS can be used to compute the connected components of an undirected graph in linear time.

☆ Depth-first search (DFS) explores a graph aggressively, backtracking only when necessary.

☆ DFS can be implemented in linear time using a stack data structure (or recursion).

☆ A topological ordering of a directed graph assigns distinct numbers to the vertices, with every edge traveling from a smaller number to a bigger one.

☆ A directed graph has a topological ordering if and only if it is a directed acyclic graph.

☆ DFS can be used to compute a topological ordering of a directed acyclic graph in linear time.

☆ A strongly connected component of a directed graph is a maximal subset of vertices such that there is a directed path from any vertex in the set to any other vertex in the set.

☆ DFS can be used to compute the strongly connected components of a directed graph in linear time.

☆ In the Web graph, a giant strongly connected component contains roughly 28% of the vertices and is internally richly connected.

Test Your Understanding

Problem 8.1 *(S)* Which of the following statements hold? As usual, n and m denote the number of vertices and edges, respectively, of a graph. (Choose all that apply.)

a) Breadth-first search can be used to compute the connected components of an undirected graph in $O(m + n)$ time.

b) Breadth-first search can be used to compute the lengths of shortest paths from a starting vertex to every other vertex in $O(m + n)$ time, where "shortest" means having the fewest number of edges.

c) Depth-first search can be used to compute the strongly connected components of a directed graph in $O(m + n)$ time.

d) Depth-first search can be used to compute a topological ordering of a directed acyclic graph in $O(m + n)$ time.

Problem 8.2 *(S)* What is the running time of depth-first search, as a function of n and m (the number of vertices and edges), if the input graph is represented by an adjacency matrix (and NOT adjacency lists)? You may assume the graph does not have parallel edges.

a) $\Theta(m + n)$

b) $\Theta(m + n \log n)$

c) $\Theta(n^2)$

d) $\Theta(m \cdot n)$

Problem 8.3 *(S)* This problem explores the relationship between two definitions concerning graph distances. In this problem, we consider only graphs that are undirected and connected. The *diameter* of such a graph $G = (V, E)$ is the maximum, over all vertex pairs $v, w \in V$, of the shortest-path distance between v and w.[42] Next, for a vertex v, let $l(v)$ denote the maximum, over vertices $w \in V$, of the shortest-path distance between v and w. The *radius* of a graph is the minimum value of $l(v)$ over all choices of v.

Which of the following inequalities relating the radius r to the diameter d hold in every undirected connected graph? (Choose all that apply.)

a) $r \leq \frac{d}{2}$

b) $r \leq d$

c) $r \geq \frac{d}{2}$

d) $r \geq d$

Problem 8.4 *(H)* Suppose we change the code for BFS (Section 8.2.2) to use a stack data structure rather than a queue data structure, with a pop in line 4 and a push in line 8. (Unlike the iterative DFS implementation in Section 8.4.2, vertices are still checked for prior exploration before insertion into the data structure.) Show by example that this graph search algorithm is not equivalent to DFS or BFS.

Problem 8.5 *(S)* When does a directed graph have a unique topological ordering?

a) Whenever it is directed acyclic.

b) Whenever it has a unique cycle.

c) Whenever it contains a directed path that visits every vertex exactly once.

d) None of the other options are correct.

Problem 8.6 *(S)* Consider running the TopoSort algorithm (Section 8.5) on a directed graph G that is not directed acyclic. The algorithm will not compute a topological ordering (as none exist). Does it compute an ordering that minimizes the number of edges that travel backward (Figure 8.20)? (Choose all that apply.)

---

[42]Recall from Section 8.2.5 that the shortest-path distance between v and w is the fewest number of edges in a v-w path.

a) The `TopoSort` algorithm always computes an ordering of the vertices that minimizes the number of backward edges.

b) The `TopoSort` algorithm never computes an ordering of the vertices that minimizes the number of backward edges.

c) There are examples in which the `TopoSort` algorithm computes an ordering of the vertices that minimizes the number of backward edges, and also examples in which it doesn't.

d) The `TopoSort` algorithm computes an ordering of the vertices that minimizes the number of backward edges if and only if the input graph is a directed cycle.

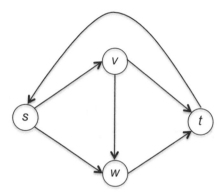

Figure 8.20: A graph with no topological ordering. In the ordering s, v, w, t, the only backward edge is (t, s).

Problem 8.7 *(S)* If you add one new edge to a directed graph G, the number of strongly connected components... (Choose all that apply.)

a) ...might or might not remain the same (depending on G and the new edge).

b) ...cannot decrease.

c) ...cannot increase.

d) ...cannot decrease by more than 1.

Problem 8.8 *(S)* Recall the `Kosaraju` algorithm from Section 8.6, which uses two passes of depth-first search to compute the strongly connected components of a directed graph. Which of the following statements are true? (Choose all that apply.)

a) The algorithm would remain correct if it used breadth-first search instead of depth-first search in both its passes.

b) The algorithm would remain correct if we used breadth-first search instead of depth-first search in its first pass.

c) The algorithm would remain correct if we used breadth-first search instead of depth-first search in its second pass.

d) The algorithm is not correct unless it uses depth-first search in both its passes.

Problem 8.9 *(S)* Recall that in the `Kosaraju` algorithm, the first pass of depth-first search operates on the reversed version of the input graph and the second on the original input graph. Which of the following statements are true? (Choose all that apply.)

a) The algorithm would remain correct if in the first pass it assigned vertex positions in increasing (rather than decreasing) order and in the second pass considered the vertices in decreasing (rather than increasing) order of vertex position.

b) The algorithm would remain correct if it used the original input graph in its first pass and used the reversed graph in its second pass.

c) The algorithm would remain correct if it used the original input graph in both passes, provided in the first pass it assigned vertex positions in increasing (rather than decreasing) order.

d) The algorithm would remain correct if it used the original input graph in both passes, provided in the second pass it considered the vertices in decreasing (rather than increasing) order of vertex position.

Challenge Problems

Problem 8.10 *(H)* An undirected graph $G = (V, E)$ is *bipartite* if its vertices V can be colored red and blue so that every edge has one red and one blue endpoint. For example, a cycle with an even number of vertices is bipartite, while one with an odd number of vertices is not (Figure 8.21). Propose an $O(m + n)$-time algorithm that determines whether or not a given graph is bipartite. (In this and the next problem, assume that the graph is represented using adjacency lists. As usual, n and m denote the number of vertices and edges, respectively.)

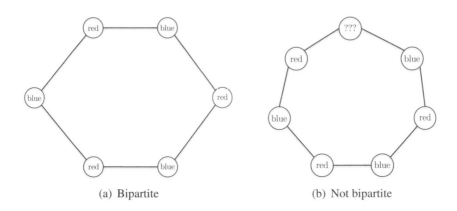

(a) Bipartite   (b) Not bipartite

Figure 8.21: Even cycles are bipartite graphs; odd cycles are not.

Problem 8.11 *(H)* The proofs of Lemma 8.7 and Theorem 8.6 suggest an $O(n^2)$-time algorithm for computing a topological ordering of a directed acyclic graph: populate an ordering from left to right through the successive extraction of source vertices. Propose an $O(m + n)$-time implementation of this idea.

Problem 8.12 *(H)* In the *2-SAT* problem, you are given a set of clauses, each of which is the disjunction (logical "or") of two literals. (A literal is a Boolean variable or the negation of a Boolean variable.) You would like to assign a value "true" or "false" to each of the variables so that all the clauses are satisfied, with at least one true literal in each clause. For example, if the input contains the three clauses $x_1 \lor x_2$, $\neg x_1 \lor x_3$, and $\neg x_2 \lor \neg x_3$, then one way to satisfy all of them is to set x_1 and x_3 to "true" and x_2 to "false."[43] Of the seven other possible truth assignments, exactly one satisfies all three clauses.

   Design an algorithm that determines whether or not a given 2-SAT instance has at least one satisfying assignment. (Your algorithm is responsible only for deciding whether or not a satisfying assignment exists; it need not exhibit such an assignment.) Your algorithm should run in $O(m + n)$ time, where m and n are the number of clauses and variables, respectively. (You can assume that the input is represented as an array of literals and an array of constraints, with pointers from each constraint to its literals and from each literal to the constraints that contain it.)

Programming Problems

Problem 8.13 Implement in your favorite programming language the `Kosaraju` algorithm from Section 8.6, and use it to compute the sizes of the five biggest strongly connected components of different directed graphs. You can implement the iterative version of depth-first search, the recursive version (though see footnote 20), or both. (See `www.algorithmsilluminated.org` for test cases and challenge data sets.)

---

[43]The symbol "$\lor$" stands for the logical "or" operation, while "$\neg$" denotes the negation of a Boolean variable.

Chapter 9

Dijkstra's Shortest-Path Algorithm

We've arrived at another one of computer science's greatest hits: Dijkstra's shortest-path algorithm.[1] This algorithm works in any directed graph with nonnegative edge lengths, and it computes the lengths of shortest paths from a starting vertex to all other vertices. After formally defining the problem and mentioning some applications (Section 9.1), we describe the algorithm (Section 9.2), its proof of correctness (Section 9.3), and a straightforward implementation (Section 9.4). In the next chapter, we'll see a blazingly fast implementation of the algorithm that takes advantage of the heap data structure. Chapter 18 describes algorithms for more general shortest path problems (with negative edge lengths, multiple starting vertices, or both).

9.1   The Single-Source Shortest Path Problem

9.1.1   Problem Definition

Dijkstra's algorithm solves the *single-source shortest path problem.*[2]

Problem: Single-Source Shortest Paths

Input: A directed graph $G = (V, E)$, a starting vertex $s \in V$, and a nonnegative *length* ℓ_e for each edge $e \in E$.

Output: $dist(s, v)$ for every vertex $v \in V$.

Recall that the term $dist(s, v)$ denotes the length of a shortest path from s to v. (If there is no path at all from s to v, $dist(s, v)$ is defined as $+\infty$.) By the *length* of a path, we mean the sum of the lengths of its edges. For instance, in a graph in which every edge has length 1, the length of a path is simply the number of edges in it. A *shortest* path from a vertex v to a vertex w is one with minimum length (among all v-w paths).

For example, if the graph represents a road network and the length of each edge represents the expected travel time from one end to the other, the single-source shortest path problem is the problem of computing driving times from an origin (the starting vertex) to all possible destinations.

---

[1]Discovered by Edsger W. Dijkstra in 1956 ("in about twenty minutes," he said in an interview many years later). Several other researchers independently discovered similar algorithms in the late 1950s.

[2]The term "source" in the name of the problem refers to the given starting vertex. We've already used the term "source vertex" to mean a vertex of a directed graph with no incoming edges (Section 8.5.2). To stay consistent with our terminology in Chapter 8, we'll stick with "starting vertex" in this chapter.

Quiz 9.1

Consider the following input to the single-source shortest path problem, with starting vertex s and with each edge labeled with its length:

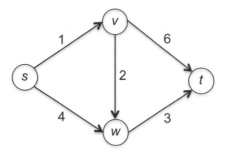

What are the shortest-path distances to s, v, w, and t, respectively?

    a) $0, 1, 2, 3$

    b) $0, 1, 3, 6$

    c) $0, 1, 4, 6$

    d) $0, 1, 4, 7$

(See Section 9.1.5 for the solution and discussion.)

9.1.2   Applications to Planning Problems

The single-source shortest path problem is obviously relevant for computing the best route through a physical network, such as a road or communication network. But the problem also shows up in disguise in applications that have nothing to do with physical networks. One recurring theme is planning problems—whenever you're confronted with a problem that boils down to computing a sequence of decisions, you should check if it's captured by the single-source shortest path problem.

When to Use a Single-Source Shortest-Path Algorithm

If your application requires the computation of a sequence of decisions, with every decision having its own independent cost, it may boil down to a single-source shortest-path computation.

For instance, the Sudoku-solving and robot-planning problems mentioned in Section 8.1.1 (page 154) fall in this category.

    For another example, imagine that you're taking a three-week course that has two different projects as deliverables. You can carry out each project whenever you want, although the time required decreases as the course proceeds and you acquire more skills and knowledge: 10 hours to complete a project during the first week, 8 during the second week, and 6 during the third week. You can even do both projects in the same week, but due to fatigue it will require an extra 3 hours to complete the second one. Naturally, your goal is to complete the course while spending as little time as possible.

You can probably guess the punchline: This problem is captured by the single-source shortest path problem! The shortest path from vertex v_{00} to vertex v_{32} in Figure 9.1(a) corresponds to the time-minimizing plan, namely completing one project in the second week and the other in the third. For the student with more endurance, requiring only 1 extra hour to complete two projects in the same week, the solution would be different: Procrastination would pay, as the time-minimizing strategy would then be to complete both projects in the final week (Figure 9.1(b)).[3]

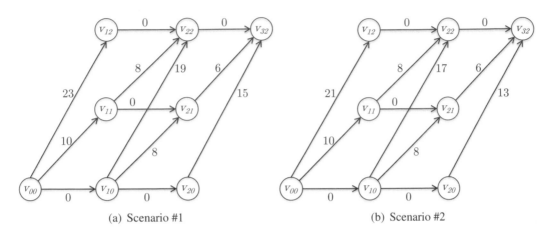

(a) Scenario #1   (b) Scenario #2

Figure 9.1: The problem of computing a time-minimizing plan for completing a course is captured by the single-source shortest path problem. A vertex v_{ij} represents the completion of exactly j projects over the first i weeks of the course. Each edge corresponds to moving forward one week in time while completing 0, 1, or 2 more projects; the edge's label indicates the amount of time (in hours) required. In (a), the shortest v_{00}-v_{32} path is $v_{00} \rightarrow v_{10} \rightarrow v_{21} \rightarrow v_{32}$. In (b), it is $v_{00} \rightarrow v_{10} \rightarrow v_{20} \rightarrow v_{32}$.

9.1.3   Some Assumptions

For concreteness, we assume throughout this chapter that the input graph is directed. Dijkstra's algorithm applies equally well to undirected graphs after small cosmetic changes (see Problem 9.7).

Our other assumption is significant, and the problem statement already spells it out:

Dijkstra's Algorithm: Key Assumption

The length of every edge is nonnegative.

In many applications, like computing driving directions, edge lengths are automatically nonnegative (barring a time machine) and there's nothing to worry about. But remember that paths in a graph can represent abstract sequences of decisions. For example, perhaps you

---

[3]For a similar but more sophisticated application of the single-source shortest path problem, see Problem 9.10.

want to compute a profitable sequence of financial transactions that involves both buying and selling. This problem corresponds to finding a shortest path in a graph with edge lengths that are both positive and negative. You should *not* use Dijkstra's algorithm in applications with negative edge lengths; see also Section 9.3.2 and Chapter 18.

9.1.4   Why Not Breadth-First Search?

We saw in Section 8.2 that one of the killer applications of breadth-first search is computing shortest-path distances from a starting vertex. Why do we need another shortest-path algorithm?

Remember that breadth-first search computes the minimum number of *edges* in a path from the starting vertex to every other vertex. This is the special case of the single-source shortest path problem in which every edge has length 1. We saw in Quiz 9.1 that, with general nonnegative edge lengths, a shortest path need not be a path with the fewest number of edges. Many applications of shortest paths, such as computing driving directions or a sequence of financial transactions, inevitably involve edges with different lengths.

But wait, you say; is the general problem really so different from this special case? Can't we think of an edge with a longer length ℓ as a path of ℓ edges that each have length 1?

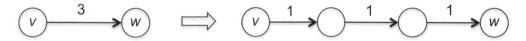

Indeed, there's no fundamental difference between an edge with a positive integer length ℓ and a path of ℓ length-1 edges. In principle, you can solve the single-source shortest path problem by expanding edges into paths of length-1 edges and applying breadth-first search to the expanded graph.

This transformation is an example of a *reduction* from one problem to another—in this case, from the single-source shortest path problem with positive integer edge lengths to the special case of the problem in which every edge has length 1.

The major problem with this reduction is that it blows up the size of the graph. The blowup is not too bad if all the edge lengths are small integers, but this is not always the case in applications. The length of an edge could even be much bigger than the number of vertices and edges in the original graph! Breadth-first search would run in time linear in the size of the expanded graph, but this is not necessarily close to linear time in the size of the original graph. Dijkstra's algorithm can be viewed as a slick simulation of breadth-first search on the expanded graph, while working only with the original input graph and running in near-linear time.

On Reductions

A problem A *reduces* to a problem B if an algorithm that solves B can be easily translated into one that solves A. For example, in Section 6.1 we saw that the problem of computing the median element of an array reduces to the problem of sorting the array. Reductions are one of the most important concepts in the study of algorithms and their limitations, and they can also have great practical utility.

> You should always be on the lookout for reductions. Whenever you encounter a seemingly new problem, always ask: Is the problem a disguised version of one you already know how to solve? Alternatively, can you reduce the general version of the problem to a special case?

9.1.5   Solution to Quiz 9.1

Correct answer: (b). No prizes for guessing that the shortest-path distance from s to itself is 0 and from s to v is 1. Vertex w is more interesting. One s-w path is the direct edge (s, w), which has length 4. But using more edges can decrease the total length: The path $s \to v \to w$ has length only $1 + 2 = 3$ and is the shortest s-w path. Similarly, each of the two-hop paths from s to t has length 7, while the zigzag path has length only $1 + 2 + 3 = 6$.

9.2   Dijkstra's Algorithm

9.2.1   Pseudocode

The high-level structure of Dijkstra's algorithm resembles that of our graph search algorithms.[4] Each iteration of its main loop processes one new vertex. The algorithm's sophistication lies in its clever rule for selecting which vertex to process next: the not-yet-processed vertex that appears to be closest to the starting vertex. The following elegant pseudocode makes this idea precise.

Dijkstra

Input: directed graph $G = (V, E)$ in adjacency-list representation, a vertex $s \in V$, a length $\ell_e \geq 0$ for each $e \in E$.
Postcondition: for every vertex v, the value $len(v)$ equals the true shortest-path distance $dist(s, v)$.

```
// Initialization
```
1 $X := \{s\}$
2 $len(s) := 0$, $len(v) := +\infty$ for every $v \neq s$
```
// Main loop
```
3 **while** there is an edge (v, w) with $v \in X, w \notin X$ **do**
4      $(a, b) :=$ such an edge minimizing $len(v) + \ell_{vw}$
5   add b to X
6      $len(b) := len(a) + \ell_{ab}$

The set X contains the vertices that the algorithm has already dealt with. Initially, X contains only the starting vertex (and, of course, $len(s) = 0$), and the set grows like a mold until it covers all the vertices reachable from s. The algorithm assigns a finite value to the len-value of a vertex at the same time it adds the vertex to X. Each iteration of the main loop augments X by one new vertex, the head of some edge (v, w) crossing from X

---

[4]When all the edges have length 1, it's equivalent to breadth-first search (as you should check).

to $V - X$ (Figure 9.2). (If there is no such edge, the algorithm halts, with $len(v) = +\infty$ for all $v \notin X$.) There can be many such edges; the `Dijkstra` algorithm chooses one (a, b) that minimizes the *Dijkstra score*, which is defined as

$$len(v) + \ell_{vw}. \tag{9.1}$$

Dijkstra scores are defined for the edges, not the vertices. A vertex $w \notin X$ may be the head of many different edges crossing from X to $V - X$, and these edges will typically have different Dijkstra scores.

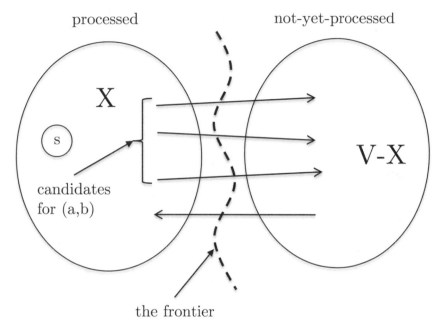

processed   not-yet-processed

X

s

candidates
for (a,b)

V-X

the frontier

Figure 9.2: Every iteration of Dijkstra's algorithm processes one new vertex, the head of an edge crossing from X to $V - X$.

You can associate the Dijkstra score for an edge (v, w) with $v \in X$ and $w \notin X$ with the hypothesis that the shortest path from s to w consists of a shortest path from s to v (which hopefully has length $len(v)$) with the edge (v, w) (which has length ℓ_{vw}) tacked on at the end. Thus, the `Dijkstra` algorithm chooses to add the as-yet-unprocessed vertex that appears closest to s, according to the already-computed shortest-path distances and the lengths of the edges crossing from X to $V - X$. While adding the chosen vertex b to X, the algorithm assigns $len(b)$ to the hypothesized shortest-path distance from s, which is the Dijkstra score $len(a) + \ell_{ab}$ of the edge (a, b). The magic of Dijkstra's algorithm, formalized in Theorem 9.1 below, is that this hypothesis is guaranteed to be correct, even if the algorithm has thus far looked at only a tiny fraction of the graph.[5]

---

[5]To compute the shortest paths themselves (and not merely their lengths), associate a pointer *predecessor*(v) with each vertex $v \in V$. When an edge (a, b) is chosen in an iteration of the main while loop (lines 4–6), assign *predecessor*(b) to a, the vertex responsible for b's selection. After the algorithm concludes, to reconstruct a shortest path from s to a vertex v, follow the *predecessor* pointers backward from v until you reach s.

9.2.2   An Example

Let's try out the `Dijkstra` algorithm on the example from Quiz 9.1, namely:

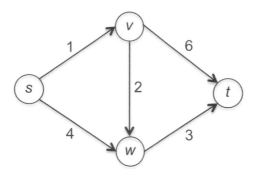

Initially, the set X contains only s, and $len(s) = 0$. In the first iteration of the main loop, there are two edges crossing from X to $V - X$ (and hence eligible to play the role of (a, b)), the edges (s, v) and (s, w). The Dijkstra scores (defined in (9.1)) for these two edges are $len(s) + \ell_{sv} = 0 + 1 = 1$ and $len(s) + \ell_{sw} = 0 + 4 = 4$. Because the former edge has the lower score, the algorithm adds its head v to X and assigns to $len(v)$ the Dijkstra score of the edge (s, v), which is 1. In the second iteration, with $X = \{s, v\}$, there are three edges to consider for the role of (a, b): (s, w), (v, w), and (v, t). Their Dijkstra scores are $0 + 4 = 4$, $1 + 2 = 3$, and $1 + 6 = 7$, respectively. Because (v, w) has the lowest Dijkstra score, w gets sucked into X and $len(w)$ is assigned the value 3 ((v, w)'s Dijkstra score). We already know which vertex gets added to X in the final iteration (the only not-yet-processed vertex t), but we still need to determine the edge that leads to its addition (to compute $len(t)$). As (v, t) and (w, t) have Dijkstra scores $1 + 6 = 7$ and $3 + 3 = 6$, respectively, $len(t)$ is set to the lower score of 6. The set X now contains all the vertices, so no edges cross from X to $V - X$ and the algorithm halts. The values $len(s) = 0$, $len(v) = 1$, $len(w) = 3$, and $len(t) = 6$ match the true shortest-path distances that we identified in Quiz 9.1.

Of course, the fact that an algorithm works correctly on a specific example does *not* imply that it is correct in general![6] In fact, the `Dijkstra` algorithm need *not* compute the correct shortest-path distances when edges can have negative lengths (Section 9.3.2). You should be initially skeptical of the `Dijkstra` algorithm and demand a proof that, at least in graphs with nonnegative edge lengths, it correctly solves the single-source shortest path problem.

*9.3   Why Is Dijkstra's Algorithm Correct?

9.3.1   A Bogus Reduction

You might be wondering why it matters whether or not edges have negative edge lengths. Can't we just force all the edge lengths to be nonnegative by adding a big number to every edge's length?

This is a great question—you should always be on the lookout for reductions to problems you already know how to solve. Alas, you cannot reduce the single-source shortest path

---

[6]Even a broken analog clock is correct two times a day…

problem with general edge lengths to the special case of nonnegative edge lengths in this way. The problem is that different paths from one vertex to another might not have the same number of edges. If we add some number to the length of each edge, then the lengths of different paths can increase by different amounts, and a shortest path in the new graph might be different than in the original graph. Here's a simple example:

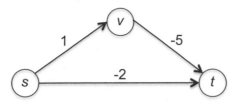

There are two paths from s to t: the direct path (which has length -2) and the two-hop path $s \rightarrow v \rightarrow t$ (which has length $1 + (-5) = -4$). The latter has the smaller (that is, more negative) length, and is the shortest s-t path.

To force the graph to have nonnegative edge lengths, we could add 5 to every edge's length:

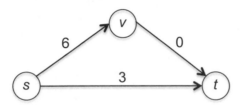

The shortest path from s to t has switched, and is now the direct s-t edge (which has length 3, better than the alternative of 6). Running a shortest-path algorithm on the transformed graph would not produce a correct answer for the original graph.

9.3.2   A Bad Example for the Dijkstra Algorithm

What happens if we try running the Dijkstra algorithm directly on a graph with some negative edge lengths, like the graph above? As always, initially $X = \{s\}$ and $len(s) = 0$, all of which is fine. In the first iteration of the main loop, however, the algorithm computes the Dijkstra scores of the edges (s, v) and (s, t), which are $len(s) + \ell_{sv} = 0 + 1 = 1$ and $len(s) + \ell_{st} = 0 + (-2) = -2$. The latter edge has the smaller score, and so the algorithm adds the vertex t to X and assigns to $len(t)$ the score -2. As we already noted, the actual shortest path from s to t (the path $s \rightarrow v \rightarrow t$) has length -4. We conclude that the Dijkstra algorithm need not compute the correct shortest-path distances in the presence of negative edge lengths.

9.3.3   Correctness with Nonnegative Edge Lengths

Proofs of correctness can feel pretty pedantic. That's why I often gloss over them for the algorithms for which readers tend to have strong and accurate intuition. Dijkstra's algorithm is different. First, the fact that it doesn't work on extremely simple graphs with negative edge lengths (Section 9.3.2) should make you nervous. Second, the Dijkstra score (9.1) might seem mysterious or even arbitrary—why is it so important? Because of these doubts, and because it is such a fundamental algorithm, we'll take the time to carefully prove its correctness (in graphs with nonnegative edge lengths).

Theorem 9.1 (Correctness of Dijkstra) *For every directed graph $G = (V, E)$, every starting vertex s, and every choice of nonnegative edge lengths, at the conclusion of the Dijkstra algorithm, $len(v) = dist(s, v)$ for every vertex $v \in V$.*

The plan is to justify the shortest-path distances computed by the Dijkstra algorithm one by one, by induction on the number of iterations of its main loop. Recall that proofs by induction follow a fairly rigid template, with the goal of establishing that an assertion $P(k)$ holds for every positive integer k (see also Appendix A). In the proof of Theorem 9.1, we will define $P(k)$ as the statement: "for the kth vertex v added to the set X in Dijkstra, $len(v) = dist(s, v)$."

On Reading Proofs

Mathematical arguments derive conclusions from assumptions. When reading a proof, always make sure you understand how each of the assumptions is used in the argument, and why the argument would break down in the absence of each assumption.

With this in mind, watch carefully for the role played in the proof of Theorem 9.1 by the two key assumptions: that edge lengths are nonnegative, and that the algorithm always chooses the edge with the smallest Dijkstra score. Any purported proof of Theorem 9.1 that fails to use both assumptions is automatically flawed.

Proof of Theorem 9.1

We proceed by induction, with $P(k)$ the assertion that the Dijkstra algorithm correctly computes the shortest-path distance of the kth vertex added to the set X. For the base case ($k = 1$), we know that the first vertex added to X is the starting vertex s. The Dijkstra algorithm assigns $len(s)$ to 0. Because every edge has a nonnegative length, the shortest path from s to itself is the empty path, with length 0. Thus, $len(s) = 0 = dist(s, s)$, which proves $P(1)$.

For the inductive step, choose $k > 1$ and assume that $P(1), P(2), \ldots, P(k-1)$ are all true—that $len(v) = dist(s, v)$ for the first $k - 1$ vertices v added to X. Let b denote the kth vertex added to X, and let (a, b) denote the edge chosen in the corresponding iteration (necessarily with a already in X). The algorithm assigns to $len(b)$ the Dijkstra score of this edge, which is $len(a) + \ell_{ab}$. We're hoping that this value is the same as the true shortest-path distance $dist(s, b)$, but is it?

We argue in two parts that it is. First, let's prove that the true distance $dist(s, b)$ cannot be larger than the algorithm's speculation $len(b)$ (that is, $dist(s, b) \leq len(b)$). Because a was already in X when the edge (a, b) was chosen, it was one of the first $k - 1$ vertices added to X. By the inductive hypothesis, the Dijkstra algorithm correctly computed a's shortest-path distance: $len(a) = dist(s, a)$. In particular, there is a path P from s to a with length exactly $len(a)$. Tacking the edge (a, b) on at the end of P produces a path P^* from s to b with length $len(a) + \ell_{ab} = len(b)$ (Figure 9.3). The length of a shortest s-b path is at most that of the candidate path P^*, so $dist(s, b)$ is at most $len(b)$.

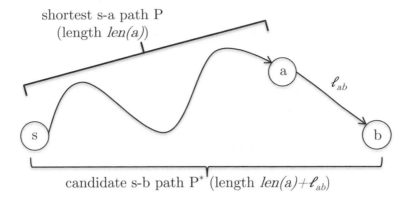

shortest s-a path P
(length *len(a)*)

a

ℓ_{ab}

s

b

candidate s-b path P* (length *len(a)+ℓ_{ab}*)

Figure 9.3: Tacking the edge (a, b) on at the end of a shortest s-a path P produces an s-b path P^* with length $len(a) + \ell_{ab}$.

Now for the reverse inequality, stating that $dist(s, b) \geq len(b)$ (and so $len(b) = dist(s, b)$, as desired). In other words, let's show that the path P^* in Figure 9.3 really is a shortest s-b path—that the length of every competing s-b path is at least $len(b)$.

Fix a competing s-b path Q. We know very little about Q. However, we *do* know that it originates at s and ends at b, and that s but not b belonged to the set X at the beginning of this iteration. Because it starts in X and ends outside X, the path Q crosses the frontier between X and $V - X$ at least once (Figure 9.4); let (y, z) denote the first edge of Q that crosses the frontier (with $y \in X$ and $z \notin X$).[7]

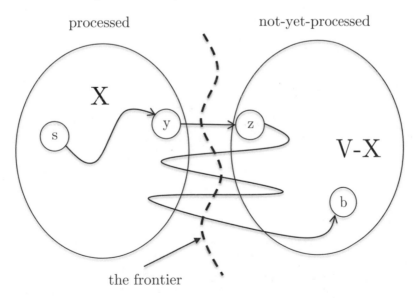

processed   not-yet-processed

X

s

y   z

V-X

b

the frontier

Figure 9.4: Every s-b path crosses at least once from X to $V - X$.

---

[7]No worries if $y = s$ or $z = b$—the argument works fine, as you should check.

To argue that the length of Q is at least $len(b)$, we consider its three pieces separately: the initial part of Q that travels from s to y, the edge (y, z), and the final part that travels from z to b. The first part can't be shorter than a shortest path from s to y, so its length is at least $dist(s, y)$. The length of the edge (y, z) is ℓ_{yz}. We don't know much about the final part of the path, which ambles among vertices that the algorithm hasn't looked at yet. But we do know—because all edge lengths are nonnegative!—that its total length is at least zero:

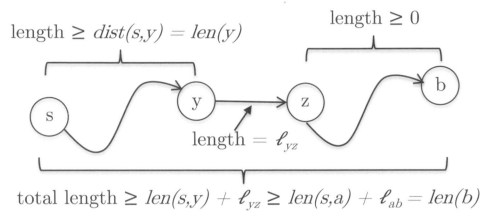

$$\text{total length} \geq len(s,y) + \ell_{yz} \geq len(s,a) + \ell_{ab} = len(b)$$

Combining our length lower bounds for the three parts of Q, we have

$$\text{length of } Q \geq \underbrace{dist(s, y)}_{\text{s-y subpath}} + \underbrace{\ell_{yz}}_{\text{edge } (y, z)} + \underbrace{0}_{\text{z-b subpath}} . \tag{9.2}$$

The last order of business is to connect our length lower bound in (9.2) to the Dijkstra scores that guide the algorithm's decisions. Because $y \in X$, it was one of the first $k - 1$ vertices added to X, and the inductive hypothesis implies that the algorithm correctly computed its shortest-path distance: $dist(s, y) = len(y)$. Thus, the inequality (9.2) translates to

$$\text{length of } Q \geq \underbrace{len(y) + \ell_{yz}}_{\text{Dijkstra score of edge } (y, z)} . \tag{9.3}$$

The right-hand side is exactly the Dijkstra score of the edge (y, z). Because the algorithm always chooses the edge with the smallest Dijkstra score, and because it chose (a, b) over (y, z) in this iteration, the former has an even smaller Dijkstra score: $len(a) + \ell_{ab} \leq len(y) + \ell_{yz}$. Plugging this inequality into (9.3) gives us what we want:

$$\text{length of } Q \geq \underbrace{len(a) + \ell_{ab}}_{\text{Dijkstra score of edge } (a, b)} = len(b).$$

This completes the second part of the inductive step, and we conclude that $len(v) = dist(s, v)$ for every vertex v that ever gets added to the set X.

For the final nail in the coffin, consider a vertex v that was never added to X. When the algorithm finished, $len(v) = +\infty$ and no edges crossed from X to $V - X$. This means no path exists from s to v in the input graph—such a path would have to cross the frontier at some point—and, hence, $dist(s, v) = +\infty$ as well. We conclude that the algorithm halts with $len(v) = dist(s, v)$ for every vertex v, whether or not v was ever added to X. This completes the proof! $\mathcal{QED}$

9.4   Implementation and Running Time

Dijkstra's shortest-path algorithm is reminiscent of our linear-time graph search algorithms in Chapter 8. A key reason why breadth- and depth-first search run in linear time (Theorems 8.2 and 8.5) is that they spend only a constant amount of time deciding which vertex to explore next (by removing the vertex from the front of a queue or stack). Alarmingly, every iteration of Dijkstra's algorithm must identify the edge crossing the frontier with the smallest Dijkstra score. Can we still implement the algorithm in linear time?

Quiz 9.2

Which of the following running times best describes a straightforward implementation of Dijkstra's algorithm for graphs in adjacency-list representation? As usual, n and m denote the number of vertices and edges, respectively.

a) $O(m + n)$

b) $O(m \log n)$

c) $O(n^2)$

d) $O(mn)$

(See below for the solution and discussion.)

Correct answer: (d). A straightforward implementation keeps track of which vertices are in X by associating a Boolean variable with each vertex. Each iteration, it performs an exhaustive search through all the edges, computes the Dijkstra score for each edge with tail in X and head outside X (in constant time per edge), and returns the crossing edge with the smallest score (or correctly identifies that no crossing edges exist). After at most $n - 1$ iterations, the Dijkstra algorithm runs out of new vertices to add to its set X. Because the number of iterations is $O(n)$ and each takes time $O(m)$, the overall running time is $O(mn)$.

Proposition 9.2 (Dijkstra Running Time (Straightforward)) *For every directed graph $G = (V, E)$, every starting vertex s, and every choice of nonnegative edge lengths, the straightforward implementation of the Dijkstra algorithm runs in $O(mn)$ time, where $m = |E|$ and $n = |V|$.*

The running time of the straightforward implementation is good but not great. It would work fine for graphs in which the number of vertices is in the hundreds or low thousands, but would choke on significantly larger graphs. Can we do better? The holy grail in algorithm design is a linear-time algorithm (or close to it), and this is what we want for the single-source shortest path problem. Such an algorithm could process graphs with millions of vertices on a commodity laptop.

We don't need a better *algorithm* to achieve a near-linear-time solution to the problem, only a better *implementation* of Dijkstra's algorithm. Data structures (queues and stacks) played a crucial role in our linear-time implementations of breadth- and depth-first search; analogously, Dijkstra's algorithm can be implemented in near-linear time with the assistance of the right data structure to facilitate the repeated minimum computations in its main loop. This data structure is called a *heap*, and it is the subject of the next chapter.

The Upshot

☆ In the single-source shortest path problem, the input consists of a graph, a starting vertex, and a length for each edge. The goal is to compute the length of a shortest path from the starting vertex to every other vertex.

☆ Dijkstra's algorithm processes vertices one by one, always choosing the not-yet-processed vertex that appears to be closest to the starting vertex.

☆ An inductive argument proves that Dijkstra's algorithm correctly solves the single-source shortest path problem whenever the input graph has only nonnegative edge lengths.

☆ Dijkstra's algorithm need not correctly solve the single-source shortest path problem when some edges of the input graph have negative lengths.

☆ A straightforward implementation of Dijkstra's algorithm runs in $O(mn)$ time, where m and n denote the number of edges and vertices of the input graph, respectively.

Test Your Understanding

Problem 9.1 *(H)* Consider a directed graph G with distinct and nonnegative edge lengths. Let s be a starting vertex and t a destination vertex, and assume that G has at least one s-t path. Which of the following statements are true? (Choose all that apply.)

   a) The shortest (meaning minimum-length) s-t path might have as many as $n - 1$ edges, where n is the number of vertices.

   b) There is a shortest s-t path with no repeated vertices (that is, with no loops).

   c) The shortest s-t path must include the minimum-length edge of G.

   d) The shortest s-t path must exclude the maximum-length edge of G.

Problem 9.2 *(S)* Consider a directed graph G with a starting vertex s, a destination t, and nonnegative edge lengths. Under what conditions is the shortest s-t path guaranteed to be unique?

   a) When all edge lengths are distinct positive integers.

   b) When all edge lengths are distinct powers of 2.

c) When all edge lengths are distinct positive integers and the graph G contains no directed cycles.

d) None of the other options are correct.

Problem 9.3 *(S)* Consider a directed graph G with nonnegative edge lengths and two distinct vertices, s and t. Let P denote a shortest path from s to t. If we add 10 to the length of every edge in the graph, then: (Choose all that apply.)

a) P definitely remains a shortest s-t path.

b) P definitely does not remain a shortest s-t path.

c) P might or might not remain a shortest s-t path (depending on the graph).

d) If P has only one edge, then P definitely remains a shortest s-t path.

Problem 9.4 *(S)* Consider a directed graph G and a starting vertex s with the following properties: no edges enter the starting vertex s; edges that leave s have arbitrary (possibly negative) lengths; and all other edge lengths are nonnegative. Does Dijkstra's algorithm correctly solve the single-source shortest path problem in this case? (Choose all that apply.)

a) Yes, for all such inputs.

b) Never, for no such inputs.

c) Maybe, maybe not (depending on the graph).

d) Only if we add the assumption that G contains no directed cycles with negative total length.

Problem 9.5 *(S)* Consider a directed graph $G = (V, E)$ and a starting vertex $s \in V$. Assume that at least one of G's edges e has a negative length $\ell_e < 0$, but that G does not contain a directed cycle $C \subseteq E$ for which the sum $\sum_{e \in C} \ell_e$ of its edges' lengths is negative. Suppose you run Dijkstra's algorithm on this input. Which of the following statements are true? (Choose all that apply.)

a) Dijkstra's algorithm might loop forever.

b) It's impossible to run Dijkstra's algorithm on a graph with negative edge lengths.

c) Dijkstra's algorithm always halts, but in some cases the shortest-path distances it computes will not all be correct.

d) Dijkstra's algorithm always halts, and in some cases the shortest-path distances it computes will all be correct.

Problem 9.6 *(H)* Continuing the previous problem, suppose now that the input graph $G = (V, E)$ does contain a negative cycle $C \subseteq E$ (with $\sum_{e \in C} \ell_e < 0$), and also a path from the starting vertex s to some vertex of this cycle. Suppose you run Dijkstra's algorithm on this input. Which of the following statements are true? (Choose all that apply.)

a) Dijkstra's algorithm might loop forever.

b) It's impossible to run Dijkstra's algorithm on a graph with a negative cycle.

c) Dijkstra's algorithm always halts, but in some cases the shortest-path distances it computes will not all be correct.

d) Dijkstra's algorithm always halts, and in some cases the shortest-path distances it computes will all be correct.

Problem 9.7 *(S)* Describe the changes to the pseudocode in Section 9.2.1 that are required to adapt the `Dijkstra` algorithm to undirected input graphs. How do these changes affect the proof of correctness in Section 9.3?

Challenge Problems

Problem 9.8 *(S)* Consider a directed graph $G = (V, E)$ with nonnegative edge lengths and a starting vertex s. Define the *bottleneck* of a path to be the maximum length of one of its edges (as opposed to the sum of the lengths of its edges). Show how to modify the `Dijkstra` algorithm to compute, for each vertex $v \in V$, the smallest bottleneck of any s-v path. Your algorithm should run in $O(mn)$ time, where m and n denote the number of edges and vertices, respectively.

Problem 9.9 *(H)* A^* *("A star") search* is a variant of Dijkstra's algorithm popular for search problems in artificial intelligence.[8],[9] Here, we assume that the input graph $G = (V, E)$ has, in addition to the usual starting vertex s and nonnegative edge length ℓ_e for each edge $e \in E$, a *goal vertex* t. The algorithm takes responsibility only for computing a shortest path from s to the specific destination t.

A^* search relies on a nonnegative *heuristic function* h, which for each vertex $v \in V$ should provide an easy-to-compute educated guess $h(v)$ for the length $dist(v, t)$ of a shortest v-t path. For example, when computing driving directions from a given origin s to a given destination t, the heuristic estimate $h(v)$ could be defined as the straight-line distance between v and t.

A^* search differs from Dijkstra's algorithm in two ways. First, it halts immediately after processing the goal vertex t. Second, the Dijkstra score of an edge (v, w) used in line 4 of the pseudocode (Section 9.2.1) is $len(v) + \ell_{vw} + h(w)$ rather than $len(v) + \ell_{vw}$. Thus, Dijkstra's algorithm (when stopped immediately after processing t) is the special case of A^* search in which h is the all-zero function.

(a) Propose an easy-to-compute heuristic function for the Sudoku-solving application mentioned in Section 8.1.1.

---

[8] The Sudoku-solving and robot-planning problems mentioned in Section 8.1.1 (page 154) are good examples of such problems.

[9] First proposed in the paper "A Formal Basis for the Heuristic Determination of Minimum Cost Paths," by Peter E. Hart, Nils J. Nilsson, and Bertram Raphael (*IEEE Transactions on Systems Science and Cybernetics*, 1968).

(b) Show that, without any further assumptions on the heuristic function h, A* search need not correctly compute the length of a shortest s-t path of G.

(c) Call a heuristic function h *admissible* if it never overestimates the remaining distance to t (that is, $h(v) \le dist(v, t)$ for every $v \in V$). Prove that, with an admissible heuristic function, A* search correctly computes the length of a shortest s-t path of G.

(d) For the problem of computing driving directions, is straight-line distance an admissible heuristic function? For Sudoku-solving, is your heuristic function from part (a) admissible?

(e) Suppose the input graph has multiple goal vertices, all equally acceptable, and the objective is to compute a shortest path from the starting vertex to some goal vertex. How would you extend A* search to this setting?

Problem 9.10 *(S)* You are given as input $2n + 1$ positive integers: n item values $x_1, x_2, \ldots, x_n$, n item costs $c_1, c_2, \ldots, c_n$, and a value target X. For example, perhaps the items represent job candidates, with values corresponding to productivity levels and costs to salaries. The goal is to compute a subset $S \subseteq \{1, 2, \ldots, n\}$ of items with the minimum-possible total cost $\sum_{i \in S} c_i$, subject to having total value $\sum_{i \in S} x_i$ at least X.[10] In our example, this corresponds to assembling the cheapest team that achieves a target overall productivity level.

Show how to solve this problem by computing single-source shortest paths in a suitably constructed directed graph with nonnegative edge lengths. The number of vertices and edges in your graph should be bounded above by a polynomial function of the number of items (n) and the target value (X).

Programming Problems

Problem 9.11 Implement in your favorite programming language the `Dijkstra` algorithm from Section 9.2, and use it to solve the single-source shortest path problem in different directed graphs. With the straightforward implementation in this chapter, what's the size of the largest problem you can solve in five minutes or less? (See www.algorithmsilluminated.org for test cases and challenge data sets.)

---

[10]This is a variant of a famous problem that we'll study at length in Chapter 16 and throughout Part IV, the *knapsack problem*.

Chapter 10

The Heap Data Structure

The remaining three chapters in this part of the book are about three of the most important and ubiquitous data structures out there—heaps, search trees, and hash tables. The goals are to learn the operations that these data structures support (along with their running times), to develop through example applications your intuition about which data structures are useful for which sorts of problems, and optionally, to learn a bit about how they are implemented under the hood.[1] We begin with *heaps*, a data structure that facilitates fast minimum or maximum computations.

10.1 Data Structures: An Overview

10.1.1 Choosing the Right Data Structure

Data structures are used in almost every major piece of software, so knowing when and how to use them is an essential skill for the serious programmer. The raison d'être of a data structure is to organize data so you can access it quickly and usefully. You've already seen a few examples. The *queue* data structure, used in our linear-time implementation of breadth-first search (Section 8.2), sequentially organizes data so that removing an object from the front or adding an object to the back takes constant time. The *stack* data structure, which was crucial in our iterative implementation of depth-first search (Section 8.4), lets you remove an object from or add an object to the front in constant time.

There are many more data structures out there—in this book, we'll see heaps, binary search trees, hash tables, bloom filters, and (in Part III) union-find. Why such a bewildering laundry list? Because *different data structures support different sets of operations, and are therefore suited for different types of programming tasks.* For example, breadth- and depth-first search have different needs, necessitating two different data structures. Our fast implementation of Dijkstra's shortest-path algorithm (in Section 10.4) has still different needs, requiring the more sophisticated heap data structure.

What are the pros and cons of different data structures, and how should you choose which one to use in a program? In general, the more operations a data structure supports, the slower the operations and the greater the space overhead. The following quote, widely attributed to Albert Einstein, is germane:

"Make things as simple as possible, but not simpler."

When implementing a program, it's important that you think carefully about exactly which operations you'll use over and over again. For example, do you care only about tracking

---

[1]Some programmers reserve the phrase *data structure* for a concrete implementation, and refer to the list of supported operations as an *abstract data type*.

which objects are stored in a data structure, or do you also want them ordered in a specific way? Once you understand your program's needs, you can follow the principle of parsimony and choose a data structure that supports all the desired operations and no superfluous ones.

Principle of Parsimony

Choose the simplest data structure that supports all the operations required by your application.

10.1.2   Taking It to the Next Level

What are your current and desired levels of expertise in data structures?

Level 0: "What's a data structure?"

Level 0 is total ignorance—someone who has never heard of a data structure and is unaware that cleverly organizing your data can dramatically improve a program's running time.

Level 1: "I hear good things about hash tables."

Level 1 is cocktail party-level awareness—at this level, you could at least have a conversation about basic data structures.[2] You've heard about a few data structures like search trees and hash tables, and are perhaps aware of some of their supported operations, but would be shaky trying to use them in a program or a technical interview.

Level 2: "This problem calls out for a heap."

With level 2, we're starting to get somewhere. This is someone who has solid literacy about basic data structures, is comfortable using them as a client in their own programs, and has a good sense of which data structures are appropriate for which types of programming tasks.

Level 3: "I use only data structures that I wrote myself."

Level 3, the most advanced level, is for hardcore programmers and computer scientists who are not content to merely use existing data structure implementations as a client. At this level, you have a detailed understanding of the guts of basic data structures, and exactly how they are implemented.

The biggest marginal empowerment comes from reaching level 2. Most programmers will, at some point, need to be educated clients of basic data structures like heaps, search trees, and hash tables. The primary goal of Chapters 10–12 is to bring you up to this level

---

[2]Speaking, as always, about sufficiently nerdy cocktail parties!

with these data structures, with a focus on the operations they support and their canonical applications. All of these data structures are readily available in the standard libraries of most modern programming languages, waiting to be deftly deployed in your own programs.

Advanced programmers do sometimes need to implement a customized version of one of these data structures from scratch. Each of Chapters 10–12 includes at least one advanced section on typical implementations of these data structures. These sections are for those of you wanting to up your game to level 3.

10.2 Supported Operations

A *heap* is a data structure that keeps track of an evolving set of objects with *keys* and can quickly identify the object with the smallest key.[3] For example, objects might correspond to employee records, with keys equal to their identification numbers. They might be the edges of a graph, with keys corresponding to edge lengths. Or they could correspond to events scheduled for the future, with each key indicating the time at which the event will occur.[4]

10.2.1   Insert and Extract-Min

The most important things to remember about any data structure are the operations it supports and the time required for each. The two most important operations supported by heaps are the INSERT and EXTRACTMIN operations.[5]

Heaps: Basic Operations

INSERT: given a heap H and a new object x, add x to H.

EXTRACTMIN: given a heap H, remove and return from H an object with the smallest key (or a pointer to it).

For example, if you invoke INSERT four times to add objects with keys 12, 7, 29, and 15 to an empty heap, the EXTRACTMIN operation will return the object with key 7. Keys need not be distinct; if there is more than one object in a heap with the smallest key, the EXTRACTMIN operation returns an arbitrary such object.

It would be easy to support only the INSERT operation, by repeatedly tacking on new objects to the end of an array or linked list (in constant time). The catch is that EXTRACTMIN would require a linear-time exhaustive search through all the objects. It's also clear how to support only EXTRACTMIN—sort the initial set of n objects by key once and for all up front (using $O(n \log n)$ preprocessing time), and then successive calls to EXTRACTMIN peel off objects from the beginning of the sorted list one by one (each in constant time). Here the catch is that any straightforward implementation of INSERT requires linear time (as you should check). The trick is to design a data structure that enables *both* operations to run super-quickly. This is exactly the raison d'être of heaps.

---

[3]Not to be confused with heap *memory*, the part of a program's memory reserved for dynamic allocation.

[4]Keys are often numerical but can belong to any totally ordered set—what matters is that for every pair of non-equal keys, one is less than the other.

[5]Data structures supporting these operations are also called *priority queues*.

Standard implementations of heaps, like the one outlined in Section 10.5, provide the following guarantee.

Theorem 10.1 (Running Time of Basic Heap Operations) *In a heap with n objects, the* INSERT *and* EXTRACTMIN *operations run in $O(\log n)$ time.*

As a bonus, in typical implementations, the constant hidden by the big-O notation is very small, and there is almost no extra space overhead.

There's also the "max-heap" variant that supports the INSERT and EXTRACTMAX operations in $O(\log n)$ time, where n is the number of objects. One way to implement this variant is to switch the direction of all the inequalities in the implementation in Section 10.5. A second way is to use a standard heap but negate the keys of objects before inserting them (which effectively transforms EXTRACTMIN into EXTRACTMAX). Neither variant of a heap supports both EXTRACTMIN and EXTRACTMAX simultaneously in $O(\log n)$ time—you have to pick which one you want.[6]

10.2.2   Additional Operations

Heaps can also support a number of less essential operations.

Heaps: Extra Operations

FINDMIN: given a heap H, return an object with the smallest key (or a pointer to it).

HEAPIFY: given an array with the objects $x_1, x_2, \ldots, x_n$, create a heap containing them.

DELETE: given a heap H and a pointer to an object x in H, delete x from H.

You could simulate a FINDMIN operation by invoking EXTRACTMIN and then applying INSERT to the result (in $O(\log n)$ time, by Theorem 10.1), but a typical heap implementation can avoid this circuitous solution and support FINDMIN directly in $O(1)$ time. You could implement HEAPIFY by inserting the n objects one by one into an empty heap (in $O(n \log n)$ total time, by Theorem 10.1), but there's a slick way to add n objects to an empty heap in a batch in total time $O(n)$ (see Problem 10.5). Finally, heaps can also support deletions of arbitrary objects—not just an object with the smallest key—in $O(\log n)$ time (see also Programming Project 10.9).

Theorem 10.2 (Running Time of Extra Heap Operations) *In a heap with n objects, the* FINDMIN, HEAPIFY, *and* DELETE *operations run in $O(1)$, $O(n)$, and $O(\log n)$ time, respectively.*

Summarizing, here's the final scorecard for heaps:

---

[6]If you want both, you can use one heap of each type (see also Section 10.3.3), or upgrade to a balanced binary search tree (see Chapter 11).

Operation	Running time
INSERT	$O(\log n)$
EXTRACTMIN	$O(\log n)$
FINDMIN	$O(1)$
HEAPIFY	$O(n)$
DELETE	$O(\log n)$

Table 10.1: Heaps: supported operations and their running times, where n denotes the current number of objects stored in the heap.

When to Use a Heap

If your application requires fast minimum (or maximum) computations on a dynamically changing set of objects, the heap is usually the data structure of choice.

10.3 Applications

The next order of business is to walk through several example applications and develop a feel for what heaps are good for. The common theme of these applications is the replacement of minimum computations, naively implemented using (linear-time) exhaustive search, with a sequence of (logarithmic-time) EXTRACTMIN operations from a heap. Whenever you see an algorithm or program with lots of linear-time minimum or maximum computations, a light bulb should go off in your head: *This algorithm calls out for a heap!*

10.3.1 Application: Sorting

For our first application, let's return to the mother of all computational problems, *sorting*.

Problem: Sorting

Input: An array of n numbers, in arbitrary order.

Output: An array of the same numbers, sorted from smallest to largest.

For example, given the input array

5	4	1	8	7	2	6	3

the desired output array is

1	2	3	4	5	6	7	8

Perhaps the simplest sorting algorithm is SelectionSort. This algorithm performs a linear scan through the input array to identify the minimum element, swaps it with the first element in the array, does a second scan over the remaining $n - 1$ elements to identify and swap into the second position the second-smallest element, and so on. Each scan takes time proportional to the number of remaining elements, so the overall running time is $\Theta(\sum_{i=1}^{n} i) = \Theta(n^2)$.[7] Because each iteration of SelectionSort computes a minimum element using exhaustive search, it calls out for a heap! The idea is simple: Insert all the elements in the input array into a heap, and populate the output array from left to right with successively extracted minimum elements. The first extraction produces the smallest element; the second the smallest remaining element (the second-smallest overall); and so on.

HeapSort

Input: array A of n distinct integers.
Output: array B with the same integers, sorted from smallest to largest.

$H :=$ empty heap
for $i := 1$ to n **do**
        INSERT $A[i]$ into H
for $i := 1$ to n **do**
        $B[i] :=$ EXTRACTMIN from H

Quiz 10.1

What's the running time of the HeapSort algorithm, as a function of the length n of the input array?

a) $O(n)$

b) $O(n \log n)$

c) $O(n^2)$

d) $O(n^2 \log n)$

(See below for the solution and discussion.)

Correct answer: (b). The work done by the HeapSort algorithm boils down to $2n$ operations on a heap containing at most n objects.[8] Because Theorem 10.1 guarantees that every heap operation requires $O(\log n)$ time, the overall running time is $O(n \log n)$.

---

[7]The sum $\sum_{i=1}^{n} i$ is at most n^2 (it has n terms, each at most n) and at least $n^2/4$ (it has $n/2$ terms that are all at least $n/2$).

[8]An even better implementation would replace the first loop with a single HEAPIFY operation, which runs in $O(n)$ time. The second loop still requires $O(n \log n)$ time, however.

Theorem 10.3 (Running Time of `HeapSort`) *For every input array of length $n \geq 1$, the running time of* `HeapSort` *is* $O(n \log n)$.

Let's take a step back and appreciate what just happened. We started with the least imaginative sorting algorithm possible, the quadratic-time `SelectionSort` algorithm. We recognized the pattern of repeated minimum computations, swapped in a heap data structure, and—boom!—out popped an $O(n \log n)$-time sorting algorithm.[9] This is a great running time for a sorting algorithm—it's even *optimal*, up to constant factors, among comparison-based sorting algorithms.[10] A neat byproduct of this observation is a proof that there's no comparison-based way to implement both the INSERT and EXTRACTMIN operations in better-than-logarithmic time: such a solution would yield a better-than-$O(n \log n)$-time comparison-based sorting algorithm, and we know this is impossible.

10.3.2 Application: Event Manager

Our second application, while a bit obvious, is both canonical and practical. Imagine you've been tasked with writing software that performs a simulation of the physical world. For example, perhaps you're contributing to a basketball video game. For the simulation, you must keep track of different events and when they should occur—the event that a player shoots the ball with a particular angle and velocity, that the ball consequently hits the back of the rim, that two players vie for the rebound at the same time, that one of these players commits an over-the-back foul on the other, and so on.

A simulation must repeatedly identify what happens next. This boils down to repeated minimum computations on the set of scheduled event times, so a light bulb should go off in your head: The problem calls out for a heap! If events are stored in a heap, with keys equal to their scheduled times, the EXTRACTMIN operation hands you the next event on a silver platter, in logarithmic time. New events can be inserted into the heap as they arise (again, in logarithmic time).

10.3.3 Application: Median Maintenance

For a less obvious application of heaps, let's consider the *median maintenance* problem. You are presented with a sequence of numbers, one by one; assume for simplicity that they are distinct. Each time you receive a new number, your responsibility is to reply with the median element of all the numbers you've seen thus far.[11] Thus, after seeing the first 11

---

[9]For clarity we described `HeapSort` using separate input and output arrays, but it can be implemented in place, with almost no additional memory. This in-place implementation is a super-practical algorithm, and is almost as fast as `QuickSort` in most applications.

[10]Recall from Section 5.6 that a *comparison-based* sorting algorithm accesses the input array only via comparisons between pairs of elements, and never directly accesses the value of an element. "General-purpose" sorting algorithms, which make no assumptions about the elements to be sorted, are necessarily comparison-based. Examples include `SelectionSort`, `InsertionSort`, `HeapSort`, and `QuickSort`. Non-examples include `BucketSort`, `CountingSort`, and `RadixSort`. Theorem 5.5 shows that no comparison-based sorting algorithm has a worst-case asymptotic running time better than $\Theta(n \log n)$.

[11]Recall from Chapter 6 that the *median* of a collection of numbers is its "middle element." In an array with odd length $2k - 1$, the median is the kth order statistic (that is, the kth-smallest element). In an array with even length $2k$, both the kth and $(k + 1)$th order statistics are considered median elements.

numbers, you should reply with the sixth-smallest one you've seen; after 12, the sixth- or seventh-smallest; after 13, the seventh-smallest; and so on.

One approach to the problem, which should seem like overkill, is to recompute the median from scratch in every iteration. We saw in Chapter 6 how to compute the median of a length-n array in $O(n)$ time, so this solution requires $O(i)$ time in each round i. Alternatively, we could keep the elements seen so far in a sorted array, so that it's easy to compute the median element in constant time. The drawback is that updating the sorted array when a new number arrives can require linear time. Can we do better?

Taking advantage of heaps, we can solve the median maintenance problem using only *logarithmic* time per round. I suggest putting the book down at this point and spending several minutes thinking about how this might be done.

The key idea is to maintain *two* heaps H_1 and H_2 while satisfying two invariants. The first invariant is that H_1 and H_2 are *balanced*, meaning they each contain the same number of elements (after an even round) or that one contains exactly one more element than the other (after an odd round). The second invariant is that H_1 and H_2 are *ordered*, meaning every element in H_1 is smaller than every element in H_2. For example, if the numbers so far have been $1, 2, 3, 4, 5$, then H_1 stores 1 and 2 and H_2 stores 4 and 5; the median element 3 is allowed to go in either one, as either the maximum element of H_1 or the minimum element of H_2. If we've seen $1, 2, 3, 4, 5, 6$, then the first three numbers are in H_1 and the second three are in H_2; both the maximum element of H_1 and the minimum element of H_2 are median elements. One twist: H_2 will be a standard heap, supporting INSERT and EXTRACTMIN, while H_1 will be the max-heap variant described in Section 10.2.1, supporting INSERT and EXTRACTMAX. This way, we can extract the median element with one heap operation, whether it's in H_1 or H_2.

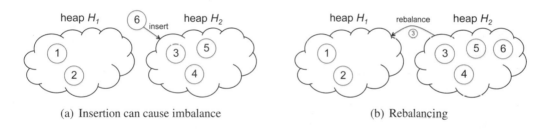

(a) Insertion can cause imbalance   (b) Rebalancing

Figure 10.1: When inserting a new element causes the heap H_2 to have two more elements than H_1, the smallest element in H_2 is extracted and re-inserted into H_1 to restore balance.

We still must explain how to update H_1 and H_2 each time a new element arrives so that they remain balanced and ordered. To figure out where to insert a new element x so that the heaps remain ordered, it's enough to compute the maximum element y in H_1 and the minimum element z in H_2.[12] If x is less than y, it must go in H_1; if it's more than z, it must go in H_2; if it's in between, it can go in either one. Do H_1 and H_2 stay balanced even after x is inserted? Yes, except for one case: In an even round $2k$, if x is inserted into the bigger heap (with k elements), this heap will contain $k + 1$ elements while the other contains only $k - 1$ elements (Figure 10.1(a)). But this imbalance is easy to fix: Extract the maximum or

---

[12]This can be done in logarithmic time by extracting and re-inserting these two elements. A better solution is to use the FINDMIN and FINDMAX operations, which run in constant time (see Section 10.2.2).

minimum element from H_1 or H_2, respectively (whichever contains more elements), and re-insert this element into the other heap (Figure 10.1(b)). The two heaps stay ordered (as you should check) and are now balanced as well. This solution uses a constant number of heap operations each round, for a running time of $O(\log i)$ in round i.

10.4 Speeding Up Dijkstra's Algorithm

Our final and most sophisticated application of heaps is a nearly linear-time implementation of Dijkstra's algorithm for the single-source shortest path problem (Chapter 9). This application vividly illustrates the beautiful interplay between the design of algorithms and the design of data structures.

10.4.1 Why Heaps?

We saw in Proposition 9.2 that the straightforward implementation of Dijkstra's algorithm requires $O(mn)$ time, where m is the number of edges and n is the number of vertices. This is fast enough to process medium-size graphs (with thousands of vertices and edges) but not big graphs (with millions of vertices and edges). Can we do better? Heaps enable a blazingly fast, near-linear-time implementation of Dijkstra's algorithm.

Theorem 10.4 (`Dijkstra` Running Time (Heap-Based)) *For every directed graph $G = (V, E)$, every starting vertex s, and every choice of nonnegative edge lengths, the heap-based implementation of `Dijkstra` runs in $O((m + n) \log n)$ time, where $m = |E|$ and $n = |V|$.*

This implementation of the algorithm is still not quite as fast as our linear-time graph search algorithms, but $O((m + n) \log n)$ is nevertheless a fantastic running time—comparable to our best sorting algorithms, and good enough to qualify as a for-free primitive.

Let's remember how Dijkstra's algorithm works (Section 9.2). The algorithm maintains a subset $X \subseteq V$ of vertices to which it has already computed shortest-path distances. In every iteration, it identifies the edge crossing the frontier (with tail in X and head in $V - X$) with the minimum Dijkstra score, where the Dijkstra score of such an edge (v, w) is the (already computed) shortest-path distance $len(v)$ from the starting vertex to v plus the length ℓ_{vw} of the edge. In other words, every iteration of the main loop performs a minimum computation, on the Dijkstra scores of the edges that cross the frontier. The straightforward implementation uses exhaustive search to carry out these minimum computations. As speeding up minimum computations from linear time to logarithmic time is the raison d'être of heaps, at this point a light bulb should go off in your head: Dijkstra's algorithm calls out for a heap!

10.4.2 The Plan

What objects should we store in a heap, and what should their keys be? Your first thought might be to store the edges of the input graph in a heap (with Dijkstra scores as keys), with an eye toward replacing the minimum computations (over edges) in the straightforward implementation with calls to EXTRACTMIN. This idea can be made to work, but the slicker and quicker implementation stores *vertices* in a heap. This might surprise you, as Dijkstra scores are defined for edges and not for vertices. On the flip side, we cared about edges'

Dijkstra scores only inasmuch as they guided us to the vertex to process next. Can we use a heap to cut to the chase and directly compute this vertex?

The concrete plan is to store the as-yet-unprocessed vertices ($V - X$ in the `Dijkstra` pseudocode) in a heap, while maintaining the following invariant.

Invariant

The key of a vertex $w \in V - X$ is the minimum Dijkstra score of an edge with tail $v \in X$ and head w, or $+\infty$ if no such edge exists.

That is, we want the equation

$$key(w) = \min_{(v,w)\in E \,:\, v\in X} \underbrace{len(v) + \ell_{vw}}_{\text{Dijkstra score}} \qquad (10.1)$$

to hold at all times for every $w \in V - X$, where $len(v)$ denotes the shortest-path distance to v computed in an earlier iteration of the algorithm (Figure 10.2).

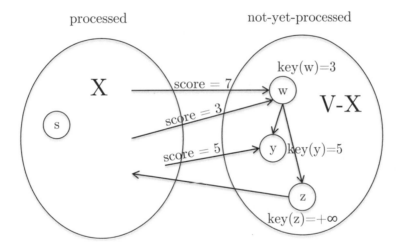

Figure 10.2: The key of a vertex $w \in V - X$ is defined as the minimum Dijkstra score of an edge with head w and tail in X.

What's going on? Imagine that we use a two-round knockout tournament to identify the edge (v, w) with $v \in X$ and $w \notin X$ with the minimum Dijkstra score. The first round comprises a local tournament for each vertex $w \in V - X$, in which the participants are the edges (v, w) with $v \in X$ and head w, and the first-round winner is the participant with the smallest Dijkstra score (if any). The first-round winners (at most one per vertex $w \in V - X$) proceed to the second round, and the final champion is the first-round winner with the lowest Dijkstra score. This champion is the same edge that would be identified by exhaustive search.

The value of the key (10.1) of a vertex $w \in V - X$ is exactly the winning Dijkstra score in the local tournament at w, so our invariant effectively implements all the first-round competitions. Extracting the vertex with the minimum key then implements the second round of the tournament, and returns on a silver platter the next vertex to process, namely the head of the crossing edge with the smallest Dijkstra score. The point is, as long as we maintain our invariant, we can implement each iteration of Dijkstra's algorithm with a single heap operation.

The pseudocode looks like this:[13]

Dijkstra (Heap-Based, Part 1)

Input: directed graph $G = (V, E)$ in adjacency-list representation, a vertex $s \in V$, a length $\ell_e \geq 0$ for each $e \in E$.
Postcondition: for every vertex v, the value $len(v)$ equals the true shortest-path distance $dist(s, v)$.

```
// Initialization
```
1 $X :=$ empty set, $H :=$ empty heap
2 $key(s) := 0$
3 **for** every $v \neq s$ **do**
4      $key(v) := +\infty$
5 **for** every $v \in V$ **do**
6   INSERT v into H // or use HEAPIFY
   `// Main loop`
7 **while** H is non-empty **do**
8      $w :=$ EXTRACTMIN(H)
9   add w to X
10     $len(w) := key(w)$
       `// update heap to maintain invariant`
11   (to be announced)

But how much work is it to maintain the invariant?

10.4.3 Maintaining the Invariant

Now it's time to pay the piper. We enjoyed the fruits of our invariant, which reduces each minimum computation required by Dijkstra's algorithm to a single heap operation. In exchange, we must show how to maintain it without excessive work.

Each iteration of the algorithm moves one vertex w from $V - X$ to X, which changes the frontier (Figure 10.3). Edges from vertices in X to w get sucked into X and no longer cross the frontier. More problematically, edges from w to other vertices of $V - X$ no longer reside entirely in $V - X$ and instead cross from X to $V - X$. Why is this a problem? Because our invariant (10.1) insists that, for every vertex $y \in V - X$, y's key equals the smallest Dijkstra score of a crossing edge ending at y. New crossing edges mean new candidates for the smallest Dijkstra score, so the right-hand side of the invariant (10.1) might decrease for some vertices y. For example, the first time a vertex w with an outgoing edge to y gets

---

[13]Initializing the set X of processed vertices to the empty set rather than to the starting vertex leads to cleaner pseudocode (cf., Section 9.2.1). The first iteration of the main loop is guaranteed to extract the starting vertex (do you see why?), which is then the first vertex added to X.

sucked into the set X, this expression for y drops from $+\infty$ to a finite number (specifically, to $len(w) + \ell_{wy}$).

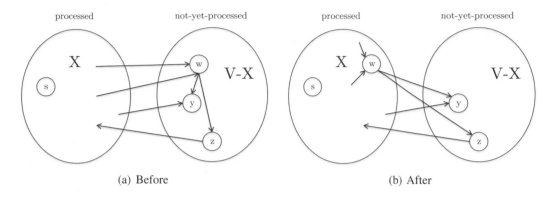

(a) Before   (b) After

Figure 10.3: When a new vertex w is moved from $V - X$ to X, edges going out of w can become crossing edges.

Every time we extract a vertex w from the heap, moving it from $V - X$ to X, we might need to decrease the key of some of the vertices remaining in $V - X$ to reflect the new crossing edges. Because all the new crossing edges emanate from w, we only need to iterate through w's list of outgoing edges and check the vertices $y \in V - X$ with an edge (w, y).[14] For each such vertex y, there are two candidates for the first-round winner in y's local tournament: either it is the same as before, or it is the new entrant (w, y). Thus, the new value of y's key should be either its old value or the Dijkstra score $len(w) + \ell_{wy}$ of the new crossing edge, whichever is smaller.

How can we decrease the key of an object in a heap? One easy way is to first remove it, using the DELETE operation described in Section 10.2.2, update its key, and then use INSERT to add it back into the heap.[15] This completes the heap-based implementation of the `Dijkstra` algorithm.

`Dijkstra` (Heap-Based, Part 2)

```
        // update heap to maintain invariant
11      for every edge (w, y) with y ∈ V − X do
12          DELETE y from H
13          key(y) := min{key(y), len(w) + ℓwy}
14          INSERT y into H
```

10.4.4   Running Time

Almost all the work performed by the heap-based implementation of the `Dijkstra` algorithm consists of heap operations (as you should check). Each of these operations

---

[14]This step is facilitated by the adjacency-list representation of the input graph.

[15]Some heap implementations export a DECREASEKEY operation, running in $O(\log n)$ time for an n-object heap. In this case, only one heap operation is needed.

takes $O(\log n)$ time, where n is the number of vertices. (The heap never contains more than n objects.)

How many heap operations does the algorithm perform? There are n operations in each of lines 6 and 8. What about in lines 12 and 14?

Quiz 10.2

How many times does `Dijkstra` execute lines 12 and 14? Select the smallest bound that applies. (As usual, n and m denote the number of vertices and edges, respectively.)

    a) $O(n)$

    b) $O(m)$

    c) $O(n^2)$

    d) $O(mn)$

(See below for the solution and discussion.)

Correct answer: (b). Lines 12 and 14 may look a little scary. In one iteration of the main loop, these two lines might be performed as many as $n - 1$ times—once per outgoing edge of w. There are n iterations, which seems to lead to a quadratic number of heap operations. This bound is accurate for dense graphs, but in general, we can do better. The reason? Let's assign responsibility for these heap operations to *edges* rather than vertices. Each edge (v, w) of the graph makes at most one appearance in line 11—when v is first extracted from the heap and moved from $V - X$ to X.[16] Thus, lines 12 and 14 are each performed at most once per edge, for a total of $2m$ operations, where m is the number of edges.

Quiz 10.2 shows that the heap-based implementation of the `Dijkstra` algorithm uses $O(m + n)$ heap operations, each taking $O(\log n)$ time. The overall running time is $O((m + n) \log n)$, as promised by Theorem 10.4. $\mathcal{QED}$

*10.5 Implementation Details

Let's take your understanding of heaps to the next level by describing how you would implement one from scratch. We'll focus on the two basic operations—INSERT and EXTRACTMIN—and how to ensure that both run in logarithmic time.

10.5.1 Heaps as Trees

There are two ways to visualize objects in a heap, as a tree (better for pictures and exposition) or as an array (better for an implementation). Let's start with trees.

A heap can be viewed as a complete rooted binary tree—every node has 0, 1, or 2 children, and every level is as packed as possible. When the number of objects stored is one

---

[16]If w is extracted before v, the edge (v, w) never makes an appearance.

less than a power of 2, every level is fully packed (Figures 10.4(a) and 10.4(b)). When the number of objects is between two such numbers, all levels are fully packed except the last, which is populated from left to right (Figure 10.4(c)).[17]

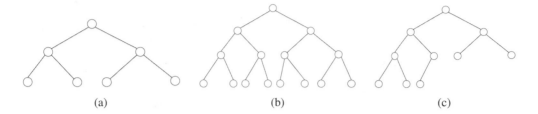

(a)   (b)   (c)

Figure 10.4: Complete binary trees with 7, 15, and 10 nodes.

A heap manages objects associated with keys and ensures that the following *heap property* holds.

The Heap Property

For every object x, the key of x is less than or equal to the keys of its children.

Duplicate keys are allowed. For example, here's a valid heap containing nine objects, including some with duplicate keys:[18]

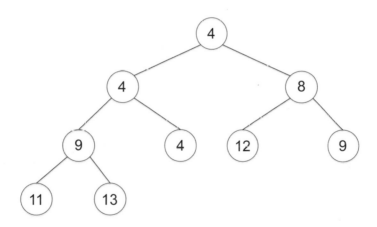

For every parent-child pair, the parent's key is at most that of the child.[19]

There's more than one way to arrange objects so that the heap property holds. Here's another heap, with the same set of keys:

---

[17]For some reason, computer scientists seem to think that trees grow downward.

[18]When we draw a heap, we show only the objects' keys. Don't forget that what a heap really stores is objects (or pointers to objects). Each object is associated with a key and possibly lots of other data.

[19]Applying the heap property iteratively to an object's children, its children's children, and so on shows that the key of each object is less than or equal to those of *all* of its direct descendants. The example above illustrates that the heap property implies nothing about the relative order of keys in different subtrees—just like in real family trees!

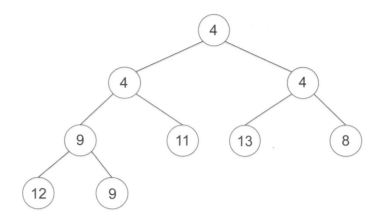

Both heaps have a "4" at the root, which is also (tied for) the smallest of all the keys. This is not an accident: because keys stay the same or decrease as you traverse a heap upward, the root's key is as small as it gets. This should sound encouraging, given that the raison d'être of a heap is fast minimum computations.

10.5.2   Heaps as Arrays

In our minds we visualize a heap as a tree, but in an implementation we use an array with length equal to the maximum number of objects we expect to store. The first element of the array corresponds to the tree's root, the next two elements to the next level of the tree (in the same order), and so on (Figure 10.5).

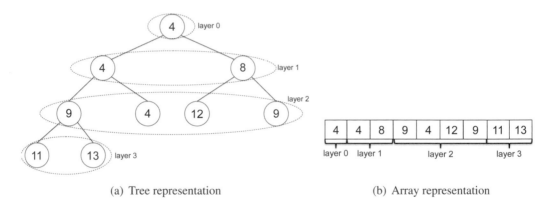

(a) Tree representation   (b) Array representation

Figure 10.5: Mapping the tree representation of a heap to its array representation.

Parent-child relationships in the tree translate nicely to the array (Table 10.2). Assuming the array positions are labeled $1, 2, \ldots, n$, where n is the number of objects, the children of the object in position i correspond to the objects in positions $2i$ and $2i + 1$ (if any). For example, in Figure 10.5, the children of the root (in position 1) are the next two objects (in positions 2 and 3), the children of the 8 (in position 3) are the objects in positions 6 and 7, and so on. Going in reverse, for a non-root object (in position $i \geq 2$), i's parent is the object in position $\lfloor i/2 \rfloor$ (i.e., $i/2$ rounded down to the nearest integer). For example, in Figure 10.5, the parent of the last object (in position 9) is the object in position $\lfloor 9/2 \rfloor = 4$.

Position of parent	$\lfloor i/2 \rfloor$ (provided $i \geq 2$)
Position of left child	$2i$ (provided $2i \leq n$)
Position of right child	$2i + 1$ (provided $2i + 1 \leq n$)

Table 10.2: Relationships between the position $i \in \{1, 2, 3, \ldots, n\}$ of an object in a heap and the positions of its parent, left child, and right child, where n denotes the number of objects in the heap.

There are such simple formulas to go from a child to its parent and back because we use only complete binary trees.[20] There is no need to explicitly store the tree; consequently, the heap data structure has minimal space overhead.[21]

10.5.3   Implementing INSERT in $O(\log n)$ Time

We'll illustrate the implementation of both the INSERT and EXTRACTMIN operations by example rather than by pseudocode.[22] The challenge is to both keep the tree complete and maintain the heap property after an object is added or removed. We'll follow the same blueprint for both operations:

1. Keep the tree complete in the most obvious way possible.

2. Play whack-a-mole to systematically squash any violations of the heap property.

Specifically, recall the INSERT operation:

given a heap H and a new object x, add x to H.

After x's addition to H, H should still correspond to a complete binary tree (with one more node than before) that satisfies the heap property. The operation should take $O(\log n)$ time, where n is the number of objects in the heap.

Let's start with our running example:

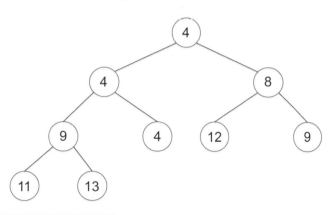

---

[20] As a bonus, in low-level languages it's possible to multiply or divide by 2 ridiculously quickly, using bit-shifting tricks.

[21] By contrast, search trees (Chapter 11) need not be complete and therefore require additional space to store explicit pointers from each node to its children.

[22] We'll keep drawing heaps as trees, but don't forget that they're stored as arrays. When we talk about going from a node to a child or its parent, we mean by applying the simple index formulas in Table 10.2.

When a new object is inserted, the most obvious way to keep the tree complete is to tack the new object on to the end of the array, or equivalently to the last level of the tree. (If the last level is already packed full, the object becomes the first at a new level.) As long as the implementation keeps track of the number n of objects (which is easy to do), this step takes constant time. For example, if we insert an object with key 7 into our running example, we obtain:

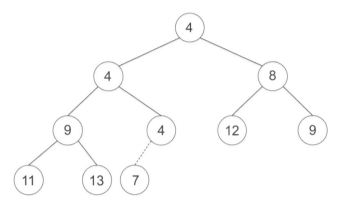

We have a complete binary tree, but does the heap property hold? There's only one place it might fail—the one new parent-child pair (the 4 and the 7). In this case we got lucky, and the new pair doesn't violate the heap property. If our next insertion is an object with key 10, then again we get lucky and immediately obtain a valid heap:

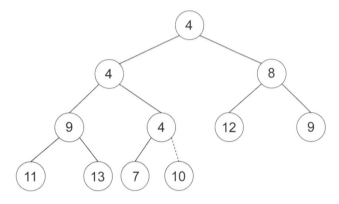

But suppose we now insert an object with key 5. After tacking it on at the end, our tree is:

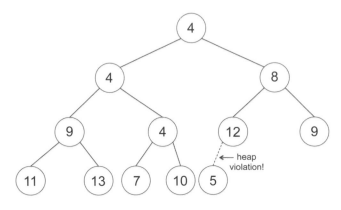

Now we have a problem: The new parent-child pair (the 12 and the 5) violates the heap property. What can we do about it? We can at least fix the problem locally by swapping the two nodes in the violating pair:

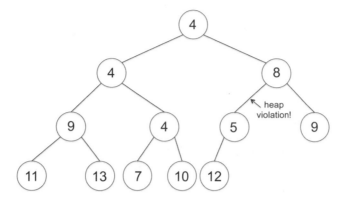

This fixes the violating parent-child pair. We're not out of the woods yet, however, as the heap violation has migrated upward to the 8 and the 5. So we do it again, and swap the nodes in the violating pair to obtain:

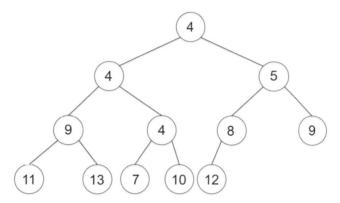

This explicitly fixes the violating pair. We've seen that such a swap has the potential to push the violation of the heap property upward, but here it doesn't happen—the 4 and 5 are already in the correct order. You might worry that a swap could also push the violation downward. But this also doesn't happen—the 8 and 12 are already in the correct order. With the heap property restored, the insertion is complete.

    In general, the INSERT operation tacks the new object on to the end of the heap, and repeatedly swaps the nodes of a violating pair.[23] At all times, there is at most one violating parent-child pair—the pair in which the new object is the child.[24] Each swap pushes the violating parent-child pair up one level in the tree. This process cannot go on forever—if the

---

[23]This swapping subroutine goes by a number of names, including `Bubble-Up`, `Sift-Up`, `Heapify-Up`, and more.

[24]At no point are there any heap violations between the new object and its children. It has no children initially, and after a swap its children comprise the node it replaced (which has a larger key, as otherwise we wouldn't have swapped) and a previous child of that node (which, by the heap property, must have the same or a still larger key). Every parent-child pair that does not involve the new object appeared in the original heap, and hence does not violate the heap property. For instance, after the two swaps in our example, the 8 and 12 are once again in a parent-child relationship, just like in the original heap.

new object makes it to the root, it has no parent and there can be no violating parent-child pair.

INSERT

1. Stick the new object at the end of the heap and increment the heap size.

2. Repeatedly swap the new object with its parent until the heap property is restored.

Because a heap is a complete binary tree, it has $\approx \log_2 n$ levels, where n is the number of objects in the heap. The number of swaps is at most the number of levels, and only a constant amount of work is required per swap. We conclude that the worst-case running time of the INSERT operation is $O(\log n)$, as desired.

10.5.4   Implementing EXTRACTMIN in $O(\log n)$ Time

Recall the EXTRACTMIN operation:

> given a heap H, remove and return from H an object with the smallest key.

The output of the operation will be the object at the root of the heap; by the heap property, it is guaranteed to be an object with the smallest key. The implementation challenge is to restore both the complete binary tree property and the heap property after ripping out the heap's root.

We again keep the tree complete in the most obvious way possible. Like INSERT in reverse, we know that the last object of the tree must wind up in an earlier position. But where should it go? Because we're extracting the root anyway, let's overwrite the old root node with what used to be the last node. For example, starting from the heap

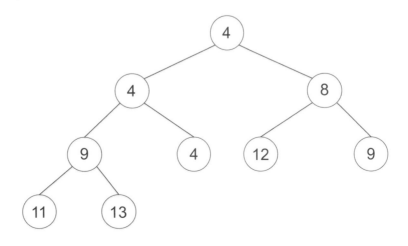

the resulting tree looks like

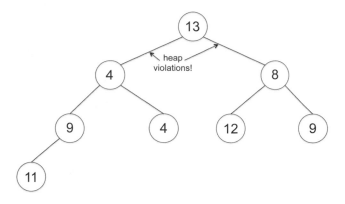

The good news is that we've restored the complete binary tree property. The bad news is that the massive promotion granted to the object with key 13 has created two violating parent-child pairs (the 13 and 4 and the 13 and 8). Do we need two swaps to correct them?

The key idea is to swap the root node with the *smaller* of its two children:

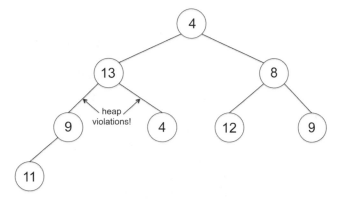

There are no longer any heap violations involving the root—the new root node is smaller than both the node it replaced (that's why we swapped) and its other child (as we swapped the smaller child).[25] The heap violations migrate downward, again involving the object with key 13 and its two (new) children. So we do it again, and swap the 13 with its smaller child:

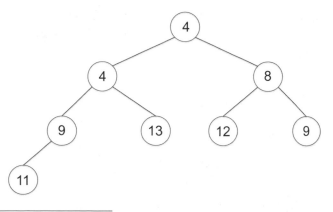

---

[25] Swapping the 13 with the 8 would fail to vaccinate the left subtree from heap violations (with violating pair 8 and 4) while allowing the disease to spread to the right subtree (with violating pairs 13 and 12, and 13 and 9).

The heap property is restored at last, and now the extraction is complete.

In general, the EXTRACTMIN operation moves the last object of a heap to the root node (by overwriting the previous root), and repeatedly swaps this object with its smaller child.[26] At all times, there are at most two violating parent-child pairs—the two pairs in which the formerly-last object is the parent.[27] Because each swap pushes this object down one level in the tree, this process cannot go on forever—it stops once the new object belongs to the last level, if not earlier.

EXTRACTMIN

1. Overwrite the object r at the root (after saving a local copy) with the last object x in the heap and decrement the heap size.

2. Repeatedly swap x with its smaller child until the heap property is restored.

3. Return the original root object r.

The number of swaps is at most the number of levels, and only a constant amount of work is required per swap. Because there are $\approx \log_2 n$ levels, we conclude that the worst-case running time of the EXTRACTMIN operation is $O(\log n)$, where n is the number of objects in the heap.

The Upshot

☆ There are many different data structures, each optimized for a different set of operations.

☆ The principle of parsimony recommends choosing the simplest data structure that supports all the operations required by your application.

☆ If your application requires fast minimum (or maximum) computations on an evolving set of objects, the heap is usually the data structure of choice.

☆ The two most important heap operations, INSERT and EXTRACT-MIN, run in $O(\log n)$ time, where n is the number of objects.

☆ Heaps also support FINDMIN in $O(1)$ time, DELETE in $O(\log n)$ time, and HEAPIFY in $O(n)$ time.

☆ The HeapSort algorithm uses a heap to sort a length-n array in $O(n \log n)$ time.

☆ Heaps can be used to implement Dijkstra's shortest-path algorithm in $O((m + n) \log n)$ time, where m and n denote the number of

---

[26]This swapping subroutine is called, among other things, Bubble-Down.

[27]Every parent-child pair that does not involve this formerly-last object appeared in the original heap, and hence does not violate the heap property. There is also no violation involving this object and its parent—initially it had no parent, and subsequently it is swapped downward with objects that have smaller keys.

edges and vertices of the graph, respectively.

☆ Heaps can be visualized as complete binary trees but are implemented as arrays.

☆ The heap property states that the key of every object is less than or equal to the keys of its children.

☆ The INSERT and EXTRACTMIN operations are implemented by keeping the tree complete in the most obvious way possible and systematically squashing any violations of the heap property.

Test Your Understanding

Problem 10.1 *(S)* Which of the following patterns in a computer program suggest that a heap data structure could provide a significant speed-up? (Check all that apply.)

a) Repeated lookups.

b) Repeated minimum computations.

c) Repeated maximum computations.

d) None of the other options.

Problem 10.2 *(S)* Suppose you implement the functionality of a priority queue (that is, the INSERT and EXTRACTMIN operations) using an array sorted from largest to smallest. What is the worst-case running time of INSERT and EXTRACTMIN, respectively? Assume you have a large enough array to accommodate all your insertions.

a) $\Theta(1)$ and $\Theta(n)$

b) $\Theta(n)$ and $\Theta(1)$

c) $\Theta(\log n)$ and $\Theta(1)$

d) $\Theta(n)$ and $\Theta(n)$

Problem 10.3 *(S)* Suppose you implement the functionality of a priority queue (that is, the INSERT and EXTRACTMIN operations) using an *unsorted* array. What is the worst-case running time of INSERT and EXTRACTMIN, respectively? Assume you have a large enough array to accommodate all your insertions.

a) $\Theta(1)$ and $\Theta(n)$

b) $\Theta(n)$ and $\Theta(1)$

c) $\Theta(1)$ and $\Theta(\log n)$

d) $\Theta(n)$ and $\Theta(n)$

Problem 10.4 *(S)* You are given a heap with n objects. Which of the following tasks can you solve using $O(1)$ INSERT and EXTRACTMIN operations and $O(1)$ additional work? (Choose all that apply.)

a) Find the object stored in the heap with the fifth-smallest key.

b) Find the object stored in the heap with the maximum key.

c) Find the object stored in the heap with the median key.

d) None of the above.

Challenge Problems

Problem 10.5 *(H)* Propose an $O(n)$-time implementation of the HEAPIFY operation (page 217), where n is the number of objects in the input array.

Problem 10.6 *(S)* Continuing Problem 9.8, show how to modify the heap-based implementation of Dijkstra's algorithm (Section 10.4) to compute, for each vertex $v \in V$, the smallest bottleneck of an s-v path. Your algorithm should run in $O((m + n) \log n)$ time, where m and n denote the number of edges and vertices, respectively.

Problem 10.7 *(H)* (Difficult.) Continuing the previous problem, we can do better. Suppose now the graph is undirected. Give a linear-time (that is, $O(m + n)$-time) algorithm to compute a minimum-bottleneck path between two given vertices.

Problem 10.8 *(H)* (Difficult.) Continuing the previous problem, what if the graph is directed? Can you compute a minimum-bottleneck path between two given vertices in less than $O((m + n) \log n)$ time?

Programming Problems

Problem 10.9 Implement in your favorite programming language the heap-based version of the `Dijkstra` algorithm from Section 10.4, and use it to solve the single-source shortest path problem in different directed graphs. With this heap-based implementation, what's the size of the largest problem you can solve in five minutes or less? (See www.algorithmsilluminated.org for test cases and challenge data sets.)

[Notes: This implementation requires the DELETE operation (see line 12 on page 225), which may force you to implement a customized heap data structure from scratch. To delete an object from a heap at a given position, follow the high-level approach of INSERT and EXTRACTMIN, using `Bubble-Up` or `Bubble-Down` as needed to squash violations of the heap property. In order to delete an object given only a pointer to it, you may also need to keep track of the current heap position of every vertex in the heap, perhaps by using a hash table (see Chapter 12).]

Chapter 11

Search Trees

A *search tree*, like a heap, is a data structure for storing an evolving set of objects associated with keys (and possibly lots of other data). It maintains a total ordering over the stored objects, and can support a richer set of operations than a heap, at the expense of increased space and, for some operations, somewhat slower running times. We'll start with the "what" (that is, supported operations) before proceeding to the "why" (applications) and the "how" (optional implementation details). To focus squarely on the most important ideas, we assume throughout this chapter that all the objects to be stored possess distinct keys.[1]

11.1 Sorted Arrays

A good way to think about a search tree is as a dynamic version of a sorted array—it can do everything a sorted array can do, while also accommodating fast insertions and deletions.

11.1.1 Sorted Arrays: Supported Operations

You can do a lot of things with a sorted array.

Sorted Arrays: Supported Operations

SEARCH: for a key k, return a pointer to the object in the data structure with key k (or report that no such object exists).

MIN (MAX): return a pointer to the object in the data structure with the smallest (respectively, largest) key.

PREDECESSOR (SUCCESSOR): given a pointer to an object in the data structure, return a pointer to the object with the closest smaller key (respectively, closest larger key). If the given object has the minimum (respectively, maximum) key, report "none."

OUTPUTSORTED: output pointers to the objects in the data structure one by one in order of their keys.

SELECT: given a number i, between 1 and the number of objects, return a pointer to the object in the data structure with the ith-smallest key.

---

[1]Problem 11.6 explores strategies for accommodating duplicate keys.

RANK: given a key k, return the number of objects in the data structure with key at most k.

Let's review how to implement each of these operations.

- The SEARCH operation uses binary search: First check if the object in the middle position of the array has the desired key. If so, return it. If not, recurse either on the left half (if the middle object's key is too large) or on the right half (if it's too small).[2] For example, to search the array

3	6	10	11	17	23	30	36

for the key 8, binary search will: examine the fourth object (with key 11); recurse on the left half (the objects with keys 3, 6, and 10); check the second object (with key 6); recurse on the right half of the remaining array (the object with key 10); conclude that the rightful position for an object with key 8 would be between the second and third objects; and report "none." As each recursive call cuts the array size by a factor of 2, there are at most $\log_2 n$ recursive calls, where n is the length of the array. Because each recursive call does a constant amount of work, the operation runs in $O(\log n)$ time.

- MIN and MAX are easy to implement in $O(1)$ time: Return a pointer to the first or last object in the array, respectively.

- To implement PREDECESSOR or SUCCESSOR, first use the SEARCH operation to recover the position in the sorted array of the object referenced by the given pointer. Then, return a pointer to the object in the previous or next position, respectively. These two operations are as fast as SEARCH—running in $O(\log n)$ time, where n is the length of the array.[3]

- The OUTPUTSORTED operation is straightforward to implement in linear time with a sorted array: Perform a single front-to-back pass over the array, outputting a pointer to each object in turn.

- SELECT is easy to implement in constant time: Given an index i, return a pointer to the object in the ith position of the array.

- The RANK operation, an approximate inverse of SELECT, can be implemented along the same lines as SEARCH (see Problem 11.3).

Summarizing, here's the final scorecard for sorted arrays:

---

[2]Readers of at least a certain age should be reminded of searching for a phone number in a phone book. If you haven't walked through the code of this algorithm before, look it up in your favorite introductory programming book or tutorial.

[3]In some programming languages (such as C++), the PREDECESSOR and SUCCESSOR operations can be implemented in $O(1)$ time using "pointer arithmetic."

Operation	Running time
SEARCH	$O(\log n)$
MIN	$O(1)$
MAX	$O(1)$
PREDECESSOR	$O(\log n)$
SUCCESSOR	$O(\log n)$
OUTPUTSORTED	$O(n)$
SELECT	$O(1)$
RANK	$O(\log n)$

Table 11.1: Sorted arrays: supported operations and their running times, where n denotes the number of objects stored in the array.

11.1.2   Unsupported Operations

Could you really ask for anything more? With a *static* data set that does not change over time, this is an impressive list of supported operations. Many real-world applications are *dynamic*, however, with the set of relevant objects evolving over time. For example, employees come and go, and the data structure that stores their records should stay up to date. For this reason, we also care about insertions and deletions.

Sorted Arrays: Unsupported Operations

INSERT: given a new object x, add x to the data structure.

DELETE: for a key k, delete the object with key k from the data structure, or report that no such object exists.[4]

These two operations aren't impossible to implement with a sorted array, but they're painfully slow—inserting or deleting an element while maintaining the sorted array property requires linear time in the worst case. Is there an alternative data structure that replicates all the functionality of a sorted array, while matching the logarithmic-time performance of a heap for the INSERT and DELETE operations?

11.2   Search Trees: Supported Operations

The raison d'être of a search tree is to support all the operations that a sorted array supports, plus insertions and deletions. All the operations except OUTPUTSORTED run in $O(\log n)$ time, where n is the number of objects in the search tree. The OUTPUTSORTED opera-

---

[4]The eagle-eyed reader may have noticed that this specification of the DELETE operation (which takes only a key as input) is less demanding than the one on page 217 for heaps (which expects a pointer to an entire object as input). Because heaps do not support fast search, a key alone does not provide enough information to quickly identify (let alone delete) an object. But in a sorted array (as well as in search trees and hash tables), it's easy to recover a pointer to an object given its key (via SEARCH).

tion runs in $O(n)$ time, and this is as good as it gets (as the operation is responsible for outputting n different pointers).

Here's the scorecard for search trees, compared with sorted arrays:

Operation	Sorted Array	Balanced Search Tree
SEARCH	$O(\log n)$	$O(\log n)$
MIN	$O(1)$	$O(\log n)$
MAX	$O(1)$	$O(\log n)$
PREDECESSOR	$O(\log n)$	$O(\log n)$
SUCCESSOR	$O(\log n)$	$O(\log n)$
OUTPUTSORTED	$O(n)$	$O(n)$
SELECT	$O(1)$	$O(\log n)$
RANK	$O(\log n)$	$O(\log n)$
INSERT	$O(n)$	$O(\log n)$
DELETE	$O(n)$	$O(\log n)$

Table 11.2: Balanced search trees vs. sorted arrays: supported operations and their running times, where n denotes the current number of objects stored in the data structure.

An important caveat: The running times in Table 11.2 are achieved by a *balanced* search tree, which is a more sophisticated version of the standard binary search tree described in Section 11.3. These running times are *not* guaranteed by an unbalanced search tree.[5]

When to Use a Balanced Search Tree

If your application requires maintaining an ordered representation of a dynamically changing set of objects, the balanced search tree (or a data structure based on one[6]) is usually the data structure of choice.[7]

Remember the principle of parsimony: Choose the simplest data structure that supports all the operations required by your application. If you need to maintain only an ordered representation of a static data set (with no insertions or deletions), use a sorted array instead of a balanced search tree; the latter would be overkill. If your data set is dynamic but you care only about fast minimum (or maximum) operations, use a heap instead of a balanced search tree.[8] These simpler data structures do less than a balanced search tree, but what they

---

[5]A preview of Sections 11.3 and 11.4: In general, search tree operations run in time proportional to the *height* of the tree, meaning the longest path length from the tree's root to one of its leaves. In a binary tree with n nodes, the height can be anywhere from $\approx \log_2 n$ (if the tree is perfectly balanced) to $n-1$ (if the nodes form a single chain). Balanced search trees do a modest amount of extra work to ensure that the height is always $O(\log n)$; this height guarantee then leads to the running time bounds in Table 11.2.

[6]For example, the `TreeMap` class in Java and the `map` class template in the C++ Standard Template Library are built on top of balanced search trees.

[7]One good place to see balanced search trees in the wild is in the Linux kernel. For example, they are used to manage the scheduling of processes, and to keep track of the virtual memory footprint of each process.

[8]And if your data set is dynamic but all you care about is the SEARCH operation, use a hash table or bloom filter (see Chapter 12).

do, they do better—faster (by a constant or logarithmic factor) and with less space (by a constant factor).

*11.3 Implementation Details

This section provides a high-level description of a typical implementation of a (not necessarily balanced) binary search tree. Section 11.4 touches on some of the extra ideas needed to implement a balanced search tree.

11.3.1   The Search Tree Property

In a binary search tree, every node corresponds to an object (with a key) and has three pointers associated with it: a parent pointer, a left child pointer, and a right child pointer. Any of these pointers can be null, indicating the absence of a parent or child. The left subtree of a node x comprises the nodes reachable from x via its left child pointer, and similarly for the right subtree. The defining *search tree property* is:[9]

The Search Tree Property

1. For every object x, objects in x's left subtree have keys smaller than that of x.

2. For every object x, objects in x's right subtree have keys larger than that of x.

The search tree property imposes a requirement for *every* node of a search tree, not just for the root:

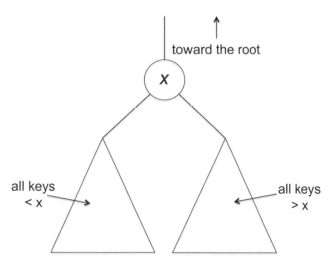

For example, here's a search tree containing objects with the keys $\{1, 2, 3, 4, 5\}$, and a table listing the destinations of the three pointers at each node:

Binary search trees and heaps differ in several ways. Heaps can be thought of as trees, but they are implemented as arrays, with no explicit pointers between objects. A search tree

---

[9]We refer to nodes of search trees and the corresponding objects interchangeably.

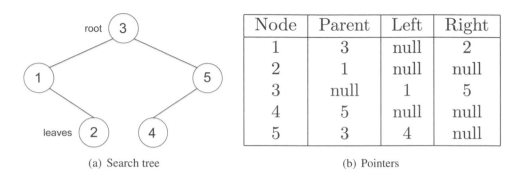

Node	Parent	Left	Right
1	3	null	2
2	1	null	null
3	null	1	5
4	5	null	null
5	3	4	null

(a) Search tree   (b) Pointers

Figure 11.1: A search tree and its corresponding parent and child pointers.

explicitly stores three pointers per object, and hence uses more space (by a constant factor). Heaps don't need explicit pointers because they always correspond to complete binary trees, while binary search trees can have an arbitrary structure.

Search trees have a different purpose than heaps. For this reason, the search tree property is incomparable to the heap property. Heaps are optimized for fast minimum computations, and the heap property—that a child's key is the same or larger than its parent's key—makes a minimum-key object easy to find (there's one at the root). Search trees are optimized for—wait for it—search, and the search tree property is defined accordingly. For example, if you are searching for an object with the key 23 in a search tree and the root's key is 17, you know that the object can reside only in the root's right subtree, and can discard the objects in the left subtree from further consideration. This should remind you of binary search, as befits a data structure whose raison d'être is to simulate a dynamically changing sorted array.

11.3.2   The Height of a Search Tree

Many different search trees exist for a given set of keys. Here's a second search tree containing objects with the keys $\{1, 2, 3, 4, 5\}$:

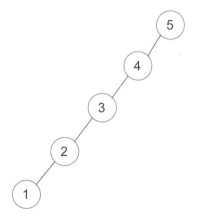

Both conditions in the search tree property hold, the second one vacuously (as there are no non-empty right subtrees).

The *height* of a tree is defined as the length of a longest path from its root to a leaf. Different search trees containing identical sets of objects can have different heights, as in our first two examples (which have heights 2 and 4, respectively). In general, a binary search tree containing n objects can have a height anywhere from

$$\approx \log_2 n \qquad \text{to} \qquad n - 1.$$

$\underbrace{\qquad\qquad}$ perfectly balanced binary tree (best-case scenario) $\underbrace{\qquad\qquad}$ chain, as above (worst-case scenario)

The rest of this section outlines how to implement all the operations of a binary search tree in time proportional to the tree's height (save OUTPUTSORTED, which runs in time linear in n). For the refinements of binary search trees that are guaranteed to have height $O(\log n)$ (see Section 11.4), this leads to the logarithmic running times reported in the scorecard in Table 11.2.

11.3.3   Implementing SEARCH in $O(height)$ Time

Let's begin with the SEARCH operation:

> for a key k, return a pointer to the object in the data structure with key k (or report that no such object exists).

The search tree property tells you exactly where to look for an object with key k. If k is less than (respectively, greater than) the root's key, such an object must reside in the root's left subtree (respectively, right subtree). To search, follow your nose: Start at the root and repeatedly go left or right (as appropriate) until you find the desired object (a successful search) or encounter a null pointer (an unsuccessful search).

For example, suppose we search for an object with key 2 in our first binary search tree:

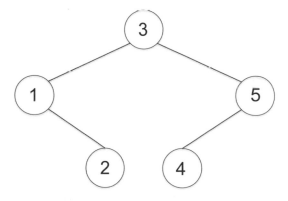

Because the root's key (3) is too big, the first step traverses the left child pointer. Because the next node's key is too small (1), the second step traverses the right child pointer, arriving at the desired object. If we search for an object with key 6, the search traverses the root's right child pointer (as the root's key is too small). Because the next node's key (5) is also too small, the search tries to follow another right child pointer, encounters a null pointer, and halts the search (unsuccessfully).

SEARCH

1. Start at the root node.

2. Repeatedly traverse left and right child pointers, as appropriate (left if k is less than the current node's key, right if k is bigger).

3. Return a pointer to the object with key k (if found) or "none" (upon reaching a null pointer).

The running time is proportional to the number of pointers followed, which is at most the height of the search tree (plus 1, if you count the final null pointer of an unsuccessful search).

11.3.4   Implementing MIN and MAX in $O(height)$ Time

The search tree property makes it easy to implement the MIN and MAX operations.

> MIN (MAX): return a pointer to the object in the data structure with the smallest (respectively, largest) key.

Keys in the left subtree of the root are smaller than the root's key, and keys in the right subtree are larger. If the left subtree is empty, the smallest key must be at the root. Otherwise, the minimum of the left subtree is also the minimum of the entire tree. This suggests following the root's left child pointer and repeating the process.

For example, in the search trees we considered earlier:

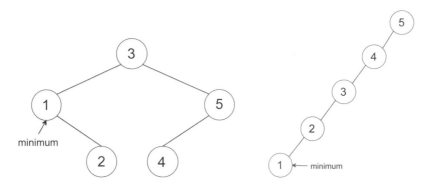

repeatedly following left child pointers leads to the object with the minimum key.

MIN (MAX)

1. Start at the root node.

2. Traverse left child pointers (right child pointers) as long as possible, until encountering a null pointer.

3. Return a pointer to the last object visited.

The running time is proportional to the number of pointers followed, which is $O(height)$.

11.3.5   Implementing PREDECESSOR in $O(height)$ Time

Next is the PREDECESSOR operation; the implementation of the SUCCESSOR operation is analogous.

> PREDECESSOR: given a pointer to an object in the data structure, return a pointer to the object with the closest smaller key. (If the object has the minimum key, report "none.")

Given an object x, where could x's predecessor reside? Not in x's right subtree, where all the keys are larger than x's key (by the search tree property). Our running example

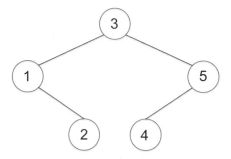

illustrates two cases. The predecessor might appear in the left subtree (as for the nodes with keys 3 and 5), or it could be an ancestor farther up in the tree (as for the nodes with keys 2 and 4).

The general pattern is: If an object x's left subtree is non-empty, the maximum of this subtree is x's predecessor[10]; otherwise, x's predecessor is the closest ancestor of x that has a smaller key than x. Equivalently, tracing parent pointers upward from x, it is the destination of the first left turn.[11] For example, in the search tree above, tracing parent pointers upward from the node with key 4 first takes a right turn (leading to a node with the bigger key 5) and then takes a left turn, arriving at the correct predecessor (3). If x has an empty left subtree and no left turns above it, then it is the minimum in the search tree and has no predecessor (like the node with key 1 in the search tree above).

PREDECESSOR

1. If x's left subtree is non-empty, return the result of MAX applied to this subtree.

2. Otherwise, traverse parent pointers upward toward the root. If the traversal visits consecutive nodes y and z with y a right child of z, return a pointer to z.

3. Otherwise, report "none."

The running time is proportional to the number of pointers followed, which in all cases is $O(height)$.

---

[10]Among the keys less than x's, the ones in x's left subtree are the closest to x's key (as you should check). Among the keys in this subtree, the maximum is the closest to x's key.

[11]Right turns lead to nodes with larger keys, which cannot be x's predecessor. The search tree property also implies that neither more distant ancestors nor non-ancestors can be x's predecessor (as you should check).

11.3.6 Implementing OUTPUTSORTED in $O(n)$ Time

Recall the OUTPUTSORTED operation:

> OUTPUTSORTED: output pointers to the objects in the data structure one by one in order of their keys.

A lazy way to implement this operation is to first use the MIN operation to output a pointer to the object with the minimum key, and then repeatedly invoke the SUCCESSOR operation to output pointers to the rest of the objects in order. A better method is to use what's called an *in-order traversal* of the search tree, which recursively processes the root's left subtree, then the root, and then the root's right subtree. This idea meshes perfectly with the search tree property, which implies that OUTPUTSORTED should first output the objects in the root's left subtree in order, followed by the object at the root, followed by the objects in the root's right subtree in order.

OUTPUTSORTED

1. Recursively call OUTPUTSORTED on the root's left subtree.

2. Output a pointer to the object at the root.

3. Recursively call OUTPUTSORTED on the root's right subtree.

For a tree containing n objects, the operation performs n recursive calls (one initiated at each node) and does a constant amount of work in each, for a total running time of $O(n)$.

11.3.7 Implementing INSERT in $O(height)$ Time

None of the operations discussed so far modify the given search tree, so they run no risk of screwing up the crucial search tree property. Our next two operations—INSERT and DELETE—make changes to the tree, and must take care to preserve the search tree property.

> INSERT: given a new object x, add x to the data structure.

The INSERT operation piggybacks on SEARCH. An unsuccessful search for an object with key k locates where such an object would have appeared. This is the appropriate place to stick a new object with key k (rewiring the old null pointer). In our running example, the correct location for a new object with key 6 is the spot where our unsuccessful search concluded:

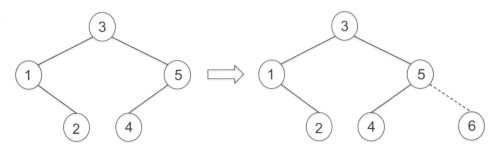

INSERT

1. Start at the root node.

2. Repeatedly traverse left and right child pointers, as appropriate (left if k is smaller than the current node's key, right if it's larger), until a null pointer is encountered.

3. Replace the null pointer with one to the new object. Set the new node's parent pointer to its parent, and its child pointers to null.

The operation preserves the search tree property because it places the new object where it should have been.[12] The running time is the same as for the SEARCH operation, which is $O(height)$.

11.3.8   Implementing DELETE in $O(height)$ Time

In most data structures, the DELETE operation is the toughest one to get right. Search trees are no exception.

> DELETE: for a key k, delete the object with key k from the search tree, or report that no such object exists.

The main challenge is to repair a tree after a node removal so that the search tree property is restored.

The first step is to invoke SEARCH to locate the object x with key k. (If there is no such object, the DELETE operation halts and reports this fact.) There are three cases, depending on whether x has 0, 1, or 2 children. If x is a leaf, it can be deleted without harm. For example, if we delete the node with key 2 from our favorite search tree:

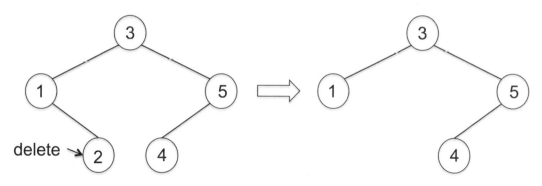

For every remaining node y, the nodes in y's subtrees are the same as before, except possibly with x removed; the search tree property continues to hold.

---

[12]More formally, let x denote the newly inserted object and consider an existing object y. If x is not a member of the subtree rooted at y, then it cannot interfere with the search tree property at y. If it is a member of the subtree rooted at y, then y was one of the nodes visited during the unsuccessful search for x. The keys of x and y were explicitly compared in this search, with x placed in y's left subtree if and only if its key is smaller than y's.

When x has one child y, we can splice it out. Deleting x leaves y without a parent and x's old parent z without one of its children. The obvious fix is to let y assume x's previous position (as z's child).[13] For example, if we delete the node with key 5 from our favorite search tree:

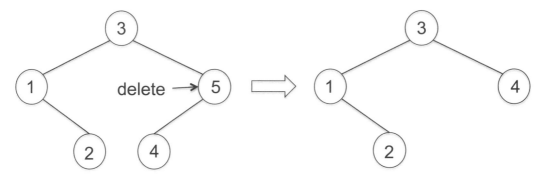

By the same reasoning as in the first case, the search tree property is preserved.

The hard case is when x has two children. Deleting x leaves *two* nodes without a parent, and it's not clear where to put them. In our running example, it's not obvious how to repair the tree after deleting its root.

The key trick is to reduce the hard case to one of the easy ones. First, use the PRE-DECESSOR operation to compute the predecessor y of x.[14] Because x has two children, its predecessor is the object in its (non-empty!) left subtree with the maximum key (see Section 11.3.5). Because the object with the maximum key is computed by following right child pointers as long as possible (see Section 11.3.4), y cannot have a right child; it might or might not have a left child.

Here's a crazy idea: *Swap x and y!* In our running example, with the root node acting as x:

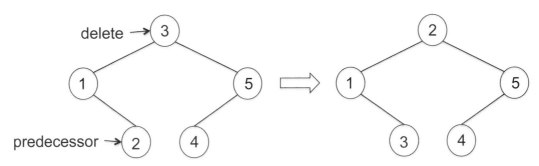

This crazy idea looks like a bad one, as we've now violated the search tree property (with the node with key 3 in the left subtree of the node with key 2). But every violation of the search tree property involves the node x, which we're going to delete anyway.[15] Because x now occupies y's previous position, it no longer has a right child. Deleting x from its new

---

[13] Insert your favorite nerdy Shakespeare joke here. . .

[14] The successor also works fine, if you prefer.

[15] For every node z other than y, the only possible new node in z's subtree is x. Meanwhile, y, as x's immediate predecessor in the sorted ordering of all keys, has a key larger than those of all the other nodes in x's old left subtree and less than those of all the nodes in x's old right subtree. Thus, the search tree condition holds for y in its new position, except with respect to x.

position falls into one of the two easy cases: We delete it if it also has no left child, and splice it out if it does have a left child. Either way, with x out of the picture, the search tree property is restored. Back to our running example:

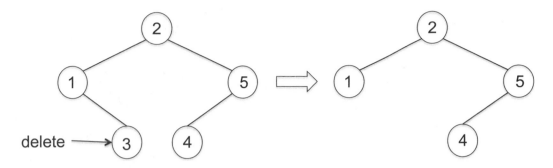

DELETE

1. Use SEARCH to locate the object x with key k. (If no such object exists, halt.)

2. If x has no children, delete x by setting the appropriate child pointer of x's parent to null. (If x was the root, the new tree is empty.)

3. If x has one child, splice x out by rewiring the appropriate child pointer of x's parent to x's child, and the parent pointer of x's child to x's parent. (If x was the root, its child becomes the new root.)

4. Otherwise, swap x with the object in its left subtree that has the biggest key, and delete x from its new position (where it has at most one child).

The operation performs a constant amount of work in addition to one SEARCH and one PREDECESSOR operation, so it runs in $O(height)$ time.

11.3.9   Augmented Search Trees for SELECT

Finally, the SELECT operation:

> SELECT: given a number i, between 1 and the number of objects, return a pointer to the object in the data structure with the ith-smallest key.

To get SELECT to run quickly, we'll *augment* the search tree by having each node keep track of information *about the structure of the tree itself*, and not just about an object.[16] Search trees can be augmented in many ways; here, we'll store at each node x an integer $size(x)$ indicating the number of nodes in the subtree rooted at x (including x itself). In our running example

---

[16]This idea can also be used to implement the RANK operation in $O(height)$ time (see Problem 11.4).

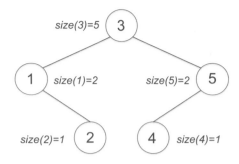

we have $size(1) = 2$, $size(2) = 1$, $size(3) = 5$, $size(4) = 1$, and $size(5) = 2$.

Quiz 11.1

Suppose the node x in a search tree has children y and z. What is the relationship between $size(x)$, $size(y)$, and $size(z)$?

a) $size(x) = \max\{size(y), size(z)\} + 1$

b) $size(x) = size(y) + size(z)$

c) $size(x) = size(y) + size(z) + 1$

d) There is no general relationship.

(See Section 11.3.10 for the solution and discussion.)

How is this additional information helpful? Imagine you're looking for the object with the 17th-smallest key (i.e., $i = 17$) in a search tree with 100 objects. Starting at the root, you can compute in constant time the sizes of its left and right subtrees. By the search tree property, every key in the left subtree is less than those at the root and in the right subtree. If the population of the left subtree is 25, these are the 25 smallest keys in the tree, including the 17th-smallest key. If its population is only 12, the right subtree contains all but the 13 smallest keys, and the 17th-smallest key is the 4th-smallest among its 87 keys. Either way, we can call SELECT recursively to locate the desired object.

SELECT

1. Start at the root and let j be the size of its left subtree. (If it has no left child pointer, then $j = 0$.)

2. If $i = j + 1$, return a pointer to the root.

3. If $i < j + 1$, recursively compute and return the ith-smallest key in the left subtree.

4. If $i > j + 1$, recursively compute and return the $(i - j - 1)$th-smallest key in the right subtree.[17]

---

[17]The structure of the recursion might remind you of our linear-time selection algorithms in Chapter 6, with the root node playing the role of the pivot element.

Because each node of the search tree stores the size of its subtree, each recursive call performs only a constant amount of work. Each recursive call proceeds further downward in the tree, so the total amount of work is $O(height)$.

Paying the piper.   We still have to pay the piper. We've exploited the additional metadata stored in the search tree, and every operation that modifies the tree must take care to keep this information up to date, in addition to preserving the search tree property. Problem 11.5 asks you to think through how to re-implement the INSERT and DELETE operations, still running in $O(height)$ time, so that all the subtree sizes remain accurate.

11.3.10   Solution to Quiz 11.1

Correct answer: (c). Every node in the subtree rooted at x is either x itself, or a node in x's left subtree, or a node in x's right subtree. We therefore have

$$size(x) = \underbrace{size(y)}_{\text{nodes in left subtree}} + \underbrace{size(z)}_{\text{nodes in right subtree}} + \underbrace{1}_{x \text{ itself}} .$$

*11.4   Balanced Search Trees

11.4.1   Working Harder for Better Balance

The running time of every binary search tree operation (save OUTPUTSORTED) is proportional to the tree's height, which can range anywhere from the best-case scenario of $\approx \log_2 n$ (for a perfectly balanced tree) to the worst-case scenario of $n - 1$ (for a chain), where n is the number of objects in the tree. Badly unbalanced search trees really can occur, for example when objects are inserted in sorted or reverse sorted order:

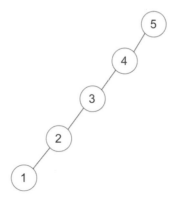

The difference between a logarithmic and a linear running time is huge, so it's a win to work a little harder in INSERT and DELETE—still $O(height)$ time, but with a larger constant factor—to guarantee that the tree's height is always $O(\log n)$.

Several different types of balanced search trees guarantee $O(\log n)$ height and, hence, achieve the operation running times stated in the scorecard in Table 11.2.[18] The devil is in the implementation details, and they can get pretty tricky for balanced search trees. Happily,

---

[18]Popular ones include red-black trees, 2-3 trees, AVL trees, splay trees, and B and B+ trees.

implementations are readily available and it's unlikely that you'll ever need to code up your own version from scratch. I encourage readers interested in what's under the hood of a balanced search tree to check out a textbook treatment or explore the open-source implementations and visualization demos that are freely available online.[19] To whet your appetite for further study, let's conclude the chapter with one of the most ubiquitous ideas in balanced search tree implementations.

11.4.2 Rotations

All the most common implementations of balanced search trees use *rotations*, a constant-time operation that performs a modest amount of local rebalancing while preserving the search tree property. For example, we could imagine transforming the chain of five objects on page 251 into a more civilized search tree by composing two local rebalancing operations:

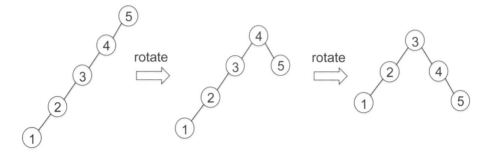

A rotation takes a parent-child pair and reverses their relationship (Figure 11.2). A *right rotation* applies when the child y is the left child of its parent x (and so y has a smaller key than x); after the rotation, x is the right child of y. When y is the right child of x, a *left rotation* makes x the left child of y.

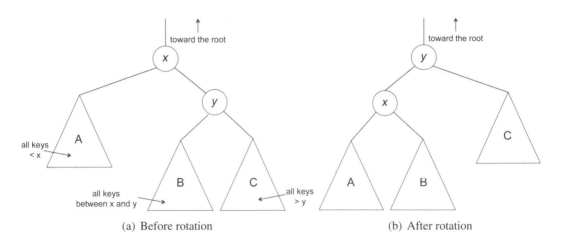

(a) Before rotation   (b) After rotation

Figure 11.2: A left rotation in action.

---

[19] Standard textbook treatments include Chapter 13 of *Introduction to Algorithms (Fourth Edition)*, by Thomas H. Cormen, Charles E. Leiserson, Ronald L. Rivest, and Clifford Stein (MIT Press, 2022); and Section 3.3 of *Algorithms (Fourth Edition)*, by Robert Sedgewick and Kevin Wayne (Addison-Wesley, 2011). See also the bonus videos at www.algorithmsilluminated.org for the basics of red-black trees.

The search tree property dictates the remaining details. For example, consider a left rotation, with y the right child of x. The search tree property implies that x's key is less than y's; that all the keys in x's left subtree ("A" in Figure 11.2) are less than that of x (and y); that all the keys in y's right subtree ("C" in Figure 11.2) are greater than that of y (and x); and that all the keys in y's left subtree ("B" in Figure 11.2) are between those of x and y. After the rotation, y inherits x's old parent and has x as its new left child. There's a unique way to put all the pieces back together while preserving the search tree property, so let's just follow our nose.

There are three free slots for the subtrees A, B, and C: y's right child pointer and both child pointers of x. The search tree property forces us to stick the smallest subtree (A) as x's left child, and the largest subtree (C) as y's right child. This leaves one slot for subtree B (x's right child pointer), and fortunately the search tree property works out: All the subtree's keys are wedged between those of x and y, and the subtree winds up in y's left subtree (where it needs to be) and x's right subtree (ditto).

A right rotation is then a left rotation in reverse (Figure 11.3).

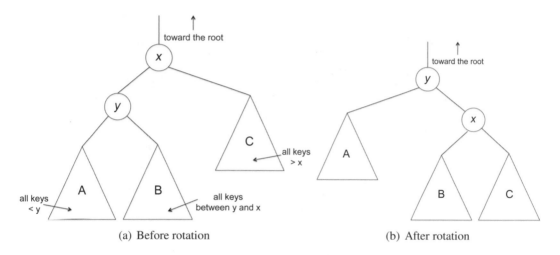

(a) Before rotation   (b) After rotation

Figure 11.3: A right rotation in action.

Because a rotation merely rewires a few pointers, it can be implemented with a constant number of operations. By construction, it preserves the search tree property.

The operations that modify the search tree—INSERT and DELETE—are the ones that must employ rotations. Without rotations, such an operation might render the tree a little more unbalanced. Because a single insertion or deletion can wreak only so much havoc, it should be plausible that a small—constant or perhaps logarithmic—number of rotations can correct any newly created imbalance and prevent the tree's height from growing beyond a small constant times $\log_2 n$, where n is the number of objects stored in the tree. This is exactly what the aforementioned balanced search tree implementations do. The extra work from rotations adds $O(height)$ overhead to the INSERT and DELETE operations, leaving their overall running times at $O(height) = O(\log n)$.

The Upshot

✰ If your application requires maintaining a totally ordered representation of an evolving set of objects, the balanced search tree is usually the data structure of choice.

✰ Balanced search trees support the operations SEARCH, MIN, MAX, PREDECESSOR, SUCCESSOR, SELECT, RANK, INSERT, and DELETE in $O(\log n)$ time, where n is the number of objects.

✰ A binary search tree has one node per object, each with a parent pointer, a left child pointer, and a right child pointer.

✰ The search tree property states that, at every node x of the tree, the keys in x's left subtree are smaller than x's key, and the keys in x's right subtree are larger than x's key.

✰ The *height* of a search tree is the length of a longest path from its root to a leaf. A binary search tree with n objects can have height anywhere from $\approx \log_2 n$ to $n - 1$.

✰ In a basic binary search tree, all the supported operations above can be implemented in $O(height)$ time. (For SELECT and RANK, after augmenting the tree to maintain subtree sizes at each node.)

✰ Balanced binary search trees do extra work in the INSERT and DELETE operations—still $O(height)$ time, but with a larger constant factor—to guarantee that the tree's height is always $O(\log n)$.

Test Your Understanding

Problem 11.1 *(S)* Which of the following statements are true? (Check all that apply.)

a) The height of a binary search tree with n nodes cannot be smaller than $\Theta(\log n)$.

b) All the operations supported by a binary search tree (except OUTPUTSORTED) run in $O(\log n)$ time.

c) The heap property is a special case of the search tree property.

d) The search tree property is a special case of the heap property.

e) Balanced binary search trees are always preferable to sorted arrays.

Problem 11.2 *(S)* You are given a binary tree with n nodes (via a pointer to its root). Each node of the tree has a *size* field, as in Section 11.3.9, but these fields have not been filled in yet. How much time is necessary and sufficient to compute the correct value for all the *size* fields?

a) $\Theta(height)$

b) $\Theta(n)$

c) $\Theta(n \log n)$

d) $\Theta(n^2)$

Problem 11.3 *(S)* For a sorted array, propose an $O(\log n)$-time implementation of the RANK operation (page 238), where n is the number of objects in the array.

Problem 11.4 *(H)* For a binary search tree augmented with subtree sizes (see page 249), propose an $O(height)$-time implementation of the RANK operation.

Problem 11.5 *(H)* For a binary search tree augmented with subtree sizes, propose $O(height)$-time implementations of the INSERT and DELETE operations that keep all subtree sizes accurate.

Challenge Problems

Problem 11.6 *(H)* This problem explores some of the subtleties in extending binary search trees to accommodate distinct objects with equal keys. Here are three possible ways to extend the search tree property (page 241), corresponding to allowing duplicate keys in left subtrees, in right subtrees, or in both:

(i) For every object x, objects in x's left (respectively, right) subtree have keys smaller than or equal to (respectively, larger than) that of x.

(ii) For every object x, objects in x's left (respectively, right) subtree have keys smaller than (respectively, larger than or equal to) that of x.

(iii) For every object x, objects in x's left (respectively, right) subtree have keys smaller than or equal to (respectively, larger than or equal to) that of x.

A fourth possible approach is to leave the search tree property alone and instead relax our standing assumption that the nodes of the tree are in one-to-one correspondence with the stored objects:

(iv) store with each tree node a distinct key k and a linked list of all the objects with key k.[20]

(a) For each of the approaches (i)–(iv) to extending binary search trees to accommodate duplicate keys, propose an $O(height)$-time implementation of the INSERT operation.

(b) Here's a version of the SEARCH operation that is indifferent between objects with the same key: given a key k, return a pointer to some object in the data structure with key k (or report that no such object exists).

For each of the approaches (i)–(iv), propose an $O(height)$-time implementation of this operation.

---

[20] Alternatively, a hash table (see Chapter 12) could be used in place of a linked list.

(c) Suppose objects have distinct names in addition to (not necessarily distinct) keys. Here's a version of the SEARCH operation in which the object identity matters: given a key k and an object name o, return a pointer to the object in the data structure with key k and name o (or report that no such object exists).

For each of the approaches (i)–(iv), propose an implementation of this operation. Are any of these approaches particularly well or ill suited to support this operation?

(d) For which of the approaches (i)–(iv) are balanced binary search trees (Section 11.4)—binary trees that satisfy the proposed version of the search tree property and are also guaranteed to have height $O(\log n)$, where n is the number of stored objects—a plausible possibility?

Problem 11.7 *(H)* In the *tree concatenation problem*, the goal is to fuse together two binary search trees T_1 and T_2 (specified by pointers to their roots) into a single one, under the assumption that every key in T_1 is less than every key in T_2. (You can also assume that all the keys are distinct.) Give an $O(\min\{h_1, h_2\})$-time algorithm for this problem, where h_1 and h_2 denote the heights of T_1 and T_2, respectively.

Problem 11.8 *(H)* For an array A containing the n integers $a_1, a_2, \ldots, a_n$, the *partial sum* defined by two array positions $i, j \in \{1, 2, \ldots, n\}$ with $i \le j$ is the sum of the numbers in A between positions i and j, inclusive: $\sum_{k=i}^{j} a_k$. Propose a data structure that is initialized with the all-zero array A and, after its initialization, supports both of the following two operations in $O(\log n)$ time:

PARTIALSUM: given array positions $i, j \in \{1, 2, \ldots, n\}$ with $i \le j$, return the corresponding partial sum $\sum_{k=i}^{j} a_k$.

UPDATE: given an array position $i \in \{1, 2, \ldots, n\}$ and a value v, reassign the integer a_i in the ith position of A to the value v.

Programming Problems

Problem 11.9 This problem uses the median maintenance problem from Section 10.3.3 to explore the relative performance of heaps and search trees.

a) Implement in your favorite programming language the heap-based solution in Section 10.3.3 to the median maintenance problem.

b) Implement a solution to the problem that instead uses a single search tree and its INSERT and SELECT operations.

Which implementation is faster?

You can use existing implementations of heaps and search trees, or you can implement your own from scratch. (See www.algorithmsilluminated.org for test cases and challenge data sets.)

Chapter 12

Hash Tables and Bloom Filters

We conclude with an incredibly useful and ubiquitous data structure known as a *hash table* (or *hash map*). Hash tables, like heaps and search trees, maintain an evolving set of objects associated with keys (and possibly lots of other data). Unlike heaps and search trees, they maintain no ordering information whatsoever. The raison d'être of a hash table is to facilitate super-fast searches, which are also called *lookups* in this context. A hash table can tell you what's there and what's not, and can do it really, really quickly (much faster than a heap or search tree). As usual, we'll start with the supported operations (Section 12.1) before proceeding to applications (Section 12.2) and some optional implementation details (Sections 12.3 and 12.4). Sections 12.5 and 12.6 cover *bloom filters*, close cousins of hash tables that use less space at the expense of occasional errors.

12.1 Supported Operations

The raison d'être of a hash table is to keep track of an evolving set of objects with keys while supporting fast lookups (by key), so that it's easy to check what's there and what's not. For example, if your company manages an ecommerce site, you might use one hash table to keep track of employees (perhaps with names as keys), another one to store past transactions (with transaction IDs as keys), and a third to remember the visitors to your site (with IP addresses as keys).

Conceptually, you can think of a hash table as an array. One thing that arrays are good for is immediate random access. Wondering what's in position number 17 of an array? Just access that position directly, in constant time. Want to change the contents in position 23? Again, easy in constant time.

Suppose you want a data structure for remembering your friends' phone numbers. If you're lucky, all your friends had unusually unimaginative parents who named their kids after positive integers, say between 1 and 10000. In this case, you can store phone numbers in a length-10000 array (which is not that big). If your best friend is named 173, store their phone number in position 173 of the array. To forget about your ex-friend 548, overwrite position 548 with a default value. This array-based solution works well, even if your friends change over time—the space requirements are modest and insertions, deletions, and lookups run in constant time.

Probably your friends have more interesting but less convenient names, like Alice, Bob, Carol, and so on. Can we still use an array-based solution? In principle, you could maintain an array with entries indexed by every possible name you might ever see (with at most, say, 25 letters). To look up Alice's phone number, you can then look in the "Alice" position of the array (Figure 12.1).

257

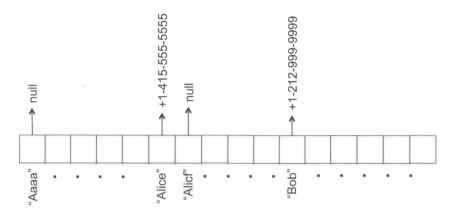

Figure 12.1: In principle, you could store your friends' phone numbers in an array indexed by strings with at most 25 characters.

Quiz 12.1

How many length-25 character strings are there? (Choose the strongest true statement.)

a) More than the number of hairs on your head.

b) More than the number of Web pages in existence.

c) More than the total amount of storage available on Earth (in bits).

d) More than the number of atoms in the universe.

(See Section 12.1.1 for the solution and discussion.)

The point of Quiz 12.1 is that the array needed for this solution is WAY TOO BIG. Is there an alternative data structure that replicates all the functionality of an array, with constant-time insertions, deletions, and lookups, and that also uses space proportional to the number of objects stored? A hash table is exactly such a data structure.

Hash Tables: Supported Operations

LOOKUP (a.k.a. SEARCH): for a key k, return a pointer to an object in the hash table with key k (or report that no such object exists).

INSERT: given a new object x, add x to the hash table.

DELETE: for a key k, delete an object with key k from the hash table, if one exists.

In a hash table, all these operations typically run in *constant* time—matching the naive array-based solution—under a couple of assumptions that generally hold in practice (described in Section 12.3). A hash table uses space linear in the number of objects stored.

This is radically less than the space required by the naive array-based solution, which is proportional to the number of all-imaginable objects that might ever need to be stored. The scorecard reads:

Operation	Typical running time
LOOKUP	$O(1)^*$
INSERT	$O(1)$
DELETE	$O(1)^*$

Table 12.1: Hash tables: supported operations and their typical running times. The asterisk (*) indicates that the running time bound holds if and only if the hash table is implemented properly (with a good hash function and an appropriate table size) and the data is non-pathological; see Section 12.3 for details.

Summarizing, hash tables don't support many operations, but what they do, they do really, really well. Whenever lookups constitute a significant amount of your program's work, a light bulb should go off in your head—the program calls out for a hash table!

When to Use a Hash Table

If your application requires fast lookups with a dynamically changing set of objects, the hash table is usually the data structure of choice.

12.1.1 Solution to Quiz 12.1

Correct answer: (c). The point of this quiz is to have fun thinking about some really big numbers, rather than to identify the correct answer per se. Let's assume that there are 26 choices for a character—ignoring punctuation, upper vs. lower case, etc. Then, there are 26^{25} 25-letter strings, which has order of magnitude roughly 10^{35}. (There are also the strings with 24 letters or less, but these are dwarfed in number by the length-25 strings.) The number of hairs on a person's head is typically around 10^5. The indexed Web has several billion pages, but the actual number of Web pages is probably around one trillion (10^{12}). The total amount of storage on Earth is hard to estimate but, at least in 2022, is surely no more than a yottabyte (10^{24} bytes, or roughly 10^{25} bits). Meanwhile, the number of atoms in the known universe is estimated to be around 10^{80}.

12.2 Applications

It's pretty amazing how many different applications boil down to repeated lookups and hence call out for a hash table. Back in the 1950s, researchers building the first compilers needed a *symbol table*, meaning a good data structure for keeping track of a program's variable and function names. Hash tables were invented for exactly this type of application. For a more modern example, imagine that a network router is tasked with blocking data packets from certain IP addresses, perhaps belonging to spammers. Every time a new data packet arrives, the router must look up whether the source IP address is in the blacklist. If so, it drops the packet; otherwise, it forwards the packet toward its destination. Again, these repeated lookups are right in the wheelhouse of hash tables.

12.2.1   Application: De-duplication

De-duplication is a canonical application of hash tables. Suppose you're processing a massive amount of data that's arriving one piece at a time, as a stream. For example:

- You're making a single pass over a huge file stored on disk, like all the transactions of a major retail company from the past year.

- You're crawling the Web and processing billions of Web pages.

- You're tracking data packets passing through a network router at a torrential rate.

- You're watching the visitors to your Web site.

In the de-duplication problem, your responsibility is to ignore duplicates and keep track only of the distinct keys seen so far. For example, you may be interested in the number of distinct IP addresses that have accessed your Web site, in addition to the total number of visits. Hash tables provide a simple solution to the de-duplication problem.

De-duplication with a Hash Table

When a new object x with key k arrives:

1. Use LOOKUP to check if the hash table already contains an object with key k.

2. If not, use INSERT to put x in the hash table.

After processing the data, the hash table contains exactly one object per key represented in the data stream.[1]

12.2.2   Application: The 2-SUM Problem

Our next example is more academic, but it illustrates how repeated lookups can show up in surprising places. The example concerns the 2-SUM problem.

Problem: 2-SUM

Input: An unsorted array A of n integers, and a target integer t.

Goal: Determine whether or not there are two numbers x, y in A satisfying $x + y = t$.

---

[1]With most hash table implementations, it's possible to iterate through the stored objects, in some arbitrary order, in linear time (see Problem 12.5). This enables further processing of the objects after the duplicates have been removed.

There are two slightly different versions of the problem, depending on whether or not x and y are required to be distinct. We'll allow $x = y$; the other case is similar (as you should check).

The 2-SUM problem can be solved by exhaustive search—by trying all possibilities for x and y and checking if any of them work. Because there are n choices for each of x and y, this is a quadratic-time ($\Theta(n^2)$) algorithm.

We can do better. The first key observation is that, for each choice of x, only one choice for y could possibly work (namely, $t - x$). So why not look specifically for this y?

2-SUM (Attempt #1)

Input: array A of n integers and a target integer t.
Output: "yes" if $A[i] + A[j] = t$ for some $i, j \in \{1, 2, 3, \ldots, n\}$, "no" otherwise.

---

for $i := 1$ to n **do**
    $y := t - A[i]$
    if A contains y **then**   // linear search
        return "yes"
return "no"

Does this help? The for loop has n iterations and it takes linear time to search for an integer in an unsorted array, so this would seem to be another quadratic-time algorithm. But remember, sorting is a for-free primitive. Why not use it, so that all the searches can take advantage of a sorted array?

2-SUM (Sorted Array Solution)

Input: array A of n integers and a target integer t.
Output: "yes" if $A[i] + A[j] = t$ for some $i, j \in \{1, 2, 3, \ldots, n\}$, "no" otherwise.

---

sort A // using a good sorting subroutine
for $i := 1$ to n **do**
    $y := t - A[i]$
    if A contains y **then**   // binary search
        return "yes"
return "no"

Quiz 12.2

What's the running time of an educated implementation of the sorted array-based algorithm for the 2-SUM problem?

a) $\Theta(n)$

b) $\Theta(n \log n)$

c) $\Theta(n^{1.5})$

d) $\Theta(n^2)$

(See Section 12.2.4 for the solution and discussion.)

The sorted array-based solution to 2-SUM is a big improvement over exhaustive search, and it showcases the elegant power of some of the algorithmic tools from Part I of the book. But we can do even better. The final insight is that this algorithm needed a sorted array only inasmuch as it needed to search it quickly. Because most of the work boils down to repeated lookups, a light bulb should go off in your head: A sorted array is overkill, and what this algorithm really calls out for is a hash table!

2-SUM (Hash Table Solution)

Input: array A of n integers and a target integer t.
Output: "yes" if $A[i] + A[j] = t$ for some $i, j \in \{1, 2, 3, \ldots, n\}$, "no" otherwise.

$H :=$ empty hash table
for $i := 1$ to n **do**
    INSERT $A[i]$ into H
for $i := 1$ to n **do**
    $y := t - A[i]$
    if H contains y **then**   // using LOOKUP
        return "yes"
return "no"

Assuming a good hash table implementation and non-pathological data, the INSERT and LOOKUP operations typically run in constant time. In this case, the hash table-based solution to the 2-SUM problem runs in *linear* time. Because any correct algorithm must generally look at every number in A at least once, this is the best-possible running time (up to constant factors).

12.2.3 Application: Searching Huge State Spaces

Hash tables are all about speeding up search. One application domain in which search is ubiquitous is game-playing, and more generally in planning problems. Think, for example, of a chess-playing program exploring the ramifications of different moves. Sequences of moves can be viewed as paths in a huge directed graph, in which vertices correspond to states of the game (positions of all the pieces and whose turn it is) and edges correspond to legal moves from one state to another. The size of this graph is astronomical (more than 10^{100} vertices), so there's no hope of writing it down explicitly and applying any of our graph search algorithms from Chapter 8. A more tractable alternative is to run a graph search algorithm like breadth-first search, starting from the current state, and explore the short-term consequences of different moves until reaching a time limit. To learn as much as possible, it's important to avoid exploring a vertex more than once, and so the search algorithm must keep track of which vertices it has already visited. As in our de-duplication application, this task is ready-made for a hash table. When the search algorithm reaches a vertex, it looks it up in a hash table. If the vertex is already there, the algorithm skips it and backtracks; otherwise, it inserts the vertex into the hash table and continues with its exploration.[2,3]

12.2.4   Solution to Quiz 12.2

Correct answer: (b). The first step can be implemented in $O(n \log n)$ time using MergeSort (see Sections 1.4–1.5) or HeapSort (see Section 10.3.1).[4] Each of the n for loop iterations can be implemented in $O(\log n)$ time via binary search. Adding everything up gives the final running time bound of $O(n \log n)$.

*12.3   Implementation: High-Level Ideas

This section covers the most important high-level ideas in a hash table implementation: hash functions (which map keys to positions in an array), collisions (different keys that map to the same position), and the most common collision-resolution strategies. Section 12.4 offers more detailed advice about implementing a hash table.

12.3.1   Two Straightforward Solutions

A hash table stores a set S of keys (and associated data), drawn from a universe U of all possible keys. For example, U might be all 2^{32} possible IPv4 addresses, all possible character strings of length at most 25, all possible chess board states, and so on. The set S could be the IP addresses that actually visited a Web page in the last 24 hours, the actual names of your friends, or the chess board states that your program explored in the last five seconds. In most applications of hash tables, the size of U is astronomical but the size of the subset S is manageable.

One conceptually straightforward way to implement the LOOKUP, INSERT, and DELETE operations is to keep track of objects in a big array, with one entry for every possible key in U. If U is a small set like all three-character strings (to keep track of airports by their three-letter codes, say), this array-based solution is a good one, with all operations running in constant time. In the many applications in which U is extremely large, this solution is absurd and unimplementable; we can realistically consider only data structures requiring space proportional to $|S|$ (rather than to $|U|$).

---

[2] In game-playing applications, the most popular graph search algorithm is called A^* *("A star") search*. The A^* search algorithm is a goal-oriented generalization of Dijkstra's algorithm (Chapter 9), which adds to the Dijkstra score (9.1) of an edge (v, w) a heuristic estimate of the cost required to travel from w to a "goal vertex." For example, if you're computing driving directions from a given origin to a given destination t, the heuristic estimate could be the straight-line distance from w to t. (See Problem 9.9 for a deeper dive on A^* search.)

[3] Take a moment to think about modern technology and speculate where else hash tables are used. It shouldn't take long to come up with some good guesses!

[4] No faster implementation is possible, at least with a comparison-based sorting algorithm (see Section 5.6 or footnote 10 in Chapter 10).

A second straightforward solution is to store objects in a linked list. The good news is that the space this solution uses is proportional to $|S|$. The bad news is that the running times of LOOKUP and DELETE also scale linearly with $|S|$—far worse than the constant-time operations that the array-based solution supports. The point of a hash table is to achieve the best of both worlds—space proportional to $|S|$ and constant-time operations (Table 12.2).

Data Structure	Space	Typical Running Time of LOOKUP
Array	$\Theta(|U|)$	$\Theta(1)$
Linked List	$\Theta(|S|)$	$\Theta(|S|)$
Hash Table	$\Theta(|S|)$	$\Theta(1)^*$

Table 12.2: Hash tables combine the best features of arrays and linked lists, with space linear in the number of objects stored and constant-time operations. The asterisk (*) indicates that the running time bound holds if and only if the hash table is implemented properly and the data is non-pathological.

12.3.2 Hash Functions

To achieve the best of both worlds, a hash table mimics the straightforward array-based solution, but with the array length n proportional to $|S|$ rather than $|U|$.[5] For now, you can think of n as roughly $2|S|$.

A *hash function* performs the translation from what we really care about—our friends' names, chess board states, etc.—to positions in the hash table. Formally, a hash function is a function from the set U of all possible keys to the set of array positions (Figure 12.2). Positions are usually numbered from 0 in a hash table, so the set of array positions is $\{0, 1, 2, \ldots, n-1\}$.

Hash Functions

A hash function $h : U \rightarrow \{0, 1, 2, \ldots, n-1\}$ assigns every key from the universe U to a position in an array of length n.

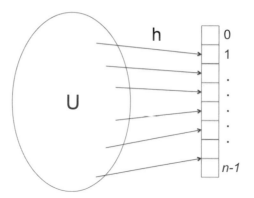

Figure 12.2: A hash function maps every possible key in the universe U to a position in $\{0, 1, 2, \ldots, n-1\}$. If $|U| > n$, two different keys must be mapped to the same position.

---

[5]But wait; isn't the set S changing over time? Yes it is, but it's not hard to periodically resize the array so that its length remains proportional to the current size of S; see also Section 12.4.2.

A hash function tells you where to start searching for an object. If you choose a hash function h with $h(\text{"Alice"}) = 17$—in which case, we say that the string "Alice" *hashes* to 17—then position 17 of the array is the place to start looking for Alice's phone number. Similarly, position 17 is the first place to try inserting Alice's phone number into the hash table.

12.3.3   Collisions Are Inevitable

You may have noticed a serious issue: What if two different keys (like "Alice" and "Bob") hash to the same position (like 23)? If you're looking for Alice's phone number but find Bob's in position 23 of the array, how do you know whether or not Alice's number is also in the hash table? If you're trying to insert Alice's phone number into position 23 but the position is already occupied, where do you put it?

When a hash function h maps two different keys k_1 and k_2 to the same position (that is, when $h(k_1) = h(k_2)$), it's called a *collision*.

Collisions

Two keys k_1 and k_2 from U *collide* under the hash function h if $h(k_1) = h(k_2)$.

Collisions cause confusion about where an object resides in the hash table, and we'd like to minimize them as much as possible. Why not design a super-smart hash function with no collisions whatsoever? Because *collisions are inevitable*. The reason is the *Pigeonhole Principle*, the intuitively obvious fact that, for every positive integer n, no matter how you stuff $n+1$ pigeons into n holes, there will be a hole with at least two pigeons. Thus whenever the number n of array positions (the holes) is less than the size of the universe U (the pigeons), every hash function (assignment of pigeons to holes)—no matter how clever—suffers from at least one collision (Figure 12.2). In most applications of hash tables, including those in Section 12.2, $|U|$ is much, much bigger than n.

Collisions are even more inevitable than the Pigeonhole Principle argument suggests. The reason is the *birthday paradox*, the subject of the next quiz.

Quiz 12.3

Consider n people with random birthdays, with each of the 366 days of the year equally likely. (Assume all n people were born in a leap year.) How large does n need to be before there is at least a 50% chance that two people have the same birthday?

a) 23

b) 57

c) 184

d) 367

(See Section 12.3.7 for the solution and discussion.)

What does the birthday paradox have to do with hashing? Imagine a hash function that assigns each key independently and uniformly at random to a position in $\{0, 1, 2, \ldots, n-1\}$. This is not a practically viable hash function (see Quiz 12.5), but such random functions are the gold standard to which we compare practical hash functions (see Section 12.3.6). The birthday paradox implies that, even for the gold standard, we're likely to start seeing collisions in a hash table of size n once a small constant times $\sqrt{n}$ objects have been inserted. For example, when $n = 10,000$, the insertion of 200 objects is likely to cause at least one collision—even though at least 98% of the array positions are completely unused!

12.3.4   Collision Resolution: Chaining

With collisions an inevitable fact of life, a hash table needs some method for resolving them. This section and the next describe the two dominant approaches, *separate chaining* (or simply *chaining*) and *open addressing*. Both approaches lead to implementations in which insertions and lookups typically run in constant time, assuming the hash table size and hash function are chosen appropriately and the data is non-pathological (cf., Table 12.1).

Buckets and Lists

Chaining is easy to implement and think about. The key idea is to default to the linked-list-based solution (Section 12.3.1) to handle multiple objects mapped to the same array position (Figure 12.3). With chaining, the positions of the array are often called *buckets*, as each can contain multiple objects. The LOOKUP, INSERT, and DELETE operations then reduce to one hash function evaluation (to determine the correct bucket) and the corresponding linked list operation.

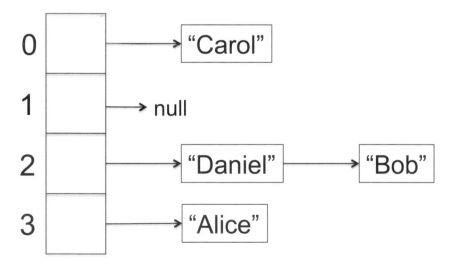

Figure 12.3: A hash table with collisions resolved by chaining, with four buckets and four objects. The strings "Bob" and "Daniel" collide in the third bucket (bucket 2). Only the keys are shown, and not the associated data (like phone numbers).

Chaining

1. Keep a linked list in each bucket of the hash table.

2. To LOOKUP, INSERT, or DELETE an object with key k, perform the corresponding operation on the linked list in the bucket $A[h(k)]$ to which k hashes; here h denotes the hash function and A the hash table's array.

Performance of Chaining

Provided the hash function h can be evaluated in constant time, the INSERT operation also takes constant time—the new object (with key k) can be inserted immediately at the front of the linked list stored in $A[h(k)]$. LOOKUP and DELETE must search through this list, which takes time proportional to the list's length. To achieve constant-time lookups in a hash table with chaining, the buckets' lists must stay short—ideally, with length at most a small constant.

List lengths (and lookup times) degrade if the hash table becomes heavily populated. For example, if $100n$ objects are stored in a hash table with array length n, a typical bucket has 100 objects to sift through. Lookup times can also degrade with a poorly chosen hash function that causes lots of collisions. For example, in the extreme case in which all the objects collide and wind up in the same bucket, the hash table devolves to a linked list and lookups can take time linear in the data set size. Section 12.4 elaborates on how to manage the size of a hash table and choose an appropriate hash function to achieve the running time bounds stated in Table 12.1.

12.3.5   Collision Resolution: Open Addressing

The second popular method for resolving collisions is *open addressing*. Open addressing is much easier to implement and understand when the hash table must support only INSERT and LOOKUP (and not DELETE); we'll focus on this case. (Plenty of hash table applications don't require the DELETE operation, including the three applications in Section 12.2.)

With open addressing, each position of the array stores 0 or 1 objects, rather than a list. (For this to make sense, the size $|S|$ of the data set cannot exceed the size n of the hash table.) Collisions create an immediate quandary for the INSERT operation: Where do we put an object with key k if a different object is already stored in position $h(k)$ of the hash table's array A?

Probe Sequences

The idea is to associate each key k with a *probe sequence* of positions, not just a single position. The first number of the sequence indicates the position to consider first; the second the next position to consider when the first is already occupied; and so on, until all options are exhausted. The object is stored in the first unoccupied position of its key's probe sequence (see Figure 12.4).

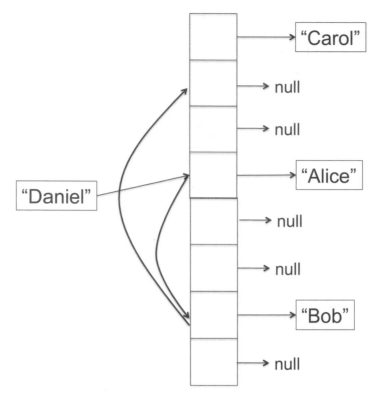

Figure 12.4: An insertion into a hash table with collisions resolved by open addressing. The first entry of the probe sequence for "Daniel" collides with "Alice," and the second with "Bob," but the third entry is an unoccupied position.

Open Addressing

1. INSERT: Given an object with key k, iterate through the probe sequence associated with k, storing the object in the first empty position found.

2. LOOKUP: Given a key k, iterate through the probe sequence associated with k until encountering the desired object (in which case, return a pointer to it) or an empty position (in which case, report "none").[6]

Linear Probing

There are several ways to use one or more hash functions to define a probe sequence. The simplest is *linear probing*. This method uses one hash function h, and defines the probe sequence for a key k as $h(k)$, followed by $h(k) + 1$, followed by $h(k) + 2$, and so on (wrapping around to the beginning upon reaching the last position). That is, the hash function indicates the starting position for an insertion or lookup, and the operation scans to the right (wrapping around if needed) until it finds the desired object or an empty position.

---

[6]If you encounter an empty position i, you can be confident that no object with key k is in the hash table. Such an object would have been stored either at position i or at an earlier position in k's probe sequence.

Double Hashing

A more sophisticated method is *double hashing*, which uses two hash functions.[7] The first tells you the first position of the probe sequence, and the second indicates the offset for subsequent positions. For example, if $h_1(k) = 17$ and $h_2(k) = 23$, the first place to look for an object with key k is position 17; failing that, position 40; failing that, position 63; failing that, position 86; and so on. For a different key k', the probe sequence could look quite different. For example, if $h_1(k') = 42$ and $h_2(k') = 27$, the probe sequence would be 42, followed by 69, followed by 96, followed by 123, and so on.

Performance of Open Addressing

With chaining, the running time of a lookup is governed by the lengths of buckets' lists; with open addressing, it's the typical number of probes required to find either an empty slot or the sought-after object. It's harder to understand hash table performance with open addressing than with chaining, but it should be intuitively clear that performance suffers as the hash table gets increasingly full—if very few slots are empty, it will usually take a probe sequence a long time to find one—or when a poor choice of hash function causes lots of collisions (see also Quiz 12.4). With an appropriate hash table size and hash function, open addressing achieves the running time bounds stated in Table 12.1 for the INSERT and LOOKUP operations; see Section 12.4 for additional details.

12.3.6   What Makes for a Good Hash Function?

No matter which collision-resolution strategy we employ, hash table performance degrades with the number of collisions. How can we choose a hash function so that there aren't too many collisions?

Bad Hash Functions

There are a zillion different ways to define a hash function, and the choice matters. For example, what happens to hash table performance with a dumbest-possible choice of a hash function?

Quiz 12.4

Consider a hash table with length $n \geq 1$, and let h be the hash function with $h(k) = 0$ for every key $k \in U$. Suppose a data set S is inserted into the hash table, with $|S| \leq n$. What is the worst-case running time of LOOKUP?

a) $\Theta(1)$ with chaining, $\Theta(1)$ with open addressing.

b) $\Theta(1)$ with chaining, $\Theta(|S|)$ with open addressing.

c) $\Theta(|S|)$ with chaining, $\Theta(1)$ with open addressing.

---

[7]There are several quick-and-dirty ways to define two hash functions from a single hash function h. For example, if keys are nonnegative integers represented in binary, define h_1 and h_2 from h by tacking on a new digit (either '0' or '1') to the end of the given key k: $h_1(k) = h(2k)$ and $h_2(k) = h(2k+1)$.

d) $\Theta(|S|)$ with chaining, $\Theta(|S|)$ with open addressing.

(See Section 12.3.7 for the solution and discussion.)

Pathological Data Sets and Hash Function Kryptonite

None of us would ever implement the dumb hash function in Quiz 12.4. Instead, we'd work hard to design a smart hash function guaranteed to cause few collisions, or better yet we'd look up such a function in a book like this one. Unfortunately, I can't tell you such a function. My excuse? *Every hash function, no matter how smart, has its own kryptonite,* in the form of a huge data set for which all objects collide and with hash table performance deteriorating as in Quiz 12.4.

> **Pathological Data Sets**
>
> For *every* hash function $h : U \to \{0, 1, 2, \ldots, n-1\}$, there exists a set S of keys of size $|U|/n$ such that $h(k_1) = h(k_2)$ for every $k_1, k_2 \in S$.[8]

This may sound crazy, but it's just a generalization of our Pigeonhole Principle argument from Section 12.3.3. Fix an arbitrarily smart hash function h. If h perfectly partitioned the keys in U among the n positions, each position would have exactly $|U|/n$ keys assigned to it; otherwise, for some position, even more than $|U|/n$ keys would be assigned to it. (For example, if $|U| = 200$ and $n = 25$, h must assign at least eight different keys to the same position.) In any case, there is a position $i \in \{0, 1, 2, \ldots, n-1\}$ to which the hash function h assigns at least $|U|/n$ distinct keys. If the keys in a data set S happen to be all those assigned to this position i, all the objects in the data set collide.

The data set S above is "pathological" in that it was constructed with the sole purpose of foiling the chosen hash function. Why should we care about such an artificial data set? The main reason is that it explains the asterisks in our running time bounds for hash table operations in Tables 12.1 and 12.2. Unlike most of the algorithms and data structures we've seen so far, there is no hope for a good running time guarantee that holds with absolutely no assumptions about the input. The best we can hope for is a good guarantee that applies to all "non-pathological" data sets, meaning data sets defined independently of the chosen hash function.[9]

The good news is that, with a well-crafted hash function, there's usually no need to worry about pathological data sets in practice. Security applications constitute an important exception to this rule, however.[10]

---

[8]In most applications of hash tables, $|U|$ is way bigger than n, in which case a data set of size $|U|/n$ is huge!

[9]There are also randomized solutions, in the spirit of the randomized QuickSort algorithm in Chapter 5. Specifically, a technique called *universal hashing* guarantees that for *every* data set, a random choice of a hash function (from a small but carefully chosen set of functions) typically causes few collisions. For details and examples, see Problem 12.7.

[10]An interesting case study is described in the paper "Denial of Service via Algorithmic Complexity Attacks," by Scott A. Crosby and Dan S. Wallach (*Proceedings of the 12th USENIX Security Symposium*, 2003). Crosby and Wallach showed how to bring a hash table-based network intrusion system to its knees through the clever construction of a pathological data set.

Random Hash Functions

Pathological data sets show that no one hash function is guaranteed to have a small number of collisions for every data set. The best we can hope for is a hash function that has few collisions for all "non-pathological" data sets.[11]

An extreme approach to decorrelating the choice of hash function and the data set is to choose a random function, meaning a function h for which, for each key $k \in U$, the value of $h(k)$ is chosen independently and uniformly at random from the array positions $\{0, 1, 2, \ldots, n-1\}$. The function h is chosen once and for all when the hash table is initially created. Intuitively, we'd expect such a random function to typically spread out the objects of a data set S roughly evenly across the n positions, provided S is defined independently of h. As long as the number n of buckets is at least a small constant times the data set size $|S|$, this would result in a manageable number of collisions.

Quiz 12.5

Why is it impractical to use a completely random choice of a hash function? (Choose all that apply.)

a) Actually, it is practical.

b) It is not deterministic.

c) It would take too much space to store.

d) It would take too much time to evaluate.

(See Section 12.3.7 for the solution and discussion.)

Good Hash Functions

A "good" hash function is one that enjoys the benefits of a random function without suffering from either of its drawbacks.

Hash Function Desiderata

1. Cheap to evaluate, ideally in $O(1)$ time.

2. Easy to store, ideally with $O(1)$ memory.

3. Mimics a random function by spreading non-pathological data sets roughly evenly across the positions of the hash table.

What Does a Good Hash Function Look Like?

While a detailed description of state-of-the-art hash functions is outside the scope of this book, you might be hungry for something more concrete than the desiderata above.

---

[11]The dumb hash function in Quiz 12.4 leads to terrible performance for *every* data set, pathological or otherwise.

For example, consider keys that are integers between 0 and some large number M.[12] A natural first stab at a hash function is to take a key's value modulo the number n of buckets:

$$h(k) = k \bmod n,$$

where $k \bmod n$ is the result of repeatedly subtracting n from k until the result is an integer between 0 and $n - 1$.

The good news is that this function is cheap to evaluate and requires no storage (beyond remembering n).[13] The bad news is that many real-world sets of keys are not uniformly distributed in their least significant bits. For example, if $n = 1000$ and all the keys have the same last three digits (base 10)—perhaps salaries at a company that are all multiples of 1000, or prices of cars that all end in "999"—then all the keys are hashed to the same position. Using only the most significant bits can cause similar problems—think, for example, about the country and area codes of phone numbers.

The next idea is to scramble a key before applying the modulus operation:

$$h(k) = (ak + b) \bmod n,$$

where a and b are integers in $\{1, 2, \ldots, n - 1\}$. This function is again cheap to compute and easy to store (just remember a, b, and n). For well-chosen a, b, and n, this function is probably good enough to use in a quick-and-dirty prototype. For mission-critical code, however, it's often essential to use more sophisticated hash functions, which are discussed further in Section 12.4.3.

To conclude, the two most important things to know about hash function design are:

Take-Aways

1. Experts have invented hash functions that are cheap to evaluate and easy to store, and that behave like random functions for all practical purposes.

2. Designing such a hash function is extremely tricky; you should leave it to experts if at all possible.

12.3.7   Solutions to Quizzes 12.3—12.5

Solution to Quiz 12.3

Correct answer: (a). Believe it or not, all you need is 23 people in a room before you've got at least a 50-50 chance that two have the same birthday. You can do (or look up) the appropriate probability calculation, or convince yourself of this with some simple simulations.

With 367 people, there would be a 100% chance of two people with the same birthday (by the Pigeonhole Principle). But already with 57 people, the probability is roughly 99%.[14] And with 184? 99.99...%, with a large number of nines.

---

[12]To apply this idea to non-numerical data like strings, it's necessary to first convert the data to integers. For example, in Java, the `hashCode` method implements such a conversion.

[13]There are much faster ways to compute $k \bmod n$ than repeated subtraction!

[14]Which leads to a good and reliable party trick for not-so-nerdy cocktail parties of at least this size.

Most people find the answer counterintuitive, and much smaller than they expected. This is why the example is known as the "birthday paradox."[15] More generally, on a planet in which there are k days each year, the chance of duplicate birthdays hits 50% with $\Theta(\sqrt{k})$ people.[16]

Solution to Quiz 12.4

Correct answer: (d). If collisions are resolved with chaining, the hash function h hashes every object in S to the same bucket: bucket 0. The hash table is then nothing more than the simple linked-list solution (Section 12.3.1), with $\Theta(|S|)$ time required for the LOOKUP operation.

For the case of open addressing, assume that the hash table uses linear probing. (The story is the same for more complicated strategies like double hashing.) The lucky first object of S will be assigned to position 0 of the array, the next object to position 1, and so on. The LOOKUP operation is then nothing more than a linear search through the first $|S|$ positions of an unsorted array, which requires $\Theta(|S|)$ time.

Solution to Quiz 12.5

Correct answers: (c),(d). A random function from U to $\{0, 1, 2, \ldots, n-1\}$ is effectively a lookup table of length $|U|$ with $\log_2 n$ bits per entry. When the universe is very large (as in most applications), writing down or evaluating such a function is out of the question.

We could try defining the hash function on a need-to-know basis, assigning a random value to $h(k)$ the first time the key k is encountered. But then evaluating $h(k)$ requires first checking whether it has already been defined. This boils down to a lookup for k, which is the problem we're supposed to be solving!

*12.4 Further Implementation Details

This section is for readers who want to implement a custom hash table from scratch. There's no silver bullet in hash table design, so I can only offer high-level guidance. The most important lessons are: (i) manage your hash table's load; (ii) use a well-tested modern hash function; and (iii) test several competing implementations to determine the best one for your particular application.

12.4.1 Load vs. Performance

The performance of a hash table degrades as its population increases: with chaining, buckets' lists grow longer; with open addressing, it gets harder to locate an empty slot.

---

[15]"Paradox" is a misnomer here; there's no logical inconsistency, just another illustration of how most people's brains are not wired to have good intuition about probability.

[16]The reason is that n people represent not just n opportunities for duplicate birthdays, but $\binom{n}{2} \approx n^2/2$ different opportunities (one for each pair of people). Two people have the same birthday with probability $1/k$, and you expect to start seeing collisions once the number of collision opportunities is roughly k (which happens when $n = \Theta(\sqrt{k})$).

The Load of a Hash Table

We measure the population of a hash table via its *load*:

$$\text{load of a hash table} = \frac{\text{number of objects stored}}{\text{array length } n}. \tag{12.1}$$

For example, in a hash table with chaining, the load is the average population in one of the table's buckets.

Quiz 12.6

Which hash table strategy is feasible for loads larger than 1?

a) Both chaining and open addressing.

b) Neither chaining nor open addressing.

c) Only chaining.

d) Only open addressing.

(See Section 12.4.5 for the solution and discussion.)

Idealized Performance with Chaining

In a hash table with chaining, the running time of a LOOKUP or DELETE operation scales with the lengths of buckets' lists. In the best-case scenario, the hash function spreads the objects perfectly evenly across the buckets. With a load of α, this idealized scenario results in at most $\lceil \alpha \rceil$ objects per bucket.[17] The LOOKUP and DELETE operations then take only $O(\lceil \alpha \rceil)$ time, and so are constant-time operations provided $\alpha = O(1)$.[18] Because good hash functions spread most data sets roughly evenly across buckets, this best-case performance is approximately matched by practical chaining-based hash table implementations (with a good hash function and with non-pathological data).[19]

---

[17]As usual, the notation $\lceil x \rceil$ denotes the "ceiling" function, which rounds its argument up to the nearest integer.

[18]We bother to write $O(\lceil \alpha \rceil)$ instead of $O(\alpha)$ only to handle the case in which α is close to 0. The running time of every operation is always $\Omega(1)$, no matter how small α is—if nothing else, there is one hash function evaluation to be accounted for. Alternatively, we could also write $O(1 + \alpha)$ or $O(\max\{1, \alpha\})$ in place of $O(\lceil \alpha \rceil)$.

[19]Here's a more mathematical argument for readers who remember basic probability (see also Appendix B). A good hash function mimics a random function, so let's go ahead and assume that the hash function h independently assigns each key to one of the n buckets uniformly at random. (See Section 12.6.1 for further discussion of this heuristic assumption.) Suppose that the key k is mapped to position i by h. Under our assumption, for every other key k', the probability that h also maps k' to the position i is $1/n$. Thus, for every data set S, in total over the keys distinct from k that are represented in S, the expected number of keys that share k's bucket is at most $|S|/n$ (a.k.a. the load α). (Technically, this statement follows from linearity of expectation and the "decomposition blueprint" described in Section 5.5.2.) Therefore, assuming that all stored objects have distinct keys, the expected running time of a LOOKUP for an object with key k is $O(\lceil \alpha \rceil)$.

Idealized Performance with Open Addressing

In a hash table with open addressing, the running time of a LOOKUP or INSERT operation scales with the number of probes required to locate an empty slot (or the sought-after object). When the hash table's load is α, an α fraction of its slots are full and the remaining $1 - \alpha$ fraction are empty. In the best-case scenario, each probe is uncorrelated with the hash table's contents and has a $1 - \alpha$ chance of locating an empty slot. In this idealized scenario, the expected number of probes required is $1/(1 - \alpha)$.[20] If α is bounded away from 1—like 70%, for example—the idealized running time of all operations is $O(1)$. This best-case performance is approximately matched by practical hash tables implemented with double hashing or other sophisticated probe sequences. With linear probing, objects tend to clump together in consecutive slots, resulting in slower operation times: roughly $1/(1 - \alpha)^2$, even in the idealized case.[21] This is still $O(1)$ time provided the load α is significantly less than 100%.

Collision-Resolution Strategy	Idealized Running Time of LOOKUP
Chaining	$O\left(\lceil\alpha\rceil\right)$
Double hashing	$O\left(1/(1 - \alpha)\right)$
Linear probing	$O\left(1/(1 - \alpha)^2\right)$

Table 12.3: Idealized performance of a hash table as a function of its load α and its collision-resolution strategy. All three running time bounds are $O(1)$ provided the hash table load α is kept well below 1.[22]

12.4.2   Managing the Load of Your Hash Table

Insertions and deletions change the numerator in (12.1), and a hash table implementation should update the denominator to keep pace. A good rule of thumb is to periodically resize the hash table's array so that the table's load stays below 70% (or perhaps even less, depending on the application and your collision-resolution strategy). Then, with a well-chosen hash function and non-pathological data, all of the most common collision-resolution strategies typically lead to constant-time hash table operations.

The simplest way to implement array resizing is to keep track of the table's load and, whenever it reaches 70%, to double the number n of buckets. All the objects are then rehashed into the new, larger hash table (which now has load 35%). Optionally, if a sequence of deletions brings the load down far enough, the array can be downsized accordingly to

---

[20] This resembles a coin-flipping experiment: if a coin has probability p of coming up "heads," what is the average number of flips required to see your first "heads"? (For us, $p = 1 - \alpha$.) As discussed in Section 6.2—or search Wikipedia for "geometric random variable"—the answer is $1/p$.

[21] This highly non-obvious result was first derived by Donald E. Knuth, the father of the analysis of algorithms. It made quite an impression on him: "I first formulated the following derivation in 1962... Ever since that day, the analysis of algorithms has in fact been one of the major themes in my life." (Donald E. Knuth, *The Art of Computer Programming, Volume 3 (2nd edition)*, Addison-Wesley, 1998, page 536.)

[22] For more details on how the performance of different collision-resolution strategies varies with the hash table load, see the bonus videos at www.algorithmsilluminated.org.

save space (with all remaining objects rehashed into the smaller table). Such resizes can be time-consuming, but in most applications they are infrequent.

12.4.3   Choosing Your Hash Function

Designing good hash functions is a difficult and dark art. It's easy to propose reasonable-looking hash functions that end up being subtly flawed, leading to poor hash table performance. For this reason, I advise against designing your own hash functions from scratch. Fortunately, clever programmers have devised a number of well-tested and publicly available hash functions that you can use in your own work.

Which hash function should you use? Ask ten programmers this question, and you'll get at least eleven different answers. Because different hash functions fare better on different data distributions, you should compare the performance of several state-of-the-art hash functions in your particular application and runtime environment. As of this writing (in 2022), hash functions that are good starting points for further exploration include `FarmHash`, `MurmurHash3`, `SpookyHash`, and `MD5`. These are all *non-cryptographic* hash functions, and are not designed to protect against adversarial attacks like that of Crosby and Wallach (see footnote 10).[23] *Cryptographic* hash functions are more complicated and slower to evaluate than their non-cryptographic counterparts, but they do protect against such attacks.[24] A good starting point here is the hash function `SHA-1` and its newer relatives like `SHA-256` and `Keccak-256`.

12.4.4   Choosing Your Collision-Resolution Strategy

For collision resolution, is it better to use chaining or open addressing? With open addressing, is it better to use linear probing, double hashing, or something else? As usual, when I present you with multiple solutions to a problem, the answer is "it depends." For example, chaining takes more space than open addressing (to store the pointers in the linked lists), so the latter might be preferable when space is a first-order concern. Deletions are more complicated with open addressing than with chaining, so chaining might be preferable in applications with lots of deletions.

Comparing linear probing with more complicated open addressing implementations like double hashing is also tricky. Linear probing results in bigger clumps of consecutive objects in the hash table and therefore more probes than more sophisticated approaches; however, this cost can be offset by its friendly interactions with the runtime environment's memory hierarchy. As with the choice of a hash function, for mission-critical code, there's no substitute for coding up multiple competing implementations and seeing which works best for your application.

---

[23]The function `MD5` was originally designed to be a cryptographic hash function, but it is no longer considered secure.

[24]All hash functions, even cryptographic ones, suffer from pathological data sets (Section 12.3.6). Cryptographic hash functions have the special property that it's computationally infeasible to reverse engineer a pathological data set, in roughly the same sense that it's computationally infeasible to factor large integers and break the RSA public-key cryptosystem.

12.4.5   Solution to Quiz 12.6

Correct answer: (c). Because hash tables with open addressing store at most one object per array position, they can never have a load larger than 1. Once the load is 1, it's not possible to insert any more objects.

An arbitrary number of objects can be inserted into a hash table with chaining, although performance degrades as more are inserted. For example, if the load is 100, the average length of a bucket's list is also 100.

12.5   Bloom Filters: The Basics

Bloom filters are close cousins of hash tables.[25] They are ridiculously space-efficient but, in exchange, they occasionally make errors. This section covers what bloom filters are good for and how they are implemented, while Section 12.6 maps out the trade-off curve between a filter's space usage and its frequency of errors.

12.5.1   Supported Operations

The raison d'être of a bloom filter is essentially the same as that of a hash table: super-fast insertions and lookups, so that you can quickly remember what you've seen and what you haven't. Why should we bother with another data structure with the same set of operations? Because bloom filters are preferable to hash tables in applications in which space is at a premium and the occasional error is not a dealbreaker.

Like hash tables with open addressing, bloom filters are much easier to implement and understand when they support only INSERT and LOOKUP (and no DELETE). We'll focus on this case.

Bloom Filters: Supported Operations

LOOKUP: for a key k, return "yes" if k has been previously inserted into the bloom filter and "no" otherwise.

INSERT: add a new key k to the bloom filter.

Bloom filters are very space-efficient; in a typical use case, they might require only 8 bits per insertion. This is pretty incredible, as 8 bits are nowhere near enough to remember even a 32-bit key or a pointer to an object! This is the reason why the LOOKUP operation in a bloom filter returns only a "yes"/"no" answer, whereas in a hash table the operation returns a pointer to the sought-after object (if found). This is also why the INSERT operation now takes only a key, rather than (a pointer to) an object.

Bloom filters can make mistakes, in contrast to all the other data structures we've studied. There are two different kinds of mistakes: false negatives, in which LOOKUP returns "false" even though the queried key was inserted previously; and false positives, in which LOOKUP returns "true" even though the queried key was never inserted in the past. We'll see in

---

[25]Named after their inventor; see the paper "Space/Time Trade-offs in Hash Coding with Allowable Errors," by Burton H. Bloom (*Communications of the ACM*, 1970).

Section 12.5.3 that basic bloom filters never suffer from false negatives, but they can have "phantom elements" in the form of false positives. Section 12.6 shows that the frequency of false positives can be controlled by tuning the space usage appropriately. A typical bloom filter implementation might have an error rate of around 1% or 0.1%.

The running times of both the INSERT and LOOKUP operations are as fast as those in a hash table. Even better, these operations are *guaranteed* to run in constant time, independent of the bloom filter implementation and the data set.[26] The implementation and data set do affect the filter's error rate, however.

Summarizing the advantages and disadvantages of bloom filters over hash tables:

Bloom Filters Vs. Hash Tables

1. **Pro:** More space efficient.

2. **Pro:** Guaranteed constant-time operations for every data set.

3. **Con:** Can't store pointers to objects.

4. **Con:** Deletions are complicated, relative to a hash table with chaining.

5. **Con:** Non-zero false positive probability.

The scorecard for the basic bloom filter reads:

Operation	Running time
LOOKUP	$O(1)^{\dagger}$
INSERT	$O(1)$

Table 12.4: Basic bloom filters: supported operations and their running times. The dagger ($\dagger$) indicates that the LOOKUP operation suffers from a controllable but non-zero probability of false positives.

Bloom filters should be used in place of hash tables in applications in which their advantages matter and their disadvantages are not dealbreakers.

When to Use a Bloom Filter

If your application requires fast lookups with a dynamically changing set of objects, space is at a premium, and a small number of false positives can be tolerated, the bloom filter is usually the data structure of choice.

12.5.2   Applications

Next are three applications with repeated lookups in which it can be important to save space and false positives are not a dealbreaker.

---

[26]Provided hash function evaluations take constant time and that a constant number of bits is used per inserted key.

Spell checkers.   Back in the 1970s, bloom filters were used to implement spell checkers. In a preprocessing step, every word in a dictionary was inserted into a bloom filter. Spell-checking a document boiled down to one LOOKUP operation per word in the document, and flagging any words for which the operation returned "no."

In this application, a false positive corresponds to an illegal word that the spell checker inadvertently accepts. Such errors are not ideal. Space was at a premium in the early 1970s, however, so at that time it was a win to use bloom filters.

Forbidden passwords.   An old application that remains relevant today is keeping track of forbidden passwords—passwords that are too common or too easy to guess. Initially, all forbidden passwords are inserted into a bloom filter; additional forbidden passwords can be inserted later, as needed. When a user tries to set or reset their password, the system looks up the proposed password in the bloom filter. If the LOOKUP returns "yes," the user is asked to try again with a different password. Here, a false positive translates to a strong password that the system rejects. Provided the error rate is not too large, say at most 1% or 0.1%, this is not a big deal. Once in a while, some user will need one extra attempt to find a password acceptable to the system.

Internet routers.   Many of today's killer applications of bloom filters take place in the core of the Internet, where routers process data packets that arrive at a torrential rate. The more these routers can do, the better. For example, an ideal router would be able to compare the source IP address of each arriving packet to those in a list of blocked IP addresses; keep track of cache contents to avoid spurious cache lookups; maintain statistics that facilitate identifying denial-of-service attacks; and so on. These applications all boil down to repeated lookups, with the rate of packet arrivals demanding super-fast operations and limited router memory putting space at a premium. All of them are right in the wheelhouse of a bloom filter.

12.5.3   Implementation

Looking under the hood of a bloom filter reveals an elegant implementation. The data structure maintains an n-bit string, or equivalently a length-n array A in which each entry is either 0 or 1. (All entries are initialized to 0.) The structure also uses m hash functions $h_1, h_2, \ldots, h_m$, each mapping the universe U of all possible keys to the set $\{0, 1, 2, \ldots, n - 1\}$ of array positions. The parameter m is proportional to the number of bits that the bloom filter uses per insertion, and is typically a small constant (like 5).[27]

Every time a key is inserted into a bloom filter, each of the m hash functions plants a flag by setting the corresponding bit of the array A to 1.

Bloom Filter: INSERT (given key k)

for $i := 1$ to m **do**
$\qquad A[h_i(k)] := 1$

---

[27] Sections 12.3.6 and 12.4.3 provide guidance for choosing one hash function. Footnote 7 describes a quick-and-dirty way of deriving two hash functions from one; the same idea can be used to derive m hash functions from one. An alternative approach, inspired by double hashing, is to use two hash functions h and h' to define $h_1, h_2, \ldots, h_m$ via the formula $h_i(k) = (h(k) + (i - 1) \cdot h'(k)) \bmod n$.

For example, if $m = 3$ and $h_1(k) = 23$, $h_2(k) = 17$, and $h_3(k) = 5$, inserting k causes the 5th, 17th, and 23rd bits of the array to be set to 1 (Figure 12.5).

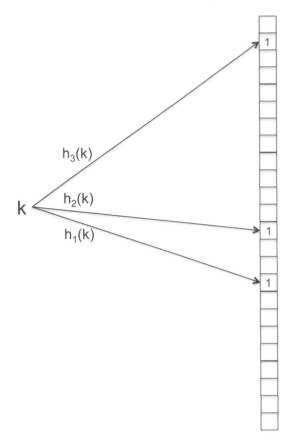

Figure 12.5: Inserting a new key k into a bloom filter sets the bits in positions $h_1(k), h_2(k), \ldots, h_m(k)$ to 1.

In the LOOKUP operation, a bloom filter looks for the footprint that would have been left by k's insertion.

Bloom Filter: LOOKUP (given key k)

    for $i := 1$ to m **do**
        if $A[h_i(k)] = 0$ **then**
            return "no"
    return "yes"

We can now see why bloom filters can't suffer from false negatives. When a key k is inserted, the relevant m bits are set to 1. Over the bloom filter's lifetime, bits can change from 0 to 1 but never the reverse. Thus, these m bits remain 1 forevermore. Every subsequent LOOKUP for k is guaranteed to return the correct answer "yes."

We can also see how false positives arise. Suppose that $m = 3$ and the four keys k_1, k_2, k_3, k_4 have the following hash values:

Key	Value of h_1	Value of h_2	Value of h_3
k_1	23	17	5
k_2	5	48	12
k_3	37	8	17
k_4	32	23	2

Suppose we insert k_2, k_3, and k_4 into the bloom filter (Figure 12.6). These three insertions cause a total of nine bits to be set to 1, including the three bits in k_1's footprint (5, 17, and 23). At this point, the bloom filter can no longer distinguish whether or not k_1 has been inserted. Even if k_1 was never inserted into the filter, a LOOKUP for it will return "yes," which is a false positive.

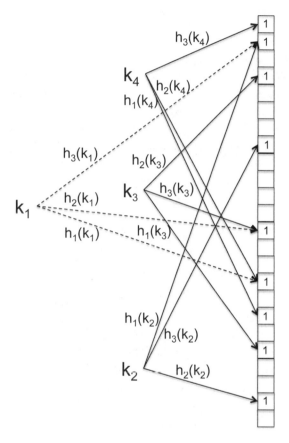

Figure 12.6: False positives: A bloom filter can contain the footprint of a key k_1 even if k_1 was never inserted.

Intuitively, as we make the bloom filter size n bigger, the number of overlaps between the footprints of different keys should decrease, in turn leading to fewer false positives. But the first-order goal of a bloom filter is to save on space. Is there a sweet spot where both n and the frequency of false positives are small simultaneously? The answer is not obvious and requires some mathematical analysis, undertaken in the next section.[28]

---

[28]Spoiler alert: The answer is yes. For example, using 8 bits per key typically leads to a false positive probability of roughly 2% (assuming well-crafted hash functions and a non-pathological data set).

*12.6 Bloom Filters: Heuristic Analysis

The goal of this section is to understand the quantitative trade-off between the space consumption and the frequency of false positives of a bloom filter. That is, how rapidly does the frequency of false positives of a bloom filter decrease as a function of its array length?

If a bloom filter uses a length-n bit array and stores (the footprints of) a set S of keys, the per-key storage in bits is

$$b = \frac{n}{|S|}.$$

We're interested in the case in which b is smaller than the number of bits needed to explicitly store a key or a pointer to an object (which is typically 32 or more). For example, b could be 8 or 16.

12.6.1 Heuristic Assumptions

The relationship between the per-key storage b and the frequency of false positives is not easy to guess, and working it out requires some probability calculations. To understand them, all you need to remember from probability theory is:

> The probability that two independent events both occur equals the product of their individual probabilities.

For example, the probability that two independent tosses of a fair 6-sided die are "4" followed by an odd number is $\frac{1}{6} \cdot \frac{3}{6} = \frac{1}{12}$.[29]

To greatly simplify the calculations, we'll make two unjustified assumptions—the same ones we used in passing in our heuristic analyses of hash table performance (Section 12.4.1).

Unjustified Assumptions

1. For every key $k \in U$ and hash function h_i used in the bloom filter, $h_i(k)$ is uniformly distributed, with each of the n array positions equally likely.

2. All of the $h_i(k)$'s, ranging over all keys $k \in U$ and hash functions $h_1, h_2, \ldots, h_m$, are independent random variables.

The first assumption says that, for each key k, each hash function h_i, and each array position $q \in \{0, 1, 2, \ldots, n - 1\}$, the probability that $h_i(k) = q$ is exactly $1/n$. The second assumption implies that, for every pair of keys k_1, k_2 and hash functions h_i, h_j, the probability that $h_i(k_1) = q$ and also $h_j(k_2) = r$ is the product of the individual probabilities, also known as $1/n^2$.[30]

Both assumptions would be legitimate if we randomly chose each of the bloom filter's hash functions independently from the set of all possible hash functions, as in Section 12.3.6. Completely random hash functions are unimplementable (recall Quiz 12.5), so in practice a

---

[29]See also Appendix B and the additional resources available at www.algorithmsilluminated.org.

[30]Unless of course both $k_1 = k_2$ and $i = j$, in which case the probability is either 0 (if $q \neq r$) or 1 (if $q = r$).

fixed, "random-like" function is used. This means that in reality, *our heuristic assumptions are false*. With fixed hash functions, every value $h_i(k)$ is completely determined, with no randomness whatsoever. This is why we call the analysis "heuristic."

On Heuristic Analyses

What possible use is a mathematical analysis based on false premises? Ideally, the conclusion of the analysis remains valid in practical situations even though the heuristic assumptions are not satisfied. For bloom filters, the hope is that, provided the data is non-pathological and well-crafted "random-like" hash functions are used, the frequency of false positives behaves *as if* the hash functions were completely random.

You should always be suspicious of a heuristic analysis, and be sure to test its conclusions with a concrete implementation. Happily, empirical studies demonstrate that the frequency of false positives in bloom filters in practice is comparable to the prediction of our heuristic analysis.

12.6.2   The Fraction of Bits Set to 1

We begin with a preliminary calculation.

Quiz 12.7

Suppose a data set S is inserted into a bloom filter that uses m hash functions and a length-n bit array. Under our heuristic assumptions, what is the probability that the array's first bit is set to 1?

a) $\left(\frac{1}{n}\right)^{|S|}$

b) $\left(1 - \frac{1}{n}\right)^{|S|}$

c) $\left(1 - \frac{1}{n}\right)^{m|S|}$

d) $1 - \left(1 - \frac{1}{n}\right)^{m|S|}$

(See Section 12.6.5 for the solution and discussion.)

There is nothing special about the first bit of the bloom filter. By symmetry, the answer to Quiz 12.7 is also the probability that the 7th, or the 23rd, or the 42nd bit is set to 1.

12.6.3   The False Positive Probability

The solution to Quiz 12.7 is messy. To clean it up, we can use the fact that e^x is a good approximation of $1 + x$ when x is close to 0, where $e \approx 2.718\ldots$ is the base of the natural logarithm. This fact is evident from a plot of the two functions:

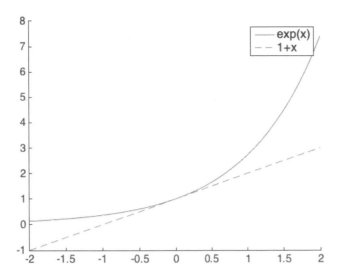

For us, the relevant value of x is $x = -\frac{1}{n}$, which is close to 0 (ignoring the uninteresting case of tiny n). Thus, among friends, we can use the quantity

$$1 - \left(e^{-1/n}\right)^{m|S|} \text{ as a proxy for } 1 - \left(1 - \tfrac{1}{n}\right)^{m|S|}.$$

We can further simplify the left-hand side to

$$1 - e^{-m|S|/n} = \underbrace{1 - e^{-m/b}}_{\text{estimate of probability that a given bit is 1}},$$

where $b = n/|S|$ denotes the number of bits used per insertion.

Fine, but what about the frequency of false positives? A false positive occurs for a key k not in S if all the m bits $h_1(k), \ldots, h_m(k)$ in its footprint are set to 1 after inserting the keys in S.[31] Because the probability that a given bit is 1 is approximately $1 - e^{-m/b}$, the probability that all m of these bits are set to 1 is approximately

$$\underbrace{\left(1 - e^{-\frac{m}{b}}\right)^m}_{\text{estimate of false positive frequency}}. \tag{12.2}$$

As a sanity check, let's examine this estimate for extreme values of b. As the bloom filter grows arbitrarily large (with $b \to \infty$) and is increasingly empty, the estimate (12.2) goes to 0, as we would hope (because e^{-x} goes to 1 as x goes to 0). Conversely, when b is very small, the estimate of the chance of a false positive is large ($\approx 63.2\%$ when $b = m = 1$, for example).[32]

---

[31] For simplicity, we're assuming that each of the m hash functions hashes k to a different position (as is usually the case).

[32] In addition to our two heuristic assumptions, this analysis cheated twice. First, $e^{-1/n}$ isn't exactly equal to $1 - \frac{1}{n}$, but it's close. Second, even with our heuristic assumptions, the values of two different bits of a bloom filter are not independent—knowing that one bit is 1 makes it slightly more likely that a different bit is 0—but they are close. Both cheats are close approximations of reality (given the heuristic assumptions), and it can be verified both mathematically and empirically that they lead to an accurate conclusion.

12.6.4   The Punchline

We can use our precise estimate (12.2) of the false positive rate to understand the trade-off between space and accuracy. In addition to the per-key space b, the estimate in (12.2) depends on m, the number of hash functions that the bloom filter uses. The value of m is under complete control of the bloom filter designer, so why not set it to minimize the estimated frequency of errors? That is, holding b fixed, we can choose m to minimize (12.2). Calculus can identify the best choice of m, by setting the derivative of (12.2) with respect to m to 0 and solving for m. You can do the calculations in the privacy of your own home, with the end result being that $(\ln 2) \cdot b \approx 0.693 \cdot b$ is the optimal choice for m. This is not an integer, so round it up or down to get the ideal number of hash functions. For example, when $b = 8$, the number of hash functions m should be either 5 or 6.

We can now specialize the error estimate in (12.2) with the optimal choice of $m = (\ln 2) \cdot b$ hash functions to produce the estimate

$$\left(1 - e^{-\ln 2}\right)^{(\ln 2) \cdot b} = \left(\frac{1}{2}\right)^{(\ln 2) \cdot b}.$$

This is exactly what we wanted all along—a formula that spits out the expected frequency of false positives as a function of the amount of space we're willing to use.[33] The formula decreases *exponentially* with the per-key space b, which is why there is a sweet spot at which both the bloom filter size and its frequency of false positives are small simultaneously. For example, with only 8 bits per key stored ($b = 8$), this estimate is slightly over 2%. What if we take $b = 16$ (see Problem 12.3)?

12.6.5   Solution to Quiz 12.7

Correct answer: (d). We can visualize the insertion of the keys in S into the bloom filter as the throwing of darts at a dartboard with n regions, with each dart equally likely to land in each region. Because the bloom filter uses m hash functions, each insertion corresponds to the throwing of m darts, for a total of $m|S|$ darts overall. A dart hitting the ith region corresponds to setting the ith bit of the bloom filter to 1.

By the first heuristic assumption, for every $k \in S$ and $i \in \{1, 2, \ldots, m\}$, the probability that the corresponding dart hits the first region (that is, that $h_i(k) = 0$) is $\frac{1}{n}$. Thus, the dart *misses* the first region (that is, $h_i(k)$ is *not* 0) with the remaining probability $1 - \frac{1}{n}$. By the second heuristic assumption, different darts are independent. Thus, the probability that *every* dart misses the first region—that $h_i(k) \neq 0$ for *every* $k \in S$ and $i \in \{1, 2, \ldots, m\}$— is the product of the individual probabilities, which is $(1 - \frac{1}{n})^{m|S|}$. With the remaining $1 - (1 - \frac{1}{n})^{m|S|}$ probability, some dart hits the first region (that is, the first bit of the bloom filter is set to 1).

The Upshot

★ If your application requires fast lookups on an evolving set of objects, the hash table is usually the data structure of choice.

---

[33]Equivalently, if you have a target false positive rate of $\epsilon > 0$, you should choose the per-key space to be at least $b \approx 1.44 \log_2 \frac{1}{\epsilon}$ bits. As expected, the smaller the target error rate ϵ, the larger the space requirements.

* Hash tables support the INSERT and LOOKUP operations, and in some cases the DELETE operation. With a well-implemented hash table and non-pathological data, all operations typically run in $O(1)$ time.

* A hash table uses a hash function to translate from objects' keys to positions in an array.

* Two keys k_1, k_2 collide under a hash function h if $h(k_1) = h(k_2)$. Collisions are inevitable, and a hash table needs a method for resolving them, such as chaining or open addressing.

* A good hash function is cheap to evaluate and easy to store, and mimics a random function by spreading non-pathological data sets roughly evenly across the positions of the hash table's array.

* Experts have published good hash functions that you can use in your own work.

* A hash table should be resized periodically to keep its load small (for example, less than 70%).

* For mission-critical code, there's no substitute for trying out multiple competing hash table implementations.

* Bloom filters also support the INSERT and LOOKUP operations in constant time, and are preferable to hash tables in applications in which space is at a premium and the occasional false positive is not a dealbreaker.

Test Your Understanding

Problem 12.1 *(S)* Which of the following is *not* a property you would expect a well-designed hash function to have?

a) The hash function should spread out every data set roughly evenly across its range.

b) The hash function should be easy to compute (constant time or close to it).

c) The hash function should be easy to store (constant space or close to it).

d) The hash function should spread out most data sets roughly evenly across its range.

Problem 12.2 *(S)* A good hash function mimics the gold standard of a random function for all practical purposes, so it's interesting to investigate collisions with a random function. If the locations of two different keys $k_1, k_2 \in U$ are chosen independently and uniformly at random across n array positions (with all possibilities equally likely), what is the probability that k_1 and k_2 will collide?

a) 0

b) $\frac{1}{n}$

c) $\frac{2}{n(n-1)}$

d) $\frac{1}{n^2}$

Problem 12.3 *(S)* We interpreted our heuristic analysis of bloom filters in Section 12.6 by specializing it to the case of 8 bits of space per key inserted into the filter. Suppose we were willing to use twice as much space (16 bits per insertion). What can you say about the corresponding false positive rate, according to our heuristic analysis, assuming that the number m of hash functions is set optimally? (Choose the strongest true statement.)

a) The false positive rate would be less than 1%.

b) The false positive rate would be less than 0.1%.

c) The false positive rate would be less than 0.01%.

d) The false positive rate would be less than 0.001%.

Problem 12.4 *(S)* The 3-SUM problem extends the 2-SUM problem in the obvious way:

Problem: 3-SUM

Input: An unsorted array A of n integers, and a target integer t.

Goal: Determine whether or not there are three (not necessarily distinct) numbers x, y, z in A satisfying $x + y + z = t$.

Give an $O(n^2)$-time algorithm for this problem. (You can assume that every hash table operation requires $O(1)$ time.)

Problem 12.5 *(H)* This problem investigates the following hash table operation:

OUTPUTUNSORTED: output pointers to the objects stored in the hash table one by one, in some arbitrary order.

(a) Propose an implementation of OUTPUTUNSORTED for hash tables implemented with chaining. The operation should run in $O(n + m)$ time, where n is the length of the hash table's array and m is the number of stored objects.

(b) Propose an implementation of OUTPUTUNSORTED for hash tables implemented with open addressing. The operation should run in $O(n)$ time. (Recall that with open addressing, m must be at most n.)

(c) Show how to augment a hash table (with chaining or open addressing) so that the OUTPUTUNSORTED operation can be implemented in $O(m)$ time (even if m is much less than n). The running time of the INSERT, LOOKUP, and DELETE operations should degrade by at most a constant factor.

Problem 12.6 *(H)* Propose how to use a hash table to compute, given a text file with n words, the 10 most frequently occurring words. Assuming that the INSERT and LOOKUP operations run in $O(1)$ time, your solution should run in $O(n)$ time.

Challenge Problems

Problem 12.7 *(H)* This problem and the next assume familiarity with probability, random variables, and expectation (at the level of Appendix B). The goal of this problem is to explore universal hashing (as mentioned in footnote 9).

Fix a universe U of possible keys and a number n of buckets for a hash table. Recall that a hash function is a function from U to $\{0, 1, 2, \ldots, n-1\}$. A set H of such functions is called *universal* if every pair $x, y \in U$ of distinct keys collides under at most a $1/n$ fraction of the hash functions in H. Equivalently, for every such pair x, y, the probability that x and y collide under a randomly chosen function from H is at most $1/n$:

$$\mathbf{Pr}_{h \in H}[h(x) = h(y)] \leq \frac{1}{n}.$$

Confronted with a new definition like universal hashing, you should immediately ask two questions: what are some interesting examples, and what are some applications?

(a) Prove that the set of all functions from U to $\{0, 1, 2, \ldots, n-1\}$ is universal.

(b) The set in part (a) is way too big to be practically useful (see Quiz 12.5); here's a much smaller one.

Assume that $U = \{0, 1\}^k$ is the set of all k-bit strings and that $n = 2^\ell$ is a power of 2, so that the inputs and outputs of a hash function both correspond to 0-1 vectors (of lengths k and ℓ, respectively). Every $\ell \times k$ 0-1 matrix M can then be interpreted as a hash function h_M, through matrix-vector multiplication: $h_M(x) = M \cdot x$.[34] For example (with $k = 4$ and $\ell = 2$),

$$\underbrace{\begin{bmatrix} 0 & 1 & 0 & 1 \\ 0 & 0 & 1 & 1 \end{bmatrix}}_{M} \cdot \underbrace{\begin{bmatrix} 0 \\ 1 \\ 0 \\ 1 \end{bmatrix}}_{x} = \underbrace{\begin{bmatrix} 0 \\ 1 \end{bmatrix}}_{M \cdot x (=h_M(x))}.$$

Such a hash function can be described by only $k \cdot \ell = \log_2 |U| \cdot \log_2 n$ bits.[35] Prove that the set H of all such functions (corresponding to all possible $\ell \times k$ 0-1 matrices M) is universal.

---

[34] Here x is viewed as a 0-1 vector of length k, and all additions are modulo 2. In the context of 0s and 1s, "addition modulo 2" simply means that $1 + 1 = 0$ (and as usual $0 + 0 = 0$ and $1 + 0 = 0 + 1 = 1$).

[35] In comparison, describing an arbitrary hash function requires $|U| \log_2 n$ bits.

(c) Fix a data set S of m distinct keys drawn from the universe U. Let H be a universal set of hash functions (from U to $\{0, 1, 2, \ldots, n-1\}$). Consider a hash table with chaining, with the hash function h chosen uniformly at random from the set H. Prove that, for every key $x \in S$ in the data set, in expectation over the random choice of the hash function $h \in H$, the time required to perform a LOOKUP for x is that of one hash function evaluation plus $O(\lceil m/n \rceil)$ additional work.

Problem 12.8 *(H)* For this problem, we'll consider applications of hash tables in which the entire data set is available in advance of the table's initialization.[36] To compensate for this strong assumption, we'll pursue the ambitious goal of setting up a linear-size hash table-esque data structure that has *no collisions at all*.[37]

Assume the existence of a subroutine that takes as input a data set S and a hash table array length n and returns as output a hash function (from U to $\{0, 1, 2, \ldots, n-1\}$) that causes fewer than $|S|^2/n$ collisions among the pairs of elements of S.[38,39]

Given a size-m data set S, use this subroutine as a black box to design a data structure with the following properties:

1. Total space: $O(m)$.

2. Guaranteed running time of the LOOKUP operation: two hash function evaluations, plus $O(1)$ additional work.

Programming Problems

Problem 12.9 Implement in your favorite programming language the hash table-based solution to the 2-SUM problem in Section 12.2.2. For example, you could generate a list S of one million random integers between -10^{11} and 10^{11}, and count the number of targets t between -10000 and 10000 for which there are distinct $x, y \in S$ with $x + y = t$.

You can use existing implementations of hash tables, or you can implement your own from scratch. In the latter case, compare your performance under different collision-resolution strategies, such as chaining versus linear probing. (See www. algorithmsilluminated.org for test cases and challenge data sets.)

---

[36] For example, the 2-SUM problem (Section 12.2.2) falls into this category, as do the spell-checking and password-checking applications mentioned in Section 12.5.2.

[37] This goal is closely related to that of *perfect hashing*.

[38] For example, if h maps four elements of S to the bucket 0, this bucket contributes $\binom{4}{2} = 6$ collisions to the total.

[39] How would you ever implement such a subroutine? Simply choose a small number of hash functions independently and randomly from a universal set (such as the 0-1 matrices from Problem 12.7(b))—almost always, at least one of them will have the sought-after property. (Hint for the proof: in the spirit of footnote 16, use linearity of expectation to argue that the expected number of collisions caused by such a randomly chosen hash function is $\approx |S|^2/2n$.)

Part III

Greedy Algorithms and Dynamic Programming

Chapter 13

Introduction to Greedy Algorithms

Much of the beauty in the design and analysis of algorithms stems from the interplay between general algorithm design principles and the instantiation of these principles to solve concrete computational problems. There's no silver bullet in algorithm design—no universal technique that can solve every computational problem you'll encounter. But there *are* several general design paradigms that can help you solve problems from many different application domains. Teaching you these paradigms and their most famous instantiations is one of the major goals of this book.

13.1 The Greedy Algorithm Design Paradigm

13.1.1 Algorithm Design Paradigms

What's an "algorithm design paradigm"? Section 3.1 provided our first example, the divide-and-conquer paradigm. That paradigm went like this:

The Divide-and-Conquer Paradigm

1. *Divide* the input into smaller subproblems.

2. *Conquer* the subproblems recursively.

3. *Combine* the solutions for the subproblems into a solution for the original problem.

We saw numerous instantiations of this paradigm in Part I of this book: the MergeSort and QuickSort algorithms, Karatsuba's $O(n^{1.59})$-time algorithm for multiplying two n-digit integers, Strassen's $O(n^{2.71})$-time algorithm for multiplying two $n \times n$ matrices, and more.

Chapters 13–15 are about the *greedy* algorithm design paradigm. What is a greedy algorithm, exactly? Much blood and ink have been spilled over this question, so we'll content ourselves with an informal definition.[1]

The Greedy Paradigm

Construct a solution iteratively, via a sequence of myopic decisions, and hope that everything works out in the end.

---

[1]To investigate formal definitions of greedy algorithms, start with the paper "(Incremental) Priority Algorithms," by Allan Borodin, Morten N. Nielsen, and Charles Rackoff (*Algorithmica*, 2003).

The best way to get a feel for greedy algorithms is through examples. We'll see several over the next few chapters.[2]

13.1.2   Themes of the Greedy Paradigm

Here are a few themes to watch for in our examples. (You might want to re-read this section after going through one or more examples, so that it's less abstract.) First, for many problems, it's surprisingly easy to come up with one or even multiple greedy algorithms that might plausibly work. This is both a bug and a feature—greedy algorithms can be a great cure for writer's block when you're stuck on a problem, but it can be hard to assess which greedy approach is the most promising. Second, the running time analysis is often a one-liner. For example, many greedy algorithms boil down to sorting plus a linear amount of extra processing. Using MergeSort (Chapter 1) or HeapSort (Chapter 10) as a subroutine, the running time would then be $O(n \log n)$, where n is the number of objects to be sorted. Finally, it's often difficult to figure out whether a proposed greedy algorithm actually returns the correct output for every possible input. The fear is that one of the algorithm's irrevocable myopic decisions will come back to haunt you and, with full hindsight, be revealed as a terrible idea. And even when a greedy algorithm *is* correct, proving it can be difficult.[3]

Features and Bugs of the Greedy Paradigm

1. Easy to come up with one or more greedy algorithms.

2. Easy to analyze the running time.

3. Hard to establish correctness.

One of the reasons why it can be hard to prove the correctness of greedy algorithms is that most such algorithms are *not* correct, meaning there exist inputs for which the algorithm fails to produce the desired output. If you remember only one thing about greedy algorithms, it should be this.

Warning

Most greedy algorithms are not always correct.

This point is especially difficult to accept for clever greedy algorithms that you invented yourself. You might believe, in your heart of hearts, that your natural greedy algorithm must

---

[2]Dijkstra's shortest-path algorithm can be viewed as a greedy algorithm—in each iteration, the algorithm irrevocably and myopically commits to an estimate of the shortest-path distance to one additional vertex, never revisiting the decision. As we saw in Theorem 9.1, in graphs with only nonnegative edge lengths, everything works out in the end and all the shortest-path distance estimates are correct.

[3]All three themes are a big contrast to the divide-and-conquer paradigm. It's often tricky to come up with a good divide-and-conquer algorithm for a problem, and when you do, there's usually a "Eureka!" moment when you know that you've cracked the problem. Analyzing the running times of divide-and-conquer algorithms can be difficult, due to the tug-of-war between the forces of proliferating subproblems and shrinking work-per-subproblem. (All of Chapter 4 is devoted to this topic.) Finally, proofs of correctness for divide-and-conquer algorithms are usually straightforward inductive arguments.

always solve the problem correctly. More often than not, this belief is unfounded.[4]

Now that my conscience is clear, let's look at some cherry-picked examples of problems that *can* be solved correctly with a judiciously designed greedy algorithm.

13.2   A Scheduling Problem

Our first case study concerns *scheduling*, in which the goal is to schedule tasks on one or more shared resources to optimize some objective. For example, a resource could represent a computer processor (with tasks corresponding to jobs), a classroom (with tasks corresponding to lectures), or your calendar for the day (with tasks corresponding to meetings).

13.2.1   The Setup

In scheduling, the tasks to be completed are usually called *jobs*, and jobs can have different characteristics. Suppose that each job j has a known *length* ℓ_j, which is the amount of time required to process the job (for example, the length of a lecture or meeting). Also, each job has a *weight* w_j, with higher weights corresponding to higher-priority jobs.

13.2.2   Completion Times

A *schedule* specifies an order in which to process the jobs. In a problem instance with n jobs, there are $n! = n \cdot (n-1) \cdot (n-2) \cdots 2 \cdot 1$ different schedules. That's a lot of schedules! Which one should we prefer?

Next, we need to define an *objective function* that assigns a numerical score to every schedule and quantifies what we want. First, a preliminary definition:

Completion Times

The *completion time* $C_j(\sigma)$ of a job j in a schedule σ is the sum of the lengths of the jobs preceding j in σ, plus the length of j itself.

In other words, a job's completion time in a schedule is the total time that elapses before the job has been fully processed.

Quiz 13.1

Consider a problem instance that has three jobs with $\ell_1 = 1$, $\ell_2 = 2$, and $\ell_3 = 3$, and suppose they are scheduled in this order (with job 1 first). What are the completion times of the three jobs in this schedule? (The job weights are irrelevant for this question, so we have not specified them.)

a) 1, 2, and 3

b) 3, 5, and 6

---

[4]A not-always-correct greedy algorithm can still serve as a super-fast heuristic algorithm for a problem, a point we'll return to in Chapter 20.

c) 1, 3, and 6

d) 1, 4, and 6

(See Section 13.2.4 for the solution and discussion.)

13.2.3 Objective Function

What makes for a good schedule? We'd obviously like jobs' completion times to be small, but trade-offs between jobs are inevitable—in any schedule, jobs scheduled early will have short completion times while those scheduled toward the end will have long completion times.

One way to make trade-offs between the jobs is to minimize the *sum of weighted completion times*. In math, this objective function translates to

$$\min_{\sigma} \sum_{j=1}^{n} w_j C_j(\sigma), \tag{13.1}$$

where the minimization is over all $n!$ possible schedules σ, and $C_j(\sigma)$ denotes job j's completion time in the schedule σ. This is equivalent to minimizing the weighted average of the jobs' completion times, with the averaging weights proportional to the w_j's.

For example, consider the three jobs in Quiz 13.1 and suppose their weights are $w_1 = 3$, $w_2 = 2$, and $w_3 = 1$. If we schedule the first job first, the second job second, and the third job third, the sum of the weighted completion times is

$$\underbrace{3 \cdot 1}_{\text{job \#1}} + \underbrace{2 \cdot 3}_{\text{job \#2}} + \underbrace{1 \cdot 6}_{\text{job \#3}} = 15.$$

By checking all $3! = 6$ possible schedules, you can verify that this is the schedule that minimizes the sum of weighted completion times. How can we solve this problem in general, given as input an arbitrary set of job lengths and weights?

Problem: Minimizing the Sum of Weighted Completion Times

Input: A set of n jobs with positive lengths $\ell_1, \ell_2, \ldots, \ell_n$ and positive weights $w_1, w_2, \ldots, w_n$.

Output: A job sequence that minimizes the sum of weighted completion times (13.1).

With $n!$ different schedules, computing the best one by exhaustive search is out of the question for all but the tiniest instances. We need a smarter algorithm.[5]

---

[5]For example, $n!$ is bigger than 3.6 million when $n = 10$, bigger than 2.4 quintillion when $n = 20$, and bigger than the estimated number of atoms in the known universe when $n \geq 60$. Thus no conceivable improvement in computer technology would transmute exhaustive search into a viable algorithm.

13.2.4   Solution to Quiz 13.1

Correct answer: (c). We can visualize a schedule by stacking the jobs on top of one another, with time increasing from bottom to top (Figure 13.1). The completion time of a job is the time corresponding to its topmost edge. For the first job, its completion time is just its length, which is 1. The second job must wait for the first job to complete, so its completion time is the sum of the lengths of the first two jobs, which is 3. The third job doesn't even start until time 3, and then it takes 3 more time units to complete, so its completion time is 6.

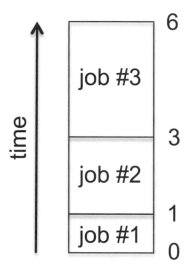

Figure 13.1: The completion times of the three jobs are 1, 3, and 6.

13.3   Developing a Greedy Algorithm

Greedy algorithms seem like a good fit for the problem of scheduling jobs to minimize the weighted sum of completion times. The output has an iterative structure, with jobs processed one by one. Why not use a greedy algorithm that iteratively decides which job should go next?

The first step of our plan is to solve two special cases of the general problem. Our solutions to these will suggest what a greedy algorithm might look like in the general case. We'll then narrow the field to a single candidate algorithm and prove that this candidate correctly solves the problem. The process by which we arrive at this algorithm is more important to remember than the algorithm itself; it's a repeatable process that you can use in your own applications.

13.3.1   Two Special Cases

Let's think positive and posit that there actually is a correct greedy algorithm for the problem of minimizing the weighted sum of completion times. What would it look like? For starters, what if you knew that all the jobs had the same length (but possibly different weights)? What if they all had the same weight (but possibly different lengths)?

Quiz 13.2

(1) If all job lengths are identical, should we schedule smaller- or larger-weight jobs earlier?

(2) If all job weights are identical, should we schedule shorter or longer jobs earlier?

  a) larger/shorter

  b) smaller/shorter

  c) larger/longer

  d) smaller/longer

(See Section 13.3.3 for the solution and discussion.)

13.3.2 Dueling Greedy Algorithms

In the general case, jobs can have different weights and different lengths. Whenever our two rules-of-thumb—to prefer shorter jobs and higher-weight jobs—luckily coincide for a pair of jobs, we know which one to schedule first (the shorter, higher-weight one). But what if the two rules give conflicting advice? What should we do with one short low-weight job and one long high-weight job?

What's the simplest greedy algorithm that might work? Each job has two parameters, and the algorithm must look at both. The best-case scenario would be to come up with a formula that compiles each job's length and weight into a single *score*, so that scheduling jobs from highest to lowest score is guaranteed to minimize the sum of weighted completion times. If such a formula exists, our two special cases imply that it must have two properties: (i) holding the length fixed, it should be increasing in the job's weight; and (ii) holding the weight fixed, it should be decreasing in the job's length. (Remember, higher scores are better.) Take a minute to brainstorm some formulas that have both of these properties.

* * * * * * * * * * * * *

Perhaps the simplest function that is increasing in weight and decreasing in length is the difference between the two:

$$\text{proposal \#1 for score of job } j: \quad w_j - \ell_j.$$

This score might be negative, but that poses no obstacle to sequencing the jobs from highest to lowest score.

There are plenty of other options. For example, the ratio of the two parameters is another candidate:

$$\text{proposal \#2 for score of job } j: \quad \frac{w_j}{\ell_j}.$$

These two scoring functions lead to two different greedy algorithms.

GreedyDiff

Schedule the jobs in decreasing order of $w_j - \ell_j$
(breaking ties arbitrarily).

GreedyRatio

Schedule the jobs in decreasing order of $\frac{w_j}{\ell_j}$
(breaking ties arbitrarily).

Thus, already, our first case study illustrates the first theme of the greedy paradigm (Section 13.1.2): It is often easy to propose multiple competing greedy algorithms for a problem.

Which of the two algorithms, if any, is correct? A quick way to rule out one of them is to find an instance in which the two algorithms output different schedules, with different objective function values. For whichever algorithm fares worse in this example, we can conclude that it is not always optimal.

Both algorithms do the right thing in our two special cases, with equal-weight or equal-length jobs. The simplest way to rule out one of them would be to devise a problem instance with two jobs, with different weights and lengths, such that the jobs' ordering by difference is the opposite of their ordering by ratio. One example is:

	Job #1	Job #2
Length	$\ell_1 = 5$	$\ell_2 = 2$
Weight	$w_1 = 3$	$w_2 = 1.$

The first job has the larger ratio ($3/5$ vs. $1/2$) but the smaller (more negative) difference (-2 vs. -1). Thus the GreedyDiff algorithm schedules the second job first, while GreedyRatio does the opposite.

Quiz 13.3

What is the sum of weighted completion times in the schedules output by the GreedyDiff and GreedyRatio algorithms, respectively?

a) 22 and 23

b) 23 and 22

c) 17 and 17

d) 17 and 11

(See Section 13.3.3 for the solution and discussion.)

We've made progress by ruling out the GreedyDiff algorithm from further consideration. (See Problem 13.4 for an alternative way to arrive at this conclusion.) However, the outcome of Quiz 13.3 does *not* immediately imply that the GreedyRatio algorithm is always optimal. For all we know, there are other cases in which the algorithm outputs a suboptimal schedule. You should always be skeptical about an algorithm that does not come with a proof of correctness, even if the algorithm does the right thing in some toy examples, and extra-skeptical of greedy algorithms.

In our case, the `GreedyRatio` algorithm *is*, in fact, guaranteed to minimize the sum of weighted completion times.

Theorem 13.1 (Correctness of `GreedyRatio`) *For every set of positive job weights* $w_1, w_2, \ldots, w_n$ *and positive job lengths* $\ell_1, \ell_2, \ldots, \ell_n$, *the* `GreedyRatio` *algorithm outputs a schedule with the minimum-possible sum of weighted completion times.*

This assertion is not obvious and you should not trust it until I supply you with a proof. Consistent with the third theme of the greedy paradigm (Section 13.1.2), this proof occupies the entire next section.

The remaining theme of the greedy paradigm is the ease of running time analysis (Section 13.1.2). That's certainly the case here. All the `GreedyRatio` algorithm does is sort the jobs by ratio, which requires $O(n \log n)$ time, where n is the number of jobs in the input.

13.3.3   Solutions to Quizzes 13.2–13.3

Solution to Quiz 13.2

Correct answer: (a). First suppose that all n jobs have the same length, say length 1. Then, every schedule has exactly the same set of completion times—$\{1, 2, 3, \ldots, n\}$—and the only question is which job gets which completion time. Because a higher weight indicates a higher priority, we might expect that the higher-weight jobs should receive the smaller completion times, and this is in fact the case. For example, you wouldn't want to schedule a job with weight 10 third (with completion time 3) and one with weight 20 fifth (with completion time 5); you'd be better off exchanging the positions of these two jobs, which would decrease the sum of weighted completion times by 20 (as you should check).

The second case, in which all jobs have equal weights, is a little more subtle. Here, you want to favor shorter jobs. For example, consider two unit-weight jobs with lengths 1 and 2. If you schedule the shorter job first, the completion times are 1 and 3, for a total of 4. In the opposite order, the completion times are 2 and 3, for an inferior total of 5. In general, the job scheduled first contributes to the completion times of *all* the jobs, as all jobs must wait for the first one to finish. All else being equal, scheduling the shortest job first minimizes this negative impact. The second job contributes to all the completion times other than that of the first job, so the second-shortest job should be scheduled next, and so on.

Solution to Quiz 13.3

Correct answer: (b). The `GreedyDiff` algorithm schedules the second job first. The completion time of this job is $C_2 = \ell_2 = 2$ while that of the other job is $C_1 = \ell_2 + \ell_1 = 7$. The sum of weighted completion times is then

$$w_1 \cdot C_1 + w_2 \cdot C_2 = 3 \cdot 7 + 1 \cdot 2 = 23.$$

The `GreedyRatio` algorithm schedules the first job first, resulting in completion times $C_1 = \ell_1 = 5$ and $C_2 = \ell_1 + \ell_2 = 7$ and a sum of weighted completion times of

$$3 \cdot 5 + 1 \cdot 7 = 22.$$

The `GreedyDiff` algorithm fails to compute an optimal schedule for this example, and we can therefore conclude that it is not always correct.

13.4 Proof of Correctness

Divide-and-conquer algorithms usually have formulaic correctness proofs, consisting of a straightforward induction. Not so with greedy algorithms, for which correctness proofs are more art than science—be prepared to throw in the kitchen sink. To the extent that there are recurring themes in correctness proofs of greedy algorithms, we will emphasize them as we go along.

The proof of Theorem 13.1 includes a vivid example of one such theme: *exchange arguments*. The key idea is to prove that every feasible solution can be improved (or at least made no worse) by modifying it to look more like the output of the greedy algorithm.[6]

13.4.1 High-Level Plan

We proceed to the proof of Theorem 13.1. Fix a set of jobs, with positive weights $w_1, w_2, \ldots, w_n$ and lengths $\ell_1, \ell_2 \ldots, \ell_n$. We must show that the `GreedyRatio` algorithm produces a schedule that minimizes the sum of weighted completion times (13.1). We start with two assumptions.

Two Assumptions

(1) The jobs are indexed in nonincreasing order of weight-length ratio:

$$\frac{w_1}{\ell_1} \geq \frac{w_2}{\ell_2} \geq \cdots \geq \frac{w_n}{\ell_n}. \tag{13.2}$$

(2) There are no ties between ratios: $\frac{w_i}{\ell_i} \neq \frac{w_j}{\ell_j}$ whenever $i \neq j$.

The first assumption is without loss of generality, merely an agreement among friends to minimize our notational burden. (Reordering the jobs in the input doesn't affect the problem, so we can reorder and reindex the jobs so that (13.2) holds.) The second assumption does restrict the allowable inputs, and Problem 13.5 asks you to show that Theorem 13.1 holds more generally with this assumption dropped and ties between jobs allowed. Together, the two assumptions imply that jobs are indexed in strictly decreasing order of weight-length ratio.

---

[6]Exchange arguments are only one way among many to prove that a greedy algorithm is correct. For example, in Theorem 9.1, our correctness proof for Dijkstra's algorithm used induction rather than an exchange argument. Both induction and exchange arguments play a role in our correctness proofs for Huffman's greedy coding algorithm (Chapter 14) and for Prim's and Kruskal's minimum spanning tree algorithms (Chapter 15).

The high-level plan is to proceed by contradiction. Recall that in this type of proof, you assume the *opposite* of what you want to prove, and then build on this assumption with a sequence of logically correct steps that culminates in a patently false statement. Such a contradiction implies that the assumption can't be true, which proves the desired statement.

To begin, we assume that the GreedyRatio algorithm produces a schedule σ of the given jobs that is *not* optimal. Thus, there is an optimal schedule σ^* of these jobs with a strictly smaller sum of weighted completion times. The inspired idea is to use the differences between σ and σ^* to explicitly construct a schedule that is *even better than σ^**; this will contradict our assumption that σ^* is an optimal schedule.

13.4.2 Exchanging Jobs

Suppose, for contradiction, that the GreedyRatio algorithm produces the schedule σ and that there is an optimal schedule σ^* with a strictly smaller sum of weighted completion times. The GreedyRatio algorithm schedules jobs in nonincreasing order of weight-length ratios and so, on account of assumptions (1) and (2), schedules job 1 first, followed by job 2, and so on all the way up to job n (Figure 13.2).

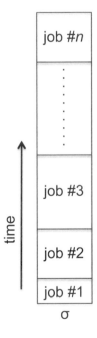

Figure 13.2: The greedy schedule σ, with jobs scheduled in order of nonincreasing weight-length ratio.

Because the optimal schedule σ^* is not the same as σ, it does *not* schedule the jobs in nonincreasing order of weight-length ratios, and thus at some point schedules a job j with a higher ratio immediately after a job i with a lower ratio (that is, with $i > j$); see Figure 13.3(a). How can we use this fact to exhibit another schedule σ' that is even better than σ^*, thereby furnishing a contradiction?

The key idea is to perform an *exchange*. We define a new schedule σ' that is identical to σ^* except that the jobs i and j are processed in the opposite order, with j now processed

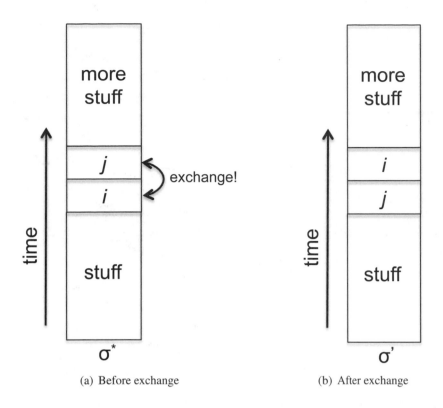

(a) Before exchange   (b) After exchange

Figure 13.3: Obtaining the new schedule σ' from the allegedly optimal schedule σ^* by exchanging a pair of consecutive jobs i, j with $i > j$.

immediately before i (Figure 13.3(b)). The jobs before both i and j ("stuff" in Figure 13.3) are the same in both σ^* and σ' (and in the same order), and likewise for the jobs that follow both i and j ("more stuff").

13.4.3   Cost-Benefit Analysis

What are the ramifications of the exchange illustrated in Figure 13.3?

Quiz 13.4

What effect does the exchange have on the completion time of: (i) a job other than i or j; (ii) the job i; and (iii) the job j?

   a) (i) Not enough information to answer; (ii) goes up; (iii) goes down.

   b) (i) Not enough information to answer; (ii) goes down; (iii) goes up.

   c) (i) Unaffected; (ii) goes up; (iii) goes down.

   d) (i) Unaffected; (ii) goes down; (iii) goes up.

(See Section 13.4.4 for the solution and discussion.)

Solving Quiz 13.4 puts us in a great position to complete the contradiction by showing how to transform σ^* into a "too-good-to-be-true" schedule. The cost of exchanging consecutive jobs i and j is that i's completion time C_i goes up by the length ℓ_j of job j, which increases the objective function (13.1) by $w_i \cdot \ell_j$. The benefit is that j's completion time C_j goes down by the length ℓ_i of job i, which decreases the objective function (13.1) by $w_j \cdot \ell_i$.

Summarizing,

$$\underbrace{\sum_{k=1}^{n} w_k C_k(\sigma')}_{\text{objective fn value of } \sigma'} = \underbrace{\sum_{k=1}^{n} w_k C_k(\sigma^*)}_{\text{objective fn value of } \sigma^*} + \underbrace{w_i \ell_j - w_j \ell_i}_{\text{effect of exchange}} . \tag{13.3}$$

Now is the time to use the fact that σ^* scheduled i and j in the "wrong order," with $i > j$. Our standing assumptions (1) and (2) imply that jobs are indexed in strictly decreasing order of weight-length ratio, so

$$\frac{w_i}{\ell_i} < \frac{w_j}{\ell_j} .$$

After clearing denominators, this translates to

$$\underbrace{w_i \ell_j}_{\text{cost of exchange}} < \underbrace{w_j \ell_i}_{\text{benefit of exchange}} .$$

Because the benefit of the exchange exceeds the cost, equation (13.3) tells us that

objective function value of σ' < objective function value of σ^*.

But this is nuts—σ^* was supposed to be an optimal schedule, with the smallest possible sum of weighted completion times! We've arrived at the desired contradiction, which completes the proof of Theorem 13.1 in the case of jobs with distinct weight-length ratios. $\mathcal{QED}$

13.4.4   Solution to Quiz 13.4

Correct answer: (c). First, jobs k other than i and j couldn't care less about i and j being swapped. This is easiest to see for a job k processed before i and j in σ^* (as part of the "stuff" in Figure 13.3). Because the exchange occurs after k completes, it has no effect on k's completion time. For a job k processed after i and j in σ^* (as part of the "more stuff" in Figure 13.3), the set of jobs completed before k is exactly the same in σ^* and in σ'. The completion time of a job depends only on the set of jobs preceding it (and not on their order), so job k is none the wiser and completes at the same time in both schedules.

As for job i, its completion time goes up in σ'. It must wait for the same jobs as before ("stuff"), and now job j as well, so its completion time increases by ℓ_j. Similarly, job j waits for the same jobs to complete as before, except that in σ' it no longer waits for i. Job j's completion time therefore decreases by ℓ_i.

The Upshot

☆ Greedy algorithms construct solutions iteratively, via a sequence of myopic decisions, and hope that everything works out in the end.

☆ It is often easy to propose one or more greedy algorithms for a

★ Most greedy algorithms are not always correct.

★ Even when a greedy algorithm is always correct, proving it can be difficult.

★ Given tasks with lengths and weights, greedily ordering them from highest to lowest weight-length ratio minimizes the weighted sum of completion times.

★ Exchange arguments are among the most common techniques used in correctness proofs for greedy algorithms. The idea is to show that every feasible solution can be improved by modifying it to look more like the output of the greedy algorithm.

Test Your Understanding

Problem 13.1 *(H)* You are given as input n jobs, each with a length ℓ_j and a deadline d_j. Define the *lateness* $\lambda_j(\sigma)$ of a job j in a schedule σ as the difference $C_j(\sigma) - d_j$ between the job's completion time and deadline, or as 0 if $C_j(\sigma) \le d_j$. (See page 293 for the definition of a job's completion time in a schedule.) This problem considers the objective of minimizing the maximum lateness, $\max_{j=1}^{n} \lambda_j(\sigma)$.

Which of the following greedy algorithms always produces a schedule that minimizes the maximum lateness? Feel free to assume that there are no ties.

a) Schedule the jobs in increasing order of deadline d_j.

b) Schedule the jobs in increasing order of length ℓ_j.

c) Schedule the jobs in increasing order of the product $d_j \cdot \ell_j$.

d) None of the other answers are correct.

Problem 13.2 *(H)* Continuing Problem 13.1, consider instead the objective of minimizing the *total* lateness, $\sum_{j=1}^{n} \lambda_j(\sigma)$.

Which of the following greedy algorithms always produces a schedule that minimizes the total lateness? Feel free to assume that there are no ties.

a) Schedule the jobs in increasing order of deadline d_j.

b) Schedule the jobs in increasing order of length ℓ_j.

c) Schedule the jobs in increasing order of the product $d_j \cdot \ell_j$.

d) None of the other answers are correct.

Problem 13.3 *(H)* You are given as input n jobs, each with a start time s_j and a finish time t_j. Two jobs *conflict* if they overlap in time—if one of them starts between the start and finish times of the other. In this problem, the goal is to select a maximum-size subset of jobs that have no conflicts. (For example, given three jobs consuming the intervals $[0, 3]$, $[2, 5]$, and $[4, 7]$, the optimal solution consists of the first and third jobs.) The plan is to design an iterative greedy algorithm that, in each iteration, irrevocably adds a new job j to the solution-so-far and removes from future consideration all jobs that conflict with j.

Which of the following greedy algorithms is guaranteed to compute an optimal solution? Feel free to assume that there are no ties.

a) At each iteration, choose the remaining job with the earliest finish time.

b) At each iteration, choose the remaining job with the earliest start time.

c) At each iteration, choose the remaining job that requires the least time (that is, with the smallest value of $t_j - s_j$).

d) At each iteration, choose the remaining job with the fewest number of conflicts with other remaining jobs.

Problem 13.4 *(S)* For the problem of minimizing the sum of weighted completion times (page 294):

(a) Argue that doubling the weight of every job in the input does not change the set of optimal schedules.

(b) Use (a) to argue that the `GreedyDiff` algorithm (page 297) cannot possibly be correct on all inputs.

Challenge Problems

Problem 13.5 *(S)* Prove Theorem 13.1 in its full generality: The `GreedyRatio` algorithm (page 297) always computes a schedule with the minimum-possible sum of weighted completion times, even if there are jobs with identical weight-length ratios.

Problem 13.6 *(H)* Consider modifying the problem of minimizing the sum of weighted completion times (page 294) in three ways:

1. Jobs have equal priority, meaning that $w_j = 1$ for every job j.

2. Each job j has a positive length ℓ_j and a nonnegative *release date* r_j. A feasible schedule can process a job only at or after its release date.

3. Jobs can be *preempted*, meaning stopped in the middle of processing and restarted later. A job with length ℓ_j is considered complete once it has been processed for ℓ_j units of time overall.

The goal is to schedule the jobs to minimize the sum of their (unweighted) completion times. For example, for the input

	Job #1	Job #2
Length	$\ell_1 = 4$	$\ell_2 = 2$
Release Date	$r_1 = 0$	$r_2 = 1$

the optimal schedule processes the first job (partially) from time 0 to time 1, the second job (completely) from time 1 to time 3, and the rest of the first job from time 3 to time 6 (for a sum of completion times of $6 + 3 = 9$).

Design a greedy algorithm that always returns a feasible schedule with the minimum-possible sum of completion times. Prove that your algorithm is correct.

Programming Problems

Problem 13.7 Implement in your favorite programming language the `GreedyDiff` and `GreedyRatio` algorithms from Section 13.3 for the problem of minimizing the weighted sum of completion times. Run both algorithms on several examples. How much better are the schedules computed by the `GreedyRatio` algorithm than those by the `GreedyDiff` algorithm? (See `www.algorithmsilluminated.org` for test cases and challenge data sets.)

Chapter 14

Huffman Codes

Everybody loves compression. The number of photos you can store on your smartphone? It depends on how much you can compress the files with little or no loss. The time required to download a file? The more you compress, the faster the download. *Huffman coding* is a widely-used method for lossless compression. For example, every time you import or export an MP3 audio file, your computer uses Huffman codes. In this chapter, we'll learn about the optimality of Huffman codes, as well as a blazingly fast greedy algorithm for computing them.

14.1 Codes

14.1.1 Fixed-Length Binary Codes

Let's set the stage before we proceed to a problem definition or algorithm. An *alphabet* Σ is a finite non-empty set of symbols. For example, Σ might be a set of 64 symbols that includes all 26 letters (both upper and lower case) plus punctuation and some special characters. A *binary code* for an alphabet is a way of writing each of its symbols as a distinct binary string (i.e., as a sequence of bits, meaning 0s and 1s). For example, with an alphabet of 64 symbols, a natural encoding is to associate each symbol with one of the $2^6 = 64$ length-6 binary strings, with each string used exactly once. This is an example of a *fixed-length* binary code, which uses the same number of bits to encode each symbol. This is roughly how ASCII codes work, for instance.

Fixed-length codes are a natural solution, but we can't get complacent. As always, it's our duty to ask the question: *Can we do better?*

14.1.2 Variable-Length Codes

When some symbols of the alphabet occur much more frequently than others, variable-length codes can be more efficient than fixed-length ones. Allowing variable-length codes introduces a complication, however, which we illustrate by example. Consider a four-symbol alphabet, say $\Sigma = \{A, B, C, D\}$. One natural fixed-length code for this alphabet is:

Symbol	Encoding
A	00
B	01
C	10
D	11

Suppose we wanted to get away with fewer bits in our code by using a 1-bit encoding for some of the symbols. For example, we could try:

Symbol	Encoding
A	0
B	01
C	10
D	1

This shorter code can only be better, right?

Quiz 14.1

With the variable-length binary code above, what is the string "001" an encoding of?

a) AB

b) CD

c) AAD

d) Not enough information to answer

(See Section 14.1.6 for the solution and discussion.)

The point of Quiz 14.1 is that, with variable-length codes and no further precautions, it can be unclear where one symbol starts and the next one begins. This problem does not arise with fixed-length codes. If every symbol is encoded using 6 bits, the second symbol always starts with the 7th bit, the third symbol with the 13th bit, and so on. With variable-length codes, we must impose a constraint to prevent ambiguity.

14.1.3   Prefix-Free Codes

We can eliminate all ambiguity by insisting that a code be *prefix-free*. This means that, for each pair of distinct symbols $a, b \in \Sigma$, the encoding of a is not a prefix of that of b, and vice versa. Every fixed-length code is automatically prefix-free. The variable-length code in the preceding section is not: The encoding of "A" is a prefix of that of "B," and similarly with "D" and "C."

With a prefix-free code, encodings are unambiguous and can be decoded in the obvious way. If the first 5 bits of a sequence match the encoding of a symbol a, then a was definitely the first symbol encoded—because the code is prefix-free, there's no way these 5 bits could correspond to (a prefix of) the encoding of any other symbol. If the next 7 bits match the encoding of b, then b was the second symbol encoded, and so on.

Here's an example of a prefix-free code for the alphabet $\Sigma = \{A, B, C, D\}$ that is not fixed-length:

Symbol	Encoding
A	0
B	10
C	110
D	111

Because "0" is used to encode A, the encodings of the other three symbols must start with a "1." Because B is encoded as "10," the encodings of C and D begin with "11."

14.1.4   The Benefits of Prefix-Free Codes

Variable-length prefix-free codes can be more efficient than fixed-length codes when the symbols have very different frequencies. For example, suppose we have the following statistics about symbol frequencies in our application (perhaps from past experience or from preprocessing the file to be encoded):

Symbol	Frequency
A	60%
B	25%
C	10%
D	5%

Let's compare the performance of our fixed-length and variable-length prefix-free codes:

Symbol	Fixed-length code	Variable-length prefix-free code
A	00	0
B	01	10
C	10	110
D	11	111

By "performance," we mean the average number of bits used to encode a symbol, with symbols weighted according to their frequencies. The fixed-length code always uses 2 bits, so this is also its average per-symbol length. What about the variable-length code? We might hope that it's better, given that it uses only 1 bit most of the time (60%) and resorts to 3 bits only in rare cases (15%).

Quiz 14.2

What is the average number of bits per symbol used by the variable-length code above?

  a) 1.5

  b) 1.55

  c) 2

  d) 2.5

(See Section 14.1.6 for the solution and discussion.)

14.1.5   Problem Definition

The preceding example shows that the best binary code for the job depends on the symbol frequencies. This means we have a super-cool algorithmic problem on our hands, which is the subject of the rest of this chapter.

> **Problem: Optimal Prefix-Free Codes**
>
> **Input:** A nonnegative frequency p_a for each symbol a of an alphabet Σ of size $n \geq 2$.
>
> **Output:** A prefix-free binary code with the minimum-possible average encoding length:
> $$\sum_{a \in \Sigma} p_a \cdot (\text{number of bits used to encode } a).$$

How would you know in advance how frequent different symbols are? In some applications, there's plenty of data or domain knowledge. For example, any genomicist can tell you the typical frequency of each nucleobase (As, Cs, Gs, and Ts) in human DNA. In the case of encoding an MP3 file, the encoder computes symbol frequencies explicitly when preparing an initial digital version of the file (perhaps following an analog-to-digital conversion), and then uses an optimal prefix-free code to compress the file further.

The problem of computing an optimal prefix-free code looks intimidating at first encounter. The number of possible codes grows exponentially with the alphabet size n, so even for modest values of n there is no hope of exhaustively searching through all of them.[1] But surprisingly, the problem can be solved efficiently using a slick greedy algorithm.

14.1.6   Solutions to Quizzes 14.1–14.2

Solution to Quiz 14.1

Correct answer: (d). The proposed variable-length code creates ambiguity, and more than one sequence of symbols would lead to the encoding "001." One possibility is AB (encoded as "0" and "01," respectively), and another is AAD (encoded as "0," "0," and "1"). Given only the encoding, there's no way of knowing which meaning was intended.

Solution to Quiz 14.2

Correct answer: (b). Expanding out the weighted average, we have

$$\text{average \# of bits per symbol} = \underbrace{1 \cdot .6}_{\text{``A''}} + \underbrace{2 \cdot .25}_{\text{``B''}} + \underbrace{3 \cdot (.1 + .05)}_{\text{``C'' and ``D''}} = 1.55.$$

For this set of symbol frequencies, the variable-length code uses 22.5% fewer bits than the fixed-length code (on average)—a significant savings.

14.2   Codes as Trees

The "prefix-free" constraint in the optimal prefix-free code problem sounds a little scary. When putting together a code, how can we ensure that it's prefix-free? Crucial to reasoning about the problem is a method of associating codes with labeled binary trees.

---

[1]For example, there are $n!$ different prefix-free codes that encode one symbol using one bit ("0"), another using two bits ("10"), another using three bits ("110"), and so on.

14.2.1 Three Examples

The connection between codes and trees is easiest to explain through examples. Our fixed-length code

Symbol	Encoding
A	00
B	01
C	10
D	11

can be represented via a complete binary tree with four leaves:

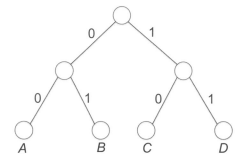

Every edge connecting a node to its left or right child is labeled with a "0" or "1," respectively. The leaves of the tree are labeled with the four symbols of the alphabet. Every path from the root to a labeled node traverses two edges. We can interpret the labels of these two edges as an encoding of the leaf's symbol. For example, because the path from the root to the node labeled "B" traverses a left child edge ("0") followed by a right child edge ("1"), we can interpret the path as encoding the symbol B by 01. This matches B's encoding in our fixed-length code. The same is true for the other three symbols, as you should check.

Next, recall our first (non-prefix-free) variable-length code:

Symbol	Encoding
A	0
B	01
C	10
D	1

This code can be represented using a different labeled binary tree:

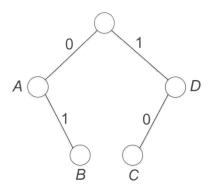

Once again there are four nodes labeled with the symbols of the alphabet—the two leaves and
their parents. This tree defines an encoding for each symbol via the sequence of edge labels
on the path from the root to the node labeled with that symbol. For example, going from the
root to the node labeled "A" requires traversing only one left child edge, corresponding to
the encoding "0." The encodings defined by this tree match those in the table above, as you
should verify.

Finally, we can represent our prefix-free variable-length code

Symbol	Encoding
A	0
B	10
C	110
D	111

with the tree

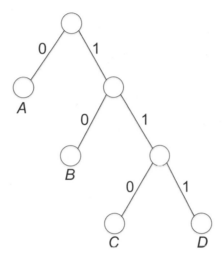

More generally, *every* binary code can be represented as a binary tree with left and right
child edges labeled with "0" and "1," respectively, and with each symbol of the alphabet
used as the label for exactly one node.[2] Conversely, every such tree defines a binary code,
with the edge labels on the paths from the root to the labeled nodes providing the symbol
encodings. The number of edges in a path equals the number of bits used to encode the
corresponding symbol, so we have the following proposition. (The *depth* of a node in a tree
is the number of edges on the path to it from the root.)

Proposition 14.1 (Encoding Length and Node Depth) *For every binary code, the encoding length in bits of a symbol $a \in \Sigma$ equals the depth of the node with label a in the
corresponding tree.*

For example, in the prefix-free code above, the level-1 leaf corresponds to the symbol
with a 1-bit encoding (A), the level-2 leaf to the symbol with a 2-bit encoding (B), and the
level-3 leaves to the two symbols with 3-bit encodings (C and D).

---

[2]Suppose the largest number of bits used to encode a symbol is ℓ. Form a complete binary tree with 2^{ℓ}
leaves. The encoding of each symbol a defines a path through the tree starting from the root, and the final
node of this path (which may be a leaf or an internal node) should be labeled with a. Finally, repeatedly prune
unlabeled leaves until none remain.

14.2.2   Which Trees Represent Prefix-Free Codes?

We've seen that binary trees can represent all binary codes, prefix-free or not. There's a dead giveaway when the code corresponding to a tree is not prefix-free.

For a clue, look at our three examples. The first and third trees, corresponding to the two prefix-free codes, look quite different from one another. But both share one property: Only the leaves are labeled with alphabet symbols. By contrast, two non-leaves are labeled in the second tree.

In general, the encoding of a symbol a is a prefix of that of another symbol b if and only if the node labeled a is an ancestor of the node labeled b. A labeled internal node is an ancestor of the (labeled) leaves in its subtree and leads to a violation of the prefix-free constraint.[3] Conversely, because no leaf can be the ancestor of another, a tree with labels only at the leaves defines a prefix-free code. Decoding a sequence of bits reduces to following your nose: Traverse the tree from top to bottom, taking a left or right turn whenever the next input bit is a 0 or 1, respectively. When a leaf is reached, its label indicates the next symbol in the sequence and the process restarts from the root with the remaining input bits. For example, with our third code, decoding the input "010111" results in three root-leaf traversals, terminating in A, then B, and finally D (see Figure 14.1).

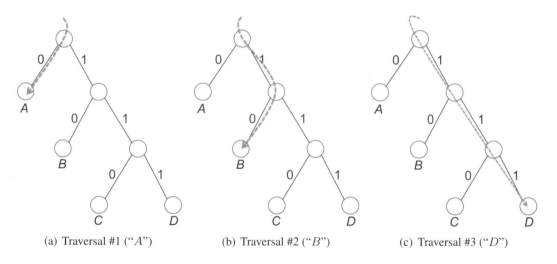

(a) Traversal #1 ("A")   (b) Traversal #2 ("B")   (c) Traversal #3 ("D")

Figure 14.1: Decoding the string "010111" to "ABD" by repeated root-leaf traversals.

14.2.3   Problem Definition (Rephrased)

We can now restate the optimal prefix-free code problem in a particularly crisp form. By a Σ-*tree*, we mean a binary tree with leaves labeled in one-to-one correspondence with the symbols of Σ. As we've seen, prefix-free binary codes for an alphabet Σ correspond to Σ-trees.

For a Σ-tree T and symbol frequencies $\mathbf{p} = \{p_a\}_{a \in \Sigma}$, we denote by $L(T, \mathbf{p})$ the average depth of a leaf in T, with the contribution of each leaf weighted according to the frequency

---

[3]We can assume that every leaf of the tree has a label, as removing unlabeled leaves does not change the code defined by the tree.

of its label:

$$L(T, \mathbf{p}) = \sum_{a \in \Sigma} p_a \cdot (\text{depth of the leaf labeled } a \text{ in } T). \tag{14.1}$$

Proposition 14.1 implies that $L(T, \mathbf{p})$ is exactly the average encoding length of the code that corresponds to T, which is what we want to minimize. We can therefore rephrase the optimal prefix-free code problem as a problem purely about binary trees.

Problem: Optimal Prefix-Free Codes (Rephrased)

Input: A nonnegative frequency p_a for each symbol a of an alphabet Σ of size $n \geq 2$.

Output: A Σ-tree with the minimum-possible average leaf depth (14.1).

14.3   Huffman's Greedy Algorithm

14.3.1   Building Trees Through Successive Mergers

Huffman's big idea back in 1951 was to tackle the optimal prefix-free code problem using a bottom-up approach.[4] "Bottom-up" means starting with n nodes (where n is the size of the alphabet Σ), each labeled with a different symbol of Σ, and building up a tree through successive mergers. For example, if $\Sigma = \{A, B, C, D\}$, we start with what will be the leaves of the tree:

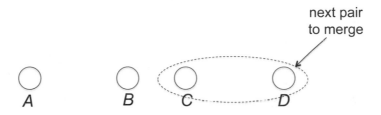

Our first merger might be of the nodes labeled "C" and "D," implemented by introducing one new unlabeled internal node with left and right children corresponding to C and D, respectively:

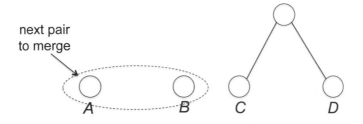

---

[4]This was for David A. Huffman's term paper in a class, believe it or not, and it superseded the (suboptimal) divide-and-conquer-esque top-down algorithm previously invented by Huffman's graduate advisor, Robert M. Fano.

In effect, this merger commits to a tree in which the leaves labeled "C" and "D" are siblings (i.e., have the same parent).

Next we might do the same thing with A and B, committing further to a tree in which the leaves labeled "A" and "B" are siblings:

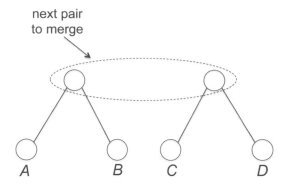

At this point, only two groups are left to merge. Merging them produces a full-blown binary tree:

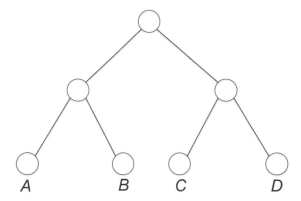

This binary tree is the same one used to represent the fixed-length code in Section 14.2.1.

Alternatively, in the second iteration we could merge the node labeled "B" with the tree containing "C" and "D":

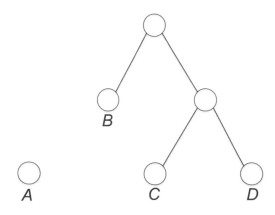

The final merge is again forced on us and produces the binary tree used to represent the variable-length prefix-free code in Section 14.2.1:

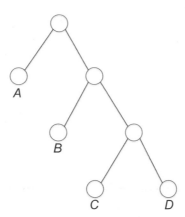

In general, Huffman's greedy algorithm maintains a *forest*, which is a collection of one or more binary trees. The leaves of the trees are in one-to-one correspondence with the symbols of Σ. Each iteration of the algorithm chooses two of the trees in the current forest and merges them by making their roots the left and right children of a new unlabeled internal node. The algorithm halts when only one tree remains.

Quiz 14.3

How many mergers will Huffman's greedy algorithm perform before halting? (Let $n = |\Sigma|$ denote the number of symbols.)

  a) $n - 1$

  b) n

  c) $\frac{(n+1)n}{2}$

  d) Not enough information to answer

(See Section 14.3.7 for the solution and discussion.)

14.3.2   Huffman's Greedy Criterion

For a given set of symbol frequencies $\{p_a\}_{a \in \Sigma}$, which pair of trees should we merge in each iteration? Each merger increments the depths of all the leaves in the two participating trees and, hence, the encoding lengths of the corresponding symbols. For example, in the penultimate merge above, the depth of the nodes labeled "C" and "D" increases from 1 to 2, and the depth of the node labeled "B" increases from 0 to 1. Every merger thus increases the objective function that we want to minimize: the average leaf depth (14.1). Every iteration of Huffman's greedy algorithm myopically performs the merge that increases this objective function the least.

Huffman's Greedy Criterion

Merge the pair of trees that causes the minimum-possible increase in the average leaf depth.

By how much does a merger increase the average leaf depth? For every symbol a in one of the two participating trees, the depth of the corresponding leaf goes up by 1 and so the contribution of the corresponding term in the sum (14.1) goes up by p_a. Thus, merging two trees T_1 and T_2 increases the average leaf depth by the sum of the frequencies of the participating symbols:

$$\sum_{a \in T_1} p_a + \sum_{a \in T_2} p_a, \tag{14.2}$$

where the summations are over all the alphabet symbols for which the corresponding leaf belongs to T_1 or T_2, respectively. Huffman's greedy criterion then dictates that we merge the pair of trees for which the sum (14.2) is as small as possible.

14.3.3 Pseudocode

As advertised, Huffman's algorithm builds a Σ-tree bottom-up, and in every iteration it merges the two trees that have the smallest sums of corresponding symbol frequencies. (Below, "argmin" returns the name of the minimum element in a set, breaking ties arbitrarily.)

Huffman

Input: a nonnegative frequency p_a for each symbol a of an
alphabet Σ.
Output: a Σ-tree with the minimum-possible average leaf depth,
representing a prefix-free binary code with the minimum-possible
average encoding length.

```
// Initialization
```
for each $a \in \Sigma$ **do**
    $T_a :=$ tree containing one node, labeled "a" $P(T_a) := p_a$
$\mathcal{F} := \{T_a\}_{a \in \Sigma}$ `// invariant:` $\forall T \in \mathcal{F}, P(T) = \sum_{a \in T} p_a$
```
// Main loop
```
while $\mathcal{F}$ contains at least two trees **do**
    $T_1 := \text{argmin}_{T \in \mathcal{F}} P(T)$ `// smallest frequency sum`
    $T_2 := \text{argmin}_{T \in \mathcal{F}, T \neq T_1} P(T)$ `// second-smallest`
    remove T_1 and T_2 from $\mathcal{F}$
    `// roots of` T_1, T_2 `become left, right`
        `children of a new internal node`
    $T_3 :=$ merger of T_1 and T_2
    $P(T_3) := P(T_1) + P(T_2)$ `// maintains invariant`
    add T_3 to $\mathcal{F}$
return the unique tree in $\mathcal{F}$

14.3.4 Example

For example, let's return to our four-symbol alphabet with the same frequencies as in Quiz 14.2:

Symbol	Frequency
A	.60
B	.25
C	.10
D	.05

Initially, the `Huffman` algorithm creates a forest of four trees, T_A, T_B, T_C, T_D, each containing one node labeled with a different alphabet symbol. The first iteration of the algorithm merges the nodes that correspond to the two symbols with the smallest frequencies—in this case, "C" and "D." After this iteration, the algorithm's forest contains only three trees, with the following sums of symbol frequencies:

Tree	Sum of Symbol Frequencies
tree containing A	.60
tree containing B	.25
tree containing C and D	$.05 + .10 = .15$

The second two trees have the smallest sums of symbol frequencies, so these are the trees merged in the second iteration. In the third iteration, the forest $\mathcal{F}$ contains only two trees; they are merged to produce the final output, which is exactly the tree used to represent the variable-length prefix-free code in Section 14.2.1:

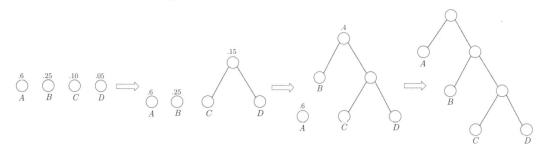

14.3.5   A Larger Example

To ensure that Huffman's greedy algorithm is crystal clear, let's see how the final tree takes shape in a larger example:

Symbol	Frequency
A	3
B	2
C	6
D	8
E	2
F	6

If it bothers you that the symbol frequencies don't add up to 1, feel free to divide each of them by 27; it doesn't change the problem.

As usual, the first step merges the two symbols with the smallest frequencies, namely "B" and "E":

The five trees left in the forest are

Tree	Sum of Symbol Frequencies
tree containing A	3
tree containing C	6
tree containing D	8
tree containing F	6
tree containing B and E	$2 + 2 = 4$

and the algorithm next merges the first and last of these:

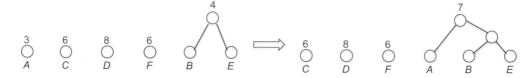

The four remaining trees are

Tree	Sum of Symbol Frequencies
tree containing C	6
tree containing D	8
tree containing F	6
tree containing A, B and E	$4 + 3 = 7$

Next the algorithm merges the nodes labeled "C" and "F":

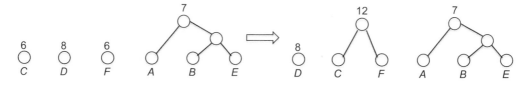

and three trees remain:

Tree	Sum of Symbol Frequencies
tree containing D	8
tree containing C and F	$6 + 6 = 12$
tree containing A, B and E	7

The penultimate merge is of the first and third trees:

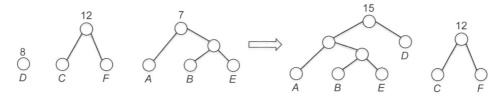

and the final merge produces the output of the algorithm:

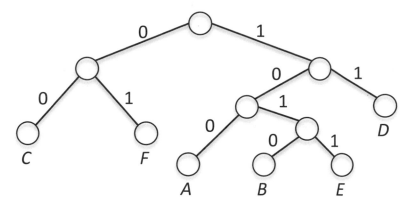

This tree corresponds to the following prefix-free code:

Symbol	Encoding
A	100
B	1010
C	00
D	11
E	1011
F	01

14.3.6   Running Time

A straightforward implementation of the Huffman algorithm runs in $O(n^2)$ time, where n is the number of symbols. As noted in Quiz 14.3, each merge decreases the number of trees in $\mathcal{F}$ by 1, resulting in $n-1$ iterations of the main loop. Each iteration is responsible for identifying the two current trees with the smallest sums of symbol frequencies; this can be done by exhaustive search over the $O(n)$ trees of $\mathcal{F}$. The rest of the work—initialization, updating $\mathcal{F}$, rewiring pointers when merging two trees—contributes only $O(n)$ operations to the overall running time bound, for a total of $O(n^2)$.

Readers who remember Chapter 10 should spot an opportunity to do better. Recall that the raison d'être of the heap data structure is to speed up repeated minimum computations so that each computation takes logarithmic rather than linear time. The work performed in each iteration of the main loop in the Huffman algorithm is dominated by two minimum computations, so a light bulb should go off in your head: This algorithm calls out for a heap! Using a heap to speed up these minimum computations decreases the running time from $O(n^2)$ to $O(n \log n)$, which qualifies as a blazingly fast implementation.[5]

We can do even better. The Huffman algorithm can be implemented by sorting the symbols in order of increasing frequency and then performing a linear amount of additional processing. This implementation eschews heaps in favor of an even simpler data structure: a

---

[5]The objects in the heap correspond to the trees of $\mathcal{F}$. The key associated with an object is the sum of the frequencies of the symbols that correspond to the tree's leaves. In each iteration, the trees T_1 and T_2 can be removed from the heap using two successive EXTRACTMIN operations, and the merged tree T_3 added with one INSERT operation (with T_3's key set to the sum of the keys of T_1 and T_2).

queue (actually, two queues). (See Problem 14.6 for details.) The n symbols can be sorted by frequency in $O(n \log n)$ time (using MergeSort or HeapSort, for example), so the running time of this implementation is $O(n \log n)$. Moreover, in the special cases in which sorting is possible in linear time, this implementation of the Huffman algorithm also runs in linear time.[6]

14.3.7 Solution to Quiz 14.3

Correct answer: (a). The initial forest has n trees, where n is the number of alphabet symbols. Each merge replaces a pair of trees with a single tree and, hence, decreases the number of trees by 1. The algorithm halts once one tree remains, which is after $n - 1$ mergers.

*14.4 Proof of Correctness

The Huffman algorithm correctly solves the optimal prefix-free code problem.

Theorem 14.2 (Correctness of Huffman) *For every alphabet Σ and nonnegative symbol frequencies $\{p_a\}_{a \in \Sigma}$, the* Huffman *algorithm outputs a prefix-free code with the minimum-possible average encoding length.*

Equivalently, the algorithm outputs a Σ-tree with the minimum-possible average leaf depth (14.1).

14.4.1 High-Level Plan

The proof of Theorem 14.2 blends two common strategies for correctness proofs of greedy algorithms, both mentioned in Section 13.4: induction and exchange arguments.

We'll proceed by induction on the size of the alphabet, with two ideas required to implement the inductive step. Fix from now on an input, with alphabet Σ and symbol frequencies $\mathbf{p}$, and let a and b denote the symbols with the smallest and second-smallest frequencies, respectively. Consider the first iteration of the Huffman algorithm, in which it merges the leaves that correspond to a and b. The algorithm has then effectively committed to a Σ-tree in which (the leaves corresponding to) a and b are siblings. The first main idea is to prove that, among all such trees, the Huffman algorithm outputs an optimal one.

Main Idea #1

Prove that the output of the Huffman algorithm minimizes the average leaf depth over all Σ-trees in which a and b are siblings.

This step boils down to showing that the problem of computing an optimal Σ-tree in which a and b are siblings is equivalent to that of computing an optimal Σ'-tree, where Σ' is the same as Σ except with a and b fused into a single symbol. Because Σ' is a smaller alphabet than Σ, we can complete the proof using induction.

---

[6]For example, recall from Section 5.6 that, if every element to be sorted is an integer with magnitude at most n^{10} (say), the RadixSort algorithm can be used to sort them in $O(n)$ time.

This first idea is not enough. If every Σ-tree with a and b as siblings is suboptimal, it does us no good to optimize over them. The second main idea resolves this worry and proves that it's always safe to commit to a tree in which the two lowest-frequency symbols correspond to sibling leaves.

Main Idea #2

Prove that there is an optimal Σ-tree in which a and b are siblings.

The idea here is to show that every Σ-tree can be massaged into an equally good or better Σ-tree in which a and b are siblings, by exchanging the labels a and b with the labels x and y of two leaves in the tree's deepest level. Intuitively, it's a net win to demote the smaller-frequency symbols a and b to the deepest level of the tree while promoting the higher-frequency symbols x and y closer to the root.

If both main ideas can be implemented, the inductive step and Theorem 14.2 follow easily. The first idea implies that the `Huffman` algorithm solves the problem optimally over a restricted family of Σ-trees, those in which a and b are siblings. The second guarantees that an optimal tree of this restricted type is, in fact, optimal for the original problem.

14.4.2   The Details

For the formal proof, we turn to our old friend (or is it nemesis?), induction. Recall from Appendix A that proofs by induction follow a fairly rigid template, using a base case and an inductive step to establish that an assertion $P(k)$ holds for arbitrarily large positive integers k. We'll take $P(k)$ as the statement:

> "the `Huffman` algorithm correctly solves the optimal prefix-free code problem whenever the alphabet size is at most k."

For us, the natural base case is the statement $P(2)$. (The optimal prefix-free code problem is uninteresting with a one-symbol alphabet.) To carry out the inductive step (for some $k > 2$), we'll assume that $P(2), P(3), \ldots, P(k-1)$ are all true (i.e., the inductive hypothesis)—and prove that $P(k)$ is consequently true as well.

The `Huffman` algorithm is optimal for two-symbol alphabets: The algorithm uses 1 bit to encode each symbol (0 for one symbol and 1 for the other), which is the minimum possible. This proves the base case.

For the inductive step, assume that $k > 2$ and fix an alphabet Σ of size k and nonnegative symbol frequencies $\mathbf{p} = \{p_x\}_{x \in \Sigma}$. For the rest of the proof, we denote by a and b the two symbols of Σ with the smallest and second-smallest frequencies, respectively. (Break ties arbitrarily.)

The First Main Idea, Restated

To implement the first and more difficult main idea from Section 14.4.1, define

$$\mathcal{T}_{ab} = \left\{ \begin{array}{l} \Sigma\text{-trees in which } a \text{ and } b \text{ are the left and right} \\ \text{children of a common parent, respectively} \end{array} \right\}.$$

The Huffman algorithm outputs a tree of $\mathcal{T}_{ab}$, and we want to prove that it is an optimal such tree:

(*) among all trees in $\mathcal{T}_{ab}$, the Huffman algorithm outputs one with the minimum-possible average leaf depth.

As a reminder, the average leaf depth of a Σ-tree T with respect to the symbol frequencies $\mathbf{p}$ is

$$L(T, \mathbf{p}) = \sum_{x \in \Sigma} p_x \cdot (\text{depth of the leaf labeled } x \text{ in } T).$$

This quantity is the same as the average encoding length of the corresponding prefix-free code.

Applying the Inductive Hypothesis to a Residual Problem

The inductive hypothesis applies only to alphabets with less than k symbols. So derive Σ' from Σ by fusing the symbols a and b—the symbols with the smallest and second-smallest frequencies—into a single "meta-symbol" ab. There is a one-to-one correspondence between Σ'-trees and the restricted set $\mathcal{T}_{ab}$ of Σ-trees (Figure 14.2). Every Σ'-tree T' can be transformed into a Σ-tree $T \in \mathcal{T}_{ab}$ by replacing the leaf labeled "ab" with an unlabeled node that has children labeled "a" and "b." We denote this mapping $T' \mapsto T$ by $\beta(T')$. Conversely, every tree $T \in \mathcal{T}_{ab}$ can be turned into a Σ'-tree T' by sucking the leaves labeled a and b into their (common) parent and labeling the resulting "meta-node" with "ab." We denote this inverse mapping $T \mapsto T'$ by $\alpha(T)$.

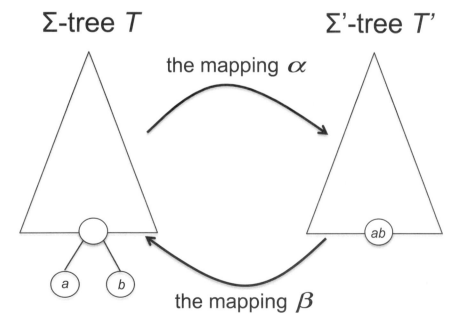

Figure 14.2: There is a one-to-one correspondence between Σ'-trees and the Σ-trees in which a and b are the left and right children of a common parent.

The frequencies $\mathbf{p'} = \{p'_x\}_{x \in \Sigma'}$ we assign to the symbols of Σ' match those of Σ, except with the frequency p'_{ab} of the new symbol ab defined as the sum $p_a + p_b$ of the frequencies of the two symbols it represents.

The first iteration of the `Huffman` algorithm merges the leaves labeled "a" and "b" and thereafter treats them as an indivisible unit with total frequency $p_a + p_b$. This means the final output of the algorithm is the same as if it had been restarted from scratch with the input Σ' and $\mathbf{p'}$, with the resulting Σ'-tree translated by the mapping β back to a Σ-tree of $\mathcal{T}_{ab}$.

Proposition 14.3 (Preservation of Behavior of `Huffman`) *The output of the `Huffman` algorithm with input Σ and $\mathbf{p}$ is $\beta(T')$, where T' is the output of the `Huffman` algorithm with input Σ' and $\mathbf{p'}$.*

Additional Properties of the Correspondence

The correspondence between Σ'-trees and the Σ-trees in $\mathcal{T}_{ab}$ given by the mappings α and β (Figure 14.2) also preserves the average leaf depth, up to a constant that is independent of the choice of tree.

Proposition 14.4 (Preservation of Average Leaf Depth) *For every Σ-tree T of $\mathcal{T}_{ab}$ with symbol frequencies $\mathbf{p}$ and corresponding Σ'-tree $T' = \alpha(T)$ and symbol frequencies $\mathbf{p'}$,*

$$L(T, \mathbf{p}) = L(T', \mathbf{p'}) + \underbrace{p_a + p_b}_{\text{independent of } T} .$$

Proof: Leaves of T not labeled a or b occupy the same position in T'. Their symbols have the same frequencies in $\mathbf{p}$ and $\mathbf{p'}$, so these leaves contribute the same amount to the average leaf depth of both trees. The total frequency of a and b in $\mathbf{p}$ is the same as that of ab in $\mathbf{p'}$, but the depth of the corresponding leaves is one larger. Thus, the contribution of a and b to the average leaf depth of T is $p_a + p_b$ larger than the contribution of ab to the average leaf depth of T'. $\mathcal{QED}$

Because the correspondence between Σ'-trees and the Σ-trees in $\mathcal{T}_{ab}$ preserves the average leaf depth (up to the tree-independent constant $p_a + p_b$), it associates an optimal Σ'-tree with an optimal Σ-tree in $\mathcal{T}_{ab}$:

$$\text{best } \Sigma\text{-tree in } \mathcal{T}_{ab} \;\underset{\beta}{\overset{\alpha}{\rightleftharpoons}}\; \text{best } \Sigma'\text{-tree}$$

$$\text{second-best } \Sigma\text{-tree in } \mathcal{T}_{ab} \;\underset{\beta}{\overset{\alpha}{\rightleftharpoons}}\; \text{second-best } \Sigma'\text{-tree}$$

$$\vdots$$

$$\text{worst } \Sigma\text{-tree in } \mathcal{T}_{ab} \;\underset{\beta}{\overset{\alpha}{\rightleftharpoons}}\; \text{worst } \Sigma'\text{-tree.}$$

Corollary 14.5 (Preservation of Optimal Solutions) *A Σ'-tree T^* minimizes $L(T', \mathbf{p'})$ over all Σ'-trees T' if and only if the corresponding Σ-tree $\beta(T^*)$ minimizes $L(T, \mathbf{p})$ over all Σ-trees T in $\mathcal{T}_{ab}$.*

Implementing the First Main Idea

We now have all our ducks in a row for proving the statement (*), that among all trees of $\mathcal{T}_{ab}$, the Huffman algorithm outputs one with the minimum-possible average leaf depth:

1. By Proposition 14.3, the output of the Huffman algorithm with input Σ and $\mathbf{p}$ is $\beta(T')$, where T' is the output of the Huffman algorithm with input Σ' and $\mathbf{p}'$.

2. Because $|\Sigma'| < k$, the inductive hypothesis implies that the output T' of the Huffman algorithm with input Σ' and $\mathbf{p}'$ is optimal.

3. By Corollary 14.5, the Σ-tree $\beta(T')$ is optimal among trees of $\mathcal{T}_{ab}$ for the original problem with input Σ and $\mathbf{p}$.

Implementing the Second Main Idea

The second part of the inductive step is easier and based on an exchange argument. Here, we want to prove that the Huffman algorithm did not make a mistake by committing to a tree in which the two smallest-frequency symbols are siblings:

(†) There is a tree of $\mathcal{T}_{ab}$ that minimizes the average leaf depth $L(T, \mathbf{p})$ over all Σ-trees T.

To prove (†), consider an arbitrary Σ-tree T. We can complete the proof by exhibiting a tree $T^* \in \mathcal{T}_{ab}$ in which a and b are siblings such that $L(T^*, \mathbf{p}) \leq L(T, \mathbf{p})$. Without loss of generality, each node of T either is a leaf or has two children.[7] Thus, there are two leaves with a common parent that inhabit the deepest level of T, say with left child x and right child y. For clarity, assume that the leaf pairs $\{a, b\}$ and $\{x, y\}$ do not overlap.[8] Construct the Σ-tree $T^* \in \mathcal{T}_{ab}$ by exchanging the labels of the leaves labeled "a" and "b" with the labels of the leaves labeled "x" and "y":

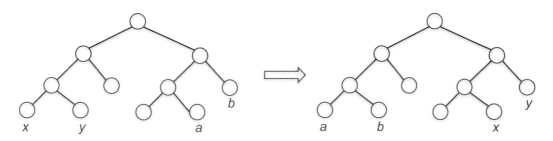

How does the average leaf depth change? Expanding the definition (14.1) and canceling the terms that correspond to leaves other than a, b, x, y, we have

$$L(T) - L(T^*) = \sum_{z \in \{a, b, x, y\}} p_z \cdot (\text{depth of } z \text{ in } T - \text{depth of } z \text{ in } T^*).$$

---

[7]An internal node with only one child can be spliced out to give another Σ-tree with smaller average leaf depth.

[8]If the leaf pairs overlap (for example, with $a = y$), the same exchange argument can be applied to the leaves outside their intersection (for example, b and x).

Depths in T^* can be rewritten in terms of depths in T. For example, the depth of a in T^* is the same as the depth of x in T, the depth of y in T^* is the same as the depth of b in T, and so on. We can therefore sneakily rearrange terms to obtain

$$L(T) - L(T^*) = \underbrace{(p_x - p_a)}_{\geq 0} \cdot \underbrace{(\text{depth of } x \text{ in } T - \text{depth of } a \text{ in } T)}_{\geq 0}$$
$$+ \underbrace{(p_y - p_b)}_{\geq 0} \cdot \underbrace{(\text{depth of } y \text{ in } T - \text{depth of } b \text{ in } T)}_{\geq 0}$$
$$\geq 0.$$

The rearrangement makes it obvious that the difference on the left-hand side is nonnegative. The terms $p_x - p_a$ and $p_y - p_b$ are nonnegative because a and b were chosen as the symbols with the smallest frequencies (and, by assumption, x and y are distinct from a and b). The other two terms on the right-hand side are nonnegative because x and y were chosen from the deepest level of T. We conclude that the average leaf depth of $T^* \in \mathcal{T}_{ab}$ is at most that of T. Because every Σ-tree is equaled or bettered by a tree of $\mathcal{T}_{ab}$, $\mathcal{T}_{ab}$ contains a tree that is optimal among all Σ-trees. This wraps up the proof of (†).

To recap, the statement (*) implies that, with the input Σ and $\mathbf{p}$, the Huffman algorithm outputs an optimal tree from the restricted set $\mathcal{T}_{ab}$. By (†), this tree must be optimal for the original problem. This completes the proof of the inductive step and of Theorem 14.2. $\mathcal{QED}$

The Upshot

☆ Prefix-free variable-length binary codes can have smaller average encoding lengths than fixed-length codes when different alphabet symbols have different frequencies.

☆ Prefix-free codes can be visualized as binary trees in which the leaves are in one-to-one correspondence with the alphabet symbols. Encodings correspond to root-leaf paths, with left and right child edges interpreted as 0s and 1s, respectively, while the average encoding length corresponds to the average leaf depth.

☆ Huffman's greedy algorithm maintains a forest, with leaves in correspondence to alphabet symbols, and in each iteration greedily merges the pair of trees that causes the minimum-possible increase in the average leaf depth.

☆ Huffman's algorithm is guaranteed to compute a prefix-free code with the minimum-possible average encoding length.

☆ Huffman's algorithm can be implemented in $O(n \log n)$ time, where n is the number of symbols.

☆ The proof of correctness uses an exchange argument to show the existence of an optimal solution in which the two smallest-frequency symbols are siblings, and induction to show that the algorithm computes such a solution.

Test Your Understanding

Problem 14.1 *(S)* Consider the following symbol frequencies for a five-symbol alphabet:

Symbol	Frequency
A	.32
B	.25
C	.2
D	.18
E	.05

What is the average encoding length of an optimal prefix-free code?

a) 2.23

b) 2.4

c) 3

d) 3.45

Problem 14.2 *(S)* Consider the following symbol frequencies for a five-symbol alphabet:

Symbol	Frequency
A	.16
B	.08
C	.35
D	.07
E	.34

What is the average encoding length of an optimal prefix-free code?

a) 2.11

b) 2.31

c) 2.49

d) 2.5

Problem 14.3 *(H)* What is the maximum number of bits that Huffman's greedy algorithm might use to encode a single symbol? (As usual, $n = |\Sigma|$ denotes the alphabet size.)

a) $\log_2 n$

b) $\ln n$

c) $n - 1$

d) n

Problem 14.4 *(H)* Which of the following statements about Huffman's greedy algorithm are true? Assume that the symbol frequencies sum to 1. (Choose all that apply.)

a) A symbol with frequency at least 0.4 will never be encoded with two or more bits.

b) A symbol with frequency at least 0.5 will never be encoded with two or more bits.

c) If all symbol frequencies are less than 0.33, all symbols will be encoded with at least two bits.

d) If all symbol frequencies are less than 0.5, all symbols will be encoded with at least two bits.

Problem 14.5 *(H)* Consider an alphabet Σ, symbol frequencies $\mathbf{p}$, and two symbols $x, y \in \Sigma$ with $p_x < p_y$. Could there be an optimal prefix-free code in which x's encoding is shorter than y's?

Challenge Problems

Problem 14.6 *(S)* Give an implementation of Huffman's greedy algorithm that uses a single invocation of a sorting subroutine, followed by a linear amount of additional work.

Problem 14.7 *(H)* A *ternary code* for an alphabet is a way of writing each of its symbols as a distinct ternary string (i.e., as a sequence of 0s, 1s, and 2s). Design a greedy algorithm that, given an alphabet and symbol frequencies as input, outputs a prefix-free ternary code with the minimum-possible average encoding length. Prove that your algorithm is correct.

Programming Problems

Problem 14.8 Implement in your favorite programming language the Huffman algorithm from Section 14.3 for the optimal prefix-free code problem. How much faster is the heap-based implementation (outlined in footnote 5) than the straightforward quadratic-time implementation?[9] How much faster is the implementation in Problem 14.6 than the heap-based implementation? (See www.algorithmsilluminated.org for test cases and challenge data sets.)

---

[9] Don't forget to check if the heap data structure is built in to your favorite programming language, such as the PriorityQueue class in Java.

Chapter 15

Minimum Spanning Trees

This chapter applies the greedy algorithm design paradigm to a famous graph problem, the *minimum spanning tree (MST)* problem. The MST problem is a uniquely great playground for the study of greedy algorithms, in which almost any greedy algorithm that you can think of turns out to be correct. After reviewing graphs and defining the problem formally (Section 15.1), we'll discuss the two best-known MST algorithms—Prim's algorithm (Section 15.2) and Kruskal's algorithm (Section 15.5). Both algorithms admit blazingly fast implementations, using the heap and union-find data structures, respectively. Section 15.8 outlines an application of Kruskal's algorithm in machine learning, to single-link clustering.

15.1 Problem Definition

The minimum spanning tree problem is about connecting a bunch of objects as cheaply as possible. The objects and connections could represent something physical, like computer servers and communication links between them. Or maybe each object is a representation of a document (say, as a vector of word frequencies), with connections corresponding to pairs of "similar" documents. The problem arises naturally in several application domains, including computer networking (try a Web search for "spanning tree protocol") and machine learning (see Section 15.8).

15.1.1 Graphs

Objects and connections between them are most naturally modeled with graphs (Chapter 7). To review, a graph $G = (V, E)$ has two ingredients, a set V of vertices, and a set E of edges:

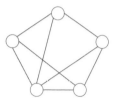

This chapter considers only undirected graphs, in which each edge e is an unordered pair of vertices.[1] The numbers $|V|$ and $|E|$ of vertices and edges are usually denoted by n and m, respectively. This chapter assumes that the input graph is represented using adjacency lists (Section 7.4), with an array of vertices, an array of edges, pointers from each edge to its two endpoints, and pointers from each vertex to its incident edges.

---

[1]There is an analog of the MST problem for directed graphs, which is known as both the *minimum-cost arborescence problem* and the *optimum branching problem*. There are also fast algorithms for this problem, but they lie a bit beyond the scope of this book.

15.1.2 Spanning Trees

The input in the minimum spanning tree problem is an undirected graph $G = (V, E)$ in which each edge e has a real-valued cost c_e. (For example, c_e could indicate the cost of connecting two computer servers.) The goal is to compute a spanning tree of the graph with the minimum-possible sum of edge costs. By a *spanning tree* of G, we mean a subset $T \subseteq E$ of edges that satisfies two properties. First, T should not contain a cycle (this is the "tree" part).[2] Second, for every pair $v, w \in V$ of vertices, T should include a path between v and w (this is the "spanning" part).[3]

Quiz 15.1

What is the minimum sum of edge costs of a spanning tree of the following graph? (Each edge is labeled with its cost.)

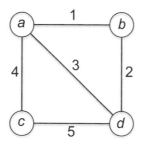

a) 6

b) 7

c) 8

d) 9

(See Section 15.1.3 for the solution and discussion.)

It makes sense only to talk about spanning trees of connected graphs $G = (V, E)$, meaning graphs in which it's possible to travel from any vertex $v \in V$ to any other vertex $w \in V$ using a path of edges in E; see also page 144. (If there is no path in E between the vertices v and w, there certainly isn't one in any subset $T \subseteq E$ of edges, either.) For this reason, throughout this chapter we assume that the input graph is a connected graph.

MST Assumption

The input graph is connected, with at least one path between each pair of vertices.

---

[2] A *cycle* in a graph $G = (V, E)$ is a path that loops back to where it began—an edge sequence $e_1 = (v_0, v_1), e_2 = (v_1, v_2), \ldots, e_k = (v_{k-1}, v_k)$ with $v_k = v_0$.

[3] For convenience, we typically allow a path $(v_0, v_1), (v_1, v_2), \ldots, (v_{k-1}, v_k)$ in a graph to include repeated vertices or, equivalently, to contain one or more cycles. Don't let this bother you: You can always convert such a path into a cycle-free path with the same endpoints v_0 and v_k by repeatedly splicing out subpaths between different visits to the same vertex (see Figure 15.1 on the next page).

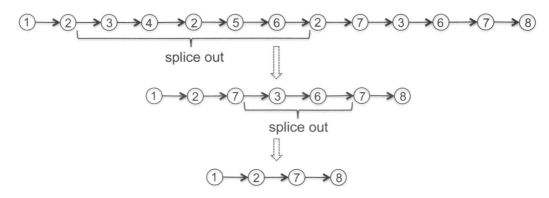

Figure 15.1: A path with repeated vertices can be converted into a path with no repeated vertices and the same endpoints.

It's easy enough to compute the minimum spanning tree of a four-vertex graph like the one in Quiz 15.1; what about in general?

Problem: Minimum Spanning Tree (MST)

Input: A connected undirected graph $G = (V, E)$ and a real-valued cost c_e for each edge $e \in E$.

Output: A spanning tree $T \subseteq E$ of G with the minimum-possible sum $\sum_{e \in T} c_e$ of edge costs.[4]

We can assume that the input graph has at most one edge between each pair of vertices. Why? Because all but the cheapest of a set of parallel edges can be thrown out without changing the problem.

Like minimizing the sum of weighted completion times (Chapter 13) or the optimal prefix-free code problem (Chapter 14), the number of possible solutions can be exponential in the size of the problem.[5] Could there be an algorithm that magically homes in on the minimum-cost needle in the haystack of spanning trees?

15.1.3   Solution to Quiz 15.1

Correct answer: (b). The minimum spanning tree comprises the edges (a, b), (b, d), and (a, c):

---

[4]For graphs that are not connected, we could instead consider the minimum spanning *forest* problem, in which the goal is to find a maximal acyclic subgraph with the minimum-possible sum of edge costs. This problem can be solved by first computing the connected components of the input graph in linear time using breadth- or depth-first search (see Section 8.3) and then applying an algorithm for the MST problem to each component separately.

[5]For example, *Cayley's formula* is a famous result from combinatorics stating that the n-vertex complete graph (in which all the $\binom{n}{2}$ possible edges are present) has exactly n^{n-2} different spanning trees. This is bigger than the estimated number of atoms in the known universe when $n \geq 50$.

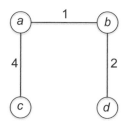

The sum of the edges' costs is 7. The edges do not include a cycle, and they can be used to travel from any vertex to any other vertex.

Here are two spanning trees with an inferior total cost of 8:

The three edges (a, b), (b, d), and (a, d) have a smaller total cost of 6:

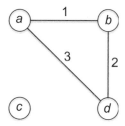

but these edges do not form a spanning tree. In fact, they fail on both counts: They form a cycle and there is no way to use them to travel from c to any other vertex.

15.2 Prim's Algorithm

Our first algorithm for the minimum spanning tree problem is *Prim's algorithm*, which is named after Robert C. Prim, who discovered the algorithm in 1957. The algorithm closely resembles Dijkstra's shortest-path algorithm (which we saw in Chapter 9), so it shouldn't surprise you that Edsger W. Dijkstra independently arrived at the same algorithm shortly thereafter, in 1959. Only later was it realized that the algorithm had been discovered over 25 years earlier, by Vojtěch Jarník in 1930. For this reason, the algorithm is also called *Jarník's algorithm* and the *Prim-Jarník algorithm*.[6]

15.2.1 Example

Next we'll step through Prim's algorithm on a concrete example, the same one from Quiz 15.1:

---

[6]History buffs should check out the paper "On the History of the Minimum Spanning Tree Problem," by Ronald L. Graham and Pavol Hell (*Annals of the History of Computing*, 1985).

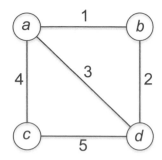

It might seem weird to go through an example of an algorithm before you've seen its code, but trust me: After you understand the example, the pseudocode will practically write itself.

Prim's algorithm begins by choosing an arbitrary vertex—let's say vertex b in our example. (In the end, it won't matter which one we pick.) The plan is to construct a tree one edge at a time, starting from b and growing like a mold until the tree spans the entire vertex set. In each iteration, we'll greedily add the cheapest edge that extends the reach of the tree-so-far.

The algorithm's initial (empty) tree spans only the starting vertex b. There are two options for expanding its reach: the edge (a, b) and the edge (b, d).

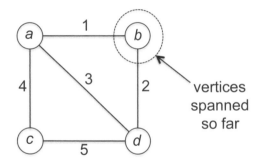

The former is cheaper, so the algorithm chooses it. The tree-so-far spans the vertices a and b.

In the second iteration, three edges would expand the tree's reach: (a, c), (a, d), and (b, d).

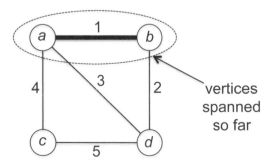

The cheapest of these is (b, d). After its addition, the tree-so-far spans a, b, and d. Both endpoints of the edge (a, d) have been sucked into the set of vertices spanned so far; adding this edge in the future would create a cycle, so the algorithm does not consider it further.

In the final iteration, there are two options for expanding the tree's reach to c, the edges (a, c) and (c, d):

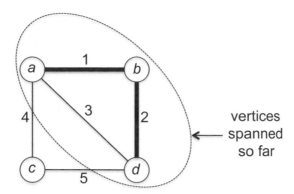

Prim's algorithm chooses the cheaper edge (a, c), resulting in the same minimum spanning tree identified in Quiz 15.1:

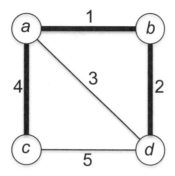

15.2.2   Pseudocode

In general, Prim's algorithm grows a spanning tree from a starting vertex one edge at a time, with each iteration extending the reach of the tree-so-far by one additional vertex. As a greedy algorithm, the algorithm always chooses the cheapest edge that does the job.

Prim

Input: connected undirected graph $G = (V, E)$ in adjacency-list representation and a cost c_e for each edge $e \in E$.
Output: the edges of a minimum spanning tree of G.

```
// Initialization
```
$X := \{s\}$ // s is an arbitrarily chosen vertex
$T := \emptyset$ // invariant: the edges in T span X
```
// Main loop
```
while there is an edge (v, w) with $v \in X, w \notin X$ **do**
    $(a, b) :=$ a minimum-cost such edge
    add vertex b to X
    add edge (a, b) to T
return T

The sets T and X keep track of the edges chosen and the vertices spanned so far. The algorithm seeds X with an arbitrarily chosen starting vertex s; as we'll see, the algorithm is correct no matter which vertex it chooses.[7] Each iteration is responsible for adding one new edge to T. To avoid redundant edges and ensure that the edge addition extends the reach of T, the algorithm considers only the edges that "cross the frontier," with one endpoint in each of X and $V - X$ (Figure 15.2). If there are many such edges, the algorithm greedily chooses the cheapest one. After $n - 1$ iterations (where n is the number of vertices), X contains all the vertices and the algorithm halts. Under our assumption that the input graph G is connected, there's no way for the algorithm to get stuck; if there were ever an iteration with no edges of G crossing between X and $V - X$, we could conclude that G is not connected (because it contains no path from any vertex in X to any vertex in $V - X$).

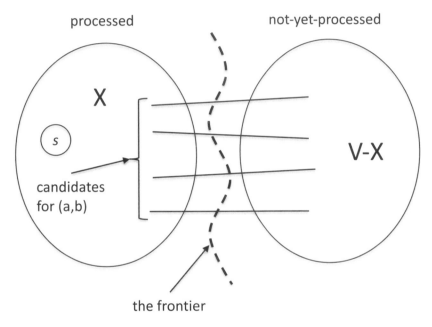

Figure 15.2: Every iteration of Prim's algorithm chooses one new edge that crosses from X to $V - X$.

The algorithm `Prim` computes the minimum spanning tree in the four-vertex five-edge graph of Quiz 15.1, which means approximately...nothing. The fact that an algorithm works correctly on a specific example does *not* imply that it is correct in general! You should be initially skeptical of the `Prim` algorithm and demand a proof of correctness.

Theorem 15.1 (Correctness of `Prim`) *For every connected graph $G = (V, E)$ and real-valued edge costs, the `Prim` algorithm returns a minimum spanning tree of G.*

See Section 15.4 for a proof of Theorem 15.1.

---

[7]The MST problem definition makes no reference to a starting vertex, so it might seem weird to artificially introduce one here. One big benefit is that a starting vertex allows us to closely mimic Dijkstra's shortest-path algorithm (which is saddled with a starting vertex by the problem it solves, the single-source shortest path problem). And it doesn't really change the problem: Connecting every pair of vertices is the same thing as connecting some vertex s to every other vertex. (To get a v-w path, paste together paths from v to s and from s to w.)

15.2.3   Straightforward Implementation

As is typical of greedy algorithms, the running time analysis of Prim's algorithm (assuming a straightforward implementation) is far easier than its correctness proof.

Quiz 15.2

Which of the following running times best describes a straightforward implementation of Prim's minimum spanning tree algorithm for graphs in adjacency-list representation? As usual, n and m denote the number of vertices and edges, respectively, of the input graph.

a) $O(m + n)$

b) $O(m \log n)$

c) $O(n^2)$

d) $O(mn)$

(See below for the solution and discussion.)

Correct answer: (d). A straightforward implementation keeps track of which vertices are in X by associating a Boolean variable with each vertex. In each iteration, it performs an exhaustive search through all the edges to identify the cheapest one with one endpoint in each of X and $V - X$. After $n - 1$ iterations, the algorithm runs out of new vertices to add to its set X and halts. Because the number of iterations is $O(n)$ and each takes $O(m)$ time, the overall running time is $O(mn)$.

Proposition 15.2 (Prim Running Time (Straightforward)) *For every graph $G = (V, E)$ and real-valued edge costs, the straightforward implementation of* Prim *runs in $O(mn)$ time, where $m = |E|$ and $n = |V|$.*

*15.3   Speeding Up Prim's Algorithm via Heaps

15.3.1   The Quest for Near-Linear Running Time

The running time of the straightforward implementation of Prim's algorithm (Proposition 15.2) is nothing to sneeze at—it's a polynomial function of the problem size, while exhaustive search through all of a graph's spanning trees can take an exponential amount of time (see footnote 5). This implementation is fast enough to process medium-size graphs (with thousands of vertices and edges) in a reasonable amount of time, but not big graphs (with millions of vertices and edges). Remember the mantra of any algorithm designer worth their salt: Can we do better? The holy grail in algorithm design is a linear-time algorithm (or close to it), and this is what we want for the MST problem.

We don't need a better *algorithm* to achieve a near-linear-time solution to the problem, just a better *implementation* of Prim's algorithm. The key observation is that the straightforward implementation performs minimum computations, over and over, using exhaustive search. Any method for computing repeated minimum computations faster than exhaustive search would translate to a faster implementation of Prim's algorithm.

We know from Chapter 10 that there is, in fact, a data structure whose raison d'être is fast minimum computations: the *heap* data structure. Thus, a light bulb should go off in your head: Prim's algorithm calls out for a heap!

15.3.2   The Heap Data Structure

In Chapter 10, we learned that a heap maintains an evolving set of objects with keys and supports several fast operations; we'll need three.

Heaps: Three Supported Operations

INSERT: given a heap H and a new object x, add x to H.

EXTRACTMIN: given a heap H, remove and return from H an object with the smallest key (or a pointer to it).

DELETE: given a heap H and a pointer to an object x in H, delete x from H.

For example, if you invoke INSERT four times to add objects with keys 12, 7, 29, and 15 to an empty heap, the EXTRACTMIN operation will return the object with key 7.

Standard implementations of heaps (like the one outlined in Section 10.5) provide the following guarantee.

Theorem 15.3 (Running Time of Three Heap Operations) *In a heap with n objects, the* INSERT, EXTRACTMIN, *and* DELETE *operations run in* $O(\log n)$ *time.*

As a bonus, in typical implementations, the constant hidden by the big-O notation and the amount of space overhead are relatively small.[8]

15.3.3   How to Use Heaps in Prim's Algorithm

Heaps enable a blazingly fast, near-linear-time implementation of Prim's algorithm, similar to the heap-based implementation of Dijkstra's shortest-path algorithm in Section 10.4.

Theorem 15.4 (Prim Running Time (Heap-Based)) *For every graph $G = (V, E)$ and real-valued edge costs, the heap-based implementation of Prim runs in $O((m + n) \log n)$ time, where $m = |E|$ and $n = |V|$.*[9]

The running time bound in Theorem 15.4 is only a logarithmic factor more than the time required to read the input. The minimum spanning tree problem thus qualifies as a for-free primitive (see page 23), joining the likes of sorting, computing the connected components of a graph, and the single-source shortest path problem.

---

[8]For the goals of this section, it's not important to remember what heaps look like under the hood. We'll simply be educated clients of them, taking advantage of their logarithmic-time operations.

[9]Under our standing assumption that the input graph is connected, m is at least $n - 1$ and we can therefore simplify $O((m + n) \log n)$ to $O(m \log n)$ in the running time bound.

In the heap-based implementation of Prim's algorithm, the objects in the heap correspond to the as-yet-unprocessed vertices ($V - X$ in the Prim pseudocode).[10,11] The key of a vertex $w \in V - X$ is defined as the minimum cost of an incident crossing edge (Figure 15.3).

Invariant

The key of a vertex $w \in V - X$ is the minimum cost of an edge (v, w) with $v \in X$, or $+\infty$ if no such edge exists.

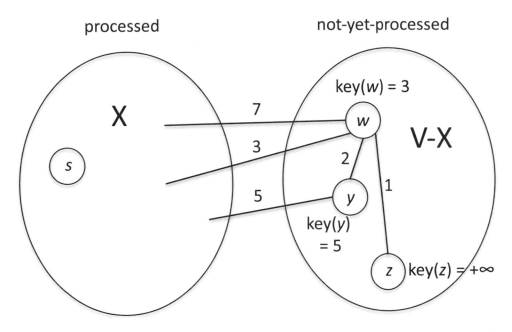

Figure 15.3: The key of a vertex $w \in V - X$ is defined as the minimum cost of an edge (v, w) with $v \in X$ (or $+\infty$, if no such edge exists).

To interpret these keys, imagine using a two round knockout tournament to identify the minimum-cost edge (v, w) with $v \in X$ and $w \notin X$. The first round comprises a local tournament for each vertex $w \in V - X$, where the participants are the edges (v, w) with $v \in X$ and the first-round winner is the cheapest participant (or $+\infty$, if there are no such edges). The first-round winners (at most one per vertex $w \in V - X$) proceed to the second round, and the final champion is the cheapest first-round winner. Thus, the key of a vertex $w \in V - X$ is exactly the winning edge cost in the local tournament at w. Extracting the vertex with the minimum key then implements the second round of the tournament and returns on a silver platter the next addition to the solution-so-far. As long as we pay the piper and maintain the invariant, keeping objects' keys up to date, we can implement each iteration of Prim's algorithm with a single heap operation.

---

[10]We refer to vertices of the input graph and the corresponding objects in the heap interchangeably.

[11]Your first thought might be to store the *edges* of the input graph in a heap, with an eye toward replacing the minimum computations (over edges) in the straightforward implementation with calls to ExtractMin. This idea can be made to work, but the slicker and quicker implementation stores vertices in a heap.

15.3.4   Pseudocode

The pseudocode then looks like this:

Prim (Heap-Based)

Input: connected undirected graph $G = (V, E)$ in adjacency-list representation and a cost c_e for each edge $e \in E$.
Output: the edges of a minimum spanning tree of G.

```
// Initialization
```
1 $X := \{s\}, T := \emptyset, H :=$ empty heap
2 **for** every $v \neq s$ **do**
3   **if** there is an edge $(s, v) \in E$ **then**
4          $key(v) := c_{sv}, winner(v) := (s, v)$
5   **else**   // v has no crossing incident edges
6          $key(v) := +\infty, winner(v) := NULL$
7   INSERT v into H
```
// Main loop
```
8 **while** H is non-empty **do**
9      $w :=$ EXTRACTMIN(H)
10   add w to X
11   add $winner(w)$ to T
```
// update heap to maintain invariant
```
12   **for** every edge (w, y) with $y \in V - X$ **do**
13   **if** $c_{wy} < key(y)$ **then**
14   DELETE y from H
15             $key(y) := c_{wy}, winner(y) := (w, y)$
16   INSERT y into H
17 return T

Each not-yet-processed vertex w records in its *winner* and *key* fields the identity and cost of the winner of its local tournament—the cheapest edge incident to w that crosses the frontier (i.e., edges (v, w) with $v \in X$). Lines 2–7 initialize these values for all the vertices other than s so that the invariant is satisfied and insert these vertices into a heap. Lines 9–11 implement one iteration of the main loop of Prim's algorithm. The invariant ensures that the local winner of the extracted vertex is the cheapest edge crossing the frontier, which is the correct edge to add next to the tree-so-far T. The next quiz illustrates how an extraction can change the frontier, necessitating updates to the keys of vertices still in $V - X$ to maintain the invariant.

Quiz 15.3

In Figure 15.3, suppose the vertex w is extracted and moved to the set X. What should be the new values of y and z's keys, respectively?

a) 1 and 2

b) 2 and 1

c) 5 and $+\infty$

d) $+\infty$ and $+\infty$

(See Section 15.3.6 for the solution and discussion.)

Lines 12–16 of the pseudocode pay the piper and perform the necessary updates to the keys of the vertices remaining in $V - X$. When w is moved from $V - X$ to X, edges of the form (w, y) with $y \in V - X$ cross the frontier for the first time; these are the new contestants in the local tournaments at the vertices of $V - X$. (We can ignore the fact that edges of the form (v, w) with $v \in X$ get sucked into X and no longer cross the frontier, as we're not responsible for maintaining keys for vertices in X.) For a vertex $y \in V - X$, the new winner of its local tournament is either the defending champion (stored in $winner(y)$) or the new contestant (w, y). Line 12 iterates through the new contestants.[12] Line 13 checks whether an edge (w, y) is the new winner in y's local tournament; if it is, lines 14–16 update y's key and $winner$ fields and the heap H accordingly.[13]

15.3.5   Running Time Analysis

The initialization phase (lines 1–7) performs $n - 1$ heap operations (one INSERT per vertex other than s) and $O(m)$ additional work, where n and m denote the number of vertices and edges, respectively.[14] There are $n - 1$ iterations of the main while loop (lines 8–16), so lines 9–11 contribute $O(n)$ heap operations and $O(n)$ additional work to the overall running time. Bounding the total time spent in lines 12–16 is the tricky part; the key observation is that *each edge of G is examined in line 12 exactly once*, in the iteration in which the first of its endpoints gets sucked into X (i.e., plays the role of w). When an edge is examined, the algorithm performs two heap operations (in lines 14 and 16) and $O(1)$ additional work, so the total contribution of lines 12–16 to the running time (over all while loop iterations) is $O(m)$ heap operations plus $O(m)$ additional work. Tallying up, the final scorecard reads

$$O(m + n) \text{ heap operations} + O(m + n) \text{ additional work.}$$

The heap never stores more than $n - 1$ objects, so each heap operation runs in $O(\log n)$ time (Theorem 15.3). The overall running time is $O((m+n)\log n)$, as promised by Theorem 15.4. *QED*

15.3.6   Solution to Quiz 15.3

Correct answer: (b). After the vertex w is moved from $V - X$ to X, the new picture is:

---

[12]This is the main step in which it's so convenient to have the input graph represented via adjacency lists—the edges of the form (w, y) can be accessed directly via w's array of incident edges.

[13]Some heap implementations export a DECREASEKEY operation, in which case lines 14–16 can be implemented with one heap operation rather than two.

[14]This initialization phase can actually be implemented in linear time using the HEAPIFY operation described in Problem 10.5.

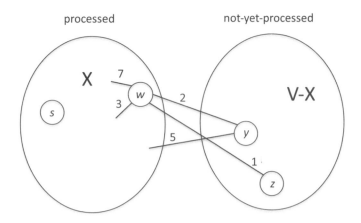

Edges of the form (v, w) with $v \in X$ get sucked into X and no longer cross the frontier (as with the edges with costs 3 and 7). The other edges incident to w, (w, y) and (w, z), get partially yanked out of $V - X$ and now cross the frontier. For both y and z, these new incident crossing edges are cheaper than all their old ones. To maintain the invariant, both of their keys must be updated accordingly: y's key from 5 to 2, and z's key from $+\infty$ to 1.

*15.4 Prim's Algorithm: Proof of Correctness

Proving the correctness of Prim's algorithm (Theorem 15.1) is a bit easier when all the edge costs are distinct. Among friends, let's adopt this assumption for this section. With a little more work, Theorem 15.1 can be proved in its full generality (see Problem 15.5).

The proof breaks down into two steps. The first step identifies a property, called the "minimum bottleneck property," possessed by the output of Prim's algorithm. The second step shows that, in a graph with distinct edge costs, a spanning tree with this property must be a minimum spanning tree.[15]

15.4.1 The Minimum Bottleneck Property

We can motivate the minimum bottleneck property by analogy with Dijkstra's shortest-path algorithm. The only major difference between Prim's and Dijkstra's algorithms is the criterion used to choose a crossing edge in each iteration. Dijkstra's algorithm greedily chooses the eligible edge that minimizes the distance (i.e., the *sum* of edge lengths) from the starting vertex s and, for this reason, computes shortest paths from s to every other vertex (provided edge lengths are nonnegative). Prim's algorithm, by always choosing the eligible edge with minimum individual cost, is effectively striving to minimize the *maximum* edge cost along every path.[16]

---

[15]A popular if more abstract alternative approach to proving the correctness of Prim's (and Kruskal's) algorithm is to use what's known as the "Cut Property" of MSTs; see Problem 15.7 for details.

[16]This observation is related to a mystery that might be troubling you: Why is Dijkstra's algorithm correct only with nonnegative edge lengths, while Prim's algorithm is correct with arbitrary (positive or negative) edge costs? A key ingredient in the correctness proof for Dijkstra's algorithm (Section 9.3) is "path monotonicity," meaning that tacking on additional edges at the end of a path can only make it worse. Tacking a negative-length edge onto a path would decrease its overall length, so nonnegative edge lengths are necessary for path monotonicity. For Prim's algorithm, the relevant measure is the *maximum* cost of an edge in a path, and this measure cannot decrease as additional (positive- or negative-cost) edges are tacked onto the path.

The minimum bottleneck property makes this idea precise. Given a graph with real-valued edge costs, define the *bottleneck* of a path P as the maximum cost $\max_{e \in P} c_e$ of one of its edges.

The Minimum Bottleneck Property (MBP)

For a graph $G = (V, E)$ with real-valued edge costs, an edge $(v, w) \in E$ satisfies the *minimum bottleneck property (MBP)* if it is a minimum-bottleneck v-w path.

In other words, an edge (v, w) satisfies the MBP if and only if there is no v-w path consisting solely of edges with cost less than c_{vw}. In our running example:

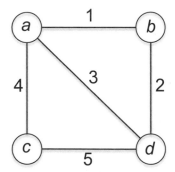

the edge (a, d) does not satisfy the MBP (every edge on the path $a \to b \to d$ is cheaper than (a, d)), nor does the edge (c, d) (every edge on the path $c \to a \to d$ is cheaper than (c, d)). The other three edges do satisfy the MBP, as you should check.[17]

The next lemma implements the first step of our proof plan by relating the output of Prim's algorithm to the MBP.

Lemma 15.5 (`Prim` Achieves the MBP) *For every connected graph $G = (V, E)$ and real-valued edge costs, every edge chosen by the* `Prim` *algorithm satisfies the MBP.*

Proof: Consider an edge (a, b) chosen in an iteration of the `Prim` algorithm, with $a \in X$ and $b \in V - X$. By the algorithm's greedy rule,

$$c_{ab} \leq c_{xy} \tag{15.1}$$

for every edge $(x, y) \in E$ with $x \in X$ and $y \in V - X$.

To prove that (a, b) satisfies the MBP, consider an arbitrary a-b path P. Because $a \in X$ and $b \notin X$, the path P crosses at some point from X to $V - X$, say via the edge (x, y) with $x \in X$ and $y \in V - X$ (Figure 15.4). The bottleneck of P is at least c_{xy}, which by inequality (15.1) is at least c_{ab}. Because P was arbitrary, the edge (a, b) is a minimum-bottleneck a-b path. $\mathcal{QED}$

We set out to solve the minimum spanning tree problem, not to achieve the minimum bottleneck property. But I'd never waste your time; in graphs with distinct edge costs, the latter automatically implies the former.[18]

---

[17]As we'll see, it's no accident that the edges satisfying the MBP in this example are precisely the edges in the minimum spanning tree.

[18]The converse of Theorem 15.6 (on the next page) is also true, even with non-distinct edge costs: Every edge of an MST satisfies the MBP (Problem 15.4).

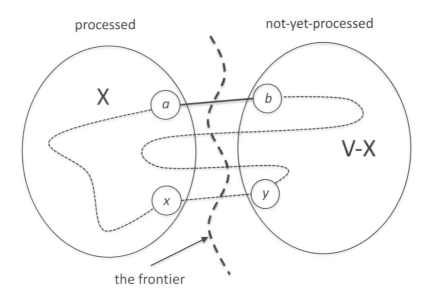

Figure 15.4: Every a-b path crosses at least once from X to $V - X$. The dotted lines represent one such path.

Theorem 15.6 (MBP Implies MST) *Let $G = (V, E)$ be a graph with distinct real-valued edge costs, and T a spanning tree of G. If every edge of T satisfies the minimum bottleneck property, T is a minimum spanning tree.*

The bad news is that the proof of Theorem 15.6 has several steps. The good news is that we can reuse all of them to also establish the correctness of another important MST algorithm, Kruskal's algorithm (Theorem 15.11 in Section 15.5).[19]

15.4.2   Fun Facts About Spanning Trees

To warm up for the proof of Theorem 15.6, we'll prove some simple and useful facts about undirected graphs and their spanning trees. First, some terminology. A graph $G = (V, E)$— not necessarily connected—naturally falls into "pieces," the connected components of the graph. More formally, recall from Section 8.3 that a connected component is a maximal subset $S \subseteq V$ of vertices such that there is a path in G from any vertex in S to any other vertex in S. For example, the connected components of the graph in Figure 15.5(a) are $\{1, 3, 5, 7, 9\}$, $\{2, 4\}$, and $\{6, 8, 10\}$. A graph is connected, with a path between every pair of vertices, if and only if it has a single connected component.

Now imagine starting from an empty graph (with vertices but no edges) and adding edges to it one by one. What changes when a new edge is added? One possibility is that the new edge fuses two connected components into one (Figure 15.5(b)). We call this a *type-F edge addition* ('F' for "fusion"). Another possibility is that the new edge closes a pre-existing path, creating a cycle (Figure 15.5(c)). We call this a *type-C edge addition* ('C' for "cycle"). Our first lemma states that every edge addition (v, w) is either type C or type F

---

[19]Theorem 15.6 does not hold as stated in graphs with non-distinct edge costs. (For a counterexample, consider a triangle with one edge with cost 1 and two edges with cost 2 each.) Nevertheless, Prim's and Kruskal's algorithms remain correct with arbitrary real-valued edge costs (see Problem 15.5).

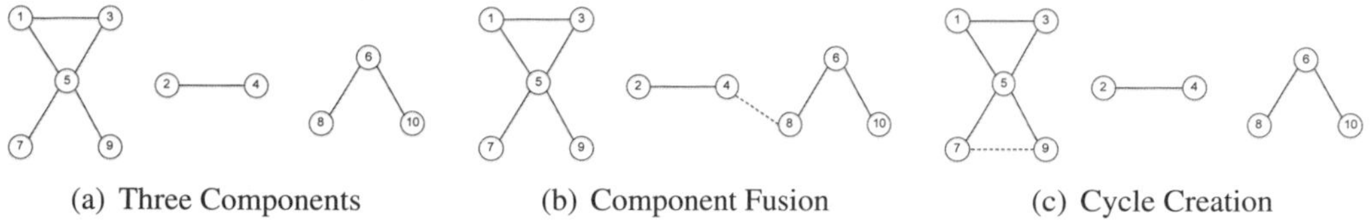

(a) Three Components   (b) Component Fusion   (c) Cycle Creation

Figure 15.5: In (a), a graph with vertex set $\{1, 2, 3, \ldots, 10\}$ and three connected components. In (b), adding the edge $(4, 8)$ fuses two components into one. In (c), adding the edge $(7, 9)$ creates a new cycle.

(and not both), depending on whether the graph already has a v-w path. If this statement seems obvious to you, feel free to skip the proof and move on.

Lemma 15.7 (Cycle Creation/Component Fusion) *Let $G = (V, E)$ be an undirected graph and $v, w \in V$ two distinct vertices such that $(v, w) \notin E$.*

(a) *(Type C) If v and w are in the same connected component of G, adding the edge (v, w) to G creates at least one new cycle and does not change the number of connected components.*

(b) *(Type F) If v and w are in different connected components of G, adding the edge (v, w) to G does not create any new cycles and decreases the number of connected components by 1.*

Proof: For part (a), if v and w are in the same connected component of G, there is a v-w path P in G. After the edge addition, $P \cup \{(v, w)\}$ forms a new cycle. The connected components remain exactly the same, with the new edge (v, w) swallowed up by the connected component that already contains both its endpoints.

For part (b), let S_1 and S_2 denote the (distinct) connected components of G that contain v and w, respectively. First, after the edge addition, the connected components S_1 and S_2 fuse into a single component $S_1 \cup S_2$, decreasing the number of components by 1. (For vertices $x \in S_1$ and $y \in S_2$, you can produce an x-y path in the new graph by pasting together an x-v path in G, the new edge (v, w), and a w-y path in G.) Second, suppose for contradiction that the edge addition *did* create a new cycle C. This cycle must include the new edge (v, w). But then $C - \{(v, w)\}$ would be a v-w path in G, contradicting our assumption that v and w are in different connected components. $\mathcal{QED}$

With Lemma 15.7 at our disposal, we can quickly deduce some interesting facts about spanning trees.

Corollary 15.8 (Spanning Trees Have Exactly $n - 1$ Edges) *Every spanning tree of an n-vertex graph has $n - 1$ edges.*

Proof: Let T be a spanning tree of a graph $G = (V, E)$ with n vertices. Start from the empty graph with vertex set V and add the edges of T one by one. Because T has no cycles, every edge addition is of type F and decreases the number of connected components by 1 (Lemma 15.7):

The process starts with n connected components (with each vertex in its own component) and ends with 1 (because T is a spanning tree), so the number of edge additions must be $n - 1$. $\mathcal{QED}$

There are two ways a subgraph can fail to be a spanning tree: by containing a cycle or by failing to be connected. A subgraph with $n - 1$ edges—a candidate for a spanning tree, by Corollary 15.8—fails one of the conditions only if it fails both.

Corollary 15.9 (Connectedness and Acyclicity Go Together) *Let* $G = (V, E)$ *be a graph and* $T \subseteq E$ *a subset of* $n - 1$ *edges, where* $n = |V|$. *The graph* (V, T) *is connected if and only if it contains no cycles.*

Proof: Reprise the edge addition process from Corollary 15.8. If each of the $n - 1$ edge additions has type F, then Lemma 15.7(b) implies that the process concludes with a single connected component and no cycles (i.e., a spanning tree).

Otherwise, there is a type-C edge addition, which by Lemma 15.7(a) creates a cycle and also fails to decrease the number of connected components:

In this case, the process starts with n connected components and the $n - 1$ edge additions decrease the number of connected components at most $n - 2$ times, leaving the final graph (V, T) with at least two connected components. We conclude that (V, T) is neither connected nor acyclic. $\mathcal{QED}$

We can similarly argue that the output of Prim's algorithm is a spanning tree. (We're not yet claiming that it's a *minimum* spanning tree.)

Corollary 15.10 (`Prim` Outputs a Spanning Tree) *For every connected input graph, the* `Prim` *algorithm outputs a spanning tree.*

Proof: Throughout the algorithm, the vertices of X form one connected component of (V, T) and each vertex of $V - X$ is isolated in its own connected component. Each of the $n - 1$ edge additions involves a vertex w of $V - X$ and hence has type F, so the final result is a spanning tree. $\mathcal{QED}$

15.4.3 Proof of Theorem 15.6 (MBP Implies MST)

The proof of Theorem 15.6 is where we use our standing assumption that edges' costs are distinct.

Proof of Theorem 15.6: We proceed by contradiction. Let T be a spanning tree in which every edge satisfies the MBP, and suppose that a minimum spanning tree T^* has a strictly smaller sum of edge costs. Inspired by our proof of Theorem 13.1, the plan is to exchange one edge for another to produce a spanning tree T' with total cost even less than T^*, thereby contradicting the alleged optimality of T^*.

The trees T and T^* must be different and each has $n - 1$ edges, where $n = |V|$ (by Corollary 15.8). Thus, T contains at least one edge $e_1 = (v, w)$ that is not in T^*. Adding e_1 to T^* creates a cycle C that contains e_1 (Lemma 15.7(a)):

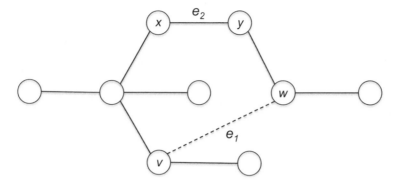

As an edge of T, e_1 satisfies the MBP, so there is at least one edge $e_2 = (x, y)$ in the v-w path $C - \{e_1\}$ with cost at least c_{vw}. Under our assumption that edges' costs are distinct, the cost of e_2 must be strictly larger: $c_{xy} > c_{vw}$.

Now derive T' from $T^* \cup \{e_1\}$ by removing the edge e_2:

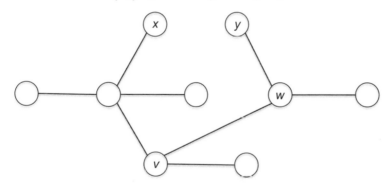

Because T^* has $n - 1$ edges, so does T'. Because T^* is connected, so is T'. (Removing an edge from a cycle undoes a type-C edge addition, which by Lemma 15.7(a) has no effect on the number of connected components.) Corollary 15.9 then implies that T' is also acyclic and hence a spanning tree. Because the cost of e_2 is larger than that of e_1, T' has a lower total cost than T^*; this contradicts the supposed optimality of T^* and completes the proof. *QED*

15.4.4   Putting It All Together

We now have the ingredients to immediately deduce the correctness of Prim's algorithm in graphs with distinct edge costs.

Proof of Theorem 15.1: Corollary 15.10 proves that the output of Prim's algorithm is a spanning tree. Lemma 15.5 implies that every edge of this spanning tree satisfies the MBP. Theorem 15.6 guarantees that this spanning tree is a minimum spanning tree. *QED*

15.5 Kruskal's Algorithm

This section describes a second algorithm for the minimum spanning tree problem, *Kruskal's algorithm.*[20] With our blazingly fast heap-based implementation of Prim's algorithm, why should we care about Kruskal's algorithm? Three reasons. One, it's a first-ballot hall-of-fame algorithm, so every seasoned programmer and computer scientist should know about it. Properly implemented, it is competitive with Prim's algorithm in both theory and practice. Two, it provides an opportunity to study a new and useful data structure, the *disjoint-set* or *union-find* data structure. Three, there are some very cool connections between Kruskal's algorithm and widely-used clustering algorithms (see Section 15.8).

15.5.1 Example

As with Prim's algorithm, it's helpful to see an example of Kruskal's algorithm in action before proceeding to its pseudocode. Here's the input graph:

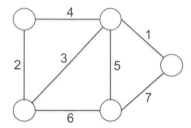

Kruskal's algorithm, like Prim's algorithm, greedily constructs a spanning tree one edge at a time. But rather than growing a single tree from a starting vertex, Kruskal's algorithm can grow multiple trees in parallel, content for them to coalesce into a single tree only at the end of the algorithm. So, while Prim's algorithm was constrained to choose the cheapest edge crossing the current frontier, Kruskal's algorithm is free to choose the cheapest remaining edge in the entire graph. Well, not quite: Cycles are a no-no, so it chooses the cheapest edge that doesn't create a cycle.

In our example, Kruskal's algorithm starts with an empty edge set T and, in its first iteration, greedily considers the cheapest edge (the edge with cost 1) and adds it to T. The second iteration follows suit with the next-cheapest edge (the edge with cost 2). At this point, the solution-so-far T looks like:

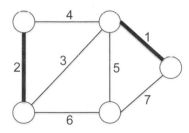

The two edges chosen so far are disjoint, so the algorithm is effectively growing two trees in parallel. The next iteration considers the edge with cost 3. Its inclusion does not create a cycle and also happens to fuse the two trees-so-far into one:

---

[20]Discovered by Joseph B. Kruskal in the mid-1950s—roughly the same time that Prim and Dijkstra were rediscovering what is now called Prim's algorithm.

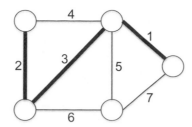

The algorithm next considers the edge with cost 4. Adding this edge to T would create a cycle (with the edges with costs 2 and 3), so the algorithm is forced to skip it. The next-best option is the edge with cost 5; its inclusion does not create a cycle and, in fact, results in a spanning tree:

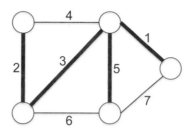

The algorithm skips the edge with cost 6 (which would create a triangle with the edges with costs 3 and 5) as well as the final edge, with cost 7 (which would create a triangle with the edges with costs 1 and 5). The final output above is the minimum spanning tree of the graph (as you should check).

15.5.2   Pseudocode

With our intuition solidly in place, the following pseudocode won't surprise you.

Kruskal

Input: connected undirected graph $G = (V, E)$ in adjacency-list representation and a cost c_e for each edge $e \in E$.
Output: the edges of a minimum spanning tree of G.

```
// Preprocessing
```
$T := \emptyset$
sort edges of E by cost   `// e.g., using MergeSort`[21]
```
// Main loop
```
for each $e \in E$, in nondecreasing order of cost **do**
    if $T \cup \{e\}$ is acyclic **then**
        $T := T \cup \{e\}$
return T

---

[21] The abbreviation "e.g." stands for *exempli gratia* and means "for example."

Kruskal's algorithm considers the edges of the input graph one by one, from cheapest to most expensive, so it makes sense to sort them in nondecreasing order of cost in a preprocessing step (using your favorite sorting algorithm, such as MergeSort or HeapSort). Ties between edges can be broken arbitrarily. The main loop zips through the edges in this order, adding an edge to the solution-so-far provided it doesn't create a cycle.[22]

It's not obvious that the `Kruskal` algorithm returns a spanning tree, let alone a minimum one. But it does!

Theorem 15.11 (Correctness of `Kruskal`) *For every connected graph $G = (V, E)$ and real-valued edge costs, the `Kruskal` algorithm returns a minimum spanning tree of G.*

We've already done most of the heavy lifting in our correctness proof for Prim's algorithm (Theorem 15.1). Section 15.7 supplies the remaining details of the proof of Theorem 15.11.

15.5.3   Straightforward Implementation

How would you actually implement Kruskal's algorithm and, in particular, the cycle-checking required in each iteration?

Quiz 15.4

Which of the following running times best describes a straightforward implementation of Kruskal's MST algorithm for graphs in adjacency-list representation? As usual, n and m denote the number of vertices and edges, respectively, of the input graph.

a) $O(m \log n)$

b) $O(n^2)$

c) $O(mn)$

d) $O(m^2)$

(See below for the solution and discussion.)

Correct answer: (c). In the preprocessing step, the algorithm sorts the edge array of the input graph, which has m entries. With a good sorting algorithm (like MergeSort), this step contributes $O(m \log n)$ work to the overall running time.[23] This work will be dominated by that done by the main loop of the algorithm, which we analyze next.

The main loop has m iterations. Each iteration is responsible for checking whether the edge $e = (v, w)$ under examination can be added to the solution-so-far T without creating

---

[22]One easy optimization: You can stop the algorithm early once $|V| - 1$ edges have been added to T, as at this point T is already a spanning tree (by Corollary 15.9).

[23]Why $O(m \log n)$ instead of $O(m \log m)$? Because there's no difference between the two expressions. The number of edges of an n-vertex connected graph with no parallel edges is at least $n - 1$ (achieved by a tree) and at most $\binom{n}{2} = \frac{n(n-1)}{2}$ (achieved by a complete graph). Thus $\log m$ lies between $\log(n - 1)$ and $2 \log n$ for every connected graph with no parallel edges, which justifies using $\log m$ and $\log n$ interchangeably inside a big-O expression.

a cycle. By Lemma 15.7, adding e to T creates a cycle if and only if T already contains a v-w path. The latter condition can be checked in linear time using any reasonable graph search algorithm, like breadth- or depth-first search starting from v (see Chapter 8). And by "linear time," we mean linear in the size of the graph (V, T) which, as an acyclic graph with n vertices, has at most $n - 1$ edges. The per-iteration running time is therefore $O(n)$, for an overall running time of $O(mn)$.

Proposition 15.12 (Kruskal Running Time (Straightforward)) *For every graph* $G = (V, E)$ *and real-valued edge costs, the straightforward implementation of* Kruskal *runs in* $O(mn)$ *time, where* $m = |E|$ *and* $n = |V|$.

*15.6   Speeding Up Kruskal's Algorithm via Union-Find

As with Prim's algorithm, we can reduce the running time of Kruskal's algorithm from the reasonable polynomial bound of $O(mn)$ (Proposition 15.12) to the blazingly fast near-linear bound of $O(m \log n)$ through the deft use of a data structure. None of the data structures discussed previously in this book are right for the job; we'll need a new one, called the *union-find* data structure. (Also known as the *disjoint-set* data structure.)

Theorem 15.13 (Kruskal Running Time (Union-Find-Based)) *For every graph* $G = (V, E)$ *and real-valued edge costs, the union-find-based implementation of* Kruskal *runs in* $O((m + n) \log n)$ *time, where* $m = |E|$ *and* $n = |V|$.[24]

15.6.1   The Union-Find Data Structure

Whenever a program does a significant computation over and over again, it's a clarion call for a data structure to speed up those computations. Prim's algorithm performs minimum computations in each iteration of its main loop, so the heap data structure is an obvious match. Each iteration of Kruskal's algorithm performs a cycle check or, equivalently, a path check. (Adding an edge (v, w) to the solution-so-far T creates a cycle if and only if T already contains a v-w path.) What kind of data structure would allow us to quickly identify whether the solution-so-far contains a path between a given pair of vertices?

The raison d'être of the union-find data structure is to maintain a partition of a static set of objects.[25] In the initial partition, each object is in its own set. These sets can merge over time, but they can never split:

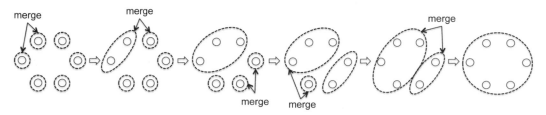

---

[24] Again, under our standing assumption that the input graph is connected, we can simplify the $O((m + n) \log n)$ bound to $O(m \log n)$.

[25] A *partition* of a set X of objects is a way of splitting them into one or more groups. More formally, it is a collection $S_1, S_2, \ldots, S_p$ of non-empty subsets of X such that each object $x \in X$ belongs to exactly one of the subsets.

In our application of speeding up Kruskal's algorithm, the objects will correspond to the vertices of the input graph and the sets in the partition to the connected components of the solution-so-far T:

Checking whether T already contains a v-w path then boils down to checking whether v and w belong to the same set of the partition (i.e., to the same connected component).

The union-find data structure supports two operations for accessing and modifying its partition, the—wait for it—UNION and FIND operations.

Union-Find: Supported Operations

INITIALIZE: given an array X of objects, create a union-find data structure with each object $x \in X$ in its own set.

FIND: given a union-find data structure and an object x in it, return the name of the set that contains x.

UNION: given a union-find data structure and two objects $x, y \in X$ in it, merge the sets that contain x and y into a single set. (If x and y are already in the same set of the partition, this operation has no effect.)

With a good implementation, the UNION and FIND operations both take time logarithmic in the number of objects.[26]

Theorem 15.14 (Running Time of Union-Find Operations) *In a union-find data structure with n objects, the* INITIALIZE, FIND, *and* UNION *operations run in* $O(n)$, $O(\log n)$, *and* $O(\log n)$ *time, respectively.*

Summarizing, here's the scorecard:

Operation	Running time
INITIALIZE	$O(n)$
FIND	$O(\log n)$
UNION	$O(\log n)$

Table 15.1: The union-find data structure: supported operations and their running times, where n denotes the number of objects.

---

[26]These bounds are for the quick-and-dirty implementation in Section 15.6.4. There are better implementations but they are overkill for the present application. See the bonus videos at www.algorithmsilluminated.org for an in-depth look at state-of-the-art union-find data structures. (Highlights include "union-by-rank," "path compression," and the "inverse Ackermann function." It's amazing stuff!)

We first show how to implement Kruskal's algorithm given a union-find data structure with logarithmic-time operations, and then outline an implementation of such a data structure.

15.6.2   Pseudocode

The main idea for speeding up Kruskal's algorithm is to use a union-find data structure to keep track of the connected components of the solution-so-far. Each vertex is in its own connected component at the beginning of the algorithm and, accordingly, a union-find data structure is born with each object in a different set. Whenever a new edge (v, w) is added to the solution-so-far, the connected components of v and w fuse into one, and one UNION operation suffices to update the union-find data structure accordingly. Checking whether an edge addition (v, w) would create a cycle is equivalent to checking whether v and w are already in the same connected component. This reduces to two FIND operations.

Kruskal (Union-Find-Based)

Input: connected undirected graph $G = (V, E)$ in adjacency-list
  representation and a cost c_e for each edge $e \in E$.
Output: the edges of a minimum spanning tree of G.

```
// Initialization
```
$T := \emptyset$
$U := \text{INITIALIZE}(V)$ `// union-find data structure`
sort edges of E by cost   `// e.g., using MergeSort`
```
// Main loop
```
for each $(v, w) \in E$, in nondecreasing order of cost **do**
    if $\text{FIND}(U, v) \neq \text{FIND}(U, w)$ **then**
        `// no v-w path in T, so OK to add (v,w)`
        $T := T \cup \{(v, w)\}$
        `// update due to component fusion`
        $\text{UNION}(U, v, w)$
return T

The algorithm maintains the invariant that, at the beginning of a loop iteration, the sets of the union-find data structure U correspond to the connected components of (V, T). Thus, the condition $\text{FIND}(U, v) \neq \text{FIND}(U, w)$ is met if and only if v and w are in different connected components of (V, T), or equivalently, if and only if adding (v, w) to T does not create a cycle. We conclude that the union-find-based implementation of Kruskal is faithful to its original implementation, with both versions producing the same output.

15.6.3   Running Time Analysis

The running time analysis of the union-find-based implementation of Kruskal's algorithm is straightforward. Initializing the union-find data structure takes $O(n)$ time. As in the original implementation, the sorting step requires $O(m \log n)$ time (see Quiz 15.4). There are m iterations of the main loop and each uses two FIND operations (for a total of $2m$).

There is one UNION operation for each edge added to the output which, as an acyclic graph, has at most $n - 1$ edges (Corollary 15.8). Provided the FIND and UNION operations run in $O(\log n)$ time, as assured by Theorem 15.14, the total running time is:

preprocessing	$O(n) + O(m \log n)$
$2m$ FIND operations	$O(m \log n)$
$n - 1$ UNION operations	$O(n \log n)$
+ remaining bookkeeping	$O(m)$
total	$O((m + n) \log n).$

This matches the running time bound promised in Theorem 15.13. $\mathscr{QED}$

15.6.4   Quick-and-Dirty Implementation of Union-Find

The Parent Graph

Under the hood, a union-find data structure is implemented as an array and can be visualized as a collection of directed trees. The array has one position for each object $x \in X$. Each array entry has a *parent* field that stores the array index of some object $y \in X$ (with $y = x$ allowed). We can then picture the current state of the data structure as a directed graph—the *parent graph*—with vertices corresponding to (indices of) objects $x \in X$ and a directed edge (x, y), called a *parent edge*, whenever $parent(x) = y$.[27] For example, if X has six objects and the current state of the data structure is:

Index of object x	$parent(x)$
1	4
2	1
3	1
4	4
5	6
6	6

then the parent graph is a pair of disjoint trees, with each root pointing back to itself:

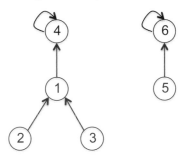

In general, the sets in the partition maintained by the data structure will correspond to the trees in the parent graph, with each set inheriting the name of its root object. The trees are not necessarily binary, as there is no limit to the number of objects that can have the same parent. In the example above, the first four objects belong to a set named "4," and the last two to a set named "6."

---

[27]The parent graph exists only in our minds. Do not confuse it with the actual (undirected) input graph in Kruskal's algorithm.

INITIALIZE and FIND

The intended semantics of the parent graph already dictate how the INITIALIZE and FIND operations should be implemented.

INITIALIZE

1. For each $i = 1, 2, \ldots, n$, initialize *parent*(i) to i.

The INITIALIZE operation clearly runs in $O(n)$ time. The initial parent graph consists of isolated vertices with self-loops:

For the FIND operation, we leap from parent to parent until we arrive at a root object, which can be identified by its self-loop.

FIND

1. Starting from x's position in the array, repeatedly traverse parent edges until reaching a position j with *parent*$(j) = j$.

2. Return j.

If FIND is invoked for the third object in our running example (page 352), the operation checks position 3 (with *parent*$(3) = 1$), then position 1 (with *parent*$(1) = 4$), and finally returns the position 4 (a root, as *parent*$(4) = 4$).

Define the *depth* of an object x as the number of parent edge traversals performed by FIND from x. In our running example, the fourth and sixth objects have depth 0, the first and fifth objects have depth 1, and the second and third objects have depth 2. The FIND operation performs $O(1)$ work per parent edge traversal, so its worst-case running time is proportional to the largest depth of any object—equivalently, to the largest *height* of one of the trees in the parent graph.

Quiz 15.5

What's the running time of the FIND operation, as a function of the number n of objects?

a) $O(1)$

b) $O(\log n)$

c) $O(n)$

d) Not enough information to answer

(See Section 15.6.5 for the solution and discussion.)

UNION

When the UNION operation is invoked with objects x and y, the two trees T_1 and T_2 of the parent graph containing them must be merged into a single tree. The simplest solution is to demote the root of one of the trees and promote that of the other. For example, if we choose to demote T_1's root, it is installed as a child of an object in the other tree T_2, meaning its *parent* field is reassigned from its own array index to that of an object in T_2. The promoted root (from T_2) continues to serve as the root of the merged tree. There are several ways to fuse the two trees in this way, such as:

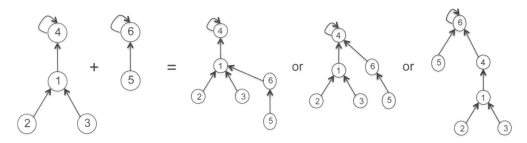

To complete the implementation, we must make two decisions:

1. Which of the two roots do we promote?

2. Under which object do we install the demoted root?

Suppose we install the root of a tree T_1 under an object z of another tree T_2. What are the consequences for the running time of a FIND operation? For an object in T_2, none: The operation traverses exactly the same set of parent edges as before. For an object x that previously inhabited T_1, the FIND operation traverses the same path as before (from x to the old root r of T_1), plus the new parent edge from r to z, plus the parent edges from z to the root of T_2:

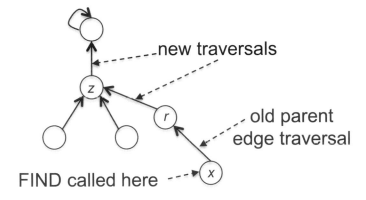

That is, the depth of every object in T_1 increases by 1 (for the new parent edge) plus the depth of z.

The answer to the second question is now clear: Install the demoted root directly under the (depth-0) promoted root so that the occupants of T_1 suffer a depth increase of only 1.

Quiz 15.6

Suppose we arbitrarily choose which root to promote. What's the running time of the FIND operation as a function of the number n of objects?

a) $O(1)$

b) $O(\log n)$

c) $O(n)$

d) Not enough information to answer

(See Section 15.6.5 for the solution and discussion.)

The solution to Quiz 15.6 demonstrates that, to achieve the desired logarithmic running time, we need another idea. If we demote the root of T_1, then T_1's occupants are pushed one step further from the new root; otherwise, T_2's occupants suffer the same fate. It seems only fair to minimize the number of objects suffering a depth increase, which means we should demote the root of the smaller tree (breaking ties arbitrarily).[28] To pull this off, we need easy access to the populations of the two trees. So, along with the *parent* field, the data structure stores with each array entry a *size* field, initialized to 1 in INITIALIZE. When two trees are merged, the *size* field of the promoted root is updated accordingly, to the combined size of the two trees.[29]

UNION

1. Invoke FIND twice to locate the positions i and j of the roots of the parent graph trees that contain x and y, respectively. If $i = j$, return.

2. If $size(i) \geq size(j)$, set $parent(j) := i$ and $size(i) := size(i) + size(j)$.

3. If $size(i) < size(j)$, set $parent(i) := j$ and $size(j) := size(i) + size(j)$.

In our running example (page 352), this implementation of UNION promotes the root 4 and demotes the root 6, resulting in:

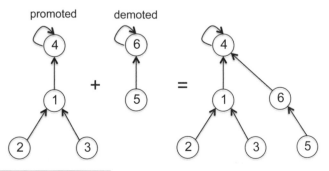

---

[28]This implementation choice goes by the name *union-by-size*. Another good idea is *union-by-rank*, which demotes the root of the tree with the smaller height (breaking ties arbitrarily). Union-by-rank is discussed at length in the bonus videos at www.algorithmsilluminated.org.

[29]There is no need to keep the *size* field accurate after a root has been demoted to a non-root.

A UNION operation performs two FIND operations and $O(1)$ additional work, so its running time matches that of FIND. Which is...?

Quiz 15.7

With the implementation of UNION above, what's the running time of the FIND (and, hence, UNION) operation, as a function of the number n of objects?

    a) $O(1)$

    b) $O(\log n)$

    c) $O(n)$

    d) Not enough information to answer

(See Section 15.6.5 for the solution and discussion.)

With the solution to Quiz 15.7, we conclude that our quick-and-dirty implementation of a union-find data structure fulfills the running time guarantees promised by Theorem 15.14 and Table 15.1.

15.6.5   Solutions to Quizzes 15.5–15.7

Solution to Quiz 15.5

Correct answer: (c or d). The worst-case running time of FIND is proportional to the biggest height of a tree of the parent graph. How big can this be? The answer depends on how we implement the UNION operation; in this sense, answer (d) is correct. A poor implementation can lead to a tree with height as large as $n - 1$:

In this sense, answer (c) is also correct.

Solution to Quiz 15.6

Correct answer: (c). With arbitrary promotion and demotion decisions, a sequence of $n - 1$ UNION operations can produce the height-$(n - 1)$ tree shown in the solution to Quiz 15.5, with each operation installing the tree-so-far underneath a previously isolated object.

Solution to Quiz 15.7

Correct answer: (b). Every object x begins with depth 0. Only one type of event can increment x's depth: a UNION operation in which the root of x's tree in the parent graph gets demoted. By our promotion criterion, this happens only when x's tree is merged with another tree that is at least as big. In other words:

whenever x's depth is incremented, the population of x's tree at least doubles.

Because the population cannot exceed the total number n of objects, the depth of x cannot be incremented more than $\log_2 n$ times. Because the running time of FIND is proportional to the depth of an object, its worst-case running time is $O(\log n)$.

*15.7   Kruskal's Algorithm: Proof of Correctness

This section proves the correctness of Kruskal's algorithm (Theorem 15.11) under the assumption that edges' costs are distinct. Theorem 15.11 can be proved in its full generality with a bit more work (see Problem 15.5).

The first order of business is to show that the algorithm's output is connected (and, as it's clearly acyclic, a spanning tree). To this end, the next lemma shows that once an edge (v, w) is processed by `Kruskal`, the solution-so-far (and, hence, the final output) necessarily contains a v-w path.

Lemma 15.15 (Connecting Adjacent Vertices) *Let T be the set of edges chosen by* `Kruskal` *up to and including the iteration that examines the edge $e = (v, w)$. Then, v and w are in the same connected component of the graph (V, T).*

Proof: In the terminology of Lemma 15.7, adding e to the solution-so-far is either a type-C or type-F edge addition. In the first case, v and w already belong to the same connected component prior to e's examination. In the second case, the algorithm will add the edge (v, w) to its solution-so-far (by Lemma 15.7(b), this doesn't create a cycle), directly connecting v and w and fusing their connected components into one. $\mathcal{QED}$

The following corollary extends Lemma 15.15 from individual edges to multi-hop paths.

Corollary 15.16 (From Edges to Paths) *Let P be a v-w path in G, and T the set of edges chosen by* `Kruskal` *up to and including the last iteration that examines an edge of P. Then, v and w are in the same connected component of the graph (V, T).*

Proof: Denote the edges of P by $(x_0, x_1), (x_1, x_2), \ldots, (x_{p-1}, x_p)$, where x_0 is v and x_p is w. By Lemma 15.15, immediately after the iteration that processes the edge (x_{i-1}, x_i), the vertices x_{i-1} and x_i lie in the same connected component of the solution-so-far. This remains true as more edges are included in subsequent iterations. After all the edges of P have been processed, all its vertices—and, in particular, its endpoints v and w—belong to the same connected component of the solution-so-far (V, T). $\mathcal{QED}$

The next step argues that `Kruskal` outputs a spanning tree.

Lemma 15.17 (`Kruskal` Outputs a Spanning Tree) *For every connected input graph, the `Kruskal` algorithm outputs a spanning tree.*

Proof: The algorithm explicitly ensures that its final output T is acyclic. To prove that its output is also connected, we can argue that all its vertices belong to the same connected component of (V, T). Fix a pair v, w of vertices; because the input graph is connected, it contains a v-w path P. By Corollary 15.16, once the `Kruskal` algorithm has processed every edge of P, its endpoints v and w belong to the same connected component of the solution-so-far (and, hence, of the final output (V, T)). $\mathcal{QED}$

To apply Theorem 15.6, we must prove that every edge chosen by the `Kruskal` algorithm satisfies the minimum bottleneck property (MBP). (Recall from Section 15.4 what this means: An edge $e = (v, w)$ in a graph G satisfies the MBP if and only if every v-w path in G has an edge with cost at least c_e.)

Lemma 15.18 (`Kruskal` Achieves the MBP) *For every connected graph $G = (V, E)$ and real-valued edge costs, every edge chosen by the `Kruskal` algorithm satisfies the MBP.*

Proof: We prove the equivalent contrapositive statement, that the output of `Kruskal` never includes an edge that fails to satisfy the MBP. Let $e = (v, w)$ be such an edge, and P a v-w path in G in which every edge has cost less than c_e. Because `Kruskal` scans through the edges in order of nondecreasing cost, the algorithm processes every edge of P before e. Corollary 15.16 now implies that, by the time `Kruskal` reaches the edge e, its endpoints v and w already belong to the same connected component of the solution-so-far T. Adding e to T would create a cycle (Lemma 15.7(a)), so `Kruskal` excludes the edge from its output. $\mathcal{QED}$

Putting it all together proves Theorem 15.11 for the case of graphs with distinct edge costs:

Proof of Theorem 15.11: Lemma 15.17 proves that the output of Kruskal's algorithm is a spanning tree. Lemma 15.18 implies that every edge of this spanning tree satisfies the MBP. Theorem 15.6 guarantees that this spanning tree is a minimum spanning tree. $\mathcal{QED}$

15.8 Application: Single-Link Clustering

Unsupervised learning is a branch of machine learning and statistics that strives to understand large collections of data points by finding hidden patterns in them. Each data point could represent a person, an image, a document, a genome sequence, and so on. For example, a data point corresponding to a 100-by-100 pixel color image might be a 30000-dimensional vector, with 3 coordinates per pixel recording the intensities of red, green, and blue in that pixel.[30] This section highlights a connection between one of the most basic algorithms in unsupervised learning and Kruskal's minimum spanning tree algorithm.

---

[30] *Supervised* learning focuses on prediction rather than pattern-finding per se. Here, each data point also has a label (e.g., 1 if the image is of a cat and 0 otherwise), and the goal is to accurately predict the labels of as-yet-unseen data points.

15.8.1   Clustering

One widely-used approach to unsupervised learning is *clustering*, in which the goal is to partition the data points into "coherent groups" (called *clusters*) of "similar points" (Figure 15.6). To make this more precise, suppose we have a *similarity function* f that assigns a nonnegative real number to each pair of data points. We assume that f is *symmetric*, meaning $f(x, y) = f(y, x)$ for every pair x, y of data points. We can then interpret points x, y with a small value of $f(x, y)$ as "similar," and those with a large value as "dissimilar."[31] For example, if the data points are vectors with a common dimension, like in the image example above, $f(x, y)$ could be defined as the Euclidean (i.e., straight-line) distance between x and y.[32] For another example, Section 17.1 defines *Needleman-Wunsch distance*, which is a symmetric similarity function designed for genome sequences. In an ideal clustering, data points in the same cluster are relatively similar while those in different clusters are relatively dissimilar.

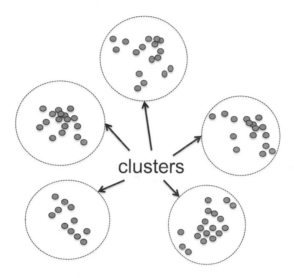

Figure 15.6: In an ideal clustering, data points in the same cluster are relatively similar while those in different clusters are relatively dissimilar.

Let k denote the number of clusters desired. Sensible values for k range from 2 to a large number, depending on the application. For example, if the goal is to cluster blog posts about U.S. politics into groups of "left-leaning" and "right-leaning" posts, it makes sense to choose $k = 2$. If the goal is to cluster a diverse collection of images according to their subject, a larger value of k should be used. When unsure about the best value for k, you can try several different choices and select your favorite among the resulting partitions.

15.8.2   Bottom-Up Clustering

The main idea in *bottom-up* or *agglomerative* clustering is to begin with every data point in its own cluster, and then successively merge pairs of clusters until exactly k remain.

---

[31]With these semantics, it's arguably more accurate to call f a *dissimilarity* function.

[32]If $x = (x_1, x_2, \ldots, x_d)$ and $y = (y_1, y_2, \ldots, y_d)$ are d-dimensional vectors, the precise formula is $f(x, y) = \sqrt{\sum_{i=1}^{d}(x_i - y_i)^2}$.

Bottom-Up Clustering (Generic)

Input: a set X of data points, a symmetric similarity function f, and a positive integer $k \in \{1, 2, 3, \ldots, |X|\}$.
Output: a partition of X into k non-empty sets.

```
C := ∅          // keeps track of current clusters
for each x ∈ X do
    add {x} to C        // each point in own cluster
// Main loop
while C contains more than k clusters do
    remove clusters S₁, S₂ from C       // details TBA
    add S₁ ∪ S₂ to C                    // merge clusters
return C
```

Each iteration of the main loop decreases the number of clusters in C by 1, so there are a total of $|X| - k$ iterations (Figure 15.7).[33]

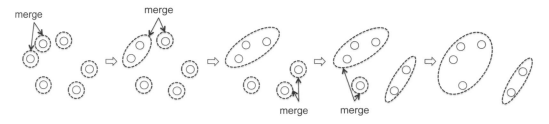

Figure 15.7: In bottom-up clustering, each point begins in its own cluster and pairs of clusters are successively merged until only k clusters remain.

Our generic bottom-up clustering algorithm does not specify which pair of clusters to merge in each iteration. Can we use a greedy approach? If so, greedy with respect to what criterion?

The next step is to derive a similarity function F for pairs of clusters from the given function f for pairs of data points. For example, one of the simplest choices for F is the best-case similarity between points in the different clusters:

$$F(S_1, S_2) = \min_{x \in S_1, y \in S_2} f(x, y). \tag{15.2}$$

Other reasonable choices for F include the worst-case or average similarity between points in the different clusters. In any case, once the function F is chosen, the generic bottom-up clustering algorithm can be specialized to greedily merge the "most similar" pair of clusters in each iteration:

---

[33]Bottom-up clustering is only one of several common approaches to clustering. For example, *top-down* algorithms begin with all the data points in a single cluster and successively split clusters in two until there are exactly k clusters. Other algorithms, like *k-means clustering*, maintain k clusters from beginning to end.

Bottom-Up Clustering (Greedy)

```
// Main loop
```
while C contains more than k clusters **do**
    remove from C the clusters S_1, S_2 that minimize $F(S_1, S_2)$
```
    // e.g., with F as in (15.2)
```
    add $S_1 \cup S_2$ to C
return C

Single-link clustering refers to greedy bottom-up clustering with the best-case similarity function (15.2). Do you see any connections between single-link clustering and Kruskal's minimum spanning tree algorithm (Section 15.5)? Take some time to think about it.

      *   *   *   *   *   *   *   *   *   *   *   *   *

Kruskal's algorithm begins with the empty edge set and each vertex isolated in its own connected component, just as single-link clustering begins with each data point in its own cluster. Each iteration of Kruskal's algorithm that adds a new edge fuses two connected components into one, just as each iteration of single-link clustering merges two clusters into one. Kruskal's algorithm repeatedly adds the cheapest new edge that does not create a cycle, fusing the components containing its endpoints, just as single-link clustering repeatedly merges the pair of clusters containing the most similar pair of data points in different clusters. Thus, Kruskal's algorithm corresponds to single-link clustering, with vertices substituting for data points and connected components for clusters. The one difference is that single-link clustering stops once there are k clusters, while Kruskal's algorithm continues until only one connected component remains. We conclude that *single-link clustering is the same as Kruskal's algorithm, stopped early.*

Single-Link Clustering via Kruskal's Algorithm

1. Define a complete undirected graph $G = (X, E)$ from the data set X and similarity function f, with vertex set X and one edge $(x, y) \in E$ with cost $c_{xy} = f(x, y)$ for each vertex pair $x, y \in X$.

2. Run Kruskal's algorithm with the input graph G until the solution-so-far T contains $|X| - k$ edges or, equivalently, until the graph (X, T) has k connected components.

3. Compute the connected components of (X, T) and return the corresponding partition of X.

The Upshot

☆ A spanning tree of a graph is an acyclic subgraph that contains a path between each pair of vertices.

☆ In the minimum spanning tree (MST) problem, the input is a connected undirected graph with real-valued edge costs and the goal is to compute a spanning tree with the minimum-possible sum of edge costs.

☆ Prim's algorithm constructs an MST one edge at a time, starting from an arbitrary vertex and growing like a mold until the entire vertex set is spanned. In each iteration, it greedily chooses the cheapest edge that expands the reach of the solution-so-far.

☆ When implemented with a heap data structure, Prim's algorithm runs in $O(m \log n)$ time, where m and n denote the number of edges and vertices of the input graph, respectively.

☆ Kruskal's algorithm also constructs an MST one edge at a time, greedily choosing the cheapest edge whose addition does not create a cycle in the solution-so-far.

☆ When implemented with a union-find data structure, Kruskal's algorithm runs in $O(m \log n)$ time.

☆ The first step in the proofs of correctness for Prim's and Kruskal's algorithms is to show that each algorithm chooses only edges satisfying the minimum bottleneck property (MBP).

☆ The second step is to use an exchange argument to prove that a spanning tree in which every edge satisfies the MBP must be an MST.

☆ Single-link clustering is a greedy bottom-up clustering method in unsupervised learning and it corresponds to Kruskal's algorithm, stopped early.

Test Your Understanding

Problem 15.1 *(H)* Consider a connected undirected graph $G = (V, E)$ in which every edge $e \in E$ has a distinct and nonnegative cost. Let T be an MST and P a shortest path from some vertex s to some other vertex t. Now suppose the cost of every edge e of G is increased by 1 and becomes $c_e + 1$. Call this new graph G'. Which of the following is true about G'?

a) T must be an MST and P must be a shortest s-t path.

b) T must be an MST but P may not be a shortest s-t path.

c) T may not be an MST but P must be a shortest s-t path.

d) T may not be an MST and P may not be a shortest s-t path.

Problem 15.2 *(H)* Consider the following algorithm that attempts to compute an MST of a connected undirected graph $G = (V, E)$ with distinct edge costs by running Kruskal's algorithm "in reverse":

Kruskal (Reverse Version)

$T := E$
sort edges of E in decreasing order of cost
for each $e \in E$, in order **do**
    if $T - \{e\}$ is connected **then**
        $T := T - \{e\}$
return T

Which of the following statements is true?

a) The output of the algorithm will never have a cycle, but it might not be connected.

b) The output of the algorithm will always be connected, but it might have cycles.

c) The algorithm always outputs a spanning tree, but it might not be an MST.

d) The algorithm always outputs an MST.

Problem 15.3 *(H)* Which of the following problems reduce (in the sense of page 201) to the minimum spanning tree problem in a straightforward way? (Choose all that apply.)

a) The maximum-cost spanning tree problem. That is, among all spanning trees T of a connected graph with edge costs, compute one with the maximum-possible sum $\sum_{e \in T} c_e$ of edge costs.

b) The minimum-product spanning tree problem. That is, among all spanning trees T of a connected graph with strictly positive edge costs, compute one with the minimum-possible product $\prod_{e \in T} c_e$ of edge costs.

c) The single-source shortest-path problem. In this problem, the input comprises a connected undirected graph $G = (V, E)$, a nonnegative length ℓ_e for each edge $e \in E$, and a designated starting vertex $s \in V$. The required output is, for every possible destination $v \in V$, the minimum total length of a path from s to v.

d) Given a connected undirected graph $G = (V, E)$ with positive edge costs, compute a minimum-cost set $F \subseteq E$ of edges such that the graph $(V, E - F)$ is acyclic.

Challenge Problems

Problem 15.4 *(S)* Prove the converse of Theorem 15.6: If T is an MST of a graph with real-valued edge costs, every edge of T satisfies the minimum bottleneck property.

Problem 15.5 *(S)* Prove the correctness of Prim's and Kruskal's algorithms (Theorems 15.1 and 15.11) in full generality, for graphs in which edges' costs need not be distinct.

Problem 15.6 *(H)* Prove that in a connected undirected graph with distinct edge costs, there is a unique MST.

Problem 15.7 *(S)* An alternative approach to proving the correctness of Prim's and Kruskal's algorithms is to use what's called the *Cut Property* of MSTs. Assume throughout this problem that edges' costs are distinct.

A *cut* of an undirected graph $G = (V, E)$ is a partition of its vertex set V into two non-empty sets, A and B.

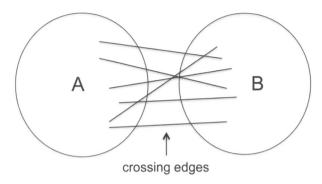

crossing edges

An edge of G *crosses* the cut (A, B) if it has one endpoint in each of A and B.

The Cut Property

Let $G = (V, E)$ be a connected undirected graph with distinct real-valued edge costs. If an edge $e \in E$ is the cheapest edge crossing a cut (A, B), e belongs to every MST of G.[34]

In other words, one way to justify an algorithm's inclusion of an edge e in its solution is to produce a cut of G for which e is the cheapest crossing edge.[35]

  (a) Prove the Cut Property.

  (b) Use the Cut Property to prove that Prim's algorithm is correct.

  (c) Repeat (b) for Kruskal's algorithm.

Problem 15.8 *(H)* Consider a connected undirected graph with distinct real-valued edge costs. A *minimum bottleneck spanning tree (MBST)* is a spanning tree T with the minimum-possible bottleneck (i.e., the minimum maximum edge cost $\max_{e \in T} c_e$).

  (a) (Difficult) Give a linear-time algorithm for computing the bottleneck of an MBST.

  (b) Does this imply a linear-time algorithm for computing the total cost of an MST?

---

[34]Readers who have solved Problem 15.6 might want to rephrase the conclusion to "...e belongs to *the* MST of G."

[35]There's also the *Cycle Property*, which asserts that if an edge e is the costliest on some cycle C, every MST excludes e. You should check that the Cycle Property is equivalent to the converse of Theorem 15.6, which is proved in Problem 15.4.

Programming Problems

Problem 15.9 Implement in your favorite programming language the Prim and Kruskal algorithms. For bonus points, implement the heap-based version of Prim (Section 15.3) and the union-find-based version of Kruskal (Section 15.6). Does one of the algorithms seem reliably faster than the other? (See www.algorithmsilluminated.org for test cases and challenge data sets.)

Chapter 16

Introduction to Dynamic Programming

There's no silver bullet in algorithm design, and the two algorithm design paradigms we've studied so far (divide-and-conquer and greedy algorithms) do not cover all the computational problems you will encounter. The second half of this part of the book will teach you a third design paradigm: the *dynamic programming* paradigm. Dynamic programming is a particularly empowering technique to acquire, as it often leads to efficient solutions beyond the reach of anyone other than serious students of algorithms.

In my experience, most people initially find dynamic programming difficult and counterintuitive. Even more than with other design paradigms, dynamic programming takes practice to perfect. But dynamic programming is relatively formulaic—certainly more so than greedy algorithms—and can be mastered with sufficient practice. This chapter and the next two provide this practice through a half-dozen detailed case studies, including several algorithms belonging to the greatest hits compilation. You'll learn how these famous algorithms work, but even better, you'll add to your programmer toolbox a general and flexible algorithm design technique that you can apply to problems that come up in your own projects. Through these case studies, the power and flexibility of dynamic programming will become clear—it's a technique you simply have to know.

Pep Talk

It is totally normal to feel confused the first time you see dynamic programming. Confusion should not discourage you. It does not represent an intellectual failure on your part, only an opportunity to get even smarter.

16.1 The Weighted Independent Set Problem

I'm not going to tell you what dynamic programming is just yet. Instead, we'll devise from scratch an algorithm for a tricky and concrete computational problem, which will force us to develop a number of new ideas. After we've solved the problem, we'll zoom out and identify the ingredients of our solution that exemplify the general principles of dynamic programming. Then, armed with a template for developing dynamic programming algorithms and an example instantiation, we'll tackle increasingly challenging applications of the paradigm.

16.1.1 Problem Definition

To describe the problem, let $G = (V, E)$ be an undirected graph. An *independent set* of G is a subset $S \subseteq V$ of mutually non-adjacent vertices: for every $v, w \in S$, $(v, w) \notin E$.

Equivalently, an independent set does not contain both endpoints of any edge of G. For example, if vertices represent people and edges pairs of people who dislike each other, the independent sets correspond to groups of people who all get along. Or, if the vertices represent classes you're thinking about taking and there is an edge between each pair of conflicting classes, the independent sets correspond to feasible course schedules (assuming you can't be in two places at once).

Quiz 16.1

How many different independent sets does a complete graph with 5 vertices have?

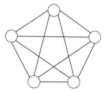

How about a cycle with 5 vertices?

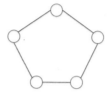

a) 1 and 2 (respectively)

b) 5 and 10

c) 6 and 11

d) 6 and 16

(See Section 16.1.4 for the solution and discussion.)

We can now state the *weighted independent set (WIS)* problem:

Problem: Weighted Independent Set (WIS)

Input: An undirected graph $G = (V, E)$ and a nonnegative weight w_v for each vertex $v \in V$.

Output: An independent set $S \subseteq V$ of G with the maximum-possible sum $\sum_{v \in S} w_v$ of vertex weights.

An optimal solution to the WIS problem is called a *maximum-weight independent set (MWIS)*. For example, if vertices represent courses, vertex weights represent units, and edges represent conflicts between courses, the MWIS corresponds to the feasible course schedule with the heaviest load (in units).

The WIS problem is challenging even in the super-simple case of *path graphs*. For example, an input to the problem might look like this (with vertices labeled by their weights):

This graph has 8 independent sets: the empty set, the four singleton sets, the first and third vertices, the first and fourth vertices, and the second and fourth vertices. The last of these has the largest total weight of 8. The number of independent sets of a path graph grows exponentially with the number of vertices (do you see why?), so there is no hope of solving the problem via exhaustive search, except in the tiniest of instances.

16.1.2   The Natural Greedy Algorithm Fails

For many computational problems, greedy algorithms are a great place to start brainstorming. Such algorithms are usually easy to come up with, and even when one fails to solve the problem (as is often the case), the manner in which it fails can help you better understand the intricacies of the problem.

For the WIS problem, perhaps the most natural greedy algorithm is an analog of Kruskal's algorithm: Perform a single pass over the vertices, from best (highest weight) to worst (lowest weight), adding a vertex to the solution-so-far if it doesn't conflict with a previously chosen vertex. Given an input graph $G = (V, E)$ with vertex weights, the pseudocode is:

WIS: A Greedy Approach

$S := \emptyset$
sort vertices of V by weight
for each $v \in V$, in nonincreasing order of weight **do**
    if $S \cup \{v\}$ is an independent set of G **then**
        $S := S \cup \{v\}$
return S

Simple enough. But does it work?

Quiz 16.2

What is the total weight of the output of the greedy algorithm when the input graph is the four-vertex path graph above? Is this the maximum possible?

a) 6; no

b) 6; yes

c) 8; no

d) 8; yes

(See Section 16.1.4 for the solution and discussion.)

Chapters 13–15 spoiled us with a plethora of cherry-picked correct greedy algorithms, but don't forget the warning back on page 292: Greedy algorithms are usually *not* correct.

16.1.3   A Divide-and-Conquer Approach?

The divide-and-conquer algorithm design paradigm (Section 13.1.1) is always worth a shot for problems in which there's a sensible way to break the input into smaller subproblems. For the WIS problem with an input path graph $G = (V, E)$, the natural high-level approach is (ignoring the base case):

WIS: A Divide-and-Conquer Approach

$G_1 :=$ first half of G
$G_2 :=$ second half of G
$S_1 :=$ recursively solve the WIS problem on G_1
$S_2 :=$ recursively solve the WIS problem on G_2
combine S_1, S_2 into a solution S for G
return S

The devil is in the details of the combine step. Returning to our running example:

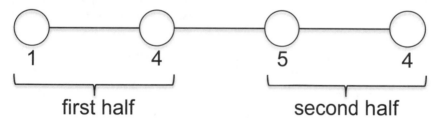

the first and second recursive calls return the second and third vertices as the optimal solutions to their respective subproblems. The union of their solutions is *not* an independent set due to the conflict at the boundary between the two solutions. It's easy to see how to defuse such a border conflict when the input graph has only four vertices; when it has hundreds or thousands of vertices, not so much.[1]

Can we do better than a greedy or divide-and-conquer algorithm?

16.1.4   Solutions to Quizzes 16.1–16.2

Solution to Quiz 16.1

Correct answer: (c). The complete graph has no non-adjacent vertices, so every independent set has at most one vertex. Thus, there are six independent sets: the empty set and the five singleton sets. The cycle has the same six independent sets that the complete graph does, plus some independent sets of size 2. (Every subset of three or more vertices has a pair of adjacent vertices.) It has five size-2 independent sets (as you should verify), for a total of eleven.

---

[1]The problem can be solved in $O(n^2)$ time by a divide-and-conquer algorithm that makes *four* recursive calls rather than two, where n is the number of vertices. (Do you see how to do this?) Our dynamic programming algorithm for the problem will run in $O(n)$ time.

Solution to Quiz 16.2

Correct answer: (a). The first iteration of the greedy algorithm commits to the maximum-weight vertex, which is the third vertex (with weight 5). This eliminates the adjacent vertices (the second and fourth ones, both with weight 4) from further consideration. The algorithm is then stuck selecting the first vertex and it outputs an independent set with total weight 6. This is not optimal, as the second and fourth vertices constitute an independent set with total weight 8.

16.2 A Linear-Time Algorithm for WIS in Paths

16.2.1 Optimal Substructure and Recurrence

To quickly solve the WIS problem in path graphs, we'll need to up our game. Key to our approach is the following thought experiment: Suppose someone handed us an optimal solution on a silver platter. What must it look like? Ideally, this thought experiment would show that an optimal solution must be constructed in a prescribed way from optimal solutions to smaller subproblems, thereby narrowing down the field of candidates to a manageable number.[2]

More concretely, let $G = (V, E)$ denote the n-vertex path graph with edges (v_1, v_2), (v_2, v_3), ..., (v_{n-2}, v_{n-1}), (v_{n-1}, v_n), and suppose that each vertex $v_i \in V$ has a non-negative weight w_i. Assume that $n \geq 2$; otherwise, the answer is obvious. Suppose we magically knew an MWIS $S \subseteq V$ with total weight W. What can we say about it? Here's a tautology: S either contains the final vertex v_n, or it doesn't. Let's examine these cases in reverse order.

Case 1: $v_n \notin S$. Suppose the optimal solution S happens to exclude v_n. Obtain the $(n-1)$-vertex path graph G_{n-1} from G by plucking off the last vertex v_n and the last edge (v_{n-1}, v_n). Because S does not include the last vertex of G, it contains only vertices of G_{n-1} and can be regarded as an independent set of G_{n-1} (still with total weight W). And S is not just any old independent set of G_{n-1}—it's a *maximum-weight* such set. For if S^* were an independent set of G_{n-1} with total weight $W^* > W$, then S^* would also constitute an independent set of total weight W^* in the larger graph G. This would contradict the supposed optimality of S. In other words:

> once you know that an MWIS excludes the last vertex, you know exactly what
> it looks like—an MWIS of the smaller graph G_{n-1}.

Case 2: $v_n \in S$. Suppose S includes the last vertex v_n. As an independent set, S cannot include two consecutive vertices from the path, so it excludes the penultimate vertex: $v_{n-1} \notin S$. Obtain the $(n-2)$-vertex path graph G_{n-2} from G by plucking off the last two vertices and edges:[3]

---

[2]There's no circularity in performing a thought experiment about the very object we're trying to compute. As we'll see, such thought experiments can light up a trail that leads directly to an efficient algorithm.

[3]When $n = 2$, we interpret G_0 as the empty graph (with no vertices or edges). The only independent set of G_0 is the empty set, which has total weight 0.

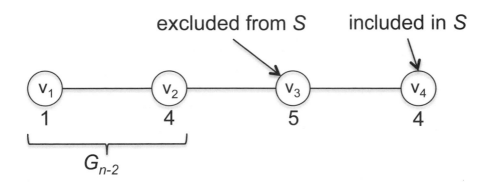

Because S contains v_n and G_{n-2} does not, we can't regard S as an independent set of G_{n-2}. But after removing the last vertex from S, we can: $S - \{v_n\}$ contains neither v_{n-1} nor v_n and hence can be regarded as an independent set of the smaller graph G_{n-2} (with total weight $W - w_n$). Moreover, $S - \{v_n\}$ must be an MWIS of G_{n-2}. For suppose S^* were an independent set of G_{n-2} with total weight $W^* > W - w_n$. Because G_{n-2} (and hence S^*) excludes the penultimate vertex v_{n-1}, blithely adding the last vertex v_n to S^* would not create any conflicts, and so $S^* \cup \{v_n\}$ would be an independent set of G with total weight $W^* + w_n > (W - w_n) + w_n = W$. This would contradict the supposed optimality of S. In other words:

> once you know that an MWIS includes the last vertex, you know exactly what it looks like—an MWIS of the smaller graph G_{n-2}, supplemented with the final vertex v_n.

Summarizing, two and only two candidates are vying to be an MWIS:

Lemma 16.1 (WIS Optimal Substructure) *Let S be an MWIS of a path graph G with $n \geq 2$ vertices. Let G_i denote the subgraph of G comprising its first i vertices and $i - 1$ edges. Then, S is either:*

(i) an MWIS of G_{n-1}; or

(ii) an MWIS of G_{n-2}, supplemented with G's final vertex v_n.

Lemma 16.1 singles out the only two possibilities for an MWIS, so whichever option has larger total weight is an optimal solution. We therefore have a recursive formula—a *recurrence*—for the total weight of an MWIS:

Corollary 16.2 (WIS Recurrence) *With the assumptions and notation of Lemma 16.1, let W_i denote the total weight of an MWIS of G_i. (When $i = 0$, interpret W_i as 0.) Then*

$$W_n = \max\{\underbrace{W_{n-1}}_{Case\ 1}, \underbrace{W_{n-2} + w_n}_{Case\ 2}\}.$$

More generally, for every $i = 2, 3, \ldots, n$,

$$W_i = \max\{W_{i-1}, W_{i-2} + w_i\}.$$

The more general statement in Corollary 16.2 follows by invoking the first statement, for each $i = 2, 3, \ldots, n$, with G_i playing the role of the input graph G.

16.2.2   A Naive Recursive Approach

Lemma 16.1 is good news—we've narrowed down the field to just two candidates for the optimal solution! So, why not try both options and return the better of the two? This leads to the following pseudocode, in which the graphs G_{n-1} and G_{n-2} are defined as before:

A Recursive Algorithm for WIS

Input: a path graph G with vertex set $\{v_1, v_2, \ldots, v_n\}$ and a nonnegative weight w_i for each vertex v_i.
Output: a maximum-weight independent set of G.

---

1 **if** $n = 0$ **then**   // base case #1
2   return the empty set
3 **if** $n = 1$ **then**   // base case #2
4   return $\{v_1\}$
  // recursion when $n \geq 2$
5 $S_1 :=$ recursively compute an MWIS of G_{n-1}
6 $S_2 :=$ recursively compute an MWIS of G_{n-2}
7 return S_1 or $S_2 \cup \{v_n\}$, whichever has higher weight

---

A straightforward proof by induction shows that this algorithm is guaranteed to compute a maximum-weight independent set.[4] What about the running time?

Quiz 16.3

What is the asymptotic running time of the recursive WIS algorithm, as a function of the number n of vertices? (Choose the strongest correct statement.)

a) $O(n)$

b) $O(n \log n)$

c) $O(n^2)$

d) none of the above

(See Section 16.2.5 for the solution and discussion.)

16.2.3   Recursion with a Cache

Quiz 16.3 shows that our recursive WIS algorithm is no better than exhaustive search. The next quiz contains the key to unlocking a radical running time improvement. Think about it carefully before reading the solution.

---

[4]The proof proceeds by induction on the number n of vertices. The base cases ($n = 0, 1$) are clearly correct. For the inductive step ($n \geq 2$), the inductive hypothesis guarantees that S_1 and S_2 are indeed MWISs of G_{n-1} and G_{n-2}, respectively. Lemma 16.1 implies that the better of S_1 and $S_2 \cup \{v_n\}$ is an MWIS of G, and this is the output of the algorithm.

Quiz 16.4

Each of the (exponentially many) recursive calls of the recursive WIS algorithm is responsible for computing an MWIS of a specified input graph. Ranging over all of the calls, how many *distinct* input graphs are ever considered?

a) $\Theta(1)$

b) $\Theta(n)$

c) $\Theta(n^2)$

d) $2^{\Theta(n)}$

(See Section 16.2.5 for the solution and discussion.)

Quiz 16.4 implies that the exponential running time of our recursive WIS algorithm stems solely from its absurd redundancy, solving the same subproblems from scratch over, and over, and over, and over again. Here's an idea: The first time we solve a subproblem, why not save the result in a cache once and for all? Then, if we encounter the same subproblem later, we can look up its solution in the cache in constant time.[5]

Blending caching into the pseudocode on page 372 is easy. The results of past computations are stored in a globally visible length-$(n + 1)$ array A, with $A[i]$ storing an MWIS of G_i, where G_i comprises the first i vertices and the first $i - 1$ edges of the original input graph (and G_0 is the empty graph). In line 6, the algorithm now first checks whether the array A already contains the relevant solution S_1; if not, it computes S_1 recursively as before and caches the result in A. Similarly, the new version of line 7 either looks up or recursively computes and caches S_2, as needed.

Each of the $n + 1$ subproblems is now solved from scratch only once. Caching surely speeds up the algorithm, but by how much? Properly implemented, the running time drops from exponential to *linear*. This dramatic speedup will be easier to see after we reformulate our top-down recursive algorithm as a bottom-up iterative one—and the latter is usually what you want to implement in practice, anyway.

16.2.4   An Iterative Bottom-Up Implementation

As part of figuring out how to incorporate caching into our recursive WIS algorithm, we realized that there are exactly $n + 1$ relevant subproblems, corresponding to all possible prefixes of the input graph (Quiz 16.4).

WIS in Path Graphs: Subproblems

Compute W_i, the total weight of an MWIS of the prefix graph G_i.

(For each $i = 0, 1, 2, \ldots, n$.)

---

[5]This technique of caching the result of a computation to avoid redoing it later is sometimes called *memoization*.

For now, we focus on computing the total weight of an MWIS for a subproblem. Section 16.3 shows how to also identify the vertices of an MWIS.

Now that we know which subproblems are the important ones, why not cut to the chase and systematically solve them one by one? The solution to a subproblem depends on the solutions to two smaller subproblems. To ensure that these two solutions are readily available, it makes sense to work bottom-up, starting with the base cases and building up to ever-larger subproblems.

WIS

Input: a path graph G with vertex set $\{v_1, v_2, \ldots, v_n\}$ and a nonnegative weight w_i for each vertex v_i.
Output: the total weight of a maximum-weight independent set of G.

$A :=$ length-$(n + 1)$ array   `// subproblem solutions`
$A[0] := 0$ `// base case #1`
$A[1] := w_1$ `// base case #2`
for $i := 2$ to n **do**
     `// use recurrence from Corollary 16.2`
     $A[i] := \max\{\underbrace{A[i-1]}_{\text{Case 1}}, \underbrace{A[i-2]+w_i}_{\text{Case 2}}\}$
return $A[n]$ `// solution to largest subproblem`

The length-$(n + 1)$ array A is indexed from 0 to n. By the time an iteration of the main loop must compute the subproblem solution $A[i]$, the values $A[i-1]$ and $A[i-2]$ of the two relevant smaller subproblems have already been computed in previous iterations (or in the base cases). Thus, each loop iteration takes $O(1)$ time, for a blazingly fast running time of $O(n)$.

For example, for the input graph

you should check that the final array values are:

prefix length i

0	1	2	3	4	5	6
0	3	3	4	9	9	14

At the conclusion of the WIS algorithm, each array entry $A[i]$ stores the total weight of an MWIS of the graph G_i that comprises the first i vertices and $i - 1$ edges of the input graph. This follows from an inductive argument similar to the one in footnote 4. The base cases $A[0]$ and $A[1]$ are clearly correct. When computing $A[i]$ with $i \geq 2$, by induction, the values $A[i-1]$ and $A[i-2]$ are indeed the total weights of MWISs of G_{i-1} and G_{i-2}, respectively. Corollary 16.2 then implies that $A[i]$ is computed correctly, as well. In the example above, the total weight of an MWIS in the original input graph is the value in the final array entry (14), corresponding to the independent set consisting of the first, fourth, and sixth vertices.

Theorem 16.3 (Properties of WIS) *For every path graph and nonnegative vertex weights, the WIS algorithm runs in linear time and returns the total weight of a maximum-weight independent set.*

16.2.5   Solutions to Quizzes 16.3–16.4

Solution to Quiz 16.3

Correct answer: (d). Superficially, the recursion pattern looks similar to that of $O(n \log n)$-time divide-and-conquer algorithms like MergeSort, with two recursive calls followed by an easy combine step. But there's a big difference: The MergeSort algorithm throws away half the input before recursing, while our recursive WIS algorithm throws away only one or two vertices (perhaps out of thousands or millions). Both algorithms have recursion trees with branching factor 2.[6] The former has roughly $\log_2 n$ levels and, hence, only a linear number of leaves. The latter has no leaves until levels $n/2$ and later, which implies that it has at least $2^{n/2}$ leaves. (See Problem 16.4 for a sharper lower bound.) We conclude that the running time of the recursive algorithm grows exponentially with n.

Solution to Quiz 16.4

Correct answer: (b). How does the input graph change upon passage to a recursive call? Either one or two vertices and edges are plucked off the end of the graph. Thus, an invariant throughout the recursion is that every recursive call is given some *prefix* G_i as its input graph, where G_i denotes the first i vertices and $i - 1$ edges of the original input graph (and G_0 denotes the empty graph):

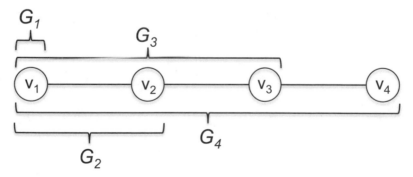

There are only $n + 1$ such graphs ($G_0, G_1, G_2, \ldots, G_n$), where n is the number of vertices in the input graph. Therefore, only $n + 1$ distinct subproblems ever get solved across the exponential number of different recursive calls.

---

[6]Recall from Section 1.5 or 4.4 that every recursive algorithm can be associated with a recursion tree, in which the nodes of the tree correspond to all the algorithm's recursive calls. The root of the tree corresponds to the initial call to the algorithm (with the original input), with one child at the next level for each of its recursive calls. The leaves at the bottom of the tree correspond to the recursive calls that trigger a base case and make no further recursive calls.

16.3 A Reconstruction Algorithm

The `WIS` algorithm in Section 16.2.4 computes only the *weight* possessed by an MWIS of a path graph, not an MWIS itself. A simple hack is to modify the `WIS` algorithm so that each array entry $A[i]$ records both the total weight of an MWIS of the ith subproblem G_i *and* the vertices of an MWIS of G_i that realizes this value.

A better approach, which saves both time and space, is to use a postprocessing step to reconstruct an MWIS from the tracks in the mud left by the `WIS` algorithm in its subproblem array A. For starters, how do we know whether the last vertex v_n of the input graph G belongs to an MWIS? The key is again Lemma 16.1, which states that two and only two candidates are vying to be an MWIS of G: an MWIS of the graph G_{n-1}, and an MWIS of the graph G_{n-2}, supplemented with v_n. Which one is it? The one with larger total weight. How do we know which one that is? Just look at the clues left in the array A! The final values of $A[n-1]$ and $A[n-2]$ record the total weights of MWISs of G_{n-1} and G_{n-2}, respectively. So:

1. If $A[n-1] \geq A[n-2] + w_n$, an MWIS of G_{n-1} is also an MWIS of G_n.

2. If $A[n-2] + w_n \geq A[n-1]$, supplementing an MWIS of G_{n-2} with v_n yields an MWIS of G_n.

In the first case, we know to exclude v_n from our solution and can continue the reconstruction process from v_{n-1}. In the second case, we know to include v_n in our solution, which forces us to exclude v_{n-1}. The reconstruction process then resumes from v_{n-2}. (If there is a tie, with $A[n-2] + w_n = A[n-1]$, both options lead to an optimal solution.)

WIS Reconstruction

Input: the array A computed by the `WIS` algorithm for a path
  graph G with vertex set $\{v_1, v_2, \dots, v_n\}$ and a nonnegative
  weight w_i for each vertex v_i.
Output: a maximum-weight independent set of G.

$S := \emptyset$ // vertices in an MWIS
$i := n$
while $i \geq 2$ **do**
   if $A[i-1] \geq A[i-2] + w_i$ **then**   // Case 1 wins
     $i := i - 1$ // exclude v_i
   else   // Case 2 wins
     $S := S \cup \{v_i\}$ // include v_i
     $i := i - 2$ // exclude v_{i-1}
  if $i = 1$ **then**   // base case #2
    $S := S \cup \{v_1\}$
  return S

`WIS Reconstruction` does a single backward pass over the array A and spends $O(1)$ time per loop iteration, so it runs in $O(n)$ time. The inductive proof of correctness is similar to that for the `WIS` algorithm (Theorem 16.3).[7]

For example, for the input graph

the `WIS Reconstruction` algorithm includes v_6 (forcing v_5's exclusion), includes v_4 (forcing v_3's exclusion), excludes v_2, and includes v_1:

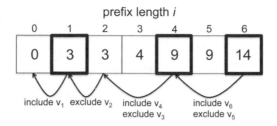

16.4   The Principles of Dynamic Programming

16.4.1   A Three-Step Recipe

Guess what? With `WIS`, we just designed our first dynamic programming algorithm! The general dynamic programming paradigm can be summarized by a three-step recipe. It is best understood through examples; we have only one so far, so I encourage you to revisit this section after we finish a few more case studies.

The Dynamic Programming Paradigm

1. Identify a relatively small collection of subproblems.

2. Show how to quickly and correctly solve "larger" subproblems given the solutions to "smaller" ones.

3. Show how to quickly and correctly infer the final solution from the solutions to all of the subproblems.

After these three steps are implemented, the corresponding dynamic programming algorithm writes itself: Systematically solve all the subproblems one by one, working from "smallest" to "largest," and extract the final solution from those of the subproblems.

In our solution to the WIS problem in n-vertex path graphs, we implemented the first step by identifying a collection of $n + 1$ subproblems. For $i = 0, 1, 2, \ldots, n$, the ith subproblem is to compute the total weight of an MWIS of the graph G_i consisting of the first i vertices and $i - 1$ edges of the input graph (where G_0 denotes the empty graph). There is an obvious

---

[7]The keen reader might complain that it's wasteful to recompute comparisons of the form $A[i - 1]$ vs. $A[i - 2] + w_i$, which have already been made by the `WIS` algorithm. If that algorithm is modified to cache the comparison results (in effect, remembering which case of the recurrence was used to fill in each array entry), these results can be looked up rather than recomputed in the `WIS Reconstruction` algorithm. This idea will be particularly important for some of the harder problems studied in Chapters 17 and 18.

way to order the subproblems from "smallest" to "largest," namely $G_0, G_1, G_2, \ldots, G_n$. The recurrence in Corollary 16.2 is a formula that implements the second step by showing how to compute the solution to the ith subproblem in $O(1)$ time from the solutions to the $(i-2)$th and $(i-1)$th subproblems. The third step is easy: Return the solution to the largest subproblem, which is the same as the original problem.

16.4.2 Desirable Subproblem Properties

The key that unleashes the potential of dynamic programming for solving a problem is the identification of the right collection of subproblems. What properties do we want them to satisfy? Assuming we perform at least a constant amount of work solving each subproblem, the number of subproblems is a lower bound on the running time of our algorithm. Thus, we'd like the number of subproblems to be as low as possible—our WIS solution used only a linear number of subproblems, which is usually the best-case scenario. Similarly, the time required to solve a subproblem (given solutions to smaller subproblems) and to infer the final solution will factor into the algorithm's overall running time.

For example, suppose an algorithm solves at most $f(n)$ different subproblems (working systematically from "smallest" to "largest"), using at most $g(n)$ time for each, and performs at most $h(n)$ postprocessing work to extract the final solution (where n denotes the input size). The algorithm's running time is then at most

$$\underbrace{f(n)}_{\text{\# subproblems}} \times \underbrace{g(n)}_{\substack{\text{time per subproblem} \\ \text{(given previous solutions)}}} + \underbrace{h(n)}_{\text{postprocessing}} . \qquad (16.1)$$

The three steps of the recipe call for keeping $f(n)$, $g(n)$, and $h(n)$, respectively, as small as possible. In the basic `WIS` algorithm, without the `WIS Reconstruction` postprocessing step, we have $f(n) = O(n)$, $g(n) = O(1)$, and $h(n) = O(1)$, for an overall running time of $O(n)$. If we include the reconstruction step, the $h(n)$ term jumps to $O(n)$, but the overall running time $O(n) \times O(1) + O(n) = O(n)$ remains linear.

16.4.3 A Repeatable Thought Process

When devising your own dynamic programming algorithms, the heart of the matter is figuring out the magical collection of subproblems. After that, everything else falls into place in a fairly formulaic way. But how would you ever come up with them? If you have a black belt in dynamic programming, you might be able to just stare at a problem and intuitively know what the subproblems should be. White belts, however, still have a lot of training to do. In our case studies, rather than plucking subproblems from the sky, we'll carry out a thought process that naturally leads to a collection of subproblems (as we did for the WIS problem). This process is repeatable and you can mimic it when you apply the dynamic programming paradigm to problems that arise in your own projects.

The main idea is to reason about the structure of an optimal solution, identifying the different ways it might be constructed from optimal solutions to smaller subproblems. This thought experiment can lead to both the identification of the relevant subproblems and a recurrence (analogous to Corollary 16.2) that expresses the solution of a subproblem as a function of the solutions of smaller subproblems. A dynamic programming algorithm can then fill in an array with subproblem solutions, proceeding from smaller to larger subproblems and using the recurrence to compute each array entry.

16.4.4   Dynamic Programming vs. Divide-and-Conquer

There may seem to be some similarities between the divide-and-conquer algorithm design paradigm (Section 3.1) and dynamic programming, especially the latter's top-down recursive formulation (Sections 16.2.2–16.2.3). Both paradigms recursively solve smaller subproblems and combine the results into a solution to the original problem. Here are six major differences between typical uses of the two paradigms:

1. Each recursive call of a typical divide-and-conquer algorithm commits to a single way of dividing the input into smaller subproblems.[8] Each recursive call of a dynamic programming algorithm keeps its options open, considering multiple ways of defining smaller subproblems and choosing the best of them.[9]

2. Because each recursive call of a dynamic programming algorithm tries out multiple choices of smaller subproblems, subproblems generally recur across different recursive calls; caching subproblem solutions is then a no-brainer optimization. In most divide-and-conquer algorithms, all the subproblems are distinct and there's no point in caching their solutions.[10]

3. Most of the canonical applications of the divide-and-conquer paradigm replace a straightforward polynomial-time algorithm for a task with a faster divide-and-conquer version.[11] The killer applications of dynamic programming are polynomial-time algorithms for optimization problems for which straightforward solutions (like exhaustive search) require an exponential amount of time.

4. In a divide-and-conquer algorithm, subproblems are chosen primarily to optimize the running time; correctness often takes care of itself.[12] In dynamic programming, subproblems are usually chosen with correctness in mind, come what may with the running time.[13]

5. Relatedly, a divide-and-conquer algorithm generally recurses on subproblems with size at most a constant fraction (like 50%) of the input. Dynamic programming has no

---

[8]For example, in the MergeSort algorithm, every recursive call divides its input array into its left and right halves. The QuickSort algorithm invokes a partitioning subroutine to choose how to split the input array in two, and then commits to this division for the remainder of its execution.

[9]For example, in the `WIS` algorithm, each recursive call chooses between a subproblem with one fewer vertex and one with two fewer vertices.

[10]For example, in the MergeSort and QuickSort algorithms, every subproblem corresponds to a different subarray of the input array.

[11]For example, the MergeSort algorithm brings the running time of sorting a length-n array down from the straightforward bound of $O(n^2)$ to $O(n \log n)$. Other examples include Karatsuba's algorithm (which improves the running time of multiplying two n-digit numbers from $O(n^2)$ to $O(n^{1.59})$) and Strassen's algorithm (for multiplying two $n \times n$ matrices in $O(n^{2.81})$ rather than $O(n^3)$ time).

[12]For example, the QuickSort algorithm always correctly sorts the input array, no matter how good or bad its chosen pivot elements are.

[13]Our dynamic programming algorithm for the knapsack problem in Section 16.5 is a good example.

qualms about recursing on subproblems that are barely smaller than the input (like in the `WIS` algorithm), if necessary for correctness.

6. The divide-and-conquer paradigm can be viewed as a special case of dynamic programming, in which each recursive call commits to a fixed collection of subproblems to solve recursively. As the more sophisticated paradigm, dynamic programming applies to a wider range of problems than divide-and-conquer, but it is also more technically demanding to apply (at least until you've had sufficient practice).

Confronted with a new problem, which paradigm should you use? If you see a divide-and-conquer solution, by all means use it. If all your divide-and-conquer attempts fail—and especially if they fail because the combine step always seems to require redoing a lot of computation from scratch—it's time to try dynamic programming.

16.4.5 Why "Dynamic Programming"?

You might be wondering where the weird moniker "dynamic programming" came from; the answer is no clearer now that we know how the paradigm works than it was before.

The first point of confusion is the anachronistic use of the word "programming." In modern times it refers to coding, but back in the 1950s "programming" usually meant "planning." (For example, it has this meaning in the phrase "television programming.") What about "dynamic"? For the full story, I refer you to the father of dynamic programming himself, Richard E. Bellman, writing about his time working at the RAND Corporation:

> The 1950's were not good years for mathematical research. We had a very interesting gentleman in Washington named Wilson. He was Secretary of Defense, and he actually had a pathological fear and hatred of the word, research. I'm not using the term lightly; I'm using it precisely. His face with suffuse, he would turn red, and he would get violent if people used the term, research, in his presence. You can imagine how he felt, then, about the term, mathematical. The RAND Corporation was employed by the Air Force, and the Air Force had Wilson as its boss, essentially. Hence, I felt I had to do something to shield Wilson and the Air Force from the fact that I was really doing mathematics inside the RAND Corporation. What title, what name, could I choose? In the first place I was interested in planning, in decision making, in thinking. But planning, is not a good word for various reasons. I decided therefore to use the word, "programming." ... ["Dynamic"] has a very interesting property as an adjective, and that is it's impossible to use the word, dynamic, in the pejorative sense. Try thinking of some combination that will possibly give it a pejorative meaning. It's impossible. Thus, I thought dynamic programming was a good name. It was something not even a Congressman could object to. So I used it as an umbrella for my activities.[14]

---

[14]Richard E. Bellman, *Eye of the Hurricane: An Autobiography*, World Scientific, 1984, page 159.

16.5   The Knapsack Problem

Our second case study concerns the well-known *knapsack problem*. Following the same thought process we used to develop the `WIS` algorithm in Section 16.2, we'll arrive at the famous dynamic programming solution to the problem.

16.5.1   Problem Definition

An instance of the knapsack problem is specified by $2n + 1$ positive integers, where n is the number of "items" (which are labeled arbitrarily from 1 to n): a value v_i and a size s_i for each item i, and a knapsack capacity C.[15] The responsibility of an algorithm is to select a subset of the items. The total value of the items should be as large as possible while still fitting in the knapsack, meaning their total size should be at most C.

Problem: Knapsack

Input: Item values $v_1, v_2, \ldots, v_n$, item sizes $s_1, s_2, \ldots, s_n$, and a knapsack capacity C. (All positive integers.)

Output: A subset $S \subseteq \{1, 2, \ldots, n\}$ of items with the maximum-possible sum $\sum_{i \in S} v_i$ of values, subject to having total size $\sum_{i \in S} s_i$ at most C.

Quiz 16.5

Consider an instance of the knapsack problem with knapsack capacity $C = 6$ and four items:

Item	Value	Size
1	3	4
2	2	3
3	4	2
4	4	3

What is the total value of an optimal solution?

   a) 6

   b) 7

   c) 8

   d) 10

(See Section 16.5.7 for the solution and discussion.)

I could tell you a cheesy story about a knapsack-wielding burglar who breaks into a house and wants to make off quickly with the best pile of loot possible, but this would do a

---

[15]It's actually not important that the item values are integers (as opposed to arbitrary positive real numbers). It *is* important that the item sizes are integers, as we'll see in due time.

disservice to the problem, which is actually quite fundamental. Whenever you have a scarce resource that you want to use in the smartest way possible, you're talking about a knapsack problem. On which goods and services should you spend your paycheck to get the most value? Given an operating budget and a set of job candidates with differing productivities and requested salaries, whom should you hire? These are examples of knapsack problems.

16.5.2 Optimal Substructure and Recurrence

To apply the dynamic programming paradigm to the knapsack problem, we must figure out the right collection of subproblems. As with the WIS problem, we'll arrive at them by reasoning about the structure of optimal solutions and identifying the different ways they can be constructed from optimal solutions to smaller subproblems. Another deliverable of this exercise will be a recurrence for quickly computing the solution to a subproblem from those of two smaller subproblems.

Consider an instance of the knapsack problem with item values $v_1, v_2, \ldots, v_n$, item sizes $s_1, s_2, \ldots, s_n$, and knapsack capacity C, and suppose someone handed us on a silver platter an optimal solution $S \subseteq \{1, 2, \ldots, n\}$ with total value $V = \sum_{i \in S} v_i$. What must it look like? As with the WIS problem, we start with a tautology: S either contains the last item (item n) or it doesn't.[16]

Case 1: $n \notin S$. Because the optimal solution S excludes the last item, it can be regarded as a feasible solution (still with total value V and total size at most C) to the smaller problem consisting of only the first $n - 1$ items (and knapsack capacity C). Moreover, S must be an optimal solution to the smaller subproblem: If there were a solution $S^* \subseteq \{1, 2, \ldots, n-1\}$ with total size at most C and total value greater than V, it would also constitute such a solution in the original instance. This would contradict the supposed optimality of S.

Case 2: $n \in S$. The trickier case is when the optimal solution S makes use of the last item n. This case can occur only when $s_n \leq C$. We can't regard S as a feasible solution to a smaller problem with only the first $n - 1$ items, but we can after removing item n. Is $S - \{n\}$ an optimal solution to a smaller subproblem?

Quiz 16.6

Which of the following statements hold for the set $S - \{n\}$? (Choose all that apply.)

a) It is an optimal solution to the subproblem consisting of the first $n-1$ items and knapsack capacity C.

b) It is an optimal solution to the subproblem consisting of the first $n-1$ items and knapsack capacity $C - v_n$.

---

[16]The WIS problem in path graphs is inherently sequential, with the vertices ordered along the path. This naturally led to subproblems that correspond to prefixes of the input. The items in the knapsack problem are not inherently ordered, but to identify the right collection of subproblems, it's helpful to mimic our previous approach and *pretend* they're ordered in some arbitrary way. A "prefix" of the items then corresponds to the first i items in our arbitrary ordering (for some $i \in \{0, 1, 2, \ldots, n\}$). Many other dynamic programming algorithms use this same trick.

c) It is an optimal solution to the subproblem consisting of the first $n-1$ items and knapsack capacity $C - s_n$.

d) It might not be feasible if the knapsack capacity is only $C - s_n$.

(See Section 16.5.7 for the solution and discussion.)

This case analysis shows that two and only two candidates are vying to be an optimal knapsack solution:

Lemma 16.4 (Knapsack Optimal Substructure) *Let S be an optimal solution to a knapsack problem with $n \geq 1$ items, item values $v_1, v_2, \ldots, v_n$, item sizes $s_1, s_2, \ldots, s_n$, and knapsack capacity C. Then, S is either:*

(i) an optimal solution for the first $n-1$ items with knapsack capacity C; or

(ii) an optimal solution for the first $n-1$ items with knapsack capacity $C - s_n$, supplemented with the last item n.

The solution in (i) is always an option for the optimal solution. The solution in (ii) is an option if and only if $s_n \leq C$; in this case, s_n units of capacity are effectively reserved in advance for item n.[17] The option with the larger total value is an optimal solution, leading to the following recurrence:

Corollary 16.5 (Knapsack Recurrence) *With the assumptions and notation of Lemma 16.4, let $V_{i,c}$ denote the maximum total value of a subset of the first i items with total size at most c. (When $i = 0$, interpret $V_{i,c}$ as 0.) For every $i = 1, 2, \ldots, n$ and $c = 0, 1, 2, \ldots, C$,*

$$V_{i,c} = \begin{cases} \underbrace{V_{i-1,c}}_{\text{Case 1}} & \text{if } s_i > c \\[2em] \max\{\underbrace{V_{i-1,c}}_{\text{Case 1}}, \underbrace{V_{i-1,c-s_i} + v_i}_{\text{Case 2}}\} & \text{if } s_i \leq c. \end{cases}$$

Because both c and items' sizes are integers, the residual capacity $c - s_i$ in the second case is also an integer.

16.5.3   The Subproblems

The next step is to define the collection of relevant subproblems and solve them systematically using the recurrence identified in Corollary 16.5. For now, we focus on computing the total value of an optimal solution for each subproblem. As for the WIS problem in path graphs, we'll be able to reconstruct the items in an optimal solution to the original problem from this information.

Back in the WIS problem in path graphs, we used only one parameter i to index subproblems, where i was the length of the prefix of the input graph. For the knapsack

---

[17]This is analogous to, for the WIS problem in path graphs, excluding the penultimate vertex of the graph to reserve space for the final vertex.

problem, we can see from Lemma 16.4 and Corollary 16.5 that subproblems should be parameterized by *two* indices: the length i of the prefix of available items and the available knapsack capacity c. (Here, there are two dimensions in which a subproblem can grow smaller; in the WIS problem in path graphs, there was only one.) Ranging over all relevant values of the two parameters, we obtain our subproblems:

Knapsack: Subproblems

Compute $V_{i,c}$, the total value of an optimal knapsack solution with the first i items and knapsack capacity c.

(For each $i = 0, 1, 2, \ldots, n$ and $c = 0, 1, 2, \ldots, C$.)

The largest subproblem (with $i = n$ and $c = C$) is exactly the same as the original problem. Because all item sizes and the knapsack capacity C are positive integers, and because capacity is always reduced by the size of some item (to reserve space for it), the only residual capacities that can ever come up are the integers between 0 and C.

16.5.4   A Dynamic Programming Algorithm

Given the subproblems and recurrence, a dynamic programming algorithm for the knapsack problem practically writes itself.

Knapsack

Input: item values $v_1, \ldots, v_n$, item sizes $s_1, \ldots, s_n$, and a knapsack capacity C (all positive integers).
Output: the maximum total value of a subset $S \subseteq \{1, 2, \ldots, n\}$ with $\sum_{i \in S} s_i \leq C$.

```
// subproblem solutions (indexed from 0)
```
$A := (n + 1) \times (C + 1)$ two-dimensional array
```
// base case (i = 0)
```
for $c := 0$ to C **do**
    $A[0][c] = 0$
```
// systematically solve all subproblems
```
for $i := 1$ to n **do**
    for $c := 0$ to C **do**
```
        // use recurrence from Corollary 16.5
```
        if $s_i > c$ **then**
            $A[i][c] := A[i-1][c]$
        else
            $A[i][c] := \max\{\underbrace{A[i-1][c]}_{\text{Case 1}}, \underbrace{A[i-1][c-s_i] + v_i}_{\text{Case 2}}\}$
return $A[n][C]$ ```// solution to largest subproblem```

The array A is now two-dimensional to reflect the two indices i and c used to parameterize the subproblems. By the time an iteration of the double for loop must compute the subproblem solution $A[i][c]$, the values $A[i-1][c]$ and $A[i-1][c-s_i]$ of the two relevant smaller subproblems have already been computed in the previous iteration of the outer loop (or in the base case). We conclude that the algorithm spends $O(1)$ time solving each of the $(n+1)(C+1) = O(nC)$ subproblems, for an overall running time of $O(nC)$.[18,19]

Finally, as with WIS, the correctness of Knapsack follows by induction on the number of items, with the recurrence in Corollary 16.5 used to justify the inductive step.

Theorem 16.6 (Properties of Knapsack) *For every instance of the knapsack problem, the Knapsack algorithm returns the total value of an optimal solution and runs in $O(nC)$ time, where n is the number of items and C is the knapsack capacity.*

16.5.5   Example

Recall the four-item example from Quiz 16.5, with $C = 6$:

Item	Value	Size
1	3	4
2	2	3
3	4	2
4	4	3

Because $n = 4$ and $C = 6$, the array A in the Knapsack algorithm can be visualized as a table with 5 columns (corresponding to $i = 0, 1, \ldots, 4$) and 7 rows (corresponding to $c = 0, 1, \ldots, 6$). The final array values are:

residual capacity c	$i=0$	$i=1$	$i=2$	$i=3$	$i=4$
6	0	3	3	7	8
5	0	3	3	6	8
4	0	3	3	4	4
3	0	0	2	4	4
2	0	0	0	4	4
1	0	0	0	0	0
0	0	0	0	0	0

prefix length i

---

[18] In the notation of (16.1), $f(n, C) = O(nC)$, $g(n, C) = O(1)$, and $h(n, C) = O(1)$.

[19] The running time bound of $O(nC)$ is impressive only if C is small, for example, if $C = O(n)$ or ideally even smaller. In Part IV of the book we'll see the reason for the not-so-blazingly fast running time—there is a precise sense in which the knapsack problem is a difficult problem.

The Knapsack algorithm computes these entries column by column (working left to right), and within a column from bottom to top. To fill in an entry of the ith column, the algorithm compares the entry immediately to the left (corresponding to case 1) to v_i plus the entry one column to the left and s_i rows down (case 2). For example, for the array entry $A[2][5]$ the better option is to skip the second item and inherit the "3" immediately to the left, while for $A[3][5]$ the better option is to include the third item and achieve 4 (for v_3) plus the 2 in the entry $A[2][3]$.

16.5.6   Reconstruction

The Knapsack algorithm computes only the total value of an optimal solution, not the optimal solution itself. As with the WIS algorithm, we can reconstruct an optimal solution by tracing back through the filled-in array A. Starting from the largest subproblem in the upper-right corner, the reconstruction algorithm checks which case of the recurrence was used to compute the array entry $A[n][C]$. If it was case 1, the algorithm omits item n and resumes reconstruction from the entry $A[n-1][C]$. If it was case 2, the algorithm includes item n in its solution and resumes reconstruction from the entry $A[n-1][C-s_n]$. In more detail:

Knapsack Reconstruction

Input: the array A computed by the Knapsack algorithm with item values $v_1, v_2, \ldots, v_n$, item sizes $s_1, s_2, \ldots, s_n$, and knapsack capacity C.

Output: an optimal knapsack solution.

```
S := ∅                // items in an optimal solution
c := C                         // remaining capacity
// work backward from biggest subproblem
for i := n downto 1 do
    if s_i ≤ c and A[i − 1][c − s_i] + v_i ≥ A[i − 1][c] then
        S := S ∪ {i}          // Case 2 wins, include i
        c := c − s_i              // reserve space for it
    // else skip i, capacity stays the same
return S
```

The Knapsack Reconstruction postprocessing step runs in $O(n)$ time (with $O(1)$ work per iteration of the main loop), which is much faster than the $O(nC)$ time used to fill in the array in the Knapsack algorithm.

In the notation of (16.1), postprocessing the filled-in array with the Knapsack Reconstruction algorithm increases the $h(n, C)$ term from $O(1)$ to $O(n)$. Happily, the overall asymptotic running time $O(nC) \times O(1) + O(n) = O(nC)$ remains exactly the same.

For instance, tracing back through the array from the example on page 385 yields the optimal solution $\{3, 4\}$:

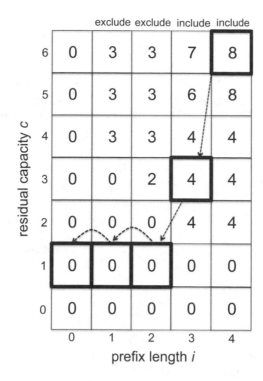

16.5.7   Solutions to Quizzes 16.5–16.6

Solution to Quiz 16.5

Correct answer: (c). Because the knapsack capacity is 6, there is no room to choose more than two items. The most valuable pair of items is the third and fourth ones (with total value 8), and these fit in the knapsack (with total size 5).

Solution to Quiz 16.6

Correct answer: (c). The most obviously false statement is (b), which doesn't even typecheck (C is in units of size, v_n in units of value). For example, v_n could be bigger than C, in which case $C - v_n$ is negative and meaningless. For (d), because S is feasible for the original problem, its total size is at most C; after n is removed from S, the total size drops to at most $C - s_n$ and, hence, $S - \{n\}$ is feasible for the reduced capacity. Answer (a) is a natural guess but is also incorrect.[20]

In (c), we are effectively reserving s_n units of capacity for item n's inclusion, which leaves a residual capacity of $C - s_n$. The items of $S - \{n\}$ constitute a feasible solution to the smaller subproblem (with knapsack capacity $C - s_n$) with total value $V - v_n$. If there were a better solution $S^* \subseteq \{1, 2, \ldots, n - 1\}$, with total value $V^* > V - v_n$ and total size at most $C - s_n$, then $S^* \cup \{n\}$ would have total size at most C and total value $V^* + v_n > (V - v_n) + v_n = V$. This would contradict the supposed optimality of S for the original problem.

---

[20]For example, suppose $C = 2$ and consider two items, with $v_1 = s_1 = 1$ and $v_2 = s_2 = 2$. The optimal solution S is $\{2\}$. $S - \{2\}$ is the empty set, but the only optimal solution to the subproblem consisting of the first item and knapsack capacity 2 is $\{1\}$.

The Upshot

✩ Dynamic programming follows a three-step recipe: (i) identify a relatively small collection of subproblems; (ii) show how to quickly solve "larger" subproblems given the solutions to "smaller" ones; and (iii) show how to quickly infer the final solution from the solutions to all the subproblems.

✩ A dynamic programming algorithm that solves at most $f(n)$ different subproblems, using at most $g(n)$ time for each, and performs at most $h(n)$ postprocessing work to extract the final solution runs in $O(f(n) \cdot g(n) + h(n))$ time, where n denotes the input size.

✩ The right collection of subproblems and a recurrence for systematically solving them can be identified by reasoning about the structure of an optimal solution and the different ways it might be constructed from optimal solutions to smaller subproblems.

✩ Typical dynamic programming algorithms fill in an array with the values of subproblems' solutions, and then trace back through the filled-in array to reconstruct the solution itself.

✩ An independent set of an undirected graph is a subset of mutually non-adjacent vertices.

✩ In n-vertex path graphs, a maximum-weight independent set can be computed using dynamic programming in $O(n)$ time.

✩ In the knapsack problem, given n items with values and sizes and a knapsack capacity C (all positive integers), the goal is to select the maximum-value subset of items with total size at most C.

✩ The knapsack problem can be solved using dynamic programming in $O(nC)$ time.

Test Your Understanding

Problem 16.1 *(S)* Consider the input graph

where vertices are labeled with their weights. What are the final array entries of the `WIS` algorithm from Section 16.2, and which vertices belong to the MWIS?

Problem 16.2 *(S)* Consider an instance of the knapsack problem with five items:

Item	Value	Size
1	1	1
2	2	3
3	3	2
4	4	5
5	5	4

and knapsack capacity $C = 9$. What are the final array entries of the `Knapsack` algorithm from Section 16.5, and which items belong to the optimal solution?

Problem 16.3 *(H)* Which of the following statements hold? (Choose all that apply.)

a) The `WIS` and `WIS Reconstruction` algorithms of Sections 16.2 and 16.3 always return a solution that includes a maximum-weight vertex.

b) When vertices' weights are distinct, the `WIS` and `WIS Reconstruction` algorithms never return a solution that includes a minimum-weight vertex.

c) If a vertex v does not belong to an MWIS of the prefix G_i comprising the first i vertices and $i - 1$ edges of the input graph, it does not belong to any MWIS of $G_{i+1}, G_{i+2}, \ldots, G_n$ either.

d) If a vertex v does not belong to an MWIS of G_{i-1} or G_i, it does not belong to any MWIS of $G_{i+1}, G_{i+2}, \ldots, G_n$ either.

Problem 16.4 *(H)* For the naive recursive algorithm for the WIS problem in path graphs (Section 16.2.2), prove that the number of leaves of its recursion tree (see footnote 6) is at least the nth Fibonacci number, where n is the number of vertices in the input graph.[21]

Problem 16.5 *(H)* Consider the following variation of the knapsack problem:

Problem: Double-Knapsack

Input: Item values $v_1, v_2, \ldots, v_n$, item sizes $s_1, s_2, \ldots, s_n$, and capacities C_1 and C_2 of *two* knapsacks. (All positive integers.)

Output: Two disjoint subsets $S_1, S_2 \subseteq \{1, 2, \ldots, n\}$ of items with the maximum-possible total value $\sum_{i \in S_1 \cup S_2} v_i$, subject to $\sum_{i \in S_1} s_i \leq C_1$ and $\sum_{i \in S_2} s_i \leq C_2$.

Here are two possible algorithmic approaches:

(1) Use the `Knapsack` algorithm from Section 16.5 to pick a maximum-value solution S_1 that fits in the first knapsack, and then use it again on the remaining items to pick a maximum-value solution S_2 that fits in the second knapsack.

---
[21]The *Fibonacci numbers* are the numbers in the sequence $1, 1, 2, 3, 5, 8, \ldots$, with each successive number defined as the sum of the previous two. The nth Fibonacci number is very closely approximated by $(\phi^n)/\sqrt{5}$, where $\phi = 1.618\ldots$ is the golden ratio. Thus, the lower bound proved in this problem is considerably larger than the bound of $2^{n/2} = (\sqrt{2})^n = (1.414\ldots)^n$ from the solution to Quiz 16.3.

(2) Use the `Knapsack` algorithm to pick a maximum-value solution S that would fit in a knapsack with capacity $C_1 + C_2$, then partition S arbitrarily into two sets S_1 and S_2 with total sizes at most C_1 and C_2, respectively.

Which of the following statements are true? (Choose all that apply.)

a) Algorithm (1) is guaranteed to produce an optimal solution to the double-knapsack problem but algorithm (2) is not.

b) Algorithm (2) is guaranteed to produce an optimal solution to the double-knapsack problem but algorithm (1) is not.

c) Algorithm (1) is guaranteed to produce an optimal solution to the double-knapsack problem when $C_1 = C_2$.

d) Neither algorithm is guaranteed to produce an optimal solution to the double-knapsack problem.

Challenge Problems

Problem 16.6 *(H)* This problem outlines an approach to solving the WIS problem in graphs more complicated than paths. Consider an arbitrary undirected graph $G = (V, E)$ with nonnegative vertex weights, and an arbitrary vertex $v \in V$ with weight w_v. Obtain H from G by removing v and its incident edges. Obtain K from H by removing v's neighbors and their incident edges:

Let W_G, W_H, and W_K denote the total weight of an MWIS in G, H, and K, respectively, and consider the formula

$$W_G = \max\{W_H, W_K + w_v\}.$$

Which of the following statements are true? (Choose all that apply.)

a) The formula is not always correct in path graphs.

b) The formula is always correct in path graphs but not always correct in trees (that is, in connected acyclic graphs).

c) The formula is always correct in trees but not always correct in arbitrary graphs.

d) The formula is always correct in arbitrary graphs.

e) The formula leads to a linear-time dynamic programming algorithm for the WIS problem in trees.

f) The formula leads to a linear-time dynamic programming algorithm for the WIS problem in arbitrary graphs.

Problem 16.7 *(H)* This problem describes four generalizations of the knapsack problem. In each, the input consists of item values $v_1, v_2, \ldots, v_n$, item sizes $s_1, s_2, \ldots, s_n$, and additional problem-specific data (all positive integers). Which of these generalizations can be solved by dynamic programming in time polynomial in the number n of items and the largest number M that appears in the input? (Choose all that apply.)

a) Given a positive integer capacity C, compute a subset of items with the maximum-possible total value subject to having total size *exactly* C. (If no such set exists, the algorithm should correctly detect that fact.)

b) Given a positive integer capacity C and an item budget $k \in \{1, 2, \ldots, n\}$, compute a subset of items with the maximum-possible total value subject to having total size at most C *and at most k items.*

c) The double-knapsack problem from Problem 16.5: Given capacities C_1 and C_2 of two knapsacks, compute disjoint subsets S_1, S_2 of items with the maximum-possible total value $\sum_{i \in S_1} v_i + \sum_{i \in S_2} v_i$, subject to the knapsack capacities: $\sum_{i \in S_1} s_i \leq C_1$ and $\sum_{i \in S_2} s_i \leq C_2$.

d) Given capacities $C_1, C_2, \ldots, C_m$ of m knapsacks, where m could be as large as n, compute disjoint subsets $S_1, S_2, \ldots, S_m$ of items with the maximum-possible total value $\sum_{i \in S_1} v_i + \sum_{i \in S_2} v_i + \cdots + \sum_{i \in S_m} v_i$, subject to the knapsack capacities: $\sum_{i \in S_1} s_i \leq C_1, \sum_{i \in S_2} s_i \leq C_2, \ldots$, and $\sum_{i \in S_m} s_i \leq C_m$.

Programming Problems

Problem 16.8 Implement in your favorite programming language the WIS and WIS Reconstruction algorithms. (See www.algorithmsilluminated.org for test cases and challenge data sets.)

Problem 16.9 Implement in your favorite programming language the Knapsack and Knapsack Reconstruction algorithms. (See www.algorithmsilluminated. org for test cases and challenge data sets.)

Chapter 17

Advanced Dynamic Programming

This chapter continues the dynamic programming boot camp with two more case studies: the sequence alignment problem (Section 17.1) and the problem of computing a binary search tree with the minimum-possible average search time (Section 17.2). In both cases, the structure of optimal solutions is more complex than in last chapter's case studies, with a subproblem solution depending on those from more than two smaller subproblems. After finishing this chapter, ask yourself: Could you have ever solved either problem without first studying dynamic programming?

17.1 Sequence Alignment

17.1.1 Motivation

If you take a course in computational genomics, the first few lectures will likely be devoted to the *sequence alignment* problem.[1] In this problem, the input consists of two strings that represent portions of one or more genomes, over the alphabet—no prizes for guessing!—$\{A, C, G, T\}$. The strings need not have the same length. For example, the input might be the strings $AGGGCT$ and $AGGCA$. Informally, the problem is to determine how similar the two strings are; we'll make this precise in the next section.

Why would you want to solve this problem? Here are two reasons among many. First, suppose you're trying to figure out the function of a region of a complex genome, like the human genome. One approach is to look for a similar region in a better-understood genome, like the mouse genome, and conjecture that the similar regions play the same or similar roles. A totally different application of the problem is to make inferences about a phylogenetic tree—which species evolved from which, and when. For example, you might be wondering if species B evolved from species A and then species C from B, or if B and C evolved independently from A. Genome similarity can be used as a proxy for proximity in a phylogenetic tree.

17.1.2 Problem Definition

Our example strings $AGGGCT$ and $AGGCA$ are obviously not identical, but they still intuitively feel more similar than not. How can we formalize this intuition? One idea is to notice that these two strings can be "nicely aligned":

$$
\begin{array}{cccccc}
A & G & G & G & C & T \\
A & G & G & - & C & A
\end{array}
$$

---

[1] The presentation in this section draws inspiration from Section 6.6 of *Algorithm Design*, by Jon Kleinberg and Éva Tardos (Pearson, 2005).

where the "−" indicates a gap inserted between two letters of the second string, which seems to be missing a '*G*'. The two strings agree in four of the six columns; the only flaws in the alignment are the gap and the mismatch between the A and T in the final column.

In general, an *alignment* is a way of inserting gaps into one or both input strings so that they have equal length:

$$\underbrace{\overbrace{\rule{0pt}{0pt}\hspace{3cm}}^{X + \text{gaps}}}_{}$$
$$\underbrace{\overbrace{\rule{0pt}{0pt}\hspace{3cm}}^{Y + \text{gaps}}}_{\text{common length } \ell}$$

We can then define the similarity of two strings according to the quality of their nicest alignment. But what makes an alignment "nice"? Is it better to have one gap and one mismatch, or three gaps and no mismatches?

Let's assume that such questions have already been answered experimentally, in the form of known *penalties* for gaps and mismatches that are provided as part of the input (along with the two strings). These specify the penalties an alignment incurs in each of its columns; the total penalty of an alignment is the sum of its columns' penalties. For example, the alignment of $AGGGCT$ and $AGGCA$ above would suffer a penalty of α_{gap} (the provided cost of a gap) plus a penalty of α_{AT} (the provided cost of an A-T mismatch). The sequence alignment problem is, then, to compute an alignment that minimizes the total penalty.

Problem: Sequence Alignment

Input: Two strings X, Y over the alphabet $\Sigma = \{A, C, G, T\}$, a penalty α_{xy} for each symbol pair $x, y \in \Sigma$, and a nonnegative gap penalty $\alpha_{gap} \geq 0$.[2]

Output: An alignment of X and Y with the minimum-possible total penalty.

One way to interpret the minimum-penalty alignment is as the "most plausible explanation" of how one of the strings might have evolved into the other. We can think of a gap as undoing a deletion that occurred sometime in the past, and a mismatch as undoing a mutation.

The minimum penalty of an alignment of two strings is a famous enough concept to have its own name: the *Needleman-Wunsch* or *NW score* of the strings.[3] Two strings are then deemed "similar" if and only if their NW score is relatively small.

Quiz 17.1

Suppose there is a penalty of 1 for each gap and a penalty of 2 for matching two different symbols in a column. What is the NW score of the strings $AGTACG$ and $ACATAG$?

---

[2]While it's natural to assume that all penalties are nonnegative with $\alpha_{xx} = 0$ for all $x \in \Sigma$ and $\alpha_{xy} = \alpha_{yx}$ for all $x, y \in \Sigma$, our dynamic programming algorithm requires only that the gap penalty is nonnegative. (Do you see why a negative gap penalty—that is, a reward for gaps—would make the problem completely uninteresting?)

[3]Named after its inventors, Saul B. Needleman and Christian D. Wunsch, and published in the paper "A general method applicable to the search for similarities in the amino acid sequence of two proteins" (*Journal of Molecular Biology*, 1970).

a) 3

b) 4

c) 5

d) 6

(See Section 17.1.8 for the solution and discussion.)

The NW score would be useless to genomicists without an efficient procedure for calculating it. The number of alignments of two strings grows exponentially with their combined length, so outside of uninterestingly small instances, exhaustive search won't complete in our lifetimes. Dynamic programming will save the day; by repeating the same type of thought experiment we used for the WIS problem in path graphs and the knapsack problem, we'll arrive at an efficient algorithm for computing the NW score.[4]

17.1.3   Optimal Substructure

Rather than be unduly intimidated by how fundamental the sequence alignment problem is, let's follow our usual dynamic programming recipe and see what happens. If you've already reached black-belt status in dynamic programming, you might be able to guess the right collection of subproblems; of course, I don't expect you to be at that level after only two case studies.

Suppose someone handed us on a silver platter a minimum-penalty alignment of two strings. What must it look like? In how many different ways could it have been built up from optimal solutions to smaller subproblems? In the WIS problem in path graphs and the knapsack problem, we zoomed in on a solution's last decision—does the last vertex of the path or the last item of a knapsack instance belong to the solution? To continue the pattern, it would seem that we should zoom in on the last column of the alignment:

$$
\begin{array}{cccccc}
A & G & G & G & C & T \\
A & G & G & - & C & A
\end{array}
$$

$$\underbrace{}_{\text{rest of alignment}} \quad \underbrace{}_{\substack{\text{last} \\ \text{column}}}$$

In our first two case studies, the final vertex or item was either in or out of the solution—two different possibilities. In the sequence alignment problem, how many relevant possibilities are there for the contents of the final column?

Quiz 17.2

Let $X = x_1, x_2, \ldots, x_m$ and $Y = y_1, y_2, \ldots, y_n$ be two input strings, with each symbol x_i or y_j in $\{A, C, G, T\}$. How many relevant possibilities are there for the contents of the final column of an optimal alignment?

a) 2

---

[4]Algorithms have shaped the development of computational genomics as a field. If there *wasn't* an efficient algorithm for computing the NW score, Needleman and Wunsch surely would have proposed a different and more tractable definition of genome similarity!

> b) 3
>
> c) 4
>
> d) mn
>
> (See Section 17.1.8 for the solution and discussion.)

Following our first two case studies, the next step shows, by a case analysis, that there are only three candidates for an optimal alignment—one candidate for each of the possibilities for the contents of the last column. This will lead to a recurrence, which can be computed by exhaustive search over the three possibilities, and a dynamic programming algorithm that uses this recurrence to systematically solve all the relevant subproblems.

Consider an optimal alignment of two non-empty strings $X = x_1, x_2, \ldots, x_m$ and $Y = y_1, y_2, \ldots, y_n$. Let $X' = x_1, x_2, \ldots, x_{m-1}$ and $Y' = y_1, y_2, \ldots, y_{n-1}$ denote X and Y, respectively, with the last symbol plucked off.

Case 1: x_m and y_n matched in last column of alignment.   Suppose an optimal alignment does not use a gap in its final column, preferring to match the final symbols x_m and y_n of the input strings. Let P denote the total penalty incurred by this alignment. We can view the rest of the alignment (excluding the final column) as an alignment of the remaining symbols—an alignment of the shorter strings X' and Y':

$$
\underbrace{
\begin{array}{l}
\text{————————} X' + \text{gaps} \text{————————} \; x_m \\
\text{————————} Y' + \text{gaps} \text{————————} \; y_n
\end{array}
}_{\text{rest of alignment}}
$$

This alignment of X' and Y' has total penalty P minus the penalty $\alpha_{x_m y_n}$ that was previously paid in the last column. And it's not just any old alignment of X' and Y'—it's an *optimal* such alignment. For if some other alignment of X' and Y' had smaller total penalty $P^* < P - \alpha_{x_m y_n}$, appending to it a final column matching x_m and y_n would produce an alignment of X and Y with total penalty $P^* + \alpha_{x_m y_n} < (P - \alpha_{x_m y_n}) + \alpha_{x_m y_n} = P$, contradicting the optimality of the original alignment of X and Y.

In other words, once you know that an optimal alignment of X and Y matches x_m and y_n in its last column, you know exactly what the rest of it looks like: an optimal alignment of X' and Y'.

Case 2: x_m matched with a gap in last column of alignment.   In this case, because y_n does not appear in the last column, the induced alignment is of X' and the original second string Y:

$$
\underbrace{
\begin{array}{l}
\text{————————} X' + \text{gaps} \text{————————} \; x_m \\
\text{————————} Y + \text{gaps} \text{————————} \; [\text{gap}].
\end{array}
}_{\text{rest of alignment}}
$$

Moreover, the induced alignment is an optimal alignment of X' and Y; the argument is analogous to that in case 1 (as you should verify).

Case 3: y_n matched with a gap in last column of alignment. Symmetrically, in this case, the induced alignment is of X and Y':

$$
\underbrace{
\begin{array}{c}
\text{———————— } X + \text{gaps ———————— [gap]} \\
\text{———————— } Y' + \text{gaps ———————— } y_n.
\end{array}
}_{\text{rest of alignment}}
$$

Moreover, as in the first two cases, it is an optimal such alignment (as you should verify).

The point of this case analysis is to narrow down the possibilities for an optimal solution to three and only three candidates.

Lemma 17.1 (Sequence Alignment Optimal Substructure) *An optimal alignment of two non-empty strings $X = x_1, x_2, \ldots, x_m$ and $Y = y_1, y_2, \ldots, y_n$ is either:*

   (i) *an optimal alignment of X' and Y', supplemented with a match of x_m and y_n in the final column;*

   (ii) *an optimal alignment of X' and Y, supplemented with a match of x_m and a gap in the final column;*

   (iii) *an optimal alignment of X and Y', supplemented with a match of a gap and y_n in the final column,*

where X' and Y' denote X and Y, respectively, with the final symbols x_m and y_n removed.

What if X or Y is the empty string?

Quiz 17.3

Suppose one of the two input strings (Y, say) is empty. What is the NW score of X and Y?

   a) 0

   b) $\alpha_{gap} \cdot (\text{length of } X)$

   c) $+\infty$

   d) undefined

(See Section 17.1.8 for the solution and discussion.)

17.1.4   Recurrence

Quiz 17.3 handles the base case of an empty input string. For non-empty input strings, of the three options in Lemma 17.1, the one with the smallest total penalty is an optimal solution. These observations lead to the following recurrence, which computes the best of the three options by exhaustive search:

Corollary 17.2 (Sequence Alignment Recurrence) *With the assumptions and notation of Lemma 17.1, let $P_{i,j}$ denote the total penalty of an optimal alignment of $X_i = x_1, x_2, \ldots, x_i$, the first i symbols of X, and $Y_j = y_1, y_2, \ldots, y_j$, the first j symbols of Y. (If $j = 0$ or $i = 0$, interpret $P_{i,j}$ as $i \cdot \alpha_{gap}$ or $j \cdot \alpha_{gap}$, respectively.) Then*

$$P_{m,n} = \min\{\underbrace{P_{m-1,n-1} + \alpha_{x_m y_n}}_{Case\ 1}, \underbrace{P_{m-1,n} + \alpha_{gap}}_{Case\ 2}, \underbrace{P_{m,n-1} + \alpha_{gap}}_{Case\ 3}\}.$$

More generally, for every $i = 1, 2, \ldots, m$ and $j = 1, 2, \ldots, n$,

$$P_{i,j} = \min\{\underbrace{P_{i-1,j-1} + \alpha_{x_i y_j}}_{Case\ 1}, \underbrace{P_{i-1,j} + \alpha_{gap}}_{Case\ 2}, \underbrace{P_{i,j-1} + \alpha_{gap}}_{Case\ 3}\}.$$

The more general statement in Corollary 17.2 follows by invoking the first statement, for each $i = 1, 2, \ldots, m$ and $j = 1, 2, \ldots, n$, with X_i and Y_j playing the role of the input strings X and Y.

17.1.5   The Subproblems

As in the knapsack problem, the subproblems in the recurrence (Corollary 17.2) are indexed by two different parameters, i and j. Knapsack subproblems can shrink in two different senses (by removing an item or removing knapsack capacity), and so it goes with sequence alignment subproblems (by removing a symbol from the first or the second input string). Ranging over all relevant values of the two parameters, we obtain our collection of subproblems:[5]

Sequence Alignment: Subproblems

Compute $P_{i,j}$, the minimum total penalty of an alignment of the first i symbols of X and the first j symbols of Y.

(For each $i = 0, 1, 2, \ldots, m$ and $j = 0, 1, 2, \ldots, n$.)

The largest subproblem (with $i = m$ and $j = n$) is exactly the same as the original problem.

17.1.6   A Dynamic Programming Algorithm

All the hard work is done. We have our subproblems. We have our recurrence for solving a subproblem given solutions to smaller subproblems. Nothing can stop us from using it to solve all the subproblems systematically, beginning with the base cases and working up to the original problem.

---

[5] Or, thinking recursively, each recursive call plucks off the last symbol from the first input string, the last symbol from the second input string, or both. The only subproblems that can arise in this way are for prefixes of the original input strings.

NW

Input: strings $X = x_1, x_2, \ldots, x_m$ and $Y = y_1, y_2, \ldots, y_n$ over the
alphabet $\Sigma = \{A, C, G, T\}$, a penalty α_{xy} for each $x, y \in \Sigma$, and a
gap penalty $\alpha_{gap} \geq 0$.
Output: the NW score of X and Y.

```
// subproblem solutions (indexed from 0)
```
$A := (m+1) \times (n+1)$ two-dimensional array
```
// base case #1  (j = 0)
```
for $i := 0$ to m **do**
  $A[i][0] = i \cdot \alpha_{gap}$
```
// base case #2  (i = 0)
```
for $j := 0$ to n **do**
  $A[0][j] = j \cdot \alpha_{gap}$
```
// systematically solve all subproblems
```
for $i := 1$ to m **do**
  for $j := 1$ to n **do**
```
      // use recurrence from Corollary 17.2
```
$$A[i][j] := \min \left\{ \begin{array}{ll} A[i-1][j-1] + \alpha_{x_i y_j} & \text{(Case 1)} \\ A[i-1][j] + \alpha_{gap} & \text{(Case 2)} \\ A[i][j-1] + \alpha_{gap} & \text{(Case 3)} \end{array} \right\}$$

return $A[m][n]$ `// solution to largest subproblem`

As in the knapsack problem, because subproblems are indexed by two different parameters,
the algorithm uses a two-dimensional array to store subproblem solutions and a double
for loop to populate it. By the time a loop iteration must compute the subproblem solution $A[i][j]$, the values $A[i-1][j-1]$, $A[i-1][j]$, and $A[i][j-1]$ of the three relevant
smaller subproblems have already been computed and are ready and waiting to be looked
up in constant time. This means the algorithm spends $O(1)$ time solving each of the
$(m+1)(n+1) = O(mn)$ subproblems, for an overall running time of $O(mn)$.[6] Like our
previous dynamic programming algorithms, correctness of the NW algorithm can be proved
by induction; the induction is on the value of $i + j$ (the subproblem size), with the recurrence
in Corollary 17.2 justifying the inductive step.

Theorem 17.3 (Properties of NW) *For every instance of the sequence alignment problem,
the NW algorithm returns the correct NW score and runs in $O(mn)$ time, where m and n are
the lengths of the two input strings.*

For an example of the NW algorithm in action, check out Problem 17.1. While this
algorithm does not run in linear or near-linear time, it is fast enough to process pairs of
strings with many thousands of characters.[7]

---

[6]In the notation of (16.1), $f(m, n) = O(mn)$, $g(m, n) = O(1)$, and $h(m, n) = O(1)$.

[7]Can we do better? In special cases, yes (see Problem 17.7). For the general problem, cutting-edge research
predicated on the "Strong Exponential Time Hypothesis (SETH)" suggests that the answer might be "no"; see
Section 23.5 for further details.

17.1.7   Reconstruction

There are no surprises in reconstructing an optimal alignment from the array values that the NW algorithm computes. Working backward, the algorithm first checks which case of the recurrence was used to fill in the array entry $A[m][n]$ corresponding to the largest subproblem (resolving ties arbitrarily).[8] If it was case 1, the last column of the optimal alignment matches x_m and y_n and reconstruction resumes from the entry $A[m-1][n-1]$. If it was case 2 or 3, the last column of the alignment matches either x_m (in case 2) or y_n (in case 3) with a gap and the process resumes from the entry $A[m-1][n]$ (in case 2) or $A[m][n-1]$ (in case 3). When the reconstruction algorithm hits a base case, it completes the alignment by prepending the appropriate number of gaps to the string that has run out of symbols. Because the algorithm performs $O(1)$ work per iteration and each iteration decreases the sum of the lengths of the remaining prefixes, its running time is $O(m+n)$. We leave the detailed pseudocode to the interested reader.

17.1.8   Solution to Quizzes 17.1–17.3

Solution to Quiz 17.1

Correct answer: (b). Here's one alignment with two gaps and one mismatch, for a total penalty of 4:

$$\begin{array}{ccccccc} A & - & G & T & A & C & G \\ A & C & A & T & A & - & G \end{array}$$

Here's one with four gaps and no mismatches, also with a total penalty of 4:

$$\begin{array}{ccccccc} A & - & - & G & T & A & C & G \\ A & C & A & - & T & A & - & G \end{array}$$

No alignment has total penalty 3 or less. Why not? Because the input strings have the same length, every alignment inserts the same number of gaps in each, and so the total number of gaps is even. An alignment with four or more gaps has total penalty at least 4. The alignment with zero gaps has four mismatches and a total penalty of 8. Every alignment that inserts only one gap in each string results in at least one mismatch, for a total penalty of at least 4.

Solution to Quiz 17.2

Correct answer: (b). Consider an optimal alignment of the strings X and Y:

$$\underbrace{\begin{array}{c} \text{———— } X + \text{gaps ————} \\ \text{———— } Y + \text{gaps ————} \end{array}}_{\text{common length } \ell}$$

What could reside in the upper-right corner, in the last column of the first row? It could be a gap, or it could be a symbol. If it's a symbol, it must be from X (because it's in the

---

[8]Depending on the implementation details, this information may have been cached by the NW algorithm, in which case it can be looked up. (See also footnote 7 of Chapter 16.) If not, the reconstruction algorithm can recompute the answer from scratch in $O(1)$ time.

top row) and it must be X's last symbol x_m (because it's in the last column). Similarly, the lower-right corner must be either a gap or the last symbol y_n of the second string Y.

With two choices for each of the two entries in the last column, there would seem to be four possible scenarios. But one of them is irrelevant! It's pointless to have two gaps in the same column—there's a nonnegative penalty per gap, so removing them produces a new alignment that is as good or better. This leaves us with three relevant possibilities for the contents of the last column of an optimal alignment: (i) x_m and y_n are matched; (ii) x_m is matched with a gap; or (iii) y_n is matched with a gap.

Solution to Quiz 17.3

Correct answer: (b). If Y is empty, the optimal alignment inserts enough gaps into Y so that it has the same length as X. This incurs a penalty of α_{gap} per gap, for a total penalty of α_{gap} times the length of X.

*17.2 Optimal Binary Search Trees

In Chapter 11 we studied binary search trees, which maintain a total ordering over an evolving set of objects and support a rich set of fast operations. In Chapter 14 we defined prefix-free codes and designed a greedy algorithm for computing the best-on-average code for a given set of symbol frequencies. Next we consider the analogous problem for search trees—computing the best-on-average search tree given statistics about the frequencies of different searches. This problem is more challenging than the optimal prefix-free code problem, but it is no match for the power of the dynamic programming paradigm.

17.2.1 Binary Search Tree Review

Recall from Chapter 11 that a binary search tree is a data structure that acts like a dynamic version of a sorted array. Every node of the tree corresponds to an object (associated with a key and possibly lots of other data) and has left and right child pointers, either of which can be null. The defining search tree property is:

The Search Tree Property

For every object x:

1. Objects in x's left subtree (i.e., those reachable via x's left child pointer) have keys smaller than that of x.

2. Objects in x's right subtree (i.e., those reachable via x's right child pointer) have keys larger than that of x.

Throughout this section, we assume, for simplicity, that no two objects have the same key. For example, here's one possible search tree containing five objects with the keys $\{1, 2, 3, 4, 5\}$:

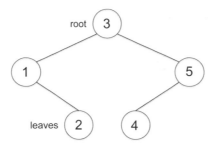

The point of the search tree property is to reduce searching for an object with a given key to following your nose, reminiscent of binary search in a sorted array. For example, suppose you're looking for an object with key 17. If the object at the root of the tree has the key 23, you know that the object you're looking for is in the root's left subtree. If the root's key is 12, you know to recursively search for the object in the right subtree.

17.2.2   Average Search Time

The *search time* for a key k in a binary search tree T is the number of nodes visited while searching for the node with key k (including that node itself). Equivalently, the search time is one plus the depth of the corresponding node in the tree. In the tree above, the key "3" has a search time of 1, the keys "1" and "5" have search times of 2, and the keys "2" and "4" have search times of 3.

Different search trees for the same set of objects result in different search times. For example, here's a second search tree containing objects with the keys $\{1, 2, 3, 4, 5\}$:

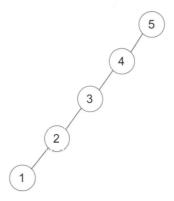

where the "1" now has a search time of 5.

Of all the search trees for a given set of objects, which is the "best"? We asked this question in Chapter 11 and the answer there was a perfectly balanced tree:

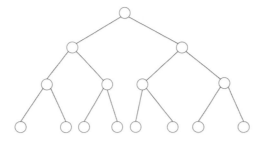

The rationale? A perfectly balanced tree minimizes the length of the longest root-leaf path ($\approx \log_2 n$ for n objects) or, equivalently, the maximum search time. Balanced binary search tree data structures, such as red-black trees, are explicitly designed to keep the search tree close to perfectly balanced (see Section 11.4).

Minimizing the maximum search time makes sense when you don't have advance knowledge about which searches are more likely than others. But what if you have statistics about the frequencies of different searches?[9]

Quiz 17.4

Consider the following two search trees that store objects with keys 1, 2, and 3:

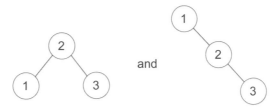

and

and the search frequencies:

Key	Search Frequency
1	.8
2	.1
3	.1

What are the average search times in the two trees, respectively?

a) 1.9 and 1.2

b) 1.9 and 1.3

c) 2 and 1

d) 2 and 3

(See Section 17.2.9 for the solution and discussion.)

17.2.3   Problem Definition

Quiz 17.4 shows that the best binary search tree for the job depends on the search frequencies, with unbalanced trees potentially superior to balanced trees when the search frequencies are not uniform. This observation suggests a cool opportunity for algorithm design: Given the search frequencies for a set of keys, what's the best binary search tree?

---

[9]For example, imagine you implement a spell checker as a binary search tree that stores all the correctly spelled words. Spell-checking a document reduces to looking up each of its words in turn, with unsuccessful searches corresponding to misspelled words. You can estimate the frequencies of different searches by counting the number of occurrences of different words (both correctly and incorrectly spelled) in a sufficiently large set of representative documents.

Problem: Optimal Binary Search Trees

Input: A sorted list of keys $k_1, k_2, \ldots, k_n$ and a nonnegative frequency p_i for each key k_i.

Output: The binary search tree T containing the keys $\{k_1, k_2, \ldots, k_n\}$ with the minimum-possible weighted search time:

$$\sum_{i=1}^{n} p_i \cdot \underbrace{\left(\text{search time for } k_i \text{ in } T\right)}_{=(k_i\text{'s depth in } T)+1}. \tag{17.1}$$

Three comments. First, the names of the keys are not important, so among friends let's just call them $\{1, 2, \ldots, n\}$. Second, the problem formulation does not assume that the p_i's sum to 1 (hence the phrasing "weighted" search time instead of "average" search time). If this bothers you, feel free to normalize the frequencies by dividing each of them by their sum $\sum_{i=1}^{n} p_i$—this doesn't change the problem. Third, the problem as stated is unconcerned with unsuccessful searches, meaning searches for a key other than one in the given set $\{k_1, k_2, \ldots, k_n\}$. You should check that our dynamic programming solution extends to the case in which unsuccessful search times are also counted, provided the input specifies the frequencies of such searches.

The optimal binary search tree problem bears some resemblance to the optimal prefix-free code problem (Chapter 14). In both problems, the input specifies a set of frequencies over symbols or keys, the output is a binary tree, and the objective function is related to minimizing the average depth. The difference lies in the constraint that the binary tree must satisfy. In the optimal prefix-free code problem, the sole restriction is that symbols appear only at the leaves. A solution to the optimal binary search tree problem must satisfy the more demanding search tree property (page 400). This is why greedy algorithms aren't good enough for the latter problem (see Problem 17.3); we'll need to up our game and apply the dynamic programming paradigm.

17.2.4   Optimal Substructure

The first step, as always with dynamic programming, is to understand the ways in which an optimal solution might be built up from optimal solutions to smaller subproblems. As a warm-up, suppose we took a (doomed-to-fail) divide-and-conquer approach to the optimal binary search tree problem. Every recursive call of a divide-and-conquer algorithm commits to a single split of its input into one or more smaller subproblems. Which split should we use? A first thought might be to install the object with the median key at the root, and then recursively compute the left and right subtrees. With non-uniform search frequencies, however, there's no reason to expect the median to be a good choice for the root (see Quiz 17.4). The choice of root has unpredictable repercussions further down the tree, so how could we know in advance the right way to split the problem into two smaller subproblems? If only we had clairvoyance and knew which key should appear at the root, we might then be able to compute the rest of the tree recursively.

If only we knew the root. This is starting to sound familiar. In the WIS problem in path graphs (Section 16.2.1), if only you knew whether the last vertex belonged to an optimal solution, you would know what the rest of it looked like. In the knapsack problem (Section 16.5.2), if only you knew whether the last item belonged to an optimal solution, you would know what the rest of it looked like. In the sequence alignment problem (Section 17.1.3), if only you knew the contents of the final column of an optimal alignment, you would know what the rest of it looked like. How did we overcome our ignorance? By trying all the possibilities—two possibilities in the WIS and knapsack problems, and three in the sequence alignment problem. Reasoning by analogy, perhaps our solution to the optimal binary search tree problem should *try all the possible roots*.

With this in mind, the next quiz asks you to guess what type of optimal substructure lemma might be true for the optimal binary search tree problem.

Quiz 17.5

Suppose an optimal binary search tree for the keys $\{1, 2, \ldots, n\}$ and frequencies $p_1, p_2, \ldots, p_n$ has the key r at its root, with left subtree T_1 and right subtree T_2:

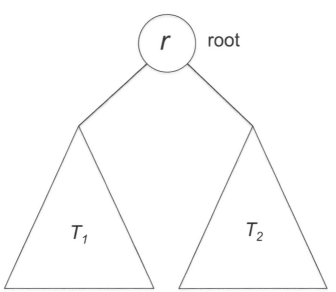

Of the following four statements, choose the strongest one that you suspect is true.

a) Neither T_1 nor T_2 need be optimal for the keys it contains.

b) At least one of T_1, T_2 is optimal for the keys it contains.

c) Each of T_1, T_2 is optimal for the keys it contains.

d) T_1 is an optimal binary search tree for the keys $\{1, 2, \ldots, r - 1\}$, and similarly T_2 for the keys $\{r + 1, r + 2, \ldots, n\}$.

(See Section 17.2.9 for the solution and discussion.)

As usual, formalizing the optimal substructure boils down to a case analysis, with one case for each possibility of what an optimal solution might look like. Consider an optimal binary search tree T with keys $\{1, 2, \ldots, n\}$ and frequencies $p_1, p_2, \ldots, p_n$. Any of the n keys might appear at the root of an optimal solution, so there are n different cases. We can reason about all of them in one fell swoop.

Case r: The root of T has key r.   Let T_1 and T_2 denote the left and right subtrees of the root. The search tree property implies that the residents of T_1 are the keys $\{1, 2, \ldots, r-1\}$, and similarly for T_2 and $\{r+1, r+2, \ldots, n\}$. Moreover, T_1 and T_2 are both valid search trees for their sets of keys (i.e., both T_1 and T_2 satisfy the search tree property). We next show that both are *optimal* binary search trees for their respective subproblems, with the frequencies $p_1, p_2, \ldots, p_{r-1}$ and $p_{r+1}, p_{r+2}, \ldots, p_n$ inherited from the original problem.[10]

Suppose, for contradiction, that at least one of the subtrees—T_1, say—is not an optimal solution to its corresponding subproblem. This means there is a different search tree T_1^* with keys $\{1, 2, \ldots, r-1\}$ and with strictly smaller weighted search time:

$$\sum_{k=1}^{r-1} p_k \cdot (k\text{'s search time in } T_1^*) < \sum_{k=1}^{r-1} p_k \cdot (k\text{'s search time in } T_1). \tag{17.2}$$

From our previous case studies, we know what we must do next: Use the inequality (17.2) to exhibit a search tree for the original problem superior to T, thereby contradicting the purported optimality of T. We can obtain such a tree T^* by performing surgery on T, cutting out its left subtree T_1 and pasting T_1^* in its place:

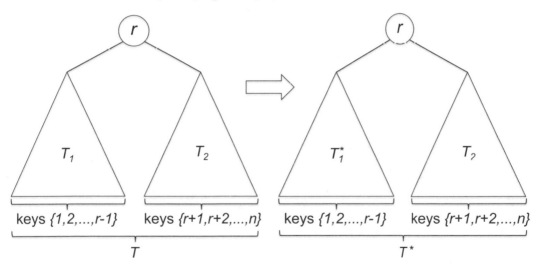

The final step is to compare the weighted search times in T^* and T. Splitting the sum in (17.1) into two parts, the keys $\{1, 2, \ldots, r-1\}$ and the keys $\{r, r+1, \ldots, n\}$, we can write these search times as

$$\sum_{k=1}^{r-1} p_k \cdot \underbrace{(k\text{'s search time in } T^*)}_{=1+(\text{search time in } T_1^*)} + \sum_{k=r}^{n} p_k \cdot (k\text{'s search time in } T^*)$$

---

[10]No worries if $r = 1$ or $r = n$; in that case, one of the two subtrees is empty, and the empty tree is trivially optimal for the empty set of keys.

and

$$\sum_{k=1}^{r-1} p_k \cdot \underbrace{(k\text{'s search time in } T)}_{=1+(\text{search time in } T_1)} + \sum_{k=r}^{n} p_k \cdot \underbrace{(k\text{'s search time in } T)}_{\text{same as in } T^* \text{ (as } k \geq r)},$$

respectively. Because the trees T^* and T have the same root r and the same right subtree T_2, the search times for the keys $r, r+1, \ldots, n$ are the same in both trees. A search for a key in $\{1, 2, \ldots, r-1\}$ first visits the root r and then recursively searches the left subtree. Thus, the search time for such a key is one more in T^* than in T_1^*, and one more in T than in T_1. This means the weighted search times in T^* and T can be written as

$$\underbrace{\sum_{k=1}^{r-1} p_k \cdot (k\text{'s search time in } T_1^*) + \sum_{k=1}^{r-1} p_k}_{\text{left-hand side of (17.2)}} + \sum_{k=r}^{n} p_k \cdot (k\text{'s search time in } T^*)$$

and

$$\underbrace{\sum_{k=1}^{r-1} p_k \cdot (k\text{'s search time in } T_1) + \sum_{k=1}^{r-1} p_k}_{\text{right-hand side of (17.2)}} + \sum_{k=r}^{n} p_k \cdot (k\text{'s search time in } T^*),$$

respectively. The second and third terms are the same in both expressions. Our assumption (17.2) is that the first term is smaller in the first expression than in the second, which implies that the weighted search time in T^* is smaller than that in T. This furnishes the promised contradiction and completes the proof of the key claim that T_1 and T_2 are optimal binary search trees for their respective subproblems.

Lemma 17.4 (Optimal BST Optimal Substructure) *If T is an optimal binary search tree with keys $\{1, 2, \ldots, n\}$, frequencies $p_1, p_2, \ldots, p_n$, root r, left subtree T_1, and right subtree T_2, then:*

(a) *T_1 is an optimal binary search tree for the keys $\{1, 2, \ldots, r-1\}$ and frequencies $p_1, p_2, \ldots, p_{r-1}$; and*

(b) *T_2 is an optimal binary search tree for the keys $\{r+1, r+2, \ldots, n\}$ and frequencies $p_{r+1}, p_{r+2}, \ldots, p_n$.*

In other words, once you know the root of an optimal binary search tree, you know exactly what its left and right subtrees look like.

17.2.5   Recurrence

Lemma 17.4 narrows down the possibilities for an optimal binary search tree to n and only n candidates, where n is the number of keys in the input (i.e., the number of options for the root). The best of these n candidates must be an optimal solution.

Corollary 17.5 (Optimal BST Recurrence) *With the assumptions and notation of Lemma 17.4, let $W_{i,j}$ denote the weighted search time of an optimal binary search tree with*

*the keys $\{i, i+1, \ldots, j\}$ and frequencies $p_i, p_{i+1}, \ldots, p_j$. (If $i > j$, interpret $W_{i,j}$ as 0.)
Then*

$$W_{1,n} = \sum_{k=1}^{n} p_k + \underbrace{\min_{r \in \{1,2,\ldots,n\}} \{W_{1,r-1} + W_{r+1,n}\}}_{\text{Case } r}. \tag{17.3}$$

More generally, for every $i, j \in \{1, 2, \ldots, n\}$ with $i \leq j$,

$$W_{i,j} = \sum_{k=i}^{j} p_k + \underbrace{\min_{r \in \{i,i+1,\ldots,j\}} \{W_{i,r-1} + W_{r+1,j}\}}_{\text{Case } r}.$$

The more general statement in Corollary 17.5 follows by invoking the first statement, for each $i, j \in \{1, 2, \ldots, n\}$ with $i \leq j$, with the keys $\{i, i+1, \ldots, j\}$ and their frequencies playing the role of the original input.

The "min" in the recurrence (17.3) implements the exhaustive search through the n different candidates for an optimal solution. The term $\sum_{k=1}^{n} p_k$ is necessary because installing the optimal subtrees under a new root adds 1 to all their keys' search times.[11] As a sanity check, note that this extra term is needed for the recurrence to be correct even when there is only one key (and the weighted search time is the frequency of that key).

17.2.6   The Subproblems

In the knapsack problem (Section 16.5.3), subproblems were indexed by two parameters because the "size" of a subproblem was two-dimensional (with one parameter tracking the prefix of items and the other tracking the remaining knapsack capacity). Similarly, in the sequence alignment problem (Section 17.1.5), there was one parameter tracking the prefix of each of the two input strings. Eyeballing the recurrence in Corollary 17.5, we see that subproblems are again indexed by two parameters (i and j), but this time for different reasons. Subproblems of the form $W_{1,r-1}$ in the recurrence (17.3) are defined by prefixes of the set of keys (as usual), but subproblems of the form $W_{r+1,n}$ are defined by *suffixes* of the keys. To be prepared for both cases, we must keep track of both the first (smallest) and last (largest) keys that belong to a subproblem.[12] We therefore end up with a two-dimensional set of subproblems, despite the seemingly one-dimensional input.

Ranging over all relevant values of the two parameters, we obtain our collection of subproblems.

---

[11] In more detail, consider a tree T with root r and left and right subtrees T_1 and T_2. The search times for the keys $\{1, 2, \ldots, r-1\}$ in T are one more than in T_1, and those for the keys $\{r+1, r+2, \ldots, n\}$ in T are one more than in T_2. Thus, the weighted search time (17.1) can be written as

$$\sum_{k=1}^{r-1} p_k \cdot (1 + k\text{'s search time in } T_1) + p_r \cdot 1 + \sum_{k=r+1}^{n} p_k \cdot (1 + k\text{'s search time in } T_2),$$

which cleans up to $\sum_{k=1}^{n} p_k +$ (weighted search time in T_1) + (weighted search time in T_2).

[12] Or, thinking recursively, each recursive call throws away either one or more of the smallest keys, or one or more of the largest keys. The subproblems that can arise in this way correspond to the contiguous subsets of the original set of keys—sets of the form $\{i, i+1, \ldots, j\}$ for some $i, j \in \{1, 2, \ldots, n\}$ with $i \leq j$. For example, a recursive call might be given a prefix of the original input $\{1, 2, \ldots, 100\}$, such as $\{1, 2, \ldots, 22\}$, but some of its own recursive calls will be on suffixes of its input, such as $\{18, 19, 20, 21, 22\}$.

Optimal BST: Subproblems

Compute $W_{i,j}$, the minimum weighted search time of a binary search tree with keys $\{i, i+1, \ldots, j\}$ and frequencies $p_i, p_{i+1}, \ldots, p_j$.

(For each $i, j \in \{1, 2, \ldots, n\}$ with $i \le j$.)

The largest subproblem (with $i = 1$ and $j = n$) is exactly the same as the original problem.

17.2.7   A Dynamic Programming Algorithm

With the subproblems and recurrence in hand, you should expect the dynamic programming algorithm to write itself. The one detail to get right is the order in which to solve the subproblems. The simplest way to define "subproblem size" is as the number of keys in the input. Therefore, it makes sense to first solve all the subproblems with a single-key input, then the subproblems with two keys in the input, and so on. In the following pseudocode, the variable s controls the current subproblem size. For an example of the algorithm in action, see Problem 17.4.

OptBST

Input: keys $\{1, 2, \ldots, n\}$ with nonnegative frequencies $p_1, p_2, \ldots, p_n$.
Output: the minimum weighted search time (17.1) of a binary search tree with the keys $\{1, 2, \ldots, n\}$.

```
// subproblems (i indexed from 1, j from 0)
```
$A := (n + 1) \times (n + 1)$ two-dimensional array
```
// base cases (i = j + 1)
```
for $i := 1$ to $n + 1$ **do**
    $A[i][i - 1] := 0$
```
// systematically solve all subproblems
```
for $s := 0$ to $n - 1$ **do**   // s=subproblem size-1
    for $i := 1$ to $n - s$ **do**   // i+s plays role of j
```
        // use recurrence from Corollary 17.5
```
        $A[i][i + s] :-$
            $\sum_{k=i}^{i+s} p_k + \min_{r=i}^{i+s}\{\underbrace{A[i][r-1] + A[r+1][i+s]}_{\text{Case } r}\}$
return $A[1][n]$ `// solution to largest subproblem`

In the loop iteration responsible for computing the subproblem solution $A[i][i + s]$, all the terms of the form $A[i][r - 1]$ and $A[r + 1][i + s]$ correspond to solutions of smaller subproblems computed in earlier iterations of the outer for loop (or in the base cases). These values are ready and waiting to be looked up in constant time.

Pictorially, we can visualize the array A in the OptBST algorithm as a two-dimensional table, with each iteration of the outer for loop corresponding to a diagonal and with the inner for loop filling in the diagonal's entries from "southwest" to "northeast":

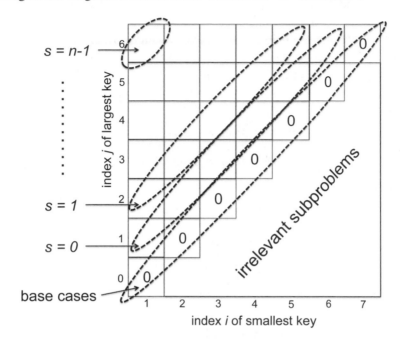

During the computation of an array entry $A[i][i + s]$, all the relevant terms of the form $A[i][r - 1]$ and $A[r + 1][i + s]$ lie on (previously computed) lower diagonals.

As with all our dynamic programming algorithms, the correctness of the OptBST algorithm follows by induction (on the subproblem size), with the recurrence in Corollary 17.5 justifying the inductive step.

What about the running time? Don't be fooled into thinking that the line of pseudocode performed in each loop iteration translates into a constant number of primitive computer operations. Computing the sum $\sum_{k=i}^{i+s} p_k$ and exhaustively searching through the $s + 1$ cases of the recurrence takes $O(s) = O(n)$ time.[13] There are $O(n^2)$ iterations (one per subproblem), for an overall running time of $O(n^3)$.[14]

Theorem 17.6 (Properties of OptBST) *For every set* $\{1, 2, \ldots, n\}$ *of keys and nonnegative frequencies* $p_1, p_2, \ldots, p_n$, *the OptBST algorithm runs in* $O(n^3)$ *time and returns the minimum weighted search time of a binary search tree with keys* $\{1, 2, \ldots, n\}$.

Analogous to our other case studies, an optimal binary search tree can be reconstructed by tracing back through the final array A computed by the OptBST algorithm.[15]

---

[13]Can you think of an optimization that avoids computing the sum $\sum_{k=i}^{i+s} p_k$ from scratch for each of the subproblems?

[14]In the notation of (16.1), $f(n) = O(n^2)$, $g(n) = O(n)$, and $h(n) = O(1)$. This is our first case study in which the per-subproblem work $g(n)$ is not bounded by a constant.

[15]If the OptBST algorithm is modified to cache the roots that determine the recurrence values for each subproblem (i.e., the value of r such that $A[i][i + s] = A[i][r - 1] + A[r + 1][i + s]$), the reconstruction algorithm runs in $O(n)$ time (as you should verify). Otherwise, it must recompute these roots and runs in $O(n^2)$ time.

17.2.8   Improving the Running Time

The cubic running time of the OptBST algorithm certainly does not qualify as blazingly fast. The first piece of good news is that the algorithm is way faster than exhaustively searching through all (exponentially many) binary search trees. The algorithm is fast enough to solve problems with n in the hundreds in a reasonable amount of time, but not problems with n in the thousands. The second piece of good news is that a slight tweak to the algorithm brings its running time down to $O(n^2)$.[16] This is fast enough to solve problems with n in the thousands and perhaps even tens of thousands in a reasonable amount of time.

17.2.9   Solution to Quizzes 17.4–17.5

Solution to Quiz 17.4

Correct answer: (b). For the first search tree, the "1" contributes $.8 \times 2 = 1.6$ to the average search time (because its frequency is .8 and its search time is 2), the "2" contributes $.1 \times 1 = .1$, and the "3" contributes $.1 \times 2 = .2$, for a total of $1.6 + .1 + .2 = 1.9$.

The second search tree has a larger maximum search time (3 instead of 2), but the lucky case of a search for the root is now much more likely. The "1" now contributes $.8 \times 1 = .8$ to the average search time, the "2" contributes $.1 \times 2 = .2$, and the "3" contributes $.1 \times 3 = .3$, for a total of $.8 + .2 + .3 = 1.3$.

Solution to Quiz 17.5

Correct answer: (d). Our vision is of a dynamic programming algorithm that tries all possibilities for the root, recursively computing or looking up the optimal left and right subtrees for each possibility. This strategy would be hopeless unless the left and right subtrees of an optimal binary search tree were guaranteed to be optimal in their own right for the corresponding subproblems. Thus, for our approach to succeed, the answer should be either (c) or (d). Moreover, by the search tree property, given the root r we know the demographics of its two subtrees—the keys less than r belong to the root's left subtree, and those greater than r to its right subtree.

---

[16]Here's the idea. First, compute in advance all sums of the form $\sum_{k=i}^{j} p_k$; this can be done in $O(n^2)$ time (do you see how?). Then, along with each subproblem solution $A[i][j]$, store the choice of the root $r(i,j)$ that minimizes $A[i][r-1] + A[r+1][j]$ or, equivalently, the root of an optimal search tree for the subproblem. (If there are multiple such roots, use the smallest one.)

The key lemma is an easy-to-believe (but tricky-to-prove) monotonicity property: Adding a new maximum (respectively, minimum) element to a subproblem can only make the root of an optimal search tree larger (respectively, smaller). Intuitively, any change in the root should be in service of rebalancing the total frequency of keys between its left and right subtrees.

Assuming this lemma, for every subproblem with $i < j$, the optimal root $r(i,j)$ is at least $r(i,j-1)$ and at most $r(i+1,j)$. (If $i = j$, then $r(i,j)$ must be i.) Thus, there's no point in exhaustively searching all the roots between i and j—the roots between $r(i,j-1)$ and $r(i+1,j)$ suffice. In the worst case, there could be as many as n such roots. In aggregate over all $\Theta(n^2)$ subproblems, however, the number of roots examined is

$$\sum_{i=1}^{n-1} \sum_{j=i+1}^{n} (r(i+1,j) - r(i,j-1) + 1),$$

which after cancellations is only $O(n^2)$ (as you should check). For further details, see the paper "Optimum Binary Search Trees," by Donald E. Knuth (*Acta Informatica*, 1971).

The Upshot

✰ In the sequence alignment problem, the input comprises two strings and penalties for gaps and mismatches, and the goal is to compute an alignment of the two strings with the minimum-possible total penalty.

✰ The sequence alignment problem can be solved using dynamic programming in $O(mn)$ time, where m and n are the lengths of the input strings.

✰ Subproblems correspond to prefixes of the two input strings. There are three different ways in which an optimal solution can be built from optimal solutions to smaller subproblems, resulting in a recurrence with three cases.

✰ In the optimal binary search tree problem, the input is a set of n keys and nonnegative frequencies for them, and the goal is to compute a binary search tree containing these keys with the minimum-possible weighted search time.

✰ The optimal binary search tree problem can be solved using dynamic programming in $O(n^3)$ time, where n is the number of keys. A slight tweak to the algorithm reduces the running time to $O(n^2)$.

✰ Subproblems correspond to contiguous subsets of the input keys. There are n different ways in which an optimal solution can be built from optimal solutions to smaller subproblems, resulting in a recurrence with n cases.

Test Your Understanding

Problem 17.1 *(S)* For the sequence alignment input in Quiz 17.1, what are the final array entries of the NW algorithm from Section 17.1?

Problem 17.2 *(H)* The Knapsack algorithm from Section 16.5 and the NW algorithm from Section 17.1 both fill in a two-dimensional array using a double for loop. Suppose we reverse the order of the for loops—literally cutting and pasting the second loop in front of the first, without changing the pseudocode in any other way. Are the resulting algorithms well defined and correct?

a) Neither algorithm remains well defined and correct after reversing the order of the for loops.

b) Both algorithms remain well defined and correct after reversing the order of the for loops.

c) The `Knapsack` algorithm remains well defined and correct after reversing the order of the for loops, but the `NW` algorithm does not.

d) The `NW` algorithm remains well defined and correct after reversing the order of the for loops, but the `Knapsack` algorithm does not.

Problem 17.3 *(S)* In the optimal binary search tree problem, the definition of the weighted search time (17.1) suggests placing high-frequency keys close to the root of the search tree. Why not follow a greedy approach, placing the highest-frequency key at the root and completing the tree recursively?

GreedyBST

Input: keys $\{i, i+1, \ldots, j\}$ with nonnegative frequencies $p_i, p_{i+1}, \ldots, p_j$.
Output: a binary search tree with keys $\{i, i+1, \ldots, j\}$.

---

if the input is empty **then**
     return the empty search tree
$r := \text{argmax}_{k=i}^{j}\, p_k$ `// root=highest-frequency key`
`// recursively compute left, right subtrees`
$T_1 := \text{GreedyBST}(\{i, i+1, \ldots, r-1\}, p_i, p_{i+1}, \ldots, p_{r-1})$
$T_2 := \text{GreedyBST}(\{r+1, r+2, \ldots, j\}, p_{r+1}, p_{r+2}, \ldots, p_j)$
return the search tree with root r, left subtree T_1, and right subtree T_2

(The outermost call to `GreedyBST` is given as input the full set $\{1, 2, \ldots, n\}$ of keys and their frequencies.) Show by example that the `GreedyBST` algorithm does not always return a search tree with the minimum-possible weighted search time.

Problem 17.4 *(S)* Consider an instance of the optimal binary search tree problem with keys $\{1, 2, \ldots, 7\}$ and the following frequencies:

Symbol	Frequency
1	20
2	5
3	17
4	10
5	20
6	3
7	25

What are the final array entries of the `OptBST` algorithm from Section 17.2?

Problem 17.5 *(H)* Recall the `WIS` algorithm (Section 16.2), the `NW` algorithm (Section 17.1), and the `OptBST` algorithm (Section 17.2). The space requirements of these algorithms are proportional to the number of subproblems: $\Theta(n)$, where n is the number of vertices; $\Theta(mn)$, where m and n are the lengths of the input strings; and $\Theta(n^2)$, where n is the number of keys, respectively.

Suppose we only want to compute the value of an optimal solution and don't care about reconstruction. How much space do you then really need to run each of the three algorithms, respectively?

a) $\Theta(1)$, $\Theta(1)$, and $\Theta(n)$

b) $\Theta(1)$, $\Theta(n)$, and $\Theta(n)$

c) $\Theta(1)$, $\Theta(n)$, and $\Theta(n^2)$

d) $\Theta(n)$, $\Theta(n)$, and $\Theta(n^2)$

Challenge Problems

Problem 17.6 *(S)* The following problems all take as input two strings X and Y, with lengths m and n, over some alphabet Σ. Which of them can be solved in $O(mn)$ time? (Choose all that apply.)

a) Consider the variation of sequence alignment in which, instead of a single gap penalty α_{gap}, you are given two positive numbers a and b. The penalty for inserting k gaps in a row is now defined as $ak + b$, rather than $k \cdot \alpha_{gap}$. The other penalties (for matching two symbols) are defined as before. The goal is to compute the minimum-possible penalty of an alignment under this new cost model.

b) Compute the length of a longest common subsequence of X and Y. (A subsequence need not comprise consecutive symbols. For example, the longest common subsequence of "abcdef" and "afebcd" is "abcd.")[17]

c) Assume that X and Y have the same length n. Determine whether there exists a permutation f, mapping each $i \in \{1, 2, \ldots, n\}$ to a distinct value $f(i) \in \{1, 2, \ldots, n\}$, such that $X_i = Y_{f(i)}$ for every $i = 1, 2, \ldots, n$.

d) Compute the length of a longest common substring of X and Y. (A substring is a subsequence comprising consecutive symbols. For example, "bcd" is a substring of "abcdef," while "bdf" is not.)

Problem 17.7 *(H)* In the sequence alignment problem, suppose you knew that the input strings were relatively similar, in the sense that there is an optimal alignment that uses at most k gaps, where k is much smaller than the lengths m and n of the strings. Show how to compute the NW score in $O((m + n)k)$ time.

Problem 17.8 *(H)* There are seven kinds of Tetris pieces.[18] Design a dynamic programming algorithm that, given $x_1, x_2, \ldots, x_7$ copies of each respective piece, determines whether you can tile a 10-by-n board with exactly those pieces (placing them however and wherever you want—not necessarily in Tetris order). The running time of your algorithm should be polynomial in n.

---

[17] A dynamic programming algorithm for the longest common subsequence problem underlies the `diff` command familiar to users of Unix and Git.

[18] See `https://tetris.fandom.com/wiki/Tetromino`.

Programming Problems

Problem 17.9 Implement in your favorite programming language the NW and OptBST algorithms, along with their reconstruction algorithms. For OptBST, include Knuth's optimization (see footnote 16). For your reconstruction algorithms, take advantage of the optimization suggested in footnote 7 of Chapter 16. (See www.algorithmsilluminated.org for test cases and challenge data sets.)

Chapter 18

Shortest Paths Revisited

This chapter centers around two famous dynamic programming algorithms for computing shortest paths in a graph. Both are slower but more general than Dijkstra's shortest-path algorithm (covered in Chapter 9). The Bellman-Ford algorithm (Section 18.2) solves the single-source shortest path problem with negative edge lengths; it also has the benefit of being "more distributed" than Dijkstra's algorithm and, for this reason, has deeply influenced the way in which traffic is routed in the Internet. The Floyd-Warshall algorithm (Section 18.4) also accommodates negative edge lengths and computes shortest-path distances from *every* origin to every destination.

18.1 Shortest Paths with Negative Edge Lengths

18.1.1 The Single-Source Shortest-Path Problem

In the single-source shortest path problem, the input consists of a directed graph $G = (V, E)$ with a real-valued length ℓ_e for each edge $e \in E$ and a designated origin $s \in V$, which is called either the *source vertex* or the *starting vertex*. The *length* of a path is the sum of the lengths of its edges. The responsibility of an algorithm is to compute, for every possible destination v, the minimum length $dist(s, v)$ of a directed path in G from s to v. (If no such path exists, $dist(s, v)$ is defined as $+\infty$.) For example, the shortest-path distances from s in the graph

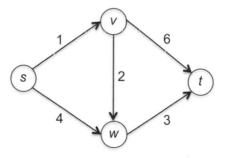

are $dist(s, s) = 0$, $dist(s, v) = 1$, $dist(s, w) = 3$, and $dist(s, t) = 6$.

Problem: Single-Source Shortest Paths (Preliminary Version)

Input: A directed graph $G = (V, E)$, a starting vertex $s \in V$, and a real-valued length ℓ_e for each edge $e \in E$.

Output: the shortest-path distance $dist(s, v)$ for every vertex $v \in V$.

We can assume that the input graph has no parallel edges: If there are multiple edges with the same beginning and end, we can throw away all but the shortest one without changing the problem.

For example, if every edge e has unit length $\ell_e = 1$, a shortest path minimizes the hop count (i.e., number of edges) between its origin and destination.[1] Or, if the graph represents a road network and the length of each edge the expected travel time from one end to the other, the single-source shortest path problem is the problem of computing driving times from an origin (the starting vertex) to all possible destinations.

Section 10.4 described a blazingly fast heap-based implementation of Dijkstra's algorithm (Chapter 9), which solves the special case of the single-source shortest path problem in which every edge length ℓ_e is nonnegative. The running time of this implementation is $O((m + n) \log n)$, where m and n denote the number of edges and vertices of the input graph, respectively (Theorem 10.4). Dijkstra's algorithm, great as it is, is *not* always correct in graphs with negative edge lengths. It fails even in a trivial example like:

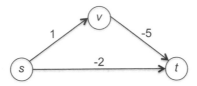

If we want to accommodate negative edge lengths, we'll need a new shortest-path algorithm.[2]

18.1.2   Negative Cycles

Who cares about negative edge lengths? In many applications, like computing driving directions, edge lengths are automatically nonnegative (barring a time machine) and there's nothing to worry about. But remember that paths in a graph can represent abstract sequences of decisions. For example, perhaps you want to compute a profitable sequence of financial transactions that involves both buying and selling. This problem corresponds to finding a shortest path in a graph with edge lengths that are both positive and negative.

With negative edge lengths, we must be careful about what we even *mean* by "shortest-path distance." It's clear enough in the three-vertex example above, with $dist(s, s) = 0$, $dist(s, v) = 1$, and $dist(s, t) = -4$. What about in a graph like the following?

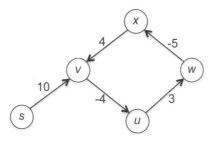

---

[1] As we saw in Section 8.2, this special case of the single-source shortest path problem can be solved in linear time using breadth-first search.

[2] Recall from Section 9.3 that you cannot reduce the single-source shortest path problem with general edge lengths to the special case of nonnegative edge lengths by adding a large positive constant to the length of every edge. In the three-vertex example above, adding 5 to every edge length would change the shortest path from $s \to v \to t$ to $s \to t$.

The issue is that this graph has a *negative cycle*, meaning a directed cycle in which the sum of its edges' lengths is negative. What might we mean by a "shortest s-v path"?

Option #1: Allow cycles.   The first option is to allow s-v paths that include one or more cycles. But then, in the presence of a negative cycle, a "shortest path" need not even exist! For example, in the graph above, there is a one-hop s-v path with length 10. Tacking a cycle traversal on at the end produces a five-hop s-v path with total length 8. Adding a second traversal increases the number of hops to 9 but decreases the overall length to 6. . . and so on, ad infinitum. Thus, there is no shortest s-v path, and the only sensible definition of $dist(s, v)$ is $-\infty$.

Option #2: Forbid cycles.   What if we consider only paths without cycles? With no repeat vertices allowed, we have only a finite number of paths to worry about. The "shortest s-v path" would then be whichever one has the smallest length. This definition makes perfect sense, but there's a more subtle problem: In the presence of a negative cycle, this version of the single-source shortest path problem is what's called an "NP-hard problem." Part IV of the book discusses such problems at length (and see, in particular, Theorem 19.1); for now, all you need to know is that NP-hard problems, unlike almost all the problems we've studied so far in this book, do not seem to admit any algorithm that is guaranteed to be correct and to run in polynomial time.[3]

Both options are disasters, so should we give up? Never! Even if we concede that negative cycles are problematic, we can aspire to solve the single-source shortest path problem in instances that have no negative cycles, such as the three-vertex example on page 416. This brings us to the revised version of the single-source shortest path problem.

Problem: Single-Source Shortest Paths (Revised Version)

Input: A directed graph $G = (V, E)$, a starting vertex $s \in V$, and a real-valued length ℓ_e for each edge $e \in E$.

Output: One of the following:

    (i) the shortest-path distance $dist(s, v)$ for every vertex $v \in V$; or

    (ii) a declaration that G contains a negative cycle.

Thus, we're after an algorithm that either computes the correct shortest-path distances or offers a compelling excuse for its failure (in the form of a negative cycle). Any such algorithm returns the correct shortest-path distances in every input graph that has no negative cycles.[4]

Suppose a graph has no negative cycles. What does that buy us?

---

[3]More precisely, any polynomial-time algorithm for any NP-hard problem would disprove the famous "P $\neq$ NP" conjecture and resolve what is arguably the most important open question in all of computer science. See Part IV of the book for the full story.

[4]For example, suppose the edges of the input graph and their lengths represent financial transactions and their costs, with vertices corresponding to different asset portfolios. Then, a negative cycle corresponds to an arbitrage opportunity. In many cases there will be no such opportunities; if there is one, you'd be very happy to identify it!

Quiz 18.1

Consider an instance of the single-source shortest path problem with n vertices, m edges, a starting vertex s, and no negative cycles. Assume that $m \geq n$. Which of the following is true? (Choose the strongest true statement.)

a) For every vertex v reachable from s, there is a shortest s-v path with at most $n - 1$ edges.

b) For every vertex v reachable from s, there is a shortest s-v path with at most n edges.

c) For every vertex v reachable from s, there is a shortest s-v path with at most m edges.

d) There is no finite upper bound (as a function of n and m) on the fewest number of edges in a shortest s-v path.

(See Section 18.1.3 for the solution and discussion.)

18.1.3 Solution to Quiz 18.1

Correct answer: (a). If you give me a path P between the starting vertex s and some destination vertex v containing at least n edges, I can give you back another s-v path P' with fewer edges than P and length no longer than that of P. This assertion, which is proved in the next paragraph, implies that any s-v path can be converted into an s-v path with at most $n - 1$ edges without increasing its length; hence, there is a shortest s-v path with at most $n - 1$ edges.

To see why this assertion is true, observe that a path P with at least n edges visits at least $n + 1$ vertices and thus makes a repeat visit to some vertex w.[5] Splicing out the cyclic subpath between successive visits to w produces a path P' with the same endpoints as P but fewer edges; see also Figure 15.1 and footnote 3 in Chapter 15. The length of P' is the same as that of P, less the sum of the edge lengths in the spliced-out cycle. *Because the input graph has no negative cycles*, this sum is nonnegative and the length of P' is less than or equal to that of P.

18.2 The Bellman-Ford Algorithm

The Bellman-Ford algorithm solves the single-source shortest path problem in graphs with negative edge lengths in the sense that it either computes the correct shortest-path distances or correctly determines that the input graph has a negative cycle.[6] This algorithm will follow

---

[5]This is equivalent to the Pigeonhole Principle: No matter how you stuff $n + 1$ pigeons into n holes, there will be a hole with at least two pigeons. (Last seen in our discussion of hash tables in Chapter 12.)

[6]This algorithm was discovered independently by many different people in the mid-to-late 1950s, including Richard E. Bellman and Lester R. Ford, Jr., though ironically Alfonso Shimbel appears to have been the first. History buffs should check out the paper "On the History of the Shortest Path Problem," by Alexander Schrijver (*Documenta Mathematica*, 2012).

naturally from the design pattern that we used in our other dynamic programming case studies.

18.2.1   The Subproblems

As always with dynamic programming, the most important step is to understand the different ways that an optimal solution might be built up from optimal solutions to smaller subproblems. Formulating the right measure of subproblem size can be tricky for graph problems. Your first guess might be that subproblems should correspond to subgraphs of the original input graph, with subproblem size equal to the number of vertices or edges in the subgraph. This idea worked well for the WIS problem in path graphs (Section 16.2), in which the vertices were inherently ordered and it was relatively clear which subgraphs to focus on (prefixes of the input graph). With a general graph, however, there is no intrinsic ordering of the vertices or edges, and few clues about which subgraphs are the relevant ones.

The Bellman-Ford algorithm takes a different tack, one inspired by the inherently sequential nature of the *output* of the single-source shortest path problem (i.e., of paths). Intuitively, you might expect that a prefix P' of a shortest path P would itself be a shortest path, albeit to a different destination:

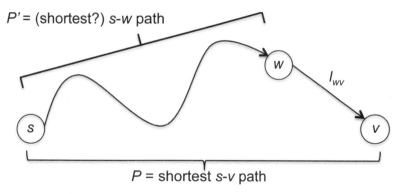

P' = (shortest?) s-w path

P = shortest s-v path

Yet even assuming that this is true (which it is, as we'll see), in what sense is the prefix P' solving a "smaller" subproblem than the original path P? With negative edge lengths, the length of P' might even be larger than that of P. What we do know is that P' contains fewer *edges* than P, which motivates the inspired idea behind the Bellman-Ford algorithm: Introduce a hop count parameter i that artificially restricts the number of edges allowed in a path, with "bigger" subproblems having larger edge budgets i. Then, a path prefix can indeed be viewed as a solution to a smaller subproblem.

For example, consider the graph

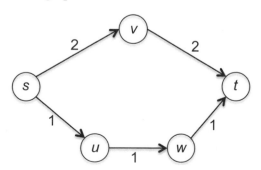

and, for the destination t, the subproblems corresponding to successive values of the edge budget i. When i is 0 or 1, there are no s-t paths with i edges or less, and no solutions to the corresponding subproblems. The shortest-path distance subject to the hop count constraint is effectively $+\infty$. When i is 2, there is a unique s-t path with at most i edges ($s \to v \to t$), and the value of the subproblem is 4. If we bump up the edge budget i to 3 (or more), the path $s \to u \to w \to t$ becomes eligible and lowers the shortest-path distance from 4 to 3.

Bellman-Ford Algorithm: Subproblems

Compute $L_{i,v}$, the length of a shortest path with at most i edges from s to v in G, with cycles allowed. (If no such path exists, define $L_{i,v}$ as $+\infty$.)

(For each $i \in \{0, 1, 2, \ldots\}$ and $v \in V$.)

Paths with cycles are allowed as solutions to a subproblem. If a path uses an edge multiple times, each use counts against its hop count budget. An optimal solution might well traverse a negative cycle over and over, but eventually it will exhaust its (finite) edge budget. For a fixed destination v, the set of allowable paths grows with i, and so $L_{i,v}$ either stays the same or decreases as i increases.

Unlike our previous dynamic programming case studies, every subproblem works with the full input (rather than a prefix or subset of it); the genius of these subproblems lies in how they control the allowable size of the output.

As stated, the parameter i could be an arbitrarily large positive integer and there is an infinite number of subproblems. The solution to Quiz 18.1 hints that perhaps not all of them are important. Shortly, we'll see that there's no reason to bother with subproblems in which i is greater than n, the number of vertices, which implies that there are $O(n^2)$ relevant subproblems.[7]

18.2.2   Optimal Substructure

With our clever choice of subproblems in hand, we can study how optimal solutions must be built up from optimal solutions to smaller subproblems. Consider an input graph $G = (V, E)$ with starting vertex $s \in V$, and fix a subproblem, which is defined by a destination vertex $v \in V$ and a hop count constraint $i \in \{1, 2, 3, \ldots\}$. Suppose P is an s-v path with at most i edges, and moreover is a shortest such path. What must it look like? If P doesn't even bother to use up its edge budget, the answer is easy.

Case 1: P has $i-1$ or fewer edges.   In this case, the path P can immediately be interpreted as a solution to the smaller subproblem with edge budget $i - 1$ (still with destination v). The path P must be an optimal solution to this smaller subproblem, as any shorter s-v path with at most $i - 1$ edges would also be a superior solution to the original subproblem, contradicting the purported optimality of P.

---

[7]If this strikes you as a lot of subproblems, don't forget that the single-source shortest path problem is really n different problems rolled up into one (with one problem per destination vertex). There's only a linear number of subproblems per value in the output, which is as good or better than all our other dynamic programming algorithms.

If the path P uses its full edge budget, we follow the pattern of several previous case studies and pluck off the last edge of P to obtain a solution to a smaller subproblem.

Case 2: P has i edges.   Let L denote the length of P. Let P' denote the first $i - 1$ edges of P, and (w, v) its final hop:

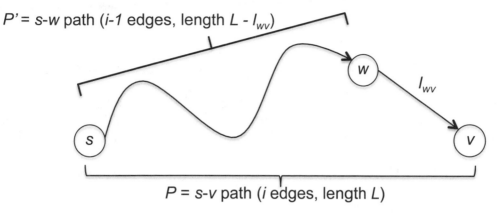

The prefix P' is an s-w path with at most $i - 1$ edges and length $L - \ell_{wv}$.[8] There cannot be a shorter such path: If P^* were an s-w path with at most $i - 1$ edges and length $L^* < L - \ell_{wv}$, appending the edge (w, v) to P^* would produce an s-v path with at most i edges and length $L^* + \ell_{wv} < (L - \ell_{wv}) + \ell_{wv} = L$, contradicting the optimality of P for the original subproblem.[9]

This case analysis narrows down the possibilities for an optimal solution to a subproblem to a small number of candidates.

Lemma 18.1 (Bellman-Ford Optimal Substructure) *Let $G = (V, E)$ be a directed graph with real-valued edge lengths and starting vertex $s \in V$. Suppose $i \geq 1$ and $v \in V$, and let P be a shortest s-v path in G with at most i edges, with cycles allowed. Then, P is either:*

(i) a shortest s-v path with at most $i - 1$ edges; or

(ii) for some $w \in V$, a shortest s-w path with at most $i - 1$ edges, supplemented with the edge $(w, v) \in E$.

How many candidates, exactly?

Quiz 18.2

How many candidates are there for an optimal solution to a subproblem with the destination v? (Let n denote the number of vertices in the input graph. The in- and out-degree of a vertex is the number of incoming and outgoing edges, respectively.)

---

[8]The path P' has *exactly* $i - 1$ edges. However, we want to establish its superiority to all competing s-w paths with $i - 1$ edges *or fewer*.

[9]If P^* already includes the vertex v, adding the edge (w, v) to it creates a cycle; this is not an issue for the proof, as our subproblem definition permits paths with cycles.

a) 2

b) 1 + the in-degree of v

c) 1 + the out-degree of v

d) n

(See Section 18.2.9 for the solution and discussion.)

18.2.3 Recurrence

As usual, the next step is to compile our understanding of optimal substructure into a recurrence that implements exhaustive search over the possible candidates for an optimal solution. The best of the candidates identified in Lemma 18.1 must be an optimal solution.

Corollary 18.2 (Bellman-Ford Recurrence) *With the assumptions and notation of Lemma 18.1, let $L_{i,v}$ denote the minimum length of an s-v path with at most i edges, with cycles allowed. (If there are no such paths, then $L_{i,v} = +\infty$.) For every $i \geq 1$ and $v \in V$,*

$$L_{i,v} = \min \left\{ \begin{array}{cc} L_{i-1,v} & \textit{(Case 1)} \\ \min_{(w,v)\in E}\{L_{i-1,w} + \ell_{wv}\} & \textit{(Case 2)} \end{array} \right\}. \qquad (18.1)$$

The outer "min" in the recurrence implements the exhaustive search over Case 1 and Case 2. The inner "min" implements the exhaustive search inside Case 2 over all possible choices for the final hop of a shortest path. If $L_{i-1,v}$ and all the relevant $L_{i-1,w}$'s are $+\infty$, then v is unreachable from s in i or fewer hops, and we interpret the recurrence as computing $L_{i,v} = +\infty$.

18.2.4 When Should We Stop?

With so much dynamic programming experience now under your belt, your Pavlovian response to the recurrence in Corollary 18.2 might be to write down a dynamic programming algorithm that uses it repeatedly to systematically solve every subproblem. Presumably, the algorithm would start by solving the smallest subproblems (with edge budget $i = 0$), followed by the next-smallest subproblems (with $i = 1$), and so on. One little issue: In the subproblems defined in Section 18.2.1, the edge budget i can be an arbitrarily large positive integer, which means there's an infinite number of subproblems. How do we know when to stop?

A good stopping criterion follows from the observation that the solutions to a given batch of subproblems, with a fixed edge budget i and v ranging over all possible destinations, depend only on the solutions to the previous batch of subproblems (with edge budget $i - 1$). Thus, if one batch of subproblems ever has exactly the same optimal solutions as the previous one (with Case 1 of the recurrence winning for every destination), these optimal solutions will remain the same forevermore.

Lemma 18.3 (Bellman-Ford Stopping Criterion) *Under the assumptions and notation of Corollary 18.2, if for some $k \geq 0$*

$$L_{k+1,v} = L_{k,v} \quad \textit{for every destination } v,$$

then:

(a) $L_{i,v} = L_{k,v}$ *for every* $i \geq k$ *and destination* v; *and*

(b) *for every destination* v, $L_{k,v}$ *is the correct shortest-path distance* $dist(s, v)$ *from* s *to* v *in* G.

Proof: By assumption, the input to the recurrence in (18.1) in the $(k + 2)$th batch of subproblems (i.e., the $L_{k+1,v}$'s) is the same as it was for the $(k+1)$th batch (i.e., the $L_{k,v}$'s). Thus, the output of the recurrence (the $L_{k+2,v}$'s) will also be the same as it was for the previous batch (the $L_{k+1,v}$'s). Repeating this argument as many times as necessary shows that the $L_{i,v}$'s remain the same for all batches $i \geq k$. This proves part (a).

For part (b), suppose for contradiction that $L_{k,v} \neq dist(s, v)$ for some destination v. Because $L_{k,v}$ is the minimum length of an s-v path with at most k hops, there must be an s-v path with $i > k$ hops and length smaller than $L_{k,v}$. But then $L_{i,v} < L_{k,v}$, contradicting part (a) of the lemma. $\mathcal{QED}$

Lemma 18.3 promises that it's safe to stop as soon as subproblem solutions stabilize, with $L_{k+1,v} = L_{k,v}$ for some $k \geq 0$ and all $v \in V$. But will this ever happen? In general, no. *If the input graph has no negative cycles*, however, subproblem solutions are guaranteed to stabilize by the time i reaches n, the number of vertices.

Lemma 18.4 (Bellman-Ford with No Negative Cycles) *Under the assumptions and nota-tion of Corollary 18.2, and also assuming that the input graph* G *has no negative cycles,*

$$L_{n,v} = L_{n-1,v} \quad \textit{for every destination } v,$$

where n *is the number of vertices in the input graph.*

Proof: The solution to Quiz 18.1 implies that, for every destination v, there is a shortest s-v path with at most $n - 1$ edges. In other words, increasing the edge budget i from $n - 1$ to n (or to any bigger number) has no effect on the minimum length of an s-v path. $\mathcal{QED}$

Lemma 18.4 shows that if the input graph does not have a negative cycle, subproblem solutions stabilize by the nth batch. Or, equivalently, in contrapositive form: If subproblem solutions *fail* to stabilize by the nth batch, the input graph *does* have a negative cycle.

In tandem, Lemmas 18.3 and 18.4 tell us the last batch of subproblems that we need to bother with: the batch with $i = n$. If subproblem solutions stabilize (with $L_{n,v} = L_{n-1,v}$ for all $v \in V$), Lemma 18.3 implies that the $L_{n-1,v}$'s are the correct shortest-path distances. If subproblem solutions don't stabilize (with $L_{n,v} \neq L_{n-1,v}$ for some $v \in V$), the contrapositive of Lemma 18.4 implies that the input graph G contains a negative cycle, in which case the algorithm is absolved from computing shortest-path distances. (Recall the problem definition in Section 18.1.2.)

18.2.5   Pseudocode

The justifiably famous Bellman-Ford algorithm now writes itself: Use the recurrence in Corollary 18.2 to systematically solve all the subproblems, up to an edge budget of $i = n$, where n denotes the number of vertices.

Bellman–Ford

Input: directed graph $G = (V, E)$ in adjacency-list representation, a starting vertex $s \in V$, and a real-valued length ℓ_e for each $e \in E$.
Output: $dist(s, v)$ for every vertex $v \in V$, or a declaration that G contains a negative cycle.

```
// subproblem array
// (i indexed from 0, v indexes V)
```
$A := (|V| + 1) \times |V|$ two-dimensional array
```
// base cases (i = 0)
```
$A[0][s] := 0$
for each $v \neq s$ **do**
$\quad A[0][v] := +\infty$
```
// systematically solve all subproblems
```
for $i := 1$ to $|V|$ **do**   `// subproblem size`
$\quad$ stable := TRUE   `// for early stopping`
$\quad$ **for** $v \in V$ **do**
```
      // use recurrence from Corollary 18.2
```
$\quad\quad A[i][v] := \min\{\underbrace{A[i-1][v]}_{\text{Case 1}}, \underbrace{\min_{(w,v)\in E}\{A[i-1][w] + \ell_{wv}\}}_{\text{Case 2}}\}$
$\quad\quad$ **if** $A[i][v] \neq A[i-1][v]$ **then**
$\quad\quad\quad$ stable := FALSE
$\quad$ **if** stable = TRUE **then**   `// done by Lemma 18.3`
$\quad\quad$ return $\{A[i-1][v]\}_{v \in V}$
```
// failed to stabilize in |V| iterations
```
return "negative cycle"   `// correct by Lemma 18.4`

The double for loop reflects the two parameters used to define subproblems, the edge budget i and the destination vertex v. By the time a loop iteration must compute the subproblem solution $A[i][v]$, all values of the form $A[i-1][v]$ or $A[i-1][w]$ have already been computed in the previous iteration of the outer for loop (or in the base cases) and are ready and waiting to be looked up in constant time.

Induction (on i) shows that the Bellman–Ford algorithm solves every subproblem correctly, with $A[i][v]$ assigned the correct value $L_{i,v}$; the recurrence in Corollary 18.2 justifies the inductive step. If subproblem solutions stabilize, the algorithm returns the correct shortest-path distances (by Lemma 18.3). If not, the algorithm correctly declares that the input graph contains a negative cycle (by Lemma 18.4).

18.2.6 Example

For an example of the Bellman–Ford algorithm in action, consider the following input graph:

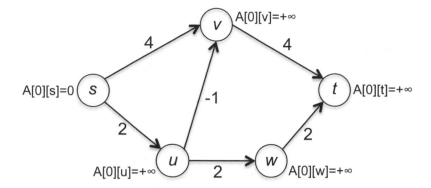

The vertices are labeled with the solutions to the first batch of subproblems (with $i = 0$).

Each iteration of the algorithm evaluates the recurrence (18.1) at each vertex, using the values computed in the previous iteration. In the first iteration, the recurrence evaluates to 0 at s (s has no incoming edges, so Case 2 of the recurrence is vacuous); to 2 at u (because $A[0][s] + \ell_{su} = 2$); to 4 at v (because $A[0][s] + \ell_{sv} = 4$); and to $+\infty$ at w and t (because $A[0][u]$ and $A[0][v]$ are both $+\infty$):

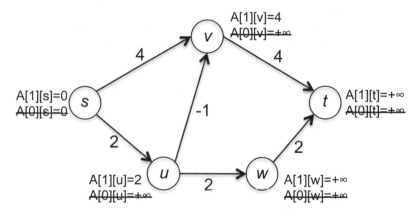

In the next iteration, both s and u inherit solutions from the previous iteration. The value at v drops from 4 (corresponding to the one-hop path $s \to v$) to 1 (corresponding to the two-hop path $s \to u \to v$). The new values at w and t are 4 (because $A[1][u] + \ell_{uw} = 4$) and 8 (because $A[1][v] + \ell_{vt} = 8$):

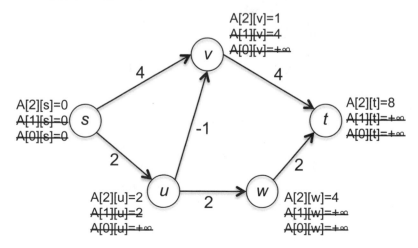

Note that the decrease in shortest-path distance to v in this iteration does not propagate to t immediately, only in the next iteration.

In the third iteration, the value at t drops to 5 (because $A[2][v] + \ell_{vt} = 5$, which is better than both $A[2][t] = 8$ and $A[2][w] + \ell_{wt} = 6$) and the other four vertices inherit solutions from the previous iteration:

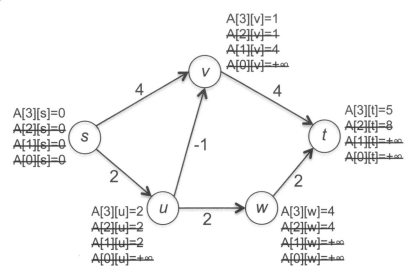

Nothing changes in the fourth iteration:

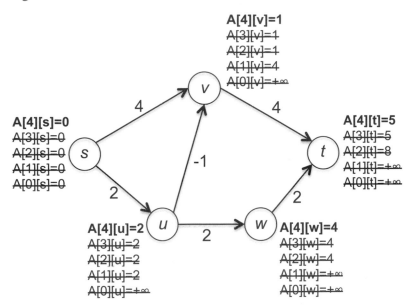

and at this point the algorithm halts with the correct shortest-path distances.[10]

18.2.7 Running Time

The running time analysis of the `Bellman-Ford` algorithm is more interesting than those of our other dynamic programming algorithms.

---

[10]For an example of the algorithm in action on an input graph with a negative cycle, see Problem 18.1.

Quiz 18.3

What's the running time of the `Bellman-Ford` algorithm, as a function of m (the number of edges) and n (the number of vertices)? (Choose the strongest true statement.)

   a) $O(n^2)$

   b) $O(mn)$

   c) $O(n^3)$

   d) $O(mn^2)$

(See Section 18.2.9 for the solution and discussion.)

Summarizing everything we now know about the `Bellman-Ford` algorithm:

Theorem 18.5 (Properties of `Bellman-Ford`) *For every input graph* $G = (V, E)$ *with* n *vertices,* m *edges, real-valued edge lengths, and a starting vertex* s, *the* `Bellman-Ford` *algorithm runs in* $O(mn)$ *time and either:*

(i) returns the shortest-path distance from s to every destination $v \in V$; or

(ii) detects that G contains a negative cycle.

As usual, shortest paths can be reconstructed by tracing back through the final array A computed by the `Bellman-Ford` algorithm.[11]

18.2.8   Internet Routing

The Bellman-Ford algorithm solves a more general problem than Dijkstra's algorithm (because it accommodates negative edge lengths). Its second advantage is that it is more "distributed" than Dijkstra's algorithm, and for this reason has played the more prominent role in the evolution of Internet routing protocols.[12] Evaluating the recurrence (18.1) at a vertex v requires information only about vertices directly connected to v: the vertices w with an edge (w, v). This suggests that the Bellman-Ford algorithm might be implementable even at an Internet scale, with each machine communicating only with its immediate neighbors and performing only local computations, blissfully unaware of what's going on in the rest of the network. Indeed, the Bellman-Ford algorithm directly inspired the early Internet routing

---

[11]For reconstruction purposes, it's a good idea to add one line of code that caches with each vertex v the most recent predecessor w that triggered a Case 2-update of the form $A[i][v] := A[i-1][w] + \ell_{wv}$. (For example, with the input graph in Section 18.2.6, the vertex v's predecessor would be initialized to null, reset to s after the first iteration, and reset again to u after the second iteration.) You can then use the final batch of predecessors to reconstruct a shortest s-v path in $O(n)$ time, by starting at v and following the predecessor trail back to s. As a bonus, because each batch of subproblem solutions and predecessors depends only on those from the previous batch, both the forward and reconstruction passes require only $O(n)$ space (analogous to Problem 17.5). See the bonus video at www.algorithmsilluminated.org for more details.

[12]The Bellman-Ford algorithm was discovered long before the Internet was a gleam in anyone's eye—over 10 years before the ARPANET, which was the earliest precursor to the Internet.

protocols RIP and RIP2—yet another example of how algorithms shape the world as we know it.[13]

18.2.9   Solutions to Quizzes 18.2–18.3

Solution to Quiz 18.2

Correct answer: (b). The optimal substructure lemma (Lemma 18.1) is stated as if there were two candidates for an optimal solution, but Case 2 comprises several subcases, one for each possible final hop (w, v) of an s-v path. The possible final hops are the incoming edges at v. Thus, Case 1 contributes one candidate and Case 2 a number of candidates equal to the in-degree of v. This in-degree could be as large as $n - 1$ in a directed graph (with no parallel edges), but is generally much smaller, especially in sparse graphs.

Solution to Quiz 18.3

Correct answer: (b). The Bellman-Ford algorithm solves $(n + 1) \cdot n = O(n^2)$ different subproblems, where n is the number of vertices. *If* the algorithm performed only a constant amount of work per subproblem (like in all our previous dynamic programming algorithms aside from OptBST), the running time of the algorithm would also be $O(n^2)$. But solving a subproblem for a destination v boils down to computing the recurrence in Corollary 18.2 which, by Quiz 18.2, involves exhaustive search through $1 + \text{in-deg}(v)$ candidates, where $\text{in-deg}(v)$ is the number of incoming edges at v.[14] Because the in-degree of a vertex could be as large as $n - 1$, this would seem to give a running time bound of $O(n)$ per-subproblem, for an overall running time bound of $O(n^3)$.

We can do better. Zoom in on a fixed iteration of the outer for loop of the algorithm, with some fixed value of i. The total work performed over all iterations of the inner for loop is proportional to

$$\sum_{v \in V} (1 + \text{in-deg}(v)) = n + \underbrace{\sum_{v \in V} \text{in-deg}(v)}_{=m}.$$

The sum of the in-degrees also goes by a simpler name: m, the number of edges. To see this, imagine removing all the edges from the input graph and adding them back in, one by one. Each new edge adds 1 to the overall edge count, and also adds 1 to the in-degree of exactly one vertex (the head of that edge).

Thus, the total work performed in each of the outer for loop iterations is $O(m + n) = O(m)$.[15] There are at most n such iterations and $O(n)$ work is performed outside the double

---

[13]"RIP" stands for "Routing Information Protocol." If you're looking to nerd out, the nitty-gritty details of the RIP and RIP2 protocols are described in RFCs 1058 and 2453, respectively. ("RFC" stands for "request for comments" and is the primary mechanism by which changes to Internet standards are vetted and communicated.) Bonus videos at www.algorithmsilluminated.org describe some of the engineering challenges involved.

[14]Assuming that the input graph is represented using adjacency lists—in particular, that an array of incoming edges is associated with each vertex—this exhaustive search can be implemented in time proportional to $1 + \text{in-deg}(v)$.

[15]Technically, this statement assumes that the number m of edges is at least a constant times n, as would be the case if, for example, every vertex v was reachable from the starting vertex s. Do you see how to tweak the algorithm to obtain a per-iteration time bound of $O(m)$ without this assumption?

for loop, leading to an overall running time bound of $O(mn)$. In sparse graphs, where m is linear or near-linear in n, this time bound is much better than the more naive bound of $O(n^3)$.

18.3   The All-Pairs Shortest Path Problem

18.3.1   Problem Definition

Why be content computing shortest-path distances from only one vertex? For example, an algorithm for computing driving directions should accommodate any possible origin; this corresponds to the *all-pairs shortest path problem*. We continue to allow negative edge lengths and negative cycles in the input graph.

Problem: All-Pairs Shortest Paths

Input: A directed graph $G = (V, E)$ with n vertices and m edges, and a real-valued length ℓ_e for each edge $e \in E$.

Output: One of the following:

   (i) the shortest-path distance $dist(v, w)$ for every ordered vertex pair $v, w \in V$; or

   (ii) a declaration that G contains a negative cycle.

There is no starting vertex in the all-pairs shortest path problem. In case (i), the algorithm is responsible for outputting n^2 numbers.

One important application of algorithms for the all-pairs shortest path problem is to computing the transitive closure of a binary relation. The latter problem is equivalent to the all-pairs reachability problem: Given a directed graph, identify all vertex pairs v, w for which the graph contains at least one v-w path (i.e., for which the hop-count shortest-path distance is finite).

18.3.2   Reduction to Single-Source Shortest Paths

If you're on the lookout for reductions (as you should be; see page 201), you might already see how to apply your ever-growing algorithmic toolbox to the all-pairs shortest path problem. One natural approach is to make repeated use of a subroutine that solves the single-source shortest path problem (like the Bellman-Ford algorithm).

Quiz 18.4

How many invocations of a single-source shortest path subroutine are needed to solve the all-pairs shortest path problem? (As usual, n denotes the number of vertices.)

   a) 1

> b) $n-1$
>
> c) n
>
> d) n^2
>
> (See Section 18.3.3 for the solution and discussion.)

Plugging in the Bellman-Ford algorithm (Theorem 18.5) for the single-source shortest path subroutine in Quiz 18.4 gives an $O(mn^2)$-time algorithm for the all-pairs shortest path problem, where m and n denote the number of edges and vertices of the input graph, respectively. Dijkstra's algorithm can substitute for the Bellman-Ford algorithm if edges' lengths are nonnegative, in which case the running time improves to $O(mn \log n)$. In sparse graphs (with $m = O(n)$ or close to it), this approaches the best we could hope for (as merely writing down the output already requires quadratic time).

Can we do better? The running time bound of $O(mn^2)$ is particularly problematic in dense graphs. For example, if $m = \Theta(n^2)$, the running time is *quartic* in n—a running time we haven't seen before and, hopefully, will never see again!

18.3.3   Solution to Quiz 18.4

Correct answer: (c). One invocation of the single-source shortest path subroutine will compute shortest-path distances from a single vertex s to every vertex of the graph (n numbers in all, out of the n^2 required). Invoking the subroutine once for each of the n choices for the starting vertex s computes shortest-path distances for every possible origin and destination. (If the input graph has a negative cycle, it will be detected by one of the invocations of the single-source shortest path subroutine.)

18.4   The Floyd-Warshall Algorithm

This section solves the all-pairs shortest path problem from scratch and presents our final case study of the dynamic programming algorithm design paradigm. The end result is another selection from the greatest hits compilation, the Floyd-Warshall algorithm.[16]

18.4.1   The Subproblems

Graphs are complex objects. Coming up with the right set of subproblems for a dynamic programming solution to a graph problem can be tricky. The ingenious idea behind the subproblems in the Bellman-Ford algorithm for the single-source shortest path problem (Section 18.2.1) is to always work with the original input graph and impose an artificial constraint on the number of edges allowed in the solution to a subproblem. The edge budget then serves as a measure of subproblem size, and a prefix of an optimal solution to a subproblem can be interpreted as a solution to a smaller subproblem (with the same origin but a different destination).

---

[16]Named after Robert W. Floyd and Stephen Warshall, but also discovered independently by a number of other researchers in the late 1950s and early 1960s.

The big idea in the Floyd-Warshall algorithm is to go one step further and artificially restrict the *identities of the vertices* that are allowed to appear in a solution. To define the subproblems, consider an input graph $G = (V, E)$ and arbitrarily assign its vertices the names $1, 2, \ldots, n$ (where $n = |V|$). Subproblems are then indexed by prefixes $\{1, 2, \ldots, k\}$ of the vertices, with k serving as the measure of subproblem size, as well as an origin v and destination w.

Floyd-Warshall Algorithm: Subproblems

Compute $L_{k,v,w}$, the minimum length of a path in the input graph G that:

(i)   begins at v and ends at w;

(ii) uses only vertices from $\{1, 2, \ldots, k\}$ as internal vertices[17]; and

(iii) does not contain a directed cycle.

(If no such path exists, define $L_{k,v,w}$ as $+\infty$.)

(For each $k \in \{0, 1, 2, \ldots, n\}$ and $v, w \in V$.)

There are $(n + 1) \cdot n \cdot n = O(n^3)$ subproblems, which is a linear number for each of the n^2 values in the output. The batch of largest subproblems (with $k = n$) corresponds to the original problem. For a fixed origin v and destination w, the set of allowable paths grows with k, and so $L_{k,v,w}$ either stays the same or decreases as k increases.

For example, consider the graph

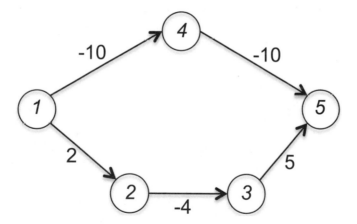

and, for the origin 1 and the destination 5, the subproblems corresponding to successive values of the prefix length k. When k is 0, 1, or 2, there are no paths from 1 to 5 such that every internal vertex belongs to the prefix $\{1, 2, \ldots, k\}$, and the subproblem's solution is $+\infty$. When $k = 3$, the path $1 \to 2 \to 3 \to 5$ becomes the unique eligible path; it has length $2 + (-4) + 5 = 3$. (The two-hop path is disqualified because it includes vertex 4 as an internal vertex. The three-hop path qualifies even though the vertex 5 does not belong to

---

[17]Every vertex of a path other than its endpoints qualifies as an *internal* vertex.

the prefix $\{1,2,3\}$; as the destination, that vertex is granted an exemption.) When $k=4$ (or larger), the subproblem solution is the length of the true shortest path $1 \to 4 \to 5$, which is -20.

In the next section, we'll see that the payoff of defining subproblems in this way is that there are only two candidates for the optimal solution to a subproblem, depending on whether it makes use of the last allowable vertex k.[18] This leads to a dynamic programming algorithm that performs only $O(1)$ work per subproblem and is therefore faster than n invocations of the Bellman-Ford algorithm (with running time $O(n^3)$ rather than $O(mn^2)$, where as usual m and n denote the number of edges and vertices, respectively).[19]

18.4.2   Optimal Substructure

Consider an input graph $G = (V, E)$ with vertices labeled 1 to n, and fix a subproblem, defined by an origin vertex v, a destination vertex w, and a prefix length $k \in \{1, 2, \ldots, n\}$. Suppose P is a v-w path with no cycles and all internal vertices in $\{1, 2, \ldots, k\}$, and moreover is a shortest such path. What must it look like? A tautology: The last allowable vertex k either appears as an internal vertex of P, or it doesn't.

Case 1: Vertex k is not an internal vertex of P.   In this case, the path P can immediately be interpreted as a solution to a smaller subproblem with prefix length $k-1$, still with origin v and destination w. The path P must be an optimal solution to the smaller subproblem; any superior solution would also be superior for the original subproblem, contradicting the assumed optimality of P.

Case 2: Vertex k is an internal vertex of P.   In this case, the path P can be interpreted as the amalgamation of *two* solutions to smaller subproblems: the prefix P_1 of P that travels from v to k, and the suffix P_2 of P that travels from k to w.

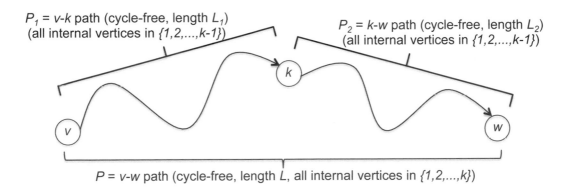

The vertex k appears in P only once (because P has no cycles!) and therefore is not an internal vertex of P_1 or P_2. Thus, we can view P_1 and P_2 as solutions to smaller subproblems,

---

[18]By contrast, the number of candidate solutions to a subproblem in the Bellman-Ford algorithm depends on the in-degree of the destination (Quiz 18.2).

[19]Ignore the uninteresting case in which m is much smaller than n; see also footnote 15.

with origins v and k and destinations k and w, respectively, and with all internal vertices in $\{1, 2, \ldots, k-1\}$.[20,21]

You can guess the next step: We want to prove that P_1 and P_2 are, in fact, *optimal* solutions to these smaller subproblems. Let L, L_1, and L_2 denote the lengths of P, P_1, and P_2, respectively. Because P is the union of P_1 and P_2, $L = L_1 + L_2$.

Suppose, for contradiction, that P_1 is not an optimal solution to its subproblem; the argument for P_2 is analogous. Then, there is a cycle-free path P_1^* from v to k with internal vertices in $\{1, 2, \ldots, k-1\}$ and length $L_1^* < L_1$. But then the concatenation of P_1^* and P_2 would be a cycle-free path P^* from v to w with internal vertices in $\{1, 2, \ldots, k\}$ and length $L_1^* + L_2 < L_1 + L_2 = L$, contradicting the assumed optimality of P.

Quiz 18.5

Do you see any bugs in the argument above? (Choose all that apply.)

 a) The concatenation P^* of P_1^* and P_2 need not have origin v.

 b) P^* need not have destination w.

 c) P^* need not have internal vertices only in $\{1, 2, \ldots, k\}$.

 d) P^* need not be cycle-free.

 e) P^* need not have length less than L.

 f) Nope, no bugs.

(See Section 18.4.6 for the solution and discussion.)

Is the bug fatal, or do we just need to work a little harder? Suppose the concatenation P^* of P_1^* and P_2 contains a cycle. By repeatedly splicing out cycles (as in Figure 15.1 and footnote 3 in Chapter 15), we can extract from P^* a cycle-free path $\widehat{P}$ with the same origin (v) and destination (w), and with the same or fewer internal vertices. The length of this cycle-free path $\widehat{P}$ equals the length L^* of P^*, less the sum of the lengths of the edges in the spliced-out cycles.

If the input graph has no negative cycles, cycle-splicing cannot increase a path's length (and $\widehat{P}$'s length would be at most L^*). In this case, we've salvaged the proof: $\widehat{P}$ is a cycle-free v-w path with internal vertices in $\{1, 2, \ldots, k\}$ and length at most $L^* < L$, contradicting the assumed optimality of the original path P. We can then conclude that the vertex k does, in fact, split the optimal solution P into optimal solutions P_1 and P_2 to their respective smaller subproblems.

We're not responsible for computing shortest-path distances for input graphs with a negative cycle. (Recall the problem definition in Section 18.3.) Let's declare victory with the following optimal substructure lemma.

---

[20]This argument explains why the Floyd-Warshall subproblems, in contrast to the Bellman-Ford subproblems, impose the cycle-free condition (iii).

[21]This approach to identifying optimal substructure would *not* work well for the single-source shortest path problem, as the suffix path P_2 would have the wrong origin vertex.

Lemma 18.6 (Floyd-Warshall Optimal Substructure) *Let $G = (V, E)$ be a directed graph with real-valued edge lengths and no negative cycles, with $V = \{1, 2, \ldots, n\}$. Suppose $k \in \{1, 2, \ldots, n\}$ and $v, w \in V$, and let P be a minimum-length cycle-free v-w path in G with all internal vertices in $\{1, 2, \ldots, k\}$. Then, P is either:*

(i) a minimum-length cycle-free v-w path with all internal vertices in $\{1, 2, \ldots, k-1\}$; or

(ii) the concatenation of a minimum-length cycle-free v-k path with all internal vertices in $\{1, 2, \ldots, k-1\}$ and a minimum-length cycle-free k-w path with all internal vertices in $\{1, 2, \ldots, k-1\}$.

Or, in recurrence form:

Corollary 18.7 (Floyd-Warshall Recurrence) *With the assumptions and notation of Lemma 18.6, let $L_{k,v,w}$ denote the minimum length of a cycle-free v-w path with all internal vertices in $\{1, 2, \ldots, k\}$. (If there are no such paths, then $L_{k,v,w} = +\infty$.) For every $k \in \{1, 2, \ldots, n\}$ and $v, w \in V$,*

$$L_{k,v,w} = \min \left\{ \begin{array}{ll} L_{k-1,v,w} & \text{(Case 1)} \\ L_{k-1,v,k} + L_{k-1,k,w} & \text{(Case 2)} \end{array} \right\}. \tag{18.2}$$

18.4.3   Pseudocode

Suppose we know that the input graph has no negative cycles, in which case Lemma 18.6 and Corollary 18.7 apply. We can use the recurrence to systematically solve all the subproblems, from smallest to largest. To get started, what are the solutions to the base cases (with $k = 0$ and no internal vertices allowed)?

Quiz 18.6

Let $G = (V, E)$ be an input graph. What is $L_{0,v,w}$ in the case where: (i) $v = w$; (ii) (v, w) is an edge of G; and (iii) $v \neq w$ and (v, w) is not an edge of G?

a) $0, 0,$ and $+\infty$

b) $0, \ell_{vw},$ and ℓ_{vw}

c) $0, \ell_{vw},$ and $+\infty$

d) $+\infty, \ell_{vw},$ and $+\infty$

(See Section 18.4.6 for the solution and discussion.)

The Floyd-Warshall algorithm computes the base cases using the solution to Quiz 18.6 and the rest of the subproblems using the recurrence in Corollary 18.7. The final for loop in the pseudocode checks whether the input graph contains a negative cycle and is explained in Section 18.4.4. See Problems 18.4 and 18.5 for examples of the algorithm in action.

Floyd–Warshall

Input: directed graph $G = (V, E)$ in adjacency-list or adjacency-matrix representation, and a real-valued length ℓ_e for each edge $e \in E$.

Output: $dist(v, w)$ for every vertex pair $v, w \in V$, or a declaration that G contains a negative cycle.

---

label the vertices $V = \{1, 2, 3, \ldots, n\}$ arbitrarily
// subproblems (k indexed from 0, v, w from 1)
$A := (n + 1) \times n \times n$ three-dimensional array
// base cases ($k = 0$), as in Quiz 18.6
for $v := 1$ to n **do**   // origin
   for $w := 1$ to n **do**   // destination
      if $v = w$ **then**
         $A[0][v][w] := 0$
      else if (v, w) is an edge of G **then**
         $A[0][v][w] := \ell_{vw}$
      else
         $A[0][v][w] := +\infty$
// systematically solve all subproblems
for $k := 1$ to n **do**   // subproblem size
   for $v := 1$ to n **do**   // origin
      for $w := 1$ to n **do**   // destination
         // use recurrence from Corollary 18.7
         $A[k][v][w] :=$
           $\min\{\underbrace{A[k-1][v][w]}_{\text{Case 1}}, \underbrace{A[k-1][v][k] + A[k-1][k][w]}_{\text{Case 2}}\}$
// check for a negative cycle
for $v := 1$ to n **do**
   if $A[n][v][v] < 0$ **then**
      return "negative cycle"   // see Lemma 18.8
return $\{A[n][v][w]\}_{v,w \in V}$

The algorithm uses a three-dimensional array of subproblems and a corresponding triple for loop because subproblems are indexed by three parameters (an origin, a destination, and a prefix of vertices). It's important that the outer loop is indexed by the subproblem size k, so that all of the relevant terms $A[k-1][v][w]$ are available for constant-time look up in each inner loop iteration. (The relative order of the second and third for loops doesn't matter.) There are $O(n^3)$ subproblems, where n denotes the number of vertices, and the algorithm performs $O(1)$ work for each one.[22] It performs $O(n^2)$ work outside the triple for loop, and

---

[22]Unlike most of our graph algorithms, the Floyd-Warshall algorithm is equally fast and easy-to-implement for graphs represented with an adjacency matrix (where the (v, w) entry of the matrix is ℓ_{vw} if $(v, w) \in E$ and $+\infty$ otherwise) as for graphs represented with adjacency lists.

so its overall running time is $O(n^3)$.[23] Induction (on k) and the correctness of the recurrence (Corollary 18.7) imply that, when the input graph has no negative cycles, the algorithm correctly computes the shortest-path distances between each pair of vertices.[24]

18.4.4   Detecting a Negative Cycle

What about when the input graph has a negative cycle? How do we know whether we can trust the solutions to the final batch of subproblems? The "diagonal" entries of the subproblem array are the tell.[25]

Lemma 18.8 (Detecting a Negative Cycle) *The input graph $G = (V, E)$ has a negative cycle if and only if, at the conclusion of the* Floyd-Warshall *algorithm, $A[n][v][v] < 0$ for some vertex $v \in V$.*

Proof: If the input graph G does not have a negative cycle, then: (i) Floyd-Warshall correctly computes all shortest-path distances; and (ii) there is no path from a vertex v to itself shorter than the empty path (which has length 0). Thus $A[n][v][v] = 0$ for all $v \in V$ at the end of the algorithm.

To prove the other direction, assume that G has a negative cycle. This implies that G has a negative cycle with no repeated vertices other than its start and end. (Do you see why?) Let C denote an arbitrary such cycle. The Floyd-Warshall algorithm need not compute the correct shortest-path distances, but it is still the case that each array entry $A[k][v][w]$ is *at most* the minimum length of a cycle-free v-w path with internal vertices restricted to $\{1, 2, \ldots, k\}$ (as you should check, by induction on k).

Of the vertices in the negative cycle C, suppose that k has the largest label. Let $v \neq k$ be some other vertex of C:

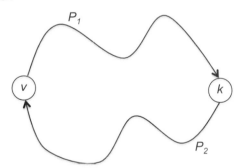

The two sides P_1 and P_2 of the cycle are cycle-free v-k and k-v paths with internal vertices restricted to $\{1, 2, \ldots, k-1\}$, so $A[k-1][v][k]$ and $A[k-1][k][v]$ are at most their respective lengths. Thus $A[k][v][v]$, which (by the recurrence) is at most $A[k-1][v][k] + A[k-1][k][v]$, is at most the length of the cycle C, which is less than zero. Thus $A[n][v][v]$, which (by the recurrence) is at most $A[k][v][v]$, is also negative. $\mathcal{QED}$

---

[23]Because the solutions to a batch of subproblems depend only on those from the previous batch, the algorithm can be implemented using $O(n^2)$ space (analogous to Problem 17.5).

[24]Had I shown you the Floyd-Warshall algorithm before your boot camp in dynamic programming, your response might have been: "That's an impressively elegant algorithm, but how could I ever have come up with it myself?" Now that you've achieved a black-belt (or at least brown-belt) level of skill in the art of dynamic programming, I hope your reaction is: "How could I *not* have come up with this algorithm myself?"

[25]For a different approach, see Problem 18.6.

18.4.5   Summary and Open Questions

Summarizing everything we now know about the `Floyd-Warshall` algorithm:

Theorem 18.9 (Properties of `Floyd-Warshall`) *For every input graph* $G = (V, E)$ *with* n *vertices and real-valued edge lengths, the* `Floyd-Warshall` *algorithm runs in* $O(n^3)$ *time and either:*

   (i) returns the shortest-path distances between each pair $v, w \in V$ *of vertices; or*

   (ii) detects that G *contains a negative cycle.*

As usual, shortest paths can be reconstructed by tracing back through the final array A computed by the `Floyd-Warshall` algorithm.[26]

How should we feel about the cubic running time of the Floyd-Warshall algorithm? We're stuck with a quadratic number of values to report, but there's a big gap between cubic and quadratic running times. Can we do better? Nobody knows! One of the biggest open questions in the field of algorithms is whether there is an algorithm for the all-pairs shortest path problem on n-vertex graphs that runs in, say, $O(n^{2.99})$ time.[27]

18.4.6   Solutions to Quizzes 18.5–18.6

Solution to Quiz 18.5

Correct answer: (d). The concatenation P^* of P_1^* and P_2 definitely starts at v (because P_1^* does) and ends at w (because P_2 does). The internal vertices of P^* are the same as those of P_1^* and of P_2, plus the new internal vertex k. Because all of the internal vertices of P_1^* and P_2 belong to $\{1, 2, \ldots, k-1\}$, all of the internal vertices of P^* belong to $\{1, 2, \ldots, k\}$. The length of the concatenation of two paths is the sum of their lengths, so P^* does indeed have length $L_1^* + L_2 < L$. The issue is that the concatenation of two cycle-free paths need not be cycle-free. For example, in the graph

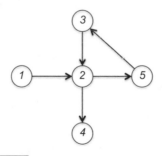

---

[26]Analogous to the Bellman-Ford algorithm (footnote 11), it's a good idea to maintain with each vertex pair v, w the last hop of a minimum-length cycle-free v-w path with internal vertices restricted to $\{1, 2, \ldots, k\}$. (If Case 1 of the recurrence wins for the vertex pair v, w in the kth batch of subproblems, the last hop for the pair remains the same. If Case 2 wins, the last hop for v, w is reassigned to the most recent last hop for k, w.) Reconstruction for a given vertex pair then requires only $O(n)$ time.

[27]We can do better than the Floyd-Warshall algorithm for graphs that are not very dense. For example, a clever trick reduces the all-pairs shortest path problem (with negative edge lengths) to one invocation of the Bellman-Ford algorithm followed by $n - 1$ invocations of Dijkstra's algorithm. This reduction, which is called Johnson's algorithm and described in the bonus videos at `www.algorithmsilluminated.org`, runs in $O(mn) + (n-1) \cdot O(m \log n) = O(mn \log n)$ time. (As usual, m denotes the number of edges.) This running time is subcubic in n except when m is very close to quadratic in n.

concatenating the path $1 \to 2 \to 5$ with the path $5 \to 3 \to 2 \to 4$ produces a path that contains the directed cycle $2 \to 5 \to 3 \to 2$.

Solution to Quiz 18.6

Correct answer: (c). If $v = w$, the only v-w path with no internal vertices is the empty path (with length 0). If $(v, w) \in E$, the only such path is the one-hop path $v \to w$ (with length ℓ_{vw}). If $v \neq w$ and $(v, w) \notin E$, there are no v-w paths with no internal vertices and $L_{0,v,w} = +\infty$.

The Upshot

☆ It is not obvious how to define shortest-path distances in a graph with a negative cycle.

☆ In the single-source shortest path problem, the input consists of a directed graph with edge lengths and a starting vertex. The goal is either to compute the length of a shortest path from the starting vertex to every other vertex or to detect that the graph has a negative cycle.

☆ The Bellman-Ford algorithm is a dynamic programming algorithm that solves the single-source shortest path problem in $O(mn)$ time, where m and n are the number of edges and vertices of the input graph, respectively.

☆ The key idea in the Bellman-Ford algorithm is to parameterize sub-problems by an edge budget i (in addition to a destination) and consider only paths with i or fewer edges.

☆ The Bellman-Ford algorithm has played a prominent role in the evolution of Internet routing protocols.

☆ In the all-pairs shortest path problem, the input consists of a directed graph with edge lengths. The goal is to either compute the length of a shortest path from every vertex to every other vertex, or detect that the graph has a negative cycle.

☆ The Floyd-Warshall algorithm is a dynamic programming algorithm that solves the all-pairs shortest path problem in $O(n^3)$ time, where n is the number of vertices of the input graph.

☆ The key idea in the Floyd-Warshall algorithm is to parameterize subproblems by a prefix of k vertices (in addition to an origin and a destination) and consider only cycle-free paths with all internal vertices in $\{1, 2, \ldots, k\}$.

Test Your Understanding

Problem 18.1 *(S)* For the input graph

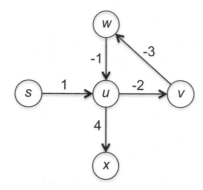

what are the final array entries of the `Bellman-Ford` algorithm from Section 18.2?

Problem 18.2 *(S)* Lemma 18.3 shows that once the subproblem solutions stabilize in the Bellman-Ford algorithm (with $L_{k+1,v} = L_{k,v}$ for every destination v), they remain the same forevermore (with $L_{i,v} = L_{k,v}$ for all $i \geq k$ and $v \in V$). Is this also true on a per-vertex basis? That is, is it true that, whenever $L_{k+1,v} = L_{k,v}$ for some $k \geq 0$ and destination v, $L_{i,v} = L_{k,v}$ for all $i \geq k$? Provide either a proof or a counterexample.

Problem 18.3 *(H)* Consider a directed graph $G = (V, E)$ with n vertices, m edges, a starting vertex $s \in V$, real-valued edge lengths, and no negative cycles. Suppose you know that every shortest path in G from s to another vertex has at most k edges. How quickly can you solve the single-source shortest path problem? (Choose the strongest statement that is guaranteed to be true.)

a) $O(m + n)$

b) $O(kn)$

c) $O(km)$

d) $O(mn)$

Problem 18.4 *(S)* For the input graph

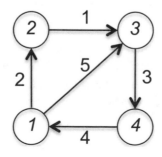

what are the final array entries of the `Floyd-Warshall` algorithm from Section 18.4?

Problem 18.5 *(S)* For the input graph

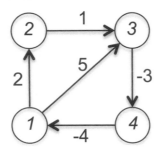

what are the final array entries of the `Floyd-Warshall` algorithm?

Challenge Problems

Problem 18.6 *(S)* The `Floyd-Warshall` algorithm runs in $O(n^3)$ time on graphs with n vertices and m edges, whether or not the input graph contains a negative cycle. Modify the algorithm so that it solves the all-pairs shortest path problem in $O(mn)$ time for input graphs with a negative cycle and $O(n^3)$ time otherwise. (You may assume that $m \geq n$, but do not assume that the input graph necessarily has a directed path from every vertex to every other vertex.)

Problem 18.7 *(H)* Which of the following problems can be solved in $O(n^3)$ time, where n is the number of vertices in the input graph? (Choose all that apply.)

a) Given a directed graph $G = (V, E)$ with nonnegative edge lengths, compute the maximum length of a shortest path between any pair of vertices (that is, $\max_{v,w \in V} dist(v, w)$).

b) Given a directed acyclic graph with real-valued edge lengths, compute the length of a longest path between any pair of vertices.

c) Given a directed graph with nonnegative edge lengths, compute the length of a longest cycle-free path between any pair of vertices.

d) Given a directed graph with real-valued edge lengths, compute the length of a longest cycle-free path between any pair of vertices.

Programming Problems

Problem 18.8 Implement in your favorite programming language the `Bellman-Ford` and `Floyd-Warshall` algorithms. For the all-pairs shortest path problem, how much faster is the Floyd-Warshall algorithm than n invocations of the Bellman-Ford algorithm? For bonus points, implement the space optimizations and linear-time reconstruction algorithms outlined in footnotes 11, 23, and 26. (See `www.algorithmsilluminated.org` for test cases and challenge data sets.)

Part IV

Algorithms for NP-Hard Problems

Chapter 19

What Is NP-Hardness?

Introductory books on algorithms, as well as the first three parts of this book, suffer from selection bias. They focus on computational problems that are solvable by clever, fast algorithms—after all, what's more fun and empowering to learn than an ingenious algorithmic short-cut? The good news is that many fundamental and practically relevant problems fall into this category: sorting, graph search, shortest paths, Huffman codes, minimum spanning trees, sequence alignment, and so on. But it would be fraudulent to teach you only this cherry-picked collection of problems while ignoring the spectre of computational intractability that haunts the serious algorithm designer or programmer. Sadly, there are many important computational problems, including ones likely to show up in your own projects, for which no fast algorithms are known. Even worse, we can't expect any future algorithmic breakthroughs for these problems, as they are widely believed to be intrinsically difficult and unsolvable by any fast algorithm.

Newly aware of this stark reality, two questions immediately come to mind. First, how can you recognize such hard problems when they appear in your own work, so that you can adjust your expectations accordingly and avoid wasting time looking for a too-good-to-be-true algorithm? Second, when such a problem is important to your application, how should you revise your ambitions, and what algorithmic tools can you apply to achieve them? This part of the book will equip you with thorough answers to both questions.

19.1 MST vs. TSP: An Algorithmic Mystery

Hard computational problems can look a lot like easy ones, and telling them apart requires a trained eye. To set the stage, let's rendezvous with a familiar friend (the minimum spanning tree problem) and meet its more demanding cousin (the traveling salesman problem).

19.1.1 The Minimum Spanning Tree Problem

One famous computational problem solvable by a blazingly fast algorithm is the *minimum spanning tree (MST)* problem (covered in Chapter 15).

Problem: Minimum Spanning Tree (MST)

Input: A connected undirected graph $G = (V, E)$ and a real-valued cost c_e for each edge $e \in E$.

Output: A spanning tree $T \subseteq E$ of G with the minimum-possible sum $\sum_{e \in T} c_e$ of edge costs.

Recall that a graph $G = (V, E)$ is *connected* if, for every pair $v, w \in V$ of vertices, the graph contains a path from v to w. A *spanning tree* of G is a subset $T \subseteq E$ of edges such that the subgraph (V, T) is both connected and acyclic. For example, in the graph

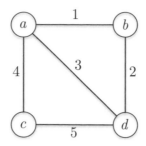

the minimum spanning tree comprises the edges (a, b), (b, d), and (a, c), for an overall cost of 7.

A graph can have an exponential number of spanning trees (see footnote 5 of Chapter 15), but the MST problem can nevertheless be solved by clever fast algorithms, such as Prim's and Kruskal's algorithms. Deploying appropriate data structures (heaps and union-find, respectively), these two algorithms have blazingly fast implementations, with a running time of $O((m + n) \log n)$, where m and n are the number of edges and vertices of the input graph, respectively.

19.1.2   The Traveling Salesman Problem

Another famous problem, absent from previous parts of the book but prominent in Part IV, is the *traveling salesman problem (TSP)*. Its definition is almost the same as that of the MST problem, except with *tours*—simple cycles that span all vertices—playing the role of spanning trees.

Problem: Traveling Salesman Problem (TSP)

Input: A complete undirected graph $G = (V, E)$ and a real-valued cost c_e for each edge $e \in E$.[1]

Output: A tour $T \subseteq E$ of G with the minimum-possible sum $\sum_{e \in T} c_e$ of edge costs.

Formally, a *tour* is a cycle that visits every vertex exactly once (with two edges incident to each vertex).

Quiz 19.1

In an instance $G = (V, E)$ of the TSP with $n \geq 3$ vertices, how many distinct tours $T \subseteq E$ are there? (In the answers below, $n! = n \cdot (n - 1) \cdot (n - 2) \cdots 2 \cdot 1$ denotes the factorial function.)

---

[1]In a *complete* graph, all $\binom{n}{2}$ possible edges are present. The assumption that the graph is complete is without loss of generality, as an arbitrary input graph can be harmlessly turned into a complete graph by adding in all the missing edges and giving them very high costs.

a) 2^n

b) $\frac{1}{2}(n-1)!$

c) $(n-1)!$

d) $n!$

(See Section 19.1.4 for the solution and discussion.)

If all else fails, the TSP can be solved by exhaustively enumerating all of the (finitely many) tours and remembering the best one. Try exhaustive search out on a small example.

Quiz 19.2

What is the minimum sum of edge costs of a tour of the following graph? (Each edge is labeled with its cost.)

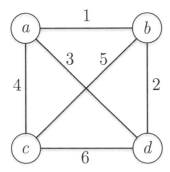

a) 12

b) 13

c) 14

d) 15

(See Section 19.1.4 for the solution and discussion.)

The TSP can be feasibly solved by exhaustive search for only the smallest of instances. *Can we do better?* Could there be, analogous to the MST problem, an algorithm that magically homes in on the minimum-cost needle in the exponential-size haystack of traveling salesman tours? Despite the superficial similarity of the statements of the two problems, the TSP appears to be far more difficult to solve than the MST problem.

19.1.3 Trying and Failing to Solve the TSP

I could tell you a cheesy story about, um, a traveling salesman, but this would do a disservice to the TSP, which is actually quite fundamental. Whenever you have a bunch of tasks to complete in a sequence, with the cost or time for carrying out a task dependent on the preceding task, you're talking about the TSP in disguise.

For example, tasks could represent cars to be assembled in a factory, with the time required to assemble a car equal to a fixed cost (for assembly) plus a setup cost that depends on how different the factory configurations are for this and the previous car. Assembling all the cars as quickly as possible boils down to minimizing the sum of the setup costs, which is exactly the TSP.

For a very different application, imagine that you've collected a bunch of overlapping fragments of a genome and would like to reverse engineer their most plausible ordering. Given a "plausibility measure" that assigns a cost to each fragment pair (for example, derived from the length of their longest common substring), this ordering problem also boils down to the TSP.[2]

Seduced by the practical applications and aesthetic appeal of the TSP, many of the greatest minds in optimization have, since at least the early 1950s, devoted a tremendous amount of effort and computation to solving large-scale instances of the TSP.[3] Despite the decades and intellectual firepower involved:

Fact

As of this writing (in 2022), there is no known fast algorithm for the TSP.

What do we mean by a "fast" algorithm? Back in Section 1.6, we agreed that:

> A "fast algorithm" is an algorithm whose worst-case running time grows
> slowly with the input size.

And what do we mean by "grows slowly"? For much of this book, the holy grail has been algorithms that run in linear or almost-linear time. Forget about such blazingly fast algorithms—for the TSP, no one even knows of an algorithm that always runs in $O(n^{100})$ time on n-vertex instances, or even $O(n^{10000})$ time.

There are two competing explanations for the dismal state-of-the-art: (i) there is a fast algorithm for the TSP but no one's been smart enough to find it yet; or (ii) no such algorithm exists. We do not know which explanation is correct, though most experts believe in the second one.

Speculation

No fast algorithm for the TSP exists.

As early as 1967, Jack Edmonds wrote:

---

[2]Both applications are arguably better modeled as traveling salesman *path* problems, in which the goal is to compute a minimum-cost cycle-free path that visits every vertex (without going back to the starting vertex). Any algorithm solving the TSP can be easily converted into one solving the path version of the problem, and vice versa (Problem 19.7).

[3]Readers curious about the history or additional applications of the TSP should check out the first four chapters of the book *The Traveling Salesman Problem: A Computational Study*, by David L. Applegate, Robert E. Bixby, Vašek Chvátal, and William J. Cook (Princeton University Press, 2006).

I conjecture that there is no good algorithm for the traveling saleman [sic] problem. My reasons are the same as for any mathematical conjecture: (1) It is a legitimate mathematical possibility, and (2) I do not know.[4]

Unfortunately, the curse of intractability is not confined to the TSP. We'll see that many other practically relevant problems are similarly afflicted.

19.1.4   Solutions to Quizzes 19.1–19.2

Solution to Quiz 19.1

Correct answer: (b). There is an intuitive correspondence between vertex orderings (of which there are $n!$) and tours (which visit the vertices once each, in some order), so answer (d) is a natural guess. However, this correspondence counts each tour in $2n$ different ways: once for each of the n choices of the initial vertex and once for each of the two directions of traversing the tour. Thus, the total number of tours is $n!/2n = \frac{1}{2}(n-1)!$. For example, with $n = 4$, there are three distinct tours:

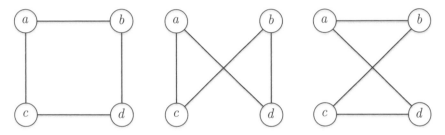

Solution to Quiz 19.2

Correct answer: (b). We can enumerate tours by starting with the vertex a and trying all six possible orderings of the other three vertices, with the understanding that the tour finishes by traveling from the last vertex back to a. (Actually, this enumeration counts each tour twice, once in each direction.) The results:

Vertex Ordering	Cost of Corresponding Tour
a, b, c, d or a, d, c, b	15
a, b, d, c or a, c, d, b	13
a, c, b, d or a, d, b, c	14

The shortest tour is the second one, with a total cost of 13.

19.2   Possible Levels of Expertise

Some computational problems are easier than others. The point of the theory of NP-hardness is to classify, in a precise sense, problems as either "computationally easy" (like the MST problem) or "computationally difficult" (like the TSP). Part IV of this book is aimed both

---

[4]From the paper "Optimum Branchings," by Jack Edmonds (*Journal of Research of the National Bureau of Standards, Series B*, 1967). By a "good" algorithm, Edmonds means an algorithm with a running time bounded above by some polynomial function of the input size.

at readers looking for a white-belt primer on the topic and at those pursuing black-belt expertise. This section offers guidance on how to approach the rest of the book, as a function of your goals and constraints.

What are your current and desired levels of expertise in recognizing and tackling NP-hard problems?[5]

(Level 0:) "What's an NP-hard problem?"

Level 0 is total ignorance—you've never heard of NP-hardness and are unaware that many practically relevant computational problems are widely believed to be unsolvable by any fast algorithm. If I've done my job, this book should be accessible even to level-0 readers.

(Level 1:) "Oh, the problem is NP-hard? I guess we should either reformulate the problem, scale down our ambitions, or invest a lot more resources into solving it."

Level 1 represents cocktail-party-level awareness and at least an informal understanding of what NP-hardness means.[6] For example, are you managing a software project with an algorithmic or optimization component? If so, you should acquire at least level-1 knowledge, in case one of your team members bumps into an NP-hard problem and wants to discuss the possible next steps. To raise your level to 1, study Sections 19.3, 19.4, and 19.6.

(Level 2:) "Oh, the problem is NP-hard? Give me a chance to apply my algorithmic expertise and see how far I can get."

The biggest marginal empowerment for software engineers comes from reaching level 2, and acquiring a rich toolbox for developing practically useful algorithms for solving or approximating NP-hard problems. Serious programmers should shoot for this level (or above). Happily, all the algorithmic paradigms that we developed for polynomial-time solvable problems in Parts I–III are also useful for making headway on NP-hard problems. The goal of Chapters 20 and 21 is to bring you up to level 2; see also Section 19.4 for an overview and Chapter 24 for a detailed case study of the level-2 toolbox in action in a high-stakes application.

(Level 3:) "Tell me about your computational problem. [... listens carefully ...] My condolences, your problem is NP-hard."

At level 3, you can quickly recognize NP-hard problems when they arise in practice (at which point you can switch to applying your level-2 skills). You know several famous NP-hard problems and also how to prove that additional problems are NP-hard. Specialists in algorithms should master these skills. For example, I frequently draw on level-3 knowledge when advising colleagues, students, or engineers in industry on algorithmic problems. Chapter 22 provides a boot camp for upping your game to level 3; see also Section 19.5 for an overview.

---

[5] What's up with the term "NP"? See Section 19.6.

[6] Speaking, as always, about sufficiently nerdy cocktail parties!

(Level 4:) "Allow me to explain the P $\neq$ NP conjecture to you on this whiteboard."

Level 4, the most advanced level, is for budding theoreticians and anyone seeking a rigorous mathematical understanding of NP-hardness and the P vs. NP question. If that qualifier doesn't scare you off, the optional Chapter 23 is for you.

19.3 Easy and Hard Problems

An oversimplification of the "easy vs. hard" dichotomy proposed by the theory of NP-hardness is:

easy	$\leftrightarrow$	can be solved with a polynomial-time algorithm;
hard	$\leftrightarrow$	requires exponential time in the worst case.

This summary of NP-hardness overlooks several important subtleties (see Section 19.3.9). But ten years from now, if you remember only a few words about the meaning of NP-hardness, these are good ones.

19.3.1 Polynomial-Time Algorithms

To segue into the definition of an "easy" problem, let's recap the running times of some of the famous algorithms that we studied in Parts I–III:

Problem	Algorithm	Running Time
Sorting	MergeSort	$O(n \log n)$
Strong Components	Kosaraju	$O(m + n)$
Shortest Paths	Dijkstra	$O((m + n) \log n)$
MST	Kruskal	$O((m + n) \log n)$
Sequence Alignment	NW	$O(mn)$
All-Pairs Shortest Paths	Floyd-Warshall	$O(n^3)$

The exact meaning of n and m is problem-specific, but in all cases they are closely related to the input size.[7] The key takeaway from this table is that, while the running times of these algorithms vary, *all of them are bounded above by some polynomial function of the input size*. In general:

Polynomial-Time Algorithms

A *polynomial-time algorithm* is an algorithm with worst-case running time $O(n^d)$, where n denotes the input size and d is a constant (independent of n).

The six algorithms listed above are all polynomial-time algorithms (with reasonably small exponents d).[8] Do all natural algorithms run in polynomial time? No. For example, for many problems, exhaustive search runs in time exponential in the input size. There's something special about the clever polynomial-time algorithms that we've studied so far.

---

[7]In sorting, n denotes the length of the input array; in the four graph problems, n and m denote the number of vertices and edges, respectively; and in the sequence alignment problem, n and m denote the lengths of the two input strings.

[8]Remember that a logarithmic factor can be bounded above (sloppily) by a linear factor; for example, if $T(n) = O(n \log n)$, then $T(n) = O(n^2)$ as well.

19.3.2   Polynomial vs. Exponential Time

Don't forget that any exponential function eventually grows much faster than any polynomial function. There's a huge difference between typical polynomial and exponential running times, even for very small instances. The following plot (of the polynomial function $100n^2$ versus the exponential function 2^n) is representative:

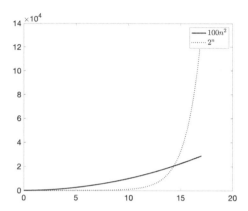

Moore's law asserts that the computing power available for a given price doubles every 1–2 years. Does this mean that the difference between polynomial-time and exponential-time algorithms will disappear over time? Actually, the exact opposite is true! Our computational ambitions grow with our computational power, and as time goes on we consider increasingly large input sizes and suffer an increasingly big gulf between polynomial and exponential running times.

Imagine that you have a fixed time budget, like an hour or a day. How does the solvable input size scale with additional computing power? With a polynomial-time algorithm, it increases by a constant factor (such as from $1,000,000$ to $1,414,213$) with every doubling of your computing power.[9] With an algorithm that runs in time proportional to 2^n, where n is the input size, each doubling of computing power increases the solvable input size by only one (such as from $1,000,000$ to $1,000,001$)!

19.3.3   Easy Problems

The theory of NP-hardness defines "easy" problems as those solvable by a polynomial-time algorithm, or equivalently by an algorithm for which the solvable input size (for a fixed time budget) scales multiplicatively with increasing computational power:[10]

Polynomial-Time Solvable Problems

A computational problem is *polynomial-time solvable* if there is a polynomial-time algorithm that solves it correctly for every input.

---

[9]With a linear-time algorithm, you could solve problems that are twice as big; with a quadratic-time algorithm, $\sqrt{2} \approx 1.414$ times as big; with a cubic-time algorithm, $\sqrt[3]{2} \approx 1.26$ as big; and so on.
[10]This definition was proposed independently by Alan Cobham and Jack Edmonds (see footnote 4) in the mid-1960s.

For example, the six problems listed at the beginning of this section are all polynomial-time solvable.

Technically, a (useless-in-practice) algorithm that runs in $O(n^{100})$ time on size-n inputs counts as a polynomial-time algorithm, and a problem solved by such an algorithm qualifies as polynomial-time solvable. Turning this statement around, if a problem like the TSP is *not* polynomial-time solvable, there is not even an $O(n^{100})$-time or $O(n^{10000})$-time algorithm that solves it (!).

Courage, Definitions, and Edge Cases

The identification of "easy" with "polynomial-time solvable" is imperfect; a problem might be solved in theory (by an algorithm that technically runs in polynomial time) but not in reality (by an empirically fast algorithm), or vice versa. Anyone with the guts to write down a precise mathematical definition (like polynomial-time solvability) to express a messy real-world concept (like "easy to solve via computer in the physical world") must be ready for friction between the binary nature of the definition and the fuzziness of reality. The definition will inevitably include or exclude some edge cases that you wish had gone the other way, but this is no excuse to ignore or dismiss a good definition. Polynomial-time solvability has been unreasonably effective at classifying problems as "easy" or "hard" in a way that accords with empirical experience. With a half-century of evidence behind us, we can confidently say that natural polynomial-time solvable problems typically can be solved with practical general-purpose algorithms, and that problems believed to not be polynomial-time solvable typically require significantly more work and domain expertise.

19.3.4   Relative Intractability

Suppose we suspected that a problem like the TSP is "not easy," meaning unsolvable by any polynomial-time algorithm (no matter how large the polynomial). How would we amass evidence that this is, in fact, the case? The most convincing argument, of course, would be an airtight mathematical proof. But the status of the TSP remains in limbo to this day: No one has found a polynomial-time algorithm that solves it, nor has anyone found a proof that no such algorithm exists.

How can we develop a theory that usefully differentiates "tractable" and "intractable" problems despite our deficient understanding of what algorithms can do? The brilliant conceit behind the theory of NP-hardness is to classify problems based on their *relative* (rather than absolute) difficulty and to declare a problem as "hard" if it is "at least as hard as" an overwhelming number of other unsolved problems.

19.3.5   Hard Problems

The many failed attempts at solving the TSP (Section 19.1.3) provide circumstantial evidence that the problem may not be polynomial-time solvable.

Weak Evidence of Hardness

A polynomial-time algorithm for the TSP would solve a problem that has resisted the efforts of hundreds (if not thousands) of brilliant minds over many decades.

Can we do better, meaning build a more compelling case of intractability? This is where the magic and power of NP-hardness comes in. The big idea is to show that a problem like the TSP is at least as hard as a vast array of unsolved problems from many different scientific fields—in fact, all problems for which you quickly know a solution when you see one. Such an argument would imply that a hypothetical polynomial-time algorithm for the TSP would automatically solve all these other unsolved problems, as well!

Strong Evidence of Hardness

A polynomial-time algorithm for the TSP would solve *thousands* of problems that have resisted the efforts of *tens (if not hundreds) of thousands* of brilliant minds over many decades.

In effect, the theory of NP-hardness shows that thousands of computational problems (including the TSP) are variations of the same problem in disguise, all destined to suffer identical computational fates. If you're trying to devise a polynomial-time algorithm for an NP-hard problem like the TSP, you're inadvertently attempting to also come up with such algorithms for these thousands of related problems.[11]

We call a problem *NP-hard* if there is strong evidence of intractability in the sense above:

NP-Hardness (Main Idea)

A problem is *NP-hard* if it is at least as difficult as every problem with easily recognized solutions.

This idea will be made 100% precise in Section 23.3.4; until then, we'll work with a provisional definition of NP-hardness that is phrased in terms of a famous mathematical conjecture, the "P ≠ NP conjecture."

19.3.6   The P ≠ NP Conjecture

Perhaps you've heard of the P ≠ NP conjecture. What is it, exactly? Section 23.4 provides the precise mathematical statement; for now, we'll settle for an informal version that should resonate with anyone who's had to grade student homework:

---

[11]Playing devil's advocate, hundreds (if not thousands) of brilliant minds have likewise failed to prove the other direction, that the TSP is *not* polynomial-time solvable. Symmetrically, doesn't this suggest that perhaps no such proof exists? The difference is that we seem far better at proving solvability (with fast algorithms known for countless problems) than unsolvability. Thus, if the TSP were polynomial-time solvable, it would be odd that we haven't yet found a polynomial-time algorithm for it; if not, no surprise that we haven't yet figured out how to prove it.

The P $\neq$ NP Conjecture (Informal Version)

Checking an alleged solution to a problem can be fundamentally easier than coming up with your own solution from scratch.

The "P" and "NP" in the conjecture refer to problems that can be solved from scratch in polynomial time and those whose solutions can be checked in polynomial time, respectively; for formal definitions, see Chapter 23.

For example, checking someone's proposed solution to a Sudoku or KenKen puzzle sure seems easier than working it out yourself. Or, in the context of the TSP, it's easy to verify that someone's proposed traveling salesman tour is good (with a total cost of, say, at most 1000) by adding up the costs of its edges; it's not so clear how you would quickly come up with your own such tour from scratch. Thus, intuition strongly suggests that the P $\neq$ NP conjecture is true.[12,13]

19.3.7 Provisional Definition of NP-Hardness

Provisionally, we'll call a problem NP-hard if, assuming that the P $\neq$ NP conjecture *is* true, it cannot be solved by any polynomial-time algorithm.

NP-Hard Problem (Provisional Definition)

A computational problem is *NP-hard* if a polynomial-time algorithm solving it would refute the P $\neq$ NP conjecture.

Thus, any polynomial-time algorithm for any NP-hard problem (such as the TSP) would automatically imply that the P $\neq$ NP conjecture is false and trigger an algorithmic bounty that seems too good to be true: a polynomial-time algorithm for every single problem for which solutions can be recognized in polynomial time. In the likely event that the P $\neq$ NP conjecture is true, no NP-hard problem is polynomial-time solvable, not even with an algorithm that runs in $O(n^{100})$ or $O(n^{10000})$ time on size-n inputs.

19.3.8 Randomized and Quantum Algorithms

Our definition of polynomial-time solvability on page 449 contemplates only deterministic algorithms. As we know, randomization can be a powerful tool in algorithm design (for example, in the QuickSort algorithm). Can randomized algorithms escape the binds of NP-hardness?

More generally, what about much-hyped quantum algorithms? (As it turns out, randomized algorithms can be viewed as a special case of quantum algorithms.) It's true that large-scale, general-purpose quantum computers (if realized) would be a game-changer

---

[12]We'll see in Problem 23.2 that the P $\neq$ NP conjecture is equivalent to Edmonds's conjecture (page 445) stating that the TSP cannot be solved in polynomial time.

[13]Why isn't it "obvious" that the P $\neq$ NP conjecture is true? Because the space of polynomial-time algorithms is unfathomably rich, with many ingenious inhabitants. (Remember Strassen's mind-blowing subcubic matrix multiplication algorithm from Section 3.3?) Proving that none of the infinitely many candidate algorithms solve the TSP seems pretty intimidating!

for a handful of problems, including the extremely important problem of factoring large integers. However, the factoring problem is not known or believed to be NP-hard, and experts conjecture that even quantum computers cannot solve NP-hard problems in polynomial time. The challenges posed by NP-hardness are not going away anytime soon.[14]

19.3.9   Subtleties

The oversimplified discussion at the beginning of this section (page 448) suggested that a "hard" problem would require exponential time to solve in the worst case. Our provisional definition in Section 19.3.7 says something different: An NP-hard problem is one that, assuming the $P \neq NP$ conjecture, cannot be solved by any polynomial-time algorithm.

The first discrepancy between the two definitions is that NP-hardness rules out polynomial-time solvability only if the $P \neq NP$ conjecture is true (and this remains an open question). If the conjecture is false, almost all the NP-hard problems discussed in this book are, in fact, polynomial-time solvable.

The second discrepancy is that, even in the likely event that the $P \neq NP$ conjecture is true, NP-hardness implies only that super-polynomial (as opposed to exponential) time is required in the worst case to solve the problem.[15] However, for most natural NP-hard problems, including all those studied in this book, experts generally believe that exponential time is indeed required in the worst case. This belief is formalized by the "Exponential Time Hypothesis," a stronger form of the $P \neq NP$ conjecture (see Section 23.5).[16]

Finally, while 99% of the problems that you'll come across will be either "easy" (polynomial-time solvable) or "hard" (NP-hard), a few rare examples appear to lie in between. Thus, our "dichotomy" between easy and hard problems covers most, but not all, practically relevant computational problems.[17]

19.4   Algorithmic Strategies for NP-Hard Problems

Suppose you've identified a computational problem on which the success of your project rests. Perhaps you've spent the last several weeks throwing the kitchen sink at it—all the algorithm design paradigms you know, every data structure in the book, all the for-free primitives (page 23)—but nothing works. Finally, you realize that the issue is not a

---

[14] A majority of experts believe that every polynomial-time randomized algorithm can be *derandomized* and turned into an equivalent polynomial-time deterministic algorithm (perhaps with a larger polynomial in the running time bound). If true, the $P \neq NP$ conjecture would automatically apply to randomized algorithms as well.

By contrast, a majority of experts believe that quantum algorithms *are* fundamentally more powerful than classical algorithms (but not powerful enough to solve NP-hard problems in polynomial time). Isn't it amazing—and exciting—how much we still don't know?

[15] Examples of running time bounds that are super-polynomial but subexponential in the input size n include $n^{\log_2 n}$ and $2^{\sqrt{n}}$.

[16] None of the computational problems studied in this book require more than exponential time to solve, but other problems do. One famous example is the "halting problem," which can't be solved in any finite (let alone exponential) amount of time; see also Section 23.1.2.

[17] Two important problems that are believed to be neither polynomial-time solvable nor NP-hard are factoring (finding a non-trivial factor of an integer or determining that none exist) and the graph isomorphism problem (determining whether two graphs are identical up to a renaming of the vertices). Subexponential-time (but not polynomial-time) algorithms are known for both problems.

deficiency of ingenuity on your part, it's the fact that the problem is NP-hard. Now you have an explanation of why your weeks of effort have come to naught, but that doesn't diminish the problem's significance to your project. What should you do?

19.4.1   General, Correct, Fast (Pick Two)

The bad news is that NP-hard problems are ubiquitous; right now, one might well be lurking in your latest project. The good news is that NP-hardness is not a death sentence. NP-hard problems can often (but not always) be solved in practice, at least approximately, through sufficient investment of resources and algorithmic sophistication.

NP-hardness throws down the gauntlet to the algorithm designer and tells you where to set your expectations. You should not expect a general-purpose and always-fast algorithm for an NP-hard problem, akin to those we've seen for problems such as sorting, shortest paths, or sequence alignment. Unless you're lucky enough to face only unusually small or well-structured inputs, you're going to have to work pretty hard to solve the problem, and possibly also make some compromises.

What kinds of compromises? NP-hardness rules out algorithms with the following three desirable properties (assuming the P $\neq$ NP conjecture):

Three Properties (You Can't Have Them All)

1. *General-purpose.* The algorithm accommodates all possible inputs of the computational problem.

2. *Correct.* For every input, the algorithm correctly solves the problem.

3. *Fast.* For every input, the algorithm runs in polynomial time.

Accordingly, you can choose from among three types of compromises: compromising on generality, compromising on correctness, and compromising on speed. All three strategies are useful and common in practice.

The rest of this section elaborates on these three algorithmic strategies; Chapters 20 and 21 are deep dives into the latter two. As always, our focus is on powerful and flexible algorithm design principles that apply to a wide range of problems. You should take these principles as a starting point and run with them, guided by whatever domain expertise you have for the specific problem that you need to solve.

19.4.2   Compromising on Generality

One strategy for making progress on an NP-hard problem is to give up on general-purpose algorithms and focus instead on special cases of the problem relevant to your application. In the best-case scenario, you can identify domain-specific constraints on inputs and design an algorithm that is always correct and always fast on this subset of inputs. Graduates of the dynamic programming boot camp in Part III have already seen two examples of this strategy.

Weighted independent set.   Recall from Section 16.1 that, in this problem, the input is an undirected graph $G = (V, E)$ and a nonnegative weight w_v for each vertex $v \in V$; the goal is to compute an independent set $S \subseteq V$ with the maximum-possible sum $\sum_{v \in S} w_v$

of vertex weights, where an *independent set* is a subset $S \subseteq V$ of mutually non-adjacent vertices (with $(v, w) \notin E$ for every $v, w \in S$). For example, if edges represent conflicts (between people, courses, etc.), independent sets correspond to conflict-free subsets.

The weighted independent set problem is NP-hard in general, as we'll see in Section 22.5. The special case of the problem in which G is a path graph (with vertices $v_1, v_2, \ldots, v_n$ and edges $(v_1, v_2), (v_2, v_3), \ldots, (v_{n-1}, v_n)$) can be solved in linear time using a dynamic programming algorithm (see Section 16.2). This algorithm can be extended to accommodate all acyclic graphs (see Problem 16.6).

Knapsack.   Recall from Section 16.5 that, in this problem, the input is specified by $2n + 1$ positive integers: n item values $v_1, v_2, \ldots, v_n$, n item sizes $s_1, s_2, \ldots, s_n$, and a knapsack capacity C. The goal is to compute a subset $S \subseteq \{1, 2, \ldots, n\}$ of items with the maximum-possible sum $\sum_{i \in S} v_i$ of values, subject to having total size $\sum_{i \in S} s_i$ at most C. In other words, the objective is to make use of a scarce resource in the most valuable way possible. For example, given an operating budget and a set of job candidates with differing productivity levels and requested salaries, whom should you hire?

The knapsack problem is NP-hard, as we'll see in Section 22.8 and Problem 22.7. There is an $O(nC)$-time dynamic programming algorithm for the problem (see Section 16.5); this is a polynomial-time algorithm in the special case in which C is bounded by a polynomial function of n.

A Polynomial-Time Algorithm for Knapsack?

Why doesn't the $O(nC)$-time algorithm for the knapsack problem refute the P $\neq$ NP conjecture? Because this is not a polynomial-time algorithm. The input size—the number of keystrokes needed to specify the input to a computer—scales with the number of *digits* in a number, not the *magnitude* of a number. It doesn't take a million keystrokes to communicate the number "1,000,000"—only 7 (or 20 if you're working base-2). For example, in an instance with n items, knapsack capacity 2^n, and all item values and sizes at most 2^n, the input size is $O(n^2)$—$O(n)$ numbers with $O(n)$ digits each—while the running time of the dynamic programming algorithm is exponentially larger (proportional to $n \cdot 2^n$).

The algorithmic strategy of designing fast and correct algorithms (for special cases) uses the entire algorithmic toolbox that we developed in Parts I–III. For this reason, no chapter of Part IV is dedicated to this strategy. We will, however, encounter along the way further examples of polynomial-time solvable special cases of NP-hard problems, including the traveling salesman, satisfiability, and graph coloring problems (see Problems 19.8 and 8.12).

19.4.3   Compromising on Correctness

The second algorithmic strategy, which is particularly popular in time-critical applications, is to insist on generality and speed at the expense of correctness. Algorithms that are not always correct are sometimes called *heuristic algorithms*.[18]

Ideally, a heuristic algorithm is "mostly correct." This could mean one or both of two things:

Relaxations of Correctness

1. The algorithm is correct on "most" inputs.[19]

2. The algorithm is "almost correct" on every input.

The second property is easiest to interpret for optimization problems, in which the goal is to compute a feasible solution (like a traveling salesman tour) with the best objective function value (like the minimum total cost). "Almost correct" then means that the algorithm outputs a feasible solution with objective function value close to the best possible, like a traveling salesman tour with total cost not much more than that of an optimal tour.

Your existing algorithmic toolbox for designing fast exact algorithms is directly useful for designing fast heuristic algorithms. For example, Sections 20.1–20.3 describe greedy heuristics for problems ranging from scheduling to influence maximization in social networks. These heuristic algorithms come with proofs of "approximate correctness" guaranteeing that, for every input, the objective function value of the algorithm's output is within a modest constant factor of the best-possible objective function value.[20]

Sections 20.4–20.5 augment your toolbox with the *local search* algorithm design paradigm. Local search and its generalizations are unreasonably effective in practice at tackling many NP-hard problems, including the TSP, even though local search algorithms rarely possess compelling approximate correctness guarantees.

19.4.4   Compromising on Worst-Case Running Time

The final strategy is appropriate for applications in which you cannot afford to compromise on correctness and are therefore unwilling to consider heuristic algorithms. Every correct algorithm for an NP-hard problem must run in super-polynomial time on some inputs (assuming the $P \neq NP$ conjecture). The goal, therefore, is to design an algorithm that is as fast as possible—at a minimum, one that improves dramatically on naive exhaustive search. This could mean one or both of two things:

Relaxations of Polynomial Running Time

1. The algorithm typically runs quickly (for example, in polynomial time) on the inputs that are relevant to your application.

2. The algorithm is faster than exhaustive search on every input.

---

[18]To this point, we've seen only one example of a mostly-but-not-always-correct solution: bloom filters (Sections 12.5–12.6).

[19]For example, one typical implementation of a bloom filter has a 2% false positive rate, with 98% of lookups answered correctly (see Section 12.6).

[20]Some authors call such algorithms "approximation algorithms" while reserving the term "heuristic algorithms" for algorithms that lack such proofs of approximate correctness.

In the second case, we should still expect the algorithm to run in exponential time on some inputs—after all, the problem is NP-hard. For example, Section 21.1 employs dynamic programming to beat exhaustive search for the TSP, reducing the running time from $O(n!)$ to $O(n^2 \cdot 2^n)$, where n is the number of vertices. Section 21.2 combines randomization with dynamic programming to beat exhaustive search for the problem of finding long paths in graphs (with running time $O((2e)^k \cdot m)$ rather than $O(n^k)$, where n and m denote the number of vertices and edges in the input graph, k the target path length, and $e = 2.718\ldots$).

Making progress on relatively large instances of NP-hard problems typically requires additional tools that do not possess better-than-exhaustive-search running time guarantees but are unreasonably effective in many applications. Sections 21.3–21.5 outline how to stand on the shoulders of experts who, over several decades, have developed remarkably potent solvers for mixed integer programming ("MIP") and satisfiability ("SAT") problems. Many NP-hard optimization problems (such as the TSP) can be encoded as mixed integer programming problems. Many NP-hard feasibility-checking problems (such as checking for a conflict-free assignment of classes to classrooms) are easily expressed as satisfiability problems. Whenever you face an NP-hard problem that can be easily specified as a MIP or SAT problem, try applying the latest and greatest solvers to it. There's no guarantee that a MIP or SAT solver will solve your particular instance in a reasonable amount of time—the problem is NP-hard, after all—but they constitute cutting-edge technology for tackling NP-hard problems in practice.

19.4.5   Key Takeaways

If you're shooting for level-1 knowledge of NP-hardness (Section 19.2), the most important things to remember are:

Three Facts About NP-Hard Problems

1. *Ubiquity:* Practically relevant NP-hard problems are everywhere.

2. *Intractability:* Under a widely believed mathematical conjecture, no NP-hard problem can be solved by any algorithm that is always correct and always runs in polynomial time.

3. *Not a death sentence:* NP-hard problems can often (but not always) be solved in practice, at least approximately, through sufficient investment of resources and algorithmic sophistication.

19.5   Proving NP-Hardness: A Simple Recipe

How can you recognize NP-hard problems when they arise in your own work, so that you can adjust your ambitions accordingly and abandon the search for an algorithm that is general-purpose, correct, and fast? Nobody wins if you spend weeks or months of your life inadvertently trying to refute the P $\neq$ NP conjecture.

First, know a collection of simple and common NP-hard problems (like the 19 problems in Chapter 22); in the simplest scenario, your application will literally boil down to one of these problems. Second, sharpen your ability to spot reductions between computational problems. Reducing one problem to another can spread computational tractability from the latter to the former. Turning this statement on its head, such a reduction can also spread computational *intractability* in the opposite direction, from the former problem to the latter. Thus, to show that a computational problem that you care about is NP-hard, all you need to do is reduce a known NP-hard problem to it.

The rest of this section elaborates on these points and provides one simple example; for a deep dive, see Chapter 22.

19.5.1   Reductions

Any problem B that is at least as hard as an NP-hard problem A is itself NP-hard. The phrase "at least as hard as" can be formalized using *reductions*.

Reductions

A problem A *reduces* to another problem B if an algorithm that solves B can be easily translated into one that solves A (Figure 19.1).

When discussing NP-hard problems, "easily translate" means that problem A can be solved using at most a polynomial (in the input size) number of invocations of a subroutine that solves problem B, along with a polynomial amount of additional work (outside of the subroutine calls).

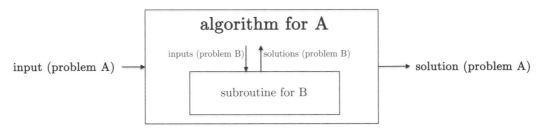

Figure 19.1: If the problem A reduces to the problem B, then A can be solved using a polynomial (in the input size) number of calls to a subroutine for B, plus a polynomial amount of additional work.

19.5.2   Using Reductions to Design Fast Algorithms

Seasoned algorithm designers are always on the lookout for reductions—why solve a problem from scratch if you don't have to? Examples from Parts I–III related to the problems listed in Section 19.3.1 include:

Familiar Examples of Reductions

1. (Section 6.1.2) Finding the median of an array of integers reduces to the problem of sorting the array. (Sort the array and return the middle element.)

2. (Section 18.3.2) The all-pairs shortest path problem reduces to the single-

source shortest path problem. (Invoke a single-source shortest-path algorithm once for each possible choice of a starting vertex.)

3. (Problem 17.6) The longest common subsequence problem reduces to the
   sequence alignment problem. (Invoke a sequence alignment algorithm with
   a very large penalty for matching two different symbols.)

These reductions take after the light side of the force and serve the honorable mission of
creating new fast algorithms from old ones, thereby advancing the frontier of computational
tractability. For example, the first reduction translates the `MergeSort` algorithm into
an $O(n \log n)$-time median-finding algorithm or, more generally, any $T(n)$-time sorting
algorithm into an $O(T(n))$-time median-finding algorithm, where n is the array length.
The second reduction translates any $T(m,n)$-time algorithm for the single-source shortest
path problem into an $O(n \cdot T(m,n))$-time algorithm for the all-pairs shortest path problem, where m and n denote the number of edges and vertices, respectively; and the third
a $T(m,n)$-time algorithm for the sequence alignment problem into an $O(T(m,n))$-time
algorithm for the longest common subsequence problem, where m and n denote the lengths
of the two input strings.

Quiz 19.3

Suppose that a problem A can be solved by invoking a subroutine for a problem B
at most $T_1(n)$ times and performing at most $T_2(n)$ additional work (outside of
the subroutine calls), where n denotes the input size. Provided with a subroutine
that solves problem B in time at most $T_3(n)$ on size-n inputs, how much time do
you need to solve problem A? (Choose the strongest true statement. Assume that
a program must use at least s primitive operations to construct a size-s input to a
subroutine call.)

a) $T_1(n) + T_2(n) + T_3(n)$

b) $T_1(n) \cdot T_2(n) + T_3(n)$

c) $T_1(n) \cdot T_3(n) + T_2(n)$

d) $T_1(n) \cdot T_3(T_2(n)) + T_2(n)$

(See Section 19.5.5 for the solution and discussion.)

Whenever the functions $T_1(n)$, $T_2(n)$, and $T_3(n)$ in Quiz 19.3 are each bounded by
a polynomial function of n, so are their sums, products, and compositions.[21] For this

---

[21]For example, if $T_1(n) \le a_1 n^{d_1}$ and $T_2(n) \le a_2 n^{d_2}$, where a_1, a_2, d_1, and d_2 are positive constants
(independent of n), then

$$T_1(n) \cdot T_2(n) \le (a_1 a_2) n^{(d_1+d_2)}$$

and

$$T_1(T_2(n)) \le (a_1 a_2^{d_1}) n^{(d_1 d_2)}.$$

reason, Quiz 19.3 implies that whenever a problem A reduces to another problem B, any polynomial-time algorithm for B can be translated into one for A:

Reductions Spread Tractability

If problem A reduces to problem B and B can be solved by a polynomial-time algorithm, then A can also be solved by a polynomial-time algorithm (Figure 19.2).

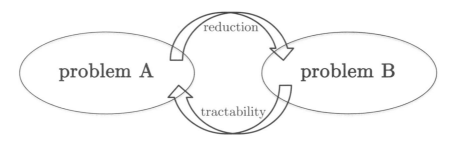

Figure 19.2: Spreading tractability from B to A: If problem A reduces to problem B and B is computationally tractable, then A is also computationally tractable.

19.5.3   Using Reductions to Spread NP-Hardness

The theory of NP-hardness follows the dark side of the force, nefariously using reductions to spread the curse of computational intractability (in the opposite direction of Figure 19.2). Let's turn the preceding boxed statement on its head. Suppose that a problem A reduces to another problem B. Suppose further that A is NP-hard, meaning that a polynomial-time algorithm for A would refute the P $\neq$ NP conjecture. Well, a polynomial-time algorithm for B would automatically lead to one for A (because A reduces to B); this, in turn, would refute the P $\neq$ NP conjecture. In other words, B is also NP-hard!

Reductions Spread Intractability

If problem A reduces to problem B and A is NP-hard, then B is also NP-hard (Figure 19.3).

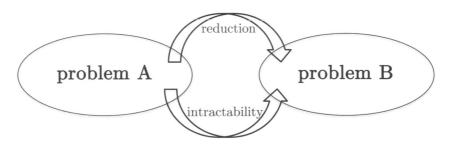

Figure 19.3: Spreading intractability in the opposite direction, from A to B: If problem A reduces to problem B and A is computationally intractable, then B is also computationally intractable.

We therefore have a remarkably simple two-step recipe for proving that a problem is NP-hard:

How to Prove a Problem Is NP-Hard

To prove that a problem B is NP-hard:

1. Choose an NP-hard problem A.

2. Prove that A reduces to B.

Carrying out the first step requires knowledge of some known NP-hard problems; Chapter 22 will get you started. The second step builds on your already-developed skills in finding reductions between problems; these will be honed further through practice in Chapter 22. Let's get the gist of how this recipe works by revisiting a familiar problem: the single-source shortest path problem, with negative edge lengths allowed.

19.5.4   NP-Hardness of Cycle-Free Shortest Paths

Recall from Section 18.1.1 that in the single-source shortest path problem, the input consists of a directed graph $G = (V, E)$, a real-valued length ℓ_e for each edge $e \in E$, and a starting vertex $s \in V$. The length of a path is the sum of the lengths of its edges. The goal is to compute, for every possible destination $v \in V$, the minimum length $dist(s, v)$ of a directed path in G from s to v. (If no such path exists, $dist(s, v)$ is defined as $+\infty$.) Negative edge lengths are allowed.[22] For example, the shortest-path distances from s in the graph

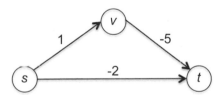

are $dist(s, s) = 0$, $dist(s, v) = 1$, and $dist(s, t) = -4$.

Negative Cycles

How should we define shortest-path distances in a graph like the following?

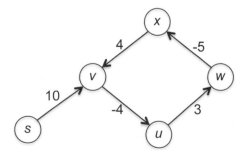

---

[22]Dijkstra's algorithm (Chapter 9) solves the single-source shortest path problem in graphs with only nonnegative edge lengths in blazingly fast fashion. But recall from Section 18.1.1 that negative edge lengths naturally arise in some applications, for example when computing an optimal sequence of financial transactions.

This graph has a *negative cycle*, meaning a directed cycle for which the sum of the edge lengths is negative. There is a one-hop s-v path with length 10. Tacking a cycle traversal at the end produces a five-hop s-v path with total length 8. Adding a second traversal decreases the overall length to 6, and so on. If we allow paths with cycles, then this graph has no shortest s-v path.

The Cycle-Free Shortest Path Problem

An obvious alternative is to forbid paths with cycles, insisting that every vertex is visited at most once.

Problem: Cycle-Free Shortest Paths (CFSP)

Input: A directed graph $G = (V, E)$, a starting vertex $s \in V$, and a real-valued length ℓ_e for each edge $e \in E$.

Output: For every $v \in V$, the minimum length of a cycle-free s-v path in G (or $+\infty$, if there is no s-v path in G).

Unfortunately, this version of the problem is NP-hard.

Theorem 19.1 (NP-Hardness of Cycle-Free Shortest Paths) *The cycle-free shortest path problem is NP-hard.*

This result explains why the Bellman-Ford algorithm (Section 18.2)—along with every other polynomial-time shortest-path algorithm—solves only a special case of the problem (input graphs without negative cycles, in which shortest paths are automatically cycle-free). Theorem 19.1 shows that, assuming the P $\neq$ NP conjecture, no such algorithm can compute correct cycle-free shortest-path distances in general.

The Directed Hamiltonian Path Problem

We can prove Theorem 19.1 by following the two-step recipe in Section 19.5.3. For the first step, we'll use a famous NP-hard problem known as the *directed Hamiltonian path* problem.

Problem: Directed Hamiltonian Path (DHP)

Input: A directed graph $G = (V, E)$, a starting vertex $s \in V$, and an ending vertex $t \in V$.

Output: "Yes" if G contains an s-t path visiting every vertex $v \in V$ exactly once (called an s-t *Hamiltonian path*), and "no" otherwise.

For example, of the two directed graphs

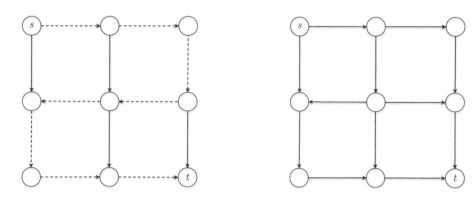

the first has an s-t Hamiltonian path (the dashed edges) while the second does not.

Proof of Theorem 19.1

Section 22.6 proves that the directed Hamiltonian path problem is NP-hard (again using the two-step recipe in Section 19.5.3). For now, we'll take its NP-hardness on faith and move on to the second step of the recipe, in which we reduce a known NP-hard problem (in this case, directed Hamiltonian path) to the problem of interest (cycle-free shortest paths).

Lemma 19.2 (Reduction from DHP to CFSP) *The directed Hamiltonian path problem reduces to the cycle-free shortest path problem.*

Proof: How can we use a subroutine for the cycle-free shortest path problem to solve the directed Hamiltonian path problem (recall Figure 19.1)? Suppose we're given an instance of the latter problem, specified by a directed graph $G = (V, E)$, a starting vertex $s \in V$, and an ending vertex $t \in V$. The assumed cycle-free shortest path subroutine is awaiting a graph (and we have one to offer, our own input graph G) and a starting vertex s (ditto). It's not prepared for an ending vertex, but we can keep mum about t. The subroutine is expecting to receive real-valued edge lengths, however, so we'll have to make some up. We can trick the subroutine into thinking that long paths (like an s-t Hamiltonian path) are actually short by giving each edge a negative length. Summarizing, the reduction is (Figure 19.4):

---

1. Assign every edge $e \in E$ a length $\ell_e = -1$.

2. Compute cycle-free shortest paths using the assumed subroutine, reusing the same input graph G and starting vertex s.

3. If the length of a shortest cycle-free path from s to t is $-(|V| - 1)$, return "yes." Otherwise, return "no."

To prove that this reduction is correct, we must show that it returns "yes" whenever the input graph G contains an s-t Hamiltonian path, and "no" otherwise. In the constructed cycle-free shortest paths instance, the minimum length of a cycle-free s-t path equals -1 times the maximum number of hops in a cycle-free s-t path of the original input graph G. A cycle-free s-t path uses $|V| - 1$ hops if it's an s-t Hamiltonian path (to visit all $|V|$ vertices), and fewer otherwise. So, if G has an s-t Hamiltonian path, the cycle-free shortest-path

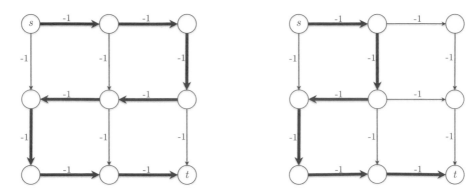

Figure 19.4: Example of the reduction in the proof of Lemma 19.2. The s-t Hamiltonian path in the first graph translates to a cycle-free s-t path with length -8. The second graph has no s-t Hamiltonian path, and the minimum length of a cycle-free s-t path is -6.

distance from s to t in the constructed instance is $-(|V|-1)$; otherwise, it is bigger (that is, less negative). Either way, the reduction returns the correct answer.

By the two-step recipe, Lemma 19.2 and the NP-hardness of the directed Hamiltonian path problem prove Theorem 19.1. Chapter 22 presents many more examples of this recipe in action.

19.5.5   Solution to Quiz 19.3

Correct answer: (d). At first blush, the answer seems to be (c): Each of the at most $T_1(n)$ calls to the subroutine performs at most $T_3(n)$ operations; beyond these calls, the algorithm performs at most $T_2(n)$ operations, for an overall running time of at most $T_1(n) \cdot T_3(n) + T_2(n)$.

This reasoning is correct for most natural reductions between problems, including the three examples in Section 19.5.2. Technically, however, a reduction might, given a size-n input, invoke a subroutine for B on inputs *larger* than n. For example, imagine a reduction that takes as input a graph and, for whatever reason, adds some additional vertices or edges to it before invoking the subroutine for B. What's the worst that could happen? Because the reduction performs at most $T_2(n)$ operations outside of the subroutine calls, it has time only to write down inputs of problem B of size at most $T_2(n)$. Thus, each of the $T_1(n)$ invocations of B requires at most $T_3(T_2(n))$ operations, for an overall running time of $T_1(n) \cdot T_3(T_2(n)) + T_2(n)$.

19.6   Rookie Mistakes and Acceptable Inaccuracies

NP-hardness is a pretty technical topic but, at the same time, highly relevant for practicing algorithm designers and serious programmers. Outside of textbooks and research papers, computer scientists often take liberties with the precise mathematical definitions in the interest of easier communication. Some types of inaccuracies will mark you as a clueless newbie, while others are culturally acceptable. How would you ever know which is which? Because I'm going to tell you, right now.

Rookie Mistake #1

Thinking that "NP" stands for "not polynomial."

You don't need to remember what "NP" actually stands for as long as you avoid this rookie mistake.[23]

Rookie Mistake #2

Saying that a problem is "an NP problem" or "in NP" instead of "NP-hard."

Readers who persevere through Section 23.3 will learn that being "an NP problem" or "in NP" is actually a *good* thing, not a bad thing.[24] So don't forget the "-hard" after the "NP."

Rookie Mistake #3

Thinking that NP-hardness doesn't matter because NP-hard problems can generally be solved in practice.

It's true that NP-hardness is not a death sentence and that NP-hard problems have been tamed, using sufficient human and computational investment, in many practical applications; see Chapter 24 for an in-depth case study. But there are plenty of other applications in which computational problems have been modified or even abandoned because of the challenges posed by NP-hardness. (Naturally, people report their successes in tackling NP-hard problems much more eagerly than their failures!) If it really were true that no problems are hard in practice, why would heuristic algorithms be so common? For that matter, how could modern ecommerce even exist?[25]

Rookie Mistake #4

Thinking that advances in computer technology will rescue us from NP-hardness.

Moore's law and correspondingly larger input sizes only exacerbate the issue, with an increasingly big gulf between running times that are polynomial and those that are not (Section 19.3.2). Quantum computers enable algorithms that improve on exhaustive search but appear inadequate for solving any NP-hard problem in polynomial time (Section 19.3.8).

Rookie Mistake #5

Devising a reduction in the wrong direction.

---

[23] So, what *does* it stand for? Section 23.3 provides the historical context, but in case the suspense is killing you... "nondeterministic polynomial time."

[24] Specifically, it means that if someone handed you a solution on a silver platter (like a completed Sudoku puzzle), you could verify its validity in polynomial time.

[25] Ecommerce relies on cryptosystems like RSA, the security of which depends on the computational intractability of factoring large integers. A polynomial-time algorithm for any NP-hard problem would, via reductions, immediately lead to a polynomial-time factoring algorithm.

A reduction from one problem A to another problem B spreads NP-hardness from A to B, not the other way around (compare Figures 19.2 and 19.3). Because we're so accustomed to designing reductions that spread tractability rather than intractability, this is the hardest mistake to avoid. Whenever you think you've proved that a problem is NP-hard, go back and triple-check that your reduction goes in the correct direction—the same direction in which you're attempting to spread intractability.

Acceptable Inaccuracies

Next are three statements that are culturally acceptable despite being unproven or technically incorrect. None of these will shake anyone's confidence in your understanding of NP-hardness.

Acceptable Inaccuracy #1

Assuming that the P $\neq$ NP conjecture is true.

The status of the P $\neq$ NP conjecture remains open, though most experts are believers. While we wait for our mathematical understanding to catch up to our intuition, many treat the conjecture as a law of nature.

Acceptable Inaccuracy #2

Using the terms "NP-hard" and "NP-complete" interchangeably.

"NP-completeness" is a specific type of NP-hardness; the details are technical and deferred to Section 23.3. The algorithmic implications are the same either way: Whether NP-complete or NP-hard, the problem is not polynomial-time solvable (assuming the P $\neq$ NP conjecture).

Acceptable Inaccuracy #3

Conflating NP-hardness with requiring exponential time in the worst case.

This is the oversimplified interpretation of NP-hardness from the beginning of Section 19.3. This conflation is technically inaccurate (see Section 19.3.9) but faithful to how most experts think about NP-hardness; no one will bat an eye if you make it yourself.

The Upshot

☆ A polynomial-time algorithm is one with worst-case running time $O(n^d)$, where n denotes the input size and d is a constant.

☆ A computational problem is polynomial-time solvable if there is a polynomial-time algorithm that solves it correctly for every input.

☆ The theory of NP-hardness equates "easy" with polynomial-time solvable. Oversimplifying, a "hard" problem is one requiring exponential time to solve in the worst case.

☆ Informally, the P $\neq$ NP conjecture asserts that checking a solution to a problem can be easier than coming up with your own from scratch.

☆ Provisionally, a computational problem is NP-hard if a polynomial-time algorithm solving it would refute the P $\neq$ NP conjecture.

☆ A polynomial-time algorithm for any NP-hard problem would automatically solve thousands of problems that have resisted the efforts of countless brilliant minds over many decades.

☆ NP-hard problems are ubiquitous.

☆ To make progress on an NP-hard problem, the algorithm designer must compromise on generality, correctness, or speed.

☆ Fast heuristic algorithms run quickly but are not always correct. The greedy and local search paradigms are particularly useful for designing such algorithms.

☆ Dynamic programming can improve on exhaustive search for several NP-hard problems.

☆ Mixed integer programming and satisfiability solvers constitute cutting-edge technology for tackling NP-hard problems in practice.

☆ Problem A reduces to problem B if A can be solved using a polynomial number of calls to a subroutine solving B and a polynomial amount of additional work.

☆ Reductions spread tractability: If problem A reduces to problem B and B can be solved by a polynomial-time algorithm, then A can also be solved by a polynomial-time algorithm.

☆ Reductions spread intractability, in the opposite direction: If problem A reduces to problem B and A is NP-hard, then B is also NP-hard.

☆ To prove that a problem B is NP-hard: (i) choose an NP-hard problem A; (ii) prove that A reduces to B.

Test Your Understanding

Problem 19.1 *(S)* Suppose that a computational problem B that you care about is NP-hard. Which of the following are true? (Choose all that apply.)

a) NP-hardness is a "death sentence"; you shouldn't bother trying to solve the instances of B that are relevant for your application.

b) If your boss criticizes you for failing to find a polynomial-time algorithm for B, you can legitimately respond that thousands of brilliant minds have likewise tried and failed to solve B.

c) You should not try to design an algorithm that is guaranteed to solve B correctly and in polynomial time for every possible instance of the problem (unless you're explicitly trying to refute the $P \neq NP$ conjecture).

d) Because the dynamic programming paradigm is useful only for designing exact algorithms, there's no point in trying to apply it to problem B.

Problem 19.2 *(S)* Which of the following statements are true? (Choose all that apply.)

a) The MST problem is computationally tractable because the number of spanning trees of a graph is polynomial in the number n of vertices and the number m of edges.

b) The MST problem is computationally tractable because there are at most m possibilities for the total cost of a spanning tree of a graph.

c) Exhaustive search does not solve the TSP in polynomial time because a graph has an exponential number of traveling salesman tours.

d) The TSP is computationally intractable because a graph has an exponential number of traveling salesman tours.

Problem 19.3 *(S)* Which of the following statements are true? (Choose all that apply.)

a) If the $P \neq NP$ conjecture is true, NP-hard problems can never be solved in practice.

b) If the $P \neq NP$ conjecture is true, no NP-hard problem can be solved by an algorithm that is always correct and that always runs in polynomial time.

c) If the $P \neq NP$ conjecture is false, NP-hard problems can always be solved in practice.

d) If the $P \neq NP$ conjecture is false, some NP-hard problems are polynomial-time solvable.

Problem 19.4 *(S)* Which of the following statements are implied by the $P \neq NP$ conjecture? (Choose all that apply.)

a) Every algorithm that solves an NP-hard problem runs in super-polynomial time in the worst case.

b) Every algorithm that solves an NP-hard problem runs in exponential time in the worst case.

c) Every algorithm that solves an NP-hard problem always runs in super-polynomial time.

d) Every algorithm that solves an NP-hard problem always runs in exponential time.

Problem 19.5 *(S)* Suppose that a problem A reduces to another problem B. Which of the following statements are always true? (Choose all that apply.)

a) If A is polynomial-time solvable, then B is also polynomial-time solvable.

b) If B is NP-hard, then A is also NP-hard.

c) B also reduces to A.

d) B cannot reduce to A.

e) If the problem B reduces to another problem C, then A also reduces to C.

Problem 19.6 *(S)* Assume that the P $\neq$ NP conjecture is true. Which of the following statements about the knapsack problem (Sections 16.5 and 19.4.2) are correct? (Choose all that apply.)

a) The special case in which all item sizes are positive integers less than or equal to n^5, where n is the number of items, can be solved in polynomial time.

b) The special case in which all item values are positive integers less than or equal to n^5, where n is the number of items, can be solved in polynomial time.

c) The special case in which all item values, all item sizes, and the knapsack capacity are positive integers can be solved in polynomial time.

d) There is no polynomial-time algorithm for the knapsack problem in general.

Challenge Problems

Problem 19.7 *(H)* The input in the *traveling salesman path problem (TSPP)* is the same as that in the TSP, and the goal is to compute a minimum-cost cycle-free path that visits every vertex (that is, a tour without its final edge). Prove that the TSPP reduces to the TSP and vice versa.

Problem 19.8 *(H)* This problem describes a computationally tractable special case of the TSP. Consider a connected and acyclic graph $T = (V, F)$ in which each edge $e \in F$ has a nonnegative length $a_e \geq 0$. Define the corresponding *tree instance* $G = (V, E)$ of the TSP by setting the cost c_{vw} of each edge $(v, w) \in E$ equal to the length $\sum_{e \in P_{vw}} a_e$ of the (unique) v-w path P_{vw} in T. For example:

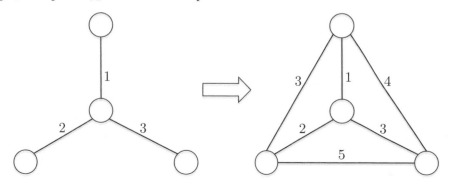

connected acyclic graph   corresponding tree instance of TSP

Design a linear-time algorithm that, given a connected acyclic graph with nonnegative edge lengths, outputs a minimum-cost traveling salesman tour of the corresponding tree instance. Prove that your algorithm is correct.

Programming Problems

Problem 19.9 Implement in your favorite programming language the exhaustive search algorithm for the TSP (as seen in Quiz 19.2). Give your implementation a spin on instances with edge costs chosen independently and uniformly at random from the set $\{1, 2, \ldots, 100\}$. How large an input size (that is, how many vertices) can your program reliably process in under a minute? What about in under an hour? (See www.algorithmsilluminated.org for test cases and challenge data sets.)

Chapter 20

Compromising on Correctness: Efficient Inexact Algorithms

You can't have it all with NP-hard problems and must give up on generality, correctness, or speed. When generality and speed are mission-critical, it's time to consider heuristic algorithms that are not always correct. The goal is then to minimize the damage and design a general-purpose and fast algorithm that is—perhaps provably, or at least empirically— "approximately correct." This chapter illustrates through examples how to use techniques both new (like local search) and old (like greedy algorithms) for this purpose. The case studies concern scheduling (Section 20.1), team selection (Section 20.2), social network analysis (Section 20.3), and the TSP (Section 20.4).

20.1 Makespan Minimization

Our first case study concerns *scheduling* and the goal of assigning tasks to shared resources to optimize some objective. For example, a resource could represent a computer processor (with tasks corresponding to jobs), a classroom (with tasks corresponding to lectures), or a workday (with tasks corresponding to meetings).

20.1.1 Problem Definition

In scheduling problems—as last seen in Chapter 13—the tasks to be completed are usually called *jobs* and the resources are called *machines*. A *schedule* specifies, for each job, one machine to process it. There are a lot of possible schedules. Which of them should we prefer?

Suppose that each job j has a known length ℓ_j, which is the amount of time required to process it (for example, the length of a lecture or meeting). We'll consider one of the most common objectives in applications, of scheduling the jobs so that they all complete as quickly as possible. The following objective function formalizes this idea by assigning a numerical score to every schedule and quantifying what we want:

The Makespan of a Schedule

1. The *load* of a machine in a schedule is the sum of the lengths of the jobs assigned to it.

2. The *makespan* of a schedule is the maximum of the machine loads.

Machine loads and the makespan are the same no matter how jobs are ordered on each machine, so schedules specify only assignments of jobs to machines and not orderings of jobs. (In Chapter 13, a schedule recorded the specific ordering of the jobs because the objective function studied there—minimizing the weighted sum of completion times—depended on it.)

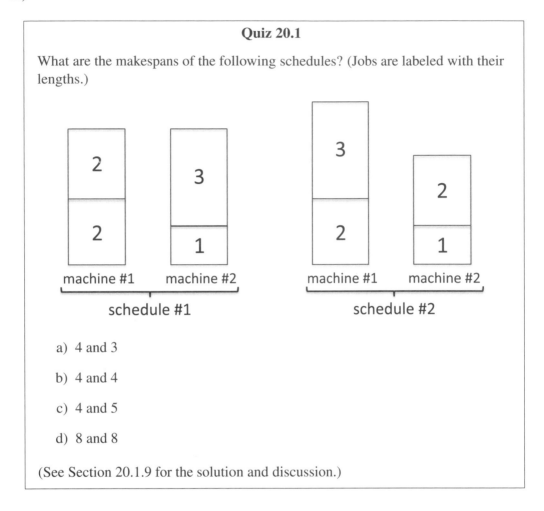

Quiz 20.1

What are the makespans of the following schedules? (Jobs are labeled with their lengths.)

schedule #1

schedule #2

a) 4 and 3

b) 4 and 4

c) 4 and 5

d) 8 and 8

(See Section 20.1.9 for the solution and discussion.)

An "optimal" schedule is then one with the minimum-possible makespan. For example, in Quiz 20.1, the first schedule is the unique one that minimizes the makespan.

Problem: Makespan Minimization

Input: A set of n jobs with positive lengths $\ell_1, \ell_2, \ldots, \ell_n$ and m identical machines.

Output: An assignment of jobs to machines that minimizes the makespan.

For example, if jobs represent parts of a computational task to be processed in parallel (such as the jobs that make up a MapReduce or Hadoop program), the schedule's makespan governs when the entire computation completes.

Minimizing the makespan is an NP-hard problem (see Problem 22.10). Could there be an algorithm that is general-purpose, fast, and "almost correct"?

20.1.2 Greedy Algorithms

For many computational problems (both easy and hard), greedy algorithms are a great place to start brainstorming. To recap the discussion in Section 13.1, the greedy algorithm design paradigm is:

The Greedy Paradigm

Construct a solution iteratively, via a sequence of myopic decisions, and hope that everything works out in the end.

The two biggest selling points of greedy algorithms are that they're usually easy to come up with and they tend to be very fast. The downside is that most greedy algorithms return an incorrect solution in some cases. But for an NP-hard problem, this flaw is shared by all fast algorithms: *No* polynomial-time algorithm is correct on all inputs (assuming, as usual, that the $P \neq NP$ conjecture is true)! Thus, the greedy paradigm is particularly apropos for the design of fast heuristic algorithms for NP-hard problems, and it plays a starring role in this chapter.

20.1.3 Graham's Algorithm

What would a greedy algorithm look like for the makespan minimization problem? Perhaps the simplest approach would be a single-pass algorithm, which assigns jobs irrevocably to machines one by one. To which machine should a job be assigned? Because we're after the most balanced schedule possible, the obvious greedy strategy is to assign a job to the machine that can best tolerate it—the machine with the *smallest* current load. This greedy algorithm is known as *Graham's algorithm*.[1]

Graham

Input: a set $\{1, 2, \ldots, m\}$ of machines and a set $\{1, 2, \ldots, n\}$ of jobs with positive lengths $\ell_1, \ell_2, \ldots, \ell_n$.
Output: an assignment of jobs to machines.

```
   // Initialization
1  for i := 1 to m do
2     J_i := ∅           // jobs assigned to machine i
3     L_i := 0           // current load of machine i
   // Main loop
4  for j := 1 to n do
5     k := argmin_{i=1}^m L_i      // least-loaded machine
6     J_k := J_k ∪ {j}             // assign current job
7     L_k := L_k + ℓ_j             // update loads
8  return J_1, J_2, ..., J_m
```

---

[1]Proposed by Ronald L. Graham in the paper "Bounds on Multiprocessing Time Anomalies" (*SIAM Journal on Applied Mathematics*, 1969).

20.1.4 Running Time

Is Graham's algorithm any good? As usual with greedy algorithms, its running time is easy to analyze. If the argmin computation in line 5 is implemented by exhaustive search through the m possibilities, each of the n iterations of the main loop runs in $O(m)$ time (implementing the J_i's as linked lists, for example). Because only $O(m)$ work is performed outside the main loop, this straightforward implementation leads to a running time of $O(mn)$.

Readers who remember Chapter 10 should recognize an opportunity for improvement. The work done by the algorithm boils down to repeated minimum computations, so a light bulb should go off in your head: This algorithm calls out for a heap data structure! Because a heap reduces the running time of a minimum computation from linear to logarithmic, its use here leads to a blazingly fast $O(n \log m)$-time implementation of the Graham algorithm. Problem 20.6 asks you to fill in the details.

20.1.5 Approximate Correctness

What about the makespan of the schedule constructed by Graham's algorithm?

Quiz 20.2

Suppose there are five machines and the list of jobs consists of twenty jobs with length 1 each, followed by a single job with length 5. What is the makespan of the schedule output by the Graham algorithm, and what is the smallest-possible makespan of a schedule of these jobs?

a) 5 and 4

b) 6 and 5

c) 9 and 5

d) 10 and 5

(See Section 20.1.9 for the solution and discussion.)

Quiz 20.2 demonstrates that the Graham algorithm does not always output an optimal schedule. This is no surprise, given that the problem is NP-hard and the algorithm runs in polynomial time. (If the algorithm *were* always correct, we would have refuted the P $\neq$ NP conjecture!) Even so, the example in Quiz 20.2 should give you pause. Could there be other, more complicated inputs for which Graham's algorithm performs still more poorly? Happily, examples of the type in Quiz 20.2 are as bad as it gets:

Theorem 20.1 (Graham: Approximate Correctness) *The makespan of the schedule output by the Graham algorithm is always at most $2 - \frac{1}{m}$ times the minimum-possible makespan, where m denotes the number of machines.*[2,3]

---

[2]To generalize the bad example in Quiz 20.2 to an arbitrary number m of machines, use $m(m-1)$ length-1 jobs followed by a single job with length m.

[3]The multiplier $2 - \frac{1}{m}$ is sometimes called the *approximation ratio* of the algorithm, which in turn is called a $(2 - \frac{1}{m})$-*approximation algorithm*.

Graham's algorithm is, therefore, an "approximately correct" algorithm for the makespan minimization problem. Think of Theorem 20.1 as an insurance policy. Even in the doomsday scenario of a contrived input like that in Quiz 20.2, the makespan of the algorithm's schedule is no more than double what you'd get by exhaustive search. For more realistic inputs, you should expect the `Graham` algorithm to overdeliver and achieve a makespan much closer to the minimum possible; see also Problem 20.1.

The next section provides the full proof of Theorem 20.1. The time-constrained or math-phobic reader might prefer some brief but accurate intuition:

Intuition for Theorem 20.1

1. The *smallest* machine load is at most the (equal) machine loads in a perfectly balanced schedule, which in turn is at most the minimum-possible makespan (as the best-case scenario is a perfectly balanced schedule).

2. By the `Graham` algorithm's greedy criterion, the largest and smallest machine loads differ by at most the length of a single job, which in turn is at most the minimum-possible makespan (as every job has to go somewhere).

3. Thus, the largest machine load in the algorithm's output is at most twice the minimum-possible makespan.

20.1.6 Proof of Theorem 20.1

For the formal proof, fix an instance comprising jobs with lengths $\ell_1, \ell_2, \ldots, \ell_n$ and m machines. Directly comparing the minimum-possible makespan M^* and the makespan M of the schedule output by the `Graham` algorithm would be messy. Instead, the analysis hinges on two easy-to-compute lower bounds on M^*—the maximum job length and the average machine load—that are easily related to M and ultimately show that $M \leq (2 - \frac{1}{m})M^*$.

The first lower bound on M^* is simple: Every job must go somewhere, so it's impossible to achieve a makespan smaller than a job length.

Lemma 20.2 (Lower Bound #1 on the Optimal Makespan) *If M^* denotes the minimum makespan of any schedule and j a job,*

$$M^* \geq \ell_j. \tag{20.1}$$

More generally, in every schedule, every job j is assigned to exactly one machine i and contributes ℓ_j to its load L_i. Thus, in every schedule, the sum of the machines' loads equals the sum of the jobs' lengths: $\sum_{i=1}^{m} L_i = \sum_{j=1}^{n} \ell_j$. In a perfect schedule, each machine has an *ideal* load, meaning an exact $\frac{1}{m}$ fraction of the total (that is, $\frac{1}{m} \sum_{j=1}^{n} \ell_j$). In any other schedule, some machines have a more-than-ideal load and others a less-than-ideal load. For example, in Quiz 20.1, in the first schedule both machines have ideal loads, while in the second schedule neither has an ideal load (with one over and the other under). The second lower bound on M^* now follows from the fact that every schedule has a machine with a load equal to or larger than the ideal load:

Lemma 20.3 (Lower Bound #2 on the Optimal Makespan) *If M^* denotes the minimum makespan of any schedule, then*

$$M^* \geq \underbrace{\frac{1}{m} \sum_{j=1}^{n} \ell_j}_{\text{ideal load}}.$$ (20.2)

The last step is to bound from above the makespan M of the Graham algorithm's schedule in terms of the two lower bounds introduced in Lemmas 20.2 and 20.3. Let i denote a machine with the largest load in this schedule (that is, with load L_i equal to M), and j the final job assigned to it (Figure 20.1(a)). Rewind the algorithm to the moment in time just before j's assignment and let $\widehat{L}_i$ denote i's load at that time. The new and final load L_i of the machine (and, hence, the makespan M) is $\ell_j + \widehat{L}_i$.

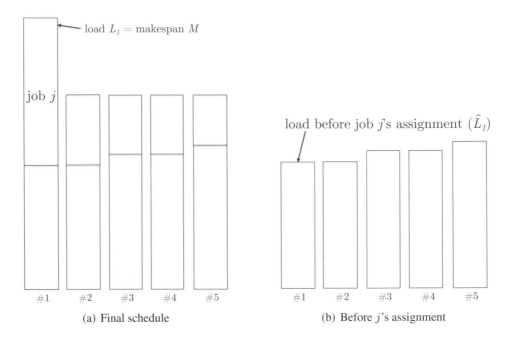

(a) Final schedule   (b) Before j's assignment

Figure 20.1: The most loaded machine was the least loaded machine immediately prior to its final job assignment.

How big could $\widehat{L}_i$ have been? By the greedy criterion of the Graham algorithm, i was the most lightly loaded machine at the time (Figure 20.1(b)). If the jobs $\{1, 2, \ldots, j-1\}$ prior to j were perfectly balanced across the machines, all machines' loads at that time would have been $\frac{1}{m} \sum_{h=1}^{j-1} \ell_h$; otherwise, the lightest load $\widehat{L}_i$ would have been even less. In any case, the final makespan $M = \ell_j + \widehat{L}_i$ is at most

$$\ell_j + \frac{1}{m} \sum_{h=1}^{j-1} \ell_h \leq \ell_j + \frac{1}{m} \sum_{h \neq j} \ell_h,$$

where on the right-hand side we have thrown in the missing (positive) terms $\ell_{j+1}/m, \ell_{j+2}/m, \ldots, \ell_n/m$ for convenience. Transferring ℓ_j/m from the first term to the second, we can write

$$M \leq \underbrace{\left(1-\frac{1}{m}\right)\cdot \ell_j}_{\leq \left(1-\frac{1}{m}\right)M^* \text{ by (20.1)}} + \underbrace{\frac{1}{m}\sum_{h=1}^{n}\ell_h}_{\leq M^* \text{ by (20.2)}} \leq \left(2-\frac{1}{m}\right)\cdot M^*, \qquad (20.3)$$

with the second inequality following from Lemma 20.2 (to bound the first term) and Lemma 20.3 (to bound the second term). This completes the proof of Theorem 20.1. $\mathcal{QED}$

20.1.7   Longest Processing Time First (LPT)

An insurance policy like the approximate correctness guarantee in Theorem 20.1 is reassuring, but it remains our duty to ask: Can we do better? Can we devise a different fast heuristic algorithm that is "even less incorrect," offering an insurance policy with a lower deductible? We can, using a familiar for-free primitive.

What goes wrong with the Graham algorithm in the contrived example of Quiz 20.2? It perfectly balances the length-1 jobs, leaving no good location for the length-5 job. If only the algorithm had considered the length-5 job first, all the other jobs would have fallen neatly into place. More generally, the second part of the intuition for Theorem 20.1 (page 475) and the final step in its proof (inequality (20.3)) both advocate for making the last job assigned to the most loaded machine (job j in (20.3)) as small as possible. This suggests the *longest processing time first (LPT)* algorithm (also proposed by Graham), which saves the smallest jobs for last.

LPT

Input/Output: as in the Graham algorithm (page 473).

---

sort the jobs from longest to shortest
run the Graham algorithm on the sorted jobs

The first step can be implemented in $O(n\log n)$ time (for n jobs) using, for example, MergeSort. If the Graham algorithm is implemented with heaps (Problem 20.6), both of these steps run in near-linear time.[4]

Quiz 20.3

Suppose there are five machines, three jobs with length 5, two with length 6, two with length 7, two with length 8, and two with length 9. What is the makespan of the schedule output by the LPT algorithm, and what is the smallest-possible makespan of a schedule of these jobs?

a) 16 and 15

---

[4]The Graham algorithm is an example of an "online algorithm": It can be used even if the jobs materialize one by one and must be scheduled immediately. The LPT algorithm is not an online algorithm; it requires advance knowledge of all the jobs to sort them by length.

> b) 17 and 15
>
> c) 18 and 15
>
> d) 19 and 15
>
> (See Section 20.1.9 for the solution and discussion.)

Again, because the makespan minimization problem is NP-hard and the LPT algorithm runs in polynomial time, we fully expected such examples demonstrating that the latter is not always optimal. But does it provide a better insurance policy than the Graham algorithm?

Theorem 20.4 (LPT: Approximate Correctness) *The makespan of the schedule output by the LPT algorithm is always at most $\frac{3}{2} - \frac{1}{2m}$ times the minimum-possible makespan, where m denotes the number of machines.*

Intuitively, sorting the jobs reduces the possible damage caused by a single job—the difference between the largest and smallest machine loads—from M^* (the minimum-possible makespan) to $M^*/2$.

The keen reader may have noticed the daylight between the bad example in Quiz 20.3 (with a makespan blowup of $19/15 \approx 1.267$) and the assurance of Theorem 20.4 (which, for $m = 5$, promises a blowup of at most $14/10 = 1.4$). With some additional arguments (outlined in Problem 20.7), the guarantee in Theorem 20.4 can be refined from $\frac{3}{2} - \frac{1}{2m}$ to $\frac{4}{3} - \frac{1}{3m}$. Consequently, the examples suggested by Quiz 20.3 are as bad as it gets for the LPT algorithm. And as with the Graham algorithm, you should expect the LPT algorithm to overdeliver for more realistic inputs.[5]

20.1.8   Proof of Theorem 20.4

The proof of Theorem 20.4 follows that of Theorem 20.1, with the improvement enabled by a variant of Lemma 20.2 that is useful when the jobs are sorted from longest to shortest.

Lemma 20.5 (Variant of Lower Bound #1) *If M^* denotes the minimum makespan of any schedule and j a job that is not among the m longest (breaking ties arbitrarily),*

$$M^* \geq 2\ell_j. \tag{20.4}$$

Proof: By the Pigeonhole Principle (page 265), every schedule must assign two of the longest $m + 1$ jobs to the same machine. Therefore, the minimum-possible makespan is at least twice the length of the $(m + 1)$th-longest job; this is at least $2\ell_j$. $\mathcal{QED}$

Now on to:

Proof of Theorem 20.4: As in the final part of the proof of Theorem 20.1, let i denote a machine that has the largest load in the LPT algorithm's schedule and j the final job assigned to it (Figure 20.1(a)). Suppose at least one other job is assigned to i (prior to j); otherwise,

---

[5]There are more sophisticated algorithms with even better approximate correctness guarantees; these technically run in polynomial time but are impractically slow. If the makespan minimization problem comes up in your own work, the LPT algorithm is an excellent starting point.

there's nothing to prove. (If j is the only job assigned to i, the algorithm's schedule has makespan ℓ_j and, by Lemma 20.2, no other schedule can be better.)

The algorithm assigns each of the first m jobs to a different machine (each empty at the time). Therefore, job j cannot be one of the first m jobs. By the LPT greedy criterion, job j cannot be one of the m longest jobs. Lemma 20.5 then tells us that $\ell_j \le M^*/2$, where M^* is the minimum-possible makespan. Plugging this improved bound (relative to Lemma 20.2) into the inequality (20.3) shows that the makespan M achieved by the LPT algorithm satisfies

$$M \le \underbrace{\left(1 - \frac{1}{m}\right) \cdot \ell_j}_{\le \left(1-\frac{1}{m}\right)\cdot(M^*/2)\text{ by (20.4)}} + \underbrace{\frac{1}{m}\sum_{h=1}^{n}\ell_h}_{\le M^*\text{ by (20.2)}} \le \left(\frac{3}{2} - \frac{1}{2m}\right) \cdot M^*.$$

QED

20.1.9   Solutions to Quizzes 20.1–20.3

Solution to Quiz 20.1

Correct answer: (c). The machine loads are $2 + 2 = 4$ and $1 + 3 = 4$ in the first schedule and $2 + 3 = 5$ and $1 + 2 = 3$ in the second. Because the makespan is the largest machine load, these schedules have makespans of 4 and 5, respectively.

Solution to Quiz 20.2

Correct answer: (c). The Graham algorithm schedules the first twenty jobs evenly across the machines (with four length-1 jobs on each). No matter how it schedules the final length-5 job, it's stuck with a makespan of 9:

Meanwhile, reserving one machine for the big job and splitting the twenty small jobs evenly between the remaining four machines creates a perfectly balanced schedule, with makespan 5:

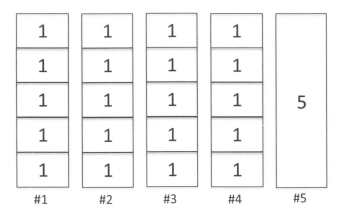

Solution to Quiz 20.3

Correct answer: (d). The optimal schedule is perfectly balanced, with the three length-5 jobs assigned to a common machine and every other machine receiving either a length-9 and length-6 job or a length-8 and length-7 job:

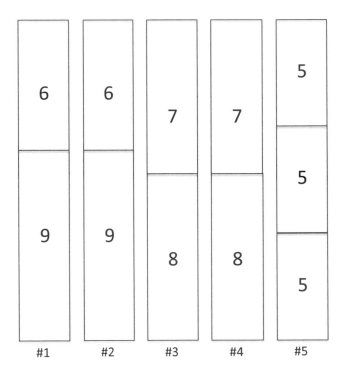

The makespan of this schedule is 15. Meanwhile, all machines already have load 14 when the time comes for the LPT algorithm to assign its final length-5 job, so it gets stuck with a final makespan of 19:

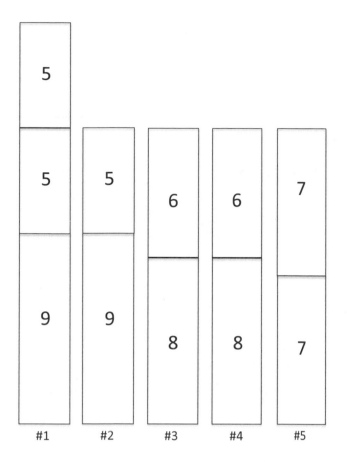

20.2 Maximum Coverage

Imagine you've been put in charge of assembling a team—maybe at your company to complete a project, or in your fantasy sports league to compete over a season. You can afford to hire only a limited number of people. Each potential team member has a combination of skills—perhaps corresponding to programming languages that they know, or positions on the field that they can play. You want a diverse team with as many different skills as possible. Whom should you pick?

20.2.1 Problem Definition

In the *maximum coverage* problem, the input comprises m subsets $A_1, A_2, \ldots, A_m$ of a ground set U, and a budget k. For example, in a team-hiring application, the ground set U corresponds to all possible skills that a team member could have, and each subset A_i corresponds to one potential team member, with the elements of the subset indicating the candidate's skills. The goal is to choose k of the subsets to maximize their *coverage*—the number of distinct ground set elements they contain. In a team-hiring problem, coverage corresponds to the number of distinct skills possessed by the team.

Problem: Maximum Coverage

Input: A collection $A_1, A_2, \ldots, A_m$ of subsets of a ground set U, and a positive integer k.

Output: A choice $K \subseteq \{1, 2, \ldots, m\}$ of k indices to maximize the coverage $f_{cov}(K)$ of the corresponding subsets, where:

$$f_{cov}(K) = \left| \cup_{i \in K} A_i \right|. \tag{20.5}$$

For example:

Quiz 20.4

Consider a ground set U with 16 elements and six subsets of it:

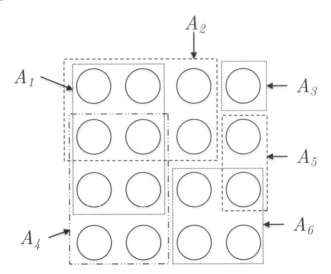

What is the largest coverage achieved by four of the subsets?

   a) 13

   b) 14

   c) 15

   d) 16

(See Section 20.2.8 for the solution and discussion.)

Maximum coverage problems are tricky because of overlaps between subsets. For example, some skills may be common (covered by many subsets) and others rare (covered by few). An ideal subset is large with few redundant elements—a team member blessed with many unique skills.

20.2.2 Further Applications

Maximum coverage problems show up all the time, and not only in team-hiring applications. For example, suppose you want to choose locations for k new firehouses in a city to maximize the number of residents who live within one mile of a firehouse. This is a maximum coverage problem in which the ground set elements correspond to residents, each subset corresponds to a possible firehouse location, and the elements of a subset correspond to the residents who live within one mile of that location.

For a more complex example, imagine you want to coax people to show up at an event, such as a concert. You need to start setting up for the event and have time to convince only k of your friends to come. But whichever friends you recruit then bring along *their* friends, and friends of friends, and so on. We can visualize this problem using a directed graph, in which vertices correspond to people and an edge directed from v to w signifies that w would follow v to the event should v attend. For example, in the graph

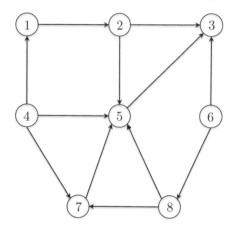

recruiting your friend 1 would ultimately trigger the attendance of four people (1, 2, 3, and 5). Your friend 6 will show up only if recruited directly, in which case four others (3, 5, 7, and 8) follow suit.

Maximizing event attendance is a maximum coverage problem. Ground set elements correspond to people—equivalently, the vertices of the graph. There is one subset per person, indicating who would ultimately follow that person to the event—equivalently, the vertices reachable by a directed path from that vertex. The total attendance triggered by the recruitment of k people is then exactly the coverage achieved by the corresponding k subsets.

20.2.3 A Greedy Algorithm

The maximum coverage problem is NP-hard (see Problem 22.8). If we don't want to give up on speed, it's time to consider heuristic algorithms. Greedy algorithms, which myopically select subsets one by one, are again the obvious place to start.

The problem is easy to solve when you can pick only one subset ($k = 1$)—go with the biggest one. Suppose $k = 2$ and you have already committed to picking the biggest of the subsets, A. What should the second subset be? What matters now are the elements in a subset *not already covered by* A, so the sensible greedy criterion is to maximize the number of newly covered elements. Extending this idea to an arbitrary budget k leads to

the following famous greedy algorithm for the maximum coverage problem, in which the
coverage function f_{cov} is defined as in (20.5):[6]

GreedyCoverage

Input: subsets $A_1, A_2, \ldots, A_m$ of a ground set U and a positive
   integer k.
Output: a set $K \subseteq \{1, 2, \ldots, m\}$ of k indices.

---

1 $K := \emptyset$ `// indices of chosen sets`
2 **for** $j := 1$ to k **do**   `// choose sets one by one`
       `// greedily increase coverage`
       `// (break ties arbitrarily)`
3     $i^* := \mathrm{argmax}_{i=1}^{m} \left[f_{cov}(K \cup \{i\}) - f_{cov}(K) \right]$
4     $K := K \cup \{i^*\}$

5 return K

For simplicity, the argmax in line 3 examines all the subsets; equivalently, it could restrict
attention to those not already chosen in previous iterations.

20.2.4   Bad Examples for the GreedyCoverage Algorithm

The GreedyCoverage algorithm is easy to implement in polynomial time.[7] Because the
maximum coverage problem is NP-hard, we should expect examples for which the algorithm
outputs a suboptimal solution (as otherwise it would refute the P $\neq$ NP conjecture). Here's
one:

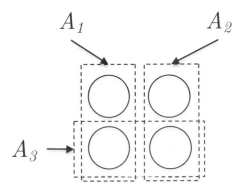

Suppose $k = 2$. The optimal solution is to pick the subsets A_1 and A_2 to cover all four
elements. The greedy algorithm (with arbitrary tie-breaking) might well pick the subset A_3

---

[6]First analyzed by Gérard P. Cornuéjols, Marshall L. Fisher, and George L. Nemhauser in the paper
"Location of Bank Accounts to Optimize Float: An Analytic Study of Exact and Approximate Algorithms"
(*Management Science*, 1977).

[7]For example, compute the argmax in line 3 by exhaustive search through the m subsets, computing the
additional coverage $f_{cov}(K \cup \{i\}) - f_{cov}(K)$ provided by a subset A_i using a single pass over A_i's elements.
A straightforward implementation leads to a running time of $O(kms)$, where s denotes the maximum size of a
subset (which is at most $|U|$).

in its first iteration, in which case it's stuck picking either A_1 or A_2 in the second iteration and covering only three of the four elements.

Are there still worse examples for the GreedyCoverage algorithm? At least for larger budgets k, the answer is yes.

Quiz 20.5

Consider the following ground set of 81 elements and five subsets of it:

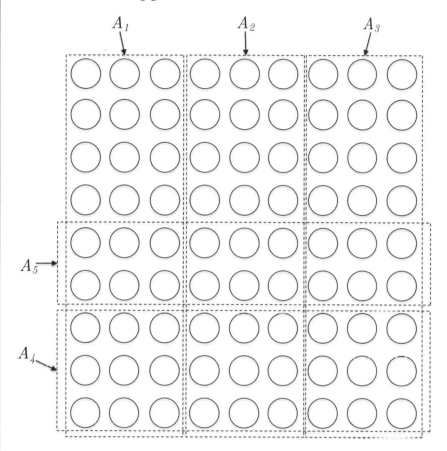

For $k = 3$, what is: (i) the maximum-possible coverage; (ii) the smallest-possible coverage of the output of the GreedyCoverage algorithm (with arbitrary tie-breaking)?

    a) 72 and 60

    b) 81 and 57

    c) 81 and 60

    d) 81 and 64

(See Section 20.2.8 for the solution and discussion.)

Thus, with $k = 2$, the GreedyCoverage algorithm might capture only 75% of the elements that could be covered, and with $k = 3$, it might fare as poorly as $\frac{57}{81} = \frac{19}{27} \approx 70.4\%$. How bad can things get? Problem 20.8(a) asks you to extend this pattern to all positive integers k, thereby showing:[8]

Proposition 20.6 (Bad Examples for GreedyCoverage) *For every positive integer k, there is an instance of the maximum coverage problem in which:*

(a) *There exist k subsets that cover the entire ground set.*

(b) *With arbitrary tie-breaking, the GreedyCoverage algorithm might cover only a $1 - (1 - \frac{1}{k})^k$ fraction of the elements.*[9]

The easiest way to get a handle on a crazy expression with one variable is to plot it. Following this advice for the function $1 - (1 - \frac{1}{x})^x$, we see that it is decreasing but seems to approach an asymptote at roughly 63.2%:

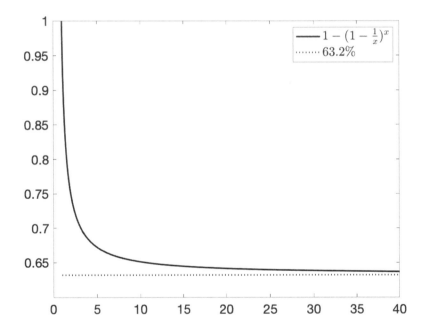

What's going on is that $1 - x$ is very well approximated by e^{-x} when x is close to 0 (as you should verify with a plot or a Taylor expansion of e^{-x}). Thus, the expression $1 - (1 - \frac{1}{k})^k$ tends to $1 - (e^{-1/k})^k = 1 - \frac{1}{e} \approx 0.632$ as k tends to infinity.[10]

20.2.5 Approximate Correctness

What's a weird number like $1 - \frac{1}{e}$ doing in proximity to the super-simple GreedyCoverage algorithm? Maybe it's an artifact of the examples we cooked up

---

[8]The reliance on arbitrary tie-breaking is convenient but not essential to these examples; see Problem 20.8(b).

[9]Note that $1 - (1 - \frac{1}{k})^k$ equals $1 - (\frac{1}{2})^2 = \frac{3}{4}$ when $k = 2$ and $1 - (\frac{2}{3})^3 = \frac{19}{27}$ when $k = 3$.

[10]Here, $e = 2.718\ldots$ denotes Euler's number.

in Quiz 20.5 and Proposition 20.6? Quite the opposite: The following approximate correctness guarantee proves that these are the worst examples for the `GreedyCoverage` algorithm, showing that it is inextricably tied to the numbers $1 - (1 - \frac{1}{k})^k$ and $1 - \frac{1}{e}$.[11,12]

Theorem 20.7 (`GreedyCoverage`: Approximate Correctness) *The coverage of the solution output by the* `GreedyCoverage` *algorithm is always at least a* $1 - (1 - \frac{1}{k})^k$ *fraction of the maximum-possible coverage, where* k *is the number of subsets chosen.*

Thus, the `GreedyCoverage` algorithm is guaranteed to cover at least 75% as many elements as an optimal solution when $k = 2$, at least 70.4% as many when $k = 3$, and at least 63.2% as many no matter how large k is. As with Theorems 20.1 and 20.4, Theorem 20.7 is an insurance policy that limits the damage in a worst-case scenario; for more realistic inputs, the algorithm is likely to overdeliver and achieve significantly higher percentages.

20.2.6   A Key Lemma

To develop your intuition for Theorem 20.7, let's revisit the example in Quiz 20.5. Why didn't the `GreedyCoverage` algorithm come up with the optimal solution? In the first iteration, it had the option of picking any of the three subsets in the optimal solution (A_1, A_2, or A_3). Unfortunately, the algorithm was tricked by a fourth, equally large subset (A_4, covering 27 elements). In the second iteration, the algorithm again had the option of picking any of A_1, A_2, or A_3, but it was tricked by the subset A_5, which covered just as many new elements (18).

In general, every miscue by the `GreedyCoverage` algorithm can be attributed to a subset that covers at least as many new elements as each of the k subsets in an optimal solution. But shouldn't this mean that the `GreedyCoverage` algorithm makes healthy progress in each iteration? This idea is formalized in the next lemma, which bounds from below the number of newly covered elements in each iteration as a function of the current coverage deficiency:

Lemma 20.8 (`GreedyCoverage` Makes Progress) *For each* $j \in \{1, 2, \ldots, k\}$, *let* C_j *denote the coverage achieved by the first* j *subsets chosen by the* `GreedyCoverage` *algorithm. For each such* j, *the* j*th subset chosen covers at least* $\frac{1}{k}(C^* - C_{j-1})$ *new elements, where* C^* *denotes the maximum-possible coverage by* k *subsets:*

$$C_j - C_{j-1} \geq \frac{1}{k}\left(C^* - C_{j-1}\right). \tag{20.6}$$

Proof: Let K_{j-1} denote the indices of the first $j - 1$ subsets chosen by the `GreedyCoverage` algorithm and $C_{j-1} = f_{cov}(K_{j-1})$ their coverage. Consider any competing set $\widehat{K}$ of k indices, with corresponding coverage $\widehat{C} = f_{cov}(\widehat{K})$.

---

[11] It gets weirder: Assuming the P $\neq$ NP conjecture, *no* polynomial-time algorithm (greedy or otherwise) can guarantee a solution with coverage larger than a $1 - \frac{1}{e}$ fraction of the maximum possible as k grows large. (This is a difficult result, due to Uriel Feige in the paper "A Threshold of $\ln n$ for Approximating Set Cover" (*Journal of the ACM*, 1998).) This fact provides a strong theoretical justification for adopting the `GreedyCoverage` algorithm as a starting point when tackling the maximum coverage problem in practice. It also implies that the number $1 - \frac{1}{e}$ is intrinsic to the maximum coverage problem rather than an artifact of one particular algorithm.

[12] We won't see the number $1 - \frac{1}{e}$ again in this book, but it recurs mysteriously often in the analysis of algorithms.

The most important inequality in the proof is:

$$\sum_{i \in \widehat{K}} \underbrace{[f_{cov}(K_{j-1} \cup \{i\}) - C_{j-1}]}_{\text{coverage increase from } A_i} \geq \underbrace{\widehat{C} - C_{j-1}}_{\text{current coverage gap}} \quad . \tag{20.7}$$

Why is it true? Let W denote the ground set elements covered by the subsets corresponding to $\widehat{K}$ but not those corresponding to K_{j-1} (Figure 20.2). On the one hand, the size of W is at least $\widehat{C} - C_{j-1}$, the right-hand side of (20.7). On the other, it is also no more than the left-hand side of (20.7): Each element of W contributes at least once to the sum—once per subset with index in $\widehat{K}$ that contains it. Therefore, the left-hand side of (20.7) is at least its right-hand side, with the size of W sandwiched between them.

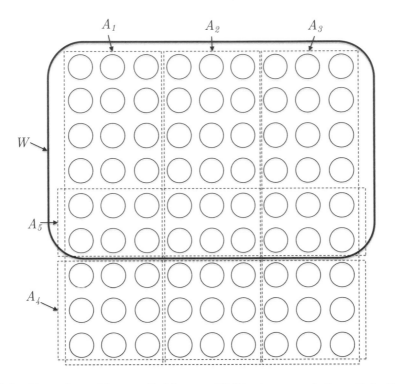

Figure 20.2: Illustration of the proof of Lemma 20.8 in the example from Quiz 20.5, with $j = 2$, $K_{j-1} = \{4\}$, $C_{j-1} = 27$, $\widehat{K} = \{1, 2, 3\}$, and $\widehat{C} = 81$. The set W is the $81 - 27 = 54$ elements covered by some subset with index in $\widehat{K}$ and no subset with index in K_{j-1}.

Next, if the k numbers summed on the left-hand side of (20.7) were equal, each would be $\frac{1}{k} \sum_{i \in \widehat{K}} [f_{cov}(K_{j-1} \cup \{i\}) - C_{j-1}]$; otherwise, the largest of them would be even bigger:

$$\underbrace{\max_{i \in \widehat{K}} [f_{cov}(K_{j-1} \cup \{i\}) - C_{j-1}]}_{\text{biggest value}} \geq \underbrace{\frac{1}{k} \sum_{i \in \widehat{K}} [f_{cov}(K_{j-1} \cup \{i\}) - C_{j-1}]}_{\text{average value}}. \tag{20.8}$$

Now instantiate $\widehat{K}$ as the indices K^* of an optimal solution, with coverage $f_{cov}(K^*) = C^*$. Chaining together inequalities (20.7) and (20.8) shows that the GreedyCoverage algorithm has at least one good option (the best of the indices in the optimal solution K^*):

$$\underbrace{\max_{i \in K^*} \left[f_{cov}(K_{j-1} \cup \{i\}) - C_{j-1} \right]}_{\text{best of the optimal indices}} \geq \underbrace{\frac{1}{k} \left(C^* - C_{j-1} \right)}_{\text{guaranteed progress}}.$$

The `GreedyCoverage` algorithm, due to its greedy criterion, selects an index that is at least this good, thereby increasing the coverage of its solution by at least $\frac{1}{k} \left(C^* - C_{j-1} \right)$. $\mathcal{QED}$

20.2.7   Proof of Theorem 20.7

We can now prove Theorem 20.7 by iterating the recurrence (20.6) from Lemma 20.8 that bounds from below the progress made by the `GreedyCoverage` algorithm in each iteration. Continuing with the same notation, the goal is to compare the coverage C_k achieved by the algorithm's solution with the maximum-possible coverage C^*.

The anticipated term $1 - \frac{1}{k}$ enters the picture as soon as we apply Lemma 20.8 (first with $j = k$):

$$C_k \geq C_{k-1} + \frac{1}{k} \left(C^* - C_{k-1} \right) = \frac{C^*}{k} + \left(1 - \frac{1}{k} \right) C_{k-1}.$$

Applying it again (now with $j = k - 1$):

$$C_{k-1} \geq \frac{C^*}{k} + \left(1 - \frac{1}{k} \right) C_{k-2}.$$

Combining the two inequalities:

$$C_k \geq \frac{C^*}{k} \left(1 + \left(1 - \frac{1}{k} \right) \right) + \left(1 - \frac{1}{k} \right)^2 C_{k-2}.$$

Applying Lemma 20.8 a third time with $j = k - 2$ and then substituting for C_{k-2}:

$$C_k \geq \frac{C^*}{k} \left(1 + \left(1 - \frac{1}{k} \right) + \left(1 - \frac{1}{k} \right)^2 \right) + \left(1 - \frac{1}{k} \right)^3 C_{k-3}.$$

The pattern continues and, after k applications of the lemma (and using that $C_0 = 0$), we wind up with

$$C_k \geq \frac{C^*}{k} \underbrace{\left(1 + \left(1 - \frac{1}{k} \right) + \left(1 - \frac{1}{k} \right)^2 + \cdots + \left(1 - \frac{1}{k} \right)^{k-1} \right)}_{\text{geometric series}}.$$

Inside the parentheses is an old friend, a geometric series. Recall from Section 4.4.8 the closed-form formula

$$1 + r + r^2 + \cdots + r^\ell = \frac{1 - r^{\ell+1}}{1 - r} \tag{20.9}$$

that holds for every $r \neq 1$. Invoking this formula with $r = 1 - \frac{1}{k}$ and $\ell = k - 1$, our lower bound on C_k transforms into

$$C_k \geq \frac{C^*}{k} \left(\frac{1 - (1 - \frac{1}{k})^k}{1 - (1 - \frac{1}{k})} \right) = C^* \left(1 - \left(1 - \frac{1}{k} \right)^k \right),$$

fulfilling the promise made by Theorem 20.7. $\mathcal{QED}$

20.2.8   Solutions to Quizzes 20.4–20.5

Solution to Quiz 20.4

Correct answer: (c). There are two ways to cover 15 of the 16 elements, by choosing A_2, A_4, A_6, and either A_3 or A_5. The large subset A_1 does not participate in any optimal solution because it is largely redundant with the other subsets.

Solution to Quiz 20.5

Correct answer: (b). The optimal solution picks the subsets A_1, A_2, and A_3 and covers all 81 elements. One possible execution of the `GreedyCoverage` algorithm picks A_4 in its first iteration, breaking a four-way tie with A_1, A_2, A_3; A_5 in its second iteration, again breaking a four-way tie with A_1, A_2, A_3; and, finally, A_1. This solution has coverage $27 + 18 + 12 = 57$.

*20.3   Influence Maximization

The `GreedyCoverage` algorithm from Section 20.2 was originally motivated by old-school applications like choosing locations for new factories. In the 21st century, generalizations of this algorithm have found new applications in many fields of computer science. This section describes a representative example in social network analysis.

20.3.1   Cascades in Social Networks

For our purposes, a *social network* is a directed graph $G = (V, E)$ in which the vertices correspond to people and a directed edge (v, w) signifies that v "influences" w. For example, perhaps w follows v in an online social network such as Twitter or Instagram.

A *cascade model* posits how information (such as a news article or meme) travels through a social network. Here's a simple one, parameterized by a directed graph $G = (V, E)$, an activation probability $p \in [0, 1]$, and a subset $S \subseteq V$ of *seed* vertices:[13]

A Simple Cascade Model

Initially, every seed vertex is "active" and all other vertices are "inactive." All edges are initially "unflipped."

While there is some active vertex v and unflipped outgoing edge (v, w):

- Flip a biased coin that comes up "heads" with probability p.

- If the coin comes up "heads," update the status of edge (v, w) to "active." If w is inactive, update its status to "active."

- If the coin comes up "tails," update the status of edge (v, w) to "inactive."

---

[13]To brush up on basic discrete probability, see the resources at `www.algorithmsilluminated.org` or Appendix B.

Once a vertex is activated (say, due to reading an article or seeing a movie), it never becomes inactive. A vertex can have multiple activation opportunities—one for each of its activated influencers. For example, maybe the first two recommendations from friends for a new movie don't register, but the third triggers you to go see it.

20.3.2   Example

In the graph

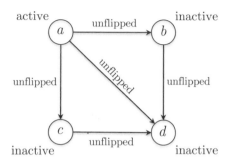

the vertex a is a seed and initially active; the rest are initially inactive. Each of the outgoing edges (a, b), (a, c), and (a, d) has a probability of p of activating the other endpoint of the edge. Suppose the coin associated with edge (a, b) comes up "heads" and the other two come up "tails." The new picture is:

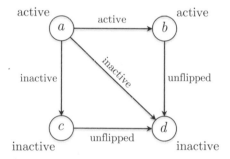

At this point, there is no hope of activating vertex c. There remains a probability of p that vertex d is activated via the unflipped edge (b, d); if this event occurs, the final state is:

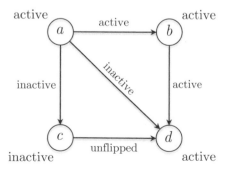

For closure and convenience, we can optionally add a postprocessing step that flips the coins of any remaining unflipped edges and updates their statuses accordingly (while leaving all vertices' statuses unchanged). In our running example, the final result might be:

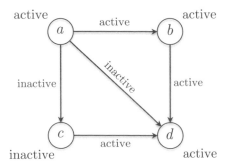

In general, with or without the postprocessing step, the vertices that wind up activated at the end of the process are precisely those reachable from a seed vertex by a directed path of activated edges.

20.3.3   The Influence Maximization Problem

In the *influence maximization* problem, the goal is to choose a limited number of seed vertices in a social network to maximize the spread of information, meaning the number of vertices that are eventually activated according to our cascade model.[14] This number is a random variable, depending on the outcomes of the coin flips in the cascade model, and we focus on its expectation.[15] Formally, let $X(S)$ denote the (random) set of vertices that are eventually activated when the vertices S are chosen as seeds, and define the *influence* of S as

$$f_{inf}(S) = \mathbf{E}[|X(S)|], \tag{20.10}$$

where the expectation is over the random coin flips in the cascade model. The influence of a set depends on both the graph and on the activation probability, with more edges or a higher probability resulting in a bigger influence.

Problem: Influence Maximization

Input: A directed graph $G = (V, E)$, a probability p, and a positive integer k.

Output: A choice $S \subseteq V$ of k vertices with the maximum-possible influence $f_{inf}(S)$ in the cascade model with activation probability p.

For example, if you're giving away k promotional copies of a product and want to choose the recipients to maximize its eventual adoption, you're facing an influence maximization problem.

Problem 20.9 asks you to show that the maximum coverage problem can be viewed as a special case of the influence maximization problem. Because the special case is NP-hard (Problem 22.8), so is the more general problem. Could there be a fast and approximately correct heuristic algorithm for the influence maximization problem?

---

[14]For much more on the influence maximization problem and its many variations, check out the paper "Maximizing the Spread of Influence Through a Social Network," by David Kempe, Jon Kleinberg, and Éva Tardos (*Theory of Computing*, 2015).

[15]The *expectation* $\mathbf{E}[Y]$ of a random variable Y is its average value, weighted by the appropriate probabilities (see Appendix B). For example, if Y can take on the values $\{0, 1, 2, \ldots, n\}$, then $\mathbf{E}[Y] = \sum_{i=0}^{n} i \cdot \mathbf{Pr}[Y = i]$.

20.3.4   A Greedy Algorithm

The influence maximization problem resembles the maximum coverage problem, with vertices playing the role of subsets and with influence (20.10) playing the role of coverage (20.5). The GreedyCoverage algorithm for the latter problem translates easily to the former, swapping in the new definition (20.10) of the objective function.

GreedyInfluence

Input: directed graph $G = (V, E)$, probability $p \in [0, 1]$, and positive integer k.
Output: a set $S \subseteq V$ of k vertices.

---

1 $S := \emptyset$ // chosen vertices
2 **for** $j := 1$ to k **do**   // choose vertices one by one
        // greedily increase influence
        // (break ties arbitrarily)
3       $v^* := \text{argmax}_{v \in V} \left[f_{inf}(S \cup \{v\}) - f_{inf}(S) \right]$
4       $S := S \cup \{v^*\}$
5 return S

Quiz 20.6

What is the running time of a straightforward implementation of the GreedyInfluence algorithm on graphs with n vertices and m edges? (Choose the strongest true statement.)

a) $O(knm)$

b) $O(knm^2)$

c) $O(knm2^m)$

d) Unclear

(See Section 20.3.8 for the solution and discussion.)

20.3.5   Approximate Correctness

Happily, our greedy heuristic algorithm remains equally approximately correct for the influence maximization problem. Because the maximum coverage problem is a special case of the influence maximization problem (Problem 20.9), this is the best-case scenario—an equally strong approximate correctness guarantee, but for a more general problem.

Theorem 20.9 (GreedyInfluence: Approximate Correctness) *The influence of the solution output by the GreedyInfluence algorithm is always at least a $1 - (1 - \frac{1}{k})^k$ fraction of the maximum-possible influence, where k is the number of vertices chosen.*

The key insight in the proof of Theorem 20.9 is to recognize the influence function (20.10) as a weighted average of coverage functions (20.5). Each of these coverage functions corresponds to the event attendance application (Section 20.2.2) with a subgraph of the social network (comprising the activated edges). We can then check that the proof of Theorem 20.7 in Sections 20.2.6 and 20.2.7 for coverage functions can be extended to weighted averages of coverage functions.

20.3.6   Influence Is a Weighted Sum of Coverage Functions

More formally, fix a directed graph $G = (V, E)$, an activation probability $p \in [0, 1]$, and a positive integer k. For convenience, we include the postprocessing step in the cascade model (see Section 20.3.2) so that every edge ends up either active or inactive. The vertices $X(S)$ activated by the seeds S are precisely those reachable from a vertex in S by a directed path of activated edges.

As a thought experiment, imagine we had telepathy and knew in advance the edges $H \subseteq E$ that would be activated—in effect, tossing all edges' coins up front rather than on a need-to-know basis. Then, the influence maximization problem would boil down to a maximum coverage problem. The ground set would be the vertices V and there would be one subset per vertex, with the subset $A_{v,H}$ containing the vertices that are reachable from v by a directed path in the subgraph (V, H) of activated edges. For example, if the graph and edge statuses are:

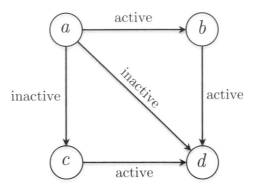

then $A_{a,H} = \{a, b, d\}$, $A_{b,H} = \{b, d\}$, $A_{c,H} = \{c, d\}$, and $A_{d,H} = \{d\}$. The influence of a set S of seeds (given the activated edges H) is then the coverage of the corresponding subsets:

$$f_H(S) := |\cup_{v \in S} A_{v,H}|. \tag{20.11}$$

Of course, we don't have advance knowledge of the subset of activated edges, and each subset $H \subseteq E$ occurs with some positive probability p_H. (Not that we'll need it, but the formula is $p_H = p^{|H|}(1 - p)^{|E|-|H|}$.) But because influence is defined as an expectation, we can express it as a weighted average of coverage functions, with weights equal to probabilities:[16]

Lemma 20.10 (Influence = Average of Coverage Functions) *For each subset $H \subseteq E$ of edges, let f_H denote the coverage function defined in (20.11) and p_H the probability that*

---

[16]For the rigor-obsessed: We're using the law of total expectation to write the expectation in (20.10) as a probability-weighted average of conditional expectations, where the conditioning is on the activated edges H.

the subset of edges activated in the cascade model is precisely H. For every subset $S \subseteq V$ of vertices,

$$f_{inf}(S) = \mathbf{E}_H[f_H(S)] = \sum_{H \subseteq E} p_H \cdot f_H(S). \tag{20.12}$$

20.3.7   Proof of Theorem 20.9

We can declare victory after proving an analog of Lemma 20.8 showing that the `GreedyInfluence` algorithm makes healthy progress in each iteration. Theorem 20.9 then follows from the exact same algebra that we used to prove Theorem 20.7 in Section 20.2.7.

Lemma 20.11 (`GreedyInfluence` Makes Progress) *For each $j \in \{1, 2, \ldots, k\}$, let I_j denote the influence achieved by the first j vertices chosen by the `GreedyInfluence` algorithm. For each such j, the jth vertex chosen increases the influence by at least $\frac{1}{k}(I^* - I_{j-1})$, where I^* denotes the maximum-possible influence of k vertices:*

$$I_j - I_{j-1} \geq \frac{1}{k}\left(I^* - I_{j-1}\right).$$

Proof: Let S_{j-1} denote the first $j-1$ vertices chosen by the `GreedyInfluence` algorithm and $I_{j-1} = f_{inf}(S_{j-1})$ their influence. Let S^* denote a set of k vertices with the maximum-possible influence I^*.

Next, consider an arbitrary subset $H \subseteq E$ of edges and the corresponding coverage function f_H defined in (20.11). Piggybacking on our hard work for coverage functions, we can translate the key inequality (20.7) in the analysis of the `GreedyCoverage` algorithm to the inequality

$$\sum_{v \in S^*} \underbrace{[f_H(S_{j-1} \cup \{v\}) - f_H(S_{j-1})]}_{\text{coverage increase from } v \text{ (under } f_H)} \geq \underbrace{f_H(S^*) - f_H(S_{j-1})}_{\text{coverage gap (under } f_H)}; \tag{20.13}$$

here S_{j-1} and S^* are playing the roles of K_{j-1} and $\widehat{K}$, and $f_H(S_{j-1})$ and $f_H(S^*)$ corre spond to C_{j-1} and $\widehat{C}$.

From Lemma 20.10, we know that influence (f_{inf}) is a weighted average of coverage functions (the f_H's). We have one inequality of the form (20.13) for each subset $H \subseteq E$ of edges; for shorthand, denote its left- and right-hand sides by L_H and R_H, respectively. The idea is to examine the analogous weighted average of these 2^m inequalities (where m denotes $|E|$).

Because multiplying both sides of an inequality by the same nonnegative number (such as a probability p_H) preserves it,

$$p_H \cdot L_H \geq p_H \cdot R_H$$

for every $H \subseteq E$. Because all 2^m inequalities go in the same direction, they add up to a combined inequality:

$$\sum_{H \subseteq E} p_H \cdot L_H \geq \sum_{H \subseteq E} p_H \cdot R_H. \tag{20.14}$$

Unpacking the right-hand side of (20.14) and using the expanded formula for f_{inf} in (20.12), we obtain

$$\sum_{H \subseteq E} p_H \left(f_H(S^*) - f_H(S_{j-1}) \right) = \sum_{H \subseteq E} p_H \cdot f_H(S^*) - \sum_{H \subseteq E} p_H \cdot f_H(S_{j-1})$$

$$= \underbrace{f_{inf}(S^*) - f_{inf}(S_{j-1})}_{\text{right-hand side of (20.14)}}.$$

The left-hand side of (20.14), after the same maneuvers, becomes

$$\underbrace{\sum_{v \in S^*} [f_{inf}(S_{j-1} \cup \{v\}) - f_{inf}(S_{j-1})]}_{\text{left-hand side of (20.14)}}.$$

Thus, inequality (20.14) translates to an analog of the key inequality (20.7) in the proof of Lemma 20.8:

$$\sum_{v \in S^*} [f_{inf}(S_{j-1} \cup \{v\}) - \underbrace{f_{inf}(S_{j-1})}_{=I_{j-1}}] \geq \underbrace{f_{inf}(S^*)}_{=I^*} - \underbrace{f_{inf}(S_{j-1})}_{=I_{j-1}}. \qquad (20.15)$$

The biggest of the k terms in the sum on the left-hand side is at least the average value (as in (20.8)), so the GreedyInfluence algorithm always has at least one good option (the best of the vertices in the optimal solution S^*):

$$\max_{v \in S^*} [f_{inf}(S_{j-1} \cup \{v\}) - I_{j-1}] \geq \frac{1}{k} (I^* - I_{j-1}).$$

The GreedyInfluence algorithm, due to its greedy criterion, selects a vertex that is at least this good, thereby increasing the influence of its solution by at least $\frac{1}{k}(I^* - I_{j-1})$. $\mathcal{QED}$

20.3.8   Solution to Quiz 20.6

Correct answers: (c),(d). There are k iterations of the main loop, each of which involves computing an argmax over the n vertices. The running time of a straightforward implementation is, therefore, $O(kn)$ times the number of operations required to compute the influence $f_{inf}(S)$ of a subset S. And how many operations is this? Unlike for the coverage objective function f_{cov}, the answer is not obvious because of the pesky expectation in (20.10). (In this sense, answer (d) is correct.) Computing this expectation naively—computing $|X(S)|$ via breadth- or depth-first search in $O(m)$ time for each of the 2^m possible outcomes of the coin flips, and averaging the results—leads to the running time bound in (c).

So is the GreedyInfluence algorithm useless in practice? Not at all. The influence $f_{inf}(S)$ of a subset S may be difficult to compute to arbitrary precision, but it is easy to estimate accurately using random sampling. In other words, given a subset S, go ahead and flip all the coins in the cascade model and see how many vertices end up activated with seed set S. After repeating this experiment many times, the average number of activated vertices will almost always be a good estimate of $f_{inf}(S)$.

20.4   The 2-OPT Heuristic Algorithm for the TSP

NP-hardness is always a drag, but at least for the NP-hard problems in Sections 20.1–20.3 (makespan minimization, maximum coverage, and influence maximization), there are fast algorithms with good approximate correctness guarantees. Alas, for many other NP-hard problems, including the TSP, such an algorithm would refute the P $\neq$ NP conjecture (see Problem 22.12). If you insist on an efficient algorithm for such a problem, the best-case scenario is a heuristic algorithm that, despite having no insurance policy, works well on many of the problem instances that arise in your application. *Local search*, along with its many variants, is one of the most powerful and flexible paradigms for devising algorithms of this type.

20.4.1   Tackling the TSP

I'm not going to tell you what local search is in general just yet. Instead, we'll devise from scratch a heuristic algorithm for the traveling salesman problem (TSP), which will force us to develop several new ideas. Then, in Section 20.5, we'll zoom out and identify the ingredients of our solution that exemplify the general principles of local search. Armed with a template for developing local search algorithms and an example instantiation, you'll be well-positioned to apply the technique in your own work.

In the TSP (Section 19.1.2), the input is a complete graph $G = (V, E)$ with real-valued edge costs, and the goal is to compute a tour—a cycle visiting every vertex exactly once—with the minimum-possible sum of edge costs. The TSP is NP-hard (see Section 22.7); if speed is mission-critical, the only option is to resort to heuristic algorithms (assuming, as usual, that the P $\neq$ NP conjecture is true).

To get a feel for the TSP, let's start with the first greedy algorithm that you might think of, along the lines of Prim's minimum spanning tree algorithm.

Quiz 20.7

The *nearest neighbor* heuristic algorithm is a greedy algorithm for the TSP which, given a complete graph with real-valued edge costs, works as follows:

1. Begin a tour at an arbitrary vertex a.

2. Repeat until all vertices have been visited:

   a) If the current vertex is v, proceed to the closest unvisited vertex (a vertex w minimizing c_{vw}).

3. Return to the starting vertex.

In the following example, what is the cost of the tour constructed by the nearest neighbor algorithm, and what is the minimum cost of a tour?

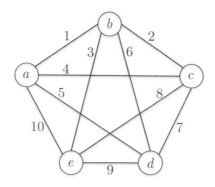

a) 29 and 23

b) 29 and 24

c) 29 and 25

d) 30 and 24

(See Section 20.4.6 for the solution and discussion.)

Quiz 20.7 shows that the nearest neighbor heuristic algorithm does not always construct a minimum-cost tour—hardly surprising, given that the TSP is NP-hard and the algorithm runs in polynomial time. More disturbingly, the greedily constructed tour remains the same even if we change the cost of the final hop (a, e) to a huge number. Unlike our greedy heuristic algorithms in Sections 20.1–20.3, the nearest neighbor algorithm can produce solutions that are worse than an optimal solution by an arbitrarily large factor. More sophisticated greedy algorithms can overcome this particular bad example, but all ultimately suffer an equally disappointing fate in more complicated TSP instances.

20.4.2   Improving a Tour with 2-Changes

Who says we have to give up as soon as we've constructed an initial tour? If there's a way to greedily tweak a tour to make it better, why not do it? What's the minimal modification that could transform one tour into a better one?

Quiz 20.8

In a TSP instance with n vertices, what is the maximum number of edges that two distinct tours can share?

a) $\log_2 n$

b) $n/2$

c) $n - 2$

d) $n - 1$

(See Section 20.4.6 for the solution and discussion.)

Quiz 20.8 suggests exploring the landscape of tours by swapping out one pair of edges for another:

This type of swap is called a *2-change*.

2-Change

1. Given a tour T, remove two edges (v, w), (u, x) of T that do not share an endpoint.

2. Add either the edges (v, x) and (u, w) or the edges (u, v) and (w, x), whichever pair leads to a new tour T'.

The first step chooses two edges with four distinct endpoints.[17] There are three different ways to pair up these four vertices, and exactly one of them creates a new tour (as in the preceding figure). Beyond this and their original pairing, the third pairing creates two disjoint cycles rather than a feasible tour:

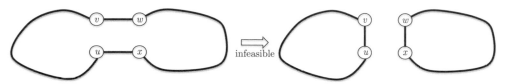

A 2-change can create a tour that is better or worse than the original one. If the newly swapped-in edges are (u, w) and (v, x):

$$\text{decrease in tour cost} = \underbrace{(c_{vw} + c_{ux})}_{\text{edges removed}} - \underbrace{(c_{uw} + c_{vx})}_{\text{edges added}}. \tag{20.16}$$

If the decrease in (20.16) is positive—if the benefit $c_{vw} + c_{ux}$ of removing the old edges outweighs the cost $c_{uw} + c_{vx}$ of adding the new ones—the 2-change produces a lower-cost tour and is called *improving*.

For example, starting from the greedily constructed tour in Quiz 20.7, there are five candidate 2-changes, three of which are improving:[18]

[figure: "possible 2-changes" with pentagon graphs and "improving 2-changes" label]

---

[17]Removing two edges with a shared endpoint is pointless; the only way to get back a feasible tour would be to put them right back in.

[18]In general, with $n \geq 4$ vertices, there are always $n(n - 3)/2$ candidate 2-changes: Choosing one of the n tour edges followed by one of the $n - 3$ tour edges with different endpoints counts every 2-change in exactly two different ways.

20.4.3   The 2-OPT Algorithm

The *2-OPT* algorithm for the TSP constructs an initial tour (for example, with the nearest neighbor algorithm) and performs improving 2-changes until none remain. In the following pseudocode, 2Change is a subroutine that takes as input a tour and two of its edges (with distinct endpoints) and returns as output the tour produced by the corresponding 2-change (as described on page 499).

2OPT

Input: complete graph $G = (V, E)$ and cost c_e for each edge $e \in E$.
Output: a traveling salesman tour.

---

1 $T :=$ initial tour   // perhaps greedily constructed
2 **while** improving 2-change $(v, w), (u, x) \in T$ exists **do**
3      $T := $ 2Change$(T, (v, w), (u, x))$
4 return T

For example, starting from the tour constructed by the nearest neighbor algorithm in Quiz 20.7, the first iteration of the 2OPT algorithm might replace the edges (a, b) and (d, e) with the edges (a, d) and (b, e):

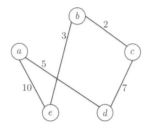

thereby lowering the tour cost from 29 to 27. From here, there are again five 2-changes to consider:

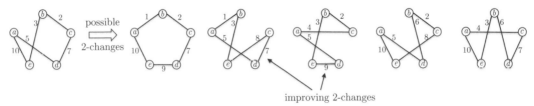

improving 2-changes

If the second iteration of the algorithm executes the first of the two improving 2-changes, replacing the edges (a, e) and (b, c) with the edges (a, b) and (c, e), the tour cost decreases further from 27 to 24. At this point, there are no improving 2-changes (one leaves the tour cost unchanged and four increase it), and the algorithm halts:

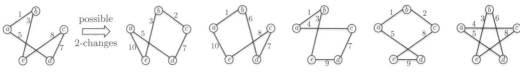

(no improving 2-changes)

20.4.4   Running Time

Does the 2OPT algorithm even halt, or could it loop forever? There are an awful lot of traveling salesman tours (Quiz 19.1), but still only finitely many. Every iteration of the 2OPT algorithm produces a tour with cost strictly smaller than the previous one, so there's no worry about the same tour showing up in two different iterations. Even in the doomsday scenario in which the algorithm searches through every possible tour, it halts within a finite amount of time.

The running time of the algorithm is governed by the number of iterations of the main while loop, times the number of operations performed per iteration. With n vertices, there are $O(n^2)$ different 2-changes to check in each iteration, leading to a per-iteration time bound of $O(n^2)$ (Problem 20.13). What about the number of iterations?

The bad news is that, in pathological examples, the 2OPT algorithm might perform an exponential (in n) number of iterations before halting. The good news is twofold. First, on more realistic inputs, the 2OPT algorithm almost always halts in a reasonable number of iterations (typically subquadratic in n). Second, because the algorithm maintains a feasible tour throughout its execution, it can be interrupted at any time.[19] You can decide in advance how long you're willing to run the algorithm (one minute, one hour, one day, etc.) and, when time expires, use the last (and best) solution that the algorithm found.

20.4.5   Solution Quality

The 2OPT algorithm can only improve upon its initial tour, but there's no guarantee that it will find an optimal solution. Already for the example in Quiz 20.7, we saw in Section 20.4.3 that the algorithm might return a tour with cost 24 instead of the optimal tour (which has cost 23). Could there be worse examples? How much worse?

The bad news is that more complicated and contrived examples show that the tour returned by the 2OPT algorithm can cost more than an optimal tour by an arbitrarily large factor. In other words, the algorithm does not have an approximate correctness guarantee akin to those in Sections 20.1–20.3. The good news is that, for the instances of the TSP that arise in practice, variants of the 2OPT algorithm routinely find tours with total cost not much more than the minimum possible. To tackle the TSP in practice on large inputs (with n in the thousands or more), the 2OPT algorithm, augmented with some of the bells and whistles covered in Section 20.5, is an excellent starting point.

20.4.6   Solutions to Quizzes 20.7–20.8

Solution to Quiz 20.7

Correct answer: (a). The nearest neighbor algorithm starts at a and greedily travels to b and then c. At this point, the tour must proceed to either d or e (as no vertex can be visited twice), with d slightly preferred (cost 7 instead of 8). Once at d, the remaining hops of the tour are forced: There is no choice but to travel to e (at a cost of 9) and then return to a (at a cost of 10). The total cost of this tour is 29 (see the left figure below). Meanwhile, the minimum total cost of a tour is 23 (see the right figure below).

---

[19]Algorithms that are interruptible in this sense are sometimes called *anytime algorithms*.

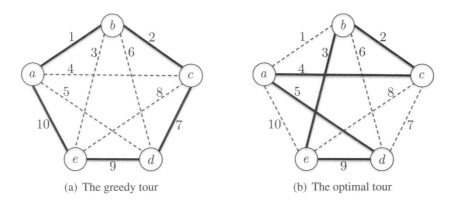

(a) The greedy tour   (b) The optimal tour

Figure 20.3: The nearest neighbor heuristic algorithm does not always construct a minimum-cost tour.

Solution to Quiz 20.8

Correct answer: (c). Because any $n - 1$ edges of a tour uniquely determine its final edge, distinct tours cannot share $n - 1$ edges. Distinct tours can share $n - 2$ edges, however:

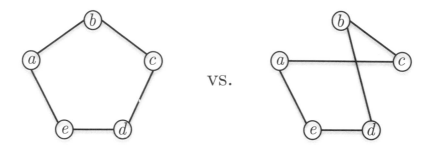

20.5   Principles of Local Search

A *local search algorithm* explores a space of feasible solutions via "local moves" that successively improve an objective function. The 2OPT algorithm for the TSP, in which local moves correspond to 2-changes, is a canonical example. This section zooms out and isolates the essential ingredients of the local search algorithm design paradigm, together with the key modeling and algorithmic decisions needed to apply it.

20.5.1   The Meta-Graph of Feasible Solutions

For a TSP instance $G = (V, E)$ with real-valued edge costs, the 2OPT algorithm can be visualized as a greedy walk through a "meta-graph" $H = (X, F)$ of feasible solutions (shown in Figure 20.4 for the running example from Quiz 20.7). The meta-graph H has one vertex $x \in X$ for each tour of G, labeled with the tour's total cost. It also has one edge $(x, y) \in F$ for each pair x, y of tours that differ in exactly two edges of G. In other words, the meta-graph edges correspond to the possible 2-changes in the TSP instance.

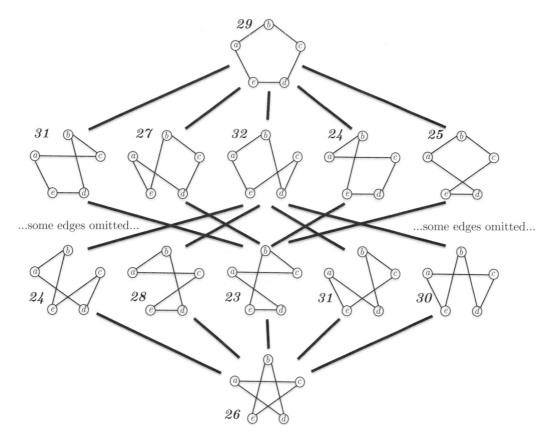

Figure 20.4: The meta-graph of feasible solutions corresponding to the TSP instance in Quiz 20.7. Vertices of the meta-graph correspond to tours, and two tours are connected by an edge of the meta-graph if and only if they differ in exactly two edges. The top tour is adjacent in the meta-graph to the five tours in the second row, and similarly for the bottom tour and the tours in the third row. Each tour in the second row is adjacent to each tour in the third row, save the one in its own column. (To avoid clutter, some of these meta-graph edges are omitted in the figure.) Each tour is labeled with its total cost.

Quiz 20.9

For a TSP instance with $n \geq 4$ vertices, how many vertices and edges does the corresponding meta-graph have? (Don't worry about the meta-graph being REALLY BIG; it exists only in our minds, never to be written out explicitly.)

a) $\frac{1}{2}(n-1)!$ and $\frac{n!(n-3)}{8}$

b) $\frac{1}{2}(n-1)!$ and $\frac{n!(n-3)}{4}$

c) $(n-1)!$ and $\frac{n!(n-3)}{4}$

d) $(n-1)!$ and $\frac{n!(n-3)}{2}$

(See Section 20.5.8 for the solution and discussion.)

We can view the 2OPT algorithm as starting at some meta-graph vertex (for example, the output of the nearest neighbor algorithm) and repeatedly traversing meta-graph edges to visit a sequence of tours with successively smaller costs. The algorithm halts when it reaches a meta-graph vertex with cost no larger than any of its neighbors in the meta-graph. The example 2OPT trajectory in Section 20.4.3 begins at the top tour in Figure 20.4 before proceeding to the second tour in the second row and halting at the first tour in the third row.

20.5.2 The Local Search Algorithm Design Paradigm

Most local search algorithms can be similarly visualized as a greedy walk in a meta-graph of feasible solutions.[20] Such algorithms differ only in the choice of meta-graph and the details of the exploration strategy.[21]

The Local Search Paradigm

1. Define your feasible solutions (equivalently, the vertices of the meta-graph).

2. Define your objective function (the numerical labels of the meta-graph vertices) and whether the goal is to maximize or minimize it.

3. Define your allowable local moves (the edges of the meta-graph).

4. Decide how to choose an initial feasible solution (a starting meta-graph vertex).

5. Decide how to choose among multiple improving local moves (the possible next steps in the meta-graph).

6. Perform local search: Starting from the initial feasible solution, iteratively improve the objective function value via local moves until reaching a *local optimum*—a feasible solution from which there is no improving local move.

The pseudocode of a generic local search algorithm closely resembles that of the 2OPT algorithm. (MakeMove takes as input a feasible solution and the description of a local move, and returns the corresponding neighboring solution.)

GenericLocalSearch

$S :=$ initial solution   // as specified in step 4
while improving local move L exists **do**
    $S := \text{MakeMove}(S, L)$ // as specified in step 5
return S // return the local optimum found

---

[20]We can even add a third dimension to the visualization, with the "height" of a meta-graph vertex specified by its objective function value. This image explains why local search is sometimes called *hill climbing*.

[21]An important variant is *gradient descent*, an ancient local search algorithm that is central to modern machine learning (e.g., neural network training). The simplest version of gradient descent is a heuristic algorithm for minimizing a differentiable objective function over Euclidean space, with improving local moves corresponding to small steps in the direction of steepest descent (that is, of the negative gradient) from the current point.

The first three steps in the local search paradigm are modeling decisions and the next two are algorithmic decisions. Let's examine each step in more detail.

20.5.3   Three Modeling Decisions

The first two steps of the local search paradigm define the problem.

Step 1: Define your feasible solutions. In the TSP, the feasible solutions of an n-vertex instance are the $\frac{1}{2}(n-1)!$ tours. In the makespan minimization problem (Section 20.1.1), the feasible solutions of an instance with m machines and n jobs are the m^n different ways of assigning jobs to machines. In the maximum coverage problem (Section 20.2.1), in an instance with m subsets and parameter k, the feasible solutions are the $\binom{m}{k}$ different ways of choosing k of the subsets.

Step 2: Define your objective function. This step is even more straightforward in our running examples. In the TSP, the objective function (to minimize) is the total cost of a tour. In the makespan minimization and maximum coverage problems, the objective functions (to minimize and maximize, respectively) are, naturally, the makespan of a schedule and the coverage of a collection of k subsets.

Steps 1 and 2 define the *global optima* of an instance—the feasible solutions with the best-possible objective function value (like the tour with cost 23 in Figure 20.4). Step 3 completes the definition of the meta-graph by specifying its edges—the permitted local moves from one feasible solution to another.

Step 3: Define your allowable local moves. In the 2OPT algorithm for the TSP, local moves correspond to 2-changes; in an instance with n vertices, the *neighborhood size*—the number of local moves available from each solution—is $n(n-3)/2$. What if you wanted to apply the local search paradigm to the makespan minimization or maximum coverage problem? For the former, the simplest definition of a local move is the reassignment of a single job to a different machine. The neighborhood size is then $n(m-1)$, where m and n denote the number of machines and jobs, respectively. For the maximum coverage problem, the simplest type of local move swaps out one of the k subsets in the current solution for a different one. With m subsets, the neighborhood size is then $k(m-k)$, with k choices to swap out and $m-k$ to swap in.

The meta-graph of feasible solutions is fully specified after steps 1–3 and so are the *local optima*—the feasible solutions from which there is no improving local move or, equivalently, the meta-graph vertices with objective function value at least as good as all their neighbors. For example, in Figure 20.4, the two local optima are the first and third tours in the third row. (The latter is also a global optimum, while the former is not.) For the makespan minimization problem, with local moves corresponding to single job reassignments, the schedule produced by the LPT algorithm in Quiz 20.3 is a local minimum, while that produced by the Graham algorithm in Quiz 20.2 is not (as you should check). For the maximum coverage problem, with local moves corresponding to subset swaps, the output of the GreedyCoverage algorithm is not a local maximum in either of the examples in Section 20.2.4.[22]

---

[22]Whenever you've got a little extra time, it's worth passing the output of a heuristic algorithm through a local search postprocessing step. After all, the solution can only get better!

Example: The 3-Change Neighborhood for the TSP

Steps 1 and 2 do not uniquely determine the decision in step 3, as multiple definitions of a "local move" might make sense for a given computational problem. For example, in the TSP, who says we can only take out and put back in two edges at a time? Why not three, or more?

A *3-change* is an operation that replaces three edges of a traveling salesman tour with three different edges in a way that produces a new tour:[23]

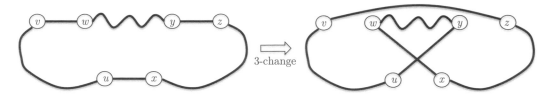

The 3OPT algorithm is the generalization of the 2OPT algorithm (Section 20.4.3) that, in each iteration of the main while loop, performs a 2-change *or a 3-change* that produces a lower-cost tour.

Quiz 20.10

Fix an instance of the TSP. Let H_2 and H_3 denote the meta-graphs corresponding to the 2OPT and 3OPT algorithms, respectively. Which of the following statements are true? (Choose all that apply.)

    a) Every edge of H_2 is also an edge of H_3.

    b) Every edge of H_3 is also an edge of H_2.

    c) Every local minimum of H_2 is also a local minimum of H_3.

    d) Every local minimum of H_3 is also a local minimum of H_2.

(See Section 20.5.8 for the solution and discussion.)

Choosing Your Neighborhood Size

When there are competing definitions of "local moves," which one should you use? This question is usually best answered empirically, by trying out several options. Quiz 20.10 does, however, illustrate a general advantage of large neighborhood sizes: More local moves means fewer lousy local optima for local search to get stuck at. The primary downside of larger neighborhood sizes is the slowdown in checking for improving local moves. For example, in the TSP, checking for an improving 2-change takes quadratic time (in the number of vertices) while checking for an improving 3-change takes cubic time. One approach to balancing these pros and cons is to use the largest neighborhood you can get away with subject to a target per-iteration running time (like one second or ten seconds).

---

[23]In a 2-change, the pair of edges removed uniquely determines the pair to be added (Section 20.4.2). This is no longer the case for 3-changes. For example, if three edges with no shared endpoints are removed, there are seven ways to pair up their six endpoints that lead to new feasible tours (as you should check).

20.5.4   Two Algorithm Design Decisions

Steps 4 and 5 of the local search paradigm supply the details missing from the generic local search algorithm in Section 20.5.2.

Step 4: Decide how to choose an initial feasible solution. Two simple ways to choose an initial solution are greedily and randomly. For example, in the TSP, the initial tour could be constructed by the nearest neighbor algorithm (Quiz 20.7), or by choosing a uniformly random order to visit the vertices. In the makespan minimization problem, the initial schedule could be constructed by the Graham or LPT algorithms, or by assigning each job independently to a uniformly random machine. For the maximum coverage problem, the initial solution could be the output of the GreedyCoverage algorithm or a uniformly random choice of k of the given subsets.

Why cast aside a perfectly good greedy heuristic algorithm in favor of a random solution? Because starting local search from a better initial solution does not necessarily lead to a better (or even equally good) local optimum. An ideal initialization procedure quickly produces a not-too-bad solution that leaves lots of opportunities for local improvement. Random initialization often fits the bill.

Step 5: Decide how to choose among multiple improving local moves. The generic local search algorithm in Section 20.5.2 does not specify how to choose one improving local move from many. The simplest approach is to enumerate local moves one by one until an improving one is found.[24] An alternative with a slower per-iteration running time but a larger per-iteration objective function improvement is to complete the enumeration and greedily execute the local move offering the biggest improvement. A third option is to encourage wider exploration of the solution space by choosing one of the improving moves at random.

20.5.5   Running Time and Solution Quality

Steps 1–5 fully specify a local search algorithm, which starts from an initial solution (chosen using the procedure from step 4) and repeatedly performs improving local moves (chosen using the procedure from step 5) until a local optimum is reached and no further improving moves are possible. What kind of performance can you expect from such an algorithm?

All the lessons learned about the 2OPT algorithm for the TSP in Sections 20.4.4–20.4.5 apply to most other local search algorithms:

Common Characteristics of Local Search

1. Guaranteed to halt. (Provided there are finitely many feasible solutions.)

2. Not guaranteed to halt in a polynomial (in the input size) number of iterations.

3. On realistic inputs, almost always halts within a tolerable number of iterations.

---

[24]The 2OPT algorithm followed this approach in the example in Section 20.4.3 (assuming that it always scanned 2-changes from left to right in the figures).

4. Can be interrupted at any time to return the last (and best) solution found.

5. Not guaranteed to return a local optimum with an objective function value that is close to the best possible.

6. On realistic inputs, often produces high-quality local optima, but sometimes produces low-quality local optima.

20.5.6   Avoiding Bad Local Optima

Low-quality local optima can impede the successful application of local search. How can you tweak a local search algorithm to better avoid them? While one fix is to increase the neighborhood size (see Section 20.5.3), perhaps the easiest workaround is to rely on randomization, choosing a random initial solution or random improving moves in each iteration. You can then run as many independent trials of your algorithm as you have time for, returning the best local optimum found by any of the trials.

A more drastic approach to avoiding bad local optima is to sometimes allow non-improving local moves. For example, in each iteration:

(i) From the current solution, choose a local move uniformly at random.

(ii) If the chosen local move is improving, perform it.

(iii) Otherwise, if the chosen local move makes the objective function worse by $\Delta \geq 0$, perform it with some probability $p(\Delta)$ that is decreasing in Δ, and otherwise do nothing. (One popular choice for the function $p(\Delta)$ is the exponential function $e^{-\lambda\Delta}$, where $\lambda > 0$ is a tunable parameter.)[25]

Local search algorithms that permit non-improving moves do not generally halt and should be interrupted after a target amount of computation time.

There's no end to the additional bells and whistles you can layer on top of the basic local search algorithm.[26] Two different genres of them are:

• *History-dependent neighborhoods.* Rather than fixing the allowable local moves once and for all, they could depend on the trajectory-so-far of the local search algorithm. For example, you might disallow local moves that seem to partially reverse the previous move, such as a 2-change using some of the same endpoints as the previous 2-change.[27] Rules of this type are particularly useful for avoiding cycles in local search algorithms that allow non-improving moves.

• *Maintaining a population of solutions.* The algorithm could maintain $k \geq 2$ feasible solutions at all times, rather than only one. Each iteration of the algorithm now generates k new feasible solutions from k old ones, for example, by keeping only the k best neighbors of the current k solutions, or by combining pairs of current solutions to create new ones.[28]

---

[25] If you've heard of the "Metropolis algorithm" or "simulated annealing," both are based on this idea.

[26] For a deep dive, check out the book *Local Search in Combinatorial Optimization*, edited by Emile Aarts and Jan Karel Lenstra (Princeton University Press, 2003).

[27] "Tabu search" and the "Lin-Kernighan variable-depth heuristic" are both related to this idea.

[28] If you've heard of "beam search" or "genetic algorithms," both are variants of this idea.

20.5.7   When Should You Use Local Search?

You know a lot of algorithm design paradigms; when is local search the first one to try? If your application checks several of the following boxes, local search is probably worth a shot.

When to Use Local Search

1. You don't have enough time to compute an exact solution.

2. You're willing to give up on running time and approximate correctness guarantees.

3. You want an algorithm that is relatively easy to implement.

4. You already have a good heuristic algorithm but want to improve its output further in a postprocessing step.

5. You want an algorithm that can be interrupted at any time.

6. State-of-the-art mixed integer programming and satisfiability solvers (discussed in Sections 21.4–21.5) aren't good enough—either because your input sizes are too big for the solvers to handle, or because your problem can't be translated easily into the format they require.

And remember, to get the most out of local search, you have to experiment—with different neighborhoods, initialization strategies, local move selection strategies, extra bells and whistles, and so on.

20.5.8   Solutions to Quizzes 20.9–20.10

Solution to Quiz 20.9

Correct answer: (a). The meta-graph has one vertex per tour, for a total of $\frac{1}{2}(n-1)!$ (see Quiz 19.1). Each vertex of the meta-graph is adjacent to $n(n-3)/2$ other vertices (see footnote 18). The total number of edges is therefore

$$\frac{1}{2} \cdot \underbrace{\frac{(n-1)!}{2}}_{\text{\# of vertices}} \cdot \underbrace{\frac{n(n-3)}{2}}_{\text{\# of incident edges}} = \frac{n!(n-3)}{8};$$

the leading "$\frac{1}{2}$" term corrects for the double-counting of each meta-graph edge (once via each endpoint).

Solution to Quiz 20.10

Correct answers: (a),(d). The 3OPT algorithm can make whatever 2-change (or 3-change) it likes in each iteration. With every local move available to 2OPT available also to 3OPT, answer (a) is correct. Thus, (d) is correct as well: If a vertex has a neighbor in H_2 with better objective function value (showing that it is not a local minimum in H_2), this same neighbor shows that the vertex is not a local minimum in H_3, either.

In the example in Figure 20.4, the first tour in the third row cannot be improved by a 2-change but can be improved by a 3-change (as you should check). This shows that (b) and (c) are both incorrect.

The Upshot

☆ In the makespan minimization problem, the goal is to assign jobs to machines to minimize the makespan (the maximum machine load).

☆ Making a single pass over the jobs and scheduling each on the currently least loaded machine produces a schedule with makespan at most twice the minimum possible.

☆ Sorting the jobs first (from longest to shortest) improves the guarantee from 2 to $4/3$.

☆ In the maximum coverage problem, the goal is to choose k of m subsets to maximize their coverage (the size of their union).

☆ Greedily selecting subsets that increase the coverage as much as possible achieves a coverage of at least 63.2% of the maximum possible.

☆ The influence of a set of initially active vertices in a directed graph is the expected number of eventually activated vertices, assuming that an activated vertex activates each of its out-neighbors with some probability p.

☆ In the influence maximization problem, the goal is to choose k vertices of a directed graph to maximize their influence.

☆ Because influence is a weighted average of coverage functions, the 63.2% guarantee carries over to the greedy algorithm that iteratively selects vertices that increase the influence the most.

☆ In the traveling salesman problem (TSP), the input is a complete graph with real-valued edge costs, and the goal is to compute a tour (a cycle visiting every vertex exactly once) with the minimum-possible sum of edge costs.

☆ A 2-change creates a new tour from an old one by swapping out one pair of edges for another.

☆ The 2-OPT algorithm for the TSP repeatedly improves an initial tour via 2-changes until no such improvements are possible.

☆ A local search algorithm takes a walk through a meta-graph in which vertices correspond to feasible solutions (labeled by objective function value) and edges to local moves.

> ☆ A local search algorithm is specified by a meta-graph, an initial solution, and a rule for selecting among improving local moves.
>
> ☆ Local search algorithms often produce high-quality solutions in a reasonable amount of time, despite lacking provable running time and approximate correctness guarantees.
>
> ☆ Local search algorithms can be tweaked to better avoid low-quality local optima, for example, by allowing randomization and non-improving local moves.

Test Your Understanding

Problem 20.1 *(S)* In the makespan minimization problem (Section 20.1.1), suppose that jobs have similar lengths (with $\ell_j \leq 2\ell_h$ for all jobs j, h) and that there is a healthy number of jobs (at least 10 times the number of machines). What can you say about the makespan of the schedule output by the Graham algorithm of Section 20.1.3? (Choose the strongest true statement.)

a) It is at most 10% larger than the minimum-possible makespan.

b) It is at most 20% larger than the minimum-possible makespan.

c) It is at most 50% larger than the minimum-possible makespan.

d) It is at most 100% larger than the minimum-possible makespan.

Problem 20.2 *(S)* The goal in the maximum coverage problem (Section 20.2.1) is to cover as many elements as possible using a fixed number of subsets; in the closely related *set cover* problem, the goal is to cover *all* the elements while using as few subsets as possible (like hiring a team with all the requisite skills at the minimum-possible cost).[29] The greedy algorithm for the maximum coverage problem (Section 20.2.3) extends easily to the set cover problem (given as input m subsets $A_1, A_2, \ldots, A_m$ of a ground set U, with $\cup_{i=1}^{m} A_i = U$):

Greedy Heuristic Algorithm for Set Cover

$K := \emptyset$ // indices of chosen sets
while $f_{cov}(K) < |U|$ **do**   // part of U uncovered
     $i^* := \text{argmax}_{i=1}^{m} [f_{cov}(K \cup \{i\}) - f_{cov}(K)]$
     $K := K \cup \{i^*\}$
return K

Let k denote the minimum number of subsets required to cover all of U. Which of the following approximate correctness guarantees holds for this algorithm? (Choose the strongest true statement.)

---

[29]This problem is NP-hard; see Problem 22.6.

a) Its solution consists of at most $2k$ subsets.

b) Its solution consists of $O(k \log |U|)$ subsets.

c) Its solution consists of $O(k \cdot \sqrt{|U|})$ subsets.

d) Its solution consists of $O(k \cdot |U|)$ subsets.

Problem 20.3 *(S)* This problem considers three greedy heuristics for the knapsack problem (Section 16.5). The input consists of n items with values $v_1, v_2, \ldots, v_n$ and sizes $s_1, s_2, \ldots, s_n$, and a knapsack capacity C.

Greedy Heuristic Algorithm #1 for Knapsack

$I := \emptyset, S := 0$ // chosen items and their size
sort and reindex the jobs so that $v_1 \geq v_2 \geq \cdots \geq v_n$
for $i := 1$ to n **do**
    if $S + s_i \leq C$ **then**   // choose item if feasible
        $I := I \cup \{i\}, S := S + s_i$
return I

Greedy Heuristic Algorithm #2 for Knapsack

$I := \emptyset, S := 0$ // chosen items and their size
sort and reindex the jobs so that $\frac{v_1}{s_1} \geq \frac{v_2}{s_2} \geq \cdots \geq \frac{v_n}{s_n}$
for $i := 1$ to n **do**
    if $S + s_i \leq C$ **then**   // choose item if feasible
        $I := I \cup \{i\}, S := S + s_i$
return I

Greedy Heuristic Algorithm #3 for Knapsack

$I_1 :=$ output of greedy heuristic algorithm #1
$I_2 :=$ output of greedy heuristic algorithm #2
return whichever of I_1, I_2 has higher total value

Which of the following statements are true? (Choose all that apply.)

a) The total value of the solution returned by the first greedy algorithm is always at least 50% of the maximum possible.

b) The total value of the solution returned by the second greedy algorithm is always at least 50% of the maximum possible.

c) The total value of the solution returned by the third greedy algorithm is always at least 50% of the maximum possible.

d) If every item size is at most 10% of the knapsack capacity (that is, $\max_{i=1}^{n} s_i \leq C/10$), the total value of the solution returned by the first greedy algorithm is at least 90% of the maximum possible.

e) If every item size is at most 10% of the knapsack capacity, the total value of the solution returned by the second greedy algorithm is at least 90% of the maximum possible.

f) If every item size is at most 10% of the knapsack capacity, the total value of the solution returned by the third greedy algorithm is at least 90% of the maximum possible.

Problem 20.4 *(S)* In the *vertex cover* problem, the input is an undirected graph $G = (V, E)$, and the goal is to identify a minimum-size subset $S \subseteq V$ of vertices that includes at least one endpoint of every edge in E.[30] (For example, perhaps the edges represent roads and the vertices intersections, and the goal is to monitor all the roads while installing security cameras at as few intersections as possible.) One simple heuristic algorithm repeatedly chooses a not-yet-covered edge and adds *both* its endpoints to its solution-so-far:

Heuristic Algorithm for Vertex Cover

$S := \emptyset$ // chosen vertices
while there is an edge $(v, w) \in E$ with $v, w \notin S$ **do**
    $S := S \cup \{v, w\}$ // add both endpoints of edge
return S

Let k denote the minimum number of vertices required to capture at least one endpoint of each edge. Which of the following approximate correctness guarantees holds for this algorithm? (Choose the strongest true statement.)

a) Its solution consists of at most $2k$ vertices.

b) Its solution consists of $O(k \log |E|)$ vertices.

c) Its solution consists of $O(k \cdot \sqrt{|E|})$ vertices.

d) Its solution consists of $O(k \cdot |E|)$ vertices.

Problem 20.5 *(S)* Which of the following statements about the generic local search algorithm in Section 20.5.2 is *not* true?

a) Its output generally depends on the choice of the initial feasible solution.

b) Its output generally depends on the method for choosing one improving local move from many.

c) It will always, eventually, halt at an optimal solution.

d) In some cases, it performs an exponential (in the input size) number of iterations before halting.

---
[30]This problem is NP-hard; see Problem 22.5.

Challenge Problems

Problem 20.6 *(H)* Propose an implementation of the `Graham` algorithm (Section 20.1.3) that uses a heap data structure and runs in $O(n \log m)$ time, where n is the number of jobs and m is the number of machines.[31]

Problem 20.7 *(H)* This problem improves Theorem 20.4 and extends the example in Quiz 20.3 to identify the best-possible approximate correctness guarantee for the `LPT` algorithm (Section 20.1.7).

(a) Let job j be the last job assigned to the most heavily loaded machine in the schedule returned by the `LPT` algorithm. Prove that if $\ell_j > M^*/3$, where M^* denotes the minimum-possible makespan, then this schedule is optimal (that is, has makespan M^*).

(b) Prove that the `LPT` algorithm always outputs a schedule with makespan at most $\frac{4}{3} - \frac{1}{3m}$ times the minimum possible, where m denotes the number of machines.

(c) Generalize the example in Quiz 20.3 to show that, for every $m \geq 1$, there is an example with m machines in which the schedule produced by the `LPT` algorithm has makespan $\frac{4}{3} - \frac{1}{3m}$ times the minimum possible.

Problem 20.8 *(H)* Recall the bad example for the `GreedyCoverage` algorithm in Quiz 20.5.

(a) Prove Proposition 20.6.

(b) Extend your examples in (a) to show that, even with best-case tie-breaking, for every constant $\epsilon > 0$, the `GreedyCoverage` algorithm does not guarantee a

$$1 - (1 - \tfrac{1}{k})^k + \epsilon$$

fraction of the maximum-possible coverage (where k denotes the number of subsets chosen).

Problem 20.9 *(H)* Show that every instance of the maximum coverage problem can be encoded as an instance of the influence maximization problem so that: (i) the two instances have the same optimal objective function value F^*; and (ii) any solution to the latter instance with influence F can be easily converted to a solution to the former instance with coverage at least F.

Problem 20.10 *(H)* The goal in the maximum coverage problem is to choose k subsets to maximize the coverage f_{cov}. The goal in the influence maximization problem is to choose k vertices to maximize the influence f_{inf}. The general version of this type of problem is: Given a set O of objects and a real-valued set function f (specifying a number $f(S)$ for each subset $S \subseteq O$), choose k objects of O to maximize f. The `GreedyCoverage` and `GreedyInfluence` algorithms extend naturally to the general problem:

---

[31] Technically, the running time will be $O(m + n \log m)$. The problem is uninteresting when $n \leq m$, however, as in that case each job can be granted a dedicated machine.

Greedy Algorithm for Set Function Maximization

$S := \emptyset$ `// chosen objects`
for $j := 1$ to k **do**   `// choose objects one by one`
    `// greedily increase objective function`
    $o^* := \text{argmax}_{o \notin S}\, [f(S \cup \{o\}) - f(S)]$
    $S := S \cup \{o^*\}$
return S

For which objective functions f does this greedy algorithm enjoy an approximate correctness guarantee akin to Theorems 20.7 and 20.9? Here are the key properties:

1. *Nonnegative:* $f(S) \geq 0$ for all $S \subseteq O$.

2. *Monotone:* $f(S) \geq f(T)$ whenever $S \supseteq T$.

3. *Submodular:*
$$f(S \cup \{o\}) - f(S) \leq f(T \cup \{o\}) - f(T)$$

   whenever $S \supseteq T$ and $o \notin S$. (Submodularity asserts a "diminishing returns" property: The marginal value of a new object o can decrease but cannot increase as other objects are acquired.)

(a) Prove that the coverage and influence functions f_{cov} and f_{inf} possess all three properties.

(b) Prove that whenever f is nonnegative, monotone, and submodular, the general greedy heuristic algorithm is guaranteed to return a set S of objects that satisfies

$$f(S) \geq \left(1 - \left(1 - \frac{1}{k}\right)^k\right) \cdot f(S^*),$$

where S^* maximizes f over all size-k subsets of O.

Problem 20.11 *(H)* Problem 20.3 investigated approximate correctness guarantees for greedy heuristic algorithms for the knapsack problem. This problem outlines a dynamic programming algorithm with a much stronger guarantee: For a user-specified error parameter $\epsilon > 0$ (like .1 or .01), the algorithm outputs a solution with total value at least $1 - \epsilon$ times the maximum possible. (Full disclosure, in case this sounds too good to be true for an NP-hard problem: The running time of the algorithm blows up as ϵ approaches 0.)

(a) In Section 16.5 we saw that the knapsack problem can be solved in $O(nC)$ time using dynamic programming, where n denotes the number of items and C the knapsack capacity. (All item values and sizes, as well as the knapsack capacity, are positive integers.) Give a different dynamic programming algorithm for the problem that runs in $O(n^2 \cdot v_{max})$ time, where v_{max} denotes the largest value of any item.

(b) To shrink the item values down to a manageable magnitude, divide each of them by $m := (\epsilon \cdot v_{max})/n$ and round each result down to the nearest integer (where ϵ is the user-specified error parameter). Prove that the total value of every feasible solution goes down by at least a factor of m and that the total value of an optimal solution goes down by at most a factor of $m/(1 - \epsilon)$. (You can assume that every item has size at most C and hence fits in the knapsack.)

(c) Propose an $O(n^3/\epsilon)$-time algorithm that is guaranteed to return a feasible solution with total value at least $1 - \epsilon$ times the maximum possible. (A heuristic algorithm with this type of guarantee is called a *fully polynomial-time approximation scheme (FPTAS)*.)

Problem 20.12 *(H)* This problem describes a commonly encountered special case of the traveling salesman problem for which there are fast heuristic algorithms with good approximate correctness guarantees. In a *metric* instance $G = (V, E)$ of the TSP, all the edge costs c_e are nonnegative and the shortest path between any two vertices is the direct one-hop path (a condition that is known as the "triangle inequality"): $c_{vw} \leq \sum_{e \in P} c_e$ for every pair $v, w \in V$ of vertices and v-w path P. (The example in Quiz 19.2 is a metric instance, while the example in Quiz 20.7 is not.) The triangle inequality typically holds in applications in which edge costs correspond to physical distances. The TSP remains NP-hard in the special case of metric instances (see Problem 22.12(a)).

Our starting point for a fast heuristic algorithm is the linear-time algorithm for tree instances described in Problem 19.8. The key idea is to reduce a general metric instance to a tree instance by computing a minimum spanning tree.

MST Heuristic for Metric TSP

$T :=$ minimum spanning tree of the input graph G
return an optimal tour of the tree instance defined by T

The first step can be implemented in near-linear time using Prim's or Kruskal's algorithm. The second step can be implemented in linear time using the solution to Problem 19.8. In the tree TSP instance constructed in the second step, the length a_e of an edge e of T is set to the cost c_e of that edge in the given metric TSP instance (with the cost of each edge (v, w) in the tree instance then defined as the total length $\sum_{e \in P_{vw}} a_e$ of the unique v-w path P_{vw} in T):

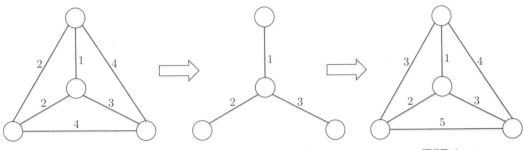

metric TSP instance   a minimum spanning tree   tree TSP instance

(a) Prove that the minimum total cost of a traveling salesman tour is at least that of a minimum spanning tree. (This step does not require the triangle inequality.)

(b) Prove that, for every instance of metric TSP, the total cost of the tour computed by the MST heuristic is at most twice the minimum possible.

Problem 20.13 *(H)* Propose an implementation of the 2OPT algorithm (Section 20.4.3) in which each iteration of the main while loop runs in $O(n^2)$ time, where n is the number of vertices.

Problem 20.14 *(S)* Most local search algorithms lack polynomial running time and approximate correctness guarantees; this problem describes a rare exception. For an integer $k \geq 2$, in the *maximum k-cut* problem, the input is an undirected graph $G = (V, E)$. The feasible solutions are the k-cuts of the graph, meaning partitions of the vertex set V into k non-empty groups $S_1, S_2, \ldots, S_k$. The objective is to maximize the number of edges with endpoints in different groups. The maximum k-cut problem is NP-hard.

For example, in the graph

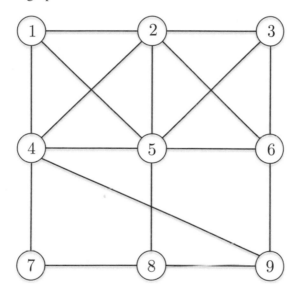

sixteen of the seventeen edges have endpoints in distinct groups of the 3-cut $(\{1, 6, 7\}, \{2, 5, 9\}, \{3, 4, 8\})$. (There's no way to do better, as two of the vertices in $\{1, 2, 4, 5\}$ must belong to a common group.)

For a k-cut $(S_1, S_2, \ldots, S_k)$, each local move corresponds to a reassignment of a single vertex from one group to another, subject to the constraint that none of the k groups can become empty.

(a) Prove that, for every initial k-cut and selection rule for choosing improving local moves, the generic local search algorithm halts within $|E|$ iterations.

(b) Prove that, for every initial k-cut and selection rule for choosing improving local moves, the generic local search algorithm halts with a k-cut with an objective function value of at least $(k - 1)/k$ times the maximum possible.

Programming Problems

Problem 20.15 Implement in your favorite programming language the nearest neighbor algorithm for the TSP (as seen in Quiz 20.7). Try out your implementation on instances with edge costs chosen independently and uniformly at random from the set $\{1, 2, \ldots, 100\}$ or, alternatively, for vertices that correspond to points chosen independently and uniformly at random from the unit square.[32] How large an input size (that is, how many vertices) can your program reliably process in under a minute? What about in under an hour? (See www.algorithmsilluminated.org for test cases and challenge data sets.)

Problem 20.16 Implement in your favorite programming language the 2OPT algorithm from Section 20.4.3. Use your implementation of the nearest neighbor algorithm from Problem 20.15 to compute the initial tour. Implement each iteration of the main loop so that it runs in quadratic time (see Problem 20.13) and experiment with different ways of selecting an improving local move. Try out your implementation on the same instances you used for Problem 20.15.[33] By how much does local search improve the total cost of the initial tour? Which of your selection rules leads to the most dramatic improvement? (See www.algorithmsilluminated.org for test cases and challenge data sets.)

---

[32] That is, the x- and y-coordinates of each point are independent and uniformly random numbers in $[0, 1]$. The cost of the edge connecting two points (x_1, y_1) and (x_2, y_2) is then defined as the Euclidean (that is, straight-line) distance between them, which is $\sqrt{(x_1 - x_2)^2 + (y_1 - y_2)^2}$. (For the nearest neighbor algorithm, you can equivalently work with squared Euclidean distances.)

[33] For points in the unit square, does it matter whether you use Euclidean or squared Euclidean distances?

Chapter 21

Compromising on Speed: Exact Inefficient Algorithms

You can't have it all with NP-hard problems. When correctness cannot be compromised and heuristic algorithms are out of the question, it's time to consider correct algorithms that do not always run in polynomial time. The goal is then to design a general-purpose and correct algorithm that is as fast as possible, and certainly faster than exhaustive search, on as many inputs as possible. Sections 21.1 and 21.2 use dynamic programming to design algorithms that are always faster than exhaustive search in two case studies: the TSP and the problem of finding a long path in a graph. Sections 21.3–21.5 introduce mixed integer programming and satisfiability solvers, which lack better-than-exhaustive-search running time guarantees but can nevertheless be highly effective at solving the instances of NP-hard problems that arise in practice.

21.1 The Bellman-Held-Karp Algorithm for the TSP

21.1.1 The Baseline: Exhaustive Search

In the TSP (Section 19.1.2), the input is a complete graph $G = (V, E)$ with real-valued edge costs and the goal is to compute a tour—a cycle visiting every vertex exactly once—with the minimum-possible sum of edge costs. The TSP is NP-hard (see Section 22.7); if correctness cannot be compromised, the only option is to resort to algorithms that run in super-polynomial (and presumably exponential) time in the worst case (assuming, as usual, that the P $\neq$ NP conjecture is true). Can algorithmic ingenuity at least improve over mindless exhaustive search? How big a speed-up can we hope for?

Solving the TSP by exhaustive search through the $\frac{1}{2}(n-1)!$ possible tours (Quiz 19.1) results in an $O(n!)$-time algorithm. The factorial function $n! = n \cdot (n-1) \cdot (n-2) \cdots 2 \cdot 1$ certainly grows more quickly than a simple exponential function like 2^n—the latter is the product of n 2's, the former the product of n terms that are mostly much bigger than 2. Just how big is it?

There's a remarkably accurate answer to this question, called *Stirling's approximation*.[1] (In it, $e = 2.718\ldots$ denotes Euler's number and, of course, $\pi = 3.14\ldots$.)

Stirling's Approximation

$$n! \approx \sqrt{2\pi n} \left(\frac{n}{e}\right)^n \tag{21.1}$$

---

[1]Remember the name but not the formula or its proof; you can always look it up on Wikipedia or elsewhere when you need it.

Stirling's approximation shows that the factorial function (with its n^n-type dependence) grows a *lot* faster than 2^n. For example, you could run to completion an $n!$-time algorithm on modern computers only for n up to maybe 15, while a 2^n-time algorithm could handle input sizes up to $n = 40$ or so. (Still not that impressive, perhaps, but you take what you can get with NP-hard problems!) Thus, solving the TSP in time closer to 2^n than $n!$ is a worthy goal.

21.1.2   Dynamic Programming

While many of the killer applications of dynamic programming are to polynomial-time solvable problems (as seen in Chapters 16–18), the paradigm is equally adept at solving NP-hard problems faster than exhaustive search, including the knapsack problem (Section 16.5), the TSP (this section), and more (Section 21.2). To recap the discussion in Section 16.4, the dynamic programming paradigm is:

The Dynamic Programming Paradigm

1. Identify a relatively small collection of subproblems.

2. Show how to quickly and correctly solve "larger" subproblems given the solutions to "smaller" ones.

3. Show how to quickly and correctly infer the final solution from the solutions to all the subproblems.

After these three steps are implemented, the corresponding dynamic programming algorithm writes itself: Systematically solve all the subproblems one by one, working from "smallest" to "largest," and extract the final solution from those of the subproblems.

For example, suppose a dynamic programming algorithm solves at most $f(n)$ different subproblems (working systematically from "smallest" to "largest"), using at most $g(n)$ time for each, and performs at most $h(n)$ postprocessing work to extract the final solution (where n denotes the input size). The algorithm's running time is then at most

$$\underbrace{f(n)}_{\text{\# subproblems}} \times \underbrace{g(n)}_{\substack{\text{time per subproblem} \\ \text{(given previous solutions)}}} + \underbrace{h(n)}_{\text{postprocessing}} . \tag{21.2}$$

When applying dynamic programming to an NP-hard problem like the TSP, we should expect at least one of the functions $f(n)$, $g(n)$, or $h(n)$ to be exponential in n. Looking back at some canonical dynamic programming algorithms, we can see that the functions $g(n)$ and $h(n)$ are almost always $O(1)$ or $O(n)$, while the number $f(n)$ of subproblems varies widely from algorithm to algorithm.[2] We should, therefore, be ready for a dynamic programming algorithm for the TSP to use an exponential number of subproblems.

---

[2]For example, the dynamic programming algorithm in Section 16.2 for the weighted independent set problem in path graphs solves $O(n)$ subproblems (where n denotes the number of vertices), while that for the knapsack problem in Section 16.5 solves $O(nC)$ subproblems (where n denotes the number of items and C the knapsack capacity). The Bellman-Ford (Section 18.2) and Floyd-Warshall (Section 18.4) shortest-path algorithms use $O(n^2)$ and $O(n^3)$ subproblems, respectively (where n denotes the number of vertices).

21.1.3   Optimal Substructure

The key that unleashes the potential of dynamic programming is the identification of the right collection of subproblems. The best way to home in on them is to think through the ways in which an optimal solution might be built up from optimal solutions to smaller subproblems.

Suppose someone handed us on a silver platter a minimum-cost traveling salesman tour T of the vertices $V = \{1, 2, \ldots, n\}$, with $n \geq 3$. What must it look like? In how many different ways could it have been built up from optimal solutions to smaller subproblems? Think of the tour T as starting and ending at the vertex 1, and zoom in on its last decision—its final edge, from some vertex j back to the starting point 1. If we only knew the identity of j, we would know what the tour looks like: a minimum-cost cycle-free path from 1 to j that visits every vertex, followed by the edge from j back to 1:[3]

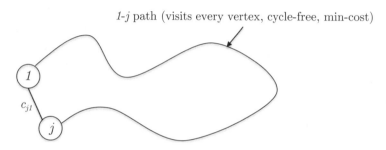

Thus, there are $n - 1$ and only $n - 1$ candidates vying to be an optimal traveling salesman tour (one for each choice $j \in \{2, 3, \ldots, n\}$ of the final vertex), and the best of these must be a minimum-cost tour:

$$\text{optimal tour cost} = \min_{j=2}^{n} \left(\begin{array}{c} \text{minimum cost of a cycle-free} \\ \text{1-}j \text{ path that visits every vertex} \end{array} + c_{j1} \right). \tag{21.3}$$

The argument grows trickier if we forge ahead. Consider an optimal solution to one of our $n - 1$ subproblems—a minimum-cost path from 1 to j that visits every vertex exactly once (equivalently, that visits every vertex and is cycle-free). What must it look like?

Quiz 21.1

Let P be a minimum-cost cycle-free path from 1 to j that visits every vertex, with final hop (k, j). Let P' denote P with its final hop (k, j) removed. Which of the following are true? (Choose all that apply.)

a) P' is a cycle-free path from 1 to k that visits every vertex of $V - \{j\}$.

b) P' is a minimum-cost path of the form in (a).

c) P' is a cycle-free path from 1 to k that visits every vertex of $V - \{j\}$ and

---

[3] Why must $T - \{(j, 1)\}$ be such a minimum-cost path? Because if there were a lower-cost cycle-free 1-j path visiting every vertex, we could plug the edge $(j, 1)$ back in to recover a lower-cost tour (contradicting the optimality of T).

> does not visit vertex j.
>
> d) P' is a minimum-cost path of the form in (c).
>
> (See Section 21.1.7 for the solution and discussion.)

The solution to Quiz 21.1 proves the following lemma.

Lemma 21.1 (TSP Optimal Substructure) *Assume that $n \geq 3$. Suppose P is a minimum-cost cycle-free path from vertex 1 to vertex j that visits every vertex of $V = \{1, 2, \ldots, n\}$, and its final hop is (k, j). The 1-k subpath P' is a minimum-cost cycle-free 1-k path that visits exactly the vertices $V - \{j\}$.*

The subproblem solved optimally by P' in Lemma 21.1 specifies the exact subset of vertices to visit. The bad news is that this will force our dynamic programming algorithm to use subproblems indexed by subsets of vertices (of which there are, unfortunately, an exponential number). The good news is that these subproblems will not specify the *order* in which to visit the vertices. For this reason, their number will scale with 2^n rather than $n!$. (For the same reason, the *memory* required by the algorithm will also scale with 2^n—unlike exhaustive search, which uses minimal memory).

21.1.4 Recurrence

Lemma 21.1 narrows down the possibilities for an optimal path from vertex 1 to a vertex j to $n - 2$ and only $n - 2$ candidates—one for each choice of the penultimate vertex k. The best of these $n - 2$ candidates must be an optimal path.

Corollary 21.2 (TSP Recurrence) *With the assumptions and notation of Lemma 21.1, let $C_{S,j}$ denote the minimum cost of a cycle-free path that begins at the vertex 1, ends at the vertex $j \in S$, and visits exactly the vertices in the subset $S \subseteq V$. Then, for every $j \in V - \{1\}$,*

$$C_{V,j} = \min_{\substack{k \in V \\ k \neq 1, j}} \left(C_{V-\{j\},k} + c_{kj} \right). \tag{21.4}$$

More generally, for every subset $S \subseteq V$ that contains 1 and at least two other vertices, and for every vertex $j \in S - \{1\}$,

$$C_{S,j} = \min_{\substack{k \in S \\ k \neq 1, j}} \left(C_{S-\{j\},k} + c_{kj} \right). \tag{21.5}$$

The second statement in Corollary 21.2 follows by applying the first statement to the vertices of S, viewed as a TSP instance in their own right (with edge costs inherited from the original instance). The "min" in the recurrences (21.4) and (21.5) implements exhaustive search over the candidates for the penultimate vertex of an optimal solution.

21.1.5 The Subproblems

Ranging over all relevant values of the parameters S and j in the recurrence (21.5), we obtain our collection of subproblems. The base cases correspond to subsets of the form $\{1, j\}$ for some $j \in V - \{1\}$.

TSP: Subproblems

Compute $C_{S,j}$, the minimum cost of a cycle-free path from vertex 1 to vertex j that visits exactly the vertices in S.

(For each $S \subseteq \{1, 2, \ldots, n\}$ containing vertex 1 and at least one other vertex, and each $j \in S - \{1\}$.)

Or, thinking recursively, each application of the recurrence (21.5) effectively removes one vertex (other than vertex 1) from further consideration. These vertex choices are arbitrary, so we must be prepared for any subset of vertices (that contains 1 and at least one other vertex).

The identity in (21.3) shows how to compute the minimum cost of a tour from the solutions to the largest subproblems (with $S = V$):

$$\text{optimal tour cost} = \min_{j=2}^{n} (C_{V,j} + c_{j1}) . \tag{21.6}$$

21.1.6   The Bellman-Held-Karp Algorithm

With the subproblems, recurrence (21.5), and postprocessing step (21.6) in hand, the dynamic programming algorithm for the TSP writes itself.

BellmanHeldKarp

Input: complete undirected graph $G = (V, E)$ with
$V = \{1, 2, \ldots, n\}$ and $n \geq 3$, and a real-valued cost c_{ij} for each
edge $(i, j) \in E$.
Output: the minimum total cost of a traveling salesman tour of G.

```
// subproblems  (1 ∈ S, |S| ≥ 2,  j ∈ V − {1})
// (only subproblems with j ∈ S are ever used)
```
$A := (2^{n-1} - 1) \times (n - 1)$ two-dimensional array

```
// base cases  (|S| = 2)
```
for $j := 2$ to n **do**
    $A[\{1, j\}][j] := c_{1j}$

```
// systematically solve all subproblems
```
for $s := 3$ to n **do**   // s=subproblem size
    for S with $|S| = s$ and $1 \in S$ **do**
        for $j \in S - \{1\}$ **do**
            // use recurrence from Corollary 21.2
            $A[S][j] := \min_{\substack{k \in S \\ k \neq 1, j}} (A[S - \{j\}][k] + c_{kj})$

```
// use (21.6) to compute the optimal tour cost
```
return $\min_{j=2}^{n} (A[V][j] + c_{j1})$

In this pseudocode, there are $2^{n-1} - 1$ choices of S to keep track of (one per non-empty subset of $\{2, 3, \ldots, n\}$), and "subproblem size" is measured by the number of vertices to visit (the size of S). For a base case with subset $S = \{1, j\}$, the only option is the one-hop 1-j path with cost c_{1j}. The subproblem array is indexed by vertex subsets S; a concrete implementation would encode these subsets by integers.[4] In the loop iteration responsible for computing the subproblem solution $A[S][j]$, all terms of the form $A[S - \{j\}][k]$ have been computed in the previous iteration of the outermost for loop (or in the base cases). These values are ready and waiting to be looked up in constant time. See Problem 21.2 for an example of this algorithm in action.[5]

The correctness of the `BellmanHeldKarp` algorithm follows by induction (on the subproblem size), with the recurrence in Corollary 21.2 justifying the inductive step and the identity (21.6) the final postprocessing step.

And the running time? The base cases and the postprocessing step take $O(n)$ time. There are $(2^{n-1} - 1)(n - 1) = O(n2^n)$ subproblems. Solving a subproblem boils down to the minimum computation in the inner loop, which takes $O(n)$ time. The overall running time is then $O(n^2 2^n)$.[6,7]

Theorem 21.3 (Properties of `BellmanHeldKarp`) *For every complete graph $G = (V, E)$ with $n \geq 3$ vertices and real-valued edge costs, the `BellmanHeldKarp` algorithm runs in $O(n^2 2^n)$ time and returns the minimum cost of a traveling salesman tour.*

The `BellmanHeldKarp` algorithm computes the total cost of an optimal tour, not an optimal tour itself. As always with dynamic programming algorithms, you can reconstruct an optimal solution in a postprocessing step that traces back through the filled-in subproblem array (Problem 21.6).

21.1.7 Solution to Quiz 21.1

Correct answers: (a),(c),(d). Because P is a cycle-free path from 1 to j visiting every vertex and with final hop (k, j), the subpath P' is a cycle-free path from 1 to k that visits all the vertices of $V - \{j\}$ but not j. Thus, (a) and (c) are both correct answers. Answer (b) is incorrect because P' might not be able to compete with the cycle-free paths from 1 to k that visit every vertex of $V - \{j\}$ and *can also* visit j:

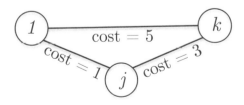

---

[4]For example, the subsets of $V - \{1\}$ can be represented using length-$(n - 1)$ bit arrays, which in turn can be interpreted as the binary expansions of the integers between 0 and $2^{n-1} - 1$.

[5]This algorithm was proposed independently by Richard E. Bellman in the paper "Dynamic Programming Treatment of the Travelling Salesman Problem" (*Journal of the ACM*, 1962) and Michael Held and Richard M. Karp in the paper "A Dynamic Programming Approach to Sequencing Problems" (*Journal of the Society for Industrial and Applied Mathematics*, 1962).

[6]In the notation of (21.2), $f(n) = O(n2^n)$, $g(n) = O(n)$, and $h(n) = O(n)$.

[7]This running time analysis assumes that the subsets S with a given size $s \geq 3$ and $1 \in S$ are enumerated in time linear in their number $\binom{n-1}{s-1}$, for example, by recursive enumeration. (If you want to venture out into the weeds on this point, look up "Gosper's hack.")

We can prove (d) by contradiction. Let C denote the total cost of P, so that the cost of P' is $C - c_{kj}$. If (d) is false, there is another cycle-free path P^* from 1 to k that visits every vertex of $V - \{j\}$, does not visit vertex j, and has cost $C^* < C - c_{kj}$. Then, appending the edge (k, j) to P^* produces a path $\widehat{P}$ from 1 to j with total cost $C^* + c_{kj} < C$:

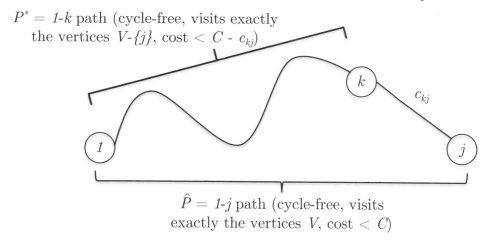

$P^* = 1\text{-}k$ path (cycle-free, visits exactly the vertices $V\text{-}\{j\}$, cost $< C$ - c_{kj})

$\widehat{P} = 1\text{-}j$ path (cycle-free, visits exactly the vertices V, cost $< C$)

Moreover, the path $\widehat{P}$ is cycle-free (because P^* is cycle-free and does not visit j) and visits every vertex of V (because P^* visits every vertex of $V - \{j\}$). This contradicts our assumption that P is a minimum-cost such path.

*21.2 Finding Long Paths by Color Coding

Graphs are omnipresent in the study of algorithms because they hit the sweet spot between expressiveness and tractability. Throughout this book, we've seen many efficient algorithms for processing graphs (graph search, connected components, shortest paths, etc.), and many application domains well modeled by graphs (road networks, the World Wide Web, social networks, etc.). This section furnishes another example, a killer application of dynamic programming and randomization to the detection of structure in biological networks.

21.2.1 Motivation

Most of the work that takes place in a cell is carried out by proteins (chains of amino acids), often acting in concert. For example, a series of proteins might transmit a signal that arrives at the cell membrane to the proteins that regulate the transcription of the cell's DNA to RNA. Understanding such signaling pathways and how they get rewired by genetic mutations is an important step in developing new drugs to combat diseases.

Interactions between proteins are naturally modeled as a graph, called a *protein-protein interaction (PPI)* network, with one vertex per protein and one edge per pair of proteins suspected to interact. The simplest signaling pathways are *linear* pathways, corresponding to paths in the PPI network. How quickly can we find them?

21.2.2 Problem Definition

The problem of finding a linear pathway of a given length in a PPI network can be cast as the following minimum-cost k-path problem, where a k-path of a graph is a (cycle-free) path of $k - 1$ edges visiting k distinct vertices.

Problem: Minimum-Cost k-Path

Input: An undirected graph $G = (V, E)$, a real-valued cost c_e for each edge $e \in E$, and a positive integer k.

Output: A k-path P of G with the minimum-possible total cost $\sum_{e \in P} c_e$. (Or if G has no k-paths, report this fact.)

The edge costs reflect the uncertainties inevitable in noisy biological data, with a higher cost indicating a lower confidence that the corresponding pair of proteins really do interact. (Missing edges effectively have a cost of $+\infty$.) In a PPI network, the minimum-cost k-path corresponds to the most plausible linear pathway of a given length. In realistic instances, k might be 10 or 20; the number of vertices might be in the hundreds or thousands.

For example, in the graph

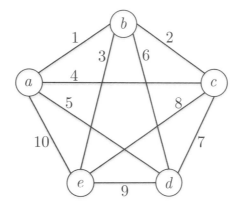

the minimum cost of a 4-path is 8 ($c \to a \to b \to e$).

The minimum-cost k-path problem is closely related to the TSP and, for this reason, is NP-hard (see Section 22.3). But can we at least improve over exhaustive search?

21.2.3   A First Stab at the Subproblems

The minimum-cost k-path problem closely resembles the TSP, with the main difference being the path length bound k. Why not use the same subproblems that served us so well in beating exhaustive search for the TSP (Section 21.1.5)? That is, given a graph $G = (V, E)$ with real-valued edge costs and a path length k:

Subproblems (A First Stab)

Compute $C_{S,v}$, the minimum cost of a cycle-free path that ends at the vertex $v \in V$ and visits exactly the vertices in S (or $+\infty$, if there is no such path).

(For each non-empty subset $S \subseteq V$ of at most k vertices and each $v \in S$.)

Because a minimum-cost k-path could start anywhere, subproblems no longer specify a starting vertex (which in the TSP was always vertex 1). The minimum cost of a k-path is the smallest of the solutions to the biggest subproblems (with $|S| = k$); if the graph has no k-paths, all such subproblem solutions will be $+\infty$.

Quiz 21.2

Suppose $k = 10$. How many subproblems are there, as a function of the number of vertices n? (Choose the strongest correct statement.)

a) $O(n)$

b) $O(n^{10})$

c) $O(n^{11})$

d) $O(2^n)$

(See Section 21.2.11 for the solution and discussion.)

Meanwhile:

Quiz 21.3

Suppose $k = 10$. What is the running time of a straightforward implementation of exhaustive search, as a function of n? (Choose the strongest correct statement.)

a) $O(n^{10})$

b) $O(n^{11})$

c) $O(2^n)$

d) $O(n!)$

(See Section 21.2.11 for the solution and discussion.)

Uh-oh… a dynamic programming algorithm that uses the subproblems on page 526 can't beat exhaustive search! And any algorithm with a running time like $O(n^{10})$ is practically useless except in the smallest of graphs. We need another idea.

21.2.4   Color Coding

Why are we using so many subproblems? Oh right, we're keeping track of the vertices S visited by a path to avoid inadvertently creating a path that visits a vertex more than once (recall Quiz 21.1 and Lemma 21.1). Can we get away with tracking less information about a path? Here's the inspired idea, given a graph $G = (V, E)$ and path length bound k:[8]

---

[8]Proposed by Noga Alon, Raphael Yuster, and Uri Zwick, in the paper "Color-Coding" (*Journal of the ACM*, 1995).

Color Coding

1. Partition the vertex set V into k groups $V_1, V_2, \ldots, V_k$ so that there is a minimum-cost k-path of G that has exactly one vertex in each group.

2. Among all paths with exactly one vertex in each group, compute one with the minimum cost.

This technique is called *color coding* because if we associate each integer of $\{1, 2, \ldots, k\}$ with a color, we can visualize the ith group V_i of the partition in the first step as the vertices colored i. The second step then seeks a minimum-cost *panchromatic path*, meaning a path in which each color is represented exactly once:

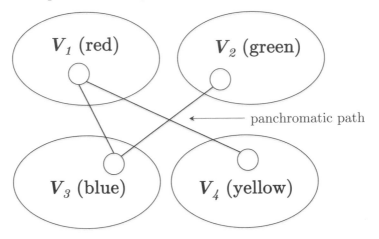

Because there are k colors, a panchromatic path must be a k-path. The converse is false, as a k-path might use some color more than once (and some other color not at all):

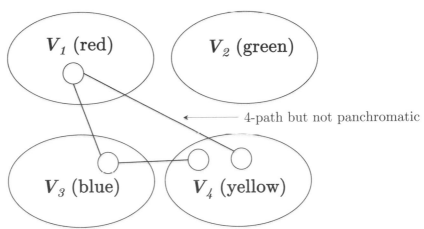

If the color-coding plan can be carried out, it would solve the minimum-cost k-path problem: The second step computes a minimum-cost panchromatic path, and the first step ensures that this is also a minimum-cost k-path in G (panchromatic or otherwise).

Skeptical? Perfectly understandable. Why should computing a minimum-cost panchromatic path be any easier than the original problem? And how on earth can we implement the first step without knowing anything about what the minimum-cost k-paths are?

21.2.5   Computing a Minimum-Cost Panchromatic Path

Restricting attention to panchromatic paths simplifies the minimum-cost k-path problem because it frees a dynamic programming algorithm to guard against repeated *colors* instead of repeated vertices. (A repeated vertex implies a repeated color but not vice versa.) Subproblems can track the colors represented in a path, along with an ending vertex, in lieu of the vertices themselves. Why is this a win? Because there are only 2^k subsets of colors, as opposed to the $\Omega(n^k)$ subsets of at most k vertices (see the solution to Quiz 21.2).

Subproblems and Recurrence

For a color subset $S \subseteq \{1, 2, \ldots, k\}$, an S-*path* is a (cycle-free) path with $|S|$ vertices and all colors of S represented. (Panchromatic paths are precisely the S-paths with $S = \{1, 2, \ldots, k\}$.) For a graph $G = (V, E)$ with edge costs and a color assignment $\sigma(v)$ (in $\{1, 2, \ldots, k\}$) to each vertex $v \in V$, the subproblems are then:

> **Minimum-Cost Panchromatic Path: Subproblems**
>
> Compute $C_{S,v}$, the minimum cost of an S-path that ends at the vertex $v \in V$ (or $+\infty$, if there is no such path).
>
> (For each non-empty subset $S \subseteq \{1, 2, \ldots, k\}$ of colors, and each vertex $v \in V$.)

The minimum cost of a panchromatic path is the smallest of the solutions to the biggest subproblems (with $S = \{1, 2, \ldots, k\}$); if the graph has no panchromatic paths, all such subproblem solutions will be $+\infty$.

An optimal path P for a subproblem with color subset S and ending vertex v must be built up from an optimal path for a smaller subproblem:

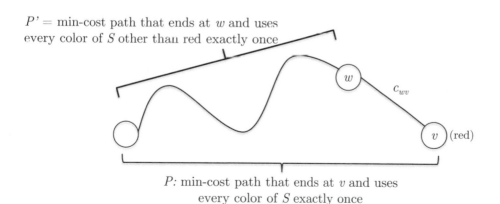

P' = min-cost path that ends at w and uses every color of S other than red exactly once

P: min-cost path that ends at v and uses every color of S exactly once

If P's final hop is (w, v), its prefix $P' = P - \{(w, v)\}$ must be a minimum-cost $(S - \{\sigma(v)\})$-path ending at w, where $\sigma(v)$ denotes v's color.[9] This optimal substructure leads immediately to the following recurrence for solving all the subproblems.

---

[9]The formal proof of this statement is almost the same as the proof of Lemma 21.1 (see page 525).

Lemma 21.4 (Min-Cost Panchromatic Path Recurrence) *Continuing with the same notation, for every subset $S \subseteq \{1, 2, \ldots, k\}$ of at least two colors and vertex $v \in V$:*

$$C_{S,v} = \min_{(w,v) \in E} \left(C_{S-\{\sigma(v)\},w} + c_{wv} \right). \tag{21.7}$$

Dynamic Programming Algorithm

In turn, this recurrence leads immediately to a dynamic programming algorithm for computing the minimum cost of a panchromatic path (or $+\infty$, if no such path exists):

PanchromaticPath

Input: undirected graph $G = (V, E)$, a real-valued cost c_{vw} for each edge $(v, w) \in E$, and a color $\sigma(v) \in \{1, 2, \ldots, k\}$ for each vertex $v \in V$.
Output: the minimum total cost of a panchromatic path of G (or $+\infty$, if no such path exists).

```
// subproblems (indexed by S ⊆ {1,...,k}, v ∈ V)
```
$A := (2^k - 1) \times |V|$ two-dimensional array
```
// base cases (|S| = 1)
```
for $i := 1$ **to** k **do**
    for $v \in V$ **do**
        if $\sigma(v) = i$ **then**
            $A[\{i\}][v] := 0$ `// via the empty path`
        else
            $A[\{i\}][v] := +\infty$ `// no such path`
```
// systematically solve all subproblems
```
for $s := 2$ **to** k **do**   `// s=subproblem size`
    for S with $|S| = s$ **do**
        for $v \in V$ with $\sigma(v) \in S$ **do**
             `// use recurrence from Lemma 21.4`
            $A[S][v] := \min_{(w,v) \in E} \left(A[S - \{\sigma(v)\}][w] + c_{wv} \right)$
```
// best of solutions to largest subproblems
```
return $\min_{v \in V} A[\{1, 2, \ldots, k\}][v]$

See Problem 21.5 for an example of the algorithm in action.

21.2.6   Correctness and Running Time

The correctness of the `PanchromaticPath` algorithm follows by induction (on the subproblem size), with the recurrence in Lemma 21.4 justifying the inductive step. With a little extra bookkeeping, a minimum-cost panchromatic path can be reconstructed in an $O(k)$-time postprocessing step (Problem 21.7).

The running time analysis echoes that of the Bellman-Ford algorithm (Section 18.2). Almost all the work performed by the algorithm occurs in its triple-for loop. Assuming the input graph is represented using adjacency lists, an innermost loop iteration that computes the value of $A[S][v]$ takes $O(\deg(v))$ time, where $\deg(v)$ denotes the degree (i.e., the number of incident edges) of the vertex v.[10] For each subset S, the combined time spent solving the associated $|V|$ subproblems is $O(\sum_{v \in V} \deg(v)) = O(m)$, where $m = |E|$ denotes the number of edges.[11] The number of different color subsets S is less than 2^k, so the overall running time of the algorithm is $O(2^k m)$.

Theorem 21.5 (Properties of `PanchromaticPath`)   *For every graph G with m edges, real-valued edge costs, and assignment of each vertex to a color in $\{1, 2, \ldots, k\}$, the `PanchromaticPath` algorithm runs in $O(2^k m)$ time and returns the minimum cost of a panchromatic path (if one exists) or $+\infty$ (otherwise).*

With running time scaling with 2^k rather than n^k, the `PanchromaticPath` algorithm improves dramatically over exhaustive search. But the problem we truly care about is the minimum-cost k-path problem without any panchromatic constraint. How does this algorithm help?

21.2.7   Randomization to the Rescue

The first step of the color-coding approach colors the vertices of the input graph so that at least one minimum-cost k-path turns panchromatic. How can we accomplish this without knowing which k-paths are the minimum-cost ones? Time to bring out another tool from our algorithmic toolbox: *randomization*. The hope is that a uniformly random coloring has a healthy chance of rendering some minimum-cost k-path panchromatic, in which case the `PanchromaticPath` algorithm will find one.

Quiz 21.4

Suppose we assign each vertex of a graph G a color from $\{1, 2, \ldots, k\}$ independently and uniformly at random. Consider a k-path P in G. What is the probability that P winds up panchromatic?

    a) $1/k$

    b) $1/k^2$

    c) $1/k!$

    d) $k!/k^k$

    e) $1/k^k$

(See Section 21.2.11 for the solution and discussion.)

---

[10] Assume that any degree-0 vertices have already been discarded harmlessly in a preprocessing step.
[11] The sum $\sum_{v \in V} \deg(v)$ of vertex degrees is twice the number of edges, with each edge contributing 1 to the degree of each of its two endpoints.

Is this probability of getting lucky—call it p—big or small? Remember that we know an extremely accurate estimate of the factorial function (Stirling's approximation on page 519). Plugging in the approximation in (21.1), with k playing the role of n:

$$p = \frac{k!}{k^k} \approx \frac{1}{k^k} \cdot \sqrt{2\pi k} \left(\frac{k}{e} \right)^k = \frac{\sqrt{2\pi k}}{e^k}. \tag{21.8}$$

Looks bad—the probability of success (that is, of turning a minimum-cost k-path panchromatic) is less than 1% already when $k = 7$. But if we experiment with a large number of independent random colorings—running the `PanchromaticPath` algorithm for each and remembering the least costly k-path found—*one* lucky coloring is all we need. How many random trials T do we need to ensure a 99% chance that one of our colorings renders a minimum-cost k-path panchromatic?

A trial succeeds with probability p, so it fails with probability $1 - p$. Because the trials are independent, their failure probabilities multiply. The probability that all T trials fail is then $(1 - p)^T$.[12] Remembering that we can bound $1 - p$ from above by e^{-p}:

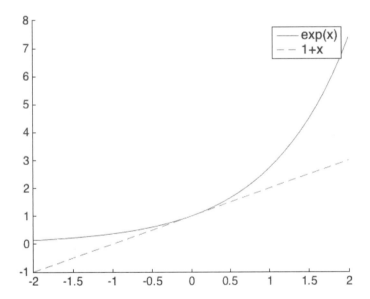

this failure probability is

$$(1 - p)^T \leq (e^{-p})^T = e^{-pT}. \tag{21.9}$$

Setting the right-hand side of (21.9) to a target δ (like .01), taking logarithms of both sides, and solving for T shows that

$$T \geq \frac{1}{p} \cdot \ln \left(\frac{1}{\delta} \right) \tag{21.10}$$

independent trials are enough to drive the failure probability down to δ. As expected, the lower the single-trial success probability or the desired failure probability, the greater the number of trials required.

Substituting our success probability p from (21.8) into (21.10) shows that:

---

[12]For background on discrete probability, see the resources at www.algorithmsilluminated.org or Appendix B.

Lemma 21.6 (Random Colorings Are Good Enough) *For every graph G, k-path P of G, and failure probability* $\delta \in (0, 1)$*: If*

$$T \geq \frac{e^k}{\sqrt{2\pi k}} \cdot \ln\left(\frac{1}{\delta}\right),$$

the probability that at least one of T uniformly random colorings turns P panchromatic is at least $1 - \delta$.

The exponential number of trials in Lemma 21.6 may look extravagant, but it's in the same ballpark as the time already required by a single invocation of the `PanchromaticPath` subroutine. When k is small relative to n—the regime relevant to the motivating application (Section 21.2.1)—the number of trials is much less than the time required to solve the minimum-cost k-path problem on n-vertex graphs by exhaustive search (which, by Quiz 21.3, scales with n^k).

21.2.8 The Final Algorithm

We now have all our ducks in a row: Lemma 21.6 promises that many independent random colorings suffice to implement the first step of the color-coding approach (page 528) and the `PanchromaticPath` algorithm takes care of the second step.

ColorCoding

Input: undirected graph $G = (V, E)$, a real-valued cost c_{vw} for each edge $(v, w) \in E$, a path length k, and a failure probability $\delta \in (0, 1)$.

Output: the minimum total cost of a k-path of G (or $+\infty$, if no such path exists), except with a failure probability of at most δ.

$C_{best} := +\infty$ // cheapest k-path found so far
// number of random trials (from Lemma 21.6)
$T := (e^k/\sqrt{2\pi k}) \ln\frac{1}{\delta}$ // round up to an integer
for $t := 1$ to T **do**   // independent trials
    for each $v \in V$ **do**   // choose random coloring
        $\sigma_t(v) :=$ random number from $\{1, 2, \ldots, k\}$
    // best panchromatic path with coloring σ_t
    $C := $ `PanchromaticPath`(G, c, σ_t) // see page 530
    if $C < C_{best}$ **then**   // found a cheaper k-path!
        $C_{best} := C$
return C_{best}

21.2.9 Running Time and Correctness

The running time of the `ColorCoding` algorithm is dominated by its $T = O((e^k/\sqrt{k})\ln\frac{1}{\delta})$ calls to the $O(2^k m)$-time `PanchromaticPath` subroutine, where m denotes the number of edges (Theorem 21.5).

To argue correctness, consider a minimum-cost k-path P^* of G, with total cost C^*.[13] For every coloring σ, the minimum cost of a panchromatic path—the output of the `PanchromaticPath` subroutine—is at least C^*. Whenever σ turns P^* panchromatic, this cost is exactly C^*. By Lemma 21.6, with probability at least $1 - \delta$, at least one of the iterations of the outer loop chooses such a coloring; in this event, the `ColorCoding` algorithm returns C^*, which is the correct answer.[14]

To summarize:

Theorem 21.7 (Properties of `ColorCoding`) *For every graph G with n vertices and m edges, real-valued edge costs, path length $k \in \{1, 2, \ldots, n\}$, and failure probability $\delta \in (0, 1)$, the `ColorCoding` algorithm runs in*

$$O\left(\frac{(2e)^k}{\sqrt{k}} m \ln\left(\frac{1}{\delta}\right)\right) \tag{21.11}$$

time and, with probability at least $1 - \delta$, returns the minimum cost of a k-path of G (if one exists) or $+\infty$ (otherwise).

How should we feel about the running time of the `ColorCoding` algorithm? The bad news is that the running time bound in (21.11) is exponential—no surprise, given that the minimum-cost k-path problem is NP-hard in general. The good news is that its exponential dependence is confined entirely to the path length k, with only linear dependence on the graph size. In fact, in the special case in which $k \leq c \ln m$ for a constant $c > 0$, the `ColorCoding` algorithm solves the minimum-cost k-path problem in polynomial time![15,16]

21.2.10   Revisiting PPI Networks

Fancy guarantees like Theorem 21.7 are nice and all, but how well does the `ColorCoding` algorithm actually work in the motivating application of finding long linear pathways in PPI networks? The algorithm is a great fit for the application, in which typical path lengths k are in the 10–20 range. (Significantly longer paths, if they exist, are challenging to interpret.) Already with circa-2007 computers, optimized implementations of the `ColorCoding` algorithm could find linear pathways of length $k = 20$ in major PPI networks with thousands

---

[13]If G has no k-paths, every invocation of `PanchromaticPath` and the `ColorCoding` algorithm will return $+\infty$ (which is the correct answer).

[14]The most famous randomized algorithm, QuickSort, has a random running time (ranging from near-linear to quadratic) but is always correct (see Chapter 5). The `ColorCoding` algorithm is the opposite: The outcomes of its coin flips determine whether it's correct but have little effect on its running time.

[15]Observe that $(2e)^{c \ln m} = m^{c \ln(2e)} \approx m^{1.693c}$, which is polynomial in the graph size.

[16]The `ColorCoding` algorithm is an example of a *fixed-parameter* algorithm, meaning one with a running time of the form $O(f(k) \cdot n^d)$, where n denotes the input size, d is a constant (independent of k and n), and k is a parameter measuring the "difficulty" of the instance. The function f must be independent of n but can have arbitrary dependence (typically exponential or worse) on the parameter k. A fixed-parameter algorithm runs in polynomial time for all instances in which k is sufficiently small relative to n.

The 21st century has seen tremendous progress in understanding which NP-hard problems and parameter choices allow for fixed-parameter algorithms. For a deep dive, check out the book *Parameterized Algorithms*, by Marek Cygan, Fedor V. Fomin, Łukasz Kowalik, Daniel Lokshtanov, Dániel Marx, Marcin Pilipczuk, Michał Pilipczuk, and Saket Saurabh (Springer, 2015).

of vertices. This was a significant advance over exhaustive search (which is useless even for $k = 5$) and the competing algorithms at that time (which failed to go much beyond $k = 10$).[17]

21.2.11   Solutions to Quizzes 21.2–21.4

Solution to Quiz 21.2

Correct answer: (b). The number of non-empty subsets $S \subseteq V$ of size at most 10 is the sum $\sum_{i=1}^{10} \binom{n}{i}$ of ten binomial coefficients. Bounding the ith summand from above by n^i and using the formula (20.9) for a geometric series shows that this sum is $O(n^{10})$. Expanding the last binomial coefficient shows that it alone is $\Omega(n^{10})$. With at most ten choices for the endpoint v for each set S, the total number of subproblems is $\Theta(n^{10})$.

Solution to Quiz 21.3

Correct answer: (a). Exhaustive search enumerates the $n \cdot (n-1) \cdot (n-2) \cdots (n-9)$ $= \Theta(n^{10})$ ordered 10-tuples of distinct vertices, computes the cost of each tuple that corresponds to a path (in $O(1)$ time, assuming access to an adjacency matrix populated by edges' costs), and remembers the best of the 10-paths it encounters. The running time of this algorithm is $\Theta(n^{10})$.

Solution to Quiz 21.4

Correct answer: (d). There are k^k different ways to color the vertices of P (with k color choices for each of the k vertices), each equally likely (with probability $1/k^k$ each). How many of these render P panchromatic? There are k choices for the vertex receiving the color 1, then $k-1$ remaining choices for the vertex receiving the color 2, and so on, for a total of $k!$ panchromatic colorings. The probability of panchromaticity is, therefore, $k!/k^k$.

21.3   Problem-Specific Algorithms vs. Magic Boxes

21.3.1   Reductions and Magic Boxes

Bespoke solutions to fundamental problems like the `BellmanHeldKarp` (Section 21.1.6) and `ColorCoding` (Section 21.2.8) algorithms are deeply satisfying. But before investing the effort necessary to design or code up a new algorithm, you should always ask yourself:

> Is this problem a special case or a thinly disguised version of one that I already know how to solve?

If the answer is "no," or even "yes, but the algorithms for the more general problem aren't good enough for this application," you've justified proceeding to problem-specific algorithm development.

Throughout this book, we've seen several problems for which the answer is "yes." For example, median-finding reduces to sorting, all-pairs shortest paths reduces to single-source

---

[17]For more details, check out the paper "Algorithm Engineering for Color-Coding with Applications to Signaling Pathway Detection," by Falk Hüffner, Sebastian Wernicke, and Thomas Zichner (*Algorithmica*, 2008).

shortest paths, and the longest common subsequence problem is a special case of the sequence alignment problem (Section 19.5.2). Such reductions transfer tractability from one problem B to another problem A:

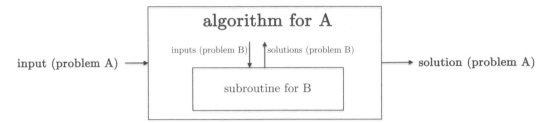

Our reductions thus far have been to problems B for which we ourselves had already designed a fast algorithm. But a reduction from a problem A to a problem B retains its power *even if you don't personally know* how to solve B efficiently. As long as someone gives you a magic box (such as an inscrutable piece of software) that solves problem B, you're good to go: To solve problem A, execute the reduction to problem B and invoke the magic box as needed.

21.3.2   MIP and SAT Solvers

A "magic box" probably sounds like pure fantasy, akin to a unicorn or the fountain of youth. Could one really exist? Sections 21.4 and 21.5 describe two of the closest approximations out there—solvers for mixed integer programming (MIP) and satisfiability (SAT) problems. By a "solver," we mean a sophisticated algorithm that has been carefully tuned and expertly implemented as ready-to-use software. MIP and SAT are very general problems, expressive enough to capture most of the problems studied in this book as special cases.

Several decades worth of engineering effort and ingenuity have been poured into state-of-the-art MIP and SAT solvers. For this reason, despite their generality, such solvers semi-reliably solve medium-size instances of NP-hard problems in a tolerable amount of time. Solver performance varies widely with the problem (and many other factors) but, as a rough guideline, you can reasonably cross your fingers and hope for inputs with size in the thousands to be solved in less than a day, and often much faster. In some applications, MIP and SAT solvers are unreasonably effective even for large instances, with input sizes in the millions.

21.3.3   What You Will and Won't Learn

The goals of Sections 21.4 and 21.5 are modest. They do not explain how MIP and SAT solvers work—that would require a whole other book. Instead, they prepare you to be an educated client of these solvers.[18]

---

[18]From 30,000 feet, the basic idea is: Recursively search the space of candidate solutions à la depth-first search, applying the clues gleaned so far to aggressively prune not-yet-examined candidates (such as candidates that cannot possibly have objective function value better than the best solution already discovered), backtracking as needed. The hope is that most of the search space gets pruned without explicit examination. To explore these ideas further, look up "branch and bound" (for MIP solvers) and "conflict-driven clause learning" (for SAT solvers).

Goals of Sections 21.4–21.5

1. Be aware that semi-reliable magic boxes called MIP and SAT solvers exist and can be unreasonably effective at tackling NP-hard problems in practice. (Not enough programmers know this!)

2. See examples of encodings of NP-hard problems as MIP and SAT problems.

3. Know where to go next to learn more.

21.3.4   A Rookie Mistake Revisited

MIP and SAT solvers routinely crack tough problems, but don't get fooled into thinking that NP-hardness doesn't matter in practice (the third rookie mistake in Section 19.6). When applying such a solver to an NP-hard problem, keep your fingers crossed and have at the ready a plan B (like a fast heuristic algorithm) in case the solver fails. And make no mistake: There will be some instances out there, including fairly small ones, that can bring your solver to its knees. You take whatever you can with NP-hard problems, and semi-reliable magic boxes are about as good as it gets.

21.4   Mixed Integer Programming Solvers

Most discrete optimization problems can be cast as mixed integer programming (MIP) problems.[19] Whenever you're faced with an NP-hard optimization problem that you can encode efficiently as a MIP problem, throwing the latest and greatest MIP solver at it is probably worth a shot.

21.4.1   Example: The Knapsack Problem

In the knapsack problem (Section 16.5), the input is specified by $2n + 1$ positive integers: n item values $v_1, v_2, \ldots, v_n$, n item sizes $s_1, s_2, \ldots, s_n$, and a knapsack capacity C. For example:

	Value	Size
Item #1	6	5
Item #2	5	4
Item #3	4	3
Item #4	3	2
Item #5	2	1
Knapsack capacity: 10		

The goal is to compute a subset of the items with the maximum-possible total value, subject to having a total size of at most the knapsack capacity. The problem specification thus spells out three things:

---

[19]This is the same anachronistic use of the word "programming" as in dynamic programming (or television programming); it refers to planning, not coding.

1. *The decisions to be made:* for each of the n items, whether to include it in the subset. One convenient way to encode these per-item binary decisions numerically is with 0-1 variables, called *decision variables*:

$$x_j = \begin{cases} 1 & \text{if item } j \text{ is included} \\ 0 & \text{if item } j \text{ is excluded.} \end{cases} \tag{21.12}$$

2. *The constraints to be respected:* the sum of the sizes of the chosen items should be at most the knapsack capacity C. This constraint is easily expressed in terms of the decision variables, with item j contributing s_j to the total size if it's included (with $x_j = 1$) and 0 if it's excluded (with $x_j = 0$):

$$\underbrace{\sum_{j=1}^{n} s_j x_j}_{\substack{\text{total size of} \\ \text{chosen subset}}} \leq C. \tag{21.13}$$

3. *The objective function:* the sum of the values of the chosen items should be as large as possible (subject to the capacity constraint). This objective function is equally easy to express (with j contributing value v_j if included and 0 if excluded):

$$\text{maximize } \underbrace{\sum_{j=1}^{n} v_j x_j}_{\substack{\text{total value of} \\ \text{chosen subset}}}. \tag{21.14}$$

Guess what? In (21.12)–(21.14), you've just seen your first example of an *integer program*. For example, in the 5-item instance described above, this integer program reads:

$$\begin{aligned} \text{maximize} \quad & 6x_1 + 5x_2 + 4x_3 + 3x_4 + 2x_5 & (21.15) \\ \text{subject to} \quad & 5x_1 + 4x_2 + 3x_3 + 2x_4 + x_5 \leq 10 & (21.16) \\ & x_1, x_2, x_3, x_4, x_5 \in \{0, 1\}. & (21.17) \end{aligned}$$

This is exactly the sort of description that can be fed directly into a magic box called a *mixed integer programming (MIP) solver*. For example, to solve the integer program in (21.15)–(21.17) using Gurobi Optimizer, the leading commercial MIP solver, you literally just call it from the command line with the following input file:

```
Maximize 6 x(1) + 5 x(2) + 4 x(3) + 3 x(4) + 2 x(5)
subject to
5 x(1) + 4 x(2) + 3 x(3) + 2 x(4) + x(5) <= 10
binary
x(1) x(2) x(3) x(4) x(5)
end
```

Magically, the solver then spits out the optimal solution (in this case, with $x_1 = 0$, $x_2 = x_3 = x_4 = x_5 = 1$, and objective function value 14).[20,21]

21.4.2   MIPs More Generally

In general, a MIP is specified by the three ingredients listed in Section 21.4.1: the decision variables, along with the values they can assume (such as 0 or 1, or any integer, or any real number); the constraints; and the objective function. The one important restriction is that both the constraints and the objective function should be *linear* in the decision variables.[22] In other words, it's OK to scale a decision variable by a constant, and it's OK to add decision variables together, but that's it. For example, in (21.15)–(21.17), you don't see any terms like x_j^2, $x_j x_k$, $1/x_j$, e^{x_j}, and so on.[23]

Problem: Mixed Integer Programming

Input: A list of (binary, integer, or real-valued) decision variables $x_1, x_2, \ldots, x_n$; a linear objective function to be maximized or minimized, specified by its coefficients $c_1, c_2, \ldots, c_n$; and m linear constraints, with each constraint i specified by its coefficients $a_{i1}, a_{i2}, \ldots, a_{in}$ and right-hand side b_i.

Output: An assignment of values to $x_1, x_2, \ldots, x_n$ that optimizes the objective function ($\sum_{j=1}^{n} c_j x_j$) subject to the m constraints ($\sum_{j=1}^{n} a_{ij} x_j \leq b_i$ for all $i = 1, 2, \ldots, m$). (Or if no assignment satisfies all the constraints, report this fact.)

Even with the linearity restriction, it's often embarrassingly simple to express NP-hard optimization problems as MIPs. For example, consider the *two-dimensional* knapsack problem, where every item j now has a *weight* w_j in addition to a value v_j and size s_j; in addition to the knapsack capacity C, there is a weight bound W. The goal is then to choose the maximum-value subset of items with total size at most C and total weight at most W. As a graduate of the *Algorithms Illuminated* dynamic programming boot camp, you could knock out an algorithm for this problem without much trouble. But you couldn't do it as quickly as you could add the constraint

$$\sum_{j=1}^{n} w_j x_j \leq W \qquad (21.18)$$

---

[20] For this toy example, the input file is easy enough to create by hand. For larger instances, you'll want to write a program that generates the input file automatically or interacts directly with the solver API.

[21] Why "mixed"? Because MIP solvers also accommodate decision variables that can take on real (not necessarily integer) values. Some authors refer to MIPs as integer linear programs (ILPs) or simply integer programs (IPs). Others reserve the latter term for MIPs in which all the decision variables are integer-valued.

A MIP in which none of the decision variables are required to be integers is called a *linear program (LP)*. State-of-the-art solvers work particularly well for LPs, and often solve thousands of them in the course of solving a single MIP. (Relatedly, linear programming is a polynomial-time solvable problem while general mixed integer programming is an NP-hard problem.)

[22] Thus, "MILP" (for mixed integer linear program) would be more precise than "MIP," though also less pleasing to the ear...

[23] State-of-the-art solvers can also accommodate limited types of nonlinearity (like quadratic terms) but are typically much faster with linear constraints and objective functions.

to the knapsack MIP (21.12)–(21.14)!

Familiar optimization problems like the maximum-weight independent set (Section 16.1), minimum makespan (Section 20.1), and maximum coverage (Section 20.2) problems are almost equally easy to express as MIPs (see Problem 21.9).[24] MIPs are also the basis for the state-of-the-art exact algorithms for the TSP (Section 19.1.2), although this application is much more sophisticated (see Problem 21.10).[25]

A problem can generally be formulated as a MIP problem in several different ways, with some formulations leading to better solver performance than others (in some cases by orders of magnitude). If your first attempt at tackling an optimization problem with a MIP solver fails, consider experimenting with alternative encodings. As with algorithms, the design of good MIP formulations takes practice; the resources in footnote 25 will get you started.

Finally, if your MIP solver is taking too long to complete no matter which formulation you try, you can interrupt it after a target amount of time and use the best feasible solution found up to that point. (MIP solvers typically generate a sequence of successively better feasible solutions, analogous to the local search algorithms of Sections 20.4–20.5, en route to an optimal solution.) Stopping early effectively turns a MIP solver into a fast heuristic algorithm.

21.4.3   MIP Solvers: Some Starting Points

Now that you're amped up to apply a MIP solver to your favorite problem, where should you start? As of this writing (in 2022), there is a huge gulf in performance between commercial and non-commercial MIP solvers. Currently, Gurobi Optimizer is generally viewed as the fastest and most robust MIP solver, with runners-up including CPLEX and FICO Xpress. University students and staff can obtain free academic licenses for these solvers (for research and educational purposes only).

If you're stuck using a non-commercial solver, good starting points include SCIP, CBC, MIPCL, and GLPK. CBC and MIPCL have more liberal licensing agreements than the other two, which are free for non-commercial use only.

You can decouple the tasks of formulating a MIP for your problem and describing that MIP to a particular solver by specifying your MIP in a high-level solver-independent modeling language, such as the Python-based CVXPY. You can then experiment easily with all the solvers supported by that language, with your high-level specification automatically compiled into the format expected by the solver.

21.5   Satisfiability Solvers

In many applications, the primary goal is to figure out whether a feasible solution exists (and, if so, to find some such solution) rather than to optimize a numerical objective function.

---

[24]For starters, a constraint of the form $\sum_{j=1}^{n} a_{ij}x_j \geq b_i$ can be represented by the equivalent constraint $\sum_{j=1}^{n}(-a_{ij})x_j \leq -b_i$, and an equality constraint $\sum_{j=1}^{n} a_{ij}x_j = b_i$ can be expressed by a pair of inequality constraints.

[25]For many more examples and tricks of the trade, check out the (free) documentation for the solvers listed in Section 21.4.3, or the textbook *Model Building in Mathematical Programming*, by H. Paul Williams (*Wiley*, 5th edition, 2013). The examples in Dan Gusfield's book *Integer Linear Programming in Computational and Systems Biology* (Cambridge, 2019) slant toward biological applications but are useful broadly for MIP (and especially Gurobi Optimizer) newbies.

Problems of this type can often be cast as satisfiability (SAT) problems. Whenever you're faced with an NP-hard problem that you can encode efficiently as a SAT problem, throwing the latest and greatest SAT solver at it is probably worth a shot.

21.5.1   Example: Graph Coloring

One of the oldest graph problems out there, studied extensively already in the 19th century, is the *graph coloring* problem. A *k-coloring* of an undirected graph $G = (V, E)$ is an assignment $\sigma(v)$ of each of its vertices $v \in V$ to a color in $\{1, 2, \ldots, k\}$ such that no edge is monochromatic (that is, $\sigma(v) \neq \sigma(w)$ whenever $(v, w) \in E$).[26] A graph with a *k*-coloring is called—wait for it—*k-colorable*.[27] For example, a wheel graph with six spokes is 3-colorable, while a wheel graph with five spokes is not (as you should check):

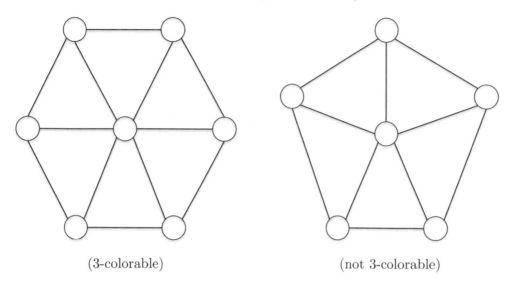

(3-colorable)   (not 3-colorable)

Problem: Graph Coloring

Input: An undirected graph $G = (V, E)$ and a positive integer k.

Output: A k-coloring of G, or a correct declaration that G is not k-colorable.

The graph coloring problem is not purely recreational. For example, the problem of assigning classes to one of k classrooms is exactly a graph coloring problem (with one vertex per class and an edge between each pair of classes that overlap in time). For a high-stakes application of graph coloring-type problems, see Chapter 24.

---

[26]The `ColorCoding` algorithm (Section 21.2.8) uses random colorings—which are generally not k-colorings—internally as a device to achieve a faster running time. In this section, the problem studied explicitly concerns k-colorings.

[27]The most famous result in all of graph theory is the "Four Color Theorem," stating that every planar graph—a graph that can be drawn on a piece of paper without any edge crossings—is 4-colorable. (The second graph above shows that four colors may be necessary.) Equivalently, as it turns out, maps need only four colors of ink to ensure that every pair of neighboring countries can be colored with different colors (assuming each country is a contiguous region).

21.5.2 Satisfiability

The non-numerical and rule-based nature of the graph coloring problem suggests expressing decision variables and constraints using the formalism of *logic* rather than arithmetic. Instead of numerical decision variables, we'll use *Boolean* variables, which can take on only the values true and false. A *truth assignment* specifies one of these two values for each variable. Constraints, which are also called *clauses*, are then logical formulas that express restrictions on the permitted truth assignments. A seemingly simple type of constraint, called a *disjunction of literals*, uses only the logical "or" (denoted by $\vee$) and logical "not" (denoted by $\neg$) operations.[28] For example, the constraint $x_1 \vee \neg x_2 \vee x_3$ is a disjunction of literals and is satisfied unless you screw up all three of its assignment requests (by setting x_1 and x_3 to false and x_2 to true):

Value of x_1	Value of x_2	Value of x_3	$x_1 \vee \neg x_2 \vee x_3$ Satisfied?
true	true	true	yes
true	true	false	yes
true	false	true	yes
false	true	true	yes
true	false	false	yes
false	true	false	no
false	false	true	yes
false	false	false	yes

In general, disjunctions of literals are easygoing creatures: one with k literals, each corresponding to a distinct decision variable, forbids one and only one of the 2^k ways to assign values to its variables.

An instance of satisfiability (SAT) is specified by its variables (restricted to be Boolean) and constraints (restricted to be disjunctions of literals).

Problem: Satisfiability

Input: A list of Boolean decision variables $x_1, x_2, \ldots, x_n$; and a list of constraints, each a disjunction of one or more literals.

Output: A truth assignment to $x_1, x_2, \ldots, x_n$ that satisfies every constraint, or a correct declaration that no such truth assignment exists.

21.5.3 Encoding Graph Coloring as SAT

Is the SAT problem, with its mere Boolean variables and disjunctions of literals, expressive enough to encode other interesting problems? For example, in the graph coloring problem, we'd ideally like one (non-Boolean) decision variable per vertex, each taking on one of k different values (one per possible color).

With a little practice, you can encode a surprisingly large number of problems as SAT.[29] For example, to encode an instance of graph coloring specified by the graph $G = (V, E)$

---

[28]"Literal" means a decision variable x_i or its negation $\neg x_i$, and "disjunction" means logical "or."

[29]In fact, the Cook-Levin theorem (Theorems 22.1 and 23.2) shows that SAT is a "universal" problem in a precise sense; see Section 23.6.3.

and integer k, we can use k variables per vertex; for each vertex $v \in V$ and color $i \in \{1, 2, \ldots, k\}$, the Boolean variable x_{vi} indicates whether vertex v is assigned the color i.

What about the constraints? For an edge $(v, w) \in E$ and color i, the constraint

$$\neg x_{vi} \lor \neg x_{wi} \tag{21.19}$$

is not satisfied precisely when both v and w are colored i. In tandem, the $|E| \cdot k$ constraints of the form (21.19) enforce that no edge is monochromatic.

We're not quite done, as all the constraints of the form (21.19) are satisfied by the all-false truth assignment (corresponding to no vertex receiving any color). But we can add one constraint

$$x_{v1} \lor x_{v2} \lor \cdots \lor x_{vk} \tag{21.20}$$

for each vertex $v \in V$ that is not satisfied precisely when v receives no color. Every k-coloring of G translates to a truth assignment that satisfies all the constraints and now, conversely, every truth assignment that satisfies all the constraints encodes one or more k-colorings of G.[30]

The system of constraints defined by (21.19) and (21.20) is exactly the sort of description that can be fed directly into a magic box called a *satisfiability (SAT) solver*. For example, to check whether a complete graph on three vertices is 2-colorable using MiniSAT, a popular open-source SAT solver, you literally just call it from the command line with the following input file:

```
p cnf 6 9
 1  4  0
 2  5  0
 3  6  0
-1 -2  0
-4 -5  0
-1 -3  0
-4 -6  0
-2 -3  0
-5 -6  0
```

Magically, the solver spits out a (correct) declaration that there is no way to satisfy all the constraints.[31,32]

---

[30]The constraints (21.20) allow vertices to receive more than one color, but the constraints (21.19) ensure that every way of choosing among the assigned colors produces a k-coloring of G.

[31]The first line of the file warns the solver that the SAT instance has six decision variables and nine constraints; the "cnf" stands for "conjunctive normal form" and indicates that each constraint is a disjunction of literals. Numbers between 1 and 6 refer to variables, with "−" indicating negation. The first three and last three variables correspond to the first color and second color, respectively. The first three and last six constraints are of the form in (21.20) and (21.19), respectively. Zeroes mark the ends of constraints.

[32]For many more applications of satisfiability, including classic applications to hardware and software verification, see the *Handbook of Satisfiability*, edited by Armin Biere, Marijn Heule, Hans van Maaren, and Toby Walsh (IOS Press, 2009). Or, if you've been wondering what Donald E. Knuth has been up to lately, check out *Satisfiability*, Fascicle 6 of Volume 4 of *The Art of Computer Programming* (Addison-Wesley, 2015). Another fun fact: SAT solvers were recently employed to break the once-secure cryptographic hash function SHA-1 (mentioned in Section 12.4.3); see "The First Collision for Full SHA-1," by Marc Stevens, Elie Bursztein, Pierre Karpman, Ange Albertini, and Yarik Markov (*Proceedings of the 37th CRYPTO Conference*, 2017).

21.5.4   SAT Solvers: Some Starting Points

As of this writing (in 2022), there are lots of good options for freely available SAT solvers. In fact, at least once every two years, SAT nerds from around the world gather and run Olympic-style competitions (complete with medals) between the latest and greatest solvers, each evaluated across a range of difficult benchmark instances. There are dozens of submissions to each competition, most of which are open-source.[33] If you want just one recommendation, MiniSAT, which combines good performance with ease of use and a permissive license (the MIT license), is a popular choice.[34]

The Upshot

☆ Solving the TSP by exhaustive search requires time scaling with $n!$, where n is the number of vertices.

☆ The Bellman-Held-Karp dynamic programming algorithm solves the TSP in $O(n^2 2^n)$ time.

☆ The key idea in the Bellman-Held-Karp algorithm is to parameterize subproblems by a subset of vertices to be visited exactly once and which of those vertices should be visited last.

☆ In the minimum-cost k-path problem, the input is an undirected graph with real-valued edge costs, and the goal is to compute a cycle-free path visiting k vertices with the minimum-possible sum of edge costs.

☆ Solving the minimum-cost k-path problem by exhaustive search requires time scaling with n^k, where n is the number of vertices.

☆ The color-coding algorithm solves the minimum-cost k-path problem in $O((2e)^k m \ln \frac{1}{\delta})$ time, where m is the number of edges and δ is a user-specified failure probability.

☆ The first key idea in the color-coding algorithm is a dynamic programming subroutine that, given an assignment of one of k colors to each vertex of the input graph, computes in $O(2^k m)$ time a minimum-cost panchromatic path.

☆ The second key idea is to experiment with $O(e^k \ln \frac{1}{\delta})$ independent and uniformly random vertex colorings; with probability at least $1-\delta$, at least one will render some minimum-cost k-path panchromatic.

☆ A mixed integer program (MIP) is specified by numerical decision variables, linear constraints, and a linear objective function.

---

[33] See www.satcompetition.org.
[34] And to up your SAT-solving game to the next level, look up "satisfiability modulo theories (SMT)" solvers, such as Microsoft's z3 solver (which is also freely available under the MIT license).

☆ Most discrete optimization problems can be formulated as MIP problems.

☆ An instance of satisfiability (SAT) is specified by Boolean decision variables and constraints that are disjunctions of literals.

☆ Most feasibility-checking problems can be formulated as SAT problems.

☆ State-of-the-art MIP and SAT solvers can semi-reliably solve medium-size instances of NP-hard problems.

Test Your Understanding

Problem 21.1 *(S)* Does the `BellmanHeldKarp` algorithm for the TSP (Section 21.1.6) refute the P $\neq$ NP conjecture? (Choose all that apply.)

a) Yes, it does.

b) No. A polynomial-time algorithm for the TSP does not necessarily refute the P $\neq$ NP conjecture.

c) No. Because the algorithm uses an exponential (in the input size) number of subproblems, it does not always run in polynomial time.

d) No. Because the algorithm might perform an exponential amount of work to solve a single subproblem, it does not always run in polynomial time.

e) No. Because the algorithm might perform an exponential amount of work to extract the final solution from the solutions to its subproblems, it does not always run in polynomial time.

Problem 21.2 *(S)* For the TSP input in Quiz 20.7 (page 497), what are the final subproblem array entries of the `BellmanHeldKarp` algorithm from Section 21.1.6?

Problem 21.3 *(S)* Consider the following proposed subproblems for an instance $G = (V, E)$ of the TSP:

Subproblems (Attempt)

Compute $C_{i,v}$, the minimum cost of a cycle-free path that begins at vertex 1, ends at vertex v, and visits exactly i vertices (or $+\infty$, if there is no such path).

(For each $i \in \{2, 3, \ldots, |V|\}$ and $v \in V - \{1\}$.)

What prevents us from using these subproblems, with i as the measure of subproblem size, to design a polynomial-time dynamic programming algorithm for the TSP? (Choose all that apply.)

a) The number of subproblems is super-polynomial in the input size.

b) Optimal solutions to bigger subproblems cannot be computed easily from optimal solutions to smaller subproblems.

c) The optimal tour cannot be computed easily from the optimal solutions to all the subproblems.

d) Nothing!

Problem 21.4 *(S)* Which of the following problems can be solved in $O(n^2 2^n)$ time for n-vertex graphs using a minor variation of the `BellmanHeldKarp` algorithm? (Choose all that apply.)

a) Given an n-vertex undirected graph, determine whether it has a Hamiltonian path (a cycle-free path with $n - 1$ edges).

b) Given an n-vertex directed graph, determine whether it has a directed Hamiltonian path (a cycle-free directed path with $n - 1$ edges).

c) Given a complete undirected graph and real-valued edge costs, compute the maximum cost of a traveling salesman tour.

d) Given a complete n-vertex directed graph (with all $n(n - 1)$ directed edges present) and real-valued edge costs, compute the minimum cost of a directed traveling salesman tour (a directed cycle that visits every vertex exactly once).

e) The cycle-free shortest path problem defined on page 462 in Section 19.5.4.

Problem 21.5 *(S)* For the instance

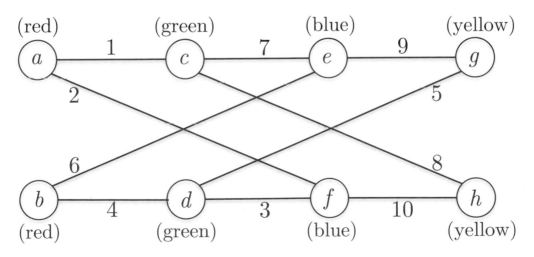

what are the final subproblem array entries of the `PanchromaticPath` algorithm from Section 21.2.5?

Problem 21.6 *(H)* Propose an implementation of a postprocessing step that reconstructs a minimum-cost traveling salesman tour from the subproblem array computed by the `BellmanHeldKarp` algorithm. Can you achieve a linear (in the number of vertices) running time, perhaps after adding some extra bookkeeping to the `BellmanHeldKarp` algorithm?

Problem 21.7 *(H)* Propose an implementation of a postprocessing step that reconstructs a minimum-cost panchromatic path from the subproblem array computed by the `PanchromaticPath` algorithm. Can you achieve a linear (in the number of colors) running time, perhaps after adding some extra bookkeeping to the `PanchromaticPath` algorithm?

Challenge Problems

Problem 21.8 *(H)* Optimize the `BellmanHeldKarp` algorithm for the TSP (Section 21.1.6) so that its memory requirement drops from $O(n \cdot 2^n)$ to $O(\sqrt{n} \cdot 2^n)$ for n-vertex instances. (You are responsible only for computing the minimum cost of a tour, not an optimal tour itself.)

Problem 21.9 *(S)* Show how to encode instances of the following problems as mixed integer programs:

(a) Maximum-weight independent set (Section 16.1).

(b) Makespan minimization (Section 20.1.1).

(c) Maximum coverage (Section 20.2.1).

Problem 21.10 *(H)* Given a TSP instance G with vertex set $V = \{1, 2, \ldots, n\}$ and edge costs c, consider the MIP

$$\text{minimize} \quad \sum_{i=1}^{n} \sum_{j \neq i} c_{ij} x_{ij} \tag{21.21}$$

$$\text{subject to} \quad \sum_{j \neq i} x_{ij} = 1 \quad \text{[for every vertex } i] \tag{21.22}$$

$$\sum_{j \neq i} x_{ji} = 1 \quad \text{[for every vertex } i] \tag{21.23}$$

$$x_{ij} \in \{0, 1\} \quad \text{[for every } i \neq j]. \tag{21.24}$$

The intent is to encode a traveling salesman tour (oriented in one of the two possible directions) with x_{ij} equal to 1 if and only if the tour visits j immediately after i. The constraints (21.22)–(21.23) enforce that each vertex has exactly one immediate predecessor and one immediate successor on the tour.

(a) Prove that, for every TSP instance G and traveling salesman tour of G, there is a feasible solution of the corresponding MIP (21.21)–(21.24) with the same objective function value.

(b) Prove that there is a TSP instance G and a feasible solution of the corresponding MIP (21.21)–(21.24) with objective function value strictly less than the minimum total cost of a traveling salesman tour of G. (Thus, this MIP has spurious feasible solutions, above and beyond the traveling salesman tours, and does not correctly encode the TSP.)

(c) Suppose we throw in the following additional constraints:

$$y_{1j} = (n-1)x_{1j} \qquad \text{[for all } j \in V - \{1\}] \qquad (21.25)$$

$$y_{ij} \leq (n-1)x_{ij} \qquad \text{[for all } i \neq j] \qquad (21.26)$$

$$\sum_{j \neq i} y_{ji} - \sum_{j \neq i} y_{ij} = 1 \qquad \text{[for all } i \in V - \{1\}] \qquad (21.27)$$

$$y_{ij} \in \{0, 1, \ldots, n-1\} \qquad \text{[for all } i \neq j], \qquad (21.28)$$

where the y_{ij}'s are additional decision variables.

Reprove (a) for the expanded MIP (21.21)–(21.28).

(d) Prove that, for every TSP instance G, every feasible solution of the corresponding expanded MIP (21.21)–(21.28) translates to a traveling salesman tour of G with the same objective function value. (As a consequence, the expanded MIP correctly encodes the TSP.)[35]

Problem 21.11 *(H)* Show how to encode an instance of the satisfiability problem as a mixed integer program.

Problem 21.12 *(H)* For a positive integer k, the *k-SAT* problem is the special case of the SAT problem in which every constraint has at most k literals. Recall from Problem 8.12 that the 2-SAT problem can be solved in $O(m+n)$ time, where m and n denote the number of constraints and variables, respectively.[36,37]

Meanwhile, the 3-SAT problem is NP-hard (Theorem 22.1). But can we at least improve over exhaustive search, which enumerates all the 2^n possible truth assignments to the n decision variables? Here's a randomized algorithm, parameterized by a number of trials T:

---

[35] Adding still more constraints, while not necessary for correctness, provides a MIP solver with more clues to work with and can result in significant speedups. For example, adding the (logically redundant) inequalities

$$x_{ij} + x_{ji} \leq 1 \quad \text{[for all } i \neq j]$$

to the expanded MIP (21.21)–(21.28) typically reduces the amount of time required to solve it. State-of-the-art MIP solvers that are tailored to the TSP, such as the Concorde TSP solver, draw from an *exponentially large* set of additional inequalities, generated lazily on an as-needed basis. (To learn more, look up the "subtour relaxation" for the TSP.)

[36] Technically, the solution to Problem 8.12 assumes that every constraint has exactly two literals. The general case (with one or two literals per constraint) reduces easily to this special case, as you should check.

[37] The satisfiability formulation in Section 21.5.3 can be viewed as a reduction from the k-coloring problem to the k-SAT problem. Through this formulation, this 2-SAT algorithm translates to a linear-time algorithm for checking whether a graph is 2-colorable. (A 2-colorable graph is also called "bipartite.") Alternatively, 2-colorability can be checked directly in linear time using breadth-first search (see Problem 8.10).

Schöning

Input: an n-variable instance of 3-SAT and a failure probability
$\delta \in (0, 1)$.
Output: with probability at least $1 - \delta$, either a truth assignment that
satisfies all the constraints or a correct declaration that none exist.

```
ta := length-n Boolean array        // truth assignment
for t := 1 to T do                  // T independent trials
    for i := 1 to n do      // random initial assignment
        ta[i] := "true" or "false"      // 50% chance each
    for k := 1 to n do          // n local modifications
        if ta satisfies all constraints then        // done!
            return ta
        else            // fix a violated constraint
            choose an arbitrary violated constraint C
            choose variable xi in C, uniformly at random
            ta[i] := ¬ta[i]             // flip its value
return "no solution"            // give up on the search
```

(a) Prove that whenever there is no truth assignment that satisfies all the constraints of the given 3-SAT instance, the Schöning algorithm returns "no solution."

(b) For this and the next three parts, restrict attention to inputs with a satisfying truth assignment (that is, a truth assignment that satisfies all the constraints). Let p denote the probability, over the coin flips of the Schöning algorithm, that an iteration of the outermost for loop discovers a satisfying assignment. Prove that, with $T = \frac{1}{p} \ln \frac{1}{\delta}$ independent random trials, the Schöning algorithm finds a satisfying assignment with probability at least $1 - \delta$.

(c) In this and the next part, let ta^* denote a satisfying assignment of the given 3-SAT instance. Prove that every variable flip made by the Schöning algorithm in its inner loop has at least a 1 in 3 chance of increasing the number of variables with the same value in both ta and ta^*.

(d) Prove that the probability that a uniformly random truth assignment agrees with ta^* on at least $n/2$ variables is at least 50%.

(e) Prove that the probability p defined in (b) is at least $1/(2 \cdot 3^{n/2})$; hence, with

$$T = 2 \cdot 3^{n/2} \ln \tfrac{1}{\delta}$$

trials, the Schöning algorithm returns a satisfying assignment with probability at least $1 - \delta$.

(f) Conclude that there is a randomized algorithm that solves the 3-SAT problem (with failure probability at most δ) in $O((1.74)^n \ln \frac{1}{\delta})$ time—exponentially faster than exhaustive search.

Discussion: This algorithm was proposed by Uwe Schöning. His paper "A Probabilistic Algorithm for k-SAT Based on Limited Local Search and Restart" (*Algorithmica*, 2002) establishes a running time bound of $O((1.34)^n \ln \frac{1}{\delta})$ for this algorithm on n-variable instances through a more careful analysis, and also extends the algorithm and analysis to the k-SAT problem for all k (with the base in the exponential running time increasing from $\approx \frac{4}{3}$ to $\approx 2 - \frac{2}{k}$). Some slightly faster algorithms (both randomized and deterministic) have been developed since, but none have achieved a running time of $O((1.3)^n)$.

Section 23.5 describes the "Exponential Time Hypothesis (ETH)" and "Strong Exponential Time Hypothesis (SETH)," both of which postulate that the flaws of the Schöning algorithm are shared by all k-SAT algorithms. The ETH is a bolder form of the P $\neq$ NP conjecture asserting that solving the 3-SAT problem requires exponential time—time $\Omega(a^n)$ for some constant $a > 1$—and hence the only improvements possible to the Schöning algorithm are to the base of the exponent. The SETH asserts that the base of the exponent of the running time of k-SAT algorithms must degrade to 2 as k grows large.

Programming Problems

Problem 21.13 Implement the `BellmanHeldKarp` algorithm for the TSP (Section 21.1.6) in your favorite programming language. As in Problem 20.15, try out your implementation on instances with edge costs chosen independently and uniformly at random from the set $\{1, 2, \ldots, 100\}$ or, alternatively, for vertices that correspond to points chosen independently and uniformly at random from the unit square (with edge costs equal to Euclidean distances). How large an input size (that is, how many vertices) can your program reliably process in under a minute? What about in under an hour? Is the biggest bottleneck time or memory? Does it help if you implement the optimization in Problem 21.8? (See `www.algorithmsilluminated.org` for test cases and challenge data sets.)

Problem 21.14 Try out one or more MIP solvers on the same types of TSP instances you considered in Problem 21.13, using the MIP formulation in Problem 21.10. How large an input size can the solver reliably process in under a minute, or under an hour? How much does the answer vary with the solver? Does it help if you add the additional inequalities from footnote 35? (See `www.algorithmsilluminated.org` for test cases and challenge data sets.)

Chapter 22

Proving Problems NP-Hard

Chapters 20 and 21 supplied you with an algorithmic toolbox for tackling NP-hard problems, be it by fast heuristic algorithms or better-than-exhaustive-search exact algorithms. How do you know when you must resort to this toolbox? If your boss hands you a computational problem and tells you it's NP-hard, fine. But what if you're the boss? Problems in the wild don't show up tattooed with their computational status, and recognizing NP-hard problems— level-3 expertise (Section 19.2)—requires a trained eye. This chapter provides this training, beginning with a single NP-hard problem (3-SAT) and concluding, after eighteen reductions, with a list of nineteen NP-hard problems, including all those studied earlier in this part of the book. You can use this list as a starting point for NP-hardness proofs, and these reductions as templates for your own.

22.1 Reductions Revisited

What is NP-hardness, again? In Section 19.3.7, we provisionally defined an NP-hard problem as one for which a polynomial-time algorithm would refute the P $\neq$ NP conjecture, which in turn we informally described as the assertion that checking a solution to a problem (like a filled-out Sudoku puzzle) can be fundamentally easier than coming up with your own from scratch. (Chapter 23 is your source for 100% rigorous definitions.) Refuting the P $\neq$ NP conjecture would immediately solve thousands of problems—including almost all those studied in this part of the book—that have resisted the efforts of countless brilliant minds over many decades. Thus, NP-hardness is strong evidence (if not an airtight proof) that a problem is intrinsically difficult and that the types of compromises described in Chapters 20 and 21 are required.

To apply the theory of NP-hardness, you don't actually have to understand any fancy mathematical definitions; this is one of the reasons why the theory has been adopted successfully far and wide, including broadly in engineering, the life sciences, and the social sciences.[1] The only prerequisite is the understanding of reductions that you already possess (Section 19.5.1):

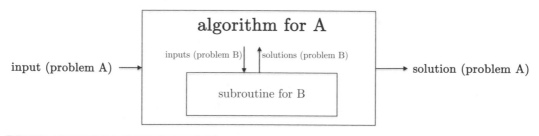

---

[1]To see what I mean, check out how many results you get back from a search for "NP-hard" or "NP-complete" in your favorite academic database!

551

Formally, a problem A *reduces* to a problem B if A can be solved using a polynomial (in the input size) number of invocations of a subroutine that solves the problem B, along with a polynomial amount of additional work (outside of the subroutine calls). We've seen several examples of reductions that spread tractability from one problem (B) to another (A). In general, if A reduces to B, a polynomial-time algorithm solving B automatically produces one for A (as in Quiz 19.3, simply run the reduction, invoking the assumed subroutine for B as needed):

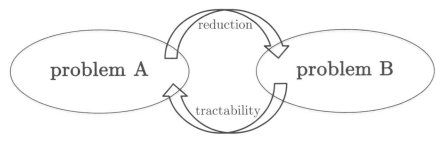

An NP-hardness proof turns this implication on its head, using a reduction for the nefarious purpose of spreading intractability from one problem to another (in the opposite direction of tractability):

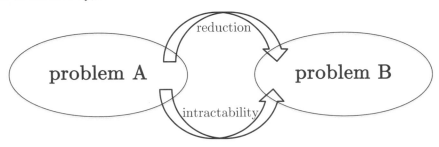

For if an NP-hard problem A reduces to B, any polynomial-time algorithm for B would automatically produce one for A, thereby refuting the P $\neq$ NP conjecture. That is, B must itself be NP-hard.

So, how do you prove that a problem is NP-hard? Just follow the simple two-step recipe.

How to Prove a Problem Is NP-Hard

To prove that a problem B is NP-hard:

1. Choose an NP-hard problem A.

2. Prove that A reduces to B.

The rest of this chapter builds up your inventory of NP-hard problems (that is, choices for A in the first step) and hones your reduction skills (to be put to work in the second step).

A typical NP-hard problem B can be proved NP-hard using any number of choices for the known NP-hard problem A in the first step. The more closely A resembles B, the simpler the details of the second step. For example, the reduction in Section 19.5.4 from the directed Hamiltonian path problem to the cycle-free shortest path problem is relatively straightforward due to the similarities between the two problems.

22.2   3-SAT and the Cook-Levin Theorem

Every application of our two-step recipe identifies one new NP-hard problem using one old one. Apply it thousands of times and you'll have a catalog of thousands of NP-hard problems. But how does the process get started in the first place? With one of the most famous and important results in all of computer science: the *Cook-Levin theorem*, which proves from scratch that the seemingly innocuous 3-SAT problem is NP-hard.[2]

Theorem 22.1 (Cook-Levin Theorem)   *The 3-SAT problem is NP-hard.*

The 3-SAT problem (introduced in Problem 21.12) is the special case of the SAT problem (Section 21.5) in which every constraint is a disjunction of at most three literals.[3,4]

Problem: 3-SAT

Input: A list of Boolean decision variables $x_1, x_2, \ldots, x_n$; and a list of constraints, each a disjunction of at most three literals.

Output: A truth assignment to $x_1, x_2, \ldots, x_n$ that satisfies every constraint, or a correct declaration that no such truth assignment exists.

For example, there's no way to satisfy all eight of the constraints

$$x_1 \vee x_2 \vee x_3 \qquad x_1 \vee \neg x_2 \vee x_3 \qquad \neg x_1 \vee \neg x_2 \vee x_3 \qquad x_1 \vee \neg x_2 \vee \neg x_3$$
$$\neg x_1 \vee x_2 \vee x_3 \qquad x_1 \vee x_2 \vee \neg x_3 \qquad \neg x_1 \vee x_2 \vee \neg x_3 \qquad \neg x_1 \vee \neg x_2 \vee \neg x_3,$$

as each of them forbids one of the eight possible truth assignments. If some constraint is removed, there is then one truth assignment left over that satisfies the other seven constraints. 3-SAT instances with and without a satisfying truth assignment are called *satisfiable* and *unsatisfiable*, respectively.

The 3-SAT problem occupies a central position in the theory of NP-hardness, both for historical reasons and because of the problem's equipoise between expressiveness and

---

[2]Proved independently around 1971 by Stephen A. Cook and Leonid Levin on opposite sides of the Iron Curtain (Toronto and Moscow, respectively), although it took awhile for Levin's work to be widely appreciated in the West. Both hinted at the possibility that many more fundamental problems would be NP-hard. This prophecy was fulfilled by Richard M. Karp, who in 1972 demonstrated the power and reach of NP-hardness by using the two-step recipe to prove that an unexpectedly diverse array of notorious problems are NP-hard. Karp's work made clear that NP-hardness was the fundamental obstacle impeding algorithmic progress in many different directions. His original list of twenty-one NP-hard problems includes most of those studied in this chapter.

Cook and Karp were awarded the ACM Turing Award—the equivalent of the Nobel Prize in computer science—in 1982 and 1985, respectively. Levin was awarded the Knuth Prize—a lifetime achievement award in theoretical computer science—in 2012. All three scientists participated in a 2021 video session celebrating the 50th anniversary of the Cook-Levin theorem; check out www.algorithmsilluminated.org for more details.

[3]Why three? Because this is the smallest value of k for which the k-SAT problem is NP-hard (see Problem 21.12).

[4]There is no contradiction between the Cook-Levin theorem and the remarkable successes of SAT solvers (Section 21.5). SAT solvers are only semi-reliable, solving some but not all SAT instances in a reasonable amount of time. They do not show that SAT is a polynomial-time solvable problem, so the P $\neq$ NP conjecture lives on!

simplicity. To this day, the 3-SAT problem remains the most common choice for the known NP-hard problem in NP-hardness proofs (that is, for the problem A in the two-step recipe).

In this chapter, we'll take the Cook-Levin theorem on faith. Standing on the shoulders of these giants, we'll assume only that a single problem (3-SAT) is NP-hard and then generate, via reductions, eighteen additional NP-hard problems. Section 23.3.5 outlines the high-level idea behind the proof of the Cook-Levin theorem and provides pointers for learning more.[5]

22.3   The Big Picture

We have a lot of problems and a lot of reductions between them to keep track of. Let's get organized.

22.3.1   A Rookie Mistake Revisited

As algorithm designers, we're accustomed to honorable reductions that spread tractability from one problem to another. Reductions nefariously spread intractability in the *opposite* direction, and for this reason, there's an overwhelming temptation to design reductions in the wrong direction (also known as the fifth rookie mistake from Section 19.6).

Quiz 22.1

Section 21.4 proves that the knapsack problem reduces to the mixed integer programming (MIP) problem. What does this imply? (Choose all that apply.)

a) If the MIP problem is NP-hard, so is the knapsack problem.

b) If the knapsack problem is NP-hard, so is the MIP problem.

c) A semi-reliable MIP solver can be translated to a semi-reliable algorithm for the knapsack problem.

d) A semi-reliable algorithm for the knapsack problem can be translated to a semi-reliable MIP solver.

(See Section 22.3.4 for the solution and discussion.)

22.3.2   Eighteen Reductions

Figure 22.1 summarizes eighteen reductions, which (assuming the Cook-Levin theorem) imply that all nineteen problems in the figure are NP-hard.[6]

Six of these reductions are either immediate or have been smuggled into previous chapters of the book.

---

[5]The proof is worth seeing at least once in your life, but almost nobody remembers the gory details. Most computer scientists are content to be educated clients of the Cook-Levin theorem, using it (and other NP-hard problems) like we do in this chapter, as a tool to prove problems NP-hard.

[6]Something stronger is true and will be explained in Chapter 23: The "search versions" of almost all of these problems are "NP-complete," and as a consequence any one of them can encode any other. The distinction between "NP-hard" and "NP-complete" is not of first-order importance to the algorithm designer: Either way, the problem is not polynomial-time solvable (assuming the P $\neq$ NP conjecture).

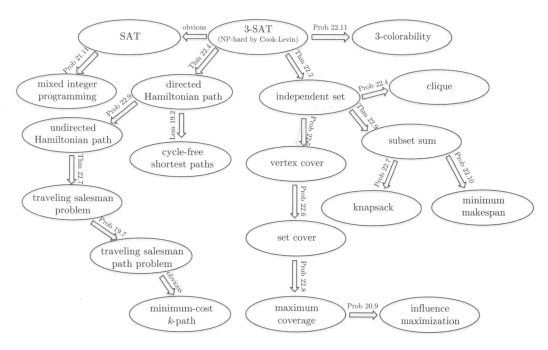

Figure 22.1: Eighteen reductions and nineteen NP-hard problems. An arrow from a problem A to a problem B indicates that A reduces to B. Computational intractability spreads in the same direction as the reductions, from the 3-SAT problem (which is NP-hard by the Cook-Levin theorem) to the other eighteen problems.

Reductions We've Already Seen

1. The 3-SAT problem is a special case of the general SAT problem (page 542) and thus trivially reduces to it.

2. The traveling salesman path problem (Problem 19.7 on page 469) trivially reduces to the minimum-cost k-path problem (page 526), as it is the special case in which the path length k equals the number of vertices.

3. Lemma 19.2 in Section 19.5.4 proves that the directed Hamiltonian path problem (page 462) reduces to the cycle-free shortest path problem (also page 462).

4. Problem 19.7 proves that the traveling salesman problem (TSP; page 443) reduces to the traveling salesman path problem.

5. Problem 20.9 proves that the maximum coverage problem (page 482) reduces to the influence maximization problem (page 492).

6. Problem 21.11 proves that the SAT problem reduces to the mixed integer programming problem (page 539).

The end-of-chapter problems cover eight of the easier reductions.

Some Easier Reductions

7. Problem 22.4: The independent set problem (page 558) reduces to the clique problem (page 575).

8. Problem 22.5: The independent set problem reduces to the vertex cover problem (Problem 20.4 on page 513).

9. Problem 22.6: The vertex cover problem reduces to the set cover problem (Problem 20.2 on page 511).

10. Problem 22.7: The subset sum problem (page 569) reduces to the knapsack problem (page 455).

11. Problem 22.8: The set cover problem reduces to the maximum coverage problem.

12. Problem 22.9: The directed Hamiltonian path problem reduces to the undirected Hamiltonian path problem (page 567).

13. Problem 22.10: The subset sum problem reduces to the makespan minimization problem (page 471).

14. Problem 22.11: The 3-SAT problem reduces to the problem of checking whether a graph is 3-colorable (page 541).[7]

We're left holding a to-do list comprising four of the more difficult reductions:

Some Harder Reductions

15. The 3-SAT problem reduces to the independent set problem (Section 22.5).

16. The 3-SAT problem reduces to the directed Hamiltonian path problem (Section 22.6).

17. The undirected Hamiltonian path problem reduces to the TSP (Section 22.7). (This one's not that difficult.)

18. The independent set problem reduces to the subset sum problem (Section 22.8).

22.3.3   Why Slog Through NP-Hardness Proofs?

I'll be honest: NP-hardness proofs can be painfully messy and problem-specific, and almost no one remembers their details. Why torture you with them over the next five sections? Because there are several good reasons to slog through a few:

---

[7]This reverses the direction of the reduction in Section 21.5.3; the intent is to spread (worst-case) intractability rather than (semi-reliable) tractability. Also, full disclosure: This reduction is somewhat harder than those in Problems 22.4–22.10.

> **Goals of Sections 22.4–22.8**
>
> 1. Fulfill previously made promises that all the problems studied in Part IV are NP-hard and hence require the compromises described in Chapters 20 and 21.
>
> 2. Provide you with a long list of known NP-hard problems for use in your own reductions (in the first step of the two-step recipe).[8]
>
> 3. Empower you with the belief that, if necessary, you could devise the reduction required to prove that a problem arising in your own work is NP-hard.

22.3.4   Solution to Quiz 22.1

Correct answers: (b),(c). A reduction from a problem A to a problem B spreads tractability from B to A and intractability in the opposite direction, from A to B (see the figures on page 552). Taking A and B as the knapsack and MIP problems, respectively, the reduction in Section 21.4 transfers tractability from the MIP problem to the knapsack problem (hence (c) is correct) and intractability in the reverse direction (hence (b) is correct).

22.4   A Template for Reductions

Typical reductions in NP-hardness proofs follow a common template. In general, a reduction from a problem A to a problem B can be sophisticated, invoking an assumed subroutine for B any polynomial number of times and processing its responses in polynomial time in arbitrarily clever ways (Section 22.1). At the other extreme, what would a simplest-imaginable reduction look like?

If we believe that the problem A is NP-hard (and that the P $\neq$ NP conjecture is true), every reduction from A to B must use the assumed subroutine for B at least once; otherwise, the reduction would constitute a stand-alone polynomial-time algorithm for A. And for typechecking purposes, the instance of problem A provided to the reduction may require preprocessing before it makes sense to feed into the subroutine for B—if, for example, the input is a graph and the subroutine is expecting a list of integers. Similarly, the subroutine's response may need postprocessing before it makes sense as the reduction's output:

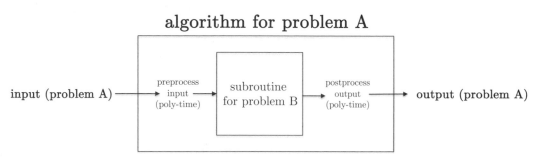

---

[8]For a *really* long list (with more than 300 NP-hard problems), check out the classic book *Computers and Intractability: A Guide to the Theory of NP-Completeness*, by Michael R. Garey and David S. Johnson (Freeman, 1979). Few computer science books from 1979 remain as useful as this one!

For our NP-hardness proofs, we'll be able to get away with these simplest-imaginable reductions:

Simplest-Imaginable Reduction from A to B

1. *Preprocessor:* Given an instance of problem A, transform it in polynomial time to an instance of problem B.

2. *Subroutine:* Invoke the assumed subroutine for B.

3. *Postprocessor:* Transform the subroutine's output in polynomial time to a correct output for the given instance of A.

The preprocessor and postprocessor are generally designed in tandem, with the former's transformation guided explicitly by the latter's needs. In all our examples, it will be obvious that the preprocessor and postprocessor run in polynomial (and, in most cases, linear) time.

The reduction in Lemma 19.2, from the directed Hamiltonian path problem to the cycle-free shortest path problem, is archetypal. That reduction uses a preprocessor that converts an instance of the former problem into one of the latter by reusing the same graph and assigning each edge a length of -1, and a postprocessor that immediately deduces the correct output from the output of the assumed cycle-free shortest path subroutine. The reductions in the next four sections are more complex variations of the same idea.

22.5 Independent Set Is NP-Hard

The first NP-hardness proof of this chapter is for the *independent set* problem, in which the input is an undirected graph $G = (V, E)$ and the goal is to compute an independent set (that is, a set of mutually non-adjacent vertices) with the maximum-possible size.[9] For example, if G is a cycle graph with n vertices, the maximum size of an independent set is $n/2$ (if n is even) or $(n - 1)/2$ (if n is odd). If edges represent conflicts between people or tasks, independent sets correspond to the conflict-free subsets.

We currently have only one NP-hard problem at our disposal, the 3-SAT problem. Thus, if we're to prove that the independent set problem is NP-hard using the two-step recipe, our hand is forced: it can only be via a reduction from the 3-SAT problem to the independent set problem. These two problems seem to have nothing to do with each other: one is about logic and the other concerns graphs. Nevertheless, the main result of this section is:

Theorem 22.2 (Reduction from 3-SAT to Independent Set) *The 3-SAT problem reduces to the independent set problem.*

Using the two-step recipe, because the 3-SAT problem is NP-hard (Theorem 22.1), so is the independent set problem.

Corollary 22.3 (NP-Hardness of Independent Set) *The independent set problem is NP-hard.*

---

[9]This problem is the special case of the weighted independent set problem (Section 16.1) in which every vertex weight is 1. Because this special case is NP-hard (as we'll see), so is the more general problem.

22.5.1   The Main Idea

The reduction from the directed Hamiltonian path problem to the cycle-free shortest path problem in Lemma 19.2 exploited the strong similarities between the two problems, both of which are about finding paths in directed graphs. The 3-SAT and independent set problems, on the other hand, appear to be totally unrelated. If we're shooting for a simplest-imaginable reduction (Section 22.4), what's our plan for the preprocessor and postprocessor? The postprocessor must somehow extract a satisfying truth assignment for a 3-SAT instance (or conclude that none exist) from a maximum-size independent set of a graph fabricated by the preprocessor. Next, we illustrate the main ideas through an example; Section 22.5.2 provides the formal description of the reduction and its proof of correctness.

To explain the reduction's preprocessor, think of a disjunction of k literals as someone's list of requests for their k favorite variable assignments. For example, the constraint $\neg x_1 \lor x_2 \lor x_3$ pleads: "could you set x_1 to false?"; "or what about x_2 to true?"; "or at least x_3 to true?" Meet at least one of their demands and they walk away happy, the constraint satisfied.

The key idea in the preprocessor is to encode an instance of the 3-SAT problem as a graph in which each vertex represents one assignment request by one constraint.[10] For example, the constraints

$$\underbrace{x_1 \lor x_2 \lor x_3}_{C_1} \qquad \underbrace{\neg x_1 \lor x_2 \lor x_3}_{C_2} \qquad \underbrace{\neg x_1 \lor \neg x_2 \lor \neg x_3}_{C_3}$$

would be represented by three groups of three vertices each:

The fourth vertex, for instance, encodes the second constraint's plea to set the variable x_1 to false (corresponding to its literal $\neg x_1$).

Looking toward the postprocessor, do subsets of these vertices encode truth assignments? Not always. The issue is that some of the requests are inconsistent and ask for opposite assignments to the same variable (like the first and fourth vertices above). But remember, the whole point of the independent set problem is to represent conflicts! The preprocessor should therefore add an edge between each vertex pair corresponding to inconsistent assignments; because every independent set must choose at most one endpoint per edge, all conflicts are then avoided. Applying this idea to our running example (with the dashed vertices indicating one particular independent set):

---

[10]Your first thought might have been to turn a 3-SAT instance with n variables into a graph with n vertices, with the 2^n vertex subsets corresponding to the 2^n possible truth assignments. Alas, this approach doesn't pan out, motivating the more clever construction used here.

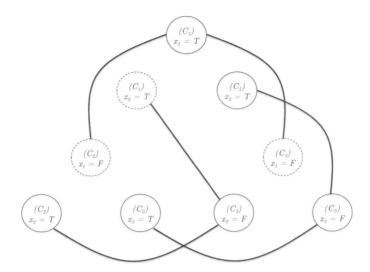

A postprocessor can now extract a satisfying truth assignment from any independent set S that contains at least one vertex in each group, simply by making all the corresponding variable assignment requests. (A variable with no requests in either direction can be safely assigned either true or false.) Because all the vertices of S are non-adjacent, none of the requests conflict, and the result is a well-defined truth assignment. Because S includes at least one vertex per group (one fulfilled request per constraint), this truth assignment satisfies all the constraints. For example, the three dashed vertices above would translate to one of the two satisfying assignments {false, true, true} or {false, true, false}.

Finally, the reduction must also recognize unsatisfiable 3-SAT instances. As we'll see in the next section, the preprocessor can make unsatisfiability obvious to the postprocessor by adding an edge between each pair of vertices that belong to the same group:

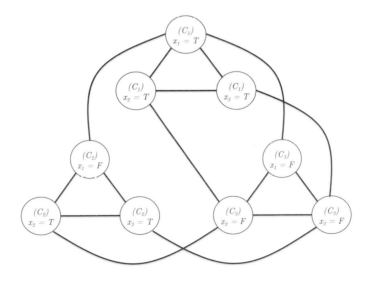

22.5.2 Proof of Theorem 22.2

The proof of Theorem 22.2 simply scales up the example and reasoning in Section 22.5.1 to general 3-SAT instances.

Description of the Reduction

Preprocessor.   Given an arbitrary 3-SAT instance, with n variables and m constraints with at most three literals each, the preprocessor constructs a corresponding graph $G = (V, E)$. It defines $V = V_1 \cup V_2 \cup \cdots \cup V_m$, where V_j is a group with one vertex per literal of the jth constraint. It defines $E = E_1 \cup E_2$, where E_1 contains one edge per pair of vertices that reside in the same group and E_2 contains one edge per pair of conflicting vertices (corresponding to requests for opposite assignments to the same variable).

Postprocessor.   If the assumed subroutine returns an independent set of the graph G constructed by the preprocessor with at least m vertices, the postprocessor returns an arbitrary truth assignment consistent with the corresponding variable assignment requests. Otherwise, the postprocessor returns "no solution."

Proof of Correctness

The crux of the correctness proof is showing that the preprocessor translates satisfiable and unsatisfiable 3-SAT instances into graphs in which the maximum size of an independent set is equal to and less than m, respectively:

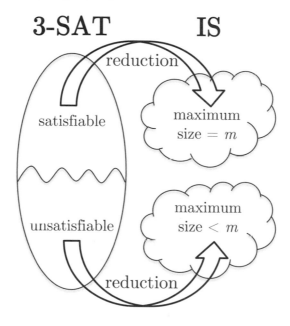

Case 1: Unsatisfiable instances.   Suppose, for the purposes of a proof by contradiction, that the reduction fails to return "no solution" for some unsatisfiable 3-SAT instance. This means that the assumed subroutine returns an independent set S of the graph $G = (V, E)$ constructed by the preprocessor that includes at least m vertices. The edges of E_1 preclude more than one vertex from a group, so S must possess exactly m vertices, with one per group. Because of the edges in E_2, at least one truth assignment is consistent with all the assignment requests corresponding to the vertices of S. Because S includes one vertex from each group, the truth assignment extracted from S by the postprocessor would satisfy every constraint. This contradicts our initial assumption that the given 3-SAT instance is unsatisfiable.

Case 2: Satisfiable instances.   Suppose the given 3-SAT instance has a satisfying truth assignment. Pick one fulfilled variable assignment request from each constraint—because the truth assignment satisfies every constraint, there must be one to pick—and let X denote the corresponding subset of m vertices. The set X is an independent set of G: It does not contain both endpoints of any edge of E_1 (as it contains only one vertex per group), nor of any edge of E_2 (as it is derived from a consistent truth assignment). With at least one size-m independent set of G out there to find, the assumed subroutine must return one—possibly X, or possibly some other size-m independent set (which in any case must have one vertex per group). As in case 1, the postprocessor then extracts from this independent set a satisfying assignment, which it returns as the reduction's (correct) output. $\mathcal{QED}$

Lest such correctness proofs strike you as overly pedantic, let's conclude this section with an example of a reduction gone awry.

Quiz 22.2

Where does the proof of Theorem 22.2 break down if the intragroup edges E_1 are omitted from the graph G? (Choose all that apply.)

a) An independent set of G no longer translates to a well-defined truth assignment.

b) A satisfiable 3-SAT instance need not translate to a graph in which the maximum size of an independent set is at least m, the number of constraints.

c) An unsatisfiable 3-SAT instance need not translate to a graph in which the maximum size of an independent set is less than m.

d) Actually, the proof still works.

(See below for the solution and discussion.)

Correct answer: (c). With an unsatisfiable 3-SAT instance, and even without the intragroup edges E_1, no independent set of G includes one vertex from each of the m groups (as the postprocessor could translate any such independent set into a satisfying assignment). However, as independent sets of G are now free to recruit multiple vertices from a group, one may well include m vertices (or more).

*22.6 Directed Hamiltonian Path Is NP-Hard

With one reduction from the 3-SAT problem to a graph problem under our belt, why not another? In the *directed Hamiltonian path (DHP)* problem (page 462), the input is a directed graph $G = (V, E)$, a starting vertex $s \in V$, and an ending vertex $t \in V$. The goal is to return an s-t path visiting every vertex of G exactly once (called an s-t *Hamiltonian path*), or correctly declare that no such path exists.[11] In contrast to most of the nineteen problems

---

[11] The problem statement on page 462 is slightly different, requiring only a "yes"/"no" answer rather than a path. Problem 22.3 asks you to show that the two versions of the problem are equivalent, with each reducing to the other.

studied in this chapter, our interest in this problem stems less from its direct applications and more from its utility in proving that other important problems (like the TSP) are NP-hard.

The main result of this section is:

Theorem 22.4 (Reduction from 3-SAT to DHP) *The 3-SAT problem reduces to the directed Hamiltonian path problem.*

Combined with the Cook-Levin theorem (Theorem 22.1) and our two-step recipe, Theorem 22.4 fulfills a promise made back in Section 19.5.4:

Corollary 22.5 (NP-Hardness of DHP) *The directed Hamiltonian path problem is NP-hard.*

22.6.1   Encoding Variables and Truth Assignments

To get away with a simplest-imaginable reduction (Section 22.4), we need a plan for the preprocessor (responsible for fabricating a directed graph from a 3-SAT instance) and the postprocessor (responsible for extracting a satisfying truth assignment from an s-t Hamiltonian path of that graph).

The first idea is to construct a graph in which an s-t Hamiltonian path is forced to make a sequence of binary decisions, which can then be interpreted as a truth assignment by the postprocessor. For example, in the diamond graph

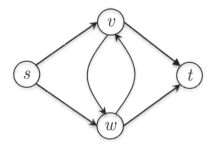

there are two s-t Hamiltonian paths: one that zig-zags downward ($s \to v \to w \to t$) and one that zig-zags upward ($s \to w \to v \to t$). Identifying down and up as "true" and "false," the s-t Hamiltonian paths encode the possible assignments to one Boolean variable.

What about more variables? The preprocessor will deploy one diamond graph per variable, chained together in a necklace. For example, the dashed s-t Hamiltonian path in the necklace graph

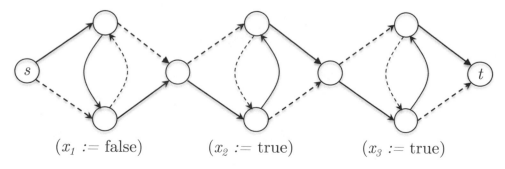

$(x_1 := \text{false})$ $(x_2 := \text{true})$ $(x_3 := \text{true})$

can be interpreted by the postprocessor as the truth assignment {false, true, true}; the rest of the s-t Hamiltonian paths similarly encode the other seven truth assignments.

22.6.2 Encoding Constraints

The preprocessor must next augment its graph to reflect the constraints of the given 3-SAT instance, so that only the satisfying truth assignments survive as s-t Hamiltonian paths. Here's an idea: Add one new vertex per constraint in such a way that visiting that vertex corresponds to satisfying the constraint. To see how this might work, consider the constraint $\neg x_1 \lor x_2 \lor x_3$ and the following graph (with the dashed edges indicating one particular s-t Hamiltonian path):

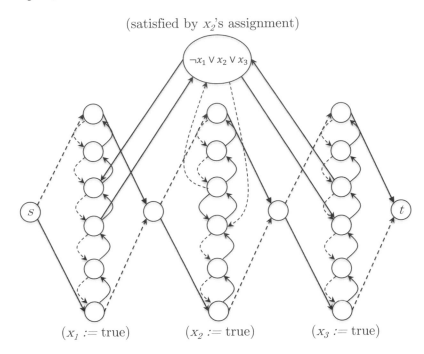

The edges between the necklace and the new constraint vertex allow visits to that vertex by s-t Hamiltonian paths only from diamonds that are traversed in a direction corresponding to a variable assignment that satisfies the constraint.[12]

For example, consider the dashed edges, an s-t Hamiltonian path. The path travels downward in each of the three diamonds, corresponding to the all-true truth assignment. Assigning x_1 to true does not satisfy the constraint $\neg x_1 \lor x_2 \lor x_3$. Accordingly, there is no way to visit the new constraint vertex from the first diamond without skipping or visiting twice some vertex. Assigning x_2 to true does satisfy the constraint, which is why the dashed path can take a quick back-and-forth day trip to the constraint vertex from the second diamond before resuming its downward journey where it left off. Because x_3's assignment also satisfies the constraint, such a day trip is possible also from the third diamond. With the constraint vertex already visited, however, the s-t Hamiltonian path instead proceeds directly down the third diamond and over to t. (There's also a second s-t Hamiltonian path

---

[12]If some variable were absent from the constraint, the corresponding diamond would have no edge to or from the constraint vertex.

corresponding to the same truth assignment, traveling straight down in the second diamond and making the day trip from the third.)

To encode a second constraint, say $x_1 \lor \neg x_2 \lor \neg x_3$, the preprocessor can add a second constraint vertex and similarly wire it to the necklace (with the dashed edges indicating one particular s-t Hamiltonian path):

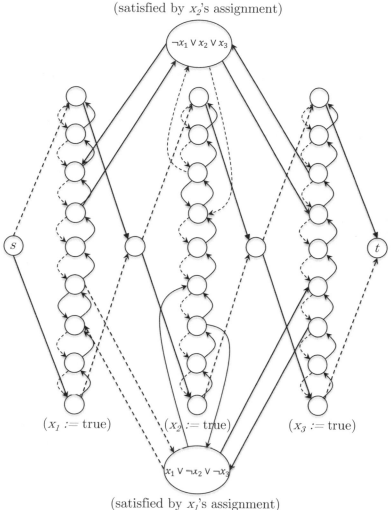

The new vertices in each diamond provide room for any s-t Hamiltonian paths that might want to make back-and-forth day trips to both constraint vertices from the same diamond. (There are no such paths above, but there would be if we changed the second constraint to, say, $x_1 \lor \neg x_2 \lor x_3$.) The dashed path is one of the two s-t Hamiltonian paths corresponding to the all-true truth assignment; the only opportunity to visit the new constraint vertex is from the first diamond. Of the other seven truth assignments, the five satisfying ones each correspond to one or more s-t Hamiltonian paths, while the other two do not.

22.6.3   Proof of Theorem 22.4

The proof of Theorem 22.4 scales up the example in Section 22.6.2 to general 3-SAT instances.

Description of the Reduction

Preprocessor.   Given a 3-SAT instance with n variables and m constraints, the preprocessor constructs a directed graph:

- Define a set V of $3mn + 4n + m + 1$ vertices: a starting vertex s; 3 external diamond vertices v_i, w_i, t_i for each variable x_i; $3m + 1$ internal diamond vertices $a_{i,1}, a_{i,2}, \ldots, a_{i,3m+1}$ for each variable x_i; and m constraint vertices $c_1, c_2, \ldots, c_m$.

- Define a set E_1 of necklace edges by connecting s to v_1 and w_1; t_i to v_{i+1} and w_{i+1} for each $i = 1, 2, \ldots, n - 1$; v_i and w_i to t_i, v_i to and from $a_{i,1}$, and w_i to and from $a_{i,3m+1}$ for each $i = 1, 2, \ldots, n$; and $a_{i,j}$ to and from $a_{i,j+1}$, for each $i = 1, 2, \ldots, n$ and $j = 1, 2, \ldots, 3m$.

- Define a set E_2 of constraint edges by connecting $a_{i,3j-1}$ to c_j and c_j to $a_{i,3j}$ whenever the jth constraint includes the literal x_i (that is, requests x_i = true); and $a_{i,3j}$ to c_j and c_j to $a_{i,3j-1}$ whenever the jth constraint includes the literal $\neg x_i$ (requesting x_i = false).

The preprocessor concludes with the graph $G = (V, E_1 \cup E_2)$; the starting and ending vertices of the constructed instance are defined as s and t_n, respectively.

Postprocessor.   If the assumed subroutine computes an s-t_n Hamiltonian path P of the graph G constructed by the preprocessor, the postprocessor returns the truth assignment in which a variable x_i is set to true if P visits the vertex v_i before w_i and to false otherwise. If the assumed subroutine responds "no solution," the postprocessor also responds "no solution."

Proof of Correctness

The crux of the correctness proof is showing that the preprocessor translates satisfiable and unsatisfiable 3-SAT instances into graphs with and without an s-t_n Hamiltonian path, respectively:

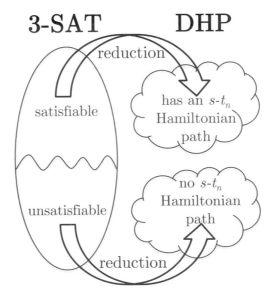

Case 1: Unsatisfiable instances.   Suppose that the reduction fails to return "no solution" for some unsatisfiable 3-SAT instance. This means that the assumed subroutine returns an s-t_n Hamiltonian path P of the graph G constructed by the preprocessor. The Hamiltonian path P must resemble those in Section 22.6.2, traversing every diamond upward or downward and also visiting every constraint vertex. To visit a constraint vertex, the path must include a back-and-forth day trip interrupting some diamond traversal in a direction that corresponds to one of the constraint's variable assignment requests.[13] The truth assignment extracted from P by the postprocessor would therefore be a satisfying assignment, contradicting the assumption that the given 3-SAT instance is unsatisfiable.

Case 2: Satisfiable instances.   Suppose the given 3-SAT instance has a satisfying truth assignment. The graph G constructed by the preprocessor then has an s-t_n Hamiltonian path: traverse each diamond in the direction suggested by this assignment (downward for variables set to true, upward for the rest), taking a back-and-forth day trip to each constraint vertex at the earliest opportunity (from the diamond corresponding to the first variable whose assignment satisfies that constraint). With at least one s-t_n Hamiltonian path of G out there to find, the assumed subroutine must return one. As in case 1, the postprocessor then extracts from this path and returns a satisfying assignment. $\mathcal{QED}$

22.7   The TSP Is NP-Hard

We now return to a problem that we care about in its own right: the traveling salesman problem (TSP) from Section 19.1.2.

22.7.1   The Undirected Hamiltonian Path Problem

The plan is to piggyback on our hard work showing that the directed Hamiltonian path problem is NP-hard (Corollary 22.5), loosely following our reduction in Section 19.5.4 from that problem to the cycle-free shortest path problem. There is an immediate typechecking error, however, because the TSP concerns undirected rather than directed graphs. The *undirected* version of the Hamiltonian path problem seems more germane.

Problem: Undirected Hamiltonian Path (UHP)

Input: An undirected graph $G = (V, E)$, a starting vertex $s \in V$, and an ending vertex $t \in V$.

Output: An s-t path of G that visits every vertex exactly once (that is, an s-t Hamiltonian path), or a correct declaration that no such path exists.

---

[13] A path that doesn't immediately return from the constraint vertex to the same diamond will be unable to visit the rest of the diamond later. For example, consider an alleged Hamiltonian path P that travels from an internal vertex $a_{i,3j-1}$ to a constraint vertex c_j without returning immediately to the vertex $a_{i,3j}$. The path P must visit $a_{i,3j}$ at some point, and can only do so via $a_{i,3j+1}$ (as P has already used up its visits to c_j and $a_{i,3j-1}$). But then P gets stuck at $a_{i,3j}$, where the only outgoing edges are to the already-visited vertices $a_{i,3j-1}$ and $a_{i,3j+1}$.

Problem 22.9 asks you to show that the undirected and directed Hamiltonian path problems are equivalent, with each reducing to the other. Corollary 22.5 thus carries over to undirected graphs as well.

Corollary 22.6 (NP-Hardness of UHP) *The undirected Hamiltonian path problem is NP-hard.*

The main result in this section is then:

Theorem 22.7 (Reduction from UHP to TSP) *The undirected Hamiltonian path problem reduces to the traveling salesman problem.*

Combining this reduction with Corollary 22.6 shows that the TSP is indeed an NP-hard problem.

Corollary 22.8 (NP-Hardness of the TSP) *The traveling salesman problem is NP-hard.*

22.7.2   Proof of Theorem 22.7

We should breathe a sigh of relief that Theorem 22.7, unlike Theorems 22.2 and 22.4, relates two intuitively similar problems, both of which more or less concern long paths in undirected graphs. Given an undirected Hamiltonian path instance, how can we convert it to an instance of the TSP, so that a Hamiltonian path (or a correct declaration that none exist) can be easily extracted from a minimum-cost traveling salesman tour? The main idea is to simulate missing edges by costly edges.

Description of the Reduction

Preprocessor. Given an undirected graph $G = (V, E)$, a starting vertex s, and an ending vertex t, the preprocessor first bridges the gap between paths that visit all vertices and cycles that visit all vertices by augmenting G with an additional vertex v_0 and edges connecting v_0 to s and t. It then assigns a cost of 0 to all edges in this augmented graph. To complete the construction of the TSP instance, the preprocessor adds in all the missing edges (to form the complete graph G' with vertex set $V \cup \{v_0\}$) and assigns each of these a cost of 1.

For example, the preprocessor translates the following graph with no s-t Hamiltonian path to a TSP instance with no zero-cost tour:

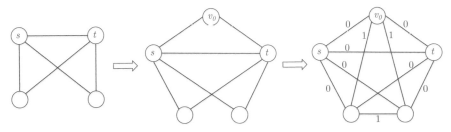

Postprocessor. If the assumed subroutine computes a zero-cost traveling salesman tour T of the graph G' constructed by the preprocessor, the postprocessor removes v_0 and its two incident edges from T and returns the resulting path. Otherwise, as in the example above, the postprocessor reports "no solution."

Proof of Correctness

To argue correctness, we'll justify this picture:

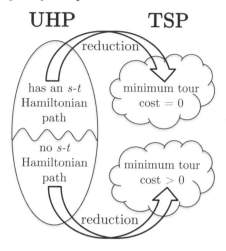

Case 1: Non-Hamiltonian instances.   Suppose that the reduction fails to return "no solution" for some undirected Hamiltonian path instance G that has no s-t Hamiltonian path. This means that the assumed subroutine returns a zero-cost tour T of the graph G' constructed by the preprocessor—a tour that avoids all the cost-1 edges in G'. Because only the edges of G and the edges (v_0, s) and (v_0, t) have cost zero in G', the two edges of T incident to v_0 must be (v_0, s) and (v_0, t), and the rest of T must be a cycle-free s-t path that visits all vertices of V while using only edges in G. Thus $T - \{(v_0, s), (v_0, t)\}$ is an s-t Hamiltonian path of G, contradicting our original assumption.

Case 2: Hamiltonian instances.   Suppose the given undirected Hamiltonian path instance has an s-t Hamiltonian path P. The TSP instance G' constructed by the preprocessor then has a zero-cost tour in $P \cup \{(v_0, s), (v_0, t)\}$. With at least one zero-cost tour out there to find, the assumed subroutine must return one. As in case 1, the postprocessor then extracts from this tour and returns an s-t Hamiltonian path of G. $\mathcal{QED}$

22.8 Subset Sum Is NP-Hard

Last in our parade of NP-hardness proofs is one for the *subset sum* problem; as a consequence, both the knapsack and makespan minimization problems are also NP-hard (see Problems 22.7 and 22.10).

Problem: Subset Sum

Input: Positive integers $a_1, a_2, \ldots, a_n$, and a positive integer t.

Output: A subset of the a_i's with sum equal to t. (Or, correctly declare that no such subset exists.)

For example, if the a_i's are all the powers of ten from 1 to 10^{100}, there is a subset with a target sum t if and only if t (written base-10) has at most 101 digits, with each digit a 0 or a 1.

All the subset sum problem worries about is a bunch of numbers; it would seem to have nothing to do with problems that concern more complex objects like graphs. Nonetheless, the main result of this section is:

Theorem 22.9 (Reduction from IS to Subset Sum) *The independent set problem reduces to the subset sum problem.*

This result, in conjunction with Corollary 22.3, shows that:

Corollary 22.10 (NP-Hardness of Subset Sum) *The subset sum problem is NP-hard.*

22.8.1 The Basic Approach

For now, let's focus on the problem of checking whether a given graph has an independent set of a given target size k, as opposed to computing a maximum-size independent set. (Any solution to the former problem extends easily to the latter: Use linear or binary search to identify the largest value of k for which the graph has a size-k independent set.)

The reduction's preprocessor must somehow metamorphose a graph and a target size into what our assumed subroutine for the subset sum problem is expecting: a bunch of positive integers.[14] The simplest-imaginable approach would define one number per vertex (along with a target t) so that independent sets of a target size k correspond to subsets of numbers that sum to t:

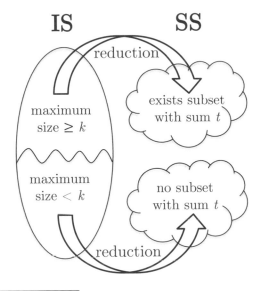

---

[14] As a special case of the knapsack problem (see Problem 22.7), the subset sum problem can be solved by dynamic programming in *pseudopolynomial* time, meaning in time polynomial in the input size and the magnitudes of the input numbers (see page 455 and Problem 20.11(a)). We should therefore expect a preprocessor to construct a subset sum instance with exponentially large numbers—an instance for which our dynamic programming algorithms offer no improvement over exhaustive search.

Problems that are both NP-hard and pseudopolynomial-time solvable are called *weakly NP-hard*, while *strongly NP-hard* problems remain NP-hard in instances with all input numbers bounded by a polynomial function of the input size. (An NP-hard problem with no numbers in the input, such as the 3-SAT problem, is automatically strongly NP-hard.) Of the nineteen problems in Figure 22.1, all but the subset sum and knapsack problems are strongly NP-hard.

22.8.2   Example: The Four-Cycle

The key idea is to use each of the lower-order digits of a number to encode whether an edge is incident to the corresponding vertex. For instance, the preprocessor could encode the vertices of the four-cycle

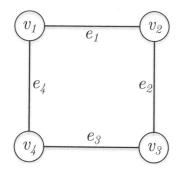

with the following five-digit numbers (written in base 10):

v_1	v_2	v_3	v_4
11,001	11,100	10,110	10,011

For example, the trailing four digits of v_2's encoding indicate that it is adjacent to e_1 and e_2 but not e_3 or e_4.

This idea shows promise. The two size-2 independent sets of the four-cycle, $\{v_1, v_3\}$ and $\{v_2, v_4\}$, correspond to two pairs of numbers with the same sum: $11{,}001 + 10{,}110 = 11{,}100 + 10{,}011 = 21{,}111$. All other subsets have different sums; for example, the sum corresponding to the non-independent set $\{v_3, v_4\}$ is $10{,}110 + 10{,}011 = 20{,}121$. A postprocessor could therefore translate any subset of numbers with sum 21,111 into a size-2 independent set of the four-cycle.

22.8.3   Example: The Five-Cycle

Suppose, however, that we try the same maneuver with the five-cycle:

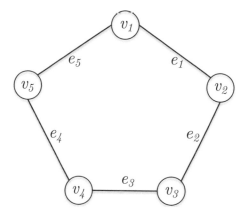

with each vertex (and its incident edges) encoded using a six-digit number. Different size-2 independent sets now correspond to pairs of numbers with different sums—211,101 and 211,110 for $\{v_1, v_3\}$ and $\{v_2, v_4\}$, for example. In general, a lower-order digit of the sum will be 0 if it corresponds to an edge with neither endpoint in the independent set, and 1 otherwise.

To correct lower-order digits that would otherwise be 0, the preprocessor can define one additional number per edge. For the five-cycle, the final list of numbers is:

v_1	v_2	v_3	v_4	v_5
110,001	111,000	101,100	100,110	100,011

e_1	e_2	e_3	e_4	e_5
10,000	1,000	100	10	1

Now, the target sum $t = 211{,}111$ can be achieved by taking the numbers corresponding to a size-2 independent set (like $\{v_1, v_3\}$ or $\{v_2, v_4\}$) along with the numbers corresponding to edges with neither endpoint in the independent set (like e_4 or e_5, respectively). There is no other way to achieve this target sum (as you should check).

22.8.4   Proof of Theorem 22.9

The proof of Theorem 22.9 scales up the example in the preceding section to general independent set instances.

Description of the Reduction

Preprocessor. Given both an undirected graph $G = (V, E)$ with vertex set $V = \{v_1, v_2, \ldots, v_n\}$ and edge set $E = \{e_1, e_2, \ldots, e_m\}$ and a target size k, the preprocessor constructs $n + m + 1$ positive integers that define an instance of the subset sum problem:

- For each vertex v_i, define the number $a_i = 10^m + \sum_{e_j \in A_i} 10^{m-j}$, where A_i denotes the edges incident to v_i. (Written in base 10, the leading digit is 1 and the jth digit after that is 1 if e_j is incident to v_i and 0 otherwise.)

- For each edge e_j, define the number $b_j = 10^{m-j}$.

- Define the target sum $t = k \cdot 10^m + \sum_{j=1}^{m} 10^{m-j}$. (Written in base 10, the digits of k followed by m 1's.)

Postprocessor. If the assumed subroutine computes a subset of $\{a_1, a_2, \ldots, a_n, b_1, b_2, \ldots, b_m\}$ with sum t, the postprocessor returns the vertices v_i that correspond to the a_i's in the subset. (For example, if handed the subset $\{a_2, a_4, a_7, b_3, b_6\}$, the postprocessor returns the vertex subset $\{v_2, v_4, v_7\}$.) If the assumed subroutine responds "no solution," the postprocessor also responds "no solution."

Outer loop. The preprocessor and postprocessor are designed to check for an independent set of a target size k. To compute a maximum-size independent set of an input graph $G = (V, E)$, the reduction checks all possible values of $k = n, n-1, n-2, \ldots, 2, 1$:

1. Invoke the preprocessor to transform G and the current value of k into an instance of the subset sum problem.

2. Invoke the assumed subroutine for the subset sum problem.

3. Invoke the postprocessor on the subroutine's output. If it returns a size-k independent set S of G, halt and return S.

Overall, the reduction invokes the subset sum subroutine at most n times and performs at most a polynomial amount of additional work.

Proof of Correctness

The reduction is correct provided that every iteration of its outer loop correctly determines, for the current value of k, whether the input graph has a size-k independent set.

Case 1: No size-k independent set.   Suppose that an iteration of the reduction's outer loop fails to return "no solution" for some graph $G = (V, E)$ that has no size-k independent set. This means that the assumed subroutine returns a subset N of the numbers $\{a_1, a_2, \ldots, a_n, b_1, b_2, \ldots, b_m\}$ constructed by the preprocessor with the target sum t. Let $S \subseteq V$ denote the vertices that correspond to the a_i's in N. To obtain a contradiction, we next argue that S is a size-k independent set of G.

In general, for every subset of s of the a_i's and any number of the b_j's, the sum (written base-10) is the digits of s followed by m digits that each belong to $\{0, 1, 2, 3\}$. (Exactly three numbers can contribute to the jth of the m trailing digits: b_j, and the two a_i's that correspond to e_j's endpoints.) Because the leading digits of the target sum t match those of k, the subset N must contain k of the a_i's; thus, S has size k. Because the m trailing digits of t are all 1, the subset N cannot contain two a_i's that correspond to the endpoints of a common edge; thus, S is an independent set of G.

Case 2: At least one size-k independent set.   Suppose the input graph $G = (V, E)$ has a size-k independent set S. The subset sum instance constructed by the preprocessor then has a subset with the target sum t: Choose the k a_i's corresponding to the vertices of S, along with the b_j's corresponding to the edges with neither endpoint in S. With at least one feasible solution out there to find, the assumed subroutine must return a subset N with sum t. As in case 1, the postprocessor then extracts from N and returns a size-k independent set of G. *QED*

The Upshot

☆ To prove that a problem B is NP-hard, follow the two-step recipe: (i) choose an NP-hard problem A; (ii) prove that A reduces to B.

☆ The 3-SAT problem is the special case of the satisfiability problem in which every constraint has at most three literals.

☆ The Cook-Levin theorem proves that the 3-SAT problem is NP-hard.

☆ Starting from the 3-SAT problem, thousands of applications of the two-step recipe have proved that thousands of problems are NP-hard.

☆ Reductions in NP-hardness proofs conform to a template: preprocess the input; invoke the assumed subroutine; postprocess the output.

☆ In the independent set problem, the input is an undirected graph and the goal is to compute a maximum-size subset of non-adjacent vertices.

☆ The 3-SAT problem reduces to the independent set problem, proving the latter NP-hard.

☆ An s-t Hamiltonian path of a graph G starts at the vertex s, ends at the vertex t, and visits every vertex of G exactly once.

☆ The 3-SAT problem reduces to the directed version of the Hamiltonian path problem, proving the latter NP-hard.

☆ The undirected version of the Hamiltonian path problem reduces to the traveling salesman problem, proving the latter NP-hard.

☆ In the subset sum problem, the goal is to compute a subset of a given set of positive integers with sum equal to a given target (or conclude that none exist).

☆ The independent set problem reduces to the subset sum problem, proving the latter NP-hard.

Test Your Understanding

Problem 22.1 *(S)* Assume that the P $\neq$ NP conjecture is true. Which of the following problems can be solved in polynomial time? (Choose all that apply.)

a) Given a connected undirected graph, compute a spanning tree with the smallest-possible number of leaves.

b) Given a connected undirected graph, compute a spanning tree with the minimum-possible maximum degree. (The degree of a vertex is the number of incident edges.)

c) Given a connected undirected graph with nonnegative edge lengths, a starting vertex s, and an ending vertex t, compute the minimum length of a cycle-free s-t path with exactly $n - 1$ edges (or $+\infty$, if no such path exists).

d) Given a connected undirected graph with nonnegative edge lengths, a starting vertex s, and an ending vertex t, compute the minimum length of a (not necessarily cycle-free) s-t path with exactly $n - 1$ edges (or $+\infty$, if no such path exists).

Problem 22.2 *(S)* Assume that the P $\neq$ NP conjecture is true. Which of the following problems can be solved in polynomial time? (Choose all that apply.)

a) Given a directed graph $G = (V, E)$ with nonnegative edge lengths, compute the longest length of a shortest path between any pair of vertices (that is, $\max_{v,w \in V} dist(v, w)$, where $dist(v, w)$ denotes the shortest-path distance from vertex v to vertex w).

b) Given a directed acyclic graph with real-valued edge lengths, compute the length of a longest path between any pair of vertices.

c) Given a directed graph $G = (V, E)$ with nonnegative edge lengths, compute the length of a longest cycle-free path between any pair of vertices (that is, $\max_{v,w \in V} maxlen(v, w)$, where $maxlen(v, w)$ denotes the length of a longest cycle-free path from v to w).

d) Given a directed graph with real-valued edge lengths, compute the length of a longest cycle-free path between any pair of vertices.

Problem 22.3 *(S)* Call the version of the directed Hamiltonian path problem on page 462, in which only a "yes"/"no" answer is required, the *decision version*. Call the version on page 562, in which an s-t Hamiltonian path itself is required (whenever one exists), the *search version*. Call the version of the TSP in Section 19.1.2 the *optimization version*, and define the *search version* of the TSP as: Given a complete graph, real-valued edge costs, and a target cost C, return a traveling salesman tour with a total cost of at most C (or correctly declare that none exist).

Which of the following are true? (Choose all that apply.)

a) The decision version of the directed Hamiltonian path problem reduces to the search version.

b) The search version of the directed Hamiltonian path problem reduces to the decision version.

c) The search version of the TSP reduces to the optimization version.

d) The optimization version of the TSP reduces to the search version.

Problem 22.4 *(H)* In the *clique* problem, the input is an undirected graph and the goal is to output a clique—a subset of mutually adjacent vertices—with the maximum-possible size. Prove that the independent set problem reduces to the clique problem, implying (by Corollary 22.3) that the latter is NP-hard.

Problem 22.5 *(H)* In the *vertex cover* problem, the input is an undirected graph $G = (V, E)$, and the goal is to identify a minimum-size subset $S \subseteq V$ of vertices that includes at least one endpoint of every edge in E. Prove that the independent set problem reduces to the vertex cover problem, implying (by Corollary 22.3) that the latter is NP-hard.

Problem 22.6 *(H)* In the *set cover* problem, the input comprises m subsets $A_1, A_2, \ldots, A_m$ of a ground set U, and the goal is to identify a minimum-size collection of subsets whose union equals U. Prove that the vertex cover problem reduces to the set cover problem, implying (by Problem 22.5) that the latter is NP-hard.

Problem 22.7 *(H)* Prove that the subset sum problem reduces to the knapsack problem (Section 16.5), implying (by Corollary 22.10) that the latter is NP-hard.

Challenge Problems

Problem 22.8 *(S)* Prove that the set cover problem reduces to the maximum coverage problem (Section 20.2.1), implying (by Problem 22.6) that the latter is NP-hard.

Problem 22.9 *(H)* Prove that the undirected Hamiltonian path problem reduces to the directed Hamiltonian path problem and vice versa. (In particular, Corollary 22.6 follows from Corollary 22.5.)

Problem 22.10 *(H)*

(a) Prove that the subset sum problem remains NP-hard in the special case in which the target sum equals half the sum of the input numbers (that is, $t = \frac{1}{2} \sum_{i=1}^{n} a_i$).[15]

(b) Prove that this special case of the subset sum problem reduces to the makespan minimization problem with two machines, implying (by (a)) that the latter is NP-hard.[16]

Problem 22.11 *(H)* Prove that the 3-SAT problem reduces to the special case of the graph coloring problem (page 541) in which the number k of allowable colors is 3, implying (by the Cook-Levin theorem) that the latter is NP-hard.[17]

Problem 22.12 *(H)* Problem 20.12 introduced the *metric* special case of the TSP, in which the edge costs c of the input graph $G = (V, E)$ are nonnegative and satisfy the triangle inequality:

$$c_{vw} \leq \sum_{e \in P} c_e$$

for every pair $v, w \in V$ of vertices and v-w path P in G. Problem 20.12 also developed a polynomial-time heuristic algorithm that, given a metric TSP instance, is guaranteed to return a tour with total cost at most twice the minimum possible. Can we do better and solve the metric special case exactly, or at least extend the heuristic algorithm's approximate correctness guarantee to the general TSP?

(a) Prove that the metric special case of the TSP is NP-hard.

(b) Assume that the P $\neq$ NP conjecture is true. Prove that there is no polynomial-time algorithm that, for every TSP instance with nonnegative edge costs (and no other assumptions), returns a tour with total cost at most 10^{100} times the minimum possible.

---

[15]This special case of the subset sum problem is often called the *partition* problem.

[16]The two-machine special case of the makespan minimization problem can be solved in pseudopolynomial time by dynamic programming (as you should check) and is therefore only weakly NP-hard (see footnote 14). A more complicated reduction shows that the general version of the problem is strongly NP-hard.

[17]The graph coloring problem can be solved in linear time when $k = 2$ (see footnote 37 in Chapter 21).

Chapter 23

P, NP, and All That

Chapters 19–22 cover everything the pure algorithm designer needs to know about NP-hard problems—the algorithmic implications of NP-hardness, algorithmic tools for making headway on NP-hard problems, and how to spot NP-hard problems in the wild. We provisionally defined NP-hardness in terms of the P $\neq$ NP conjecture and informally described this conjecture in Section 19.3.5, without any formal mathematical definitions (which we didn't need at the time). This optional chapter fills in the missing foundations.[1]

Section 23.1 outlines our plan to amass evidence of a problem's intractability by reducing a large number of problems to it. Section 23.2 distinguishes three types of computational problems: decision, search, and optimization problems. Section 23.3 defines the complexity class $\mathcal{NP}$ as the set of all search problems with efficiently recognizable solutions, formally defines NP-hard problems, and revisits the Cook-Levin theorem. Section 23.4 formally defines the P $\neq$ NP conjecture and surveys its current status. Section 23.5 describes two important conjectures that are stronger than the P $\neq$ NP conjecture—the Exponential Time Hypothesis (ETH) and Strong Exponential Time Hypothesis (SETH)—and their algorithmic implications (for example, for the sequence alignment problem). Section 23.6 concludes with a discussion of Levin reductions and NP-complete problems—universal problems that simultaneously encode all problems with efficiently recognizable solutions.

*23.1 Amassing Evidence of Intractability

In 1967, Jack Edmonds conjectured that the traveling salesman problem (TSP) cannot be solved by any polynomial-time algorithm, not even one with a running time of $O(n^{100})$ or $O(n^{10000})$ for inputs with n vertices (page 445). Absent a mathematical proof, how could we build a compelling case that this conjecture is true? The failed efforts to come up with such an algorithm by so many brilliant minds over the past seventy years constitute circumstantial evidence of intractability, but can we do better?

23.1.1 Building a Case with Reductions

The key idea is to show that a polynomial-time algorithm for the TSP would not merely solve one unsolved problem—it would solve *thousands* of them.

---

[1]This chapter is an introduction to a beautiful and mathematically deep field called *computational complexity theory*, which studies the quantity of computing resources (like time, memory, or randomness) necessary to solve different computational tasks (as a function of the input size). We'll maintain a ruthless focus on the algorithmic implications of this theory, resulting in a slightly unconventional treatment. If you want to learn more about computational complexity theory, I recommend starting with Ryan O'Donnell's excellent (and freely available) video lectures (http://www.cs.cmu.edu/~odonnell/).

Amassing Evidence That the TSP Is Intractable

1. Choose a really big collection $\mathcal{C}$ of computational problems.

2. Prove that *every* problem in $\mathcal{C}$ reduces to the TSP.[2]

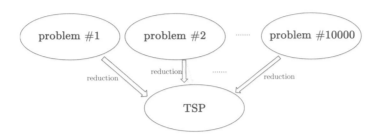

A polynomial-time algorithm for the TSP would then automatically provide one for every problem in the set $\mathcal{C}$. Said another way, if even *one* problem in the set $\mathcal{C}$ cannot be solved by a polynomial-time algorithm, neither can the TSP. The bigger the set $\mathcal{C}$, the stronger the argument that the TSP is not a polynomial-time solvable problem.

23.1.2   Choosing the Set $\mathcal{C}$ for the TSP

To make the case against the TSP's polynomial-time solvability as compelling as possible, why not reach for the stars and take $\mathcal{C}$ to be the set of *all* the computational problems in the world? Because this is too ambitious. Hard as the TSP may be, there are computational problems out there that are much, much harder. At the extreme are *undecidable* problems—problems that cannot be solved by a computer in any finite amount of time (not even in exponential time, not even in doubly-exponential time, and so on). One famous example of an undecidable problem is the *halting problem*: Given a program (say, one thousand lines of Python), determine whether it goes into an infinite loop or eventually halts. The obvious approach is to run the program and see what it does. But if the program hasn't halted after a century, how do you know if it's in an infinite loop or if it will halt tomorrow? You might hope for some shortcut smarter than rote simulation of the code, but unfortunately none exist in general.[3]

---

[2] As a reminder from Sections 19.5.1 and 22.1, a *reduction* from a problem A to a problem B is an algorithm that solves problem A while using at most a polynomial (in the input size) number of calls to a subroutine solving B and a polynomial amount of additional work. This type of reduction is sometimes called a *Cook reduction* (after Stephen Cook) or a *polynomial-time Turing reduction* (after Alan Turing), and is the most sensible one to focus on when studying algorithms. More restricted types of reductions are important for defining "NP-complete" problems; see Section 23.6.

[3] In 1936, Alan M. Turing published his paper "On Computable Numbers, with an Application to the Entscheidungsproblem" (*Proceedings of the London Mathematical Society*, 1936). I and many other computer scientists view this paper as the birth of our discipline and, for this reason, believe that Turing's name should be as widely recognized as, say, that of Albert Einstein.

What made this paper so important? Two things. First, Turing introduced a formal model of what general-purpose computers can do, now called a *Turing machine*. (Mind you, this was ten years before anyone had actually built a general-purpose computer!) Second, defining what computers can do enabled Turing to study what they *can't* do and to prove that the halting problem is undecidable. Thus, from literally day 1, computer scientists have been acutely aware of computers' limitations and the necessity of compromise when tackling hard computational problems.

The TSP no longer looks so bad—at least it can be solved in a finite (albeit exponential) amount of time via exhaustive search. No way can the halting problem reduce to the TSP, as such a reduction would translate the exponential-time algorithm for the TSP into one for the halting problem (which, per Turing, does not exist).

Going back to the drawing board, what is the largest set $\mathcal{C}$ of computational problems that might conceivably reduce to the TSP? Intuitively, the biggest set we could hope for is the set of *all problems solvable by an analogous exhaustive search algorithm*—then, among all such problems, the TSP would be the hardest one. Could there be a mathematical definition that captures this idea?

*23.2 Decision, Search, and Optimization

Before defining the set of "problems solvable by naive exhaustive-search"—the complexity class $\mathcal{NP}$—let's step back and categorize the different types of input-output formats that we've seen.

Three Types of Computational Problems

1. *Decision problem.* Output "yes" if there is a feasible solution and "no" otherwise.

2. *Search problem.* Output a feasible solution if one exists, and "no solution" otherwise.

3. *Optimization problem.* Output a feasible solution with the best-possible objective function value (or "no solution," if none exist).

Decision problems are the rarest of the three in applications, and we've seen only one example in Part IV: the original description of the directed Hamiltonian path problem (page 462), in which "feasible solutions" correspond to s-t Hamiltonian paths. Search and optimization problems are both common. Of the nineteen problems studied in Chapter 22 (see Figure 22.1), six are search problems: the 3-SAT, SAT, graph coloring, directed Hamiltonian path (the version on page 562), undirected Hamiltonian path, and subset sum problems. The other thirteen are optimization problems.[4] The definition of a "feasible solution"—such as a satisfying assignment, a Hamiltonian path, or a traveling salesman tour (perhaps with at most some target total cost)—is problem-specific. For the optimization problems, the objective function—such as minimizing the total cost or maximizing the total value—is also problem-specific.

Complexity classes usually stick with problems of only one type to avoid typechecking errors, and we'll restrict our definition of $\mathcal{NP}$ to search problems.[5] Don't worry about

---

[4]To shoehorn the cycle-free shortest path problem into this definition of an optimization problem, consider the variant in which two vertices are supplied as input and a shortest cycle-free path from the first to the second is required as output. The NP-hardness proof in Section 19.5.4 (Lemma 19.2) also applies to this version.

[5]Many books define the complexity class $\mathcal{NP}$ in terms of decision problems; this is more convenient for developing complexity theory but further removed from natural algorithmic problems. The version of the class used here is sometimes called $\mathcal{FNP}$, where the "$\mathcal{F}$" stands for "functional." All the algorithmic implications of NP-hardness, including the truth or falsity of the P $\neq$ NP conjecture, remain the same no matter which definition is used.

leaving optimization problems like the TSP out in the cold: Every optimization problem has a corresponding search version. The input to the search version also includes a target objective function value t; the goal is then to find a feasible solution with value at least t (for maximization problems) or at most t (for minimization problems), or correctly report that none exist. As we'll see, the search versions of almost all the optimization problems that we have studied reside in $\mathcal{NP}$.[6]

*23.3 $\mathcal{NP}$: Problems with Easily Recognized Solutions

We now arrive at the heart of the discussion. How can we define the set of "exhaustive-search-solvable" problems—the set of all problems that might plausibly reduce to the TSP? What are the minimal ingredients for solving a problem by naive exhaustive search?

23.3.1 Definition of the Complexity Class $\mathcal{NP}$

The big idea behind the complexity class $\mathcal{NP}$ is the *efficient recognition of purported solutions*. That is, if someone handed you an alleged feasible solution to a problem instance on a silver platter, you could quickly check whether it was indeed a feasible solution. For example, if someone hands you a filled-out Sudoku or KenKen puzzle, it's easy to check whether they followed all the rules. Or, if someone suggests a sequence of vertices in a graph, it's easy to check whether they constitute a traveling salesman tour and, if they do, whether the total cost of the tour is at most a given target t.[7]

The Complexity Class $\mathcal{NP}$

A search problem belongs to the complexity class $\mathcal{NP}$ if and only if:

1. For every instance, every candidate solution has description length (in bits, say) bounded above by a polynomial function of the input size.

2. For every instance and candidate solution, the alleged feasibility of the solution can be confirmed or denied in time polynomial in the input size.

23.3.2 Examples of Problems in $\mathcal{NP}$

The entrance requirements for membership in $\mathcal{NP}$ are so easily passed that almost all the search problems that you've seen qualify. For example, the search version of the TSP belongs to the class $\mathcal{NP}$: A tour of n vertices can be described using $O(n \log n)$ bits —roughly $\log_2 n$ bits to name each vertex—and, given a list of vertices, it's easy to check whether they

---

[6]The search version of an optimization problem reduces immediately to the original version: Either an optimal solution meets a given target objective function value t, or no feasible solutions do. More interesting is the converse: A typical optimization problem reduces to its search version via binary search over the target t (see also Problem 22.3). Such an optimization problem is polynomial-time solvable if and only if its search version is polynomial-time solvable, and similarly is NP-hard if and only if its search version is NP-hard.

[7]$\mathcal{NP}$ can equivalently be defined as the search problems that are efficiently solvable in a fictitious computational model defined by "nondeterministic Turing machines." The acronym "NP" stands for "nondeterministic polynomial time" (and not for "not polynomial"!) and refers to this alternative definition. In an algorithms context, you should always think of $\mathcal{NP}$ problems as those with efficiently recognizable solutions.

constitute a tour with total cost at most a given target t. The 3-SAT problem (Section 22.2) also belongs to $\mathcal{NP}$: Describing a truth assignment to n Boolean variables takes n bits, and checking whether one satisfies each of the given constraints is straightforward. Similarly, it's easy to check whether a proposed path is Hamiltonian, whether a proposed job schedule has a given makespan, or whether a proposed subset of vertices is an independent set, vertex cover, or clique of a given size.

Quiz 23.1

Of the nineteen problems listed in Figure 22.1, for how many does the search version belong to $\mathcal{NP}$?

   a) 16

   b) 17

   c) 18

   d) 19

(See Section 23.3.6 for the solution and discussion.)

23.3.3 $\mathcal{NP}$ Problems Are Solvable by Exhaustive Search

We originally set out to define the set of problems that are solvable by naive exhaustive search—the problems with a shot at reducing to the TSP—but instead defined the class $\mathcal{NP}$ as the search problems with efficiently recognizable solutions. The connection? Every problem in $\mathcal{NP}$ can be solved in exponential time by using naive exhaustive search to check candidate solutions one by one:

Exhaustive Search for a Generic $\mathcal{NP}$ Problem

1. Enumerate candidate solutions, one by one:

   a) If the current candidate is feasible, return it.

2. Return "no solution."

For a problem in $\mathcal{NP}$, candidate solutions require $O(n^d)$ bits to describe, where n denotes the input size and d is a constant (independent of n). Thus, the number of possible candidates (and hence of loop iterations) is $2^{O(n^d)}$.[8] By the second defining property of an NP problem, each loop iteration can be carried out in polynomial time. Exhaustive search therefore correctly solves the problem in time "only" exponential in the input size n.

---

[8]Big-O notation in an exponent suppresses constant factors (and lower order terms) in the exponent. For example, a function $T(n)$ is $2^{O(\sqrt{n})}$ if there are positive constants c and n_0 (independent of n) such that $T(n) \le 2^{c\sqrt{n}}$ for all $n \ge n_0$. (Whereas $T(n) = O(2^{\sqrt{n}})$ means that there are constants $c, n_0 > 0$ such that $T(n) \le c \cdot 2^{\sqrt{n}}$ for all $n \ge n_0$.)

23.3.4   NP-Hard Problems

The requirements for membership in the complexity class $\mathcal{NP}$ are extremely weak. All you need is the ability to recognize a correct solution—to know one when you see one. As a result, $\mathcal{NP}$ is an enormous class of search problems, capturing the overwhelming majority of those you're likely to encounter. So if *every* problem in $\mathcal{NP}$ reduces to a problem A—if A is at least as hard as every problem in $\mathcal{NP}$—a polynomial-time algorithm for A would lead directly to such algorithms for the entire gamut of $\mathcal{NP}$ problems. This constitutes strong evidence of intrinsic intractability and is exactly the formal definition of an *NP-hard* problem.

NP-Hard Problem (Formal Definition)

A computational problem is *NP-hard* if every problem in $\mathcal{NP}$ reduces to it.

Once we formally define the P $\neq$ NP conjecture in Section 23.4, we'll see that every problem that is NP-hard under this definition also satisfies the provisional definition (Section 19.3.7) used throughout Chapters 19–22. The minor switch in definition affects none of the lessons from those chapters. For example, the Cook-Levin theorem (Theorem 22.1) shows that the 3-SAT problem is NP-hard according to the formal definition (as we'll see in Section 23.3.5); reductions continue to spread NP-hardness (Problem 23.4); and as a consequence, the nineteen problems studied in Chapter 22 remain NP-hard under this new definition.[9]

23.3.5   The Cook-Levin Theorem Revisited

In Chapter 22 we were content to take the Cook-Levin theorem (Theorem 22.1) on faith and couple it with our two-step recipe to prove problems NP-hard. We're now equipped with all the definitions necessary to understand precisely what that theorem says: Every problem in $\mathcal{NP}$ reduces to the 3-SAT problem. How could this be true? The 3-SAT problem seems so simple, the class $\mathcal{NP}$ so vast.

The details of the proof get messy, but here's the gist.[10] Fix an arbitrary $\mathcal{NP}$ problem A; we must show that A reduces to the 3-SAT problem. All we know about A is that it meets the two defining requirements of an $\mathcal{NP}$ problem: (i) feasible solutions to size-n instances can be described using at most $c_1 n^{d_1}$ bits; and (ii) alleged feasible solutions to size-n instances can be verified in at most $c_2 n^{d_2}$ time (where c_1, c_2, d_1, d_2 are constants). Denote by verify$_A$ the algorithm in (ii) that checks the feasibility of a purported solution.

We'll be able to get away with a simplest-imaginable reduction (Section 22.4). The main ingredient is a preprocessor that translates instances of A with and without a feasible solution into satisfiable and unsatisfiable 3-SAT instances, respectively:

---

[9]Look in other books and you'll often see a more demanding definition of NP-hardness that requires reductions of a very specific form, called "Levin reductions." (Section 23.6.1 defines such reductions and Section 23.6.2 uses them to define "NP-complete" problems.) Only search problems are eligible for NP-hardness under this more restrictive definition; instead of "the TSP is NP-hard," one must say "the search version of the TSP is NP-hard." The more liberal definition used here, with general (Cook) reductions, better accords with the algorithmic viewpoint of this book.

[10]For a complete proof, refer to any textbook on computational complexity.

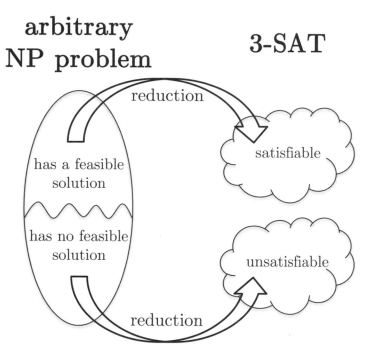

Preprocessor.   Given a size-n instance I_A of the problem A, the preprocessor constructs a 3-SAT instance I_{3SAT}:

- Define $c_1 n^{d_1}$ *solution* variables. The intent is for these variables to record bits that describe a candidate solution for I_A.

- Define $(c_2 n^{d_2})^2 = c_2^2 \cdot n^{2d_2}$ *state* variables. The intent is for these variables to encode the execution of $\texttt{verify}_A$ on the candidate solution for I_A encoded by the solution variables.

- Define constraints to enforce the semantics of the state variables. A typical constraint asserts: "the jth bit of memory after step $i + 1$ is consistent with the relevant memory contents after step i, the given instance I_A, the candidate solution to I_A encoded by the solution variables, and the code for the algorithm $\texttt{verify}_A$."

- Define constraints that ensure that the computation encoded by the state variables concludes with an assertion of the feasibility of the candidate solution encoded by the solution variables.

Why $(c_2 n^{d_2})^2$ state variables? The algorithm $\texttt{verify}_A$ performs at most $c_2 n^{d_2}$ primitive operations and, assuming a computational model in which one bit of memory can be accessed per operation, references at most $c_2 n^{d_2}$ bits of memory. Its entire computation can therefore be summarized (more or less) using a $c_2 n^{d_2} \times c_2 n^{d_2}$ table, with rows corresponding to steps i and columns to bits j of memory. Each state variable then encodes the content of one bit of memory at one point in the computation.[11]

---

[11]There are additional details here that depend on the exact computational model used and the definition of a "primitive operation." The simplest approach is to use a Turing machine (see footnote 3), in which case another batch of Boolean variables is needed at each step to encode the machine's current internal state. The proof can be made to work for any reasonable model of computation.

The consistency constraints sound complicated. But because one step of an algorithm (such as a Turing machine) is so simple, each of these logical constraints can be implemented with a small number of three-literal disjunctions (with the details depending on the precise computational model). The end result is a 3-SAT instance I_{3SAT} with a polynomial (in n) number of variables and constraints.

Postprocessor. If the assumed subroutine returns a satisfying truth assignment for the 3-SAT instance I_{3SAT} constructed by the preprocessor, the postprocessor returns the candidate solution for I_A encoded by the assignments to the solution variables. If the assumed subroutine responds that I_{3SAT} is unsatisfiable, the postprocessor reports that I_A has no feasible solutions.

Outline of correctness. The constraints of the fabricated 3-SAT instance I_{3SAT} are defined so that the satisfying truth assignments correspond to the feasible solutions to the given instance I_A (encoded by the solution variables) along with the supporting verification performed by the algorithm `verify`$_A$ (encoded by the state variables). Thus, if I_A has no feasible solutions, the instance I_{3SAT} must be unsatisfiable. Conversely, if I_A does have a feasible solution, I_{3SAT} must have a satisfying truth assignment. The assumed 3-SAT subroutine must then compute such an assignment, which will be converted by the postprocessor into a feasible solution for I_A.

23.3.6   Solution to Quiz 23.1

Correct answer: (c). The exception? The influence maximization problem. While computing the total cost of a given tour or the makespan of a given schedule is straightforward, the influence of a given subset of k vertices is defined as an expectation with exponentially many terms (see (20.10) and the solution to Quiz 20.6). Because it's unclear how to evaluate the objective function in the influence maximization problem in polynomial time, the search version of the problem does not obviously belong to $\mathcal{NP}$.

*23.4   The P $\neq$ NP Conjecture

Way back in Section 19.3.5, we informally defined the P $\neq$ NP conjecture as: Checking an alleged solution to a problem can be fundamentally easier than coming up with your own solution from scratch. We arc now, finally, in a position to state this conjecture formally.

23.4.1 $\mathcal{P}$: Polynomial-Time Solvable $\mathcal{NP}$ Problems

At least some of the problems in $\mathcal{NP}$ can be solved in polynomial time, such as the 2-SAT problem (see Problem 21.12) and the search version of the minimum spanning tree problem (see Section 19.1.1). The complexity class $\mathcal{P}$ is defined as the set of all such problems.

The Complexity Class $\mathcal{P}$

A search problem belongs to the complexity class $\mathcal{P}$ if and only if it belongs to $\mathcal{NP}$ and can be solved with a polynomial-time algorithm.

By definition, every problem in $\mathcal{P}$ also belongs to $\mathcal{NP}$:

$$\mathcal{P} \subseteq \mathcal{NP}.$$

23.4.2   Formal Definition of the Conjecture

No prizes for now guessing the formal statement of the P ≠ NP conjecture, that $\mathcal{P}$ is a strict subset of $\mathcal{NP}$:

The P ≠ NP Conjecture (Formal Version)

$$\mathcal{P} \subsetneq \mathcal{NP}.$$

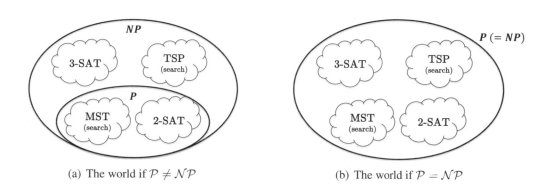

(a) The world if $\mathcal{P} \neq \mathcal{NP}$ (b) The world if $\mathcal{P} = \mathcal{NP}$

The P ≠ NP conjecture asserts the existence of a search problem with efficiently recognizable solutions (an $\mathcal{NP}$ problem) that cannot be solved by any polynomial-time algorithm—a problem for which checking an alleged feasible solution is easy, but coming up with your own from scratch is hard. If the conjecture is false, $\mathcal{P} = \mathcal{NP}$ and the efficient recognition of feasible solutions leads automatically to the efficient computation of feasible solutions (whenever they exist).

A polynomial-time algorithm for an NP-hard problem A would directly lead to one for every $\mathcal{NP}$ problem—with every problem in $\mathcal{NP}$ reducing to A, tractability would spread from A to all of $\mathcal{NP}$—proving that $\mathcal{P} = \mathcal{NP}$ and refuting the P ≠ NP conjecture. Thus, the provisional definition of an NP-hard problem in Section 19.3.7 is a logical consequence of the formal definition on page 582:

Consequence of NP-Hardness

If the P ≠ NP conjecture is true, no NP-hard problem can be solved by a polynomial-time algorithm.

23.4.3   Status of the P ≠ NP Conjecture

The P ≠ NP conjecture is arguably the most important open question in all of computer science, and also one of the deepest unsolved problems in mathematics. For example, resolving the conjecture is one of the seven "Millennium Problems" proposed in the year 2000 by the Clay Mathematics Institute; solve one of these problems and you'll earn a prize of one million US dollars.[12,13]

Most experts believe that the P $\neq$ NP conjecture is true. (Although the legendary logician Kurt Gödel conjectured, in a 1956 letter to the still more legendary John von Neumann, a statement equivalent to $\mathcal{P} = \mathcal{NP}$.) Why? For starters, humans are crafty at discovering fast algorithms. If it really were the case that every single problem in $\mathcal{NP}$ can be solved by a fast algorithm, why hasn't some super-smart engineer or scientist discovered one yet? Meanwhile, proofs delineating the limitations of algorithms have been few and far between; if $\mathcal{P} \subsetneq \mathcal{NP}$, it's no real surprise that we haven't yet figured out how to prove it.

Second, how could we reconcile $\mathcal{P} = \mathcal{NP}$ with the way the world seems to work? We all "know," from direct experience, tasks for which checking someone else's work (like a mathematical proof) takes far less time and creativity than searching a large space of candidates for your own solution. Yet $\mathcal{P} = \mathcal{NP}$ would imply that such creativity can be efficiently automated; for example, at least in principle, a proof of Fermat's Last Theorem could then be generated by an algorithm in time polynomial in the length of the proof!

The actual ramifications of $\mathcal{P} = \mathcal{NP}$ would depend on whether all $\mathcal{NP}$ problems can be solved by algorithms that are fast in practice, or merely by algorithms that technically run in polynomial time but are too slow or complicated to be implemented and used. The first and more implausible scenario would have tremendous consequences for society, including the end of cryptography and modern ecommerce as we know it (see footnote 25 in Chapter 19).[14] The second scenario would not necessarily have any practical implications; instead, it would signal that the mathematical definition of polynomial-time solvability is too liberal to accurately capture what we mean by "solvable by a fast algorithm in the physical world."

The P $\neq$ NP conjecture is a mathematical statement, and yet we're reasoning about it through anecdotes. How about some mathematical evidence for or against it? Here, we know shockingly little. It may seem bizarre that no one has been able to make much progress on such a seemingly obvious statement. The intimidating barrier is the dizzyingly rich fauna of the land of polynomial-time algorithms. If the "obvious" cubic running time lower bound for matrix multiplication is false (as shown by Strassen's algorithm in Section 3.3), who's to say that some other exotic species can't break through other "obvious" lower bounds, including the presumed ones for NP-hard problems?

Who's right: Gödel or Edmonds? You'd hope that, as the years go by, we'd be getting closer to a resolution of the P $\neq$ NP conjecture, one way or the other. Instead, as more and more mathematical approaches to the problem have proved inadequate, the solution has been receding further into the distance. We have to face the reality that we may not know the answer for a long time—certainly years, probably decades, and maybe even centuries.[15]

---

[12]The other six: the Riemann Hypothesis, the Navier-Stokes Equation, the Poincaré Conjecture, the Hodge Conjecture, the Birch and Swinnerton-Dyer Conjecture, and the Yang-Mills Existence and Mass Gap Problem. As of this writing (in 2022), only the Poincaré Conjecture has been resolved (by Grigori Perelman, in 2006, who famously refused the prize money).

[13]While one million dollars is nothing to sneeze at, it radically undersells the importance and value of the advancement in human knowledge that appears necessary to resolve a problem like the P $\neq$ NP conjecture.

[14]For a general-audience account of this possibility, see Lance Fortnow's book *A Golden Ticket* (Princeton University Press, 2013).

[15]For much more on the conjecture's broader context and current status, check out Scott Aaronson's book chapter "P $\overset{?}{=}$ NP" in *Open Problems in Mathematics*, edited by John F. Nash, Jr. and Michael Th. Rassias (Springer, 2016).

*23.5   The Exponential Time Hypothesis

23.5.1   Do NP-Hard Problems Require Exponential Time?

NP-hard problems are commonly conflated with problems that require exponential time to solve in the worst case (the third acceptable inaccuracy in Section 19.6). The P $\neq$ NP conjecture does not assert this, however, and even if true, leaves open the possibility that an NP-hard problem like the TSP could be solved in $n^{O(\log n)}$ or $2^{O(\sqrt{n})}$ time on instances with n vertices. The widely held belief that typical NP-hard problems require exponential time is codified by the *Exponential Time Hypothesis (ETH)*.[16]

The Exponential Time Hypothesis (ETH)

There is a constant $c > 1$ such that: Every algorithm that solves the 3-SAT problem requires time at least c^n in the worst case, where n denotes the number of variables.

The ETH does not preclude algorithms for the 3-SAT problem that improve over exhaustive search (which runs in time scaling with 2^n), and this is no accident: Problem 21.12 shows that there *are* much faster (if still exponential-time) algorithms for the problem. However, all the known 3-SAT algorithms require time c^n for some $c > 1$ (with the current record being $c \approx 1.308$); the ETH conjectures that this is unavoidable.

Reductions can be used to show that, if the ETH is true, many other natural NP-hard problems also require exponential time. For example, the ETH would imply that there is a constant $a > 1$ such that every algorithm for one of the NP-hard graph problems in Chapter 22 requires time at least a^n in the worst case, where n denotes the number of vertices.

23.5.2   The Strong ETH (SETH)

The Exponential Time Hypothesis is a stronger assumption than the P $\neq$ NP conjecture: If the former is true, so is the latter. Stronger assumptions lead to stronger conclusions; unfortunately, they are also more likely to be false (Figure 23.1)! Still, most experts believe the ETH is true.

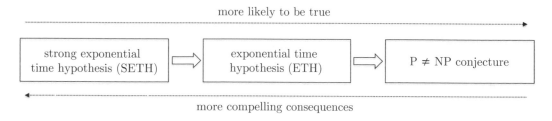

Figure 23.1: Three unproven conjectures about the computational intractability of NP-hard problems, ordered from strongest (and least plausible) to weakest (and most plausible).

---

[16]The stronger statement that *every* NP-hard problem requires exponential time is false; see Problem 23.5 for a contrived NP-hard problem that can be solved in subexponential time.

Next is an even stronger assumption that is more controversial but has remarkable algorithmic implications. What could be stronger than assuming that an NP-hard problem requires exponential time to solve? *Assuming that there is no algorithm for the problem significantly faster than exhaustive search.* This can't possibly be true for the 3-SAT problem (on account of Problem 21.12); perhaps for a different problem? We don't need to look far—the general SAT problem, with no restriction on the number of literals per constraint (page 542), is a plausible candidate.

The generality (and hence difficulty) of the k-SAT problem is nondecreasing in k, the maximum number of literals per constraint. Does the problem's difficulty strictly increase with k? For example, the randomized 3-SAT algorithm in Problem 21.12 can be extended to the k-SAT problem for every positive integer k, but its running time degrades with k as roughly $(2 - \frac{2}{k})^n$, where n is the number of variables (see the discussion on page 550). This same degradation in running time to 2^n as k increases shows up in all known k-SAT algorithms. Could it be necessary?

The Strong Exponential Time Hypothesis (SETH)

For every constant $c < 2$, there exists a positive integer k such that: Every algorithm that solves the k-SAT problem requires time at least c^n in the worst case, where n denotes the number of variables.[17]

Refuting the SETH would entail a major theoretical advance in satisfiability algorithms—a family of k-SAT algorithms (one per positive integer k), all of which run in $O((2 - \epsilon)^n)$ time, where n denotes the number of variables and $\epsilon > 0$ is a constant (independent of k and n, like .01 or .001). Such an advance might or might not be in our near future, and expert opinion on the SETH is split; in any case, everyone is prepared for it to be refuted at any time.[18]

23.5.3   Running Time Lower Bounds for Easy Problems

Why tell you about a conjecture so strong that it might well be false? Because the SETH, a conjecture about the intractability of NP-hard problems, also has striking algorithmic implications for polynomial-time solvable problems.[19]

From the SETH to Sequence Alignment

In Parts I–III of this book we aspired to ever-faster algorithms, with the holy grail a blazingly fast linear- or near-linear-time algorithm. We achieved this goal for a number of problems (especially in Parts I and II); for others (especially in Part III), we stopped short. For example, for the sequence alignment problem (Section 17.1), we declared victory with the

---

[17]While not obvious, the SETH does imply the ETH.

[18]The ETH and SETH were formulated by Russell Impagliazzo and Ramamohan Paturi in their paper "On the Complexity of k-SAT" (*Journal of Computer and System Sciences*, 2001).

[19]The ETH also has some interesting algorithmic consequences that are not known to follow from the P $\neq$ NP conjecture. For example, if the ETH is true, many NP-hard problems and parameter choices do not allow for fixed-parameter algorithms (see footnote 16 on page 534).

NW (Needleman-Wunsch) dynamic programming algorithm that runs in $O(n^2)$ time, where n denotes the length of the longer of the two input strings.

Can we do better than this quadratic-time sequence alignment algorithm? Or, how would we amass evidence that we can't? The theory of NP-hardness, developed to reason about problems that seem unsolvable in polynomial time, appears irrelevant to this question. But a relatively new area of computational complexity theory, called *fine-grained complexity*, shows that hardness assumptions for NP-hard problems (like the SETH) translate meaningfully to polynomial-time solvable problems.[20] For example, a better-than-quadratic-time algorithm for the sequence alignment problem would automatically lead to a better-than-exhaustive-search algorithm for the k-SAT problem for all k![21]

Fact 23.1 (SETH Implies That NW Is Essentially Optimal) *For every constant $\epsilon > 0$, an $O(n^{2-\epsilon})$-time algorithm for the sequence alignment problem, where n is the length of the longer input string, would refute the SETH.*

In other words, the *only avenue* for improving on the running time of the NW algorithm is to make major progress on the SAT problem! This is a stunning connection between two problems that seem wildly different.

Reductions with Exponential Blow-Up

Fact 23.1, like all our NP-hardness proofs in Chapter 22, boils down to a reduction—actually, one reduction for each positive integer k—with k-SAT playing the role of the known hard problem and sequence alignment the role of the target problem:

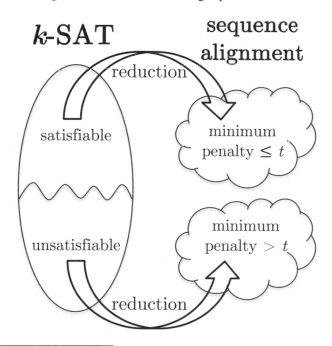

---

590 P, NP, and All That

But how can we reduce an NP-hard problem to a polynomial-time solvable one without refuting the P $\neq$ NP conjecture? Each reduction behind Fact 23.1 employs a preprocessor that translates a k-SAT instance with n variables into a sequence alignment instance that is *exponentially bigger*, with input strings that have length N in the ballpark of $2^{n/2}$.[22] The reduction also ensures that the fabricated instance has an alignment with total penalty at most a fabricated target t if and only if the given k-SAT instance is satisfiable, and that a postprocessor can easily extract a satisfiable assignment from an alignment with total penalty at most t.

Why a blow-up of $N \approx 2^{n/2}$? Because that number matches up the running times of the state-of-the-art algorithms for sequence alignment (dynamic programming) and k-SAT (exhaustive search). Composing such a reduction with an $O(N^2)$-time sequence alignment algorithm leads only to a k-SAT algorithm with running time $\approx 2^n$, the same as exhaustive search. By the same reasoning, a hypothetical $O(N^{1.99})$-time (say) sequence alignment subroutine would lead automatically (for every k) to an algorithm that solves the k-SAT problem in time roughly $O((2^{n/2})^{1.99}) = O((1.9931)^n)$. Because the base of this exponent is less than 2 (for all k), such an algorithm would refute the SETH.[23]

*23.6 NP-Completeness

A polynomial-time subroutine for an NP-hard problem like 3-SAT is all you need to solve every problem in $\mathcal{NP}$—every problem with efficiently recognizable solutions—in polynomial time. But something even stronger is true: Every problem in $\mathcal{NP}$ is *literally just a thinly disguised special case of 3-SAT*. In other words, the 3-SAT problem is *universal* among $\mathcal{NP}$ problems, in that it simultaneously encodes every single problem of $\mathcal{NP}$! This is the meaning of "NP-completeness." The search versions of almost all the problems studied in Chapter 22 are also NP-complete in this sense.

23.6.1 Levin Reductions

The idea that one search problem A is a "thinly disguised special case" of another search problem B is expressed through a highly restricted type of reduction known as a *Levin reduction*. Like the "simplest-imaginable reductions" introduced in Section 22.4, a Levin reduction carries out only the three unavoidable steps: transform in a preprocessing step a given instance of A to one of B; invoke the assumed subroutine for B; and transform in a postprocessing step the feasible solution returned by the subroutine (if any) into one for the given instance of A:[24,25]

---

[22]This exponential blow-up evokes the exponentially large numbers essential to our reduction from the independent set problem to the subset sum problem (Theorem 22.9); see footnote 14 on page 570.

[23]Problem 23.7 outlines a simpler reduction of this type for the problem of computing the diameter of a graph.

[24]Levin reductions conform to the template in Section 22.4 and, in addition: (i) both problems are required to be search problems; and (ii) the postprocessor is required to respond "no solution" if and only if the assumed subroutine does.

[25]If A and B are decision ("yes"/"no") problems rather than search problems, no postprocessing is necessary and the (binary) answer returned by the subroutine for B can be passed along unchanged as the final output. This analog of a Levin reduction for decision problems has a number of names: Karp reduction; polynomial-time many-to-one reduction; and polynomial-time mapping reduction.

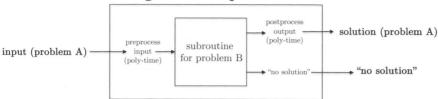

algorithm for problem A

Levin Reduction from A to B

1. *Preprocessor:* Given an instance I of problem A, transform it in polynomial time to an instance I' of problem B.

2. *Subroutine:* Invoke the assumed subroutine for B with input I'.

3. *Postprocessor (feasible case):* If the subroutine returns a feasible solution to I', transform it in polynomial time to a feasible solution to I.

4. *Postprocessor (infeasible case):* If the subroutine returns "no solution," return "no solution."

Throughout Part IV, we've inadvertently used only Levin reductions and not the full power of general (Cook) reductions. Our reduction in Theorem 22.4 from the 3-SAT problem to the directed Hamiltonian path problem (page 566) is a canonical example: Given a 3-SAT instance, the preprocessor constructs a directed graph, which is then fed into a subroutine for computing an s-t Hamiltonian path, and if the subroutine returns such a path, the postprocessor extracts from it a satisfying truth assignment.[26]

23.6.2   The Hardest Problems in $\mathcal{NP}$

A problem B is NP-hard if it is algorithmically sufficient to solve all $\mathcal{NP}$ problems in polynomial time, meaning that for every problem A in $\mathcal{NP}$ there is a (Cook) reduction from A to B (page 582). To qualify as "NP-complete," a problem B must also belong to the class $\mathcal{NP}$ and include all other $\mathcal{NP}$ problems as thinly disguised special cases.[27]

NP-Complete Problem

A computational problem B is *NP-complete* if:

1. For every problem A in $\mathcal{NP}$, there is a Levin reduction from A to B;

2. B is a member of the class $\mathcal{NP}$.

---

[26]The other three main reductions in Chapter 22 (Theorems 22.2, 22.7, and 22.9) turn into Levin reductions once the optimization problem in the original is replaced by its search version (as you should check). For example, the reduction from the undirected Hamiltonian path problem to the TSP (Theorem 22.7) requires only a subroutine for the search version of the TSP (to check whether there is a zero-cost tour).

[27]Many books define NP-completeness using decision (rather than search) problems and Karp (rather than Levin) reductions (footnote 25). The interpretation and algorithmic implications of NP-completeness are the same either way.

Because a Levin reduction is a special case of a (Cook) reduction, every NP-complete problem is automatically NP-hard. Because of the second condition, only search problems can qualify for NP-completeness. For example, the TSP is NP-hard but not NP-complete, while its search version turns out to be both NP-hard *and* NP-complete.

Of all the problems in $\mathcal{NP}$, the NP-complete problems are the hardest ones. Each such problem simultaneously encodes all search problems with efficiently recognizable solutions.

23.6.3   Existence of NP-Complete Problems

How cool is the definition of an NP-complete problem? A *single* search problem with efficiently recognizable solutions that simultaneously encodes *all* such search problems? It's amazing that such a problem could even exist!

But wait... we haven't actually seen any examples of NP-complete problems. Are there any? Could there really be such a "universal" search problem? Yes, and the Cook-Levin theorem already proves it! The reason is that its proof (Section 23.3.5) uses only a Levin reduction—a preprocessor that transforms instances of an arbitrary $\mathcal{NP}$ problem into 3-SAT instances and a postprocessor that extracts feasible solutions from satisfying truth assignments. Because the 3-SAT problem is also a member of $\mathcal{NP}$, it passes both tests for NP-completeness with flying colors.

Theorem 23.2 (Cook-Levin Theorem (Stronger Version)) *The 3-SAT problem is NP-complete.*

Proving from scratch that a problem is NP-complete is a tough task—Cook and Levin weren't awarded major prizes for nothing—but there's no need to do it more than once. Just as (Cook) reductions spread NP-hardness from one problem to another, Levin reductions spread NP-completeness (Problem 23.4):

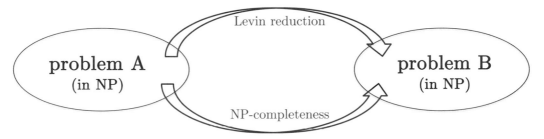

Thus, to prove that a problem is NP-complete, just follow the three-step recipe (with the third step a check that the problem indeed belongs to $\mathcal{NP}$):

How to Prove a Problem Is NP-Complete

To prove that a problem B is NP-complete:

1. Prove that B is a member of the class $\mathcal{NP}$.

2. Choose an NP-complete problem A.

3. Prove that there is a Levin reduction from A to B.

This recipe has been applied many times over, and as a result we now know that thousands of natural problems are NP-complete, including problems from all across engineering, the life sciences, and the social sciences. For example, the search versions of almost all the problems studied in Chapter 22 are NP-complete (Problem 23.3).[28] The classic book by Garey and Johnson (see footnote 8 on page 557) lists hundreds more.[29]

The Upshot

☆ To amass evidence of a problem's intractability, prove that many other seemingly difficult problems reduce to it.

☆ In a search problem, the goal is to output a feasible solution or deduce that none exist.

☆ $\mathcal{NP}$ is the set of all search problems for which feasible solutions have polynomial length and can be verified in polynomial time.

☆ A problem is NP-hard if every problem in $\mathcal{NP}$ reduces to it.

☆ $\mathcal{P}$ is the set of all $\mathcal{NP}$ problems that can be solved with a polynomial-time algorithm.

☆ The P $\neq$ NP conjecture asserts that $\mathcal{P} \subsetneq \mathcal{NP}$.

☆ The exponential time hypothesis (ETH) asserts that natural NP-hard problems like the 3-SAT problem require exponential time.

☆ The strong exponential time hypothesis (SETH) asserts that, as k grows large, no algorithm for the k-SAT problem improves significantly over exhaustive search.

☆ If the SETH is true, no algorithm for the sequence alignment problem improves significantly over the Needleman-Wunsch algorithm.

☆ A Levin reduction carries out the minimum-imaginable work: preprocess the input; invoke the assumed subroutine; postprocess the output.

---

[28]The exception? The influence maximization problem, the search version of which is not obviously in $\mathcal{NP}$ (see the solution to Quiz 23.1).

[29]The hopelessly inscrutable term "NP-complete" does a disservice to the fundamental concept that it defines, which deserves widespread appreciation and wonder. Lots of thought went into the name, however, as documented in Donald E. Knuth's article "A Terminological Proposal" (*SIGACT News*, 1974). Knuth's initial suggestions for what would become "NP-complete": "Herculean," "formidable," and "arduous." Write-in suggestions included "hard-boiled" (by Kenneth Steiglitz, as a hat tip to Cook) and "hard-ass" (by Albert R. Meyer, allegedly abbreviating "hard as satisfiability"). Meanwhile, Shen Lin suggested "PET" as a pleasingly flexible acronym, alternatively standing for: "probably exponential time," as long as the P $\neq$ NP conjecture is unresolved; "provably exponential time," if the conjecture is proved; and "previously exponential time," if the conjecture is refuted. (Now is not the time to nitpick and bring up Problem 23.5...)

> ☆ A problem B is NP-complete if it belongs to the class $\mathcal{NP}$ and, for every problem $A \in \mathcal{NP}$, there is a Levin reduction from A to B.
>
> ☆ To prove that a problem B is NP-complete, follow the three-step recipe: (i) prove that $B \in \mathcal{NP}$; (ii) choose an NP-complete problem A; and (iii) design a Levin reduction from A to B.
>
> ☆ The Cook-Levin theorem proves that the 3-SAT problem is NP-complete.

Test Your Understanding

Problem 23.1 *(S)* Which of the following statements could be true, given the current state of knowledge? (Choose all that apply.)

a) There is an NP-hard problem that is polynomial-time solvable.

b) The P $\neq$ NP conjecture is true and also the 3-SAT problem can be solved in $2^{O(\sqrt{n})}$ time, where n is the number of variables.

c) There is no NP-hard problem that can be solved in $2^{O(\sqrt{n})}$ time, where n is the size of the input.

d) Some NP-complete problems are polynomial-time solvable, and some are not polynomial-time solvable.

Problem 23.2 *(S)* Prove that Edmonds's 1967 conjecture that (the optimization version of) the TSP cannot be solved by any polynomial-time algorithm is equivalent to the P $\neq$ NP conjecture.

Problem 23.3 *(S)* Which of the eighteen reductions listed in Section 22.3.2 can be easily turned into Levin reductions between the search versions of the corresponding problems?

Challenge Problems

Problem 23.4 *(H)* This problem formally justifies the recipes on pages 552 and 592 for proving that a problem is NP-hard and NP-complete, respectively.

(a) Prove that if a problem A reduces to a problem B and B reduces to a problem C, then A reduces to C.

(b) Conclude that if an NP-hard problem reduces to a problem B, then B is also NP-hard. (Use the formal definition of NP-hardness on page 582.)

(c) Prove that if there are Levin reductions from a problem A to a problem B and from B to a problem C, then there is a Levin reduction from A to C.

(d) Conclude that if a problem B belongs to $\mathcal{NP}$ and there is a Levin reduction from an NP-complete problem to B, then B is also NP-complete.

Problem 23.5 *(S)* Call an instance of the 3-SAT problem *padded* if its list of constraints concludes with n^2 redundant copies of the single-literal constraint "x_1," where n denotes the number of Boolean variables and x_1 is the first of those variables.

In the *PADDED 3-SAT* problem, the input is the same as in the 3-SAT problem. If the given 3-SAT instance is not padded or is unsatisfiable, the goal is to return "no solution." Otherwise, the goal is to return a satisfying truth assignment for the (padded) instance.

(a) Prove that the PADDED 3-SAT problem is NP-hard (or even NP-complete).

(b) Prove that the PADDED 3-SAT problem can be solved in subexponential time, namely $2^{O(\sqrt{N})}$ time for size-N inputs.

Problem 23.6 *(H)* Assume that the Exponential Time Hypothesis (page 587) is true. Prove that there exists a problem in $\mathcal{NP}$ that is neither polynomial-time solvable nor NP-hard.[30]

Problem 23.7 *(H)* The *diameter* of an undirected graph $G = (V, E)$ is the maximum shortest-path distance between any two vertices: $\max_{v,w \in V} dist(v, w)$, where $dist(v, w)$ denotes the minimum number of edges in a v-w path of G (or $+\infty$, if no such path exists).

(a) Explain how to compute the diameter of a graph in $O(mn)$ time, where n and m denote the number of vertices and edges of G, respectively. (You can assume that n and m are at least 1.)

(b) Assume that the Strong Exponential Time Hypothesis (page 588) is true. Prove that, for every constant $\epsilon > 0$, there is no $O((mn)^{1-\epsilon})$-time algorithm for computing the diameter of a graph.

---

[30] A famous and harder-to-prove result known as Ladner's Theorem shows that the conclusion remains true assuming only the (weaker) P $\neq$ NP conjecture.

Chapter 24

Case Study: The FCC Incentive Auction

NP-hardness is not some purely academic concept—it really does govern the range of computationally feasible options when solving a real-world problem. This chapter details a recent illustration of the importance of NP-hardness, in the context of a high-stakes economic problem: the efficient reallocation of a scarce resource (wireless spectrum). The solution deployed by the U.S. government, known as the FCC Incentive Auction, drew on an amazingly wide swath of the algorithmic toolbox that you've learned in this book. As you read through its details, take the time to appreciate the mastery of algorithms you've acquired since we first struggled through Karatsuba multiplication and the MergeSort algorithm in Chapter 1—how what started as a cacophony of mysterious and unconnected tricks has resolved into a symphony of interlocking algorithm design techniques.[1,2]

24.1 Repurposing Wireless Spectrum

24.1.1 From Television to Mobile Phones

Television spread like wildfire over the United States in the 1950s. In those days, television programming was transmitted solely over the air by radio waves, sent from a station's transmitter and received by a television's antenna. To coordinate stations' transmissions and prevent interference between them, the Federal Communications Commission (FCC) divvied up the usable frequencies—the *spectrum*—into 6-megahertz (MHz) blocks called *channels*. Different stations in the same city would then broadcast on different channels. For example, "channel 14" refers to the frequencies between 470 MHz and 476 MHz; "channel 15" the frequencies between 476 MHz to 482 MHz; and so on.[3]

You know what else travels by radio waves over the air? All the data exchanged by your mobile phone and the nearest base station. For example, if Verizon Wircless is your carrier and you've been using their 4G LTE network, chances are you've been downloading and uploading data using the frequencies 746–756 MHz and 777–787 MHz, respectively. To avoid interference, the part of the spectrum reserved for cellular data does not overlap with that reserved for terrestrial (that is, over-the-air) television.

---

[1]To learn more about the FCC Incentive Auction from its lead designers—Kevin Leyton-Brown, Paul Milgrom, and Ilya Segal—dig into their paper "Economics and Computer Science of a Radio Spectrum Reallocation" (*Proceedings of the National Academy of Sciences*, 2017).

[2]For a deep dive into the connections between auctions and algorithms, check out my book *Twenty Lectures on Algorithmic Game Theory* (Cambridge University Press, 2016).

[3]The ultra high frequency (UHF) channels start at 470 MHz and go up from there in 6 MHz blocks. The very high frequency (VHF) channels use lower frequencies, 174–216 MHz (for channels 7–13) and 54–88 MHz (for channels 2–6, along with 4 MHz for miscellaneous uses like garage door openers).

Mobile and wireless data usage has been exploding throughout the 21st century, increasing by roughly an order of magnitude over the past five years alone. Transmitting more data requires more dedicated frequencies, and not all frequencies are useful for wireless communication. (For example, very high frequencies carry signals only short distances.) Spectrum is a scarce resource, and modern technology is hungry for as much as it can get.

Television may still be big, but terrestrial television is not. Roughly 85-90% of U.S. households rely exclusively on cable television (which requires no over-the-air spectrum at all) or satellite television (which uses much higher frequencies than typical wireless applications). Reserving the most valuable spectrum real estate for over-the-air television made sense in the mid-20th century; no longer in the early 21st.

24.1.2   A Recent Reallocation of Spectrum

A major reallocation of spectrum completed earlier this decade (Figure 24.1). Since the end of 2020, no television stations anywhere in the U.S. have been broadcasting over the air on what had been the highest channels, the fourteen channels between 38 and 51 (614–698 MHz). Every station that had been broadcasting on one of these channels either switched to a lower channel or ceased all terrestrial transmissions (while possibly still broadcasting via cable and satellite television). Even some of the stations that were already broadcasting on channels below 38 went off the air or migrated to different channels, to make room for their comrades dropping down from higher channels. All told, 175 stations relinquished their broadcasting licenses and roughly 1000 switched channels.[4]

The liberated 84 MHz of spectrum was reorganized and awarded to telecommunication companies like T-Mobile, Dish, and Comcast, which are using it to build out a new generation of wireless networks. (T-Mobile, for example, flipped the switch on its new nationwide 5G network in 2020.) Where there had been channels 38–51, there are now seven independent pairs of 5 MHz blocks. For example, the first pair comprises the frequencies 617–622 MHz (meant for downloading to a device) and 663–668 MHz (meant for uploading); the second 622–627 MHz and 668–673 MHz; and so on.[5]

This should all sound like a big, messy operation. For example:

- Which stations should go off the air?

- Which ones should switch channels?

- What should their new channels be?

- How much should station owners be compensated for their losses?

- Which telecoms should be awarded the newly created paired blocks of spectrum?

- What should they pay for them?

---

[4]Since the 2009 switchover from analog to exclusively digital broadcasting of terrestrial television, a logical channel (as displayed on a set-top box) can be remapped to a physical channel different from the one historically associated with that channel number. A station can therefore retain its logical channel even as its physical channel is reassigned.

[5]There's also an 11 MHz duplex gap (652–663 MHz) separating the two types of blocks, and a 3 MHz guard band (614–617 MHz) to avoid interference with channel 37 (608–614 MHz), which has long been reserved for radio astronomy and wireless medical telemetry.

These are all questions answered by the *FCC Incentive Auction*—a complex algorithm that leaned heavily on the toolbox for tackling NP-hard problems described in Part IV of this book.

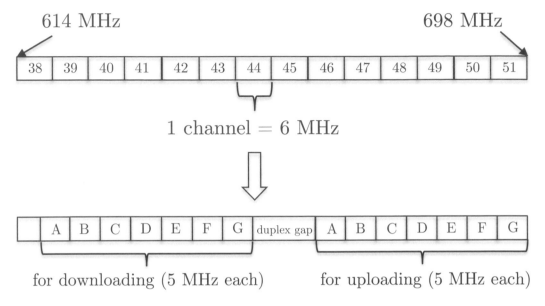

Figure 24.1: A major reorganization of spectrum: What had been the fourteen television channels between 38 and 51 (614–698 MHz) is now seven independent pairs of 5 MHz blocks, to be used by the next generation of wireless networks.

24.2   Greedy Heuristics for Buying Back Licenses

The FCC Incentive Auction had two parts: a *reverse auction* for deciding which television stations would go off the air or switch channels, and the appropriate compensation for them; and a *forward auction* for choosing who receives blocks of the newly freed spectrum, and at what prices. The U.S. government (along with many other countries) has been running forward auctions to sell spectrum licenses with great success for twenty-five years, making small tweaks to them along the way. This case study focuses on the FCC Incentive Auction's unprecedented reverse auction, wherein lay most of its innovation.

24.2.1   Four Temporary Simplifying Assumptions

The FCC confers property rights to a television broadcaster through a *broadcasting license*, which authorizes broadcasting over a channel in a specified geographic region. The FCC assumes responsibility for ensuring that each station suffers little to no interference across its broadcast area.[6]

---

[6]For the purposes of the FCC Incentive Auction, the specific channel assignment of a station was not considered part of the license owner's property rights. An act of Congress was required to authorize this interpretation and allow the auction to reassign stations' channels as needed. (Which was one of only eight bills passed by Congress in 2012, perhaps because of its veto-proof title: the "Middle Class Tax Relief and Job Creation Act.")

The goal of the reverse auction in the FCC Incentive Auction was to reclaim enough licenses from television stations to free up a target amount of spectrum (like channels 38–51). To get an initial feel for this problem, let's make some simplifying assumptions, to be removed as we go along:

Temporary Simplifying Assumptions

1. All stations that remain on the air will broadcast on a single channel (channel 14, say).

2. Two stations can broadcast on the same channel simultaneously if and only if their broadcasting areas do not overlap.

3. There is a known monetary value for each station.

4. The government can unilaterally decide which stations remain on the air.

From an economic perspective, the most valuable stations should be the ones to retain their licenses. The objective, then, would be to identify a set of non-interfering stations with the maximum-possible sum of station values. Do you recognize this optimization problem?

24.2.2   Ambushed by Weighted Independent Set

It's exactly the weighted independent set problem (Section 16.1)! Vertices correspond to stations, edges to pairs of interfering stations, and station values to vertex weights:

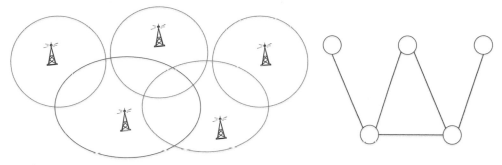

(five stations & their broadcast areas)   (corresponding graph)

We know from Corollary 22.3 that this problem is NP-hard, even when every vertex has weight 1. The problem can be solved in linear time using dynamic programming when the input graph is a tree (see Problem 16.6), but the interference patterns of television stations are not at all tree-like. For example, all stations in the same city interfere with each other, leading to a clique in the corresponding graph.

Searching Through the Algorithmic Toolbox

Now that we have diagnosed the problem as NP-hard, it's time to search for a cure in the appropriate compartment of our algorithmic toolbox. (NP-hardness is not a death sentence!) Most ambitiously, could the problem be solved exactly in a tolerable amount of time—say, under a week?

The answer depends on the size of the problem. If only thirty stations were involved, exhaustive search would work just fine. But the real problem had thousands of participating stations and tens of thousands of interference constraints—well above the pay grade of exhaustive search and the dynamic programming techniques in Sections 21.1–21.2.

The last hope for an exact algorithm would be a semi-reliable magic box for optimization problems like a MIP solver (Section 21.4). The weighted independent set problem is easily encoded as a MIP problem (Problem 21.9), and this was exactly what the FCC tried first. Unfortunately, the problem proved too big, and even the latest and greatest MIP solvers choked on it (or at least, on the more realistic multi-channel version described in Section 24.2.4). With all options exhausted for a 100% correct algorithm, the FCC had no choice but to compromise on correctness and turn to fast heuristic algorithms.

24.2.3   Greedy Heuristic Algorithms

For the weighted independent set problem, as with so many others, greedy algorithms are the perfect place to start brainstorming about fast heuristic algorithms.

The Basic Greedy Algorithm

Perhaps the simplest greedy approach to the weighted independent set problem is to mimic Kruskal's minimum spanning tree algorithm and perform a single pass over the vertices (in decreasing order of weight), adding a vertex to the output unless it destroys feasibility:

WISBasicGreedy

Input: undirected graph $G = (V, E)$ and a nonnegative weight w_v
   for each vertex $v \in V$.
Output: an independent set of G.

$S := \emptyset$
sort vertices of V from highest to lowest weight
`// Main loop`
for each $v \in V$, in nonincreasing order of weight **do**
   if $S \cup \{v\}$ is feasible **then** `// mutually non-adjacent`
      $S := S \cup \{v\}$
return S

For example, in the graph

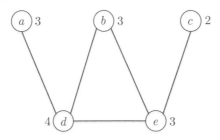

(vertices labeled with their weights)

the `WISBasicGreedy` algorithm selects the vertex d with the largest weight in its first iteration, skips the weight-3 vertices in its second, third, and fourth iterations (because each is adjacent to d), and concludes by selecting vertex c. The resulting independent set has total weight 6 and is not optimal (as the independent set $\{a, b, c\}$ has total weight 8).

Because the weighted independent set problem is NP-hard and the `WISBasicGreedy` algorithm runs in polynomial time, we were fully expecting examples of this type. But here's a more troubling case (with vertices labeled with their weights):

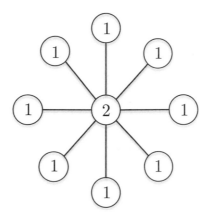

The `WISBasicGreedy` algorithm is tricked into committing to the center of the star, precluding it from taking any of the leaves. How can we discourage pitfalls of this type?

Vertex-Specific Multipliers

To avoid the miscues of the `WISBasicGreedy` algorithm, we can discriminate against vertices with many neighbors. For example, acknowledging that selecting a vertex v accrues benefit w_v while knocking out $1 + \deg(v)$ vertices from consideration (where $\deg(v)$ denotes v's degree), the algorithm's single pass could be in decreasing order of bang-per-buck $w_v/(1 + \deg(v))$ rather than of weight w_v.[7] (This greedy algorithm returns the maximum-weight independent set in our two examples.) More generally, the algorithm can compute vertex-specific multipliers however it likes in a preprocessing step before proceeding to its single pass over vertices:

WISGeneralGreedy

compute β_v for each $v \in V$ // ex: $\beta_v = 1 + \deg(v)$
$S := \emptyset$
sort vertices of V from highest to lowest value of w_v/β_v
for each $v \in V$, in nonincreasing order of w_v/β_v **do**
    if $S \cup \{v\}$ is feasible **then**   // mutually non-adjacent
        $S := S \cup \{v\}$
return S

---

[7]You might recognize this idea from Problem 20.3 and the greedy heuristic algorithm for the knapsack problem that sorts items in decreasing order of value-size ratios.

What's the best choice for the vertex-specific multipliers? No matter how smart the formula for each parameter β_v, there will be examples in which the `WISGeneralGreedy` algorithm returns a suboptimal independent set (assuming that the β_v's can be computed in polynomial time and that the P $\neq$ NP conjecture is true). The best choice depends on the problem instances that tend to show up in the application of interest, and should therefore be determined empirically using representative instances.[8]

Station-Specific Parameters in the FCC Incentive Auction

Representative instances of the weighted independent set problem, and the more general multi-channel problem described in the next section, were easy to come by in the design phase of the reverse auction. The graph—derived from the participating stations and their broadcast areas—was fully known in advance. Educated guesses could be made about the range of likely vertex weights (station values) based on historical data. With a carefully tuned choice of vertex-specific multipliers, the `WISGeneralGreedy` algorithm (and the multi-channel generalization `FCCGreedy` described in the next section) routinely returned solutions to representative instances with total weight exceeding 90% of the maximum possible.[9,10]

24.2.4   The Multi-Channel Case

Time to discard the first simplifying assumption in Section 24.2.1 and allow still-on-air stations to be assigned any one of k channels. The `WISGeneralGreedy` algorithm would seem to extend easily to the multi-channel version of the problem:[11]

FCCGreedy

compute β_v for each station v
$S := \emptyset$
sort stations from highest to lowest value of w_v/β_v
for each station v, in nonincreasing order of w_v/β_v **do**
    if $S \cup \{v\}$ is feasible **then**   `// fit on k channels`
        $S := S \cup \{v\}$
return S

---

[8]General advice for tackling NP-hard problems in a real application: Exploit as much domain-specific knowledge as you can!

[9]How were the parameters computed in the actual FCC Incentive Auction? Via the formula $\beta_v = \sqrt{\deg(v)} \cdot \sqrt{\text{pop}(v)}$, where $\deg(v)$ and $\text{pop}(v)$ denote the number of stations overlapping with and the population served by the station v, respectively. The $\sqrt{\deg(v)}$ term discriminated against stations that would block lots of other stations from remaining on the air. The point of the $\sqrt{\text{pop}(v)}$ term was more subtle (and controversial); its effect was to decrease the compensation paid by the government to small television stations that were likely to go off the air anyway. (See Section 24.4.4 for details on how the payments were determined.)

[10]The FCC was also able to obtain high-quality solutions in a reasonable amount of time by stopping a state-of-the-art MIP solver early, prior to finding an optimal solution (see page 540). The greedy approach ultimately won out on account of its easy translation to a transparent auction format (as detailed in Section 24.4).

[11]Think of k as 23, corresponding to channels 14–36. The FCC Incentive Auction also allowed UHF stations to drop down to the VHF band (channels 2–13), but most of the action took place in the UHF band.

Looks like all our other (polynomial-time) greedy algorithms, right? But let's drill down on an iteration of the main loop, which is responsible for testing whether the current station v can be added to the solution-so-far S without destroying feasibility. What makes a subset of stations "feasible"? Feasibility means that the stations can all be on the air at the same time, without interference. That is, there should be an assignment of the stations in $S \cup \{v\}$ to the k available channels so that no two stations with overlapping broadcast areas are assigned the same channel. Do you recognize this computational problem?

24.2.5   Ambushed by Graph Coloring

It's exactly the graph coloring problem (page 541)! Vertices correspond to stations, edges to pairs of stations with overlapping broadcast areas, and colors to the available channels.

As we know from Problem 22.11, the graph coloring problem is NP-hard even when $k = 3$.[12] Worse, the FCCGreedy algorithm must solve *many* instances of the graph coloring problem, one in each iteration of its main loop. How are these instances related?

Quiz 24.1

Consider the sequence of feasibility-checking instances that arises in the FCCGreedy algorithm. Which of the following statements are true? (Choose all that apply.)

a) If the instance in one iteration is feasible, so is the instance in the next iteration.

b) If the instance in one iteration is infeasible, so is the instance in the next iteration.

c) The instance in a given iteration has one more station than the instance in the previous iteration.

d) The instance in a given iteration has one more station than the most recent feasible instance.

(See Section 24.2.6 for the solution and discussion.)

Now what? Does diagnosing our feasibility-checking problem as the NP-hard graph coloring problem rule out using a greedy heuristic algorithm to approximately maximize the total value of the stations that remain on the air?

24.2.6   Solution to Quiz 24.1

Correct answer: (d). Answer (a) is obviously incorrect: The first instance is always feasible, while some of the instances toward the end of the algorithm may not be. Answer (b) is also incorrect; for example, the solution-so-far might block all newcomers in the northeastern

---

[12]Checking feasibility in the special case of a single channel (Section 24.2.2) corresponds to the trivial problem of checking 1-colorability or, equivalently, checking whether a set of vertices constitutes an independent set.

region of the U.S. while leaving its west coast wide open. Answer (c) is incorrect and (d) is correct, as the solution-so-far S changes only in an iteration in which the station set $S \cup \{v\}$ is feasible. For example, phrased in terms of graph coloring:

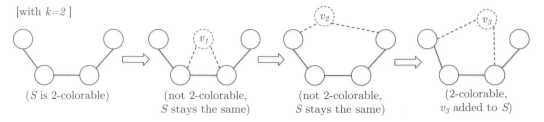

24.3 Feasibility Checking

If only we had a magic box for checking feasibility, we could run the `FCCGreedy` algorithm and, hopefully, after carefully tuning the station-specific multipliers, reliably compute feasible solutions with total value close to the maximum possible. Our dreams of magic boxes have already been thwarted once, with the original value-maximization problem proving too tough for the latest and greatest MIP solvers (Section 24.2.2). Why should we expect any more success this time around?

24.3.1 Encoding as a Satisfiability Problem

The subroutine required by the `FCCGreedy` algorithm is responsible only for feasibility checking (corresponding to checking whether a given subgraph is k-colorable), not optimization (corresponding to finding the maximum-value k-colorable subgraph of a given graph). This raises the hope for a magic box that solves the easier (if still NP-hard) feasibility-checking problem, even if none exist for the optimization problem. The pivot from optimization to feasibility checking also suggests experimenting with a different language and technology—logic and SAT solvers, rather than arithmetic and MIP solvers.

The formulation of the graph coloring problem as a satisfiability problem in Section 21.5.3 is immediately relevant here. To review, for each vertex v in the input graph and allowable color $i \in \{1, 2, \ldots, k\}$, there is a Boolean (true/false) variable x_{vi}. For each edge (u, v) of the input graph and color i, there is a constraint

$$\neg x_{ui} \vee \neg x_{vi} \tag{24.1}$$

that rules out assigning the color i to both u and v. For each vertex v of the input graph, there is a constraint

$$x_{v1} \vee x_{v2} \vee \cdots \vee x_{vk} \tag{24.2}$$

that rules out leaving v colorless.

Optionally, for each vertex v and distinct colors $i, j \in \{1, 2, \ldots, k\}$, the constraint

$$\neg x_{vi} \vee \neg x_{vj} \tag{24.3}$$

can be used to rule out assigning both color i and color j to v.[13]

---

[13] Vertices can receive multiple colors if these constraints are omitted, but every way of choosing among the assigned colors results in a k-coloring.

24.3.2   Incorporating Side Constraints

The actual FCC Incentive Auction used a formulation slightly more complicated than (24.1)–(24.3). Stations with overlapping broadcast areas interfere when assigned the same channel and, depending on several factors, may also interfere when assigned adjacent channels (like 14 and 15). A separate team at the FCC determined in advance, for each pair of stations, exactly which pairs of channel assignments would create interference. This list of forbidden pairwise channel assignments, while difficult to compile, was straightforward to incorporate into the satisfiability formulation, with one constraint of the form

$$\neg x_{uc} \lor \neg x_{vc'} \tag{24.4}$$

for each pair u, v of stations and forbidden channel assignments c, c' to them. For example, the constraint $\neg x_{u14} \lor \neg x_{v15}$ would prevent the stations u and v from being assigned channels 14 and 15, respectively. This list of interference constraints replaces the second of the simplifying assumptions in Section 24.2.1.

Another wrinkle was that not all stations were eligible for all channel assignments. For example, stations that bordered Mexico could not be assigned to a channel that would interfere with an existing station on the Mexican side of the border. To reflect these additional constraints, the decision variable x_{vi} was omitted whenever the station v was forbidden from channel i.

These tweaks to the original SAT formulation (24.1)–(24.3) illustrate a general strength of MIP and SAT solvers, relative to problem-specific algorithm design: They are often better at accommodating all kinds of idiosyncratic side constraints with minimal modifications to the basic formulation.

24.3.3   The Repacking Problem

The feasibility-checking problem in the reverse auction of the FCC Incentive Auction was almost but not quite a graph coloring problem (because of the side constraints in Section 24.3.2), so let's give it a new name: the *repacking problem*.

Problem: The Repacking Problem

Known in advance: A list V of television stations, the allowable channels C_v for each station $v \in V$, and the allowable channel pairs P_{uv} for each station pair $u, v \in V$.

Input: A subset $S \subseteq V$ of television stations.

Output: An assignment of each station $v \in S$ to a channel in C_v such that each station pair $u, v \in S$ is assigned a channel pair in P_{uv}. (Or, correctly declare that no such assignment exists.)

Call a subset of stations *packable* if the corresponding repacking instance has a feasible solution, and *unpackable* otherwise.

The FCC's algorithmic aspirations were ambitious: to solve the repacking problem reliably in a minute or less! (We'll see in Section 24.4 why the time budget was so small.)

Repacking instances in the FCC Incentive Auction had thousands of stations, tens of thousands of pairs of overlapping stations, and dozens of available channels. After the translation to satisfiability (as in Sections 24.3.1–24.3.2), the resulting instances had tens of thousands of decision variables and more than one million constraints.

That's pretty big! Still, why not throw the latest and greatest SAT solvers at them and see how they do? Unfortunately, when applied off the shelf, these solvers frequently needed ten minutes or more to solve representative repacking instances. Doing better required throwing the kitchen sink at the problem.

24.3.4   Trick #1: Presolvers (Look for an Easy Way Out)

The FCC Incentive Auction used *presolvers* to quickly ferret out instances that were obviously packable or unpackable. These presolvers exploited the nested structure of the repacking instances in the FCCGreedy algorithm (see Quiz 24.1), with each instance taking the form $S \cup \{v\}$ for a packable set of stations S and a new station v.

For example, the auction administered two quick and dirty local tests that examined only the (relatively small) neighborhood of v. Formally, call two stations *neighbors* if they appear jointly in at least one interference constraint (24.4), and let $N \subseteq S$ denote the neighbors of v in S.

1. Check if $N \cup \{v\}$ is packable; if not, halt and report "unpackable." (Correctness: Supersets of unpackable sets of stations are themselves unpackable.)

The analog in a graph coloring instance would be to check if a given vertex v and its neighbors form a k-colorable subgraph. For example (with $k = 2$):

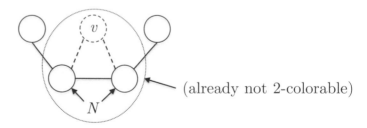

(already not 2-colorable)

2. Inherit the previously computed feasible channel assignments for the (packable) stations S. Hold the assignments of all stations in $S - N$ fixed. Check if there are channel assignments to the stations in $N \cup \{v\}$ so that the combined assignments are feasible. If so, report "packable" and return the combined channel assignments.

Whether this step succeeds generally depends on the inherited channel assignments for the stations in $S - N$. For example (with $k = 3$):

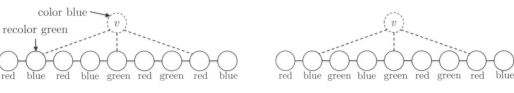

(local recoloring to obtain a 3-coloring)   (no local recoloring works)

The size of the neighborhood N was typically in the single or double digits, so each of these steps could be carried out quickly using a SAT solver. Ambiguity remained for the repacking instances that passed through both steps. Such an instance could have been packable, due to a feasible channel assignment deviating from the restricted form considered in step 2. Or it could have been unpackable, with no packing of $N \cup \{v\}$ in step 1 extendable to one of all of $S \cup \{v\}$.

24.3.5   Trick #2: Preprocess and Simplify

Every repacking instance that survived the presolvers was subjected to a preprocessing step designed to reduce its size.[14]

Removing Easy Stations

Call a station u of $S \cup \{v\}$ *easy* if, no matter what the other stations' channel assignments are, u can be assigned a channel of C_u that avoids interference with all of its neighbors. (The analog in a graph coloring instance would be a vertex whose degree is smaller than the number k of colors.)

3. Iteratively remove easy stations: (i) initialize $X := S \cup \{v\}$; (ii) while X contains an easy station u, $X := X - \{u\}$.

For example, in a graph coloring context (with $k = 3$):

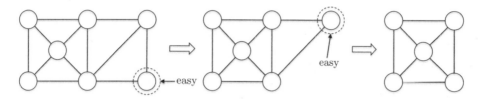

Quiz 24.2

Iteratively removing easy stations from a set $S \cup \{v\}$...

a) ...could change the set's status from packable to unpackable, or vice versa.

b) ...could change the set's status from packable to unpackable, but not from unpackable to packable.

c) ...could change the set's status from unpackable to packable, but not from packable to unpackable.

d) ...cannot change the set's packability status.

(See Section 24.3.8 for the solution and discussion.)

---

[14]This idea is similar in spirit to the for-free primitives emphasized throughout this book (see page 23). If you have a blazingly fast primitive (like sorting, computing connected components, etc.) that might simplify your problem, why not use it?

Decomposing the Problem

The next step sought to decompose the problem into smaller independent subproblems. (The analog in a graph coloring instance would be to compute a k-coloring separately for each connected component.)

4. Given a set of (non-easy) stations:

   a) Form a graph H with vertices corresponding to stations and edges to neighboring stations.

   b) Compute the connected components of H.

   c) For each connected component, solve the corresponding repacking problem.

   d) If at least one subproblem is unpackable, report "unpackable." Otherwise, report "packable" and return the union of the channel assignments computed in the subproblems.

Because stations interfere only with neighboring stations, the different subproblems do not interact in any way. The stations in X are therefore packable if and only if all the independent subproblems are packable.

Why did decomposing the problem help? The FCC Incentive Auction remained on the hook for solving all the subproblems, whose combined size was the same as that of the original problem. But whenever you have an algorithm that runs in super-linear time (as one would expect from a SAT solver), it's faster to solve an instance in pieces than all at once.[15]

24.3.6   Trick #3: A Portfolio of SAT Solvers

The toughest repacking instances survived the gauntlet of presolvers and preprocessing and awaited more sophisticated tools. While every state-of-the-art SAT solver had success on some representative instances, none met the FCC mandate of reliably solving instances in a minute or less. What next?

The designers of the reverse auction in the FCC Incentive Auction took advantage of two things: (i) the empirical observation that different SAT solvers struggle on different instances; and (ii) modern computer processors. Rather than putting all its eggs in one basket with a single SAT solver, the auction used a portfolio of *eight* carefully tuned solvers, running in parallel on an 8-core workstation.[16,17] This, finally, was sufficient algorithmic firepower to solve over 99% of the repacking instances faced by the auction within the target of one minute each. Pretty impressive for satisfiability instances with tens of thousands of variables and more than one million constraints!

---

[15]For example, consider a quadratic-time algorithm, running in time cn^2 on size-n instances for some constant $c > 0$. Solving two size-$(n/2)$ instances then takes $2 \cdot c(n/2)^2 = cn^2/2$ time, a factor-2 speedup over solving a single size-n instance.

[16]And how were these eight solvers chosen? With a greedy heuristic algorithm analogous to those for the maximum coverage (Section 20.2) and influence maximization (Section 20.3) problems! The solvers were chosen sequentially, with each new solver maximizing the marginal running time improvement on representative instances, relative to the solvers already in the portfolio.

[17]For fans of local search (Sections 20.4–20.5) distraught over its apparent absence from this case study: Several SAT solvers in this portfolio were local search algorithms—think greedier and highly parameterized versions of the randomized SAT algorithm described in Problem 21.12.

24.3.7   Tolerating Failures

Over 99% sounds pretty good, but what happened the remaining 1% of the time? Did the FCC Incentive Auction spin its wheels helplessly while eight SAT solvers fumbled around, desperate for a satisfying assignment?

   Another feature of the FCCGreedy algorithm is its tolerance of failures by its feasibility-checking subroutine. Suppose, when checking the feasibility of a set $S \cup \{v\}$, the subroutine times out and reports "I don't know." Without an assurance of feasibility (which is an ironclad constraint), the algorithm cannot risk adding v to its solution and must skip it, potentially foregoing some of the value it could have otherwise obtained. But the algorithm always finishes in a predictable amount of time with a feasible solution, and the loss in value from timeouts should be modest provided they are infrequent, as they were in the FCC Incentive Auction.

24.3.8   Solution to Quiz 24.2

Correct answer: (d). If the final set X is unpackable, so is the superset $S \cup \{v\}$. If X is packable, every feasible channel assignment to the stations of X can be extended to all of $S \cup \{v\}$, one easy station at a time (in reverse order of removal):

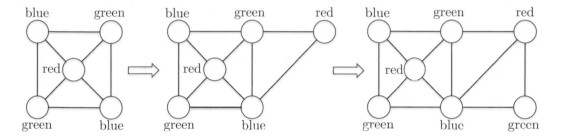

24.4   Implementation as a Descending Clock Auction

Where's the "auction" in the FCC Incentive Auction? Doesn't the FCCGreedy algorithm in Section 24.2, along with the repacking subroutine in Section 24.3, already solve the value-maximization problem to near-optimality? With at most a few thousand feasibility checks (one per participating station) and one minute spent per feasibility check, the algorithm would finish in a matter of days. Time to declare victory?

   No. Time instead to revisit and remove the last two simplifying assumptions in Section 24.2.1. Stations were not forcibly removed from the air; they relinquished their licenses voluntarily (in exchange for compensation). So why not run the FCCGreedy algorithm to figure out which stations should stay on the air and buy out the other stations at whatever price they'd be willing to accept? Because the value of a station, defined here as the minimum compensation its owner would accept for going off the air, was not known in advance. (You could ask the owner, but they would probably overstate their value in the hopes of receiving extra compensation.) How could the FCCGreedy algorithm possibly be implemented without advance knowledge of stations' values?

24.4.1   Auctions and Algorithms

Think back to auctions that you've seen in the movies or in real life—perhaps at an estate sale, an auction house, or a school fundraiser. An auctioneer asks questions of the form "who's willing to buy this tennis ball signed by Roger Federer for one hundred bucks?" and the willing buyers raise their hands. In the reverse auction of the FCC Incentive Auction, the "auctioneer" (the government) was buying rather than selling, so the questions had the form "who's willing to sell their broadcasting license for one million dollars"? A station's response to this question with offered compensation p revealed whether its value—the minimum acceptable compensation—was above or below p.

The `FCCGreedy` algorithm begins by sorting stations in nonincreasing order of w_v/β_v, where w_v is the value of station v and β_v is a station-specific parameter—an apparent nonstarter when station values are unknown.[18] Can we reimplement the algorithm so that the stations effectively sort themselves, using only auction-friendly operations of the form "is $w_v \le p$"?

24.4.2   Example

To see how this might work, assume for now that stations' values are positive integers between 1 and a known upper bound W. Assume also that there is only one free channel ($k = 1$) and that $\beta_v = 1$ for every station v. For example, suppose there are five stations and $W = 5$:

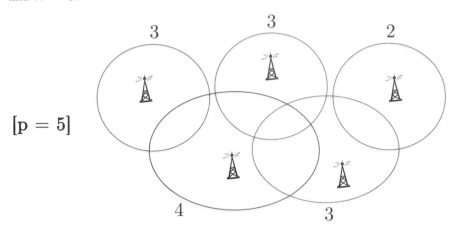

(stations labeled with their values)

The idea is to start with the highest-imaginable compensation ($p = W$) and work downward. The set S of stations to remain on the air is initially empty. In the algorithm's first iteration, each station's value is compared to the initial value of p (that is, to 5); equivalently, each broadcaster is asked if they would accept a compensation of 5 in exchange for their license. All participants accept, and the algorithm decrements p and proceeds to the next iteration. All participants again accept the reduced compensation offer (with $p = 4$). The station with value 4 refuses the offer at $p = 3$ in the next iteration, and the algorithm responds by adding it to the on-air station set S:

---

[18]In the FCC Incentive Auction, the station-specific parameters β_v *were* known in advance, as they depended only on the population served by and interference constraints of a station (see footnote 9).

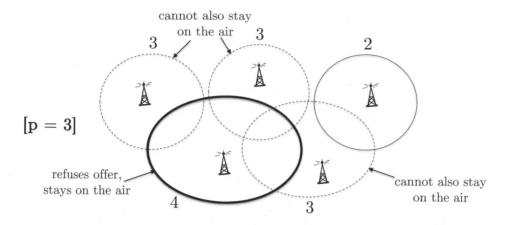

[p = 3]

cannot also stay
on the air

3   3   2

refuses offer,
stays on the air

cannot also stay
on the air

4

3

With the value-4 station now back on the air and only one channel available, the three overlapping stations are blocked and must stay off the air. In subsequent iterations, the algorithm makes decreasing offers of compensation to the only station whose fate remains unresolved, the value-2 station. That station refuses the offer at $p = 1$, at which point it is added to S and the algorithm halts:

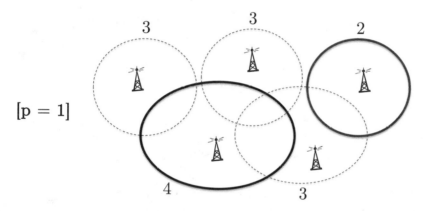

[p = 1]

3   3   2

4   3

In this example and in general, this iterative process recreates the trajectory of the `WISBasicGreedy` algorithm on the corresponding weighted independent set instance (Section 24.2.3): Stations drop out (and go back on the air) in nonincreasing order of value, subject to feasibility. Can we extend this idea to capture the full-fledged `FCCGreedy` algorithm?

24.4.3   Reimplementing the `FCCGreedy` Algorithm

The station-specific parameters β_v in the `FCCGreedy` algorithm can be emulated using station-specific offers, with compensation $\beta_v \cdot p$ offered to station v in an iteration with "base price" p. A station v with value w_v will then drop out when the base price p drops below w_v/β_v. As p gradually decreases, the resulting process faithfully simulates the `FCCGreedy` algorithm: Stations drop out (and go back on the air) in nonincreasing order of w_v/β_v, subject to feasibility. The resulting algorithm is called a *descending clock auction*, and it is the exact one used in the FCC Incentive Auction's reverse auction (with $\epsilon = 0.05$ and the β_v's defined as in footnote 9):

FCCDescendingClock

Input: set V of stations, parameter $\beta_v > 0$ for each $v \in V$,
  parameter $\epsilon \in (0, 1)$.
Output: a repackable subset $S \subseteq V$.

$p := $ LARGE NUMBER   // maximize participation
$S := \emptyset$ // stations staying on the air
$X := \emptyset$ // stations going off the air
while $S \cup X \neq V$ **do**   // still stations in limbo
    for each station $v \notin S \cup X$, in arbitrary order **do**
        // invoke feasibility checker (§24.3)
        if $S \cup \{v\}$ packable **then**   // still room for v
            offer compensation $\beta_v \cdot p$ to v
            if offer refused **then**   // because $p < w_v/\beta_v$
                $S := S \cup \{v\}$ // v goes back on air
        else   // no room for v (or timeout)
            $X := X \cup \{v\}$ // v must stay off air
    $p := (1 - \epsilon) \cdot p$ // lower offers in next round
return S

The outer loop of the FCCDescendingClock algorithm controls the value p of the "clock." This base price decreases by a small amount in each iteration (called a *round*), until all stations' fates have been sealed. Within a round, the inner loop performs a single pass over the remaining stations in an arbitrary order, with the intention of making a new, lower offer of compensation to each. But before making a lower offer to a station v, the algorithm calls on the feasibility checker from Section 24.3 to ensure that v could be accommodated on the air should it decline the offer.[19] If the feasibility checker finds that $S \cup \{v\}$ is unpackable, or if it times out, the algorithm cannot risk a refusal by v and commits to keeping v off the air. If the feasibility checker comes back with a feasible packing of the stations in $S \cup \{v\}$, the algorithm can proceed safely with the lower offer to v. The algorithm returns the final set S of stations to remain on the air, along with the channel assignments computed for them by the feasibility checker.

24.4.4   Time to Get Paid

The FCCDescendingClock algorithm determines the stations remaining on the air and their new channel assignments. It has one more responsibility: to compute the prices paid to the departing broadcasters in exchange for their licenses.[20]

---

[19]The original FCCGreedy algorithm in Section 24.2.4 invokes the feasibility checker only once per participating station. The reimplemented version, the FCCDescendingClock algorithm, requires a new batch of feasibility checks *in every round*. The FCC Incentive Auction's reverse auction ran for dozens of rounds, requiring roughly one hundred thousand feasibility checks in all. This is why the FCC granted only one minute per feasibility check. (And even with one-minute timeouts, the auction took many months to complete.)

[20]Technically, each station that remained on the air but was forced to switch channels also received a modest sum of money—far less than the typical selling price of a license—to cover the switching costs.

First, what's the initial base price p? In the FCC Incentive Auction, this value was chosen so that the opening offers would be absurdly lucrative and entice many stations to participate (participation was voluntary). For example, the opening offer to WCBS, the CBS affiliate in New York City, was 900 million dollars![21] Every broadcaster that entered the auction was contractually obligated to sell its license at the opening offer should the government request it, and similarly for every subsequent (lower) offer accepted during the auction. The government, naturally, paid the lowest agreed-upon price:

Compensation in the FCC Incentive Auction

Each broadcaster going off the air was paid the most recent (and hence lowest) offer that it accepted in the auction.

For all its complexity under the hood, the FCC Incentive Auction's reverse auction was extremely simple for the participating broadcasters. The opening offer for a license was known in advance, and each subsequent offer was automatically 95% of the previous one. As long as the current offer exceeded a broadcaster's value for its license, the obvious move was to accept it (as the broadcaster reserved the right to reject lower offers made later). Once the current offer dropped below the license's value, the obvious response was to reject the offer and go back on the air (as any subsequent offers would be even worse).

The efficacy of the feasibility checker (Section 24.3) had a first-order effect on the government's costs. No harm, no foul when the subroutine timed out with an unpackable set of stations—the `FCCDescendingClock` algorithm proceeded as it would have anyway. But whenever the feasibility checker timed out on a packable set of stations $S \cup \{v\}$, a pile of money—often in the millions of dollars—was left on the table.[22] The auction could have made a lower offer to the station v, but for the failure of its feasibility checker. You can see why the auction's designers wanted to get the subroutine's success rate up to as close to 100% as possible![23]

24.5 The Final Outcome

The FCC Incentive Auction ran for roughly a year, from March 2016 to March 2017. Nearly three thousand television stations were involved, 175 of which elected to go off the air in exchange for a total compensation of roughly ten billion dollars (an average of around fifty million dollars per license, with high variance across different regions of the country).[24] Roughly one thousand stations had their channels reassigned.

Meanwhile, the 84 MHz of freed spectrum was reorganized into seven pairs of 5 MHz blocks (one block for uploading, one for downloading). Each of the licenses for sale in the FCC Incentive Auction's forward auction corresponded to one of these seven pairs and one of 416 regions in the U.S. (called "partial economic areas"). The revenue from this forward

---

[21] And remember that selling a license only meant giving up on terrestrial broadcasting—small potatoes compared to cable and satellite television.

[22] Around 50% of the timeouts occurred with a packable set of stations.

[23] Has there ever been a more direct relationship between an algorithm's running time and huge sums of money?

[24] You can check out the full list of results at `https://auctiondata.fcc.gov/`.

auction? Twenty billion dollars![25] Most of the resulting profit was used to reduce the U.S. deficit.[26]

The FCC Incentive Auction was a smashing success, and it never would have happened without a cutting-edge algorithmic toolbox for tackling NP-hard problems—the very same toolbox that you can now, after persevering to the end of this book, claim as your own.

The Upshot

☆ The FCC Incentive Auction was a complex algorithm that procured 84 MHz of wireless spectrum used for terrestrial television and repurposed it for next-generation wireless networks.

☆ Its reverse auction decided which television stations would go off the air or switch channels, along with their compensation.

☆ Even with only one available channel, determining the most valuable non-interfering stations to keep on the air boils down to the (NP-hard) weighted independent set problem.

☆ With multiple available channels, merely checking whether a set of stations can all remain on the air without interference boils down to the (NP-hard) graph coloring problem.

☆ On representative instances, a carefully tuned greedy heuristic algorithm reliably returned solutions with near-optimal total value.

☆ Each iteration of this greedy algorithm invoked a feasibility-checking subroutine to check if there was room on the airwaves for the current station.

☆ A descending clock auction was used to implement this algorithm, with offers of compensation falling and stations dropping out over time.

---

[25]Good thing the forward auction revenue exceeded the reverse auction procurement costs—did the government just get lucky? This relates to another question: Who decided that 84 MHz was the perfect amount of spectrum to clear?

The actual FCC Incentive Auction had an additional outer loop, which searched downward for the ideal number of channels to clear (one of the reasons why the auction took so long). In its first iteration (called a "stage"), the auction ambitiously attempted to free up twenty-one channels (126 MHz), sufficient to create ten paired licenses per region for sale in the forward auction. (The twenty-one channels were 30–36 and 38–51; as noted in footnote 5, channel 37 was off limits.) This stage failed badly, with procurement costs roughly eighty-six billion dollars and forward auction revenue only around twenty-three billion dollars. The auction proceeded to a second stage with the reduced clearing target of nineteen channels (114 MHz, enough for nine paired licenses per region), resuming the reverse and forward auctions where they left off in the first stage. The auction eventually halted after the fourth stage (clearing fourteen channels, as described in this chapter)—the first one in which its revenue covered its costs.

[26]Deficit reduction was the plan all along—probably one of the main reasons the bill managed to pass Congress (see footnote 6).

☆ Using presolvers, preprocessing, and a portfolio of eight state-of-the-art SAT solvers, over 99% of the feasibility-checking instances in the FCC Incentive Auction were solved in under a minute.

☆ The FCC Incentive Auction ran for a year, removed 175 stations from the airwaves, and cleared almost ten billion U.S. dollars in profit.

Test Your Understanding

Problem 24.1 *(S)* Which of the algorithmic tools described in Chapters 20 and 21 played no role in the FCC Incentive Auction?

a) Greedy heuristic algorithms

b) Local search

c) Dynamic programming

d) MIP and SAT solvers

Problem 24.2 *(S)* In each round of the `FCCDescendingClock` algorithm in Section 24.4.3, the stations still in limbo are processed in an arbitrary order. Is the set S of stations returned by the algorithm independent of the order used in each round? (Choose whichever statements are true.)

a) Yes, provided no two station values w_v are the same and all parameters β_v are set to 1.

b) Yes, provided all parameters β_v are set to 1 and ϵ is sufficiently small.

c) Yes, provided no two station values w_v are the same, all parameters β_v are set to 1, and ϵ is sufficiently small.

d) Yes, provided no two ratios w_v/β_v are the same and ϵ is sufficiently small.

Problem 24.3 *(S)* Before making a lower offer to a station v, the `FCCDescendingClock` algorithm checks if $S \cup \{v\}$ is a packable set of stations, where S denotes the already-on-air stations. Suppose we reversed the order of these two steps:

```
offer compensation β_v · p to v
if offer refused then                  // because p < w_v/β_v
    if S ∪ {v} packable then               // room for v
        S := S ∪ {v}          // v goes back on the air
    else                               // no room for v
        X := X ∪ {v}      // v must stay off the air
```

Suppose we offer compensation to the departing broadcasters as on page 613, with each paid according to the last offer they accepted (the penultimate offer they were given). Is it still true that a broadcaster should accept every offer above its value and reject the first offer below its value?

Challenge Problems

Problem 24.4 *(H)* This problem investigates the solution quality achieved by the `WISBasicGreedy` and `WISGeneralGreedy` heuristic algorithms in Section 24.2.3 for the special case of the weighted independent set problem in graphs in which the degree $\deg(v)$ of every vertex v is at most Δ (where Δ is a nonnegative integer, such as 3 or 4).

(a) Prove that the independent set returned by the `WISBasicGreedy` algorithm always has total weight at least $1/(\Delta + 1)$ times the total weight of all the vertices in the input graph.

(b) Prove that the same guarantee holds for the `WISGeneralGreedy` algorithm with β_v set to $1 + \deg(v)$ for each vertex $v \in V$.

(c) Show by examples that, for every nonnegative integer Δ, the statements in (a) and (b) become false if $1/(\Delta + 1)$ is replaced by any larger number.

Programming Problems

Problem 24.5 Try out one or more SAT solvers on a collection of graph coloring instances, using the formulation (24.1)–(24.3). (Experiment both with and without the constraints in (24.3).) For example, you could investigate random graphs, where each edge is present independently with some probability $p \in (0, 1)$. Or, even better, derive a graph from the actual interference constraints used in the FCC Incentive Auction.[27] How large an input size can the solver reliably process in under a minute, or under an hour? How much does the answer vary with the solver?

---

[27]Available at `https://data.fcc.gov/download/incentive-auctions/Constraint_Files/`.

Appendix A

Quick Review of Proofs By Induction

Proofs by induction come up *all the time* in computer science. To cite just two examples from Part I, in Section 5.1 we use a proof by induction to argue that the QuickSort algorithm always correctly sorts its input array, and in Section 6.4 we use induction to prove that the DSelect algorithm runs in linear time.

Proofs by induction can be unintuitive, at least at first sight. The good news is that they follow a fairly rigid template, and become nearly automatic with a little practice. This appendix explains the template and provides two short examples. If you've never seen proofs by induction before, you should supplement this appendix with another source that has many more examples.[1]

A.1 A Template for Proofs by Induction

Whether you know it or not, you're probably already familiar with proofs by induction. For example, if you understand recursion, then you effectively understand induction. Or, have you ever concluded an argument with the phrase "and so on" to assert a pattern that repeats indefinitely? Fundamentally, induction is simply a translation of this rhetorical device into mathematics.

For our purposes, a proof by induction establishes an assertion $P(n)$ for every positive integer n. For example, when proving the correctness of the QuickSort algorithm in Section 5.1, we can define, for each $n \geq 1$, the assertion $P(n)$ as:

"QuickSort correctly sorts every length-n input array."

When analyzing the running time of the DSelect algorithm in Section 6.4, we can define, for each $n \geq 1$, the assertion $P(n)$ as:

"for every length-n input array, DSelect halts after performing at most $100n$ operations."

Induction allows us to prove a property of an algorithm, like correctness or a running time bound, by establishing the property for each input length in turn.

Analogous to a recursive algorithm, a proof by induction has two parts: a *base case* and an *inductive step*. The base case proves that $P(n)$ is true for all sufficiently small values of n—most commonly, simply for $n = 1$. In the inductive step, for every larger value of n, you assume that $P(1), P(2), \ldots, P(n-1)$ are all true and prove that $P(n)$ is consequently true as well.

---

[1]For instance, see the freely available book *Mathematics for Computer Science*, by Eric Lehman, F. Thomson Leighton, and Albert R. Meyer.

Base case: Prove directly that $P(1)$ is true.

Inductive step: Prove that, for every integer $n \geq 2$,

$$\text{if } \underbrace{P(1), P(2), \ldots, P(n-1) \text{ are true}}_{\textit{inductive hypothesis}} \text{ then } P(n) \text{ is true.}$$

In the inductive step, you get to *assume* that $P(k)$ has already been established for all values of k smaller than n—this is called the *inductive hypothesis*—and use this assumption to establish $P(n)$.

If you prove both the base case and the inductive step, then $P(n)$ is indeed true for every positive integer $n \geq 1$: $P(1)$ is true by the base case and, like falling dominoes, applying the inductive step over and over again shows that $P(n)$ is true for arbitrarily large values of n.

A.2   Example: A Closed-Form Formula

We can use induction to derive a closed-form formula for the sum of the first n positive integers. Let $P(n)$ denote the assertion that

$$1 + 2 + 3 + \cdots + n = \frac{(n+1)n}{2}.$$

When $n = 1$, the left-hand side is 1 and the right-hand side is $\frac{2 \cdot 1}{2} = 1$. This shows that $P(1)$ is true and completes the base case. For the inductive step, we pick an arbitrary integer $n \geq 2$ and assume that $P(1), P(2), \ldots, P(n-1)$ are all true. In particular, we can assume $P(n-1)$, which is the assertion

$$1 + 2 + 3 + \cdots + (n-1) = \frac{n(n-1)}{2}.$$

Now we can add n to both sides to derive

$$1 + 2 + 3 + \cdots + n = \frac{n(n-1)}{2} + n = \frac{n^2 - n + 2n}{2} = \frac{(n+1)n}{2},$$

which proves $P(n)$. Because we've established both the base case and the inductive step, we can conclude that $P(n)$ is true for every positive integer n.

A.3   Example: The Size of a Complete Binary Tree

Next, let's count the number of nodes in a complete binary tree with n levels. In Figure A.1, we see that with $n = 4$ levels, the number of nodes is $15 = 2^4 - 1$. Could this pattern be true in general?

For each positive integer n, let $P(n)$ be the statement:

"a complete binary tree with n levels has $2^n - 1$ nodes."

For the base case, note that a complete binary tree with 1 level has exactly one node. Because $2^1 - 1 = 1$, this proves that $P(1)$ is true. For the inductive step, fix a positive integer $n \geq 2$ and assume that $P(1), P(2), \ldots, P(n-1)$ are all true. The nodes of the complete binary

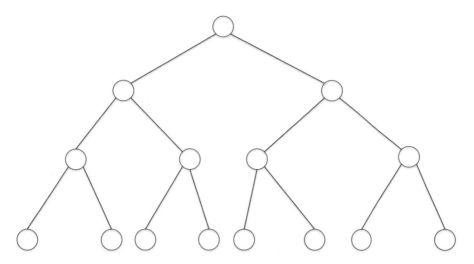

Figure A.1: A complete binary tree with 4 levels and $2^4 - 1 = 15$ nodes.

tree with n levels can be divided into three groups: (i) the root; (ii) the nodes in the left subtree of the root; and (iii) the nodes in the right subtree of the root. The left and right subtrees of the root are themselves complete binary trees, each with $n - 1$ levels. Because we are assuming that $P(n - 1)$ is true, there are exactly $2^{n-1} - 1$ nodes in each of the left and right subtrees. Adding up the nodes in the three groups, we get a total of

$$\underbrace{1}_{\text{root}} + \underbrace{2^{n-1} - 1}_{\text{left subtree}} + \underbrace{2^{n-1} - 1}_{\text{right subtree}} = 2^n - 1$$

nodes in the tree. This proves the statement $P(n)$ and, because $n \geq 2$ was arbitrary, completes the inductive step. We conclude that $P(n)$ is true for every positive integer n.

Appendix B

Quick Review of Discrete Probability

This appendix reviews five concepts from discrete probability: sample spaces, events, random variables, expectation, and linearity of expectation. Section B.6 concludes with a load-balancing example that ties all these concepts together.

We use these concepts in our analyses of a number of different algorithms and data structures, including randomized QuickSort (Section 5.5), randomized selection (Section 6.2), hash tables (Sections 12.3–12.4), bloom filters (Section 12.6), greedy influence maximization (Section 20.3), path-finding by color coding (Section 21.2), and better-than-exhaustive-search algorithms for satisfiability (Problem 21.12).

If you're seeing this material for the first time, you probably want to supplement this appendix with a more thorough treatment (see www.algorithmsilluminated.org for suggestions). If you have seen it before, don't feel compelled to read this appendix from front to back—dip in as needed wherever you need a refresher.

B.1 Sample Spaces

We're interested in random processes, in which any number of different things might happen. The *sample space* is the set Ω of all the different things that could happen—the universe in which we're going to assign probabilities, take average values, and so on.[1] For example, if our random process is the throw of a six-sided die, then $\Omega = \{1, 2, 3, 4, 5, 6\}$. Happily, in the analysis of randomized algorithms, we can almost always take Ω to be a finite set and work only with discrete probability, which is much more elementary than general probability theory.

Each element i of a sample space Ω comes with a nonnegative *probability* $p(i)$, which can be thought of as the frequency with which the outcome of the random process is i. For example, if a six-sided die is fair, then $p(i)$ is $1/6$ for each $i = 1, 2, 3, 4, 5, 6$. In general, because Ω captures everything that could possibly happen, the probabilities should sum to 1:

$$\sum_{i \in \Omega} p(i) = 1.$$

A common special case is when every element of Ω is equally likely—known as the *uniform distribution*—in which case $p(i) = 1/|\Omega|$ for every $i \in \Omega$.[2]

Sample spaces may seem like a pretty abstract concept, so let's introduce two running examples. In the first example, the random process is a throw of two standard (six-sided)

---

[1]In addition to its use in big-omega notation (Section 2.4.1), the symbol Ω is, unfortunately, the most common one for denoting a sample space.

[2]For a finite set S, $|S|$ denotes the number of elements in S.

dice. The sample space is the set of 36 different things that could happen:

$$\Omega = \underbrace{\{(1,1),(2,1),(3,1),\ldots,(5,6),(6,6)\}}_{\text{36 ordered pairs}}.$$

Assuming the dice are fair, each of these outcomes is equally likely: $p(i) = 1/36$ for every $i \in \Omega$.

The second example, more germane to algorithms, is the choice of the pivot element in the outermost call to randomized QuickSort (Section 5.4). Any element of the input array can be chosen as the pivot, so

$$\Omega = \underbrace{\{1,2,3,\ldots,n\}}_{\text{possible positions of pivot element}},$$

where n is the length of the input array. By definition, in randomized QuickSort each element is equally likely to be chosen as the pivot element, and so $p(i) = 1/n$ for every $i \in \Omega$.

B.2   Events

An *event* is a subset $S \subseteq \Omega$ of the sample space—a collection of possible outcomes of a random process. The probability $\mathbf{Pr}[S]$ of an event S is defined as you would expect, as the probability that one of the outcomes of S occurs:

$$\mathbf{Pr}[S] = \sum_{i \in S} p(i).$$

Let's get some practice with this concept using our two running examples.

Quiz B.1

Let S denote the set of outcomes for which the sum of two standard dice equals 7. What is the probability of the event S?[3]

a) $\frac{1}{36}$

b) $\frac{1}{12}$

c) $\frac{1}{6}$

d) $\frac{1}{2}$

(See Section B.2.1 for the solution and discussion.)

The second quiz concerns the choice of the random pivot element in the outermost call to QuickSort. We say that a pivot element is an "approximate median" if at least 25% of the array elements are less than the pivot, and at least 25% of the elements are greater than the pivot.

---

[3] A useful fact to know when playing the dice game craps...

Quiz B.2

Let S denote the event that the chosen pivot element in the outermost call to `QuickSort` is an approximate median. What is the probability of the event S?

    a) $\frac{1}{n}$, where n is the length of the array

    b) $\frac{1}{4}$

    c) $\frac{1}{2}$

    d) $\frac{3}{4}$

(See Section B.2.2 for the solution and discussion.)

B.2.1 Solution to Quiz B.1

Correct answer: (c). There are six outcomes in which the sum of the two dice equals 7:

$$S = \{(6,1),(5,2),(4,3),(3,4),(2,5),(1,6)\}.$$

Because every outcome of Ω is equally likely, $p(i) = 1/36$ for every $i \in S$ and so

$$\mathbf{Pr}[S] = |S| \cdot \tfrac{1}{36} = \tfrac{6}{36} = \tfrac{1}{6}.$$

B.2.2 Solution to Quiz B.2

Correct answer: (c). As a thought experiment, imagine dividing the elements in the input array into four groups: the smallest $n/4$ elements, the next-smallest $n/4$ elements, the next-smallest $n/4$ elements, and finally the largest $n/4$ elements. (As usual, we're ignoring fractions for simplicity.) Every element of the second and third groups is an approximate median: All the $n/4$ elements from the first and last groups are less than and greater than the pivot, respectively. Conversely, if the algorithm picks a pivot element from either the first or the last group, the pivot element is not an approximate median. The event S therefore corresponds to the $n/2$ elements in the second and third groups; because each element is equally likely to be chosen as the pivot element,

$$\mathbf{Pr}[S] = |S| \cdot \tfrac{1}{n} = \tfrac{n}{2} \cdot \tfrac{1}{n} = \tfrac{1}{2}.$$

B.3 Random Variables

A *random variable* is a numerical measurement of the outcome of a random process. Formally, it is a real-valued function $X : \Omega \to \mathbb{R}$ defined on the sample space Ω—the input $i \in \Omega$ to X is an outcome of the random process, and the output $X(i)$ is a numerical value.

    In our first running example, we can define a random variable that is the sum of the two dice. This random variable maps each outcome (i,j) with $i,j \in \{1,2,\ldots,6\}$ to the real number $i+j$. In our second running example, we can define a random variable that is the length of the subarray passed to the first recursive call to `QuickSort`. This random variable maps each outcome—that is, each choice of a pivot element—to the number of array elements that are less than that pivot (an integer between 0 and $n-1$, where n is the length of the input array).

Section 5.5 studies the random variable X that is the running time of randomized `QuickSort` on a given input array. Here, the state space Ω is all possible sequences of pivot elements the algorithm might choose, and $X(i)$ is the number of operations performed by the algorithm for a particular sequence $i \in \Omega$ of pivot choices.[4]

B.4   Expectation

The *expectation* or *expected value* $\mathbf{E}[X]$ of a random variable X is its average value over everything that could happen, weighted appropriately with the probabilities of different outcomes. Intuitively, if a random process is repeated over and over again, $\mathbf{E}[X]$ is the long-run average value of the random variable X. For example, if X is the value of a fair six-sided die, then $\mathbf{E}[X] = 3.5$.

In math, if $X : \Omega \to \mathbb{R}$ is a random variable and $p(i)$ denotes the probability of outcome $i \in \Omega$,

$$\mathbf{E}[X] = \sum_{i \in \Omega} p(i) \cdot X(i). \tag{B.1}$$

The next two quizzes ask you to compute the expectation of the two random variables defined in the preceding section.

Quiz B.3

What is the expectation of the sum of two dice?

   a) 6.5

   b) 7

   c) 7.5

   d) 8

(See Section B.4.1 for the solution and discussion.)

Returning to randomized `QuickSort`, how big, on average, is the length of the subarray passed to the first recursive call? Equivalently, how many elements are less than a randomly chosen pivot on average?

Quiz B.4

Which of the following values is closest to the expectation of the size of the subarray passed to the first recursive call in `QuickSort`?

   a) $\frac{n}{4}$

---

[4]Because the only randomness in randomized `QuickSort` is in the choice of pivot elements, once we fix these choices, `QuickSort` has some well-defined running time.

b) $\frac{n}{3}$

c) $\frac{n}{2}$

d) $\frac{3n}{4}$

(See Section B.4.2 for the solution and discussion.)

B.4.1 Solution to Quiz B.3

Correct answer: (b). There are several ways to see why the expectation is 7. The first way is to compute it naively, using the defining equation (B.1). With 36 possible outcomes, this is doable but tedious. A slicker way is to pair up the possible values of the sum and use symmetry. The sum is equally likely to be 2 or 12, equally likely to be 3 or 11, and so on. In each of these pairs the average value is 7, so this is also the average value overall. The third and best way is to use linearity of expectation, as covered in the next section.

B.4.2 Solution to Quiz B.4

Correct answer: (c). The exact value of the expectation is $(n-1)/2$. There is a $1/n$ chance that the subarray has length 0 (if the pivot element is the smallest element), a $1/n$ chance that it has length 1 (if the pivot element is the second-smallest element), and so on, up to a $1/n$ chance that it has length $n-1$ (if the pivot element is the largest element). By the definition (B.1) of expectation, and recalling the identity[5]

$$\sum_{i=1}^{n-1} i = \frac{n(n-1)}{2},$$

we have

$$\mathbf{E}[X] = \frac{1}{n} \cdot 0 + \frac{1}{n} \cdot 1 + \cdots + \frac{1}{n} \cdot (n-1) = \frac{1}{n} \cdot \underbrace{(1 + 2 + \cdots + (n-1))}_{=\frac{n(n-1)}{2}}$$

$$= \frac{n-1}{2}.$$

B.5   Linearity of Expectation

B.5.1 Formal Statement and Use Cases

Our final concept is a mathematical property, not a definition. *Linearity of expectation* is the property that the expectation of a sum of random variables is equal to the sum of their individual expectations. It is incredibly useful for computing the expectation of a complex random variable, like the running time of randomized `QuickSort`, when the random variable can be expressed as a weighted sum of simpler random variables.

---

[5]One way to see that $1 + 2 + \cdots + (n-1) = \frac{n(n-1)}{2}$ is to use induction on n (see Section A.2). For a sneakier proof, take two copies of the left-hand side and pair up the "1" from the first copy with the "$n-1$" from the second copy, the "2" from the first copy with the "$n-2$" from the second copy, and so on. This gives $n-1$ pairs with value n each. Because double the sum equals $n(n-1)$, the original sum equals $\frac{n(n-1)}{2}$.

Theorem B.1 (Linearity of Expectation) *Let $X_1, X_2, \ldots, X_n$ be random variables defined on the same sample space Ω, and let $a_1, a_2, \ldots, a_n$ be real numbers. Then*

$$\mathbf{E}\left[\sum_{j=1}^{n} a_j \cdot X_j\right] = \sum_{j=1}^{n} a_j \cdot \mathbf{E}[X_j]. \tag{B.2}$$

That is, you can take the sum and the expectation in either order and get the same thing. The common use case is when $\sum_{j=1}^{n} a_j X_j$ is a complex random variable (like the running time of randomized `QuickSort`) and the X_j's are simple random variables (like 0-1 random variables).[6]

For example, let X be the sum of two standard dice. We can write X as the sum of two random variables X_1 and X_2, which are the values of the first and second die, respectively. The expectation of X_1 or X_2 is easy to compute using the definition (B.1) as $\frac{1}{6}(1 + 2 + 3 + 4 + 5 + 6) = 3.5$. Linearity of expectation then gives

$$\mathbf{E}[X] = \mathbf{E}[X_1 + X_2] = \mathbf{E}[X_1] + \mathbf{E}[X_2] = 3.5 + 3.5 = 7,$$

replicating our answer in Section B.4.1 with less work.

An extremely important point is that

> *linearity of expectation holds even for random variables that are not independent.*

We won't need to formally define independence in this book, but you probably have good intuition about what it means: knowing something about the value of one random variable doesn't tell you anything new about the values of the others. For example, the random variables X_1 and X_2 above are independent because the two dice are assumed to be thrown independently.

For an example of dependent random variables, consider a pair of magnetically linked dice, where the second die always comes up with value one larger than that of the first (or 1, if the first die comes up 6). Now, knowing the value of either die tells you exactly what the value of the other die is. But we can still write the sum X of the two dice as $X_1 + X_2$, where X_1 and X_2 are the values of the two dice. It is still the case that X_1, viewed in isolation, is equally likely to be each of $\{1, 2, 3, 4, 5, 6\}$, and the same is true for X_2. Thus we still have $\mathbf{E}[X_1] = \mathbf{E}[X_2] = 3.5$ and, by linearity of expectation, $\mathbf{E}[X]$ is still 7.

Why should you be surprised? Superficially, the identity in (B.2) might look like a tautology. But if we switch from sums to *products* of random variables, the analog of Theorem B.1 generally holds only for independent random variables.[7] So linearity of expectation really is a special property about sums of random variables.

---

[6]When I teach algorithms, over many weeks of blackboard lectures, I draw a box around exactly one mathematical identity—linearity of expectation.

[7]The magnetically linked dice provide one counterexample for dependent random variables. For an even simpler counterexample, suppose X_1 and X_2 are either equal to 0 and 1 or to 1 and 0, respectively, with each outcome having 50% probability. Then $\mathbf{E}[X_1 \cdot X_2] = 0$ despite $\mathbf{E}[X_1] \cdot \mathbf{E}[X_2] = \frac{1}{4}$.

B.5.2   The Proof

The utility of linearity of expectation is matched only by the simplicity of its proof.[8]

Proof of Theorem B.1: Starting with the right-hand side of (B.2) and expanding using the definition (B.1) of expectation gives

$$\sum_{j=1}^{n} a_j \cdot \mathbf{E}[X_j] = \sum_{j=1}^{n} a_j \cdot \left(\sum_{i \in \Omega} p(i) \cdot X_j(i) \right)$$

$$= \sum_{j=1}^{n} \left(\sum_{i \in \Omega} a_j \cdot p(i) \cdot X_j(i) \right).$$

Reversing the order of summation, we have

$$\sum_{j=1}^{n} \left(\sum_{i \in \Omega} a_j \cdot p(i) \cdot X_j(i) \right) = \sum_{i \in \Omega} \left(\sum_{j=1}^{n} a_j \cdot p(i) \cdot X_j(i) \right). \qquad (B.3)$$

Because $p(i)$ is independent of $j = 1, 2, \ldots, n$, we can pull it out of the inner sum:

$$\sum_{i \in \Omega} \left(\sum_{j=1}^{n} a_j \cdot p(i) \cdot X_j(i) \right) = \sum_{i \in \Omega} p(i) \cdot \left(\sum_{j=1}^{n} a_j \cdot X_j(i) \right).$$

Finally, using again the definition (B.1) of expectation, we obtain the left-hand side of (B.2):

$$\sum_{i \in \Omega} p(i) \cdot \left(\sum_{j=1}^{n} a_j \cdot X_j(i) \right) = \mathbf{E} \left[\sum_{j=1}^{n} a_j \cdot X_j \right].$$

And that's it! Linearity of expectation is simply a reversal of a double summation. $\mathcal{QED}$

Speaking of double summations, equation (B.3) might seem opaque if you're rusty on these kinds of algebraic manipulations. For a down-to-earth way to think about it, arrange the $a_j p(i) X_j(i)$'s in a grid, with rows indexed by $i \in \Omega$, columns indexed by $j \in \{1, 2, \ldots, n\}$, and the number $a_j \cdot p(i) \cdot X_j(i)$ in the cell in the ith row and jth column:

The left-hand side of (B.3) first sums up each of the columns, and then adds up these column sums. The right-hand side first sums up the rows and then sums up these row sums. Either way, you get the sum of all the entries in the grid.

---

[8]The first time you read this proof, you should assume for simplicity that $a_1 = a_2 = \cdots = a_n = 1$.

B.6   Example: Load Balancing

To tie together all the preceding concepts, let's study an example about load balancing. Suppose we need an algorithm that assigns processes to servers, but we're feeling super-lazy. One easy solution is to simply assign each process to a random server, with each server equally likely. How well does this work?[9]

For concreteness, assume there are n processes and also n servers, where n is some positive integer. First, let's be clear on the sample space: The set Ω is all n^n possible ways of assigning the processes to the servers, with n choices for each of the n processes. By the definition of our lazy algorithm, each of these n^n outcomes is equally likely.

Now that we have a sample space, we're in a position to define random variables. One interesting quantity is server load, so let's define Y as the random variable equal to the number of processes that get assigned to the first server. (The story is the same for all the servers by symmetry, so we may as well focus on the first one.) What is the expectation of Y?

In principle, we can compute $\mathbf{E}[Y]$ by direct evaluation of the defining equation (B.1), but this is impractical for all but the smallest values of n. Fortunately, because Y can be expressed as a sum of simple random variables, linearity of expectation can save the day. Formally, for $j = 1, 2, \ldots, n$, define

$$X_j = \begin{cases} 1 & \text{if the } j\text{th process gets assigned to the first server} \\ 0 & \text{otherwise.} \end{cases}$$

Random variables that take on only the values 0 and 1 are often called *indicator* random variables because they indicate whether some event occurs (like the event that process j gets assigned to the first server).

From the definitions, we can express Y as the sum of the X_j's:

$$Y = \sum_{j=1}^{n} X_j.$$

By linearity of expectation (Theorem B.1), the expectation of Y is then the sum of the expectations of the X_j's:

$$\mathbf{E}[Y] = \mathbf{E}\left[\sum_{j=1}^{n} X_j\right] = \sum_{j=1}^{n} \mathbf{E}[X_j].$$

Because each random variable X_j is so simple, it's easy to compute its expectation directly:

$$\mathbf{E}[X_j] = \underbrace{0 \cdot \mathbf{Pr}[X_j = 0]}_{=0} + 1 \cdot \mathbf{Pr}[X_j = 1] = \mathbf{Pr}[X_j = 1].$$

Because the jth process is equally likely to be assigned to each of the n servers, $\mathbf{Pr}[X_j = 1] = 1/n$. Putting it all together, we have

$$\mathbf{E}[Y] = \sum_{j=1}^{n} \mathbf{E}[X_j] = n \cdot \frac{1}{n} = 1.$$

---

[9]This example is also relevant to our discussion of hashing in Chapter 12.

So if we care only about average server loads, our super-lazy algorithm works just fine! This example is characteristic of the role that randomization plays in algorithm design: We can often get away with really simple algorithms when we make random choices along the way.

Quiz B.5

Consider a group of k people. Assume that each person's birthday is drawn uniformly at random from the 365 possibilities. (And ignore leap years.) What is the smallest value of k such that the expected number of pairs of distinct people with the same birthday is at least one?

[Hint: Define an indicator random variable for each pair of people. Use linearity of expectation.]

    a) 20

    b) 23

    c) 27

    d) 28

    e) 366

(See below for the solution and discussion.)

Correct answer: (d). Fix a positive integer k, and denote the set of people by $\{1, 2, \ldots, k\}$. Let Y denote the number of pairs of people with the same birthday. As suggested by the hint, define one random variable X_{ij} for every choice $i, j \in \{1, 2, \ldots, k\}$ of people with $i < j$. Define X_{ij} as 1 if i and j have the same birthday and 0 otherwise. Thus, the X_{ij}'s are indicator random variables, and

$$Y = \sum_{i=1}^{k-1} \sum_{j=i+1}^{k} X_{ij}.$$

By linearity of expectation (Theorem B.1),

$$\mathbf{E}[Y] = \mathbf{E}\left[\sum_{i=1}^{k-1} \sum_{j=i+1}^{k} X_{ij}\right] = \sum_{i=1}^{k-1} \sum_{j=i+1}^{k} \mathbf{E}[X_{ij}]. \tag{B.4}$$

Because X_{ij} is an indicator random variable, $\mathbf{E}[X_{ij}] = \mathbf{Pr}[X_{ij} = 1]$. There are $(365)^2$ possibilities for the birthdays of the people i and j, and in 365 of these possibilities i and j have the same birthday. Assuming that all birthday combinations are equally likely,

$$\mathbf{Pr}[X_{ij} = 1] = \frac{365}{(365)^2} = \frac{1}{365}.$$

Plugging this in to (B.4), we have

$$\mathbf{E}[Y] = \sum_{i=1}^{k-1} \sum_{j=i+1}^{k} \frac{1}{365} = \frac{1}{365} \cdot \binom{k}{2} = \frac{k(k-1)}{730},$$

where $\binom{k}{2}$ denotes the binomial coefficient "k choose 2" (as in the solution to Quiz 3.1). The smallest value of k for which

$$\frac{k(k-1)}{730} \geq 1$$

is 28.

Epilogue: A Field Guide to Algorithm Design

With *Algorithms Illuminated* under your belt, you now possess a rich algorithmic toolbox suitable for tackling a wide range of computational problems. So rich, in fact, that you might find the sheer number of algorithms, data structures, and design paradigms daunting. When you're confronted with a new problem, what's the most effective way to put your tools to work? To give you a starting point, I'll tell you the typical recipe I use when I need to understand an unfamiliar computational problem. You should develop your own personalized recipe as you accumulate more algorithmic experience.

1. Can you avoid solving the problem from scratch? Is it a disguised version, variant, or special case of a problem that you already know how to solve? For example, can it be reduced to sorting, graph search, or a shortest-path computation?[10] If so, use the fastest and simplest algorithm sufficient for solving the problem.

2. Can you simplify the problem by preprocessing the input with a for-free primitive, such as sorting or computing connected components?

3. If you must design a new algorithm from scratch, get calibrated by identifying the line in the sand drawn by the "obvious" solution (such as exhaustive search). For the inputs that you care about, is the obvious solution already fast enough?

4. If the obvious solution is inadequate, brainstorm as many natural greedy algorithms as you can and test them on small examples. Most likely, all will fail. But the ways in which they fail will help you better understand the problem.

5. If there's an obvious way to split the input into smaller subproblems, how easy would it be to combine their solutions? If you see how to do it quickly, proceed with the divide-and-conquer paradigm.

6. Try dynamic programming. Can you argue that a solution must be built up from solutions to smaller subproblems in one of a small number of ways? Can you formulate a recurrence to quickly solve a subproblem given solutions to the smaller subproblems?

7. In the happy event that you devise a good algorithm for the problem, can you make it even better through the deft deployment of data structures? Look for significant computations that your algorithm performs over and over again (such as lookups or minimum computations). Remember the principle of parsimony: Choose the simplest data structure that supports all the operations required by your algorithm.

---

[10]If you go on to a deeper study of algorithms, you'll learn about more well-solved problems that show up in disguise all the time. A few examples include the fast Fourier transform, the maximum flow and minimum cut problems, bipartite matching, and linear and convex programming.

8. Can you make your algorithm simpler or faster using randomization? For example, if your algorithm must choose one object among many, what happens when it chooses randomly?

9. If all the preceding steps end in failure, contemplate the unfortunate but realistic possibility that there is *no* efficient algorithm for your problem. Of the NP-hard problems you know, which one most closely resembles your problem? Can you reduce this NP-hard problem to yours? What about the 3-SAT problem? Or any of the other problems in the Garey and Johnson book (page 557)?

10. Decide whether you'd rather compromise on correctness or on speed. If you prefer to retain guaranteed speed and compromise on correctness, iterate over the algorithm design paradigms again, this time looking for opportunities for fast heuristic algorithms. The greedy algorithm design paradigm stands out as the most frequently useful one for this purpose.

11. Consider also the local search paradigm, both for approximately solving the problem from scratch and for a no-downside postprocessing step to tack on to some other heuristic algorithm.

12. If you'd rather insist on guaranteed correctness while compromising on speed, return to the dynamic programming paradigm and seek out better-than-exhaustive-search (but presumably still exponential-time) exact algorithms.

13. If dynamic programming doesn't apply or your dynamic programming algorithms are too slow, cross your fingers and experiment with semi-reliable magic boxes. For an optimization problem, try formulating it as a mixed integer program and throwing a MIP solver at it. For a feasibility-checking problem, start instead with a satisfiability formulation and throw a SAT solver at it.

Hints and Solutions

Solution to Problem 1.1: The "2" is in the 7th position.

Hint for Problem 1.2: Note that the Merge subroutine can still be implemented so that the number of operations is only linear in the sum of the input array lengths.

Hint for Problem 1.3: Use the fact that $1 + 2 + \cdots + k = \frac{(k+1)k}{2}$.

Solution to Problem 1.4: **(c)**. There are $\approx \log_2 k$ iterations and each iteration takes time proportional to nk.

Solution to Problem 1.5: **(a),(b),(c),(d),(e)**.

Hint for Problem 1.6: The answer depends on k. For $k = 1$, at least n operations are required. For sufficiently large k, the following algorithm uses fewer than kn operations: (i) sort the input array A; (ii) for each $i = 1, 2, \ldots, k$, use binary search to check whether A contains t_i.

Hint for Problem 1.7: Consider computing the largest number using a knockout tournament. To whom must the second-largest number have lost?

Solution to Problem 2.1: **(a)**. Because the constant c in the exponent is inside a logarithm, it becomes part of the leading constant and gets suppressed in the big-O notation.

Hint for Problem 2.2: For (a), recall Proposition 2.4.

Solution to Problem 2.3: (d), (a), (c), (e), (b)

Solution to Problem 2.4: (e), (a), (d), (b), (c)

Solution to Problem 2.5: Exponentiation base-2 and the logarithm base-2 are inverse operations, so $2^{\log_2 n}$ is the same as n and $2^{2^{\log_2 n}}$ is the same as 2^n. Thus the correct ordering is (a), (e), (c), (b), (d).

Solution to Problem 2.6: Because $f(n) \le c \cdot g(n)$ if and only if $g(n) \ge f(n)/c$, whenever two constants $c, n_0 > 0$ prove that $f(n) = O(g(n))$, the constants $\frac{1}{c}$ and n_0 prove that $g(n) = \Omega(f(n))$. Conversely, whenever two constants $c, n_0 > 0$ prove that $g(n) = \Omega(f(n))$, the constants $\frac{1}{c}$ and n_0 prove that $f(n) = O(g(n))$.

Solution to Problem 2.7: For part (a), any two constants c and n_0 showing that $T(n) = O(f(n))$ under the alternative definition work equally well for the original definition. Conversely, if the constants c and n_0 show that $T(n) = O(f(n))$ under the original definition, the constants $2c$ and n_0 work for the alternative definition. The argument for part (b) is similar. For part (c), the definitions of big-O and little-o notation do not implement the different concepts of "less than or equal to" and "strictly less than" through the (irrelevant) choice of strict or weak inequalities in (2.1)–(2.2), but rather through their different orders of quantifiers ("there exist $c, n_0 > 0$ such that..." vs. "for all $c > 0$ there exists $n_0 > 0$ such that...").

Hint for Problem 3.1: The algorithm performs a constant number of operations per digit in the binary expansion of b.

Solution to Problem 3.2: They are 1×1 matrices with the values -2, 24, 35, 8, 65, -30, and -22, respectively.

Hint for Problem 3.3: The algorithm is similar to binary search (see also Section 4.3.2). If the middle element of the input array is bigger than both its neighbors, you're done. Otherwise, recurse on the half of the array that contains the larger neighbor.

Hint for Problem 3.4: If the middle element of the input array has value equal to its index, you're done. Otherwise, recurse on the appropriate half.

Hint for Problem 3.5: Break $\mathbf{x}$ into its first half $\mathbf{x}_1$ and second half $\mathbf{x}_2$, recursively compute $H_{k-1} \cdot \mathbf{x}_1$ and $H_{k-1} \cdot \mathbf{x}_2$, and combine the results appropriately.

Hint for Problem 3.6: Figure out how to recurse on an $\frac{n}{2} \times \frac{n}{2}$ grid after performing only $O(n)$ comparisons.

Hint for Problem 3.7: The high-level approach of the ClosestPair algorithm works here as well, though only after significant changes to the statement and proof of Lemma 3.3. Consider the first recursive call, which computes, for each point p in the left half of the point set, the closest point q_p in the left half. Call a point $q = (x, y)$ in the right half a *candidate* for such a point p if the point $\bar{q} = (\bar{x}, y)$ is closer to p than q_p is. (As usual, $\bar{x}$ denotes the largest x-coordinate among points in the left half.) Prove that every point q in the right half serves as a candidate for only $O(1)$ points in the left half. In the analog of the ClosestSplitPair subroutine, exhaustively search over all point-candidate pairs.

Solution to Problem 4.1: (d). See page 82.

Solution to Problem 4.2: (b). To falsify (a), take $a = 1$, $b = 2$, and $d = 0$ (as in binary search). To falsify (c) and (d), take $a = 4$, $b = 2$, and $d = 2$. Answer (b) is correct because b^d cannot be smaller than 1 (as $b > 1$ and $d \geq 0$).

Solution to Problem 4.3: (b). In the notation of the master method, $a = 7$, $b = 3$, and $d = 2$; using case 2, $T(n) = O(n^2)$.

Solution to Problem 4.4: (c). In the notation of the master method, $a = 9$, $b = 3$, and $d = 2$; using case 1, $T(n) = O(n^2 \log n)$.

Solution to Problem 4.5: (c). In the notation of the master method, $a = 5$, $b = 3$, and $d = 1$; using case 3, $T(n) = O(n^{\log_3 5})$.

Hint for Problem 4.6: If you mimic each step of the proof of Theorem 4.1, you shouldn't encounter any surprises.

Solution to Problem 4.7: (b). Write n as $2^{\log_2 n}$. Each application of T cuts the exponent in half. The exponent drops from $\log_2 n$ to 1 in $\approx \log_2 \log_2 n$ iterations, so $T(n) = O(\log \log n)$.

Solution to Problem 5.1: (d). Answers (a) and (b) are incorrect because `QuickSort` and `MergeSort` have incomparable strengths and weaknesses; for example, only the former works in place but only the latter is stable (page 113). Answer (c) is incorrect; see Problems 5.6–5.7. `RadixSort` shows that (d) is correct.

Solution to Problem 5.2: Every number that is bigger than everything to the left of it and smaller than everything to the right of it: 4, 5, and 9.

Solution to Problem 5.3: (c). The same as the probability that a uniformly random pivot element is not among the α fraction of the smallest elements nor the α fraction of the largest elements.

Hint for Problem 5.4: The formula that relates logarithmic functions with different bases is $\log_b n = \frac{\ln n}{\ln b}$.

Solution to Problem 5.5: (b). In the best-case scenario, the algorithm always picks the median as the pivot element. In this case, the recursion tree is essentially identical to that of `MergeSort`, which has logarithmic depth. In the worst-case scenario, the algorithm always picks the minimum or maximum element as the pivot, in which case the recursion depth is linear.

Hint for Problem 5.6: Following the proof of Theorem 5.5, prove that such an algorithm can correctly sort at most half of the $n!$ arrays using $(\log_2 n!) - 1$ comparisons or less.

Hint for Problem 5.7: Consider running a randomized comparison-based sorting algorithm on one of the $n!$ inputs in the preceding problem, chosen uniformly at random. View the randomized algorithm as a probability distribution over deterministic algorithms. By the preceding problem, averaging over the random choice of input, each of the deterministic algorithms has an expected running time of $\Omega(n \log n)$. Averaging again over the random choice of a deterministic algorithm shows that the expected running time of the randomized algorithm on a random input is also $\Omega(n \log n)$.

Solution to Problem 6.1: (a),(c). Selection reduces immediately to sorting (Section 6.1.2) but not vice versa (Theorems 5.5 and 6.6), so (a) is correct and (b) is incorrect. Answer (c) is correct because the `DSelect` algorithm runs in linear time and no algorithm can be better by more than a constant factor—even a randomized algorithm that is always correct must examine each input array element. Answer (d) is incorrect, as `RSelect` is superior to `DSelect` in practice.

Solution to Problem 6.2: (d). The same as the probability that a uniformly random pivot element is not among the $1 - \alpha$ fraction of the smallest elements nor the $1 - \alpha$ fraction of the largest elements, which is $1 - ((1 - \alpha) + (1 - \alpha)) = 2\alpha - 1$.

Solution to Problem 6.3: (a). See also the hint to Problem 5.4.

Hint for Problem 6.4: With groups of 7, following the argument from Section 6.4 leads to the recurrence $T(n) \leq T(n/7) + T(5n/7) + O(n)$, which solves to $T(n) = O(n)$. With groups of 3, following that argument leads to the recurrence $T(n) \leq T(n/3) + T(2n/3) + O(n)$ which, by a recursion tree argument, solves to $T(n) = O(n \log n)$.[11]

Hint for Problem 6.5: Use the `DSelect` algorithm to compute the ith order statistic for all values of i that are multiples of $n/8$. Check for repeated elements. Do a final pass over the array to count the number of occurrences of each remaining candidate value.

Solution to Problem 6.6: Compute the total weight W (in linear time). Initialize D_L and D_R to 0; these variables will track the total weight of discarded elements that are less than and greater than the elements of the current subarray, respectively. In the outermost recursive call, use `DSelect` to compute the (unweighted) median and `Partition` to partition the array around it (all in linear time). If the total weight on each side of the median is at most $W/2$, return it. Otherwise, recurse on the (unique) half of the array with total weight more than $W/2$, updating D_L or D_R to keep track of the total weight of the discarded elements.

In a general recursive call, use `DSelect` to compute the (unweighted) median of the remaining subarray, `Partition` the subarray around this median, and compute the total weight W_L and W_R of the subarray elements on each side. If both $W_L + D_L$ and $W_R + D_R$ are at most $W/2$, return this median (it is a weighted median of the original input array, as you should check). Otherwise, recurse on the (unique) half of the subarray with $W_L + D_L$ or $W_R + D_R$ greater than $W/2$, updating D_L or D_R accordingly.

The algorithm's running time is governed by the recurrence $T(n) \leq T(n/2) + O(n)$. By case 2 of the master method, $T(n) = O(n)$ and so the algorithm runs in linear time.

Solution to Problem 7.1: (c). There are n choices for an edge's tail, $n-1$ remaining choices for its head.

Solution to Problem 7.2: (c). Each edge contributes exactly 1 to the degrees of exactly 2 different vertices (its endpoints).

Solution to Problem 7.3: Conditions (a) and (c) are satisfied by some sparse graphs (such as a star graph) and some dense graphs (such as a complete graph with one extra edge glued on). Condition (b) is satisfied only by sparse graphs, and (d) only by dense graphs.

Solution to Problem 7.4: (c). Scan through the row corresponding to v in the adjacency matrix.

Solution to Problem 7.5: (d). You can't do better than scanning through the edge array.

Solution to Problem 8.1: All four statements are true: (a) by the `UCC` algorithm in Section 8.3; (b) by the `Augmented-BFS` algorithm in Section 8.2; (c) by the `Kosaraju` algorithm in Section 8.6; and (d) by the `TopoSort` algorithm in Section 8.5.

---

[11]Could there be a more refined analysis that proves a linear-time bound? For a deep dive on this question, see the paper "Select with Groups of 3 or 4 Takes Linear Time," by Ke Chen and Adrian Dumitrescu (arXiv:1409.3600, 2014).

Solution to Problem 8.2: (c). $\Omega(n^2)$ time is required because, in the worst case, a correct algorithm must look at each of the n^2 entries of the adjacency matrix at least once. $O(n^2)$ time is achievable, for example by constructing the adjacency list representation of the input graph in a single pass over the adjacency matrix (in $O(n^2)$ time) and running DFS with the new representation in $O(m + n) = O(n^2)$ time.

Solution to Problem 8.3: (b),(c). A triangle is a counterexample to (a) and a path to (d). Answer (b) is correct because the radius equals the shortest-path distance between some vertex pair, and the diameter is the largest such distance. For (c), let vertex x minimize $l(v)$ over all $v \in V$ (and so $r = l(x)$). The shortest-path distance between each vertex pair $v, w \in V$ is at most $2r$—pasting together a shortest v-x path and a shortest x-w path produces a v-w path with at most $2r$ edges.

Hint for Problem 8.4: Start from a corner vertex of a 3-by-3 grid.

Solution to Problem 8.5: (d). Answer (a) is incorrect because a directed acyclic graph may have many topological orderings (Section 8.5.1). Answer (b) is incorrect because such a graph has no topological orderings (Section 8.5.2). The condition in (c) guarantees only that the graph has zero or one topological orderings.

Solution to Problem 8.6: (c). Any directed acyclic graph shows that answers (b) and (d) are incorrect. For (a), there's a counterexample with three vertices.

Solution to Problem 8.7: (a),(c).

Solution to Problem 8.8: (c). Computing the "magical ordering" in the first pass of the Kosaraju algorithm requires depth-first search. (See the proof of Theorem 8.10.) In the second pass, given the magical ordering of the vertices, any instantiation of the GenericSearch algorithm (including BFS) will successfully discover the SCCs in reverse topological order.

Solution to Problem 8.9: (a),(b). The modification in (a) does not change the order in which the algorithm considers vertices in its second pass, and so it remains correct. The modification in (b) is equivalent to running the Kosaraju algorithm on the reversal of the input graph. Because a graph and its reversal have exactly the same SCCs (Quiz 8.6), the algorithm remains correct. The modifications in (c) and (d) are equivalent, as in the argument for (a) above, and do not result in a correct algorithm. For a counterexample, revisit our running example (and especially the discussion on page 185).

Hint for Problem 8.10: Designate an arbitrary starting vertex and run breadth-first search. Color vertices red or blue according to whether they belong to an even or odd layer. If both endpoints of some edge receive the same color, the input graph must have an odd cycle (why?) and cannot be bipartite.

Hint for Problem 8.11: Compute the in-degree (number of incoming edges) of each vertex. Maintain an array in which the ith entry contains a doubly-linked list of pointers to all the vertices that, taking into account the extractions thus far, have i incoming edges remaining.

When extracting a source vertex with k outgoing edges remaining, update the array in $O(k)$ time.

Hint for Problem 8.12: Show how to solve the problem by computing the strongly connected components of a suitably defined directed graph. You're on the right track if your graph has $2n$ vertices (one per literal) and $2m$ directed edges; the given 2-SAT instance will have a satisfying assignment if and only if every literal resides in a different component than its opposite.

Hint for Problem 9.1: For (a), consider a path graph. For (b), show that cutting out a cycle from an s-t path results in another s-t path; why is it relevant that edges' lengths are nonnegative? For (c) and (d), it's enough to experiment with graphs that have at most three vertices and at most three edges.

Solution to Problem 9.2: (b). Two sums of distinct powers of 2 cannot be the same. (Imagine the numbers are written in binary.) For (a) and (c), there are counterexamples with three vertices and three edges.

Solution to Problem 9.3: (c),(d). Statement (d) holds because, when P has only one edge, every path goes up in length by at least as much as P does. This also shows that (b) is false. An example similar to the one in Section 9.3.2 shows that (a) is false, and it follows that (c) is true.

Solution to Problem 9.4: (a). One approach is to go back through the proof in Section 9.3 and verify that it remains valid here. For an alternative solution, use that adding the same positive constant M to each of s's outgoing edges preserves all shortest paths (as the lengths of all the s-v paths go up by precisely M).

Solution to Problem 9.5: (c),(d). Inspection of its pseudocode shows that the `Dijkstra` algorithm does not examine whether edge lengths are positive or negative and always halts after at most $|V| - 1$ iterations of its main while loop. Thus, answers (a) and (b) are incorrect. The example in Section 9.3.2 shows that (c) is correct, and Problem 9.4 shows that (d) is correct.

Hint for Problem 9.6: For (d), note that $dist(s, v) = -\infty$ for every $v \in C$.

Solution to Problem 9.7: In line 3 of the pseudocode (page 202), every edge with one endpoint in each of X and $V - X$ should be considered. The correctness proof remains the same, with undirected edges and paths playing the previous roles of directed edges and paths.

Solution to Problem 9.8: In lines 4 and 6 of the pseudocode (page 202), respectively, replace $len(v) + \ell_{vw}$ with $\max\{len(v), \ell_{vw}\}$ and $len(a) + \ell_{ab}$ with $\max\{len(a), \ell_{ab}\}$.

Hint for Problem 9.9: For (c), make minor modifications to the proof of Theorem 9.1. For (e), if $t_1, t_2, \ldots, t_k$ denote the goal vertices, add an extra vertex t to the input graph (the new unique goal vertex), along with zero-length edges $(t_1, t), (t_2, t), \ldots, (t_k, t)$.

Solution to Problem 9.10: Introduce a starting vertex $v_{0,0}$ and a vertex $v_{i,j}$ for each $i \in \{1, 2, \ldots, n\}$ and $j \in \{0, 1, 2, \ldots, X\}$. Vertex $v_{i,j}$ is meant to represent a subset $S \subseteq \{1, 2, \ldots, i\}$ of the first i items for which the total value $\sum_{i \in S} x_i$ equals j. Vertices of the form $v_{n,j}$ have no outgoing edges. Every other vertex $v_{i,j}$ has two outgoing edges: an edge $(v_{i,j}, v_{i+1,j})$ with length 0 (representing item i's exclusion), and an edge $(v_{i,j}, v_{i+1,j+x_i})$ with length c_i (representing i's inclusion). (If $j + x_i > X$, the second edge should be interpreted as $(v_{i,j}, v_{i+1,X})$.) A shortest path P from $v_{0,0}$ to $v_{n,X}$ encodes a minimum-cost solution $S^* \subseteq \{1, 2, \ldots, n\}$ to the original problem, with item i included in S^* if and only if the path P includes an edge of the form $(v_{i,j}, v_{i+1,j+x_i})$.

Solution to Problem 10.1: (b),(c). The raison d'être of a heap is to support fast minimum computations, with HeapSort (Section 10.3.1) being a canonical application. Negating the key of every object turns a heap into a data structure that supports fast maximum computations. Heaps do not generally support fast lookups unless you happen to be looking for the object with the minimum key.

Solution to Problem 10.2: (b).

Solution to Problem 10.3: (a).

Solution to Problem 10.4: (a). Only the object with the smallest key can be extracted with one heap operation. Calling EXTRACTMIN five successive times returns the object in the heap with the fifth-smallest key. Extracting the object with the median or maximum key would require a linear number of heap operations.

Hint for Problem 10.5: Loop over the input array once, in reverse order (bottom-up in terms of the complete binary tree visualization). Upon reaching a position i containing an object x, repeatedly invoke the Bubble-Down subroutine (see footnote 26) until there are no violations of the heap property between x and its children. This process concludes with a heap (why?); how many swaps are made along the way? The loop iteration that processes position i makes at most one swap per level of the complete binary tree that is deeper than i's level. Less than n positions reside above the deepest level, so less than n swaps involve that level. Less than $n/2$ positions reside above the second-deepest level, so less than $n/2$ swaps involve that level. Less than $n/4$ swaps involve the third-deepest level, and so on. The total number of swaps is therefore less than $n + \frac{n}{2} + \frac{n}{4} + \frac{n}{8} + \cdots = 2n$. (Formally, this equation follows from the closed-form formula for geometric series; see Section 4.4.8.) Only a constant amount of time is required per swap, so the overall running time is $O(n)$.

Solution to Problem 10.6: In line 13 of the heap-based implementation of the Dijkstra algorithm (page 225), replace $len(w) + \ell_{wy}$ with $\max\{len(w), \ell_{wy}\}$.

Hint for Problem 10.7: Use linear-time selection (see Chapter 6) as a subroutine. Shoot for a recursive algorithm that cuts the input size in half in linear time.

Hint for Problem 10.8: For a deep dive on this problem, see the paper "Algorithms for Two Bottleneck Optimization Problems," by Harold N. Gabow and Robert E. Tarjan (*Journal of Algorithms*, 1988). (Spoiler alert: yes!)

Solution to Problem 11.1: (a). Statement (a) holds because there are at most 2^i nodes in the ith level of a binary tree, and hence at most $1 + 2 + 4 + \cdot + 2^i \le 2^{i+1}$ nodes in levels 0 through i combined. Accommodating n nodes requires $2^{h+1} \ge n$, where h is the tree height, so $h = \Omega(\log n)$. Statement (b) holds for balanced binary search trees but is generally false for unbalanced binary search trees (see footnote 5 in Chapter 11). Statements (c) and (d) are false because the heap and search tree properties are incomparable (see page 242). Statement (e) is false, as a sorted array is preferable to a balanced binary search tree when the set of objects to be stored is static, with no insertions or deletions (see page 240).

Solution to Problem 11.2: (b). The algorithm has the same structure as the implementation of OUTPUTSORTED (page 246).

Solution to Problem 11.3: If binary search finds an object with key k in the ith position of the array, or if it discovers that k is in between the keys of the objects in the ith and $(i+1)$th positions, the correct answer is i.

Hint for Problem 11.4: Carry out a SEARCH operation for the given key; whenever a right child pointer is traversed, pay attention to the left subtree's size.

Hint for Problem 11.5: For the INSERT operation, increment the subtree size for every node on the path between the root and the newly inserted object.

Hint for Problem 11.6: For (a), follow your nose. For (b), return the first such object found (if any). For (c), focus on comparing approach (iv) to approaches (i)–(iii). (Your answer may depend on the choice of data structure in (iv) for storing objects with a common key.) For (d), think about the extreme case of n objects, all with the same key.

Hint for Problem 11.7: Alternate traversing right child pointers of T_1 and left child pointers of T_2, until a null pointer is encountered in one of the two trees.

Hint for Problem 11.8: Assume that n is a power of 2 (tacking some superfluous zeroes on to the end of A, if necessary). Construct a perfectly balanced binary tree T, with elements of the array A in one-to-one correspondence with the leaves of T. Store with each node x of T the sum of the array elements that correspond to the leaves of x's subtree (initially zero). Compute a partial sum $\sum_{k=i}^{j} a_k$ as the difference of two prefix sums, $\sum_{k=1}^{j} a_k$ and $\sum_{k=1}^{i-1} a_k$. Computing a prefix sum is similar to the RANK operation in augmented binary search trees (Problem 11.4). Carrying out an UPDATE operation is similar to updating the subtree sizes in such trees (Problem 11.5).

Solution to Problem 12.1: (a). Pathological data sets show that property (a) is impossible and so cannot be expected (see Section 12.3.6). The other three properties are satisfied by state-of-the-art hash functions.

Solution to Problem 12.2: (b). There are n possibilities for k_1's location and n possibilities for k_2's location, for a total of n^2 outcomes. Of these, k_1 and k_2 collide in exactly n of them—the outcome in which both are assigned the first position, the outcome in which both are assigned the second position, and so on. Because every outcome is equally likely (with probability $1/n^2$ each), the probability of a collision is $n \cdot \frac{1}{n^2} = \frac{1}{n}$.

Solution to Problem 12.3: (b).

Solution to Problem 12.4: Try all possibilities for x and y, and use a hash table to look for the desired value of z (that is, for $t - x - y$).

Hint for Problem 12.5: For (a) and (b), perform a single pass over the hash table's array (and for (a), traverse each non-empty linked list encountered). For (c), under the hash table's hood, maintain a linked list of pointers to all the stored objects.

Hint for Problem 12.6: To count the frequencies of each distinct word, proceed as in the de-duplication application (Section 12.2.1). Identify the 10 most frequent words in a postprocessing step, using the OUTPUTUNSORTED operation from Problem 12.5.

Hint for Problem 12.7: For (a), there are $n^{|U|}$ functions from U to $\{0, 1, 2 \ldots, n - 1\}$; for distinct $x, y \in U$, $n^{|U|-1}$ such functions map x and y to the same number (why?). For (b), view distinct keys $x, y \in U$ as k-bit strings and choose a position i in which they differ. Prove that, for every choice of M's columns other than the ith column, there is exactly one choice for the ith column such that $h_M(x) = h_M(y)$. For (c), follow the line of argument in footnote 19; see also the bonus videos at www.algorithmsilluminated.org.

Hint for Problem 12.8: Use two levels of hash tables. Use an outer table with m buckets and fewer than m collisions. Each bucket i then uses its own inner hash table for the keys mapped to it—if a_i elements are mapped to this bucket, use an inner hash table with a_i^2 buckets and no collisions. To bound the space, relate $\sum_{i=1}^m a_i^2$ to the number of collisions in the outer hash table.

Hint for Problem 13.1: One of the greedy algorithms can be proved correct using an exchange argument, similar to the one in Section 13.4.

Hint for Problem 13.2: For each of the incorrect algorithms, there is a counterexample with only two jobs.

Hint for Problem 13.3: Let S_i denote the set of jobs with the i earliest finish times. Prove by induction on i that your greedy algorithm of choice selects the maximum-possible number of non-conflicting jobs from S_i.

Solution to Problem 13.4: For (a), the sum of weighted completion times (13.1) of every schedule doubles, so the same schedules remain optimal. For (b), doubling the job weights can change the schedule output by the GreedyDiff algorithm (for example, if initially $\ell_1 = 5$, $w_1 = 3$, $\ell_2 = 2$, and $w_2 = 1$).

Solution to Problem 13.5: Let σ denote the schedule computed by the GreedyRatio algorithm and σ^* any other schedule. Performing the swap illustrated in Figure 13.3 cannot increase the sum of weighted completion times—the sum might decrease, or it might stay the same (see (13.3)). This swap also decreases by one the number of inverted jobs, meaning the number of pairs (i, j) of jobs with $i > j$ and i processed at some point before j (why?). Repeated swapping (as in BubbleSort) transforms σ^* into σ without increasing the sum of weighted completion times; because this argument holds for every schedule σ^*, σ must be an optimal schedule.

Hint for Problem 13.6: Among the jobs that have been released, always process the one with the shortest remaining processing time (meaning the original job length minus the amount of time already spent processing it). For the correctness proof, for a schedule σ^* different from the greedy schedule σ, consider the first moment in time t at which the job j processed in σ^* differs from the job i processed in σ. Consider all the moments in time after time t at which σ^* processes job i or job j, reallocate this time so that all remaining processing on i precedes all that on j, and argue that the sum of completion times cannot increase.

Solution to Problem 14.1: (a). Achieved, for example, by the code

Symbol	Encoding
A	00
B	01
C	10
D	110
E	111

Solution to Problem 14.2: (a). Achieved, for example, by the code

Symbol	Encoding
A	110
B	1110
C	0
D	1111
E	10

Hint for Problem 14.3: For a lower bound, consider symbol frequencies that are powers of 2.

Hint for Problem 14.4: For (c), prove that a letter with frequency less than 0.33 participates in at least one merge prior to the final iteration. For (d), see Problem 14.2.

Hint for Problem 14.5: Use an exchange argument, as in the second main idea in the proof of Theorem 14.2.

Solution to Problem 14.6: Sort the symbols by frequency and insert them in increasing order into a queue Q_1. (To review the queue data structure, see footnote 9 in Chapter 8.) Initialize an empty queue Q_2. Maintain the following invariants: (i) the elements of Q_1 correspond to single-node trees in the current forest $\mathcal{F}$, stored in increasing order of frequency; (ii) the elements of Q_2 correspond to the multi-node trees of $\mathcal{F}$, stored in increasing order of sum of symbol frequencies. In each iteration of the algorithm, the trees T_1 and T_2 with the smallest sums of symbol frequencies can be identified and removed using a constant number of operations at the fronts of Q_1 and Q_2. The merger T_3 of T_1 and T_2 is inserted at the back of Q_2. (Exercise: why does invariant (ii) continue to hold?) Every queue operation (removing from the front or adding to the back) runs in $O(1)$ time, so the total running time of the $n-1$ iterations of the main loop is $O(n)$.

Hint for Problem 14.7: Assume that there is an odd number of symbols (adding a fake symbol with frequency 0, if necessary). Repeatedly merge the three trees with the smallest sums of symbol frequencies. Modify the induction and exchange arguments in the proof of Theorem 14.2, taking particular care with the latter.

Hint for Problem 15.1: To reason about T, use Corollary 15.8 or the minimum bottleneck property (page 341). To reason about P, think about two s-t paths with different numbers of edges.

Hint for Problem 15.2: Use Lemma 15.7 to prove that the output is a spanning tree. Prove that every edge that fails to satisfy the minimum bottleneck property (page 341) is excluded from the final output and use Theorem 15.6.

Hint for Problem 15.3: Three of the four problems reduce easily to the MST problem. For one of them, use the fact that $\ln(x \cdot y) = \ln x + \ln y$ for $x, y > 0$.

Solution to Problem 15.4: Suppose an edge $e = (v, w)$ of an MST T of a graph G does not satisfy the minimum bottleneck property and let P denote a v-w path in G in which every edge has cost less than c_e. Removing e from T creates two connected components, S_1 (containing v) and S_2 (containing w). The v-w path P includes an edge $e' = (x, y)$ with $x \in S_1$ and $y \in S_2$. The edge set $T' = T - \{e\} \cup \{e'\}$ is a spanning tree with total cost less than that of T, contradicting the assumption that T is an MST.

Solution to Problem 15.5: We outline the argument for Kruskal's algorithm; the argument for Prim's algorithm is similar. Let $G = (V, E)$ be a connected undirected graph with real-valued edge costs that need not be distinct. We can assume that not all edges have the same cost, and more generally that not all spanning trees have the same total cost (why?). Let $\delta_1 > 0$ denote the smallest strictly positive difference between two edges' costs. Let M^* denote the cost of an MST of G, and M the minimum cost of a suboptimal spanning tree of G. Define $\delta_2 > 0$ as $M - M^*$ and $\delta = \min\{\delta_1, \delta_2\} > 0$. Let e_i denote the ith edge of G considered by the `Kruskal` algorithm (after arbitrarily breaking ties in its sorting preprocessing step). Obtain a new graph G' from G by increasing the cost of each edge e_i from c_{e_i} to $c'_{e_i} = c_{e_i} + \delta/2^{(m-i+1)}$, where m is the number of edges. The cost of each spanning tree can only increase, and can increase by at most $\delta \cdot \sum_{i=1}^{m} 2^{-(m-i+1)} = \delta \cdot \sum_{i=1}^{m} 2^{-i} < \delta$. Because $\delta \leq \delta_2$, an MST T of G' must also be an MST of G. (Said differently, if a spanning tree T is suboptimal in G then, because δ is so small, it remains suboptimal in G'.) Because $\delta \leq \delta_1$, the edges of G' have distinct costs, with edge e_i the ith-cheapest edge of G'. The `Kruskal` algorithm examines the edges of G and G' in the same order and, therefore, outputs the same spanning tree T^* in both cases. From our proof of correctness of the `Kruskal` algorithm for graphs with distinct edge costs, we know that T^* is an MST of G' and, hence, of G as well.

Hint for Problem 15.6: Follow the proof of Theorem 15.6.

Solution to Problem 15.7: For (a), suppose for contradiction that there is an MST T that excludes $e = (v, w)$. As a spanning tree, T contains a v-w path P. Because v and w are on different sides of the cut (A, B), P includes an edge e' that crosses (A, B). By assumption, the cost of e' exceeds that of e. Thus $T' = T \cup \{e\} - \{e'\}$ is a spanning tree with cost less than that of T, a contradiction. For (b), every iteration of Prim's algorithm chooses the cheapest edge e that crosses the cut $(X, V - X)$, where X is the set of vertices spanned by the solution-so-far. The Cut Property then implies that every MST contains every edge of the algorithm's final spanning tree T, and so T is the unique MST. For (c), similarly, every edge chosen by Kruskal's algorithm is justified by the Cut Property. Each edge $e = (v, w)$ added by the algorithm is the cheapest one with endpoints in distinct connected components of the solution-so-far (as these are precisely the edges whose addition will not create a cycle). In particular, e is the cheapest edge crossing the cut (A, B), where A is v's current connected component and $B = V - A$ is the union of the other connected components.

Hint for Problem 15.8: For (a), the high-level idea is to perform a binary search for the bottleneck of an MBST. Compute the median edge cost in the input graph G using a linear-time algorithm from Chapter 6. Obtain G' from G by throwing out all the edges with cost higher than the median. Proceed by recursing on a graph with half as many edges as G. (The easy case is when G' is connected; how do you recurse if G' is not connected?) For the running time analysis, use induction or case 2 of the master method (see Theorem 4.1).

For (b), the answer appears to be no. (Every MST is an MBST but not conversely, as you should check.) The question of whether there is a deterministic linear-time algorithm for the MST problem remains open to this day; see the bonus video at www.algorithmsilluminated.org for the full story.

Solution to Problem 16.1:

0	5	5	6	12	12	16	18

and the first, fourth, and seventh vertices.

Solution to Problem 16.2: With columns indexed by i and rows by c:

c	0	1	2	3	4	5
9	0	1	3	6	8	10
8	0	1	3	6	8	9
7	0	1	3	6	7	9
6	0	1	3	6	6	8
5	0	1	3	5	5	6
4	0	1	3	4	4	5
3	0	1	2	4	4	4
2	0	1	1	3	3	3
1	0	1	1	1	1	1
0	0	0	0	0	0	0

and the second, third, and fifth items.

Hint for Problem 16.3: For (a) and (c), revisit the four-vertex example on page 368. For (d), use induction and Lemma 16.1.

Hint for Problem 16.4: Straightforward induction on n.

Hint for Problem 16.5: To assess (1), experiment with three-item examples. For (2), can you be sure that there exists such a partition of S into S_1 and S_2?

Hint for Problem 16.6: For (d), follow the proof of Lemma 16.1.

For (e), given an n-vertex tree graph G as input, designate an arbitrary vertex as the root. The subproblems are: for each vertex v of G, compute W_v, the total weight of an MWIS in the subtree of G rooted at v. Solve the subproblems bottom-up, starting from the leaves and ending at G's root. The solution to a subproblem rooted at v, with children (layer-1 vertices) A and grandchildren (layer-2 vertices) B, is the larger of

$$\sum_{u \in A} W_u \qquad \text{(Case 1)}$$

and

$$w_v + \sum_{u \in B} W_u \qquad \text{(Case 2)}.$$

The overall running time is proportional to the number of times subproblem solutions are looked up; because each of the $O(n)$ subproblem solutions is looked up at most twice (once by the parent, once by the grandparent), this is $O(n)$.

For (f), what would your subproblems be?

Hint for Problem 16.7: For (b) and (c), add a third parameter to the dynamic programming solution to the original knapsack problem in Section 16.5. For (d), how does the running time of the generalization of your solution to (c) scale with the number m of knapsacks?

Solution to Problem 17.1: With columns indexed by i and rows by j:

6	6	5	4	5	4	5	4
5	5	4	5	4	3	4	5
4	4	3	4	3	4	5	6
3	3	2	3	4	3	4	5
2	2	1	2	3	4	3	4
1	1	0	1	2	3	4	5
0	0	1	2	3	4	5	6
	0	1	2	3	4	5	6

Hint for Problem 17.2: In each loop iteration, have the necessary subproblem solutions already been computed in previous iterations (or as a base case)?

Solution to Problem 17.3: Consider three keys $\{1, 2, 3\}$ with $p_1 = .35$, $p_2 = .33$, and $p_3 = .32$.

Solution to Problem 17.4: With columns indexed by i and rows by $j = i + s$:

7	223	158	143	99	74	31	25	0
6	151	105	90	46	26	3	0	
5	142	97	84	40	20	0		
4	92	47	37	10	0			
3	69	27	17	0				
2	30	5	0					
1	20	0						
0	0							
	1	2	3	4	5	6	7	8

Hint for Problem 17.5: The idea is to reuse space once a subproblem solution is rendered irrelevant for future computations. To carry out its entire computation, the WIS algorithm must remember only the two most recent subproblems. The NW algorithm must remember subproblem solutions for the current and preceding values of i, and for all values of j (why?). What about the OptBST algorithm?

Solution to Problem 17.6: The problems in (b) and (d) can be solved using algorithms similar to NW, with one subproblem for each pair X_i, Y_j of input string prefixes. For (b), alternatively, there is an easy and direct reduction to the sequence alignment problem: given an input for the longest common subsequence problem (that is, two strings) and an efficient algorithm for the sequence alignment problem (such as the NW algorithm), invoke that algorithm with the same two input strings, a penalty of 1 per inserted gap, and a very large penalty for each mismatch of two different symbols. A longest common subsequence of the original two input strings can then be read off of the columns of the minimum-penalty alignment that contain two (identical) symbols instead of one symbol and one gap.

The problem in (a) can be solved by a generalization of the NW algorithm that keeps track of whether an inserted gap is the first in a sequence of gaps (in which case it carries a penalty of $a + b$) or not (in which case the additional penalty is a). For each pair of prefixes of the input strings, compute the total penalty of three alignments: the best one with no gaps in the final column, the best one with a gap in the upper row of the final column, and the best one with a gap in the lower row of the final column. The number of subproblems and the work-per-subproblem each blow up by a constant factor.

The problem in (c) can be solved efficiently without using dynamic programming, simply by counting the frequency of each symbol in each string. The permutation f exists if and only if every symbol occurs exactly the same number of times in each string. (Do you see why?)

Hint for Problem 17.7: Don't bother solving subproblems for prefixes X_i and Y_j with $|i - j| > k$.

Hint for Problem 17.8: The running time of your algorithm should be bounded by a polynomial function of n—a really, really big polynomial!

Solution to Problem 18.1: With columns indexed by i and rows by vertices:

x	$+\infty$	$+\infty$	5	5	5	-1
w	$+\infty$	$+\infty$	$+\infty$	-4	-4	-4
v	$+\infty$	$+\infty$	-1	-1	-1	-7
u	$+\infty$	1	1	1	-5	-5
s	0	0	0	0	0	0
	0	1	2	3	4	5

Solution to Problem 18.2: No. For a counterexample, see the previous problem.

Hint for Problem 18.3: Consider stopping a shortest-path algorithm early.

Solution to Problem 18.4: With columns indexed by k and rows by vertex pairs:

(1, 1)	0	0	0	0	0
(1, 2)	2	2	2	2	2
(1, 3)	5	5	3	3	3
(1, 4)	$+\infty$	$+\infty$	$+\infty$	6	6
(2, 1)	$+\infty$	$+\infty$	$+\infty$	$+\infty$	8
(2, 2)	0	0	0	0	0
(2, 3)	1	1	1	1	1
(2, 4)	$+\infty$	$+\infty$	$+\infty$	4	4
(3, 1)	$+\infty$	$+\infty$	$+\infty$	$+\infty$	7
(3, 2)	$+\infty$	$+\infty$	$+\infty$	$+\infty$	9
(3, 3)	0	0	0	0	0
(3, 4)	3	3	3	3	3
(4, 1)	4	4	4	4	4
(4, 2)	$+\infty$	6	6	6	6
(4, 3)	$+\infty$	9	7	7	7
(4, 4)	0	0	0	0	0
	0	1	2	3	4

Solution to Problem 18.5: With columns indexed by k and rows by vertex pairs:

(1, 1)	0	0	0	0	-4
(1, 2)	2	2	2	2	-2
(1, 3)	5	5	3	3	-1
(1, 4)	$+\infty$	$+\infty$	$+\infty$	0	-4
(2, 1)	$+\infty$	$+\infty$	$+\infty$	$+\infty$	-6
(2, 2)	0	0	0	0	-4
(2, 3)	1	1	1	1	-3
(2, 4)	$+\infty$	$+\infty$	$+\infty$	-2	-6
(3, 1)	$+\infty$	$+\infty$	$+\infty$	$+\infty$	-7
(3, 2)	$+\infty$	$+\infty$	$+\infty$	$+\infty$	-5
(3, 3)	0	0	0	0	-4
(3, 4)	-3	-3	-3	-3	-7
(4, 1)	-4	-4	-4	-4	-8
(4, 2)	$+\infty$	-2	-2	-2	-6
(4, 3)	$+\infty$	1	-1	-1	-5
(4, 4)	0	0	0	-4	-8
	0	1	2	3	4

Solution to Problem 18.6: Modify the input graph $G = (V, E)$ by adding a new source vertex s and a new zero-length edge from s to each vertex $v \in V$. The new graph G' has a negative cycle reachable from s if and only if G has a negative cycle. Run the Bellman-Ford algorithm on G' with source vertex s to check whether G contains a negative cycle. If not, run the Floyd-Warshall algorithm on G.

Hint for Problem 18.7: Longest-path problems can be reframed as shortest-path problems after multiplying all edge lengths by -1. Recall from page 417 the problem of computing shortest cycle-free paths in graphs with negative cycles and the fact that it appears to admit no polynomial-time algorithm. Does this fact have any implications for any of the four stated problems?

Solution to Problem 19.1: (b),(c). The dynamic programming algorithm for the (NP-hard) knapsack problem is a good example of why (d) is incorrect.

Solution to Problem 19.2: (c). Footnote 5 shows why (a) is incorrect. The spanning trees of a graph can all have distinct total costs (for example, if the edge costs are distinct powers of 2), so (b) is also incorrect. The logic in (d) is flawed, as the MST problem is computationally tractable even in graphs with an exponential number of spanning trees.

Solution to Problem 19.3: (b),(d). Answer (c) is incorrect because polynomial-time solvability is related to but not the same thing as solvability in practice. (Imagine an algorithm with running time $O(n^{100})$ on size-n inputs, for example.)

Solution to Problem 19.4: (a). For example, the dynamic programming algorithm for the knapsack problem shows that (c) and (d) are incorrect.

Solution to Problem 19.5: (e). For (a) and (b), the reduction goes in the wrong direction. Answer (c) is incorrect because some problems (like the halting problem mentioned in footnote 16) are strictly harder than others (like the MST problem). Answer (d) is incorrect when, for example, A and B are the single-source and all-pairs shortest path problems. The formal proof for (e) resembles the solution to Quiz 19.3.

Solution to Problem 19.6: (a),(b),(d). In (a), you can assume without loss of generality that the knapsack capacity C is at most n^6 (why?). For (b), refer to Problem 20.11. For (c), the problem is NP-hard even when the input comprises only positive integers (page 455).

Hint for Problem 19.7: To use a subroutine for the TSP to solve an instance of the TSPP, add one additional vertex, connected by a zero-cost edge to each of the original vertices. To use a subroutine for the TSPP to solve an instance of the TSP, first split an arbitrary vertex v into two copies v' and v'' (each inheriting edge costs from v, and with $c_{v'v''} = +\infty$). Then add two new vertices x, y that are each connected to all other vertices by infinite-cost edges, with the exceptions that $c_{xv'} = c_{yv''} = 0$.

Hint for Problem 19.8: Visit the vertices of G in the same order that depth-first search (from an arbitrary starting vertex) would visit the vertices of T. Prove that the total cost of the resulting tour is $2 \sum_{e \in F} a_e$, and that no tour can have a smaller total cost.

Solution to Problem 20.1: (b). To falsify (a), consider ten machines, ten jobs with length 1, ninety jobs with length $6/5$, and one job with length 2. To prove (b), use the assumptions to show that the maximum job length is at most 20% of the average machine load, and plug this into (20.3).

Solution to Problem 20.2: (b). To falsify (a), use a sixteen-element variant of the example in Quiz 20.5; the optimal solution should use two subsets and the greedy algorithm five (with worst-case tie-breaking). For (b), the first k iterations of the greedy algorithm match those of the GreedyCoverage algorithm with a budget of k. The approximate correctness guarantee for the latter algorithm (Theorem 20.7) implies that this first batch of k iterations covers at least a $1 - \frac{1}{e}$ fraction of the elements of U. The next batch of k iterations covers at least a $1 - \frac{1}{e}$ fraction of the elements that weren't covered in the first batch (why?). After t batches of k iterations each, the number of still-uncovered elements is at most $(\frac{1}{e})^t \cdot |U|$. This number is less than 1 once $t > \ln |U|$, so the algorithm completes within $O(k \log |U|)$ iterations.

Solution to Problem 20.3: (c),(e),(f). To falsify (a) and (d), take $C = 100$ and consider ten items with value 2 and size 10, together with one hundred items with value 1 and size 1. To falsify (b), consider one item with size and value equal to 100 and a second item with value 20 and size 10. To prove (c), imagine allowing the second greedy algorithm to cheat and fill up the knapsack completely using a fraction of one additional item (with value earned on a pro rata basis). Use an exchange argument to prove that the total value of this cheating solution is at least that of any feasible solution. Argue that the combined value of the solutions returned by the first two greedy algorithms is at least that of the cheating solution (and hence the better of the two is at least 50% as good). To prove (e) and (f), argue that the second greedy algorithm misses out only on the worst 10% (in terms of value-to-size ratio) of the cheating solution.

Solution to Problem 20.4: (a). Each iteration of the algorithm's main while loop chooses one edge of the input graph; let M denote the set of chosen edges. The subset S returned by the algorithm then contains $2|M|$ vertices. No two edges of M share an endpoint (why?), so every feasible solution must include at least $|M|$ vertices (one endpoint per edge of M).

Solution to Problem 20.5: (c). A local search algorithm eventually halts at a *locally* optimal solution.

Hint for Problem 20.6: Store in a heap one object per machine, with keys equal to the machines' current loads. Each machine load update boils down to an EXTRACTMIN operation followed by an INSERT operation with the updated key value.

Hint for Problem 20.7: For (a), you can ignore any jobs after job j (why?). Prove that, if $\ell_j > M^*/3$, each machine is assigned one or two of the first j jobs, with the longest jobs on their own machines and the rest paired up optimally on the remaining machines. For (b), use (20.3).

Hint for Problem 20.8: For (a), use a $k^{k-1} \times k^{k-1}$ grid of elements and $2k - 1$ subsets. For (b), replace each element with a group of N copies of it (each belonging to the same subsets as before). Eliminate ties by adding one additional copy to some of the groups. The choice of N should depend on ϵ.

Hint for Problem 20.9: For example, given an instance of the maximum coverage problem with budget k, ground set $U = \{1, 2, 3, 4\}$, and subsets $A_1 = \{1, 2\}$, $A_2 = \{3, 4\}$, and $A_3 = \{2, 4\}$, encode it using the directed graph

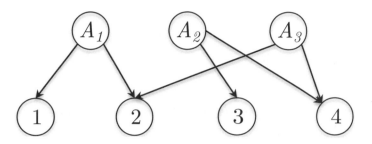

along with the activation probability $p = 1$ and the same budget k.

Hint for Problem 20.10: For (a), verify the properties directly for coverage functions and then use Lemma 20.10. For (b), the primary ingredient is a general version of Lemmas 20.8 and 20.11, and specifically the inequalities (20.7) and (20.15). Let S^* denote an optimal solution and S_{j-1} the first $j - 1$ objects chosen by the greedy algorithm. One way to view the right-hand sides of these inequalities is as the sum of the successive marginal values of the objects in $S^* - S_{j-1}$, when added to S_{j-1} one by one in an arbitrary order. The left-hand sides express the sum of the marginal values of the objects in $S^* - S_{j-1}$ when each is added to S_{j-1} in isolation. Submodularity implies that each term in the former sum is at most that in the latter. Where do nonnegativity and monotonicity show up in the proof?

Hint for Problem 20.11: For (a), each subproblem computes, for some $i \in \{0, 1, 2, \ldots, n\}$ and $x \in \{0, 1, 2, \ldots, n \cdot v_{max}\}$, the minimum total size of a subset of the first i items that has a total value of at least x (or $+\infty$, if no such subset exists). For the full solution, see the bonus videos at www.algorithmsilluminated.org.

Hint for Problem 20.12: For (a), every tour can be viewed as a Hamiltonian path (which, as a spanning tree, has total cost at least that of an MST) together with one additional edge (which, by assumption, has a nonnegative cost). For (b), use the triangle inequality to argue that all edge costs in the constructed tree TSP instance are at least as large as in the given metric TSP instance. Using the solution to Problem 19.8, conclude that the total cost of the computed tour is at most twice that of the MST T.

Hint for Problem 20.13: For example, represent the graph using an adjacency matrix (with entries encoding edges' costs) and the current tour using a doubly-linked list.

Solution to Problem 20.14: For (a), the objective function value is always an integer between 0 and $|E|$, and it increases by at least 1 in each iteration. For (b), consider a local maximum. For each vertex $v \in S_i$ and group S_j with $j \neq i$, the number of edges between v and the vertices of S_i is at most that between v and the vertices of S_j (why?). Adding up these $|V| \cdot (k - 1)$ inequalities and rearranging completes the argument.

Solution to Problem 21.1: (c).

Solution to Problem 21.2: With columns indexed by vertices of $V - \{a\}$ and rows indexed by subsets S that contain a and at least one other vertex:

$\{a,b\}$	1	N/A	N/A	N/A
$\{a,c\}$	N/A	4	N/A	N/A
$\{a,d\}$	N/A	N/A	5	N/A
$\{a,e\}$	N/A	N/A	N/A	10
$\{a,b,c\}$	6	3	N/A	N/A
$\{a,b,d\}$	11	N/A	7	N/A
$\{a,b,e\}$	13	N/A	N/A	4
$\{a,c,d\}$	N/A	12	11	N/A
$\{a,c,e\}$	N/A	18	N/A	12
$\{a,d,e\}$	N/A	N/A	19	14
$\{a,b,c,d\}$	14	13	10	N/A
$\{a,b,c,e\}$	15	12	N/A	9
$\{a,b,d,e\}$	17	N/A	13	14
$\{a,c,d,e\}$	N/A	22	21	20
$\{a,b,c,d,e\}$	23	19	18	17
	b	c	d	e

Solution to Problem 21.3: (b). Appending an edge (w, v) to a minimum-cost $(i - 1)$-hop path P from 1 to w creates a cycle if P already visits v.

Solution to Problem 21.4: (a),(b),(c),(d),(e).

Solution to Problem 21.5: With columns indexed by vertices and rows indexed by non-empty subsets of colors:

$\{R\}$	0	0	$+\infty$	$+\infty$	$+\infty$	$+\infty$	$+\infty$	$+\infty$
$\{G\}$	$+\infty$	$+\infty$	0	0	$+\infty$	$+\infty$	$+\infty$	$+\infty$
$\{B\}$	$+\infty$	$+\infty$	$+\infty$	$+\infty$	0	0	$+\infty$	$+\infty$
$\{Y\}$	$+\infty$	$+\infty$	$+\infty$	$+\infty$	$+\infty$	$+\infty$	0	0
$\{R,G\}$	1	4	1	4	$+\infty$	$+\infty$	$+\infty$	$+\infty$
$\{R,B\}$	2	6	$+\infty$	$+\infty$	6	2	$+\infty$	$+\infty$
$\{R,Y\}$	$+\infty$	$+\infty$	$+\infty$	$+\infty$	$+\infty$	$+\infty$	$+\infty$	$+\infty$
$\{G,B\}$	$+\infty$	$+\infty$	7	3	7	3	$+\infty$	$+\infty$
$\{G,Y\}$	$+\infty$	$+\infty$	8	5	$+\infty$	$+\infty$	5	8
$\{B,Y\}$	$+\infty$	$+\infty$	$+\infty$	$+\infty$	9	10	9	10
$\{R,G,B\}$	5	7	3	5	8	3	$+\infty$	$+\infty$
$\{R,G,Y\}$	9	9	$+\infty$	$+\infty$	$+\infty$	$+\infty$	9	9
$\{R,B,Y\}$	12	15	$+\infty$	$+\infty$	$+\infty$	$+\infty$	15	12
$\{G,B,Y\}$	$+\infty$	$+\infty$	16	13	14	8	8	13
$\{R,G,B,Y\}$	10	17	13	19	15	11	10	11
	a	b	c	d	e	f	g	h

Hint for Problem 21.6: Any vertex j that achieves the minimum in (21.6) appears last on some optimal tour. A vertex k that achieves the minimum in (21.4) immediately precedes j on some such tour. The rest of the tour can be similarly reconstructed in reverse order. To achieve a linear running time, modify the `BellmanHeldKarp` algorithm so that it caches for each subproblem a vertex that achieves the minimum in the recurrence (21.5) used to compute the subproblem solution.

Hint for Problem 21.7: Modify the `PanchromaticPath` algorithm so that it caches for each subproblem an edge (w, v) that achieves the minimum in the recurrence (21.7) used to compute the subproblem solution. Also, cache a vertex achieving the minimum in the last line of the pseudocode.

Hint for Problem 21.8: Throw out the solutions to the size-s subproblems after computing all the solutions to the size-$(s + 1)$ subproblems. Use Stirling's approximation (21.1) to estimate $\binom{n}{n/2}$.

Solution to Problem 21.9: (a) With x_v indicating whether vertex v is included in the solution:

$$
\begin{aligned}
\text{maximize} \quad & \sum_{v \in V} w_v x_v \\
\text{subject to} \quad & x_u + x_v \leq 1 \quad \text{[for every edge } (u, v) \in E] \\
& x_v \in \{0, 1\} \quad \text{[for every vertex } v \in V].
\end{aligned}
$$

(b) With x_{ij} indicating whether job j is assigned to machine i, and with M denoting the corresponding schedule's makespan:[12]

$$
\begin{aligned}
\text{minimize} \quad & M \\
\text{subject to} \quad & \sum_{j=1}^{n} \ell_j x_{ij} \leq M \quad \text{[for every machine } i] \\
& \sum_{i=1}^{m} x_{ij} = 1 \quad \text{[for every job } j] \\
& x_{ij} \in \{0, 1\} \quad \text{[for every machine } i \text{ and job } j] \\
& M \in \mathbb{R}.
\end{aligned}
$$

(c) With x_i indicating whether subset A_i is included in the solution, and y_e whether element e belongs to a chosen subset:[13]

$$
\begin{aligned}
\text{maximize} \quad & \sum_{e \in U} y_e \\
\text{subject to} \quad & y_e \leq \sum_{i : e \in A_i} x_i \quad \text{[for every element } e \in U] \\
& \sum_{i=1}^{m} x_i = k \\
& x_i, y_e \in \{0, 1\} \quad \text{[for every subset } A_i \text{ and element } e].
\end{aligned}
$$

Hint for Problem 21.10: For (a), orient the tour in one direction and set x_{ij} to 1 if j is the immediate successor of i and to 0 otherwise. For (b), show that a union of two (or more) disjoint directed cycles that together visit all vertices also translates to a feasible solution

---

[12] If the constraints with decision variables on both sides bother you, rewrite them as $\sum_{j=1}^{n} \ell_j x_{ij} - M \leq 0$ for every machine i. These constraints force M to be at least as large as the maximum machine load; in any optimal solution to the MIP, equality must hold (why?).

[13] The first set of constraints force $y_e = 0$ whenever none of the subsets that contain e are chosen. (And if such a subset is chosen, y_e will equal 1 in every optimal solution.)

of the MIP. For (c), if edge (i, j) is the ℓth hop of the tour (starting from vertex 1), set $y_{ij} = n - \ell$. For (d), argue that every feasible solution is of the form constructed in (c).

Hint for Problem 21.11: For example, encode the constraint $x_1 \vee \neg x_2 \vee x_3$ as $y_1 + (1 - y_2) + y_3 \geq 1$, where the y_i's are 0-1 decision variables. (Use a placeholder objective function, like the constant 0.)

Hint for Problem 21.12: For (b), recall (21.10). For (c), use that ta^* satisfies the constraint while ta does not. For (d), use that a truth assignment and its opposite are equally likely. For (f), use that a running time bound of the form $O((\sqrt{3})^n n^d \ln \frac{1}{\delta})$ for a constant d is also $O((1.74)^n \ln \frac{1}{\delta})$ (because any exponential function grows faster than any polynomial function).

Solution to Problem 22.1: (d). The undirected Hamiltonian path problem reduces to each of the problems in (a)–(c). The problem in (d) can be solved in polynomial time using a variation of the Bellman-Ford shortest-path algorithm (see Section 18.2).

Solution to Problem 22.2: (a),(b). The problems in (a) and (b) both reduce to the all-pairs shortest path problem with no negative cycles (for (b), after multiplying all edge lengths by -1), which can be solved in polynomial time using the Floyd-Warshall algorithm (see Section 18.4). The directed Hamiltonian path problem reduces to the problem in (c), proving that the latter (and the more general problem in (d)) is NP-hard.

Solution to Problem 22.3: (a),(b),(c),(d). For (b), if the assumed subroutine for the decision version says "no," report "no solution." If it says "yes," use the subroutine repeatedly to delete outgoing edges of s, never deleting an edge that would flip its answer to "no"; eventually, only one outgoing edge (s, v) will remain. Repeat the process from v.

For (d), perform binary search over the target total cost C. The running time is polynomial in the number of vertices and the number of digits required to represent the edge costs, which is polynomial in the input size; see also the discussion on page 455.

Hint for Problem 22.4: Toggle which edges are present or absent.

Hint for Problem 22.5: A subset S of vertices is a vertex cover if and only if its complement $V - S$ is an independent set.

Hint for Problem 22.6: Use one subset per vertex, containing its incident edges.

Hint for Problem 22.7: Use t as the knapsack capacity. Use a_i as both the value and size of item i.

Solution to Problem 22.8: Invoke a subroutine for the maximum coverage problem with the given set system and successively increasing budgets $k = 1, 2, \ldots, m$. The first time the subroutine returns k subsets that cover all of U, these subsets constitute an optimal solution to the given set cover instance.

Hint for Problem 22.9: To reduce the undirected version to the directed version, replace each undirected edge (v, w) with two directed edges (v, w) and (w, v). For the other direction, perform the following operation on each vertex:

Hint for Problem 22.10: For (a), add one additional number to the input. For (b), use the a_i's as job lengths.

Hint for Problem 22.11: Start with a triangle on vertices called t (for "true"), f (for "false"), and o (for "other"). Add two more vertices v_i, w_i per variable x_i in the given 3-SAT instance, and connect them in a triangle with o. In every 3-coloring, v_i and w_i either have the same colors as t and f, respectively (interpreted as $x_i := $ true) or the same colors as f and t, respectively (interpreted as $x_i := $ false). Implement a disjunction of two literals using a subgraph of the form

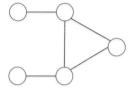

with "inputs" on the left and the "output" on the right. Fuse together two such subgraphs to implement a disjunction of three literals.

Hint for Problem 22.12: Part (b) follows immediately from the reduction in the proof of Theorem 22.7. For part (a), add 1 to each of the edge costs in this reduction.

Solution to Problem 23.1: (a),(b). For (a), for all we know, the TSP (say) can be solved in polynomial time. For (b), for all we know, $\mathcal{P} \neq \mathcal{NP}$ but the Exponential Time Hypothesis is false. For (c), see Problem 23.5. For (d), if any NP-complete problem is polynomial-time solvable, $\mathcal{P} - \mathcal{NP}$ and all such problems are polynomial-time solvable.

Solution to Problem 23.2: Because the TSP is NP-hard (Theorem 22.7), every problem in $\mathcal{NP}$ reduces to it. Hence, if Edmonds's conjecture is false (meaning there is a polynomial-time algorithm for the TSP), so is the P $\neq$ NP conjecture. Conversely, if $\mathcal{P} = \mathcal{NP}$, the search version of the TSP (which belongs to $\mathcal{NP}$) would be polynomial-time solvable. The optimization version of the TSP reduces to the search version by binary search (Problem 22.3) and would then also be polynomial-time solvable, refuting Edmonds's conjecture.

Solution to Problem 23.3: All of them (as you should check).

Hint for Problem 23.4: For (a), compose the reductions. For (c), chain together the two preprocessors and the two postprocessors. To bound the running time, argue as in the solution to Quiz 19.3.

Solution to Problem 23.5: For (a), there is a Levin reduction from 3-SAT to PADDED 3-SAT (add one new variable and the appropriate padding). For (b), check (in linear time) if the input is padded and, if so, use exhaustive search to compute a satisfying assignment or conclude that none exist. Because the size N of a padded instance is at least n^2, this exhaustive search runs in $2^{O(n)} = 2^{O(\sqrt{N})}$ time.

Hint for Problem 23.6: Borrow the trick from the previous problem, with the amount of padding super-polynomial but subexponential. Show that a polynomial-time algorithm for the padded problem would refute the Exponential Time Hypothesis. Using that the padded problem can be solved in subexponential time (why?), prove that a (Cook) reduction from the 3-SAT problem to the padded problem would also refute the Exponential Time Hypothesis.

Hint for Problem 23.7: For part (a), run breadth-first search n times, once for each choice of the starting vertex. For part (b), divide the n variables of a given k-SAT instance into two groups of size $n/2$ each. Introduce one vertex for each of the $2^{n/2}$ possible truth assignments to the variables in the first group, and likewise for the second group. Call the two sets of $2^{n/2}$ vertices A and B. Introduce one vertex for each of the m constraints, along with two additional vertices s and t; call this set of $m + 2$ vertices C and define $V = A \cup B \cup C$. (Question: How big can m be, as a function of n and k?) Include edges between each pair of vertices in C, between s and each vertex of A, and between t and each vertex of B. Complete the edge set E by connecting a vertex v of A or B to a vertex w corresponding to a constraint if and only if none of the $n/2$ variable assignments encoded by v satisfy the constraint corresponding to w. Prove that the diameter of $G = (V, E)$ is either 3 or 2, depending on whether the given k-SAT instance is satisfiable or unsatisfiable.

Solution to Problem 24.1: (c).

Solution to Problem 24.2: (c),(d). If in each round of the `FCCDescendingClock` algorithm there is at most one still-in-limbo station v that would refuse that round's offer (because for the first time, w_v exceeds $\beta_v \cdot p$), the order doesn't affect which stations remain on the air (why?).[14] When the station ratios w_v/β_v are distinct, this condition can be enforced by taking ϵ sufficiently small; hence, answers (c) and (d) are correct. If two stations are poised to drop out in the same round—because of ties between station ratios w_v/β_v or because ϵ isn't small enough—different orderings generally lead to different outputs (as you should check); hence, answers (a) and (b) are incorrect.

Solution to Problem 24.3: Not necessarily, as a broadcaster can in some cases game the system by rejecting an offer higher than its value and receiving more compensation than it would have otherwise. (For example, if the owner of an in-limbo station v learns that the set $S \cup \{v\}$ has become unpackable, the owner should always reject the next offer received.)

Hint for Problem 24.4: For (a), whenever the algorithm includes v in its solution-so-far S, it knocks out from further consideration at most Δ other vertices, each with weight at most w_v. Thus $\sum_{v \notin S} w_v \leq \sum_{v \in S} \Delta \cdot w_v$, which implies the stated bound. For (b), for $v \in S$, let $X(v)$ denote the vertices knocked out from further consideration by v's inclusion in S—that is, $u \in X(v)$ if v is the first neighbor of u added to S, or if u is v itself. By the algorithm's greedy criterion, whenever it includes v in S, $w_v \geq \sum_{u \in X(v)} w_u/(\deg(u) + 1)$. Because every vertex $u \in V$ belongs to the set $X(v)$ for exactly one vertex $v \in S$ (why?),

$$\sum_{v \in S} w_v \geq \sum_{v \in S} \sum_{u \in X(v)} \frac{w_u}{\deg(u) + 1} = \sum_{u \in V} \frac{w_u}{\deg(u) + 1} \geq \frac{\sum_{u \in V} w_u}{\Delta + 1}.$$

---

[14]Though even in this case, the compensation paid to a station going off the air might depend on the order of processing (why?).

Index

$|x|$ (absolute value), 35
$\binom{n}{2}$ (binomial coefficient), 33, 53, 146
$\lceil x \rceil$ (ceiling), 134
$\vee$ (disjunction), 542
$n!$ (factorial), 115, 293, 443, 519
$\lfloor x \rfloor$ (floor), 68
$\neg$ (logical negation), 542
$|S|$ (set size), 144
$=$ vs. $:=$, 7
$1 - \frac{1}{e}$, 486
2-OPT algorithm, 500–501
    2-change, 499
    implementation, 517, 518, 649
    improving 2-change, 499
    is interruptible, 501
    pseudocode, 500
    running time, 501
    solution quality, 501
    vs. 3-OPT, 506, 509
2-SAT, 197, 548
2-change, *see* 2-OPT algorithm
2-SUM, 260–262, 289
3-SAT
    and the Exponential Time Hypothesis, 587
    is NP-complete, *see* Cook-Levin theorem, stronger version
    is NP-hard, *see* Cook-Levin theorem
    padded, 595
    problem definition, 553
    reduces to directed Hamiltonian path, 563–567
    reduces to graph coloring, 576, 653
    reduces to independent set, 559–562
    reduction from an arbitrary $\mathcal{NP}$ problem, 582–584
    Schöning's algorithm, 548–550, 652
3-SUM, 287
63.2%, 486

A* search, 212–213, 263
Aaronson, Scott, 586
Aarts, Emile, 508
abstract data type, 214
Ackermann function, 350
acknowledgments, xvi
ACM, 39

adjacency lists, 147–148
    in graph search, 161
    input size, 150
    vs. adjacency matrix, 149
adjacency matrix, 148–149
    applications, 149
    input size, 150
    sparse representation, 150
    vs. adjacency lists, 149
Adleman, Leonard, 132
Aho, Alfred V., 5
Albertini, Ange, 543
algorithm, 2
    anytime, 501
    approximation, 456, 474
    constant-time, 28
    design paradigms, 46
    exponential-time, 449
    fast, 23, 445
    fixed-parameter, 534, 588
    heuristic, 456
    linear-time, 23
    mind-blowing, 45
    online, 477
    polynomial-time, 448
    pseudopolynomial-time, 570
    quadratic-time, 28
    quantum, 452
    randomized, 452
    subexponential-time, 453
algorithm design paradigm, 291
    divide-and-conquer, *see* divide-and-conquer algorithms
    dynamic programming, *see* dynamic programming
    greedy algorithms, *see* greedy algorithms
    local search, *see* local search
algorithm field guide, 630–631
algorithmic game theory, 596
all-pairs shortest path problem, *see* shortest paths, all-pairs
Alon, Noga, 527
alphabet, *see* code, alphabet
among friends, 11, 14, 72, 299, 340, 403
Applegate, David L., 445
applications, 2

approximation algorithm, 456, 474
approximation ratio, 474
    as an insurance policy, 475
Aquarius Records, 191
arc, *see* edge (of a graph), directed
argmax, 316
argmin, 316
asymptotic analysis, 22
asymptotic notation, 27–42
    as a sweet spot, 27
    big-O notation, *see* big-O notation
    big-O vs. big-theta notation, 38
    big-omega notation, 37
    big-theta notation, 38
    history, 39
    in seven words, 27
    little-o notation, 39
auction, *see* FCC Incentive Auction
Augmented-BFS, 164
average-case analysis, 20

backtracking, 536
Backurs, Arturs, 589
Bacon number, 153, 164
Bacon, Kevin, 154
base case (induction), 617
base case (recursion), 7
beam search, 508, *see also* local search
Bellman, Richard E., 380, 418, 524
Bellman-Ford algorithm, 418–429
    and Internet routing, 427
    correctness, 423–424
    example, 424–426
    optimal substructure, 420–421
    pseudocode, 423
    reconstruction, 427
    recurrence, 422
    running time, 426–429
    space usage, 427
    stopping criterion, 422
    subproblems, 419–420
Bellman-Held-Karp algorithm (for the TSP), 519–525
    correctness, 524
    example, 545, 649
    implementation, 550
    memory requirements, 522, 547
    optimal substructure, 521–522, 524–525
    pseudocode, 524
    reconstruction, 524, 547
    recurrence, 522
    running time, 524
    subproblems, 523
    variations, 546
BFS, *see* breadth-first search
BFS, 160

Biere, Armin, 543
big-O notation, 33–35
    as a game, 34
    English definition, 33
    high-level idea, 28
    in an exponent, 581
    mathematical definition, 34
    pictorial definition, 33
big-omega notation, 37
big-picture analysis, 21
big-theta notation, 38
binary search, 75, 238, 242
binary search tree, *see* search tree
bipartite graph, 196, 548
birthday paradox, 265, 272–273, 628
bit, 113, 306
Bixby, Robert E., 445
blazingly fast, xiii, xiv, 23, 65, 90, 91, 97, 153, 474, 607
bloom filter
    INSERT, 277, 279
    LOOKUP, 277, 280
    applications, 278–279
    has false positives, 277, 280
    has no false negatives, 280
    heuristic analysis, 282–285
    heuristic assumptions, 282
    in network routers, 279
    operation running times, 278
    raison d'être, 277
    scorecard, 278
    space-accuracy trade-off, 278, 281, 285, 287
    supported operations, 277
    vs. hash tables, 277–278
    when to use, 278
Bloom, Burton H., 277
Blum, Manuel, 132
Boolean, 542
Borodin, Allan, 291
bow tie, *see* Web graph
branch and bound, 536, *see also* MIP solvers
breadth-first search, 157–163, 330, 349
    and bipartite graphs, 196
    correctness, 163
    example, 161–162
    for computing connected components, 166–168
    for computing shortest paths, 164–165
    layers, 159, 165
    pseudocode, 160
    running time analysis, 163
Broder, Andrei, 191
broken clock, 204
brute-force search, *see* exhaustive search
BubbleSort, 11, 112, 640
BucketSort, 113

Bursztein, Elie, 543

C++, 238, 240
cache, 373
can we do better?, 5, 209, 306, 335, 444, 451, 477, 576, 577, 589
cascade model, 490
Cayley's formula, 330
cf., 83
Chen, Ke, 635
chess, 262
ChoosePivot
    median-of-three implementation, 118
    naive implementation, 98, 100
    overkill implementation, 99, 101
    randomized implementation, 102
Chvátal, Vašek, 445
clause, 542, *see also* constraint
Clay Mathematics Institute, 586
clique problem
    is NP-hard, 575, 652
    reduction from independent set, 575, 652
closest pair
    correctness, 65–67
    exhaustive search, 59
    one-dimensional case, 60
    problem definition, 59
    pseudocode, 60, 62
    running time, 62
clustering, 167, 358–361
    k-means, 360
    and Kruskal's algorithm, 361
    choosing the number of clusters, 359
    greedy criterion, 360
    informal goal, 359
    similarity function, 359
    single-link, 361
Cobham, Alan, 449
cocktail party, xv, 215, 272, 447
code
    Σ-tree, 312
    alphabet, 306
    as a tree, 309–312
    average leaf depth, 312
    average encoding length, 308
    binary, 306
    encodings as root-leaf paths, 311
    fixed-length, 306
    Huffman, *see* Huffman's algorithm
    optimal prefix-free, 308, 313
    prefix-free, 307, 312
    symbol frequencies, 308, 309
    ternary, 327
    variable-length, 306
coin flipping, 127, 275
collaborative filtering, 47

collision, *see* hash function, collision
color coding, 525–535
    and minimum-cost panchromatic paths, 529–531
    correctness, 530, 534
    example, 546, 650
    in practice, 535
    minimum-cost k-path problem, 526
    motivation, 525
    panchromatic path, 528
    pseudocode, 533
    reconstruction, 547
    recurrence, 529
    running time, 531, 533
    subproblems, 529
    with random colors, 531
compression, 306
compromising
    from day one, 578
    on correctness, 454–456, 471–518
    on generality, 454–455, 470, 548
    on speed, 454, 456–457, 519–550
computational complexity theory, 577–593
    fine-grained, 589
computational genomics, 445, 525, *see also* sequence alignment
computational geometry, 59
computational lens, 3
computationally intractable, *see* NP-hardness
conflict-driven clause learning, 536, *see also* SAT solvers
connected components
    applications, 167–168
    definition, 166
    example, 168
    in directed graphs, *see* strongly connected components
    linear-time computation, 168–170
    number of, 170
constant, 35, 74
    reverse engineering, 36, 137
constant factors, 21, 28
constraint
    in mixed integer programming, 538
    in satisfiability, 542
Cook reduction, 578
Cook, Stephen A., 553, 578
Cook, William J., 445
Cook-Levin theorem, 553–554
    50th anniversary, 553
    formal statement, 582
    history, 553
    proof sketch, 582–584
    stronger version, 592
Cormen, Thomas H., 252
Cornuéjols, Gérard P., 484

corollary, 15
counting inversions
    correctness, 49, 52
    exhaustive search, 47
    implementation, 70
    problem definition, 46
    pseudocode, 48, 49
    running time, 52
    split inversions, 51
CountingSort, 113
    stable implementation, 113
Coursera, xvi
coverage, 481, *see also* maximum coverage
    is submodular, 515
CPLEX, *see* MIP solvers
Crosby, Scott A., 270
cryptography, 276
culturally acceptable inaccuracies, 466
cut (of a graph), 364
Cut Property, *see* minimum spanning tree, Cut Property
cycle (of a graph), 329
    negative, 417
Cycle Property, *see* minimum spanning tree, Cycle Property
cycle-free shortest paths
    as an optimization problem, 579
    is NP-hard, 462, 555
    problem definition, 462
    reduction from directed Hamiltonian path, 463
Cygan, Marek, 534

DAG, *see* directed acyclic graph
Dasgupta, Sanjoy, 73
data structure
    bloom filter, *see* bloom filter
    deft deployment, 630
    disjoint-set, *see* union-find
    expertise levels, 215
    hash table, *see* hash table
    heap, *see* heap, *see* heap
    principle of parsimony, 215
    queue, 160, 214, 319
    raison d'être, 214
    scorecards, *see* scorecards
    search tree, *see* search tree
    stack, 172, 214
    union-find, *see* union-find
    vs. abstract data type, 214
de-duplication, 26, 260
decision problem, 579
decomposition blueprint, 106, 127, 274
degree (of a vertex in a graph), 151, 421
depth (of a node in a tree), 311
depth-first search, 158, 170–174, 330, 349

    correctness, 173
    example, 170
    for computing connected components, 174
    for computing strongly connected components, 183
    for topological sorting, 177–180
    iterative implementation, 172
    recursive implementation, 173
    running time analysis, 174
derandomization, 453
descending clock auction, *see* FCC Incentive Auction
design patterns, xiv
DFS, *see* depth-first search
DFS (Iterative Version), 172
DFS (Recursive Version), 173
DFS-SCC, 187
DFS-Topo, 178
diameter (of a graph), 194, 595
dictionary, *see* hash table
diff, 413
Dijkstra, 202
Dijkstra (heap-based), 224, 225
Dijkstra's shortest-path algorithm
    and A* search, 212–213, 263
    as a greedy algorithm, 292
    correctness, 206–208, 299
    Dijkstra score, 203
    example, 204
    for computing minimum bottleneck paths, 212, 236
    greedy selection rule, 203
    heap-based implementation, 222–226
    in undirected graphs, 200
    pseudocode, 202
    pseudocode (heap-based), 224, 225
    reconstructing shortest paths, 203
    resembles Prim's algorithm, 331
    running time analysis, 209
    running time analysis (heap-based), 225
    straightforward implementation, 209
    with negative edge lengths, 205, 416
Dijkstra, Edsger W., 198, 331
directed acyclic graph, 176
    has a source vertex, 176
    has a topological ordering, 176–177
discussion forum, xvi
disjunction (of literals), 542
dist, *see* shortest paths, distance
distance, *see* shortest paths, distance
divide-and-conquer, 9, 10, 45–46, 291–292, 630
    for closest pair, 60
    for counting inversions, 48
    for matrix multiplication, 55
    for sorting, 45
    proofs of correctness, 93

vs. dynamic programming, 375, 379–380
when to use, 46
double summation, 626
Draper, Don, 154
DSelect
    30-70 Lemma, 133–135
    as a knockout tournament, 129
    does not run in place, 131
    heuristic analysis, 136
    history, 132
    pseudocode, 129
    running time, 132
    running time analysis, 132–137
    vs. RSelect, 129, 132
    with groups of 3 or 7, 139
Dumitrescu, Adrian, 635
dynamic programming, xiii
    as recursion with a cache, 372
    bottom-up, 373
    for all-pairs shortest paths, see Floyd-
        Warshall algorithm
    for beating exhaustive search, 519–525, 529–
        531, 631
    for color coding, 529–531
    for graph problems, 419
    for knapsack, 455, 469, 515, 649
    for optimal binary search trees, 400–410
    for single-source shortest paths, see Bellman-
        Ford algorithm
    for the knapsack problem, 380–387
    for the sequence alignment problem, 392–399
    for the TSP, see Bellman-Held-Karp algo-
        rithm
    for weighted independent set in path graphs,
        370–377
    history, 380
    memoization, 373
    optimal substructure, 378
    ordering the input, 382
    principles, 377–378, 520
    recurrence, 379
    running time, 378, 520
    saving space, 412, 645
    subproblems, 378–379, 521
    takes practice, 366
    top-down, 372
    vs. divide-and-conquer, 375, 379–380
    when to use, 630

e (Euler's number), 486, 519
e.g., 347
Easley, David, 192
edge (of a graph), 142
    directed, 143
    length, 198, 415
    parallel, 144, 148, 330

undirected, 143
weighted, 148
Edmonds, Jack, 445, 449, 577
EdX, xvi
Egoyan, Atom, 154
Einstein, Albert, 214, 578
endpoints (of an edge), 143
equivalence class, 166
equivalence relation, 166
Erdös number, 154
Erdös, Paul, 154
ETH, see Exponential Time Hypothesis
Euclidean distance, 59, 518
event (in probability), 621
exchange argument, 299
    for minimum spanning trees, 345
    in Huffman's algorithm, 321
    in scheduling, 300
exhaustive search, 294, 309, 335, 368, 394, 410,
        581, 630
    for closest pair, 59
    for counting inversions, 47
expectation (of a random variable), 492, 494, 623
    linearity of, 624
expected value, see expectation
Exponential Time Hypothesis
    and fixed-parameter algorithms, 588
    and Schöning's algorithm, 550, 587
    definition, 587
    is false for unnatural problems, 595, 653
    vs. the P ≠ NP conjecture, 453, 587
    vs. the SETH, 588

factoring, 453, 465
Fano, Robert M., 313
fast algorithm, 23, 445
Fast Fourier Transform, 69
FCC Incentive Auction
    algorithm portfolio, 608
    and graph coloring, 603
    and greedy heuristic algorithms, 600–604
    and SAT solvers, 604–609
    and timeouts, 609
    and weighted independent set, 599
    as a descending clock auction, 609–613
    computing payments, 612, 615, 654
    feasibility checking, 604–609
    final outcome, 613
    forward auction, 598
    incentives, 613, 615, 654
    matches supply and demand, 614
    motivation, 596–598
    preprocessing, 607
    presolvers, 606
    repacking problem, 605
    representative instances, 602

reverse auction, 598
side constraints, 605
station-specific multipliers, 601–602
feasible solution
in local search, 505
to an $\mathcal{NP}$ problem, 579
Federer, Roger, 132, 610
Feige, Uriel, 487
Fermat's Last Theorem, 586
Fibonacci numbers, 389
field guide (to algorithm design), 630–631
Firth, Colin, 154
Fisher, Marshall L., 484
fixed-parameter algorithm, 534, 588
Floyd, Robert W., 132, 430
Floyd-Warshall algorithm, 430–437
    detecting a negative cycle, 436–437
    optimal substructure, 432–434
    pseudocode, 434
    reconstruction, 437
    recurrence, 434
    running time, 436
    space usage, 436
    subproblems, 430–432
Fomin, Fedor V., 534
for-free primitive, 23, 103, 155, 630
Ford Jr., Lester R., 418
forest (of trees), 315
Fortnow, Lance, 586
Four Color Theorem, 541
Fourier matrix, 69
fully polynomial-time approximation scheme (FP-
    TAS), 516

Gödel, Kurt, 586
Gabow, Harold N., 638
Garey, Michael R., 557, 593
Gauss's trick, 8, 56
Gauss, Carl Friedrich, 8
GenericSearch, 155
genetic algorithms, 508, see also local search
geometric series, 84–85, 128, 489
Git, 413
golden ratio, 389
good vs. evil, 82
Google, 3, 149
googol, 28, 262, 569, 576
Gosper's hack, 524
gradient descent, 504
Graham's algorithm, 473
    approximate correctness, 474–477
    bad example, 474, 479
    intuition, 475
    running time, 474, 514, 648
    with small jobs, 511, 647
Graham, Ronald L., 473

graph, 142
    k-colorable, 541
    adjacency lists, 147–148, 150
    adjacency matrix, 148–150, 435
    applications, 143–144
    bipartite, 196, 548
    co-authorship, 154
    complete, 146, 166, 443
    connected, 144, 443
    connected components, see connected com-
        ponents
    cut, 364
    cycle, 175, 329
    dense, 145, 430
    diameter, 194, 595
    directed, 143
    directed acyclic, see directed acyclic graph
    independent set, 366
    input size, 144
    notation, 142, 144
    number of edges, 348
    path, 146, 155, 166, 329, 368
    planar, 541
    radius, 194
    representations, 146–149
    search, 330, 349
    spanning tree, 329, 443
    sparse, 145, 429
    tour, 443
    tree, 146
    Web, see Web graph
graph coloring, 541
    and the FCC Incentive Auction, 603
    applications, 541
    as satisfiability, 542–543, 604
    is NP-hard for $k \geq 3$, 576, 653
    problem definition, 541
    reduction from 3-SAT, 576, 653
    with $k = 2$ (is linear-time solvable), 548
graph isomorphism, 453
graph search
    A*, 212–213, 263
    applications, 153–155
    breadth-first search, see breadth-first search
    depth-first search, see depth-first search
    for planning, 154
    generic algorithm, 155–158
    in game playing, 263
    problem definition, 155
greatest hits, xv
greedy algorithm, 291–293
    and brainstorming, 368, 473, 630
    as a heuristic algorithm, 293, 473, 631
    exchange argument, see exchange argument
    for clustering, 360
    for influence maximization, 493

for knapsack, 512, 648
for makespan minimization, 473, 477
for maximum coverage, 484
for optimal prefix-free codes, *see* Huffman's
    algorithm
for scheduling, 295–298
for set cover, 511, 647
for submodular function maximization, 514
for vertex cover, 513, 648
for weighted independent set, 600–602, 616,
    654
in the FCC Incentive Auction, 600–604
informal definition, 291, 473
Kruskal's algorithm, *see* Kruskal's algorithm
Prim's algorithm, *see* Prim's algorithm
proof of correctness, 299
themes, 292
usually not correct, 292, 369
`GreedyRatio`, *see* scheduling, `GreedyRatio`
guess-and-check method, 137
guiding principles, 20–23
Gurobi Optimizer, *see* MIP solvers
Gusfield, Dan, 540

Hüffner, Falk, 535
Hadamard matrix, 69
hall of fame, 90, 346
halting problem, 453, 578
Hamiltonian path (directed)
    equivalent to undirected Hamiltonian path,
        576, 652
    example, 463
    is NP-hard, 563
    problem definition (decision), 462
    problem definition (search), 562
    reduces to cycle-free shortest paths, 463
    reduction from 3-SAT, 563–567
    search vs. decision, 562, 575, 652
Hamiltonian path (undirected)
    equivalent to directed Hamiltonian path, 576,
        652
    is NP-hard, 568
    problem definition, 567
    reduces to the TSP, 568–569
Hamm, Jon, 154
Hart, Peter E., 212
hash function
    and the birthday paradox, 266
    bad, 269
    collision, 265
    collisions are inevitable, 265, 270
    cryptographic, 276, 543
    definition, 264
    desiderata, 271
    don't design your own, 276
    example, 271–272

good, 271
how to choose, 276
kryptonite, 270
multiple, 269, 279
pathological data set, 270
perfect, 289, 640
random, 271, 282
state-of-the-art, 276
universal, 270, 288, 640
hash map, *see* hash table
hash table
    DELETE, 258, 267
    INSERT, 258, 267, 268
    LOOKUP, 258, 267, 268
    OUTPUTUNSORTED, 287
    advice, 273
    applications, 259–263
    as an array, 257, 264
    bucket, 266
    collision-resolution strategies, 276
    for de-duplication, 260
    for searching a huge state space, 262
    for the 2-SUM problem, 260–262
    hash function, *see* hash function
    heuristic analysis, 274
    in compilers, 259
    in network routers, 259
    in security applications, 270
    iteration, 260, 287
    load, 274
    load vs. performance, 275
    non-pathological data set, 270
    operation running times, 259
    performance of chaining, 267, 274
    performance of open addressing, 269, 274–
        275
    probe sequence, 267
    raison d'être, 257
    resizing to manage load, 275–276
    scorecard, 259, 264, 275
    space usage, 258
    supported operations, 258
    two-level, 640
    vs. arrays, 263
    vs. bloom filters, 277
    vs. linked lists, 263
    when to use, 259
    with chaining, 266–267, 276
    with double hashing, 268–269, 275
    with linear probing, 268, 275, 276
    with open addressing, 267–269, 276
head (of an edge), 143
heap (data structure)
    DECREASEKEY, 225, 339
    DELETE, 217, 236, 336
    EXTRACTMAX, 217

EXTRACTMIN, 216, 232, 336
FINDMIN, 217
HEAPIFY, 217, 236, 638
INSERT, 216, 229, 336
    applications, 218–222
    as a tree, 226
    as an array, 228
    bubble/heapify/sift (up or down), 231, 234,
        236
    for an event manager, 220
    for median maintenance, 220, 256
    for sorting, 219
    for speeding up Dijkstra's algorithm, 222–226
    for speeding up Prim's algorithm, 336–339
    heap property, 227
    in Graham's algorithm, 474, 514, 648
    in Huffman's algorithm, 319
    in the LPT algorithm, 477
    keys, 216
    operation running times, 217, 336
    parent-child formulas, 228
    raison d'être, 216, 336
    scorecard, 217
    supported operations, 216–217
    vs. search trees, 240–242
    when to use, 217
heap (memory), 216
HeapSort, 219–220
Held, Michael, 524
Heule, Marijn, 543
heuristic algorithm, 293, 456, 631
    dynamic programming, 515
    greedy, 471–496, 600–604
    local search, *see* local search
hill climbing, *see* local search
hints, xvi, 632–654
Hoare, Tony, 92
Hopcroft, John E., 5, 132
Huffman's algorithm, 313–316
    Σ-tree, 312
    average leaf depth, 312, 322
    examples, 316–319
    for ternary codes, 327
    greedy criterion, 315
    implemented with a heap, 319
    implemented with two queues, 319, 327, 641
    obtaining symbol frequencies, 309
    proof of correctness, 320–325
    pseudocode, 316
    running time, 319
Huffman, David A., 313

i.e., 48
Impagliazzo, Russell, 588
in-place algorithm, 90
independence (in probability), 282, 625

independent set (of a graph), 366, 455
independent set problem, 558
    is NP-hard, 558
    reduces to clique, 575, 652
    reduces to subset sum, 570–573
    reduces to vertex cover, 575, 652
    reduction from 3-SAT, 559–562
    weighted, *see* weighted independent set
induction, *see* proofs, by induction
    in greedy algorithms, 299
inductive hypothesis, 618
inductive step, 617
Indyk, Piotr, 589
influence, 492
    is a weighted average of coverage functions,
        494
    is submodular, 515
influence maximization, 490–496
    and $\mathcal{NP}$, 584
    approximate correctness of greedy algorithm,
        493–496
    cascade model, 490
    generalizes maximum coverage, 492, 514,
        648
    greedy algorithm, 493
    intuition, 494
    is NP-hard, 492, 555
    problem definition, 492
    running time of greedy algorithm, 493, 496
InsertionSort, 11, 21, 112
integer multiplication, 4–9, 71–73
    grade-school algorithm, 4
    Karatsuba's algorithm, 9
    simple recursive algorithm, 7
integer programming, *see* mixed integer program-
        ming
interview questions, xv
intractable, *see* NP-hardness
invariant, 94
inversion, 46
    left vs. right vs. split, 48
IQ points, 3

Jarník's algorithm, *see* Prim's algorithm
Jarník, Vojtěch, 331
Java, 240, 272, 327
job, *see* scheduling
Johnson's algorithm, 437
Johnson, David S., 557, 593

k-coloring, 541
k-SAT, 548
    and the SETH, 588
    Schöning's algorithm, 548–550
Karatsuba, 9
    implementation, 26
    recurrence, 72

running time, 76
Karatsuba multiplication, 6–9
    in Python, 77
Karatsuba, Anatoly, 6
Karp reduction, 590, *see also* Levin reduction
Karp, Richard M., 524, 553
Karpman, Pierre, 543
Kempe, David, 492
KenKen, 452, 580
    vs. Sudoku, 112
key, 216
key-value pair, 11
Kleinberg, Jon, 45, 192, 392, 492
knapsack problem, 213, 380–387
    applications, 382
    as a mixed integer program, 538, 540
    correctness, 385
    definition, 381, 455
    dynamic programming algorithm, 384, 455,
        469, 515, 649
    example, 385–386
    generalizations, 391
    greedy algorithm, 512, 648
    is NP-hard, 575, 652
    is pseudopolynomial-time solvable, 455, 570
    measuring input size, 455
    optimal substructure, 382
    reconstruction, 386–387
    recurrence, 383
    reduction from subset sum, 575, 652
    running time, 385
    subproblems, 384
    two-dimensional, 539
Knuth Prize, 553
Knuth, Donald E., 39, 275, 410, 543, 593
Kosaraju, 187
Kosaraju's algorithm
    correctness, 189
    example, 188
    from 30,000 feet, 183
    implementation, 187, 197
    pseudocode, 187
    running time analysis, 189
    why the reversed graph?, 184–186
Kosaraju, S. Rao, 183
Kowalik, Michał, 534
Kruskal's algorithm
    achieves the minimum bottleneck property,
        358
    and clustering, 361
    cycle-checking, 349, 351
    example, 346
    in reverse, 363
    outputs a spanning tree, 357
    proof of correctness, 357–358, 364
    pseudocode (straightforward), 347

pseudocode (union-find-based), 351
    reasons to care, 346
    running time (straightforward), 348–349
    running time (union-find-based), 349
    stopping early, 348
    vs. Prim's algorithm, 346
Kruskal, Joseph B., 346
Kumar, Ravi, 191

Ladner's theorem, 595
Lehman, Eric, 617
Leighton, F. Thomson, 617
Leiserson, Charles E., 252
lemma, 15
length
    of a path, 198
    of an edge, 198, 415
Lenstra, Jan Karel, 508
Levin reduction, 590–591
    spreads NP-completeness, 592
    transitivity of, 594, 653
Levin, Leonid, 553
Leyton-Brown, Kevin, 596
Lin, Shen, 593
Lin-Kernighan heuristic, 508, *see also* local search
linear programming, 539
linear signaling pathways (in a PPI network), 525
linear-time algorithm, 23
linearity of expectation, 274, 624
    doesn't need independence, 108, 625
Linux kernel, 240
literal (in satisfiability), 542
little-o notation, 39
$\ln x$, 75
local search, 497–510
    2-OPT algorithm, *see* 2-OPT algorithm
    and gradient descent, 504
    as a walk in a graph, 504
    as no-downside postprocessing, 505, 631
    avoiding bad local optima, 508
    choosing a neighborhood, 506
    choosing an improving local move, 507
    feasible solutions, 505
    for maximum k-cut, 517, 649
    for satisfiability, 608
    for the TSP, 497–501, 506
    generic pseudocode, 504
    global optima, 505
    history-dependent neighborhoods, 508
    initialization, 507
    is interruptible, 507
    local moves, 505
    local optima, 505
    meta-graph, 502–504
    non-improving local moves, 508
    objective function, 505

overview of paradigm, 504–505
population of solutions, 508
running time, 507
solution quality, 507
vs. MIP and SAT solvers, 509
when to use, 509, 631
logarithms, 15, 74
Lokshtanov, Daniel, 534
longest common subsequence, 413, 459
reduces to sequence alignment, 645
longest common substring, 413
longest processing time first, *see* LPT algorithm
lower-order terms, 28
LPT algorithm, 477
approximate correctness, 478–479, 514, 648
bad example, 477, 480, 514, 648
intuition, 478
running time, 477

machine learning, 504
supervised learning, 358
unsupervised learning, *see* clustering
Maghoul, Farzin, 191
magic boxes, 535–537, *see also* MIP solvers, SAT
solvers
and NP-hardness, 537
when to use, 631
makespan minimization, 471–481
as a mixed integer program, 547, 651
Graham's algorithm, *see* Graham's algorithm
in practice, 472, 478
is NP-hard, 472, 576, 653
LPT algorithm, *see* LPT algorithm
machine load, 471
objective function, 471
problem definition, 472
reduction from subset sum, 576, 653
with small jobs, 511, 647
mangosteen, 112
mantra, 5
Markov, Yarik, 543
Marx, Dániel, 534
master method
a, b, and d, 73, 79
applied to RecIntMult, 76
applied to Karatsuba, 76
applied to MergeSort, 75
applied to Strassen, 77, 78
applied to binary search, 75, 78
big-theta vs. big-O, 74
does not apply, 103, 106, 136
formal statement, 74
meaning of the three cases, 82–84
more general versions, 74
proof, 80–86
master theorem, *see* master method

mathematical background, xv, 616–628
matrix multiplication
definition, 53
exponent, 79
iterative algorithm, 54
simple recursive algorithm, 56
Strassen's algorithm, 56–58, 452
the 2×2 case, 54
matrix-vector multiplication, 69
max-heap, *see* heap (data structure), EXTRACT-
MAX
maximum k-cut problem, 517, 649
maximum coverage, 481–490
applications, 483
approximate correctness of greedy algorithm,
486–489
as a mixed integer program, 547, 651
as team-hiring, 481
bad example, 482, 484–486, 490, 514, 648
greedy algorithm, 484
hardness of approximation, 487
intuition, 487
is NP-hard, 576, 652
problem definition, 482
reduction from set cover, 576, 652
running time of greedy algorithm, 484
MBP, *see* minimum spanning tree, minimum bottleneck property
median (of an array), 26, 99, 121, 220
approximate, 103, 127, 621
vs. mean, 121
weighted, 139
median-of-medians, *see* DSelect
memoization (in dynamic programming), 373
Merge, 13–14
for counting inversions, 49
running time, 14–15
MergeSort, 10–20
analysis, 16–19
as a divide-and-conquer algorithm, 45
does not run in place, 90
implementation, 70
is comparison-based, 112
motivation, 10
pseudocode, 12
recurrence, 73
running time, 15, 75
metric TSP, *see* traveling salesman problem, metric
instances
Metropolis algorithm, 508, *see also* local search
Meyer, Albert R., 593, 617
Milgrom, Paul, 596
Millennium Problems, 586
min-heap, *see* heap (data structure)
minimum bottleneck property, *see* minimum spanning tree, minimum bottleneck property

minimum spanning tree
    Cut Property, 340, 364, 642
    Cycle Property, 364, 642
    exchange argument, 345
    history, 331
    in directed graphs, 328
    in disconnected graphs, 330
    in linear time?, 643
    Kruskal's algorithm, *see* Kruskal's algorithm
    minimum bottleneck property, 340, 341, 344, 363
    MST heuristic (for the TSP), 516
    Prim's algorithm, *see* Prim's algorithm
    reductions to, 363
    uniqueness, 364
    with distinct edge costs, 340, 344
    with non-distinct edge costs, 342, 357, 363, 642
    with parallel edges, 330
minimum-bottleneck spanning tree, 364, 643
minimum-cost k-path problem, *see also* color coding
    exhaustive search, 527, 535
    is NP-hard, 526, 555
    problem definition, 526
minimum-cost panchromatic path problem, *see* color coding
MiniSAT, *see* SAT solvers
MIP, *see* mixed integer programming
MIP solvers, 537–540
    and modeling languages, 540
    and nonlinearities, 539
    are interruptible, 540
    branch and bound, 536
    example input file, 538
    for the TSP, 548, 550
    in the FCC Incentive Auction, 600, 602
    starting points, 540
    vs. local search, 509
    when to use, 537, 631
mixed integer programming, 537
    and linearity, 539
    constraints, 538
    decision variables, 538
    for knapsack, 538, 540
    for makespan minimization, 547, 651
    for maximum coverage, 547, 651
    for satisfiability, 548, 652
    for the TSP, 547, 550, 651
    for weighted independent set, 547, 651
    is NP-hard, 555
    multiple formulations, 540
    objective function, 538
    problem definition, 539
    solvers, *see* MIP solvers
mod (operator), 272

mode (of an array), 26
modulo, 272
Moore's law, 3, 22, 449, 465
MP3, 306, 309
MST, *see* minimum spanning tree
MWIS, *see* weighted independent set

$n \log n$ vs. n^2, 16, 22
Nash, John F., Jr., 586
nearest neighbors (in computational geometry), 70
Needleman, Saul B., 393
Needleman-Wunsch (NW) score, *see* sequence alignment
Nemhauser, George L., 484
network
    movie, 153
    neural, 504
    physical, 153
    road, 143
    social, 143
neural networks, 504
Nielsen, Morten N., 291
Nilsson, Nils J., 212
Nobel Prize, *see* Turing Award
node, *see* vertex (of a graph)
nondeterminism, *see* $\mathcal{NP}$
NP (acronym), 465, 580
$\mathcal{NP}$ (complexity class)
    and $\mathcal{FNP}$, 579
    and efficient recognition of solutions, 580
    and nondeterministic Turing machines, 580
    as problems solvable by naive exhaustive search, 579, 581
    does not contain the halting problem, 579
    feasible solution, 579
    formal definition, 580
    search vs. decision, 579
NP-completeness, 590–593
    formal definition, 591
    meaning, 590
    three-step recipe, 592, 594, 653
    vs. NP-hardness, 466, 591
    what's in a name?, 593
    with decision problems, 591
    with Karp reductions, 591
NP-hardness
    acceptable inaccuracies, 466
    and magic boxes, 537
    and Moore's law, 449, 465
    and reductions, 460, 551
    and subexponential-time solvability, 595, 653
    applies to randomized and quantum algorithms, 452
    as amassing evidence of intractability, 450, 577–579
    as relative intractability, 450

definition (formal), 582
definition (provisional), 452
expertise levels, 447–448
forces compromise, 454
in practice, 465
in fifteen words, 448
in other disciplines, 551
is not a death sentence, 454, 465
is ubiquitous, 454
key takeaways, 457
level-1 expertise, 448–457, 464–466
level-2 expertise, 453–457, 471–550, 596–
    616
level-3 expertise, 457–464, 551–576
level-4 expertise, 577–595
main idea, 451
of 19 problems, 554–557
of 3-SAT, see Cook-Levin theorem
oversimplified dichotomy, 448, 453, 466, 595,
    654
proofs, 556
rookie mistakes, 464–466
strong vs. weak, 570
subtleties, 453
two-step recipe, 461, 552, 594, 631, 653
vs. NP-completeness, 466, 554, 591
with Levin reductions, 582
null pointer, 241

$O(f(n))$, see big-O notation
$o(f(n))$, see little-o notation
O'Donnell, Ryan, 577
objective function, 293
$\Omega(f(n))$, see big-omega notation
optimal binary search trees, 400–410
    correctness, 409
    dynamic programming algorithm, 408
    Knuth's optimization, 410
    optimal substructure, 403–406
    problem definition, 403
    reconstruction, 409
    recurrence, 406
    running time, 409
    search frequencies, 402
    subproblems, 408
    vs. balanced binary search trees, 402
    vs. optimal prefix-free codes, 403
    weighted search time, 403
    with unsuccessful searches, 403
optimization problem, 579
    reduces to search version, 570, 575, 580, 652
order statistic, 107, 120

$\mathcal{P}$ (complexity class), 584
P $\neq$ NP conjecture, 451–452
    as a law of nature, 466
    current status, 585–586

formal definition, 585
informal version, 451
is hard to prove, 452, 586
meaning, 585
reasons to believe, 586
refutation consequences, 586
vs. the ETH, 453, 587
panchromatic path, 528
Papadimitriou, Christos, 73
Partition, 96
    proof of correctness, 97
    runs in place, 98
partition problem, see subset sum problem
path (of a graph), 329
    k-, 526
    bottleneck, 341
    cycle-free, 329
    panchromatic, 528
path graph, 368
pathological data set, 270
Paturi, Ramamohan, 588
paying the piper, 224, 251, 339
pep talk, 33, 366
Perelman, Grigori, 586
PET, 593
Pigeonhole Principle, 265, 270, 418
Pilipczuk, Marcin, 534
Pilipczuk, Michał, 534
pivot element, 91
planning (as graph search), 154
pointer, 147
polynomial vs. exponential time, 449
polynomial-time algorithm, 448
polynomial-time solvability, 450
    and reductions, 460
Pratt, Vaughan, 132
prefix-free code, see code, prefix-free
Prim's algorithm
    achieves the minimum bottleneck property,
        341
    example, 331
    greedy criterion, 333
    outputs a spanning tree, 344
    proof of correctness, 340–345, 364
    pseudocode, 333
    pseudocode (heap-based), 338
    resembles Dijkstra's shortest-path algorithm,
        331
    running time (heap-based), 336, 339
    running time (straightforward), 335
    starting vertex, 334
    straightforward implementation, 335
    vs. Dijkstra's shortest-path algorithm, 334,
        340
    vs. Kruskal's algorithm, 346
Prim, Robert C., 331

prime number, 102
primitive operation, 4, 14, 19, 21
principle of parsimony, 215, 630
priority queue, *see* heap (data structure)
probability, 274, 490, 532, 620
    independence, 282
    of an event, 621
problem
    NP-hard (formal definition), 582
    NP-hard (provisional definition), 452
    decision, 579
    easy (oversimplified), 448
    easy vs. polynomial-time solvable, 450
    hard (oversimplified), 448
    neither polynomial-time solvable nor NP-hard, 453, 595
    optimization, 579
    polynomial-time solvable, 449
    search, 579
    undecidable, 578
    universal, 592
problems vs. solutions, 3
programming, xv, 9
programming problems, xvi
proofs, xv
    by contradiction, 36, 158, 300
    by induction, 93, 137, 617–618
    of correctness, 93, 298
    on reading, 206
proposition, 15
protein-protein interaction (PPI) networks, 525
pseudocode, 9, 13
pseudopolynomial time, 570
Pyrrhic victory, 135
Pythagorean theorem, 67

$\mathscr{QED}$ (q.e.d.), 19
quantum algorithm, 452
queue (data structure), 160, 214, 319
QuickSort
    best-case scenario, 99
    handling ties, 91
    high-level description, 92
    history, 92
    implementation, 118
    is comparison-based, 112
    is not stable, 113
    median-of-three, 118
    partitioning around a pivot, 91, 93–98
    pivot element, 91
    proof of correctness, 93
    pseudocode, 98
    random shuffle, 102
    randomized, 101
    running time, 102
    running time (intuition), 103–104

running time (proof), 104–111
    runs in place, 90
    worst-case scenario, 99
quizzes, xvi

Rackoff, Charles, 291
RadixSort, 113
Raghavan, Prabhakar, 191
Rajagopalan, Sridhar, 191
random variable, 622
    geometric, 128
    independent, 625
    indicator, 627
randomized algorithms, 102, 129, 628, 631
    and NP-hardness, 452
    for 3-SAT, 548
    for color coding, 531–533
Raphael, Bertram, 212
Rassias, Michael Th., 586
rate of growth, *see* asymptotic analysis
RecIntMult, 7
    recurrence, 72
    running time, 76
RecMatMult, 56
recommendation system, 47
recurrence, 71, 371
    standard, 73
recursion, 7
recursion tree, 16, 80
reduction, 121, 201, 204, 458, 551, 630
    Cook, 578
    examples, 458
    gone awry, 562
    in the wrong direction, 465, 554
    Karp, 590
    Levin, 590–591
    many-to-one, 590
    mapping, 590
    polynomial-time Turing, 578
    preprocessor and postprocessor, 558, 591
    preserves polynomial running time, 459, 464
    simplest-imaginable, 557–558
    spreads intractability, 460, 552
    spreads tractability, 460, 536, 552
    to a magic box, 536
    transitivity of, 594, 653
    with exponential blow-up, 590, 654
reference, *see* pointer
reverse auction, *see* FCC Incentive Auction
Rivest, Ronald L., 132, 252
rookie mistakes, 84, 464–466
RSelect
    best-case scenario, 124
    expected running time, 125
    implementation, 140
    pseudocode, 122

running time analysis, 126–129
runs in place, 123
worst-case scenario, 124
RSP (rate of subproblem proliferation), *see* master method, meaning of the three cases
running time, 14, 19, 28
RWS (rate of work shrinkage), *see* master method, meaning of the three cases

sample space (in probability), 620
SAT, *see* satisfiability
SAT solvers, 540–544
    and graph coloring, 616
    and local search, 608
    and the FCC Incentive Auction, 604–609
    applications, 542
    are only semi-reliable, 553
    conflict-driven clause learning, 536
    example input file, 543
    portfolio, 608
    starting points, 544
    vs. local search, 509
    when to use, 541, 631
satisfiability
    k-SAT, *see* k-SAT
    2-SAT (is linear-time solvable), 197, 548
    3-SAT, *see* 3-SAT
    and graph coloring, 542–543, 604
    and the SETH, 588
    applications, 542
    as a mixed integer program, 548, 652
    constraints, 542
    decision variables, 542
    disjunction (of literals), 542
    is NP-hard, 555
    literal, 542
    modulo theories, 544
    problem definition, 542
    truth assignment, 542
Saurabh, Saket, 534
SCC, *see* strongly connected components
scheduling, 293, 471, *see also* makespan minimization
    GreedyDiff, 297
    GreedyRatio, 297
    completion time, 293
    correctness of GreedyRatio, 299–302
    exchange argument, 300
    greedy algorithms, 295–298
    running time, 298
    sum of weighted completion times, 294
Schrijver, Alexander, 418
Schöning's algorithm (for k-SAT), 548–550
    and the ETH, 587
    and the SETH, 588
Schöning, Uwe, 550

scorecards, 150, 217, 238, 240, 259, 264, 275, 278, 350
search problem, 579
    reduces to decision version, 562, 575, 652
search tree
    DELETE, 239, 247, 251
    INSERT, 239, 246, 251
    MAX, 237, 244
    MIN, 237, 244
    OUTPUTSORTED, 237, 246
    PREDECESSOR, 237, 245
    RANK, 238, 249, 255
    SEARCH, 237, 243
    SELECT, 237, 249–251
    SUCCESSOR, 237, 245
    2-3, 251
    applications, 240
    augmented, 249, 251, 255
    AVL, 251
    B, 251
    balanced, 240, 251–253
    height, 243
    in-order traversal, 246
    operation running times, 240
    optimal, *see* optimal binary search trees
    pointers, 241
    raison d'être, 239
    red-black, 251, 252
    rotation, 252–253
    scorecard, 240
    search tree property, 241
    splay, 251
    supported operations, 239
    vs. heaps, 240–242
    vs. sorted arrays, 237, 240
    when to use, 240
    with duplicate keys, 255
Sedgewick, Robert, 91, 252
Segal, Ilya, 596
selection
    DSelect, *see* DSelect
    RSelect, *see* RSelect
    problem definition, 120
    reduces to sorting, 121
selection bias, 442
SelectionSort, 11, 112, 219
separate chaining, *see* hash table, with chaining
sequence alignment, 392–399
    alignment, 393
    and the SETH, 589
    applications, 392
    correctness, 398
    dynamic programming algorithm (NW), 397
    gap, 393
    Needleman-Wunsch (NW) score, 393
    optimal substructure, 394

penalties, 393
problem definition, 393
reconstruction, 399
recurrence, 396
reduction from longest common subsequence, 645
running time, 398
subproblems, 397
variations, 413
set cover problem, 511
greedy algorithm, 511, 647
is NP-hard, 575, 652
reduces to maximum coverage, 576, 652
reduction from vertex cover, 575, 652
SETH, *see* Strong Exponential Time Hypothesis
Shamir, Adi, 132
Sharir, Micha, 183
Shimbel, Alfonso, 418
shortest paths
all-pairs, 429, 459
all-pairs (dense graphs), 437
all-pairs (sparse graphs), 430, 437
and Bacon numbers, 154
and Internet routing, 427
and negative cycles, 462
and transitive closure, 429
Bellman-Ford algorithm, *see* Bellman-Ford algorithm, 462
bottleneck, 212, 236
cycle-free, *see* cycle-free shortest paths
Dijkstra's algorithm, *see* Dijkstra's shortest-path algorithm
distance, 163, 198, 415
Floyd-Warshall algorithm, *see* Floyd-Warshall algorithm
history, 418
Johnson's algorithm, 437
nonnegative edge lengths, 200, *see also* Dijkstra's shortest-path algorithm
problem definition (all-pairs), 429
problem definition (single-source), 163, 198, 417
reduction from all-pairs to single-source, 429, 430
single-source, 198, 415, 459, 461
via breadth-first search, 164–165, 201
with negative cycles, 417
with negative edge lengths, 204, 416
with no negative cycles, 418
with parallel edges, 416
with unit edge lengths, 163, 201
SIGACT, 39
simulated annealing, 508, *see also* local search
single-source shortest path problem, *see* shortest paths, single-source
six degrees of separation, 192

small world property, 192
social network, 490
solutions, xvi, 632–654
solver, 536, *see also* magic box
sorted array
scorecard, 238
supported operations, 237
unsupported operations, 239
vs. search trees, 240
sorting, 458
HeapSort, *see* HeapSort
MergeSort, *see* MergeSort
MergeSort vs. QuickSort, 90
QuickSort, *see* QuickSort
applications, 11, 26
associated data, 11
by key, 11
comparison-based, 112
in linear time, 320
in place, 90
in Unix, 112
lower bound, 112, 114–115
non-comparison-based, 113
problem definition, 11, 218
randomized, 102, 114
simple algorithms, 11–12
stable, 113
with duplicates, 11
with Hungarian folk dancers, 96
spanning tree (of a graph), 329
component fusion, 342
cycle creation, 342
minimum, *see* minimum spanning tree
number of, 330
number of edges, 343
type-C vs. type-F edge addition, 342
spectrum auction, *see* FCC Incentive Auction
stack (data structure), 172, 214
pop, 172
push, 172
stack (memory), 173
starred sections, xiv, 59
Stata, Raymie, 191
Steiglitz, Kenneth, 593
Stein, Clifford, 252
Stevens, Marc, 543
Stirling's approximation, 519, 532
Strassen, 56–58, 452
running time, 77, 78
Strassen, Volker, 58
strong NP-hardness, 570
Strong Exponential Time Hypothesis
and graph diameter, 595, 654
and Schöning's algorithm, 550, 588
and sequence alignment, 589
definition, 588

vs. the ETH, 588
strongly connected components
    and the 2-SAT problem, 197
    definition, 181
    giant, 191
    in a reversed graph, 186, 189
    linear-time computation, *see* Kosaraju's algorithm
    meta-graph of, 182
    sink, 184
    source, 185
    topological ordering of, 182, 185
    via depth-first search, 181, 183
submodular function maximization, 514–515, 649
    greedy algorithm, 514
subsequence, 413
subset sum problem
    is NP-hard, 570
    is pseudopolynomial-time solvable, 570
    partition special case, 576
    problem definition, 569
    reduces to knapsack, 575, 652
    reduces to makespan minimization, 576, 653
    reduction from independent set, 570–573
substring, 413
Sudoku, 154, 212, 452, 580
    vs. KenKen, 112
superteam, 132

tabu search, 508, *see also* local search
tail (of an edge), 143
Tardos, Éva, 45, 392, 492
Tarjan, Robert E., 132, 181, 638
task scheduling, 143, 174, 175
team-hiring, *see* maximum coverage
test cases, xvi
Tetris, 413
theorem, 15
$\Theta(f(n))$, *see* big-theta notation
theta notation, *see* big-theta notation
three-step recipe, *see* NP-completeness, three-step
    recipe
Tomkins, Andrew, 191
topological ordering
    definition, 174
    existence in directed acyclic graphs, 176–177
    non-existence, 175
topological sorting, 174–180
    example, 178
    linear-time computation, 179
    problem definition, 177
    pseudocode, 178
TopoSort, 178
    correctness, 179
    in non-acyclic graphs, 181, 184
    run backward, 187

running time analysis, 179
tour (of a graph), 443
transitive closure (of a binary relation), 429
traveling salesman problem
    2-OPT algorithm, *see* 2-OPT algorithm
    2-change, 499
    3-OPT algorithm, 506
    3-change, 506
    applications, 445
    as a mixed integer program, 547, 550, 651
    Concorde solver, 548
    conjectured intractability, 446
    dynamic programming, *see* Bellman-Held-
        Karp algorithm (for the TSP)
    exhaustive search, 444, 446, 470, 579
    history, 445
    is NP-hard, 497, 568
    metric instances, 516–517, 576, 649
    MST heuristic, 516, 649
    nearest neighbor algorithm, 497, 501, 518
    number of tours, 443, 446
    on non-complete graphs, 443
    optimal substructure, 521–522, 524–525
    path version, 445, 469, 555
    problem definition, 443
    reduction from undirected Hamiltonian path,
        568–569
    search version, 575
    tree instances, 470, 647
tree, 146
    binary, 226
    chain, 243
    complete, 226
    depth (of a node), 311
    forest, 315
    height, 240, 243
    optimal binary search, *see* optimal binary
        search trees
    root, 226
    search, *see* search tree
TSP, *see* traveling salesman problem
tug-of-war, 82
Turing Award, 92, 132, 553
Turing machine, 578
    nondeterministic, 580
Turing reduction, 578
Turing, Alan M., 578
two-step recipe, *see* NP-hardness, two-step recipe

UCC, 168
    correctness, 169
    running time analysis, 169
Ullman, Jeffrey D., 5
uniform distribution, 620
union-find
    FIND, 350, 353

INITIALIZE, 350, 353
UNION, 350, 354, 355
for speeding up Kruskal's algorithm, 351–352
inverse Ackermann function, 350
operation running times, 350, 356
parent graph, 352
path compression, 350
quick-and-dirty implementation, 352–356
raison d'être, 349
scorecard, 350
state-of-the-art implementations, 350
supported operations, 350
union-by-rank, 350, 355
union-by-size, 355
Unix, 413
upshot, xiv

van Maaren, Hans, 543
Vazirani, Umesh, 73
vertex (of a graph), 142
degree, 151
in-degree, 421
out-degree, 421
reachable, 155
sink, 176
source, 176, 198
starting, 198
vertex cover problem, 513
greedy algorithm, 513, 648
is NP-hard, 575, 652
reduces to set cover, 575, 652
reduction from independent set, 575, 652
videos, xvi, 252, 275, 289, 350, 355, 427, 428, 437, 640, 643, 649
von Neumann, John, 10, 586

Wallach, Dan S., 270
Walsh, Toby, 543
Warshall, Stephen, 430
Wayne, Kevin, 91, 252
weak NP-hardness, 570
Web graph, 143, 190–192
as a sparse graph, 149
bow tie, 191
connectivity, 192
giant component, 191
size, 149, 191, 259
weighted independent set
as a mixed integer program, 547, 651
greedy algorithm, 600–602, 616, 654
in acyclic graphs, 455
in general graphs, 390
in path graphs, see weighted independent set (in path graphs)
in the FCC Incentive Auction, 599
problem definition, 367, 454
weighted independent set (in path graphs), 368

correctness, 375
dynamic programming algorithm, 374
failure of divide-and-conquer algorithms, 369
failure of greedy algorithms, 368, 370
optimal substructure, 370–371
reconstruction, 376–377
recurrence, 371
recursive algorithm, 372
running time, 374
subproblems, 373
Wernicke, Sebastian, 535
whack-a-mole, 229
why bother?, xiv, 2
Wiener, Janet, 191
Williams, H. Paul, 540
Williams, Virginia Vassilevska, 589
WIS, see weighted independent set
work, see running time
World Wide Web, see Web graph
worst-case analysis, 20
Wunsch, Christian D., 393

yottabyte, 259
YouTube, xvi
Yuster, Raphael, 527

Zichner, Thomas, 535
Zwick, Uri, 527

BOOKS BY TIM ROUGHGARDEN

Introductory

Algorithms Illuminated, Part 1: The Basics
(Soundlikeyourself Publishing, 2017)

Algorithms Illuminated, Part 2: Graph Algorithms and Data Structures
(Soundlikeyourself Publishing, 2018)

Algorithms Illuminated, Part 3: Greedy Algorithms and Dynamic Programming
(Soundlikeyourself Publishing, 2019)

Algorithms Illuminated, Part 4: Algorithms for NP-Hard Problems
(Soundlikeyourself Publishing, 2020)

Intermediate

Twenty Lectures on Algorithmic Game Theory
(Cambridge University Press, 2016)

Communication Complexity (for Algorithm Designers)
(NOW Publishers, 2016)

Advanced

Selfish Routing and the Price of Anarchy
(MIT Press, 2005)

Algorithmic Game Theory (co-edited with Noam Nisan, Éva Tardos, and Vijay V. Vazirani)
(Cambridge University Press, 2007)

Complexity Theory, Game Theory, and Economics: The Barbados Lectures
(NOW Publishers, 2020)

Beyond the Worst-Case Analysis of Algorithms (ed.)
(Cambridge University Press, 2021)